GUINNESS BOOK OF
HITS OF THE 60s

TOP

retailer and music industry news

18	LET'S TURKEY TROT (21) Little Eva — London HLU 9687
19	THE FOLK SINGER (31) Tommy Roe — H.M.V. POP 1138
20	IN DREAMS (25) Roy Orbison — London HLU 9676
21	LOOP-DE-LOOP (15) Frankie Vaughan — Philips 326566 BF
22	CUPBOARD LOVE (22) John Leyton — H.M.V. POP 1122
3	ALL ALONE AM I (23) Brenda Lee — Brunswick 05882
	END OF THE WORLD (29) Skeeter Davis — R.C.A. RCA 1328
25	MR. BASS MAN (36) Johnny Cymbal — London HLR 9682
	...IAMONDS (18) Jet Harris & ...

35	CAN'T GET USED TO LOSING (49) Andy Williams — C.B.S. AAG
36	CAN YOU FORGIVE ME (46) Karl Denver — Decca F 11608
37	DON'T SET ME FREE (—) Ray Charles — H.M.V. POP 1133
38	SAY I WON'T BE THERE (—) The Springfields — Philips 326577 BF
39	LIKE I DO (37) Maureen Evans — Oriole CB 1760
40	BOSS GUITAR (34) Duane Eddy — R.C.A. RCA 1329
41	MY KIND OF GIRL (40) Frank Sinatra and Count Basie — Reprise R 20148
42	FIREBALL (50) Don Spencer — H.M.V. POP
3	LITTLE TOWN ... (28) Del She...

I'VE NEVER BEEN GONE — Columbia DB 4977
(4) Billy Fury — Decca F 11582

FROM A JACK TO A KING
(13) Ned Miller — London HL 9658

...D OF DREAMS
...ringfields — Phili...

CHARMAI... (8) The ...

HOW DO ... (20) Gerry ...

...Y WON... (17) The ... Ronni...

WALK ... (44) The ...

SO IT WI... The Ev... — Warner Bros...

HI LILI-HI LO (24) Richard ...

...THOUSAND EYES — Liberty LIB 10069

...HEART FO...

GUINNESS BOOK OF

HITS OF THE 60s

TIM RICE JO RICE MIKE READ
PAUL GAMBACCINI

Editorial Associate: Steve Smith

SINGLES·ALBUMS·EPS·SINGLES·ALBUMS·EPS·SINGL

ACKNOWLEDGEMENTS

The four authors would like to thank many of the artists featured in this book for their interest and co-operation and also the following: Judy Craymer, Tony Gale of Pictorial Press, London, Melanie Georgi, Sheila Goldsmith, Eileen Heinink, Jan Rice, *New Musical Express, Melody Maker* and *Music Week.*

Editor: Alex E Reid
Design and layout: David Roberts

Cover design: Robert Heesom

Background photograph:
Tony Stone Associates

Colour Separation: Mayday

First edition 1984
© **GRRR Books Ltd and Guinness Superlatives Ltd 1984**

Published in Great Britain by
Guinness Superlatives Ltd
2 Cecil Court, London Road, Enfield, Middlesex

British Library Cataloguing in Publication Data

Guinness book of hits of the 60's.
1. Music, Popular (Songs, etc.) –
Great Britain – Discography
I. Rice, Tim
016.7899'1245   ML156.4.P6

ISBN 0-85112-416-X
Guinness is a registered trade mark of Guinness Superlatives Ltd.
Typeset printed and bound in Great Britain by Bemrose Confidential and Information Products Ltd, Derby.

INTRODUCTION

The sixties were different. Looking back at the 'swinging sixties' through glasses blurred by the directionless seventies and early eighties, all we see are images of youth, Carnaby Street, Antonioni films and of course the Beatles. The sixties were, for Britain at least, a decade when the energy of youth became the only qualification for success, and when the artistic capital of the world was London.

It had not started like that. Nobody expected Britain to be the centre of anything. The election of John F Kennedy as President of the United States at the age of 43 in November 1960 turned everybody's eyes to America in the expectation that their Camelot might eventually spread across the Atlantic and influence even fuddy-duddy Britain. Nobody expected Britain to be the centre of a cultural revolution of more influence in the rest of the world than anything Chairman Mao ever created in China, but it was. Nobody expected culture at all in Britain, let alone something starting in Liverpool. One Liverpool MP, Harold Wilson, announced in October 1960 that his party's 'message for the sixties' was 'a socialist-inspired scientific and technological revolution releasing energy on an enormous scale.' By the time Mr Wilson became Prime Minister in 1964 Kennedy was dead, and the most significant revolutions he presided over were at 33⅓ and 45 per minute, a fact which he recognised when he gave the Beatles their MBEs in 1965. They certainly released energy on an enormous scale.

With this book, we are continuing our series of books on the decades of the charts era which we started with **Hits of The Seventies** in 1980. This time we have been able to include not only statistics from the singles charts, but also from the LP charts, and from the EP charts which were compiled only in the 1960s. The results are, to us at least, surprising and interesting. The sixties were only a little over 3 years old when the first 'Mersey Beat' number one was achieved ('How Do You Do It' by Gerry and the Pacemakers, written by Londoner Mitch Murray) and yet the pre-Beatles favourites like Billy Fury and Adam Faith, whose careers were allegedly destroyed by the beat groups, still finished the sixties higher in the 'Most Weeks On Chart' table than all the groups except the Fab Four.

Some other unexpected facts emerge. Did you know that Roy Orbison's entire singles chart career was limited to the sixties? Who would you think was the most successful female solo act on the singles charts of the sixties? Dusty Springfield? Petula Clark? Shirley Bassey? No: it was Brenda Lee. Did you realise how staggeringly successful ballad singers were in the sixties, even against the opposition of the beat groups? In 1967, the year of flower power, Engelbert Humperdinck chalked up three monster hits and created chart records even the Beatles could not match. Other balladeers like Tom Jones, Vince Hill, Des O'Connor, Ken Dodd, Jim Reeves and Val Doonican sold records by the sackful, and Frank Sinatra's 'My Way' began its record-breaking chart run on 2 April 1969.

The charts of the sixties show very clearly success there does not always accurately reflect sales figures. The Beatles sold far more records in Britain in the sixties than did any other act; yet because they sold their records so rapidly, they did not stay very long on the charts with each single, and so they do not finish up as the top chart act of the decade. The charts reward consistency rather than spectacular success, which is why Cliff beat the Beatles and the Hollies beat the Rolling Stones.

On 1 January 1960, the charts were mainly a pale imitation of the American charts. There were some original British talents around – Lonnie Donegan, Cliff Richard, Billy Fury – but almost everyone looked to America for inspiration. By 31 December 1969, Britain had experienced its first reggae number one, its last Beatles and Stones number ones, and the first hits from David Bowie and Led Zeppelin. America looked to Britain for inspiration. In the seventies the inspiration dried up fairly quickly, and it was not until 1983 that British domination of the American charts again matched its level of 1964 and 1965. Even then, the success was led by acts like David Bowie, Rod Stewart and Police, all of whom learned their trade in the 1960s.

The purpose of this book is not to say how or why records were hits; it is merely to list the ones that were. We hope you will take note of Paddy Roberts' EP successes just as much as the Beatles' singles smashes or Cream's LP hits. We hope the book brings back memories of the sixties, settles arguments about the hits of the sixties, and encourages some of our younger readers to listen to the music of the sixties for the first time. When it was good it was very good, and when it was bad it was horrid. But all of it was exciting and interesting. The sixties **were** different.

CHART DATES IN THE SIXTIES

During the sixties, the day of the week on which the record charts were published changed more than once. This creates an apparent inconsistency in the dating system used for the singles, album and EP charts statistics in this book.

In the first edition of **The Guinness Book Of British Hit Singles,** we stated clearly that publication dates of the magazine in which the chart appeared are the dates used, which is not necessarily the date of the chart itself. This policy has continued through subsequent editions of **British Hit Singles,** and is used again in this book.

In effect, the publication dates changed four times in the sixties, as follows:

1 January 1960 to 26 February 1960
Publication date Fridays (New Musical Express).

10 March 1960 to 29 June 1967
Publication date Thursdays (Record Retailer).

5 July 1967 to 30 July 1969
Publication date Wednesdays. (Record Retailer).

9 August 1969 to date
Publication date Saturdays.
(Record Retailer/Music Week).

When we began compiling **The Guinness Book Of Hit Albums,** we decided to take a consistent line and use as the chart date for the book the Saturday of the week in which the magazine was published. This means that almost throughout the sixties, the dates used for the LP statistics by us do not coincide exactly with the singles and EP statistics dates. Thus, for example, a single which we list as hitting number one on 23 July 1964 did so in the chart published in the same magazine which showed an LP of the same title hitting number one on 25 July 1964.

From 9 August 1969, the two charts are united as Saturday charts, something which still continues. The chart date discrepancies are therefore only a problem in the Fifties and Sixties.

If you did not understand this footnote this time, we will repeat it in **Hits Of The Fifties,** and that will give you another opportunity not to understand it.

Year by Year Summaries

1960

The record of the year was Elvis Presley's 'It's Now Or Never' which topped the singles charts for 8 weeks. The only disc to approach this achievement was 'Cathy's Clown' by the Everly Brothers, whose 7 weeks at number one got the Warner Brothers label off to a cracking start in the UK with their first release, WB 1. Don and Phil had a marvellous year together, with two other Top Ten entries and one of their most-loved recordings 'Let It Be Me' peaking at what seems over 20 years later to be a surprisingly low 13. Elvis was probably more concerned with the fact that 1960 was the year he got out of the army than with the facts and figures of his chart success, but his return to civvies resulted in a massively successful year both sides of the Atlantic, indeed all over the world. His first post-army recording 'Stuck On You' made number three in the UK, his second British release 'Mess Of Blues' number two (helped enormously by the extremely popular but uncredited chart-wise 'The Girl Of My Best Friend' on the flip) and his final effort for 1960 went all the way as noted above. Only two other discs were to equal the chart topping run of 'It's Now Or Never' during the entire decade.

For all that, Elvis' chart statistics for 1960 would have been even better if copyright problems hadn't held up the UK release of 'It's Now Or Never' for over 3 months. This in turn delayed the stretch of the follow-up 'Are You Lonesome Tonight' at the top until early 1961. While the 'It's Now Or Never' hassles were being sorted out, RCA put out the US B side of 'It's Now Or Never' as an A side and it says a lot for the quality of Elvis' B sides at the time, or for his popularity, or both, that 'Mess Of Blues' got to number two. Elvis was never as popular with so many sections of the public as he was from 1960-2, yet had to be content with a mere 42 singles chart weeks in 1960. This did not even put him in the Top Ten, but in the albums list he ran out first, thanks largely to the great success of his first post-army LP 'Elvis Is Back' and the compilation 'Golden Records Vol. 2.'

Two British acts scored more weeks on the singles charts than the Everlys (61 weeks), Cliff Richard, the year's champ, 78 weeks, and Adam Faith 1 week behind with 77. Cliff had two of the ten number ones of his career (so far) in 1960 – 'Please Don't Tease,' and right at the end of 1960, 'I Love You,' both written by Bruce Welch, the first with Pete Chester. Three other top three hits and as many as 7 singles weeks for the 'Expresso Bongo' EP were just enough to edge Cliff ahead of Adam whose impressive recording career had been launched in dramatic style by the huge success of 'What Do You Want' at the end of 1959. This platter was still in the charts when Adam's second smash began its swift climb to number one and 'Poor Me' eventually won the minor honour of being the first ever topper of a *Record Retailer* (now *Music Week*) chart. Adam collected four more Top Five hits before 1960

Elvis PRESLEY, who released the record of the year 'Its Now Or Never.'
Pictorial Press, London (as are all illustrations in this section, pages 9-29, unless stated otherwise).

The EVERLY BROTHERS obtained their second number one hit in the Spring of 1960 with 'Cathy's Clown' which stayed on the singles chart for 18 weeks.

was out, narrowly failing to become the first act in chart history to have three consecutive number ones. The Everlys, Cliff and Adam all had one major chart album released in 1960, in the case of the Everlys and Faith the most successful LP of their careers.

By the end of the year, one of the most popular acts in the country was the Shadows, who, while continuing their highly successful association with Cliff Richard, branched out in their own right as a recording entity. In July they knocked their boss off the top with their first hit 'Apache' and stayed there for 5 weeks, the longest run at number one for a British act all year. Their second hit was Top 5 before 1961 came in. Instrumentals were strong in general. Johnny and the Hurricanes and Duane Eddy both kept coming up with major records and Eddy also had a great year on the album charts; the year's fourth biggest act there. His 'Because They're Young' tied with Percy Faith's US number one 'Summer Place' as the silver medallists to 'Apache' in the instrumental stakes. Both reached number two for one week. Russ Conway had lost much of his singles selling clout, but remained a big LP name, and the trad jazz boom was just gathering maximum steam, thanks largely to Acker Bilk.

Top girl was Connie Francis who couldn't quite repeat her US blitz of two number ones in the UK, but still left all rivals standing. Anthony Newley, who had entered pop music sending it up in his movie *Idle On Parade* was now taking it (fairly) seriously and had two number ones for his efforts. Norrie Paramor was without doubt singles producer of the year – in addition to his work with Cliff and the Shadows, he guided both Michael Holliday and Ricky Valance to the top. The great Lonnie Donegan had his last number one; towards the end of the year the great Roy Orbison his first. Johnny Kidd and the Pirates took one of the two records now considered by 'experts' to be genuine rock 'n' roll made in England, 'Shakin' All Over' (Cliff's 'Move It,' 1958, being the other) to the very top for just 1 week. Kidd was killed in a car smash in 1966, but at least he lived to enjoy his greatest recording successes. The great rocker Eddie Cochran was even less fortunate, killed in the UK (also in a motor accident) on Easter Sunday 1960, never to know that 'Three Steps To Heaven' was to be a UK number one. The other number one men of the year were Emile Ford (a 1959 hangover), Johnny Preston with the novelty 'Running Bear,' and Jimmy Jones with a novelty voice on 'Good Timin'.'

The summit of the album chart was nearly as uneventful as it had been in 1959 when 'South Pacific' stayed there all year. In 1960 this soundtrack album's popularity dipped to such an extent that it was only at the top for 45 weeks, allowing Elvis, Freddy Cannon (!) and the studio orchestra 101 Strings quick visits to the coveted slot. Peter Sellers (produced by George Martin) wound up second only to Elvis as album artist of the year, thanks to his classic comedy recordings 'The Best Of Sellers' and 'Songs For Swinging Sellers.' Other soundtracks did nearly as well as 'South Pacific,' notably 'Gigi' and 'Oklahoma.'

Connie FRANCIS (Top Girl of 1960) directing a policeman on a visit to London Town.

Easter Sunday was a black day for Rock'n Roll: Eddie COCHRAN was killed.

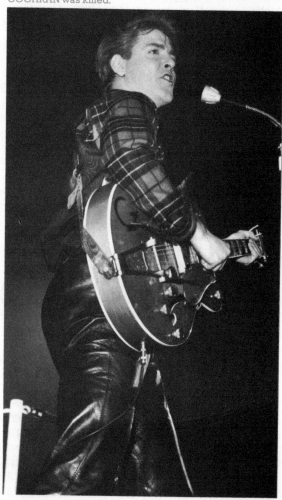

Cliff topped the first ever EP chart published in Britain in March 1960 and by the end of the year was by some distance the top EP act, ahead of predictable challengers such as Elvis and less predictable ones such as Paddy Roberts and Nina and Frederick.

1961

Elvis carried all before him in 1961. His 88 chart weeks on the singles lists was only once bettered in the entire decade – by Engelbert Humperdinck in 1967. His first three 1961 discs were all number ones, the second of these ('Wooden Heart,' which was not issued at the time as a US single) making Elvis the first artist to have three number ones with successive releases. 'Surrender' in May made it four on the trot (the first of course had been his 1960 monster, 'It's Now Or Never'). 'Wild In The Country'/'I Feel So Bad' ruined the sequence by peaking at four, but he ended the year in supreme style with the ninth topper of his already phenomenal recording career, 'His Latest Flame'/'Little Sister.' He was also way ahead in the album tally, his 91 weeks in that department owing most to the enormous popularity of the 'GI Blues' soundtrack. He had to be content to be runner-up to Cliff Richard in the EP listings.

Cliff himself had another great year without actually having a chart-topper, merely four top four singles. His backing group, if they could still be described as such, actually did even better. Their five Top Tenners (including one 1960 hangover) included their second number one 'Kon-Tiki.' On 5 October the Shadows became the first act to hit number one in all three charts simultaneously. They wound up number 3 EP act but the release of their big-selling début album came too late in the year for them to figure significantly in the final LP ratings.

Norrie Paramor as usual, was at the production controls for Cliff and the Shadows. On top of that, he launched Helen Shapiro on disc and the 14-year old girl with a woman's voice sold so many records in the year, including two number one hits, that she even pushed the still important Connie Francis into second place singles-wise. Shirley Bassey did well for the third year running, her 49 weeks including her second number one the double-sided smash 'Reach For The Stars'/'Climb Ev'ry Mountain.' Another thrush to click in '61 was Petula Clark (whose first hit was in 1954) who returned to the charts with a bang and a number one, 'Sailor', after 3 hitless years.

Others to reach the highest rung in the singles charts were Johnny Tillotson, Del Shannon (with the classic 'Runaway'), the Marcels with a manic interpretation of 'Blue Moon' – Richard Rodgers, who wrote the tune for 'Climb Ev'ry Mountain,' also co-wrote 'Blue Moon,' so he had a good pop year – and two English newcomers to the disc scene, Eden Kane and John Leyton. The latter's 'Johnny Remember Me' was given a huge boost by being featured in a TV soap *Harpers West One* – a path to record success that was to be followed many times during the next 2 decades. Beatles producer George Martin had his first number one single via

ELVIS on location

the 1930s throwback group the Temperance Seven, who in a way were part of the trad boom that peaked at the end of 1961 courtesy Acker Bilk and Kenny Ball singles-wise and Bilk and Chris Barber album-wise. Danny Williams was the lucky man with the Johnny Mercer/Henry Mancini classic 'Moon River' and the university group from Connecticut, the Highwaymen, repeated their US success with 'Michael' – both number one in the UK. Floyd Cramer, pianist on many of Presley's hits had a week at the top with 'On The Rebound' and surfaced again playing coathanger on Jimmy Dean's year-end talkie smash 'Big Bad John.' The Everly Brothers had number one hits with 'Walk Right Back,' (helped more than a little by the death-tinged flip 'Ebony Eyes') and with a revival of the 1933 Freed-Brown standard 'Temptation.' And Frankie Vaughan reached the summit with a cover of the Bacharach/Hilliard US hit for Gene McDaniels, 'Tower Of Strength.' Others to register strongly on the singles chart without the magic number one credit included Billy Fury, Bobby Darin, Bobby Vee, Duane Eddy and the Allisons (who failed to win Eurovision and failed to top the UK charts by just one place in each case). Adam Faith was still making an impact and Andy Stewart (of kilt fame) spent 53 weeks on the singles chart without getting beyond number 19.

Frank Sinatra, without making an outstanding new album (by his standards) had a great 12 months in the albums charts, partly because he switched labels to his own outfit, Reprise, which resulted in his previous companies putting out a lot of old stuff (with great success) onto the market. He was second to Elvis in this department, one place ahead of the George Mitchell Minstrels whose *Black and White Minstrel Show* was one of the TV and disc phenomena of the early 60s. Cliff and the late Buddy Holly had good album sales all year, as did the already mentioned jazz boys Barber and Bilk, and MOR king Ray Conniff. 'South Pacific' notched up another 49 chart weeks (only a few at the very top) and 'Oklahoma' and 'The King And I' made Richard Rodgers (and of course Oscar Hammerstein) even richer.

EP-wise it was Cliff, Elvis and the Shadows in that order, and though several other artists managed more than a year's worth of weeks on the EP charts, it must be said that those three names were the most important in UK pop as what was to be the Beatles chart début year began.

Prominent during the trad boom that peaked at the end of 1961, Mr. Acker BILK also starred in the film *Band of Thieves* (Above). Also involved were Carol Deene and another important figure in Sixties music, Norrie Paramor.

Chris BARBER and his JAZZ BAND.

The TORNADOS.

1962

Of course we all now know that the most significant chart event of 1962 was the appearance of Parlophone R 4949 at position 49 on the singles chart of 11 October. But at the time the Beatles were not as important as the Tornados, enjoying their second successive week at number one with 'Telstar,' and the most important event of 1962 seemed to have been the Twist. Even by the end of the year 'Love Me Do' had got no higher than number 17, and with Elvis having taken over from the Tornados on 13 December, it looked like nothing had changed – or was going to.

'Telstar' was probably Joe Meek's greatest creation. The doomed, neurotic, independent record producer made a host of memorable pop singles in the early 60s in an age when the vast majority of hits were produced by in-house A & R men employed by the major record companies that dominated the UK music business. Meek was always ahead of his time. He even owned his own label, Triumph, which only survived a few months in 1960, but which produced one Top Ten hit 'Angela Jones' by Michael Cox. In 1961 Joe's biggest hit as a producer had been John Leyton's 'Johnny Remember Me.' The Tornados were Billy Fury's backing group at the time Meek decided to record them. Their first single flopped, but the second was one of the biggest British hit singles recorded up to that point. 'Telstar' not only settled into the number one position in the UK for 5 weeks, it repeated that success in the USA, over a year before the Beatles cracked the American market. Two or three years before Phil Spector's Wall Of Sound emerged, Joe Meek's recordings were instantly recognisable by their sound alone. His production techniques, coupled with an astute choice of material (often, like 'Telstar,' composed by Meek himself) gave him a long string of chart success from 1960 until 1966 (his final hit, the year before he died, was 'Please Stay' by the Cryin' Shames).

'Telstar' was an instrumental (inspired by the communications satellite of the same name launched that year) and was the leader of a strong pack of wordless platters that hit in 1962. Two others made number one on the singles lists – the demented and irresistable assault on Tchaikowsky by B. Bumble and The Stingers, 'Nut Rocker,' and 'Wonderful Land' by the Shadows, now into their third straight big year. 'Wonderful Land' was the second of only three discs in the 60s to hold the top spot for 8 weeks. But all these instrumentals were outsold by Acker Bilk's wistful clarinet piece 'Stranger On The Shore,' a tune that the trad jazzman wrote for a TV series and which outsold any jazz recording he ever made. This single entered the charts in November 1961, and was still there in November 1962 – an unbroken run of 55 weeks in the top 50. This was easily a record then, and has only been beaten once since – by Engelbert Humperdinck (see 1967). 'Stranger On The Shore' was also a hit in the States, as was Acker's fellow jazzer Kenny Ball's 'Midnight In Moscow,' a 1962 number 2 on both sides of the pond. Bilk went all the way to number one in the US, but the best of his 55 weeks in Britain were three in second place.

Traditional jazz was still popular but its demise was hastened by the almost overnight arrival of the Twist. The Twist meant mainly Chubby Checker, and the former chicken-plucker Ernest Evans had five hit singles during 1962. Most spectacular of these was 'Let's Twist Again' which had been released in summer '61 to only moderate acclaim. When it returned to the lists in December 1961 it came back in style, for 6 months, peaking at number two. Chubby's even older 'The Twist' also re-entered the charts. Other twisters sold a lot of records thanks to this dance craze, notably Sam Cooke and Joey Dee and the Starliters. Even Elvis sub-titled 'Rock-a-Hula Baby' a 'Twist Special.'

Chubby CHECKER will always be remembered for the Twist.

11

Presley himself had a number one every time out in 1962. All four of his single releases swept all opposition aside and his 'Blue Hawaii' soundtrack and his 'Pot Luck' album both topped the LP charts. Despite these achievements (and there was no question of any waning in his popularity) he had to take second place (just) in the final album table to the George Mitchell Minstrels, and was some way behind both Acker Bilk and Chubby Checker in the singles tally.

Cliff began 1962 with his fastest selling single to date, 'The Young Ones.' This came into the chart at number one and held there for 6 weeks. Two number twos and a single destined to hit the very top in '63 followed it. As ever, Norrie Paramor produced both Cliff Richard and Shadows recordings and Norrie's achievements with these and other acts in 1962 entitled the distinguished producer/arranger/composer to be considered recording personality of the year. For 26 weeks his discs were at number one. In 1961 he had discovered Helen Shapiro (who still sold a lot of records throughout 1962) – in 1962 he delivered the goods with Frank Ifield. 'I Remember You' was number one for 7 weeks in July, August and September, and the follow-up 'Lovesick Blues' did the same for 5 weeks in November and December.

Mike Sarne (helped by Wendy Richard) launched a career that was to go well beyond the confines of the hit parade thanks to an amusing novelty entitled 'Come Outside' – a chart-topper in June and July. The great blues singer Ray Charles had his only British number one with a track from his acclaimed album 'Modern Sounds In Country and Western' – Don Gibson's 'I Can't Stop Loving You.' Only 12 records climbed to the top all year, four by Presley, four from the Norrie Paramor stable, four miscellaneous.

Other acts of great importance on the singles scene were Billy Fury, Joe Brown, Del Shannon, Roy Orbison, Bobby Vee, Pat Boone, Neil Sedaka and Karl Denver. The last-named sold well with his début album too. Others featuring prominently in the LP charts behind the Black and White Minstrels and Elvis were Cliff and the Shadows (together and also the Shadows on their own), Frank Sinatra and Buddy Holly. The success of a TV show *The Roaring Twenties* brought considerable disc fame to one of its stars, Dorothy Provine, in 1962 – mainly in the album field.

The Shadows had the not-so-important EP market sewn up, averaging over three EPs in the Top Twenty for every week of the year. Fellow Norrie Paramor stars Cliff and Helen came second and third in this department. In June Elvis Presley equalled the Shadows' 1961 achievement of heading all three sales charts at the same time.

In case you wondered – yes, 'South Pacific' was on the album chart all year. 'West Side Story' (film soundtrack) was another musical biggie.

Mike SARNE and Wendy RICHARD recorded one of the biggest novelty songs of the sixties.

Five leaping dancers plus one dustbin lid and tenement block equals *West Side Story*.

Mitzi GAYNOR was responsible for one of the most popular songs from the *South Pacific* sound track, 'I'm In Love With A Wonderful Guy'. *Ronald Grant Archive.*

1963

In 1963 it all happened. Or rather the Beatles happened and the greatest explosion of talent in British record history changed the music business irrevocably, delivering a death-blow to many distinguished careers and launching as many new ones.

The Beatles' popularity reached hysterical proportions very early in 1963, but strange to relate they had to wait until May to have a number one hit single, and they were not even the first Merseyside group to win that honour – Gerry and the Pacemakers got there on April 11 with 'How Do You Do It.'

The old guard dominated the singles charts until Gerry's big moment. The first six new chart-toppers of the year included three instrumentals (two from the Shadows, one from a Shadows breakaway combo, Jet Harris and Tony Meehan) and five of the six were Norrie Paramor productions – besides the Shads, Cliff had two and Frank Ifield one. Ifield's hit was his third number one in as many releases; he was the first British artist to achieve this. But after 11 April, the next instrumental number one was to be in November 1968, and Paramor was destined to have one more 1963 number one only (via Ifield) and then a wait until Cliff got there again in 1965.

Once the Beatles hit, they hit. Their third, fourth and fifth singles were all near-instant number ones and the sales of both 'She Loves You' and 'I Want To Hold Your Hand' were well over a million. Perhaps more significant was the fact that their début album 'Please Please Me' took over the LP chart number one spot. It stayed there 30 weeks and was only deposed by their own second album 'With The Beatles.' In their wake groups poured out of the cellars and clubs of nearly every major city. The Searchers, Gerry, The Fourmost, The Swinging Blue Jeans and Billy J Kramer from Liverpool; the Hollies and Freddie and the Dreamers from Manchester; Brian Poole and The Tremeloes, the Dave Clark Five and the Rolling Stones from London. Many, many more were to follow.

Gerry and his group hit number one with the first three singles they ever released – a feat still unequalled. They were produced, as were the Beatles and Billy J Kramer (one 1963 number one), by George Martin, who went one better than Norrie Paramor had in 1962 by being responsible for 27 weeks of the year's chart toppers. The Searchers brought even more glory Liverpool's way via 'Sweets For My Sweet' and Brian Poole kept the southern flag flying by taking his version of 'Do You Love Me' all the way, fighting off a rival recording by the Dave Clark Five in the process.

Some pre-Beatles acts survived the onslaught, but many more went to the wall. Elvis had a bad year by his standards – three of his four singles failed to make the Top Ten and his only number one 'Devil In Disguise' stayed there for a brief 7 days. Cliff and the Shadows were affected less, but by the end of 1963 it was fairly clear that for the first time a new

In 1963 the BEATLES took over all the charts. Here they relax with a couple of fans while on tour in London.

GERRY and THE PACEMAKERS on tour in Blackpool.

recording act had emerged to replace the Cliff/Shads combination as the most important in the hearts of the young record-buyers. In terms of weeks in the singles charts there was little to choose between the Beatles, Cliff, the Shadows and Frank Ifield at the year's end, but everyone knew that the world had changed.

The US music business had a ghastly time in the UK in 1963, only Elvis getting to number one with a single, and that just for 1 week.

Americans who did pull through included Del Shannon and Roy Orbison, both making superb pop records in their own highly individual style which owed nothing to the British beat boom – though Roy Orbison toured with the Beatles and Shannon covered 'From Me To You' for the US market before the Beatles themselves got there in early 1964. Brenda Lee had an excellent year with her country-tinged weepie ballads. A major femme record star of the immediate future had her first hit towards the end of 1963 – Dusty Springfield, who boldly left the successful (by pre-Beatles standards) Springfields group in the summer. The reliable Billy Fury suffered little or no loss of public affection – after all he was from Liverpool too.

1963 was also the year in which the Spector sound first made a noise – the Crystals made number two with 'Then He Kissed Me' and both they and the Ronettes had another top five single as well. It was still possible for more conventional records from the States to hit in the UK, however – Andy Williams and Ned Miller proved that point.

The weeks on chart tables for the EPs and LPs in 1963 are clearly not a true reflection of the impact made by the Mersey groups in general and by the Beatles in particular. The Beatles produced the two major albums of 1963, as discussed, but many stalwarts such as Cliff and the Shadows, Elvis Presley, Buddy Holly and Frank Ifield shifted a lot of LP product over the counters too. Even the Black and White Minstrels still had some steam left in them and good old 'South Pacific' clocked up another 45 weeks.

The EP of the year was without doubt the Beatles' 'Twist And Shout.' This sold in unprecedented quantities for an EP throughout the summer, and had it been included in the *Record Retailer* singles chart it would have got to the top or very near the top. It also would have had the effect of putting the Beatles way ahead of Cliff in the singles weeks table. As it was 'Twist And Shout' spent 16 weeks as number one EP (5 more still to come in 1964) and Brian Poole and the Tremeloes' version of the song had a free run at the singles chart, peaking at four. The Shadows had enough EPs out on the market to keep any normal act in royalties for at least three years. Needless to say, the Beatles on many occasions were number one in all three charts at once.

Frank IFIELD who from July 1962 through to July 1963 had four number one singles out of five consecutive releases.

Phil Spector's first impression on the UK charts was through the CRYSTALS.

1964

The revolution in British music that had taken place in 1963 was consolidated at home and taken to the USA in 1964. The events in the States are not the concern of this tome, but the British record-buying public for the first time ever could feel that they were at the centre of the world of popular music, that they heard first what millions around the globe would have to wait just a week or two longer to hear. The Beatles of course carried on as they had in 1963, dominating sales figures and every chart, no matter what the speed or size of the disc, but many other fine talents made their presence felt.

As it happened, it was only on the EP front that the Beatles actually spent more time on the charts than any other act. Their singles tended to sell so quickly that lengthy tenures on the best-selling lists were ruled out, and they simply did not have quite as much album product out as Jim Reeves whose death in a plane crash in July resulted in no less than nine posthumous hit albums before the end of the year. Jim was doing pretty well before his unfortunate demise, with two strong singles 'I Love You Because' and 'I Won't Forget You,' as well as two big albums to his credit, but as has happened so often, fatal disaster meant an emotional sales surge.

Despite Reeves' enormous popularity, the singles charts were beat-dominated. They were also UK-dominated, only Roy Orbison (twice) and the Supremes carving their way through the British groups to number one. Even this dismal Stateside performance was an improvement on 1963 when one solitary week of Elvis was all the colonies could manage. Elvis himself had a reasonable chart year in 1964, but owed a fair proportion of what success he had to old material issued on single for the first time. It was Orbison beyond all doubt who kept music-lovers' faith in US pop going, producing a sequence of marvellous singles that culminated in one of his biggest ever, 'Oh Pretty Woman.' His 'In Dreams' album remained on the charts for the entire year to boot. Gene Pitney also made quite an impact that had begun towards the end of '63 with his classic interpretation of Bacharach and David's 'Twenty-four Hours From Tulsa' and Motown had their first British smashes thanks to Mary Wells and the Supremes.

In January the Dave Clark Five knocked the Beatles off the top spot with 'Glad All Over.' The British media had just about cottoned on to the fact that the Beatles were big news but clearly were still in a confused state about what Dave's feat actually meant. Many assumed, ludicrously, that the Beatles were now "out" and the DC5 "in." The DC5 were fairly in for quite a while with their home public but for some reason were never as big here as they were in America, where they were to spend more and more of their time between 1964 and 1967. Despite further number one smashes from the Searchers and Billy J Kramer, and the emergence of important, talented groups such as Manfred Mann, the Animals and Kinks during

Roy ORBISON who carried the stars and stripes in UK chart throughout 1964. He had little support from his fellow Americans, although Elvis still managed a reasonable 1964.

The Tottenham Sound. The Dave CLARK FIVE had the distinction of toppling the Beatles from the top of the chart in January with 'Glad All Over.'

15

the year, it was soon evident that the only true challengers to the Beatles were the Rolling Stones, promoted initially as the antithesis of the lovable moptops that the Beatles were in danger of becoming. The Stones had minor hits in 1963, but it was not until their fourth single in Summer 1964, that they made number one, with 'It's All Over Now.' But by then they had already had a number one album with their début package, a much more important achievement. Indeed only the Beatles and Stones made number one on the LP charts all year. The final two number one singles of 1964 were by the Stones (their second) and the Beatles (their sixth).

Besides the names already mentioned, other big-selling singles acts of '64 included Cilla Black (two chart-toppers), Peter and Gordon (tops with a Lennon-McCartney song), the Bachelors (against the tide, enormously successful with old-fashioned ballads), Herman's Hermits, the Four Pennies, the Honeycombs and the Hollies. In October, Sandie Shaw became the year's second number one female vocalist (before Cilla the previous had been Helen Shapiro back in 1961) and Dusty Springfield fulfilled all the promise she had shown when her solo career had begun so well in late 1963. Cliff and the Shadows kept going with virtually no loss of popularity, but the Shadows lost much of their record sales power.

Most of the acts who sold plenty of singles seemed to have plenty album and EP clout too, so for the first time in the decade there was quite a similarity in the three final "most weeks" tables. Yet again the Beatles topped all three charts at once several times during the year, but not even that came near their staggering accomplishment in the US Hot 100 in April when they held down places 1, 2, 3, 4 and 5 simultaneously.

Dusty SPRINGFIELD fulfilled all her early promise as a solo artist. *Below* The HONEYCOMBS who featured, unusually, a girl drummer.

1965

1965, like 1964, began and ended with a Beatles single and a Beatles album at the top of the respective charts. The Beatles consolidated their position as rock's premier current act, if not as the entire entertainment business' premier current act, with almost everything they did in 1965, producing some of their greatest songs and recordings with what seemed like effortless skill. 'I Feel Fine' and 'Beatles For Sale' were in pole positions in January; in December it was 'Day Tripper'/'We Can Work It Out' and 'Rubber Soul'; there had been a wealth of great music in between.

The only two acts that really approached the Beatles for popularity and/or influence were the Rolling Stones and Bob Dylan. Indeed no act but these three and 'The Sound Of Music' soundtrack topped the album charts from 11 May 1963 until the Monkees managed it on 4 February 1967. The Stones' three 1965 smash singles were as strong a consecutive trio of releases as any act has ever issued – 'The Last Time,' 'Satisfaction' and 'Get Off Of My Cloud' – all number one,

naturally. Their first album's chart run of a year was still in progress when their second album's 37-week stretch began in January and in the autumn their third collection was only kept from the very top by Julie Andrews and the gang. Jagger and Co. twice equalled the Beatles 1963 and 1964 feat of simultaneous number ones in all three charts. And the Beatles did it again too, three times.

Dylan went electric in 1965, with electric results. Never before considered a singles artist, he had five hit singles (four Top Ten) in quick succession and his rock albums brought him a vast new audience. His back product returned to the album charts with such impact that the record his first rock album, 'Bringing It All Back Home' replaced at number one was his own much older 'Freewheelin'.' His songs were covered by a multitude of artists, notably by Manfred Mann and the Byrds, who sold even more singles than the composer himself with their versions of Dylan masterpieces. He influenced the Beatles, John Lennon in particular, just as they had influenced him.

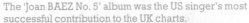

The KINKS built on their successful 1964 chart début with five top 20 singles in 1965.

Although these three acts were by some distance the most important of the period, 1965 produced many other success stories. Phil Spector had his finest hour to date with 'You've Lost That Lovin Feelin'' by the unknown Righteous Brothers, whose soulful rendition of what was to become a pop standard, coupled with Spector's masterful production, pushed aside the cover version by the much better-known Cilla Black. Elvis returned to the top of the singles heap with a track he had recorded back in 1960, the religious tear-jerker 'Crying In The Chapel,' a hit for the Orioles in 1953. There was still a reasonable demand for most of his material, but so much of it was sub-standard or had been recorded many years before, that Presley had little chance of matching the achievements of the year's Big Three.

The 'Joan BAEZ No. 5' album was the US singer's most successful contribution to the UK charts.

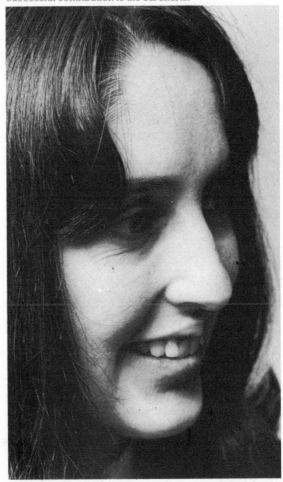

Roger Miller took a semi-novelty 'King Of The Road' to number one, and the other American chart-toppers were Sonny and Cher with 'I Got You Babe.' They made an extra-ordinary visual and musical impact when they arrived in London to promote the single. They soon found themselves with four hit singles at once, as one old record together and one other solo single each raced into the best-sellers on the coat-tails of the Spector-influenced 'I Got You Babe'.

The Everly Brothers made a most welcome return to the singles stratosphere when, helped by a tour, 'The Price Of Love' climbed to number two. Andy Williams was another US citizen who only failed by one position to top the singles list – with a song appropriately called 'Almost There.'

Other Brits to hit big on 45 included the Kinks, following on from their powerful chart début in 1964, the Moody Blues (the original pre-concept album line-up) with their only number one single 'Go Now,' the Hollies, who reached number one for the first time with their eighth hit out of eight, Unit 4 + 2 (whose writing team came up with a stunning song few acts could have matched when it came to a follow-up. The song was 'Concrete And Clay' and Unit 4 + 2 didn't), and three blues-

based acts Georgie Fame and the Blue Flames, the Animals (who not surprisingly were never quite able to match the brilliance of their 1964 monster 'House Of The Rising Sun'), and the Yardbirds, still with Eric Clapton in their ranks when they had their first hit. 1965 was the year the Who broke through, most memorably with 'My Generation.' and Wayne Fontana and the Mindbenders, Van Morrison's Them, the Fortunes and even Twinkle were all forces to be reckoned with for at least some of 1965. The weeks champs (singles) for the year, however, were the Seekers, an Australian quartet fronted by the pure voice of Judith Durham, singing melodic and definitely non-rock ballads written by Dusty Springfield's brother Tom. They had three huge singles in 1965, all of which hung around for a long time, two going all the way.

Dusty Springfield herself remained a steady singles seller, but chart-wise she was way behind Sandie Shaw, whose second '65 platter 'Long Live Love' was her second career number one. Sandie had two other Top Ten entries during the year. Jackie Trent was the only other girl to have a number one, with a song she wrote with her husband, Tony Hatch, 'Where Are You Now (My Love).' Hatch had begun the year with another smash that he had both composed and produced for a female vocalist, 'Downtown' at number two. This was internationally the greatest hit of Petula Clark's career, but her immediate follows-ups in the UK were not outstandingly successful. Dylan's close chum Joan Baez was another lady for whom 1965 was a big year, but her success was much greater in both the LP and EP formats than it was in singles.

Cliff, who had never really been away, returned to number one with a country song he had recorded in Nashville, and comedian Ken Dodd had one of the biggest records of the year with a pre-second World War ballad high on corn quotient called 'Tears.' Another big ballad number one was the more contemporary sound of 'Make It Easy On Yourself,' another in the long line of Bacharach/David 60s hits, performed by three American teen heart throbs based in Britain, the Walker Brothers. A voice that was to be enormous in the MOR stakes for the next two decades was first heard on the hit parade in 1965 – that of Tom Jones, who looked down upon the rest of the singles pile with 'It's Not Unusual' for one week in March.

Jim Reeves and Elvis still sold a good many albums, and Roy Orbison still had a good following in all departments. The Tamla-Motown sound, by now a massive force in the States, meant very little in the UK in 1965. Dylan beat the Beatles and Stones into second and third place on the album weeks table, mainly because he had so many more LPs in the shops than the British groups. He was hard to find on EP however (where the Beatles and Stones reigned supreme) except as an author eg on the brilliant Manfred Mann EP 'The One In The Middle' which owed much of its great success to Paul Jones' interpretation of Dylan's 'With God On Our Side.'

But perhaps the artist of the year was Julie Andrews. She

A buccaneering Tom JONES whose success began in 1965 with his first hit single making number one.

Starring in both Walt Disney's *Mary Poppins* and *The Sound of Music* made Julie ANDREWS a major album artist of the year. *Ronald Grant Archive.*

starred on the soundtrack album of 'Mary Poppins' which entered the charts in the third week of the year and was still there, having peaked at two, in the fifty-second. Then on 10 April 1965 the soundtrack album of 'The Sound Of Music,' also starring Julie, made its first appearance on the charts. By the end of the year it had already notched up 20 weeks at number one, at the start of what was to be the longest stay on the British LP charts by any disc, ever.

1966

In 1966, the Beatles/Dylan/Stones triumvirate was challenged by the Beach Boys who hitherto had not come near their huge US success in the UK. Now, however, they were as powerful as any other act in both single and album markets. Their major work of the year, the LP 'Pet Sounds,' was unable to break through the Beatles/Stones/Von Trapp Family number one barrier, but it came as close as any album by any other act did. They actually wound up the year's album weeks champions, and nearly repeated the feat singles-wise, losing out by one place to the highly entertaining but not highly significant pop group Dave Dee, Dozy, Beaky, Mick and Tich. The Californian surfers produced what for many was the single of the year, 'Good Vibrations.'

Dave Dee and his pals were an unpretentious combo who had first made the Top Fifty (singles) in the final weeks of 1965. In 1966, they came up with four new Top Ten singles in succession, all written by their managers, Ken Howard and Alan Blaikley. They were never to have more than fleeting visits to the LP or American charts, but proved masters of the instant single for the British fan. Another act with much of their appeal was another group from the West Country, the Troggs. Their discs, notably the immortal 'Wild Thing,' were much more basic than DDDBMT's, but were above all fun. The Troggs managed to reach number one with their second single, penned by their lead singer Reg Presley (né Ball), and also found favour in the States.

1966 was definitely a year in which rock and MOR slugged it out with honours ending more or less even. There were several huge singles that owed little to the Beatles-led revolution including number ones by Dusty Springfield, Jim Reeves and Tom Jones, and other gentler acts such as Val Doonican, Ken Dodd, Cilla Black and the Seekers were important factors in record companies' balance sheets. Even some of the rock acts were not as aggressive as yesteryear, the Kinks, Mindbenders and Manfred Mann all straying some way from their musical origins to produce in each case some of the best and biggest recordings of their careers. Manfred survived the traumatic change of lead singer (Paul Jones left, Mike d'Abo came) unscathed.

The Sinatra clan made an astonishing mark on the singles chart. Nancy, Frank's daughter, shot to number one with

In 1966 the United States fought back with the BEACH BOYS.

Nancy SINATRA with those boots.

'These Boots Are Made For Walkin'' in February, which provided her with the impetus for quite a reasonable recording career over the next 5 years. Even more unexpected was Frank's own return to disc glory with one of the biggest hits of his life, 'Strangers In The Night.' This put Frank at the top for most of June, for the first time in 12 years.

The Walker Brothers had their second number one in three outings in the spring with Scott's voice in immaculate form on 'The Sun Ain't Gonna Shine Anymore.' It looked as though the American trio were all set for superstardom (before the word was coined) but the choice of material for their subsequent singles was surprisingly misjudged and they failed to live up to their potential. Gene Pitney, operating with better songs in a similar field, had a much stronger year. Another who promised much but in the end gave us a career of only two hit singles was Crispian St Peters. Paul Jones (who quit Manfred with a number one, 'Pretty Flamingo') did well on his first solo recording.

Away from the slower, melodic stuff, several acts did very well. The Spencer Davis Group, introducing the voice of Stevie Winwood to the world, had two driving number one singles and a number two. Chris Farlowe, helped not a little by Jagger and Richard (writers) and Jagger again (producer) had his finest hour with 'Out Of Time.' (So did the Overlanders with the Beatles' 'Michelle' but Paul McCartney was nowhere near the studio when they covered the 'Rubber Soul' ballad). Back to rock – the Small Faces and their seniors in the mod-rock mould, the Who, both had great years. The Who, destined never to reach number one on the UK singles chart, were by now clearly one of rock's most important acts, though their elevation to near god-like status with 'Tommy' was still three years away.

The Motown stable at last broke through in Britain. The Four Tops put the seal on what had been a gradually improving year for the US megalabel when they raced to number one on the singles list with 'Reach Out I'll Be There.' The Supremes did well too, as did Stevie Wonder, and to a lesser extent the Temptations. The Lovin' Spoonful and the Mamas and the Papas were other popular imports from across the Atlantic, and particularly as far as albums were concerned, Herb Alpert and his Tijuana Brass. Soul greats Otis Redding, Wilson Pickett, James Brown and Ike and Tina Turner were all hitmakers in 1966, the last-named giving Phil Spector his last major success with his Wall Of Sound – 'River Deep Mountain High.'

Cliff Richard had yet another strong year, and even Elvis (né Presley) held his own with releases of slightly better quality than had been his lot in 1965. But the Beatles were still kings, just that significant step ahead of the Stones. Dylan's chart statistics were not up to his 1965 standard, but his music was until a mysterious motor-cycle accident silenced him for nearly 2 years.

The EP market was dwindling fast and facts and figures there did not mean much in 1966. 'The Sound Of Music' spent the

WALKER BROTHERS. Scott is the one at the back and the one at the front is neither John nor Gary.

1966 saw the arrival of many Motown records in the UK charts. Ahead of the pack were the FOUR TOPS.

whole year on the album chart including over half of that time at number one.

1967

1967 was "Flower Power" year, the year of peace and dope and love. The Beatles (as usual) were in the lead and at the centre of things, their album 'Sergeant Pepper's Lonely Hearts Club Band' and single 'All You Need Is Love' being two of the most important recordings to reflect this trend, which actually had several million hippies and semi-hippies believing for a while that human nature was about to be permanently improved by the youth movement.

The Beatles began 1967 with the almost forgotten experience (for them) of not having a number one hit single when a record now regarded as one of their greatest, 'Strawberry Fields Forever'/'Penny Lane' was checked at number two by the former Arnold Dorsey, now reborn as Engelbert Humperdinck. A million miles from the flowers and pot, Engelbert was the biggest-selling singles artist of the year, all done with romantic ballads and more often than not in evening dress. His stablemate and fellow balladeer Tom Jones was not far behind in singles sales and both belters were shipping hundreds of thousands of albums to the stores and thence to the fans, too. But Liverpool's finest finished the year at full steam with 'Hello Goodbye' in the middle of a 7-week stretch at the top and their double EP 'Magical Mystery Tour' on its way up to a simultaneous number two.

It was ironic that the Beatles EP should have sold so well when it did, because a week before it was released, *Record Retailer* discontinued the EP chart because of the almost total lack of interest the public and business had been showing in EPs. Despite 'Magical Mystery Tour,' which was thus forced to register on the singles chart, this was a wise decision as the demand for the four-track 45 had all but disappeared.

The Stones got a bit lost in 1967, in trouble with the law and unwisely deserting their true musical roots to follow the psychedelic trends with which they were never really at home. With Dylan incapacitated, there was no act to come near the Beatles' stature, although one brand new act did so in terms of sales.

They were a manufactured group called the Monkees, four actors signed up by Columbia Pictures to feature in a TV series about a wacky pop group that just happened to be rather like the Beatles had been in their first year of American fame. Whether the producers intended it or not, the four boys turned out to be rather talented, if not quite in the Beatles league, and they deserve a good deal of the credit for their enormous success on disc (and on TV) all over the world. Their second single 'I'm A Believer' was number one just as soon as all the instant Monkees fans could get to the shops after seeing the first programme in the series. Their two

The ROLLING STONES deserted their true musical roots in 1967 and dabbled with psychedelia.

The manufactured MONKEES take time off from filming the TV show.

albums of the year were both chart-toppers, and there even 'proved to be considerable writing talents within their ranks (notably Mike Nesmith and Micky Dolenz). What was more, one Monkee (the cute one), Davy Jones, was English. They wound up third behind Engelbert and Tom in the final singles weeks list, and third too, album-wise.

Perhaps here yet more about the incredible Hump. His first hit beat Acker Bilk's 1961-2 record of 55 consecutive weeks on the charts, 'Release Me' hanging in there for 56 weeks. His total of 97 chart weeks for 1967 was the highest by any act in 1 year in the entire decade.

The two acts to spend more time on the LP charts than the Monkees were the Beach Boys (mainly greatest hits compilations) and Herb Alpert (lotsa brass on lotsa LPs). The Beach Boys, like the Stones, did not have an inspired year and were fortunate that their superb back catalogue served them so well.

Two very important rock acts made their first mark in 1967, the Jimi Hendrix Experience and the Cream. Both had singles success, but they were obviously best understood in the longer format and as such were already some way down the route that nearly all important rock acts would take in the seventies. All the same , Jimi Hendrix, the wild man of rock, the "Black Elvis," the guitar genius, went out on tour with Engelbert and the Walker Brothers which showed that in 1967 there were still people around, even if it was only the concert promoters, who had no idea that pop and rock music was already moving in several very different directions at once.

Many other MOR acts scored in this year of mind-expanding music and substances. Petula Clark, Sandie Shaw (with her Eurovision winner 'Puppet On A String' becoming the first and still the only solo lady to have had three UK number one singles), Frank and Nancy Sinatra in tandem, the Tremeloes (sans Brian Poole), the Dave Clark Five, Long John Baldry, Vince Hill, Harry Secombe and Vikki Carr were just some of those who hit with the most innocent of material. More relevance to the revolution could be found in Scott McKenzie's tribute to the place where it all began, 'San Francisco (Be Sure To Wear Some Flowers In Your Hair)' but even that could have been warbled beautifully by Engelbert.

Procol Harum, descendants of a group that never quite made it in 1963-4, the Paramounts, had a world-wide smash with the stunning 'A Whiter Shade Of Pale' which owed a lot to Bach, the soulful voice of Gary Brooker and the obscure lyrics by Keith Reid. That certainly sounded good when one was not totally in one's skull, but more important, just as good more than 15 years later.

Soul music and Motown consolidated well. Otis Redding and Wilson Pickett retained their popularity in 1967, with newer US names such as Sam and Dave and Arthur Conley also making their presence felt. Homegrown soul from Geno Washington on albums was also tremendously popular. In November, a new act called the Foundations broke through

PROCOL HARUM in their 1967 finery.

22

with a pop-soul number one 'Baby Now That I've Found You' written by Tony Macaulay (destined to have many pop smashes in succeeding years) and John McLeod. They were replaced at number one by another Macaulay/McLeod hit by Long John Baldry. Nearly all major Motown stars could expect healthy sales with each release, with the Four Tops being particularly potent.

1967 was the début year of fame and fortune for what was to prove one of the most important acts of the rock era – the Bee Gees, whose 'Massachusetts,' their third hit, was their first number one. Keith West, on loan from his psychedelic group, Tomorrow, who never made it, had a huge hit with 'Excerpt From A Teenage Opera.' The opera never materialised.

Others that mattered were the Move, who never dabbled with anything resembling ballads, Cat Stevens, Traffic (Stevie Winwood's new outfit), the Dubliners (on album and in places where they drink) and old reliables such as the Kinks, Hollies and Cliff. Elvis had a pretty ghastly year and the great Shadows their last single hit for nearly 8 years.

And once again, 'The Sound Of Music' sat in the LP chart all year, with 13 weeks at the top. 'Dr Zhivago' was another film soundtrack everpresent. For the record, the final EP chart had 'The Beach Boys Hits' at number one.

The album sound track from *Dr Zhivago* remained on the chart for the whole of 1967. Omar Sharif and Julie Christie are shown above. *Ronald Grant Archive.*

1968

1968 ran 1967 close in the corn stakes – in fact with the rock world losing direction, producing no startling new acts or trends, it could be argued that '68 was the least memorable year of the decade. That is not to say there were no good records about.

The three acts that spent most time on the singles chart were Tom Jones, Engelbert Humperdinck and Des O'Connor, in that order, Tom and Engelbert thus reversing their 1967 placings. O'Connor, up until this point more famous as a comedian, sang the kind of big ballad that had brought the two MAM-managed artists such success, but a little more gently. He had three enormous hit singles, the second of which 'I Pretend,' written by the team that had provided Humperdinck and Jones with many of their biggest ballads, Les Reed and Barry Mason, was the most popular, reaching the very top and staying on the charts for 9 months. Jones also spent a good deal more time on the album charts than anyone else, his 135 album chart weeks in 1968 being the most any act logged in any one year in the 60s. 'Delilah' (Reed-Mason again), his first single of the year, is one of those singles that everyone thinks went to number one, but didn't. Nonetheless it is probably the song most identified with him. Engelbert too, got no further than number two with any one single, his 'A Man Without Love' being his near-miss for '68.

Also operating in the lush fields of MOR was Cliff Richard,

One Gibb and his dog. Barry and the BEE GEES began their chart success in 1967.

who celebrated his tenth anniversary in the music business by returning to the number one position for the first time since 'The Minute You're Gone' in 1965. He did this with his entry for the Eurovision Song Contest, 'Congratulations,' written by another very prolific pair of British songwriters, Phil Coulter and Bill Martin, who had also been the pens behind Sandie Shaw's Eurovision hit of 1967. Cliff, unlike Sandie, failed to win the contest (he came second to a Spanish lady named Massiel) but in terms of world-wide record sales, his disc was the smash of the show. As all Cliff's hits had been, 'Congratulations' was produced by Norrie Paramor, who hit number one again at the end of the year at the controls of the Scaffold's 'Lily The Pink.' This quasi-novelty smash was to be Paramor's 27th and final number one, a total that was unequalled until 1984 when Paul McCartney's 'Pipes Of Peace' became George Martin's 27th chart-topping production.

Other number ones as far away from hard rock as Cliff, Des and the Scaffold were singles by Esther and Abi Ofarim, Louis Armstrong (who became the oldest ever number one act) and Mary Hopkin, though Mary's huge international success 'Those Were The Days' was produced by none other than Paul McCartney, who had spotted the talented Welsh songstress on "Opportunity Knocks." Mary Hopkin's single was one of the four released when the Beatles launched their own label, Apple, in the late summer. Another of the four was 'Hey Jude,' even by Beatles standards a classic recording. This 7-minute plus epic proved to be one of their most popular songs yet and came at a perfect time, for their previous single 'Lady Madonna' (though still a number one) and their first attempt at film-making, *Magical Mystery Tour,* just before that, had not been well received in all quarters. No-one doubted in 1968 that the Beatles were still the world's number one recording act, but it was good to know that they were still capable of something like 'Hey Jude.' At the end of the year they released their first double album 'The Beatles' (better known as the White Album) which sped effortlessly to the premier position.

The Rolling Stones too had something to prove after a less than spectacularly successful 1967. They managed this with a fine single in the style of their biggest hits, 'Jumpin' Jack Flash,' (their only single of '68) and an album that went right back to their rock and blues roots, 'Beggars Banquet.'

Dave Dee, Dozy, Beaky, Mick and Tich, in their third and final year as major record sellers, had their first and only number one single with 'The Legend Of Xanadu.' The Bee Gees and the Beach Boys both had their second, the hits being for both acts something of a comeback after a period of mediocre sales. Manfred Mann had his third number one (but his first with Mike d'Abo at the mike) as did Georgie Fame. Manfred's 'Mighty Quinn' was a Bob Dylan song and soon after it hit, Dylan himself re-emerged with his first album of new material for two years, 'John Wesley Harding.' It gave Dylan his first number one album in 3 years.

Over on the album lists, 'The Sound Of Music' spent its third

The SCAFFOLD gave producer Norrie Paramor his 27th and final number one.

Mary HOPKIN recorded one of the most memorable songs about nostalgia, 'Those Were The Days'.

calendar year on the trot as an ever-present. It still managed to make guest appearances in the top slot, which was becoming a more slippery perch than ever before. A dozen acts were up there in '68. Tom Jones, Andy Williams and Val Doonican made it, as did Scott Walker, with his second solo LP since the Brothers broke up. Three acts did it with Greatest Hits collections – the Hollies, the Four Tops and Diana Ross and the Supremes. No hits package had ever gone all the way before, and the Four Tops, the first of the three to do so, scored another and more important first by being the first black act to be number one in the UK album charts.

The late Otis Redding, killed in a plane crash at the end of 1967, had no less than 121 weeks on the album chart in 1968. He became the first solo black performer to have a number one LP ('The Dock Of The Bay') and would probably have done so anyway had he lived. Jimi Hendrix and his group had a very strong album year.

Simon and Garfunkel, just two years away from their master-piece 'Bridge Over Troubled Water,' were number one with 'Bookends.' The Small Faces' 'Ogden's Nut Gone Flake' was not head of the herd for 6 weeks just because it had a circular sleeve. The first supergroup Cream, had two huge LP successes and the Moody Blues began their phenomenal run of monster concept albums.

In a year which certainly had variety, other forces on disc included Lulu (who had been doing pretty well since 1964, but '68 was her best thus far), Love Affair (who gave the press a field day when it was revealed that they had not played their instruments on their first hits), Herman's Hermits (again, hardly been away since '64), the Herd (with a young Peter Frampton, "the face of '68," in their ranks), and the Equals (with a young Eddy Grant). Joe Cocker came right to the fore in November with his stunning interpretation of the Lennon-McCartney ballad 'With A Little Help From My Friends' and the great Nina Simone's version of two songs from 'Hair' brought her to the attention of many singles buyers for the first time. Then there were fleeting hours of glory for the Casuals, Barry Ryan, Leapy Lee, Tommy James and the Shondells, Gary Puckett and the Union Gap, the 1910 Fruitgum Company . . .

Elvis made one or two singles that actually showed signs of life in the studio and on the singles chart, but had just one week on the LP chart all year, a shame shared by the George Mitchell Minstrels whose Black and White bonanza had faded.

And the music-lovers of 1968 certainly showed independence of spirit when they sent an instrumental single to number one for the first time in 5 years – Hugo Montenegro's Clint Eastwood pic theme 'The Good, The Bad And The Ugly.'

Joe COCKER's distinctive style of singing was immortalised in the film of the 1969 Rock Festival *Woodstock*.

Clint EASTWOOD in *The Good, The Bad And The Ugly*. *Ronald Grant Archive.*

1969

The final year of the sixties was just like the previous three in that 'The Sound Of Music' was on the album chart for all 52 weeks. The soundtrack LP, which was well on its way to becoming the longest-running UK chart LP of all time, failed to spend any of 1969 at the very top (its last appearance at number one turned out to be for the week of 23 November 1968) but entered the 70s with many weeks and a lot of steam left. The soundtrack of Lionel Bart's 'Oliver' was also a blockbuster in 1969.

The Seekers, who had broken up for good in 1967, finished 1969 as the LP weeks winners, thanks mainly to a retrospective album of their greatest recordings. They were a short head clear of Simon and Garfunkel who had no new release during 1969 and yet established themselves as one of the most important album acts throughout the 12 months; many of their past recordings returned to the charts, with their 1968 package 'The Graduate' soundtrack (virtually a greatest hits album) to the fore.

Cream, another group who had just called it a day, had a great send-off from their fans in the form of their first number one – for their farewell LP, 'Goodbye.' Heavyweight rock groups with a distinguished career still ahead of them made their first significant impact in 1969 – such as Jethro Tull and Led Zeppelin. The Moody Blues had their first number one album. The Rolling Stones survived the sacking and death of Brian Jones, made a triumphant appearance in a free concert in Hyde Park, released a second collection of greatest hits and had their first number one album for three and a half years when 'Let It Bleed' became number one in the week of its release in December. They obviously faced the 70s as powerful as they had ever been.

The Beatles too wound up the 60s in appropriate style – at the head of the album lists with their tenth number one LP in ten releases (not counting greatest hit collections or imports). They also notched up their 16th and 17th number one singles during 1969, taking them two ahead of Elvis in this respect. (Elvis was to catch up by 1977). Whatever the tensions within the group, the Beatles in 1969 were still in a class of their own.

Elvis himself made a magnificent comeback in 1969. He produced two of the best singles of his career ('In The Ghetto' and 'Suspicious Minds') and was unlucky in that both peaked at two. His late-1968 TV special gave him a summer 1969 soundtrack smash, and he came back all the way on the LP scene when his first decent new studio collection for years 'From Elvis In Memphis' hit the position (numero uno) he had last graced in 1962 with 'Pot Luck.' Cliff Richard had an unremarkable year, but managed to log 39 weeks on the singles chart (in this he tied with both Elvis and the Beatles) and to become the only act to be in the Top Ten singles act for every year of the 60s. Bob Dylan went country for his one release of the year, the LP 'Nashville Skyline,' which hit the top

Mark Lester as *Oliver. Ronald Grant Archive.*

A true super group, CREAM. *Left to right* Bruce, Clapton and Baker.

26

and spawned two hit singles, one 'Lay Lady Lay', his biggest since 'Like A Rolling Stone' in 1965.

Other artists to shift a lot of albums in the first year that saw albums earn more than singles for retailers and record companies were easy-listening king Ray Conniff, the unforgotten Jim Reeves, and several Motown acts.

The singles chart duration list was headed jointly by Fleetwood Mac and Frank Sinatra. Fleetwood Mac – at that point led by guitarist Peter Green and far removed from the AOR sound that a revamped line-up was to do so well with from the mid-seventies on – had three enormous hits of great variety. The first, 'Albatross' was the first guitar instrumental to reach number one since the heyday of the Shadows, and has since become a classic. The second, 'Man Of The World,' had a reflective lyric which is about all it had in common with Sinatra's 'My Way,' the disc responsible almost single-handed for the veteran's great chart year. It entered the chart in April where it stayed for 42 weeks, the third longest run of all time. In 8 subsequent returns to the chart it eventually racked a record 122 weeks.

Stevie Wonder and the Isley Brothers represented Motown in third and fourth place on the singles weeks lists, and after the already reported three-way tie between Elvis, Cliff and the Beatles, new US rock giants Creedence Clearwater Revival (two monsters in 'Proud Mary' and 'Bad Moon Rising'), the Bee Gees and Engelbert Humperdinck registered healthily, as did top singles girl Clodagh Rodgers.

Other pop acts to be there or thereabouts for all or some of the year included Amen Corner, Marmalade, the Move (1969 gave them their only number one), Peter Sarstedt and a clutch of one-hit wonders: Zager and Evans, Jane Birkin and Serge Gainsbourg (grunts and groans of French passion) and studio concoction the Archies. Tommy Roe of 1962 and 'Sheila' fame, shot back with an unexpected bang with 'Dizzy.' Bobbie Gentry went all the way with a song from *Promises Promises* a Bacharach/David musical, 'I'll Never Fall In Love Again' and the year finished with one of Britain's favourite Aussies, Rolf Harris, in the middle of a marathon six week run at the top with his tear-jerker 'Two Little Boys.' The 70s were thus ushered in with the most conservative of sounds singles-wise.

Let us not forget the good year enjoyed by old names Dean Martin, Lulu, Herman and Tremeloes. Above all, note must be made of two superb number ones by black artists, 'I Heard It Through The Grapevine' by Marvin Gaye, and reggae's first huge break-through 'Israelites' by Desmond Dekker and the Aces.

SIMON and GARFUNKEL's 'Mrs Robinson' was Anne Bancroft whose leg is seen here with a youthful Dustin Hoffman. *Ronald Grant Archive.*

Marvin GAYE had little success in the UK charts until the last year of the decade.

Comparison Statistics

Most weeks on the charts: one hundred or more weeks on each chart

Only eight acts spent over 100 weeks on each of the charts – singles, EPs and LPs – during the sixties, as follows:

	Weeks on chart			
	Singles	EPs	LPs	Total
Cliff Richard	537	432	337	1306
Elvis Presley	444	365	462	1271
Beatles	333	392	435	1160
Shadows	303	461	221	985
Beach Boys	193	108	338	639
Rolling Stones	181	154	225	560
Roy Orbison	309	101	119	529
Seekers	120	166	203	489

Shadows totals do not include weeks spent on the charts backing Cliff Richard

The annual chart champions for the sixties are as follows:

	Singles	EPs	LPs
1960	Cliff Richard	Cliff Richard	Elvis Presley
1961	Elvis Presley	Cliff Richard	Elvis Presley
1962	Mr Acker Bilk	Shadows	George Mitchell Minstrels
1963	Beatles Cliff Richard	Shadows	Cliff Richard
1964	Jim Reeves	Beatles	Jim Reeves
1965	Seekers	Beatles	Bob Dylan
1966	Dave Dee, Dozy, Beaky, Mick and Tich	Beatles	Beach Boys
1967	Engelbert Humperdinck	Seekers	Herb Alpert
1968	Tom Jones	–	Tom Jones
1969	Fleetwood Mac Frank Sinatra	–	Seekers

Cliff Richard (twice), Elvis Presley and Jim Reeves achieved champion status in two out of three categories in one year. Tom Jones, in 1968, was both singles and albums champion, and there was no EP chart to produce a champion in that category.

Cliff Richard and the Seekers won all three categories at least once, but never all in the same year.

Most hits: ten or more on each chart

Only three acts had at least ten hit singles, ten hit EPs and ten hit LPs during the sixties, as follows:

	Hit Singles	Hit EPs	Hit LPs	Total
Cliff Richard	45	23	24	92
Elvis Presley	42	15	29	86
The Beatles	23	12	13	48

(Note: The Shadows 25 singles, 19 EPs, 7 LPs, to which could be added the 18 LPs they featured on with Cliff Richard).

Number one hits in all three charts in the sixties

Number of number one hits

	Singles	LPs	EPs	Total
Beatles	17	10	8	35
Elvis Presley	11	4	5	20
Rolling Stones	8	4	3	15
Cliff Richard	7	3	4	14
Shadows	5	2	4	11
Seekers	2	1	2	5
Four Tops	1	1	1	3

The Beach Boys had number one singles and EPs in the sixties, but could only climb as high as number two on the LP charts in that decade. In the seventies, they finally hit number one on the LP charts, and are the only act outside those listed above ever to have hit the top on all three charts at any time in the history of the British charts.

Number one hits on all three charts in the same week

This feat has been performed 25 times, but by only four acts in all.

Date	Act	No. 1 Single	No. 1 LP	No. 1 EP
5 Oct 61	Shadows	Kon-Tiki	The Shadows	Shadows To The Fore
14 Jun 62	Elvis Presley	Good Luck Charm	Blue Hawaii	Follow That Dream
12 Sep 63	Beatles	She Loves You	Please Please Me	Twist And Shout
19 Sep 63	Beatles	She Loves You	Please Please Me	Twist And Shout
26 Sep 63	Beatles	She Loves You	Please Please Me	Twist And Shout
28 Nov 63	Beatles	She Loves You	Please Please Me	Twist And Shout
5 Dec 63	Beatles	She Loves You	With The Beatles	Twist And Shout
12 Dec 63	Beatles	I Want To Hold Your Hand	With The Beatles	Twist And Shout
19 Dec 63	Beatles	I Want To Hold Your Hand	With The Beatles	Twist And Shout
26 Dec 63	Beatles	I Want To Hold Your Hand	With The Beatles	Twist And Shout
2 Jan 64	Beatles	I Want To Hold Your Hand	With The Beatles	Twist And Shout
9 Jan 64	Beatles	I Want To Hold Your Hand	With The Beatles	Twist And Shout
2 Apr 64	Beatles	Can't Buy Me Love	With The Beatles	All My Loving
9 Apr 64	Beatles	Can't Buy Me Love	With The Beatles	All My Loving
16 Apr 64	Beatles	Can't Buy Me Love	With The Beatles	All My Loving
23 Jul 64	Beatles	A Hard Day's Night	A Hard Day's Night	Long Tall Sally
30 Jul 64	Beatles	A Hard Day's Night	A Hard Day's Night	Long Tall Sally
6 Aug 64	Beatles	A Hard Day's Night	A Hard Day's Night	Long Tall Sally
10 Dec 64	Beatles	I Feel Fine	Beatles For Sale	A Hard Day's Night
17 Dec 64	Beatles	I Feel Fine	Beatles For Sale	A Hard Day's Night
7 Jan 65	Beatles	I Feel Fine	Beatles For Sale	A Hard Day's Night
25 Mar 65	Rolling Stones	The Last Time	Rolling Stones No. 2	Five By Five
1 Apr 65	Rolling Stones	The Last Time	Rolling Stones No. 2	Five By Five
29 Apr 65	Beatles	Ticket To Ride	Beatles For Sale	Beatles For Sale
6 May 65	Beatles	Ticket To Ride	Beatles For Sale	Beatles For Sale

The feat of topping two of the three charts during the sixties was achieved very many times. The most significant achievement in this category was by the ROLLING STONES, who topped both the LP and EP charts with discs entitled 'Rolling Stones', for 10 consecutive weeks from 2 May 1964.

The domination of the charts by the BEATLES at the end of 1963 and the beginning of 1964 was without equal in the history of the charts. Apart from having the number one best-selling single, album and EP for 7 weeks from 28 November 1963, they also had for those entire 7 weeks the number two and number three best-selling EPs and the number two slot on the LP charts. For 3 weeks from 12 December 1963, they had the top two singles (I Want To Hold Your Hand and She Loves You), the top two LPs (With The Beatles and Please Please Me) and the top three EPs (Twist And Shout, The Beatles' Hits and The Beatles (No. 1)).

ALMOST THERE

Right: CONTRASTS: Following up his success as pin-up of page 93 in the third edition of British Hit Singles, Bill Forbes emerges from the wood as a member of the unsuccessful Contrasts.

Far right: Johnny CARR and the CADILLACS: Originally started in Bristol in 1958 as a rock 'n' roll group and had a track record of frequently changing vocalists though each one retained the name Johnny Carr. Their closest hit was in 1965 with 'Do You Love That Girl'.

Centre: Elmer GANTRY'S VELVET OPERA: Championed regularly on John Peel's BBC Radio show Top Gear, they narrowly missed the charts with the powerful 'Flames'. Members Richard Hudson and John Ford went on to join the Strawbs and subsequently Hudson-Ford while Elmer Gantry evolved into Stretch and scored with 'Why Did You Do It?'

Below: UNDERTAKERS: Representing the many Mersey groups who didn't make it. The Undertakers appeared in a 1963 documentary along with the Beatles and sang 'Mashed Potato'. After shortening their name to the Takers, lead singer Jackie Lomax went on to form the Lomax Alliance before releasing solo singles on the Apple label.

The SINGLES

The following section lists, by artist, all the acts who had hit singles during the period from 1 January 1960 to 31 December 1969, and the singles with which they found success. Each single has the following information with it; title, label and catalogue number, highest position reached and number of weeks spent on the chart.

The first nine charts of 1960 used in this book were those of the **NME** (a Top Thirty).

The **Record Retailer** Top Fifty chart began on 10 March 1960 and continued in that format for the rest of the decade.

As in all the books, in this series, if ever a week went by without a chart being published the previous week's chart was used again. The dates in this book vary slightly from the dates used in the Album section. For a full explanation of this see note on page 6.

★ Number one single
● Top Ten single

Contents

Hit singles alphabetically by artist

Date	Title Label Number	Position
3 Jul 68	● THIS GUY'S IN LOVE WITH YOU A & M AMS 727	**3** 16 wks
26 Mar 69	THIS GUY'S IN LOVE WITH YOU (re-entry) A & M AMS 727	**47** 1 wk
9 Apr 69	THIS GUY'S IN LOVE WITH YOU (2nd re-entry) A & M AMS 727	**49** 1 wk
7 May 69	THIS GUY'S IN LOVE WITH YOU (3rd re-entry) A & M AMS 727	**50** 1 wk
18 Jun 69	WITHOUT HER A & M AMS 755	**36** 5 wks

Spanish Flea, Tijuana Taxi, Casino Royale, and Without Her *credit Herb Alpert and The Tijuana Brass.* The Lonely Bull *credits only The Tijuana Brass. Alpert vocalises on* This Guy's in Love with You *and* Without Her.

AMEN CORNER

UK, male vocal/instrumental group

Date	Title Label Number	Position
26 Jul 67	GIN HOUSE BLUES Deram DM 136	**12** 10 wks
11 Oct 67	WORLD OF BROKEN HEARTS Deram DM 151	**26** 6 wks
17 Jan 68	● BEND ME SHAPE ME Deram DM 172	**3** 12 wks
31 Jul 68	● HIGH IN THE SKY Deram DM 197	**6** 13 wks
29 Jan 69	★ (IF PARADISE IS) HALF AS NICE Immediate IM 073	**1** 11 wks
25 Jun 69	● HELLO SUZIE Immediate IM 081	**4** 10 wks

AMERICAN BREED

US, male vocal/instrumental group

Date	Title Label Number	Position
7 Feb 68	BEND ME SHAPE ME Stateside SS 2078	**24** 6 wks

Moira ANDERSON

UK, female vocalist

Date	Title Label Number	Position
27 Dec 69	HOLY CITY Decca F 12989	**43** 2 wks

Chris ANDREWS

UK, male vocalist

Date	Title Label Number	Position
7 Oct 65	● YESTERDAY MAN Decca F 12236	**3** 15 wks
2 Dec 65	TO WHOM IT CONCERNS Decca F 22285	**13** 10 wks
14 Apr 66	SOMETHING ON MY MIND Decca F 22365	**45** 1 wk
28 Apr 66	SOMETHING ON MY MIND (re-entry) Decca F 22365	**41** 2 wks
2 Jun 66	WHATCHA GONNA DO NOW Decca F 22404	**40** 4 wks
25 Aug 66	STOP THAT GIRL Decca F 22472	**36** 4 wks

Bobby ANGELO and the TUXEDOS

UK, male vocal/instrumental group

Date	Title Label Number	Position
10 Aug 61	BABY SITTIN' HMV POP 892	**30** 6 wks

ANGELS

US, female vocal group

Date	Title Label Number	Position
3 Oct 63	MY BOYFRIEND'S BACK Mercury AMT 1211	**50** 1 wk

Date	Title Label Number	Position

A

ACES — See *Desmond DEKKER & the ACES*

Cliff ADAMS

UK, orchestra

Date	Title Label Number	Position
28 Apr 60	LONELY MAN THEME Pye International 7N 25056	**39** 2 wks

Jewel AKENS

US, male vocalist

Date	Title Label Number	Position
25 Mar 65	THE BIRDS AND THE BEES London HLN 9954	**29** 8 wks

Richard ALLAN

UK, male vocalist

Date	Title Label Number	Position
24 Mar 60	AS TIME GOES BY Parlophone R 4634	**44** 1 wk

ALLISONS

UK, male vocal duo

Date	Title Label Number	Position
23 Feb 61	● ARE YOU SURE Fontana H 294	**2** 16 wks
18 May 61	WORDS Fontana H 304	**34** 5 wks
15 Feb 62	LESSONS IN LOVE Fontana H 362	**30** 6 wks

ALL-STARS — See *Junior WALKER and the ALL-STARS*

Herb ALPERT

US, male instrumentalist - trumpet

Date	Title Label Number	Position
3 Jan 63	THE LONELY BULL Stateside SS 138	**22** 9 wks
9 Dec 65	● SPANISH FLEA Pye International 7 N 25335	**3** 20 wks
24 Mar 66	TIJUANA TAXI Pye International 7 N 25352	**37** 4 wks
27 Apr 67	CASINO ROYALE A & M AMS 700	**27** 14 wks

ASSOCIATION Originally called 'The Men'.

ALLISONS *Left* Bob and John from London's Parsons Green singing the British entry for the Eurovision Song Contest at Cannes on 18 March, 1961.

Frankie AVALON *Right* Originally inspired by the trumpet playing of Harry James in the 50's film *Young Man With A Horn,* he took up the instrument and by the age of 13 was playing American theatres as 'The Boy Wizard of the Horn.'

Date	Title *Label Number*	Position

ANIMALS

UK, male vocal/instrumental group

Date	Title *Label Number*	Position	
16 Apr 64	**BABY LET ME TAKE YOU HOME** *Columbia DB 7247*	21	8 wks
25 Jun 64 ★	**HOUSE OF THE RISING SUN** *Columbia DB 7301*	1	12 wks
17 Sep 64 ●	**I'M CRYING** *Columbia DB 7354*	8	10 wks
4 Feb 65 ●	**DON'T LET ME BE MISUNDERSTOOD** *Columbia DB 7445*	3	9 wks
8 Apr 65 ●	**BRING IT ON HOME TO ME** *Columbia DB 7539*	7	11 wks
15 Jul 65 ●	**WE'VE GOTTA GET OUT OF THIS PLACE** *Columbia DB 7639*	2	12 wks
28 Oct 65 ●	**IT'S MY LIFE** *Columbia DB 7741*	7	11 wks
17 Feb 66	**INSIDE - LOOKING OUT** *Decca F12332*	12	8 wks
2 Jun 66 ●	**DON'T BRING ME DOWN** *Decca F 12407*	6	8 wks

See also Eric Burdon

Paul ANKA

Canada, male vocalist

Date	Title *Label Number*	Position	
1 Jan 60	**PUT YOUR HEAD ON MY SHOULDER** *Columbia DB 4355*	17	3 wks
26 Feb 60	**IT'S TIME TO CRY** *Columbia DB 4390*	28	1 wk
31 Mar 60	**PUPPY LOVE** *Columbia DB 4434*	33	4 wks
14 Apr 60	**IT'S TIME TO CRY** (re-entry) *Columbia DB 4390*	47	1 wk
5 May 60	**PUPPY LOVE** (re-entry) *Columbia DB 4434*	37	3 wks
15 Sep 60	**HELLO YOUNG LOVERS** *Columbia DB 4504*	44	1 wk
15 Mar 62	**LOVE ME WARM AND TENDER** *RCA 1276*	19	11 wks
26 Jul 62	**A STEEL GUITAR AND A GLASS OF WINE** *RCA 1292*	41	4 wks

Richard ANTHONY

France, male vocalist

Date	Title *Label Number*	Position	
12 Dec 63	**WALKING ALONE** *Columbia DB 7133*	37	5 wks
2 Apr 64	**IF I LOVED YOU** *Columbia DB 7235*	48	1 wk
23 Apr 64	**IF I LOVED YOU** (re-entry) *Columbia DB 7235*	18	9 wks

APHRODITE'S CHILD

Greece, male vocal/instrumental group

Date	Title *Label Number*	Position	
6 Nov 68	**RAIN AND TEARS** *Mercury MF 1039*	30	7 wks

APPLEJACKS

UK, male/female vocal/instrumental group

Date	Title *Label Number*	Position	
5 Mar 64 ●	**TELL ME WHEN** *Decca F 11833*	7	13 wks
11 Jun 64	**LIKE DREAMERS DO** *Decca F 11916*	20	11 wks
15 Oct 64	**THREE LITTLE WORDS** *Decca F 11981*	23	5 wks

ARCHIES

US, male/female vocal group

Date	Title *Label Number*	Position	
11 Oct 69 ★	**SUGAR SUGAR** *RCA 1872*	1	26 wks

Louis ARMSTRONG

US, male band leader/trumpet and vocals

Date	Title *Label Number*	Position	
4 Jun 64 ●	**HELLO DOLLY** *London HLR 9878*	4	14 wks
7 Feb 68 ★	**WHAT A WONDERFUL WORLD**/ **CABARET** *HMV POP 1615*	1	29 wks
26 Jun 68	**SUNSHINE OF LOVE** *Stateside SS 2116*	41	7 wks

Cabaret was not listed with What a Wonderful World until 14 Feb 68.

Eddy ARNOLD

US, male vocalist

Date	Title *Label Number*	Position	
17 Feb 66 ●	**MAKE THE WORLD GO AWAY** *RCA 1496*	8	17 wks
26 May 66	**I WANT TO GO WITH YOU** *RCA 1519*	49	1 wk
9 Jun 66	**I WANT TO GO WITH YOU** (re-entry) *RCA 1519*	46	2 wks
28 Jul 66	**IF YOU WERE MINE MARY** *RCA 1529*	49	1 wk

P. P. ARNOLD

US, female vocalist

Date	Title *Label Number*	Position	
4 May 67	**FIRST CUT IS THE DEEPEST** *Immediate IM 047*	18	10 wks
2 Aug 67	**THE TIME HAS COME** *Immediate IM 055*	47	2 wks
24 Jan 68	**GROOVY** *Immediate IM 061*	41	4 wks
10 Jul 68	**ANGEL OF THE MORNING** *Immediate IM 067*	29	11 wks

ASSOCIATION

US, male vocal/instrumental group

Date	Title *Label Number*	Position	
22 May 68	**TIME FOR LIVING** *Warner Bros. WB 7195*	23	8 wks

Chet ATKINS

US, male instrumentalist - guitar

Date	Title *Label Number*	Position	
17 Mar 60	**TEENSVILLE** *RCA 1174*	46	1 wk
5 May 60	**TEENSVILLE** (re-entry) *RCA 1174*	49	1 wk

Winifred ATWELL

UK, female instrumentalist - piano

Date	Title *Label Number*	Position	
1 Jan 60	**PIANO PARTY** *Decca F 11183*	15	2 wks

Piano Party was a medley of the following hits: Baby Face/ Comin' Thru The Rye/ Annie Laurie/ Little Brown Jug/ Let Him Go Let Him Tarry/ Put Your Arms Around Me Honey/ I'll Be With You In Apple Blossom Time/ Shine On Me Harvest Moon/ Blue Skies/ I'll Never Say Never Again/ I'll See You In My Dreams.

Brian AUGER — See Julie DRISCOLL, Brian AUGER and the TRINITY

Frankie AVALON

US, male vocalist

Date	Title *Label Number*	Position	
22 Jan 60	**WHY** *HMV POP 688*	20	4 wks
28 Apr 60	**DON'T THROW AWAY ALL THOSE TEARDROPS** *HMV POP 727*	37	4 wks

Date	Title *Label Number*	Position		Date	Title *Label Number*	Position	

AVONS

UK, male/female vocal group

1 Jan 60	● SEVEN LITTLE GIRLS SITTING IN THE BACK SEAT *Columbia DB 4363*	3	6 wks
7 Jul 60	WE'RE ONLY YOUNG ONCE *Columbia DB 4461*	45	2 wks
27 Oct 60	FOUR LITTLE HEELS *Columbia DB 4522*	45	3 wks
26 Jan 61	RUBBER BALL *Columbia DB 4569*	30	4 wks

Bob AZZAM

Egypt, singing orchestra

26 May 60	MUSTAPHA *Decca F 21235*	23	14 wks

B

Alice BABS

Sweden, female vocalist

15 Aug 63	AFTER YOU'VE GONE *Fontana TF 409*	43	1 wk

Burt BACHARACH

US, orchestra and chorus

20 May 65	● TRAINS AND BOATS AND PLANES *London HL 9928*	4	11 wks

BACHELORS

Ireland, male vocal group

24 Jan 63	● CHARMAINE *Decca F 11559*	6	19 wks
4 Jul 63	FARAWAY PLACES *Decca F 11666*	36	3 wks
29 Aug 63	WHISPERING *Decca F 11712*	18	10 wks
23 Jan 64	★ DIANE *Decca F 11799*	1	19 wks
19 Mar 64	● I BELIEVE *Decca F 11857*	2	17 wks
4 Jun 64	● RAMONA *Decca F 11910*	4	13 wks
13 Aug 64	● I WOULDN'T TRADE YOU FOR THE WORLD *Decca F 11949*	4	16 wks
3 Dec 64	● NO ARMS CAN EVER HOLD YOU *Decca F 12034*	7	12 wks
1 Apr 65	TRUE LOVE FOR EVER MORE *Decca F 12108*	34	6 wks
20 May 65	● MARIE *Decca F 12156*	9	12 wks
28 Oct 65	IN THE CHAPEL IN THE MOONLIGHT *Decca F 12256*	27	10 wks
6 Jan 66	HELLO DOLLY *Decca F 12309*	38	4 wks
17 Mar 66	● THE SOUND OF SILENCE *Decca F 12351*	3	13 wks
7 Jul 66	CAN I TRUST YOU *Decca F 12417*	26	7 wks
1 Dec 66	WALK WITH FAITH IN YOUR HEART *Decca F 22523*	22	9 wks
6 Apr 67	OH HOW I MISS YOU *Decca F 22592*	30	8 wks
5 Jul 67	MARTA *Decca F 22634*	20	9 wks

Joan BAEZ

US, female vocalist

6 May 65	WE SHALL OVERCOME *Fontana TF 564*	26	10 wks
8 Jul 65	● THERE BUT FOR FORTUNE *Fontana TF 587*	8	12 wks
2 Sep 65	IT'S ALL OVER NOW BABY BLUE *Fontana TF 604*	22	8 wks
23 Dec 65	FAREWELL ANGELINA *Fontana TF 639*	35	3 wks
20 Jan 66	FAREWELL ANGELINA (re-entry) *Fontana TF 639*	49	1 wk
28 Jul 66	PACK UP YOUR SORROWS *Fontana TF 727*	50	1 wk

Long John BALDRY

UK, male vocalist

8 Nov 67	★ LET THE HEARTACHES BEGIN *Pye 7N 17385*	1	13 wks
28 Aug 68	WHEN THE SUN COMES SHININ' THRU *Pye 7N 17593*	29	7 wks
23 Oct 68	MEXICO *Pye 7N 17563*	15	8 wks
29 Jan 69	IT'S TOO LATE NOW *Pye 7N 17664*	21	8 wks

Kenny BALL and his JAZZMEN

UK, male band, Kenny Ball vocals and trumpet

23 Feb 61	SAMANTHA *Pye Jazz Today 7NJ 2040*	13	15 wks
11 May 61	I STILL LOVE YOU ALL *Pye Jazz 7NJ 2042*	24	6 wks
31 Aug 61	SOMEDAY *Pye Jazz 7NJ 2047*	28	6 wks
9 Nov 61	● MIDNIGHT IN MOSCOW *Pye Jazz 7NJ 2049*	2	21 wks
15 Feb 62	● MARCH OF THE SIAMESE CHILDREN *Pye Jazz 7NJ 2051*	4	13 wks
17 May 62	● THE GREEN LEAVES OF SUMMER *Pye Jazz 7NJ 2054*	7	14 wks
23 Aug 62	SO DO I *Pye Jazz 7NJ 2056*	14	8 wks
18 Oct 62	THE PAY OFF *Pye Jazz 7NJ 2061*	23	6 wks
17 Jan 63	● SUKIYAKI *Pye Jazz 7NJ 2062*	10	13 wks
25 Apr 63	CASABLANCA *Pye Jazz 7NJ 2064*	21	11 wks
13 Jun 63	RONDO *Pye Jazz 7NJ 2065*	24	8 wks
22 Aug 63	ACAPULCO 1922 *Pye Jazz 7NJ 2067*	27	6 wks
11 Jun 64	HELLO DOLLY *Pye Jazz 7NJ 2071*	30	7 wks
19 Jul 67	WHEN I'M 64 *Pye 7N 17348*	43	2 wks

BAND

Canada, male vocal/instrumental group

18 Sep 68	THE WEIGHT *Capitol CL 15559*	21	9 wks

BANDWAGON

US, male vocal group

16 Oct 68	● BREAKIN' DOWN THE WALLS OF HEARTACHE *Direction 58-3670*	4	15 wks
5 Feb 69	YOU *Direction 58-3923*	34	4 wks
28 May 69	LET'S HANG ON *Direction 58-4180*	36	6 wks

BEATLES *Above* Captured in wax.

BACHELORS *Left* John, Conleth and Declan whose big break came when they were spotted touring with Nina and Frederick in 1962. *Hey Girls!* an early biog reveals that Con likes Chinese food and pink shirts, Dec likes spaghetti and unusual ties and John likes fry-ups and blue socks.

Dave BERRY *Below* Indicates to the judges his marks out of ten for Jimmy Page's guitar work on 'The Crying Game.'

Len BARRY The former lead singer of American group the Dovells found making the Top Ten was not as easy as '1-2-3.'

Date	Title *Label Number*	Position	Date	Title *Label Number*	Position

Chris BARBER'S JAZZ BAND

UK, male band, Chris Barber trombone

Date	Title	Position	
4 Jan 62	**REVIVAL** *Columbia SCD 2166*	50	2 wks
1 Feb 62	**REVIVAL** (re-entry) *Columbia SCD 2166*	43	2 wks

BAR-KAYS

US, male vocal/instrumental group

23 Aug 67	**SOUL FINGER** *Stax 601 014*	33	7 wks

BARRON KNIGHTS

UK, male vocal/instrumental group

9 Jul 64	● **CALL UP THE GROUPS** *Columbia DB 7317*	3	13 wks
22 Oct 64	**COME TO THE DANCE** *Columbia DB 7375*	42	2 wks
25 Mar 65	● **POP GO THE WORKERS** *Columbia DB 7525*	5	13 wks
16 Dec 65	● **MERRY GENTLE POPS** *Columbia DB 7780*	9	7 wks
1 Dec 66	**UNDER NEW MANAGEMENT** *Columbia DB 8071*	15	9 wks
23 Oct 68	**AN OLYMPIC RECORD** *Columbia DB 8485*	35	4 wks

Joe BARRY

US, male vocalist

24 Aug 61	**I'M A FOOL TO CARE** *Mercury AMT 1149*	49	1 wk

John BARRY

UK, male instrumental group/orchestra

10 Mar 60	● **HIT AND MISS** *Columbia DB 4414*	10	12 wks
28 Apr 60	**BEAT FOR BEATNIKS** *Columbia DB 4446*	40	2 wks
9 Jun 60	**HIT AND MISS** (re-entry) *Columbia DB 4414*	45	1 wk
14 Jul 60	**NEVER LET GO** *Columbia DB 4480*	49	1 wk
18 Aug 60	**BLUEBERRY HILL** *Columbia DB 4480*	34	3 wks
8 Sep 60	**WALK DON'T RUN** *Columbia DB 4505*	49	1 wk
22 Sep 60	**WALK DON'T RUN** (re-entry) *Columbia DB 4505*	11	13 wks
8 Dec 60	**BLACK STOCKINGS** *Columbia DB 4554*	27	9 wks
2 Mar 61	**THE MAGNIFICENT SEVEN** *Columbia DB 4598*	48	1 wk
16 Mar 61	**THE MAGNIFICENT SEVEN** (re-entry) *Columbia DB 4598*	45	2 wks
6 Apr 61	**THE MAGNIFICENT SEVEN** (2nd re-entry) *Columbia DB 4598*	50	1 wk
8 Jun 61	**THE MAGNIFICENT SEVEN** (3rd re-entry) *Columbia DB 4598*	47	1 wk
26 Apr 62	**CUTTY SARK** *Columbia DB 4816*	35	2 wks
1 Nov 62	**JAMES BOND THEME** *Columbia DB 4898*	13	11 wks
21 Nov 63	**FROM RUSSIA WITH LOVE** *Ember S 181*	44	1 wk
19 Dec 63	**FROM RUSSIA WITH LOVE** (re-entry) *Ember S 181*	39	2 wks

Billed as the John Barry Seven on Hit and Miss, Walk Don't Run, Black Stockings, The Magnificent Seven *and* Cutty Sark. *Others John Barry Orchestra.*

Len BARRY

US, male vocalist

4 Nov 65	● **1-2-3** *Brunswick 05942*	3	14 wks
13 Jan 66	● **LIKE A BABY** *Brunswick 05949*	10	10 wks

Count BASIE — See *Frank SINATRA*

Fontella BASS

US, female vocalist

2 Dec 65	**RESCUE ME** *Chess CRS 8023*	11	10 wks
20 Jan 66	**RECOVERY** *Chess CRS 8027*	32	5 wks

Shirley BASSEY

UK, female vocalist

31 Mar 60	**WITH THESE HANDS** *Columbia DB 4422*	38	2 wks
21 Apr 60	**WITH THESE HANDS** (re-entry) *Columbia DB 4422*	31	2 wks
12 May 60	**WITH THESE HANDS** (2nd re-entry) *Columbia DB 4422*	41	2 wks
4 Aug 60	● **AS LONG AS HE NEEDS ME** *Columbia DB 4490*	2	30 wks
11 May 61	● **YOU'LL NEVER KNOW** *Columbia DB 4643*	6	17 wks
27 Jul 61	★ **REACH FOR THE STARS/ CLIMB EV'RY MOUNTAIN**	1	16 wks
23 Nov 61	**REACH FOR THE STARS/ CLIMB EV'RY MOUNTAIN** (re-entry) *Columbia DB 4685*	40	2 wks
23 Nov 61	● **I'LL GET BY** *Columbia DB 4737*	10	8 wks
15 Feb 62	**TONIGHT** *Columbia DB 4777*	21	8 wks
26 Apr 62	**AVE MARIA** *Columbia DB 4816*	34	4 wks
31 May 62	**FAR AWAY** *Columbia DB 4836*	24	12 wks
30 Aug 62	● **WHAT NOW MY LOVE** *Columbia DB 4882*	5	17 wks
28 Feb 63	**WHAT KIND OF FOOL AM I?** *Columbia DB 4974*	47	2 wks
26 Sep 63	● **I (WHO HAVE NOTHING)** *Columbia DB 7113*	6	20 wks
23 Jan 64	**MY SPECIAL DREAM** *Columbia DB 7185*	32	7 wks
9 Apr 64	**GONE** *Columbia DB 7248*	36	5 wks
15 Oct 64	**GOLDFINGER** *Columbia DB 7360*	21	9 wks
20 May 65	**NO REGRETS** *Columbia DB 7535*	39	4 wks
11 Oct 67	**BIG SPENDER** *United Artists UP 1192*	21	15 wks

BEACH BOYS

US, male vocal/instrumental group

1 Aug 63	**SURFIN' USA** *Capitol CL 15305*	34	7 wks
9 Jul 64	● **I GET AROUND** *Capitol CL 15350*	7	13 wks
29 Oct 64	**WHEN I GROW UP (TO BE A MAN)** *Capitol CL 15361*	44	2 wks
19 Nov 64	**WHEN I GROW UP (TO BE A MAN)** (re-entry) *Capitol CL 15361*	27	5 wks
21 Jan 65	**DANCE DANCE DANCE** *Capitol CL 15370*	24	6 wks
3 Jun 65	**HELP ME RHONDA** *Capitol CL 15392*	27	10 wks
2 Sep 65	**CALIFORNIA GIRLS** *Capitol CL 15409*	26	8 wks
17 Feb 66	● **BARBARA ANN** *Capitol CL 15432*	3	10 wks
21 Apr 66	● **SLOOP JOHN B** *Capitol CL 15441*	2	15 wks
28 Jul 66	● **GOD ONLY KNOWS** *Capitol CL 15459*	2	14 wks
3 Nov 66	★ **GOOD VIBRATIONS** *Capitol CL 15475*	1	13 wks
4 May 67	● **THEN I KISSED HER** *Capitol CL 15502*	4	11 wks
23 Aug 67	● **HEROES AND VILLAINS** *Capitol CL 15510*	8	9 wks
22 Nov 67	**WILD HONEY** *Capitol CL 15521*	29	6 wks

Date	Title *Label Number*	Position		Date	Title *Label Number*	Position

Date	Title *Label Number*	Position
17 Jan 68	**DARLIN'** *Capitol CL 15527*	**11** 14 wks
8 May 68	**FRIENDS** *Capitol CL 15545*	**25** 7 wks
24 Jul 68 ★	**DO IT AGAIN** *Capitol CL 15554*	**1** 14 wks
23 Dec 68	**BLUEBIRDS OVER THE MOUNTAIN** *Capitol CL 15572*	**33** 5 wks
26 Feb 69 ●	**I CAN HEAR MUSIC** *Capitol CL 15584*	**10** 13 wks
11 Jun 69 ●	**BREAK AWAY** *Capitol CL 15598*	**6** 11 wks

BEAKY — See *Dave DEE, DOZY, BEAKY, MICK and TICH*

BEATLES

UK, male vocal/instrumental group

Date	Title *Label Number*	Position
11 Oct 62	**LOVE ME DO** *Parlophone R 4949*	**17** 18 wks
17 Jan 63 ●	**PLEASE PLEASE ME** *Parlophone R 4983*	**2** 18 wks
18 Apr 63 ★	**FROM ME TO YOU** *Parlophone R 5015*	**1** 21 wks
29 Aug 63 ★	**SHE LOVES YOU** *Parlophone R 5055*	**1** 31 wks
5 Dec 63 ★	**I WANT TO HOLD YOUR HAND** *Parlophone R 5084*	**1** 21 wks
26 Mar 64 ★	**CAN'T BUY ME LOVE** *Parlophone R 5114*	**1** 14 wks
9 Apr 64	**SHE LOVES YOU** (re-entry) *Parlophone R 5055*	**42** 2 wks
14 May 64	**I WANT TO HOLD YOUR HAND** (re-entry) *Parlophone R 5084*	**48** 1 wk
11 Jun 64	**AIN'T SHE SWEET** *Polydor 52 317*	**29** 6 wks
9 Jul 64	**CAN'T BUY ME LOVE** (re-entry) *Parlophone R 5114*	**47** 1 wk
16 Jul 64 ★	**A HARD DAY'S NIGHT** *Parlophone R 5160*	**1** 13 wks
3 Dec 64 ★	**I FEEL FINE** *Parlophone R 5200*	**1** 14 wks
15 Apr 65 ★	**TICKET TO RIDE** *Parlophone R 5265*	**1** 12 wks
29 Jul 65 ★	**HELP!** *Parlophone R 5305*	**1** 14 wks
9 Dec 65 ★	**DAY TRIPPER/ WE CAN WORK IT OUT** *Parlophone R 5389*	**1** 12 wks
16 Jun 66 ★	**PAPERBACK WRITER** *Parlophone R 5452*	**1** 11 wks
11 Aug 66 ★	**YELLOW SUBMARINE/ ELEANOR RIGBY** *Parlophone R 5493*	**1** 13 wks
23 Feb 67 ●	**PENNY LANE/ STRAWBERRY FIELDS FOREVER** *Parlophone R 5570*	**2** 11 wks
12 Jul 67 ★	**ALL YOU NEED IS LOVE** *Parlophone R 5620*	**1** 13 wks
29 Nov 67 ★	**HELLO GOODBYE** *Parlophone R 5655*	**1** 12 wks
13 Dec 67 ●	**MAGICAL MYSTERY TOUR** (DOUBLE EP) *Parlophone SMMT/ MMT 1*	**2** 12 wks
20 Mar 68 ★	**LADY MADONNA** *Parlophone R 5675*	**1** 8 wks
4 Sep 68 ★	**HEY JUDE** *Apple R 5722*	**1** 16 wks
23 Apr 69 ★	**GET BACK** *Apple R 5777*	**1** 17 wks
4 Jun 69 ★	**BALLAD OF JOHN AND YOKO** *Apple R 5786*	**1** 14 wks
8 Nov 69 ●	**SOMETHING/ COME TOGETHER** *Apple R 5814*	**4** 12 wks

Get Back is 'with Billy Preston', see also Billy Preston. Tracks on Magical Mystery Tour EP; Magical Mystery Tour/ Your Mother Should Know/ I Am The Walrus/ Fool On The Hill/ Flying/ Blue Jay Way. See also Tony Sheridan and the Beatles.

Jeff BECK

UK, male vocalist/instrumentalist - guitar

Date	Title *Label Number*	Position
23 Mar 67	**HI-HO SILVER LINING** *Columbia DB 8151*	**14** 14 wks
2 Aug 67	**TALLYMAN** *Columbia DB 8227*	**30** 3 wks
28 Feb 68	**LOVE IS BLUE** *Columbia DB 8359*	**23** 7 wks

See also Donovan with the Jeff Beck Group.

BEDROCKS

UK, male vocal/instrumental group

Date	Title *Label Number*	Position
18 Dec 68	**OB-LA-DI OB-LA-DA** *Columbia DB 8516*	**20** 7 wks

BEE GEES

UK/Australia male vocal/instrumental group

Date	Title *Label Number*	Position
27 Apr 67	**NEW YORK MINING DISASTER 1941** *Polydor 56 161*	**12** 10 wks
12 Jul 67	**TO LOVE SOMEBODY** *Polydor 56 178*	**50** 1 wk
26 Jul 67	**TO LOVE SOMEBODY** (re-entry) *Polydor 56 178*	**41** 4 wks
20 Sep 67 ★	**MASSACHUSETTS** *Polydor 56 192*	**1** 17 wks
22 Nov 67 ●	**WORLD** *Polydor 56 220*	**9** 16 wks
31 Jan 68 ●	**WORDS** *Polydor 56 229*	**8** 10 wks
27 Mar 68	**JUMBO/ THE SINGER SANG HIS SONG** *Polydor 56 242*	**25** 7 wks
7 Aug 68 ★	**I'VE GOTTA GET A MESSAGE TO YOU** *Polydor 56 273*	**1** 15 wks
19 Feb 69 ●	**FIRST OF MAY** *Polydor 56 304*	**6** 11 wks
4 Jun 69	**TOMORROW TOMORROW** *Polydor 56 331*	**23** 8 wks
16 Aug 69 ●	**DON'T FORGET TO REMEMBER** *Polydor 56 343*	**2** 15 wks

Act was UK only on Don't Forget To Remember.

Harry BELAFONTE and ODETTA

US, male/female vocal duo

Date	Title *Label Number*	Position
21 Sep 61	**HOLE IN THE BUCKET** *RCA 1247*	**32** 2 wks
12 Oct 61	**HOLE IN THE BUCKET** (re-entry) *RCA 1247*	**34** 6 wks

William BELL

US, male vocalist

Date	Title *Label Number*	Position
29 May 68	**TRIBUTE TO A KING** *Stax 601 038*	**31** 7 wks

See also Judy Clay and William Bell.

Cliff BENNETT and the REBEL ROUSERS

UK, male vocal/instrumental group

Date	Title *Label Number*	Position
1 Oct 64 ●	**ONE WAY LOVE** *Parlophone R 5173*	**9** 9 wks
4 Feb 65	**I'LL TAKE YOU HOME** *Parlophone R 5229*	**42** 3 wks
11 Aug 66 ●	**GOT TO GET YOU INTO MY LIFE** *Parlophone R 5489*	**6** 11 wks

Tony BENNETT

US, male vocalist

Date	Title *Label Number*	Position
5 Jan 61	**TILL/ SERENATA** *Philips PB 1079*	**35** 2 wks
18 Jul 63	**THE GOOD LIFE** *CBS AAG 153*	**27** 13 wks
6 May 65	**IF I RULED THE WORLD** *CBS 201735*	**40** 5 wks
27 May 65	**I LEFT MY HEART IN SAN FRANCISCO** *CBS 201730*	**46** 2 wks
30 Sep 65	**I LEFT MY HEART IN SAN FRANCISCO** (re-entry) *CBS 201730*	**40** 5 wks
9 Dec 65	**I LEFT MY HEART IN SAN FRANCISCO** (2nd re-entry) *CBS 201730*	**25** 7 wks
23 Dec 65	**THE VERY THOUGHT OF YOU** *CBS 202021*	**21** 9 wks

Date	Title *Label Number*	Position		Date	Title *Label Number*	Position

Brook BENTON

US, male vocalist

6 Oct 60	**KIDDIO** *Mercury AMT 1109*	**42**	3 wks
3 Nov 60	**KIDDIO** (re-entry) *Mercury AMT 1109*	**41**	3 wks
16 Feb 61	**FOOLS RUSH IN** *Mercury AMT 1121*	**50**	1 wk
13 Jul 61	**BOLL WEEVIL SONG** *Mercury AMT 1148*	**30**	9 wks

Elmer BERNSTEIN

US, orchestra

1 Jan 60	● **STACCATO'S THEME** *Capitol CL 15101*	**4**	8 wks
10 Mar 60	**STACCATO'S THEME** (re-entry) *Capitol CL 15101*	**40**	1 wk

Chuck BERRY

US, male vocalist/guitarist

11 Jul 63	**GO GO GO** *Pye International 7N 25209*	**38**	6 wks
10 Oct 63	● **LET IT ROCK/ MEMPHIS TENNESSEE** *Pye International 7N 25218*	**6**	13 wks
19 Dec 63	**RUN RUDOLPH RUN** *Pye International 7N 25228*	**36**	6 wks
13 Feb 64	**NADINE (IS IT YOU)** *Pye International 7N 25236*	**27**	6 wks
2 Apr 64	**NADINE (IS IT YOU)** (re-entry) *Pye International 7N 25236*	**43**	1 wk
7 May 64	● **NO PARTICULAR PLACE TO GO** *Pye International 7N 25242*	**3**	12 wks
20 Aug 64	**YOU NEVER CAN TELL** *Pye International 7N 25257*	**23**	8 wks
14 Jan 65	**PROMISED LAND** *Pye International 7N 25285*	**26**	6 wks

Dave BERRY

UK, male vocalist

19 Sep 63	**MEMPHIS TENNESSEE** *Decca F 11734*	**19**	13 wks
9 Jan 64	**MY BABY LEFT ME** *Decca F 11803*	**41**	1 wk
23 Jan 64	**MY BABY LEFT ME** (re-entry) *Decca F 11803*	**37**	8 wks
30 Apr 64	**BABY IT'S YOU** *Decca F 11876*	**24**	6 wks
6 Aug 64	● **THE CRYING GAME** *Decca F 11937*	**5**	12 wks
26 Nov 64	**ONE HEART BETWEEN TWO** *Decca F 12020*	**41**	2 wks
25 Mar 65	● **LITTLE THINGS** *Decca F 12103*	**5**	12 wks
22 Jul 65	**THIS STRANGE EFFECT** *Decca F 12188*	**37**	6 wks
30 Jun 66	● **MAMA** *Decca F 12435*	**5**	16 wks

Billed as Dave Berry and The Cruisers on the first two hits.

Mike BERRY with the OUTLAWS

UK, male vocalist with male instrumental backing group

12 Oct 61	**TRIBUTE TO BUDDY HOLLY** *HMV POP 912*	**24**	6 wks
3 Jan 63	● **DON'T YOU THINK IT'S TIME** *HMV POP 1105*	**6**	12 wks
11 Apr 63	**MY LITTLE BABY** *HMV POP 1142*	**34**	7 wks

See also the Outlaws.

BEVERLEY SISTERS

UK, female vocal trio

1 Jan 60	**LITTLE DONKEY** *Decca F 11172*	**16**	1 wk
23 Jun 60	**GREEN FIELDS** *Columbia DB 4444*	**48**	1 wk
7 Jul 60	**GREEN FIELDS** (re-entry) *Columbia DB 4444*	**29**	2 wks

BIG ROLL BAND — See *Zoot MONEY and the BIG ROLL BAND*

BIG SOUND — See *Simon DUPREE and the BIG SOUND*

BIG THREE

UK, vocal/instrumental group

11 Apr 63	**SOME OTHER GUY** *Decca F 11614*	**37**	7 wks
11 Jul 63	**BY THE WAY** *Decca F 11689*	**22**	10 wks

Mr. Acker BILK

UK, male band leader, vocalist/instrumentalist - clarinet

22 Jan 60	● **SUMMER SET** *Columbia DB 4382*	**5**	19 wks
9 Jun 60	**GOODNIGHT SWEET PRINCE** *Melodisc MEL 1547*	**50**	1 wk
18 Aug 60	**WHITE CLIFFS OF DOVER** *Columbia DB 4492*	**30**	9 wks
8 Dec 60	● **BUONA SERA** *Columbia DB 4544*	**7**	18 wks
13 Jul 61	● **THAT'S MY HOME** *Columbia DB 4673*	**7**	17 wks
2 Nov 61	**STARS AND STRIPES FOREVER/ CREOLE JAZZ** *Columbia SCD 2155*	**22**	10 wks
30 Nov 61	● **STRANGER ON THE SHORE** *Columbia DB 4750*	**2**	55 wks
26 Jul 62	**GOTTA SEE BABY TONIGHT** *Columbia SCD 2176*	**24**	9 wks
27 Sep 62	**LONELY** *Columbia DB 4897*	**14**	11 wks
24 Jan 63	**A TASTE OF HONEY** *Columbia DB 4949*	**16**	9 wks

Stranger On The Shore, Lonely and A Taste Of Honey credit Mr Acker Bilk with the Leon Young String Chorale. All others Mr Acker Bilk and his Paramount Jazz Band.

Umberto BINDI

Italy, male vocalist

10 Nov 60	**IL NOSTRO CONCERTO** *Oriole CB 1577*	**47**	1 wk

BIRDS

UK, male vocal/instrumental group

27 May 65	**LEAVING HERE** *Decca F 12140*	**45**	1 wk

Jane BIRKIN and Serge GAINSBOURG

UK/France, female/male vocal duo

30 Jul 69	● **JE T'AIME. . . MOI NON PLUS** *Fontana TF 1042*	**2**	11 wks
4 Oct 69	★ **JE T'AIME. . . MOI NON PLUS** (re-issue) *Major Minor MM 645*	**1**	14 wks

Cilla BLACK *Left* "Hello Mr Epstein . . . Priscilla here! . . . Y'know, from the Cavern . . . Yeah . . . Yer left yer raincoat behind in the cloakroom luv . . . By the way, any chance of an audition?"

BEVERLEY SISTERS *Below* They originally made it in the States billed as 'England's Most Televised Act' omitting to say that not many people had a set! Babs, Joy and Teddy's only 60s hit had 'The Skye Boat Song' on the flipside.

Tony BLACKBURN *Above* The voice of Radio Caroline and Radio One surrounded by fans at a rare public appearance in 1968.

BIG THREE *Right* Before evolving into the Mugwumps and the Mamas and the Papas, Cass Elliot had an American group called the Big Three with singer songwriter Tim Rose. This is the British trio.

Date	Title Label Number	Position

Cilla BLACK
UK, female vocalist

17 Oct 63	LOVE OF THE LOVED *Parlophone R 5065*	35	6 wks
6 Feb 64	★ ANYONE WHO HAD A HEART *Parlophone R 5101*	1	17 wks
7 May 64	★ YOU'RE MY WORLD *Parlophone R 5133*	1	17 wks
6 Aug 64	● IT'S FOR YOU *Parlophone R 5162*	7	10 wks
14 Jan 65	● YOU'VE LOST THAT LOVIN' FEELIN' *Parlophone R 5225*	2	9 wks
22 Apr 65	I'VE BEEN WRONG BEFORE *Parlophone R 5265*	17	8 wks
13 Jan 66	● LOVE'S JUST A BROKEN HEART *Parlophone R 5395*	5	11 wks
31 Mar 66	● ALFIE *Parlophone R 5427*	9	12 wks
9 Jun 66	● DON'T ANSWER ME *Parlophone R 5463*	6	10 wks
20 Oct 66	A FOOL AM I *Parlophone R 5515*	13	9 wks
8 Jun 67	WHAT GOOD AM I *Parlophone R 5608*	24	7 wks
29 Nov 67	I ONLY LIVE TO LOVE YOU *Parlophone R 5652*	26	11 wks
13 Mar 68	● STEP INSIDE LOVE *Parlophone R 5674*	8	9 wks
12 Jun 68	WHERE IS TOMORROW *Parlophone R 5706*	40	3 wks
12 Feb 69	● SURROUND YOURSELF WITH SORROW *Parlophone R 5759*	3	12 wks
9 Jul 69	● CONVERSATIONS *Parlophone R 5785*	7	12 wks
13 Dec 69	IF I THOUGHT YOU'D EVER CHANGE YOUR MIND *Parlophone R 5820*	20	9 wks

Jeanne BLACK
US, female vocalist

23 Jun 60	HE'LL HAVE TO STAY *Capitol CL 15131*	41	4 wks

Tony BLACKBURN
UK, male vocalist

24 Jan 68	SO MUCH LOVE *MGM 1375*	31	4 wks
26 Mar 69	IT'S ONLY LOVE *MGM 1467*	42	3 wks

Bill BLACK'S COMBO
US, male instrumental group, Bill Black, bass

8 Sep 60	WHITE SILVER SANDS *London HLU 9090*	50	1 wk
3 Nov 60	DON'T BE CRUEL *London HLU 9212*	32	7 wks

BLACKWELLS
US, male vocal group

18 May 61	LOVE OR MONEY *London HLW 9334*	46	2 wks

Joyce BLAIR — See *Miss X*

Billy BLAND
US, male vocalist

19 May 60	LET THE LITTLE GIRL DANCE *London HL 9096*	15	10 wks

BLOOD SWEAT AND TEARS
US, male vocal/instrumental group

30 Apr 69	YOU'VE MADE ME SO VERY HAPPY *CBS 4116*	35	6 wks

Babbity BLUE
UK, female vocalist

11 Feb 65	DON'T MAKE ME *Decca F 12053*	48	2 wks

BLUE FLAMES — See *Georgie FAME*

BLUE JEANS — See *Bob B. SOXX and the BLUE JEANS*

BLUE MINK
UK/US, male/female vocal/instrumental group

15 Nov 69	● MELTING POT *Philips BF 1818*	3	15 wks

BOB and EARL
US, male vocal duo

12 Mar 69	● HARLEM SHUFFLE *Island WIP 6053*	7	13 wks

Graham BONNEY
UK, male vocalist

24 Mar 66	SUPERGIRL *Columbia DB 7843*	19	8 wks

BONNIE — See *DELANEY and BONNIE and FRIENDS featuring Eric CLAPTON*

BONZO DOG DOO-DAH BAND
UK, male vocal/instrumental group

6 Nov 68	● I'M THE URBAN SPACEMAN *Liberty LBF 15144*	5	14 wks

BOOKER T. & THE M. G.'S
US, male instrumental group

11 Dec 68	SOUL LIMBO *Stax 102*	30	9 wks
7 May 69	● TIME IS TIGHT *Stax 119*	4	18 wks
30 Aug 69	SOUL CLAP '69 *Stax 127*	35	4 wks

Date	Title Label Number	Position

Pat BOONE

US, male vocalist

Date	Title Label Number	Position	
23 Jun 60	**WALKING THE FLOOR OVER YOU** London HLD 9138	40	2 wks
14 Jul 60	**WALKING THE FLOOR OVER YOU** (re-entry) London HLD 9138	46	1 wk
4 Aug 60	**WALKING THE FLOOR OVER YOU** (2nd re-entry) London HLD 9138	39	2 wks
6 Jul 61	**MOODY RIVER** London HLD 9350	18	10 wks
7 Dec 61	● **JOHNNY WILL** London HLD 9461	4	13 wks
15 Feb 62	**I'LL SEE YOU IN MY DREAMS** London HLD 9504	27	9 wks
24 May 62	**QUANDO QUANDO QUANDO** London HLD 9543	41	4 wks
12 Jul 62	● **SPEEDY GONZALES** London HLD 9573	2	19 wks
15 Nov 62	**THE MAIN ATTRACTION** London HLD 9620	12	11 wks

David BOWIE

UK, male vocalist

6 Sep 69	**SPACE ODDITY** Philips BF 1801	48	1 wk
20 Sep 69	● **SPACE ODDITY** (re-entry) Philips BF 1801	5	13 wks

BOX TOPS

US, male vocal/instrumental group

13 Sep 67	● **THE LETTER** Stateside SS 2044	5	12 wks
20 Mar 68	**CRY LIKE A BABY** Bell 1001	15	12 wks
23 Aug 69	**SOUL DEEP** Bell 1068	22	9 wks

Jacqueline BOYER

France, female vocalist

28 Apr 60	**TOM PILLIBI** Columbia DB 4452	33	2 wks

Wilfred BRAMBELL and Harry H. CORBETT

UK, male vocal duo

28 Nov 63	**AT THE PALACE** (PARTS 1 & 2) Pye 7N 15588	25	12 wks

Los BRAVOS

Spain/Germany, male vocal/instrumental group

30 Jun 66	● **BLACK IS BLACK** Decca F 22419	2	13 wks
8 Sep 66	**I DON'T CARE** Decca F 13367	16	11 wks

Rose BRENNAN

UK, female vocalist

7 Dec 61	**TALL DARK STRANGER** Philips PB 1193	31	9 wks

Walter BRENNAN

US, male vocalist

28 Jun 62	**OLD RIVERS** Liberty LIB 55436	38	3 wks

Teresa BREWER

US, female vocalist

23 Jun 60	**HOW DO YOU KNOW IT'S LOVE** Coral Q 72396	21	11 wks

BROOK BROTHERS

UK, male vocal duo

30 Mar 61	● **WARPAINT** Pye 7N 15333	5	14 wks
24 Aug 61	**AIN'T GONNA WASH FOR A WEEK** Pye 7N 15369	13	10 wks
25 Jan 62	**HE'S OLD ENOUGH TO KNOW BETTER** Pye 7N 15409	37	1 wk
16 Aug 62	**WELCOME HOME BABY** Pye 7N 15453	33	6 wks
21 Feb 63	**TROUBLE IS MY MIDDLE NAME** Pye 7N 15498	38	4 wks

BROTHERS FOUR

US, male vocal group

23 Jun 60	**GREENFIELDS** Philips PB 1009	49	1 wk
7 Jul 60	**GREENFIELDS** (re-entry) Philips PB 1009	40	1 wk

Crazy World of Arthur BROWN

UK, male vocal/instrumental group

26 Jun 68	★ **FIRE** Track 604 022	1	14 wks

James BROWN and the FAMOUS FLAMES

US, male vocalist

23 Sep 65	**PAPA'S GOT A BRAND NEW BAG** London HL 9990	25	7 wks
24 Feb 66	**I GOT YOU** Pye International 7N 25350	29	6 wks
16 Jun 66	**IT'S A MAN'S MAN'S MAN'S WORLD** Pye International 7N 25371	13	9 wks

Joanne BROWN — See *Tony OSBORNE*

Joe BROWN

UK, male vocalist/instrumentalist - guitar

17 Mar 60	**DARKTOWN STRUTTERS BALL** Decca F 11207	34	6 wks
26 Jan 61	**SHINE** Pye 7N 15322	33	6 wks
11 Jan 62	**WHAT A CRAZY WORLD WE'RE LIVING IN** Piccadilly 7N 35024	37	2 wks
17 May 62	● **A PICTURE OF YOU** Piccadilly 7N 35047	2	19 wks

Joe BROWN He started his career as the guitarist in the ABC TV series *Boy Meets Girl* before backing such visiting American artists as Gene Vincent, Freddy Cannon, Ronnie Hawkins, and Johnny Cash at their request.

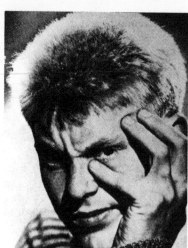

Graham BONNEY Although a one-hit artist, he wrote songs for Sacha Distel and Carol Deene and worked with Charlie Chaplin. He took time out to comment in 1965 – 'I see nothing wrong in men being obsessed with clothes and appearance – I'll bet I take longer in the bath than most girls do!'

Here's Wishing You All a Ring-a-ding Christmas and a Swinging New Year

THE Brook Brothers

BROOK BROTHERS Gee gang, here's your very own personalised Christmas card from heart-throbs Ricky and Geoff, who sure hope you had a swell 1961 type cool yule – Hey tell the crowd at the youth club that Frankie Vaughan's 'Tower of Strength' looks like being the Xmas number one!

Date	Title Label Number	Position	

Date	Title Label Number	Position	

13 Sep 62   **YOUR TENDER LOOK** *Piccadilly 7N 35058*   **31**   6 wks
15 Nov 62 ● **IT ONLY TOOK A MINUTE**   **6**   13 wks
     Piccadilly 7N 35082
7 Feb 63 ● **THAT'S WHAT LOVE WILL DO**   **3**   14 wks
     Piccadilly 7N 35106
21 Feb 63   **IT ONLY TOOK A MINUTE** (re-entry)   **50**   1 wk
     Piccadilly 7N 35082
27 Jun 63   **NATURE'S TIME FOR LOVE**   **26**   6 wks
     Piccadilly 7N 35129
26 Sep 63   **SALLY ANN** *Piccadilly 7N 35138*   **28**   9 wks
29 Jun 67   **WITH A LITTLE HELP FROM MY FRIENDS**   **32**   4 wks
     Pye 7N 17339

Joe Brown's male vocal/instrumental backing group, the Bruvvers, were credited on all hits except Shine *and* With A Little Help From My Friends.

Dave BRUBECK QUARTET

US, male instrumental group

26 Oct 61 ● **TAKE FIVE** *Fontana H 339*   **6**   15 wks
8 Feb 62   **IT'S A RAGGY WALTZ** *Fontana H 352*   **36**   3 wks
17 May 62   **UNSQUARE DANCE** *CBS AAG 102*   **14**   13 wks

Tommy BRUCE

UK, male vocalist

26 May 60 ● **AIN'T MISBEHAVIN'** *Columbia DB 4453*   **3**   16 wks
8 Sep 60   **BROKEN DOLL** *Columbia DB 4498*   **36**   4 wks
22 Feb 62   **BABETTE** *Columbia DB 4776*   **50**   1 wk

First two hits credit the Bruisers, Tommy's backing group. See also Bruisers.

BRUISERS

UK, male vocal/instrumental group

8 Aug 63   **BLUE GIRL** *Parlophone R 5042*   **31**   6 wks
26 Sep 63   **BLUE GIRL** (re-entry) *Parlophone R 5042*   **47**   1 wk

See also Tommy Bruce

BRUVVERS — See *Joe BROWN*

Dora BRYAN

UK, female vocalist

5 Dec 63   **ALL I WANT FOR CHRISTMAS IS A BEATLE** *Fontana TF 427*   **20**   6 wks

Anita BRYANT

US, female vocalist

26 May 60   **PAPER ROSES** *London HLL 9144*   **49**   1 wk
30 Jun 60   **PAPER ROSES** (re-entry) *London HLL 9144*   **45**   1 wk
14 Jul 60   **PAPER ROSES** (2nd re-entry)   **24**   2 wks
     London HLL 9144
6 Oct 60   **MY LITTLE CORNER OF THE WORLD**   **48**   2 wks
     London HLL 9171

B. BUMBLE and the STINGERS

US, male instrumental group

19 Apr 62 ★ **NUT ROCKER** *Top Rank JAR 611*   **1**   15 wks

Eric BURDON

UK, male vocalist

27 Oct 66   **HELP ME GIRL** *Decca F 12502*   **14**   10 wks
15 Jun 67   **WHEN I WAS YOUNG** *MGM 1340*   **45**   3 wks
6 Sep 67   **GOOD TIMES** *MGM 1344*   **20**   11 wks
18 Oct 67 ● **SAN FRANCISCAN NIGHTS** *MGM 1359*   **7**   10 wks
14 Feb 68   **SKY PILOT** *MGM 1373*   **40**   3 wks
15 Jan 69   **RING OF FIRE** *MGM 1461*   **35**   5 wks

Help Me Girl, When I Was Young, Good Times and Ring Of Fire are credited to Eric Burdon and the Animals. See also the Animals.

Johnny BURNETTE

US, male vocalist

29 Sep 60 ● **DREAMIN'** *London HLG 9172*   **5**   16 wks
12 Jan 61 ● **YOU'RE SIXTEEN** *London HLG 9254*   **3**   12 wks
13 Apr 61   **LITTLE BOY SAD** *London HLG 9315*   **12**   12 wks
10 Aug 61   **GIRLS** *London HLG 9388*   **37**   5 wks
17 May 62   **CLOWN SHOES** *Liberty LIB 55416*   **35**   3 wks

Prince BUSTER

Jamaica, male vocalist

23 Feb 67   **AL CAPONE** *Blue Beat BB 324*   **18**   13 wks

Max BYGRAVES

UK, male vocalist

1 Jan 60 ● **JINGLE BELL ROCK** *Decca F 11176*   **7**   2 wks
10 Mar 60 ● **FINGS AIN'T WOT THEY USED T'BE**   **5**   15 wks
     Decca F 11214
28 Jul 60   **CONSIDER YOURSELF** *Decca F 11251*   **50**   1 wk
1 Jun 61   **BELLS OF AVIGNON** *Decca F 11350*   **36**   5 wks
19 Feb 69   **YOU'RE MY EVERYTHING** *Pye 7N 17705*   **50**   1 wk
5 Mar 69   **YOU'RE MY EVERYTHING** (re-entry)   **34**   3 wks
     Pye 7N 17705

Charlie BYRD — See *Stan GETZ and Charlie BYRD*

BYRDS

US, male vocal/instrumental group

17 Jun 65 ★ **MR. TAMBOURINE MAN** *CBS 201765*   **1**   14 wks
12 Aug 65 ● **ALL I REALLY WANT TO DO** *CBS 201796*   **4**   10 wks
11 Nov 65   **TURN! TURN! TURN!** *CBS 202008*   **26**   8 wks
5 May 66   **EIGHT MILES HIGH** *CBS 202067*   **24**   9 wks
5 Jun 68   **YOU AIN'T GOIN' NOWHERE** *CBS 3411*   **45**   3 wks

Date	Title Label Number	Position

Edward BYRNES and Connie STEVENS

US, male/female vocal duo

5 May 60	**KOOKIE KOOKIE (LEND ME YOUR COMB)** Warner Bros. WB 5	**27**	8 wks

See also Connie Stevens.

BYSTANDERS

UK, male vocal/instrumental group

9 Feb 67	**98.6** *Piccadilly 7N 35363*	**45**	1 wk

C

Roy 'C'

US, male vocalist

21 Apr 66	● **SHOTGUN WEDDING** *Island WI 273*	**6**	11 wks

CADETS

UK, male/female vocal group

3 Jun 65	**JEALOUS HEART** *Pye 7N 15852*	**42**	1 wk

Hit has credit 'with Eileen Read lead vocal.'

Al CAIOLA

US, orchestra

15 Jun 61	**THE MAGNIFICENT SEVEN** *HMV POP 889*	**34**	6 wks

Glen CAMPBELL

US, male vocalist

29 Jan 69	● **WICHITA LINEMAN** *Ember EMBS 261*	**7**	13 wks
7 May 69	**GALVESTON** *Ember EMBS 263*	**14**	10 wks

See also Bobbie Gentry & Glen Campbell.

Jo-Anne CAMPBELL

US, female vocalist

8 Jun 61	**MOTORCYCLE MICHAEL** *HMV POP 873*	**41**	3 wks

Pat CAMPBELL

Ireland, male vocalist

15 Nov 69	**THE DEAL** *Major Minor MM 648*	**31**	5 wks

Ian CAMPBELL FOLK GROUP

UK, male vocal/instrumental group

11 Mar 65	**THE TIMES THEY ARE A-CHANGIN'** *Transatlantic SP 5*	**42**	2 wks
1 Apr 65	**THE TIMES THEY ARE A-CHANGIN'** (re-entry) *Transatlantic SP 5*	**47**	1 wk
15 Apr 65	**THE TIMES THEY ARE A-CHANGIN'** (2nd re-entry) *Transatlantic SP 5*	**46**	2 wks

CANNED HEAT

US, vocal/instrumental group

24 Jul 68	● **ON THE ROAD AGAIN** *Liberty LBS 15090*	**8**	15 wks
1 Jan 69	**GOING UP THE COUNTRY** *Liberty LBF 15169*	**19**	10 wks

Freddy CANNON

US, male vocalist

1 Jan 60	● **WAY DOWN YONDER IN NEW ORLEANS** *Top Rank JAR 247*	**3**	16 wks
10 Mar 60	**CALIFORNIA HERE I COME** *Top Rank JAR 309*	**33**	1 wk
17 Mar 60	**INDIANA** *Top Rank JAR 309*	**42**	1 wk
24 Mar 60	**CALIFORNIA HERE I COME** (re-entry) *Top Rank JAR 309*	**46**	1 wk
19 May 60	**THE URGE** *Top Rank JAR 369*	**18**	10 wks
20 Apr 61	**MUSKRAT RAMBLE** *Top Rank JAR 548*	**32**	5 wks
28 Jun 62	**PALISADES PARK** *Stateside SS 101*	**20**	8 wks

CARAVELLES

UK, female vocal duo

8 Aug 63	● **YOU DON'T HAVE TO BE A BABY TO CRY** *Decca F 11697*	**6**	13 wks

Pearl CARR and Teddy JOHNSON

UK, female/male vocal duo

6 Apr 61	**HOW WONDERFUL TO KNOW** *Columbia DB 4603*	**23**	11 wks

Vikki CARR

US, female vocalist

1 Jun 67	● **IT MUST BE HIM (SEUL SUR SON ETOILE)** *Liberty LIB 55917*	**2**	20 wks
30 Aug 67	**THERE I GO** *Liberty LBF 15022*	**50**	1 wk
12 Mar 69	**WITH PEN IN HAND** *Liberty LBF 15166*	**43**	1 wk
26 Mar 69	**WITH PEN IN HAND** (re-entry) *Liberty LBF 15166*	**40**	2 wks
30 Apr 69	**WITH PEN IN HAND** (2nd re-entry) *Liberty LBF 15166*	**40**	2 wks

Date	Title *Label Number*	Position

Ronnie CARROLL

UK, male vocalist

31 Mar 60	**FOOTSTEPS** *Philips PB 1004*	**36**	3 wks
22 Feb 62	**RING A DING GIRL** *Philips PB 1222*	**46**	3 wks
2 Aug 62	● **ROSES ARE RED** *Philips 326532 BF*	**3**	16 wks
15 Nov 62	**IF ONLY TOMORROW** *Philips 326550 BF*	**33**	4 wks
7 Mar 63	● **SAY WONDERFUL THINGS** *Philips 326574 BF*	**6**	14 wks

CASCADES

US, male vocal group

28 Feb 63	● **RHYTHM OF THE RAIN** *Warner Bros. WB 88*	**5**	16 wks

Johnny CASH

US, male vocalist

3 Jun 65	**IT AIN'T ME BABE** *CBS 201760*	**28**	8 wks
6 Sep 69	● **A BOY NAMED SUE** *CBS 4460*	**4**	19 wks

CASINOS

US, male vocal group

23 Feb 67	**THEN YOU CAN TELL ME GOODBYE** *President PT 123*	**28**	7 wks

Mama CASS

US, female vocalist

14 Aug 68	**DREAM A LITTLE DREAM OF ME** *RCA 1726*	**11**	12 wks
16 Aug 69	● **IT'S GETTING BETTER** *Stateside SS 8021*	**8**	15 wks

See also Mamas and the Papas.

Roy CASTLE

UK, male vocalist

22 Dec 60	**LITTLE WHITE BERRY** *Philips PB 1087*	**40**	3 wks

CASUALS

UK, male vocal/instrumental group

14 Aug 68	● **JESAMINE** *Decca F 22784*	**2**	18 wks
4 Dec 68	**TOY** *Decca F 22852*	**30**	8 wks

CATS

Holland, male instrumental group

9 Apr 69	**SWAN LAKE** *BAF 1*	**48**	1 wk
21 May 69	**SWAN LAKE** (re-entry) *BAF 1*	**50**	1 wk

CHAKACHAS

Belgium, male vocal/instrumental group

11 Jan 62	**TWIST TWIST** *RCA 1264*	**48**	1 wk

George CHAKIRIS

US, male vocalist

2 Jun 60	**HEART OF A TEENAGE GIRL** *Triumph RGM 1010*	**49**	1 wk

Richard CHAMBERLAIN

US, male vocalist

7 Jun 62	**THEME FROM DR. KILDARE (THREE STARS WILL SHINE TONIGHT)** *MGM 1160*	**12**	10 wks
1 Nov 62	**LOVE ME TENDER** *MGM 1173*	**15**	11 wks
21 Feb 63	**HI-LILI HI-LO** *MGM 1189*	**20**	9 wks
18 Jul 63	**TRUE LOVE** *MGM 1205*	**30**	6 wks

CHAMPS

US, male instrumental group

17 Mar 60	**TOO MUCH TEQUILA** *London HLH 9052*	**49**	1 wk

Gene CHANDLER

US, male vocalist

5 Jun 68	**NOTHING CAN STOP ME** *Soul City SC 102*	**41**	4 wks

Bruce CHANNEL

US, male vocalist

22 Mar 62	● **HEY! BABY** *Mercury AMT 1171*	**2**	12 wks
26 Jun 68	**KEEP ON** *Bell 1010*	**12**	16 wks

CHANTAYS

US, male instrumental group

18 Apr 63	**PIPELINE** *London HLD 9696*	**16**	14 wks

CHAQUITO

UK, male arranger/conductor Johnny Gregory under false name

27 Oct 60	**NEVER ON SUNDAY** *Fontana H 265*	**50**	1 wk

Don CHARLES

UK, male vocalist

22 Feb 62	**WALK WITH ME MY ANGEL** *Decca F 11424*	**39**	5 wks

Date	Title Label Number	Position			Date	Title Label Number	Position	

Ray CHARLES

US, male vocalist/instrumentalist,

1 Dec 60	**GEORGIA ON MY MIND** *HMV POP 792*	**47**	1 wk
15 Dec 60	**GEORGIA ON MY MIND** (re-entry) *HMV POP 792*	**24**	7 wks
19 Oct 61	● **HIT THE ROAD JACK** *HMV POP 935*	**6**	12 wks
14 Jun 62	★ **I CAN'T STOP LOVING YOU** *HMV POP 1034*	**1**	17 wks
13 Sep 62	● **YOU DON'T KNOW ME** *HMV POP 1064*	**9**	13 wks
13 Dec 62	**YOUR CHEATING HEART** *HMV POP 1099*	**13**	8 wks
28 Mar 63	**DON'T SET ME FREE** *HMV POP 1133*	**37**	3 wks
16 May 63	● **TAKE THESE CHAINS FROM MY HEART** *HMV POP 1161*	**5**	20 wks
12 Sep 63	**NO ONE** *HMV POP 1202*	**35**	7 wks
31 Oct 63	**BUSTED** *HMV POP 1221*	**21**	10 wks
24 Sep 64	**NO-ONE TO CRY TO** *HMV POP 1333*	**38**	3 wks
21 Jan 65	**MAKIN' WHOOPEE** *HMV POP 1383*	**42**	4 wks
10 Feb 66	**CRYIN' TIME** *HMV POP 1502*	**50**	1 wk
21 Apr 66	**TOGETHER AGAIN** *HMV POP 1519*	**48**	1 wk
5 Jul 67	**HERE WE GO AGAIN** *HMV POP 1595*	**38**	1 wk
19 Jul 67	**HERE WE GO AGAIN** (re-entry) *HMV POP 1595*	**45**	2 wks
20 Dec 67	**YESTERDAY** *Stateside SS 2071*	**44**	4 wks
31 Jul 68	**ELEANOR RIGBY** *Stateside SS 2120*	**36**	9 wks

Dick CHARLESWORTH and his CITY GENTS

UK, male instrumental group, Dick Charlesworth clarinet

4 May 61	**BILLY BOY** *Top Rank JAR 558*	**43**	1 wk

CHARLEY — See *JOHNNY and CHARLEY*

Chubby CHECKER

US, male vocalist

22 Sep 60	**THE TWIST** *Columbia DB 4503*	**49**	1 wk
6 Oct 60	**THE TWIST** (re-entry) *Columbia DB 4503*	**44**	1 wk
30 Mar 61	**PONY TIME** *Columbia DB 4591*	**27**	6 wks
17 Aug 61	**LET'S TWIST AGAIN** *Columbia DB 4691*	**37**	3 wks
28 Dec 61	● **LET'S TWIST AGAIN** (re-entry) *Columbia DB 4691*	**2**	27 wks
11 Jan 62	**THE TWIST** (2nd re-entry) *Columbia DB 4503*	**14**	10 wks
5 Apr 62	**SLOW TWISTIN'** *Columbia DB 4808*	**23**	8 wks
9 Aug 62	**DANCIN' PARTY** *Columbia DB 4876*	**19**	13 wks
23 Aug 62	**LET'S TWIST AGAIN** (2nd re-entry) *Columbia DB 4691*	**46**	1 wk
13 Sep 62	**LET'S TWIST AGAIN** (3rd re-entry) *Columbia DB 4691*	**49**	3 wks
1 Nov 62	**LIMBO ROCK** *Cameo-Parkway P 849*	**32**	10 wks
31 Oct 63	**WHAT DO YA SAY** *Cameo-Parkway P 806*	**37**	4 wks

See also Chubby Checker and Bobby Rydell.

Chubby CHECKER and Bobby RYDELL

US, male vocal duo

19 Apr 62	**TEACH ME TO TWIST** *Columbia DB 4802*	**45**	1 wk
20 Dec 62	**JINGLE BELL ROCK** *Cameo-Parkway C 205*	**40**	3 wks

See also Chubby Checker$ Bobby Rydell.

CHECKMATES — See *Emile FORD and the CHECKMATES*

CHECKMATES LTD.

US, male vocal/instrumental group

15 Nov 69	**PROUD MARY** *A & M AMS 769*	**30**	8 wks

CHEETAHS

UK, male vocal/instrumental group

1 Oct 64	**MECCA** *Philips BF 1362*	**36**	3 wks
21 Jan 65	**SOLDIER BOY** *Philips BF 1383*	**39**	3 wks

CHER

US, female vocalist

19 Aug 65	● **ALL I REALLY WANT TO DO** *Liberty LIB 66114*	**9**	10 wks
31 Mar 66	● **BANG BANG (MY BABY SHOT ME DOWN)** *Liberty LIB 66160*	**3**	12 wks
4 Aug 66	**I FEEL SOMETHING IN THE AIR** *Liberty LIB 12034*	**43**	2 wks
22 Sep 66	**SUNNY** *Liberty LIB 12083*	**32**	5 wks

See also Sonny and Cher.

CHEROKEES

UK, male vocal/instrumental group

3 Sep 64	**SEVEN DAFFODILS** *Columbia DB 7341*	**33**	5 wks

CHICKEN SHACK

UK, male/female vocal/instrumental group

7 May 69	**I'D RATHER GO BLIND** *Blue Horizon 57-3153*	**14**	13 wks
6 Sep 69	**TEARS IN THE WIND** *Blue Horizon 57-3160*	**29**	6 wks

CHIFFONS

US, female vocal group

11 Apr 63	**HE'S SO FINE** *Stateside SS 172*	**16**	12 wks
18 Jul 63	**ONE FINE DAY** *Stateside SS 202*	**29**	6 wks
26 May 66	**SWEET TALKIN' GUY** *Stateside SS 512*	**31**	8 wks

Neil CHRISTIAN

UK, male vocalist

7 Apr 66	**THAT'S NICE** *Strike JH 301*	**14**	10 wks

Lou CHRISTIE

US, male vocalist

24 Feb 66	**LIGHTNIN' STRIKES** *MGM 1297*	**11**	8 wks
28 Apr 66	**RHAPSODY IN THE RAIN** *MGM 1308*	**37**	2 wks
13 Sep 69	● **I'M GONNA MAKE YOU MINE** *Buddah 201 057*	**2**	17 wks
27 Dec 69	**SHE SOLD ME MAGIC** *Buddah 201 073*	**25**	8 wks

Lou CHRISTIE *Left* Lightnin' struck again and again and again for Pennsylvanian Lugee Salo. CHIFFONS *Right* The début single for Judy Craig, Barbara Lee, Patricia Bennett and Sylvia Peterson was produced by two of the Tokens. CASUALS *Middle* With leader John Tebb lurking in the background.

CHANTAYS *Right* 17-year-old South Californian schoolboys Brian Carwen, Bob Marshall, Warren Waters, Bob Stichard and Bob Welch had their Top Twenty instrumental hit in the summer of 1963.

Alma COGAN *Left* Despite her last hit being in 1961 she continued to record until her untimely death a few years later. Her output included a version of the Beatles 'Eight Days A Week' and records in French, German, Spanish, Italian and Japanese.

Date	Title Label Number	Position		Date	Title Label Number	Position	

CHUCKS
UK, male/female vocal group

| 24 Jan 63 | **LOO-BE-LOO** *Decca F 11569* | **22** | 7 wks |

Gigliola CINQUETTI
Italy, female vocalist

| 23 Apr 64 | **NON HO L'ETA PER AMARTI** *Decca F 21882* | **17** | 17 wks |

CITY GENTS — See *Dick CHARLESWORTH and his CITY GENTS*

Jimmy CLANTON
US, male vocalist

| 21 Jul 60 | **ANOTHER SLEEPLESS NIGHT** *Top Rank JAR 382* | **50** | 1 wk |

Eric CLAPTON — See *DELANEY and BONNIE and FRIENDS featuring Eric CLAPTON*

Petula CLARK
UK, female vocalist

26 Jan 61	★**SAILOR** *Pye 7N 15324*	**1**	15 wks
13 Apr 61	**SOMETHING MISSING** *Pye 7N 15337*	**44**	1 wk
13 Jul 61	●**ROMEO** *Pye 7N 15361*	**3**	15 wks
16 Nov 61	●**MY FRIEND THE SEA** *Pye 7N 15387*	**7**	13 wks
8 Feb 62	**I'M COUNTING ON YOU** *Pye 7N 15407*	**41**	2 wks
28 Jun 62	**YA YA TWIST** *Pye 7N 15448*	**14**	11 wks
20 Sep 62	**YA YA TWIST** (re-entry) *Pye 7N 15448*	**45**	2 wks
2 May 63	**CASANOVA / CHARIOT** *Pye 7N 15522*	**39**	7 wks
12 Nov 64	●**DOWNTOWN** *Pye 7N 15722*	**2**	15 wks
11 Mar 65	**I KNOW A PLACE** *Pye 7N 15772*	**17**	8 wks
12 Aug 65	**YOU BETTER COME HOME** *Pye 7N 15864*	**44**	3 wks
14 Oct 65	**ROUND EVERY CORNER** *Pye 7N 15945*	**43**	3 wks
4 Nov 65	**YOU'RE THE ONE** *Pye 7N 15991*	**23**	9 wks
10 Feb 66	●**MY LOVE** *Pye 7N 17038*	**4**	9 wks
21 Apr 66	**A SIGN OF THE TIMES** *Pye 7N 17071*	**49**	1 wk
30 Jun 66	●**I COULDN'T LIVE WITHOUT YOUR LOVE** *Pye 7N 17133*	**6**	11 wks
2 Feb 67	★**THIS IS MY SONG** *Pye 7N 17258*	**1**	14 wks
25 May 67	**DON'T SLEEP IN THE SUBWAY** *Pye 7N 17325*	**12**	11 wks
13 Dec 67	**THE OTHER MAN'S GRASS** *Pye 7N 17416*	**20**	9 wks
6 Mar 68	**KISS ME GOODBYE** *Pye 7N 17466*	**50**	1 wk

Dave CLARK FIVE
UK, male vocal/instrumental group

3 Oct 63	**DO YOU LOVE ME** *Columbia DB 7112*	**30**	6 wks
21 Nov 63	★**GLAD ALL OVER** *Columbia DB 7154*	**1**	19 wks
20 Feb 64	●**BITS AND PIECES** *Columbia DB 7210*	**2**	11 wks
28 May 64	●**CAN'T YOU SEE THAT SHE'S MINE** *Columbia DB 7291*	**10**	11 wks
13 Aug 64	**THINKING OF YOU BABY** *Columbia DB 7335*	**26**	4 wks
22 Oct 64	**ANYWAY YOU WANT IT** *Columbia DB 7377*	**25**	5 wks
14 Jan 65	**EVERYBODY KNOWS** *Columbia DB 7453*	**37**	4 wks
11 Mar 65	**REELIN' AND ROCKIN'** *Columbia DB 7503*	**24**	8 wks
27 May 65	**COME HOME** *Columbia DB 7580*	**16**	8 wks

15 Jul 65	●**CATCH US IF YOU CAN** *Columbia DB 7625*	**5**	11 wks
11 Nov 65	**OVER AND OVER** *Columbia DB 7744*	**45**	4 wks
19 May 66	**LOOK BEFORE YOU LEAP** *Columbia DB 7909*	**50**	1 wk
16 Mar 67	**YOU GOT WHAT IT TAKES** *Columbia DB 8152*	**28**	8 wks
1 Nov 67	●**EVERYBODY KNOWS** *Columbia DB 8286*	**2**	14 wks
28 Feb 68	**NO ONE CAN BREAK A HEART LIKE YOU** *Columbia DB 8342*	**28**	7 wks
18 Sep 68	●**RED BALLOON** *Columbia DB 8465*	**7**	11 wks
27 Nov 68	**LIVE IN THE SKY** *Columbia DB 8505*	**39**	6 wks
25 Oct 69	**PUT A LITTLE LOVE IN YOUR HEART** *Columbia DB 8624*	**31**	4 wks
6 Dec 69	●**GOOD OLD ROCK 'N ROLL** *Columbia DB 8638*	**7**	12 wks

Everybody Knows on DB 7435 and Everybody Knows on DB 8286 are two different songs. Good Old Rock 'N' Roll is a medley as follows: Good Old Rock 'N' Roll/ Sweet Little Sixteen/ Long Tall Sally/ Whole Lotta Shakin' Goin' On/ Blue Suede Shoes/ Lucille/ Reelin' and Rockin'/ Memphis Tennessee.

CLASSICS IV
US, male vocal/instrumental group

| 28 Feb 68 | **SPOOKY** *Liberty LBS 15051* | **46** | 1 wk |

Judy CLAY and William BELL
US, male/female vocal duo

| 20 Nov 68 | ●**PRIVATE NUMBER** *Stax 101* | **8** | 14 wks |

See also William Bell.

Jimmy CLIFF
Jamaica, male vocalist

| 25 Oct 69 | ●**WONDERFUL WORLD BEAUTIFUL PEOPLE** *Trojan TR 690* | **6** | 13 wks |

Buzz CLIFFORD
US, male vocalist

| 2 Mar 61 | **BABY SITTIN' BOOGIE** *Fontana H 297* | **17** | 13 wks |

Patsy CLINE
US, female vocalist

| 26 Apr 62 | **SHE'S GOT YOU** *Brunswick 05866* | **43** | 1 wk |
| 29 Nov 62 | **HEARTACHES** *Brunswick 05878* | **31** | 5 wks |

Jeremy CLYDE — See *Chad STUART and Jeremy CLYDE*

CLYDE VALLEY STOMPERS
UK, male instrumental group

| 9 Aug 62 | **PETER AND THE WOLF** *Parlophone R 4928* | **25** | 8 wks |

Date	Title Label Number	Position		Date	Title Label Number	Position	

Eddie COCHRAN

US, male vocalist

22 Jan 60	**HALLELUJAH I LOVE HER SO** London HLW 9022	**28**	1 wk
5 Feb 60	**HALLELUJAH I LOVE HER SO** (re-entry) London HLW 9022	**22**	3 wks
12 May 60 ★	**THREE STEPS TO HEAVEN** London HLG 9115	**1**	15 wks
6 Oct 60	**SWEETIE PIE** London HLG 9196	**38**	3 wks
3 Nov 60	**LONELY** London HLG 9196	**41**	1 wk
15 Jun 61	**WEEKEND** London HLG 9362	**15**	16 wks
30 Nov 61	**JEANNIE, JEANNIE, JEANNIE** London HLG 9460	**31**	4 wks
25 Apr 63	**MY WAY** Liberty LIB 10088	**23**	10 wks
24 Apr 68	**SUMMERTIME BLUES** Liberty LBF 15071	**34**	8 wks

Joe COCKER

UK, male vocalist

22 May 68	**MARJORINE** Regal-Zonophone RZ 3006	**48**	1 wk
2 Oct 68 ★	**WITH A LITTLE HELP FROM MY FRIENDS** Regal-Zonophone RZ 3013	**1**	13 wks
27 Sep 69 ●	**DELTA LADY** Regal-Zonophone RZ 3024	**10**	11 wks

Alma COGAN

UK, female vocalist

1 Jan 60	**WE GOT LOVE** HMV POP 670	**26**	2 wks
11 Aug 60	**TRAIN OF LOVE** HMV POP 760	**27**	5 wks
20 Apr 61	**COWBOY JIMMY JOE** Columbia DB 4607	**37**	6 wks

Shaye COGAN

US, female vocalist

| 24 Mar 60 | **MEAN TO ME** MGM 1063 | **43** | 1 wk |

Nat 'King' COLE

US, male vocalist

12 Feb 60	**TIME AND THE RIVER** Capitol CL 15111	**29**	1 wk
26 Feb 60	**TIME AND THE RIVER** (re-entry) Capitol CL 15111	**23**	2 wks
31 Mar 60	**TIME AND THE RIVER** (2nd re-entry) Capitol CL 15111	**47**	1 wk
26 May 60 ●	**THAT'S YOU** Capitol CL 15129	**10**	8 wks
10 Nov 60	**JUST AS MUCH AS EVER** Capitol CL 15163	**18**	10 wks
2 Feb 61	**THE WORLD IN MY ARMS** Capitol CL 15178	**36**	10 wks
16 Nov 61	**LET TRUE LOVE BEGIN** Capitol CL 15224	**29**	10 wks
22 Mar 62	**BRAZILIAN LOVE SONG** Capitol CL 15241	**34**	4 wks
31 May 62	**THE RIGHT THING TO SAY** Capitol CL 15250	**42**	4 wks
19 Jul 62	**LET THERE BE LOVE** Capitol CL 15257	**11**	14 wks
27 Sep 62 ●	**RAMBLIN' ROSE** Capitol CL 15270	**5**	14 wks
20 Dec 62	**DEAR LONELY HEARTS** Capitol CL 15280	**37**	3 wks

Let There Be Love *with George Shearing - see also George Shearing.*

COMETS — See *Bill HALEY and his COMETS*

Perry COMO

US, male vocalist

26 Feb 60 ●	**DELAWARE** RCA 1170	**3**	13 wks
10 May 62	**CATERINA** RCA 1283	**37**	4 wks
14 Jun 62	**CATERINA** (re-entry) RCA 1283	**45**	2 wks

Arthur CONLEY

US, male vocalist

| 27 Apr 67 ● | **SWEET SOUL MUSIC** Atlantic 584 083 | **7** | 14 wks |
| 10 Apr 68 | **FUNKY STREET** Atlantic 583 175 | **46** | 1 wk |

Jess CONRAD

UK, male vocalist

30 Jun 60	**CHERRY PIE** Decca F 11236	**39**	1 wk
26 Jan 61	**MYSTERY GIRL** Decca F 11315	**44**	1 wk
9 Feb 61	**MYSTERY GIRL** (re-entry) Decca F 11315	**18**	9 wks
11 Oct 62	**PRETTY JENNY** Decca F 11511	**50**	2 wks

CONSORTIUM

UK, male vocal group

| 12 Feb 69 | **ALL THE LOVE IN THE WORLD** Pye 7N 17635 | **22** | 9 wks |

Russ CONWAY

UK, male instrumentalist, piano

1 Jan 60 ●	**SNOW COACH** Columbia DB 4368	**8**	2 wks
1 Jan 60	**MORE AND MORE PARTY POPS** Columbia DB 4373	**11**	2 wks
10 Mar 60	**ROYAL EVENT** Columbia DB 4418	**15**	7 wks
21 Apr 60	**FINGS AIN'T WOT THEY USED T'BE** Columbia DB 4422	**47**	1 wk
19 May 60	**LUCKY FIVE** Columbia DB 4457	**14**	9 wks
29 Sep 60	**PASSING BREEZE** Columbia DB 4508	**16**	10 wks
24 Nov 60	**EVEN MORE PARTY POPS** Columbia DB 4535	**27**	9 wks
19 Jan 61	**PEPE** Columbia DB 4564	**19**	9 wks
25 May 61	**PABLO** Columbia DB 4649	**45**	2 wks
30 Nov 61 ●	**TOY BALLOONS** Columbia DB 4738	**7**	11 wks
22 Feb 62	**LESSON ONE** Columbia DB 4784	**21**	7 wks
29 Nov 62	**ALWAYS YOU AND ME** Columbia DB 4934	**33**	4 wks
3 Jan 63	**ALWAYS YOU AND ME** (re-entry) Columbia DB 4934	**35**	3 wks

See also Dorothy Squires and Russ Conway. Two of the hits were medleys as follows: More And More Party Pops: Sheik Of Araby/ Who Were You With Last Night/ Any Old Iron/ Tiptoe Through The Tulips/ If You Were The Only Girl In The World/ When I Leave The World Behind. Even More Party Pops: Ain't She Sweet/ I Can't Give You Anything But Love/ Yes We Have No Bananas/ I May Be Wrong/ Happy Days And Lonely Nights/ Glad Rag Doll.

Peter COOK

UK, male vocalist

| 15 Jul 65 | **THE BALLAD OF SPOTTY MULDOON** Decca F 12182 | **34** | 5 wks |

See also Peter Cook & Dudley Moore.

Date	Title Label Number	Position

Peter COOK and Dudley MOORE

UK, male vocal duo, Dudley Moore featured pianist

17 Jun 65	**GOODBYE-EE** *Decca F 12158*	**18**	10 wks

See also Peter Cook.

Sam COOKE

US, male vocalist

7 Jul 60	**WONDERFUL WORLD** *HMV POP 754*	**27**	8 wks
29 Sep 60	● **CHAIN GANG** *RCA 1202*	**9**	11 wks
27 Jul 61	● **CUPID** *RCA 1242*	**7**	14 wks
8 Mar 62	● **TWISTIN' THE NIGHT AWAY** *RCA 1277*	**6**	14 wks
16 May 63	**ANOTHER SATURDAY NIGHT** *RCA 1341*	**23**	12 wks
5 Sep 63	**FRANKIE AND JOHNNY** *RCA 1361*	**30**	6 wks

COOKIES

US, female vocal group

10 Jan 63	**CHAINS** *London HLU 9634*	**50**	1 wk

Tommy COOPER

UK, male vocalist

29 Jun 61	**DON'T JUMP OFF THE ROOF DAD** *Palette PG 9019*	**40**	2 wks
20 Jul 61	**DON'T JUMP OFF THE ROOF DAD** (re-entry) *Palette PG 9019*	**50**	1 wk

Harry H. CORBETT — See *Wilfred BRAMBELL and Harry H. CORBETT*

Frank CORDELL

UK, orchestra

16 Feb 61	**BLACK BEAR** *HMV POP 824*	**44**	2 wks

Louise CORDET

France, female vocalist

5 Jul 62	**I'M JUST A BABY** *Decca F 11476*	**13**	13 wks

Lynn CORNELL

UK, female vocalist

20 Oct 60	**NEVER ON SUNDAY** *Decca F 11277*	**30**	9 wks

Don COSTA

US, orchestra

13 Oct 60	**NEVER ON SUNDAY** *London HLT 9195*	**27**	9 wks
22 Dec 60	**NEVER ON SUNDAY** (re-entry) *London HLT 9195*	**41**	1 wk

Mike COTTON'S JAZZMEN

UK, male instrumental band, Mike Cotton trumpet

20 Jun 63	**SWING THAT HAMMER** *Columbia DB 7029*	**36**	4 wks

COUGARS

UK, male instrumental group

28 Feb 63	**SATURDAY NITE AT THE DUCK POND** *Parlophone R 4989*	**33**	8 wks

COUNTRYMEN

UK, male vocal group

3 May 62	**I KNOW WHERE I'M GOING** *Piccadilly 7N 35029*	**45**	2 wks

Michael COX

UK, male vocalist

9 Jun 60	● **ANGELA JONES** *Triumph RGM 1011*	**7**	13 wks
20 Oct 60	**ALONG CAME CAROLINE** *HMV POP 789*	**41**	2 wks

Floyd CRAMER

US, male instrumentalist, piano

13 Apr 61	★ **ON THE REBOUND** *RCA 1231*	**1**	14 wks
20 Jul 61	**SAN ANTONIO ROSE** *RCA 1241*	**36**	8 wks
23 Aug 62	**HOT PEPPER** *RCA 1301*	**46**	2 wks

Jimmy CRAWFORD

UK, male vocalist

8 Jun 61	**LOVE OR MONEY** *Columbia DB 4633*	**49**	1 wk
16 Nov 61	**I LOVE HOW YOU LOVE ME** *Columbia DB 4717*	**18**	10 wks

CRAZY ELEPHANT

US, male vocal group

21 May 69	**GIMME GIMME GOOD LOVIN'** *Major Minor MM 609*	**12**	13 wks

CREAM

UK, male vocal/instrumental group

20 Oct 66	**WRAPPING PAPER** *Reaction 591 007*	**34**	6 wks
15 Dec 66	**I FEEL FREE** *Reaction 591 011*	**11**	12 wks
8 Jun 67	**STRANGE BREW** *Reaction 591 015*	**17**	9 wks
5 Jun 68	**ANYONE FOR TENNIS (THE SAVAGE SEVEN THEME)** *Polydor 56 258*	**40**	3 wks
9 Oct 68	**SUNSHINE OF YOUR LOVE** *Polydor 56 286*	**25**	5 wks
15 Jan 69	**WHITE ROOM** *Polydor 56 300*	**28**	8 wks
9 Apr 69	**BADGE** *Polydor 56 315*	**18**	10 wks

CREATION *Above* They evolved from Cheshunt group the Blue Jacks to become the Mark Four in 1963 before changing to Creation in May 1966. They lasted until June 1968 when they bowed out at the John Lewis Partnership's annual binge.

Jess CONRAD *Far Left* The ex-Shepherds Bush florist who made his showbiz début as an extra in *Cockleshell Heroes* was born Gerald James but took his stage name from the adventure writer Joseph Conrad.

Bobby DARIN is best known as a singer but his hit 'Come September' was an instrumental credited to the Bobby Darin Orchestra.

DAVID and JONATHAN Prolific songwriters Roger Cook and Roger Greenaway in their guise as David and Jonathan, poised to remove the pins from their grenades.

Date	Title Label Number	Position		Date	Title Label Number	Position

CREATION

UK, male vocal/instrumental group

7 Jul 66	**MAKING TIME** *Planet PLF 116*	**49**	1 wk
3 Nov 66	**PAINTER MAN** *Planet PLF 119*	**36**	2 wks

CREEDENCE CLEARWATER REVIVAL

US, male vocal/instrumental group

28 May 69	● **PROUD MARY** *Liberty LBF 15223*	**8**	13 wks
16 Aug 69	★ **BAD MOON RISING** *Liberty LBF 15230*	**1**	15 wks
15 Nov 69	**GREEN RIVER** *Liberty LBF 15250*	**19**	11 wks

Bernard CRIBBINS

UK, male vocalist

15 Feb 62	● **HOLE IN THE GROUND** *Parlophone R 4869*	**9**	13 wks
5 Jul 62	● **RIGHT SAID FRED** *Parlophone R 4923*	**10**	10 wks
13 Dec 62	**GOSSIP CALYPSO** *Parlophone R 4961*	**25**	6 wks

CRICKETS

US, male vocal/instrumental group

15 Jan 60	**WHEN YOU ASK ABOUT LOVE** *Coral Q 72382*	**27**	1 wk
26 May 60	**BABY MY HEART** *Coral Q 72395*	**33**	4 wks
21 Jun 62	● **DON'T EVER CHANGE** *Liberty LIB 55441*	**5**	13 wks
24 Jan 63	**MY LITTLE GIRL** *Liberty LIB 10067*	**17**	9 wks
6 Jan 63	**DON'T TRY TO CHANGE ME** *Liberty LIB 10092*	**37**	4 wks
2 Jul 64	**(THEY CALL HER) LA BAMBA** *Liberty LIB 55696*	**21**	10 wks

See also Buddy Holly.

CRITTERS

US, male vocal/instrumental group

30 Jun 66	**YOUNGER GIRL** *London HL 10047*	**38**	5 wks

CROSBY, STILLS and NASH

US/UK, male vocal/instrumental group

16 Aug 69	**MARRAKESH EXPRESS** *Atlantic 584 283*	**17**	9 wks

CRUISERS — See *Dave BERRY*

CRYIN' SHAMES

UK, male vocal/instrumental group

31 Mar 66	**PLEASE STAY** *Decca F 12340*	**26**	7 wks

CRYSTALS

US, female vocal group

22 Nov 62	**HE'S A REBEL** *London HLU 9611*	**19**	13 wks
20 Jun 63	● **DA DOO RON RON** *London HLU 9732*	**5**	16 wks
19 Sep 63	● **THEN HE KISSED ME** *London HLU 9773*	**2**	14 wks
5 Mar 64	**I WONDER** *London HLU 9852*	**36**	3 wks

CUFF-LINKS

US, male vocal group

29 Nov 69	● **TRACY** *MCA MU 1101*	**4**	16 wks

Larry CUNNINGHAM and the MIGHTY AVONS

Ireland, male vocal/instrumental group

10 Dec 64	**TRIBUTE TO JIM REEVES** *King KG 1016*	**40**	8 wks
25 Feb 65	**TRIBUTE TO JIM REEVES** (re-entry) *King KG 1016*	**46**	3 wks

CUPID'S INSPIRATION

UK, male vocal/instrumental group

19 Jun 68	● **YESTERDAY HAS GONE** *Nems 56 3500*	**4**	11 wks
2 Oct 68	**MY WORLD** *Nems 56 3702*	**33**	8 wks

Adge CUTLER and the WURZELS

UK, male vocal/instrumental group

2 Feb 67	**DRINK UP THY ZIDER** *Columbia DB 8081*	**45**	1 wk

Johnny CYMBAL

US, male vocalist

14 Mar 63	**MR. BASS MAN** *London HLR 9682*	**24**	10 wks

D

Mike D'ABO — See *MANFRED MANN*

DAKOTAS

UK, male instrumental group

11 Jul 63	**THE CRUEL SEA** *Parlophone R 5044*	**18**	13 wks

See also Billy J. Kramer & the Dakotas.

Billie DAVIS swathed in ex-Brands Hatch chequered flag,
handcuffed to Mojo Stu James. (Mod cardigan-5 guineas,
John Stephen, Carnaby St – a few left).

Date	Title Label Number	Position

DALE AND GRACE

US, male/female vocal duo

| 9 Jan 64 | **I'M LEAVING IT UP TO YOU** *London HL 9807* | 42 | 2 wks |

DALE SISTERS

UK, female vocal group

| 23 Nov 61 | **MY SUNDAY BABY** *Ember S 140* | 36 | 6 wks |

Kenny DAMON

US, male vocalist

| 19 May 66 | **WHILE I LIVE** *Mercury MF 907* | 48 | 1 wk |

Johnny DANKWORTH

UK, male orchestra/group leader/instrumentalist - alto sax

| 23 Feb 61 | ● **AFRICAN WALTZ** *Columbia DB 4590* | 9 | 21 wks |

Bobby DARIN

US, male vocalist

1 Jan 60	**MACK THE KNIFE** *London HLE 8939*	19	2 wks
22 Jan 60	**MACK THE KNIFE** (re-entry) *London HLE 8939*	30	1 wk
29 Jan 60	● **LA MER (BEYOND THE SEA)** *London HLE 9034*	8	10 wks
10 Mar 60	**MACK THE KNIFE** (2nd re-entry) *London HLE 8939*	50	1 wk
31 Mar 60	● **CLEMENTINE** *London HLK 9086*	8	12 wks
21 Apr 60	**LA MER (BEYOND THE SEA)** (re-entry) *London HLE 9034*	40	2 wks
30 Jun 60	**BILL BAILEY** *London HLK 9142*	36	1 wk
14 Jul 60	**BILL BAILEY** (re-entry) *London HLK 9142*	34	1 wk
16 Mar 61	● **LAZY RIVER** *London HLK 9303*	2	13 wks
6 Jul 61	**NATURE BOY** *London HLK 9375*	24	7 wks
12 Oct 61	● **YOU MUST HAVE BEEN A BEAUTIFUL BABY** *London HLK 9429*	10	11 wks
26 Oct 61	**COME SEPTEMBER** *London HLK 9407*	50	1 wk
21 Dec 61	● **MULTIPLICATION** *London HLK 9474*	5	13 wks
19 Jul 62	● **THINGS** *London HLK 9575*	2	17 wks
4 Oct 62	**IF A MAN ANSWERS** *Capitol CL 15272*	24	6 wks
29 Nov 62	**BABY FACE** *London HLK 9624*	40	4 wks
25 Jul 63	**EIGHTEEN YELLOW ROSES** *Capitol CL 15306*	37	4 wks
13 Oct 66	● **IF I WERE A CARPENTER** *Atlantic 584 051*	9	12 wks

Come September is an instrumental credited to the Bobby Darin Orchestra.

James DARREN

US, male vocalist

11 Aug 60	**BECAUSE THEY'RE YOUNG** *Pye International 7N 25059*	29	7 wks
14 Dec 61	**GOODBYE CRUEL WORLD** *Pye International 7N 25116*	28	9 wks
29 Mar 62	**HER ROYAL MAJESTY** *Pye International 7N 25125*	36	3 wks
21 Jun 62	**CONSCIENCE** *Pye International 7N 25138*	30	6 wks

DAVE — See *SAM and DAVE*

DAVID and JONATHAN

UK, male vocal duo

| 13 Jan 66 | **MICHELLE** *Columbia DB 7800* | 11 | 6 wks |
| 7 Jul 66 | ● **LOVERS OF THE WORLD UNITE** *Columbia DB 7950* | 7 | 16 wks |

Dave DAVIES

UK, male vocalist

| 19 Jul 67 | ● **DEATH OF A CLOWN** *Pye 7N 17356* | 3 | 10 wks |
| 6 Dec 67 | **SUSANNAH'S STILL ALIVE** *Pye 7N 17429* | 20 | 7 wks |

Billie DAVIS

UK, female vocalist

7 Feb 63	● **TELL HIM** *Decca F 11572*	10	12 wks
30 May 63	**HE'S THE ONE** *Decca F 11658*	40	3 wks
9 Oct 68	**I WANT YOU TO BE MY BABY** *Decca F 12823*	33	8 wks

See also Mike Sarne.

Sammy DAVIS Jr.

US, male vocalist

| 22 Mar 62 | **WHAT KIND OF FOOL AM I?/ GONNA BUILD A MOUNTAIN** *Reprise R 20048* | 26 | 8 wks |

See also Sammy Davis Jr. and Carmen McRae, Frank Sinatra and Sammy Davis Jr.

Sammy DAVIS Jr. and Carmen McRAE

US, male/female vocal duo

| 16 Jun 60 | **HAPPY TO MAKE YOUR ACQUAINTANCE** *Brunswick 05830* | 46 | 1 wk |

See also Sammy Davis Jr., Frank Sinatra and Sammy Davis Jr.

Skeeter DAVIS

US, female vocalist

| 14 Mar 63 | **END OF THE WORLD** *RCA 1328* | 18 | 13 wks |

Desmond DEKKER Reggae's first chart-topping artist.

Doris DAY. Doris von Kappelhof – her first official engagement as a vocalist was in a Chinese restaurant at the age of 5. Her last chart engagement as a vocalist was a portion of number eight in 1964.

Joey DEE *Below* His hit was in praise of the New York lounge where the top people twisted.

Date	Title Label Number	Position		Date	Title Label Number	Position	

Spencer DAVIS GROUP

UK, male vocal/instrumental group

Date	Title Label Number	Position	
5 Nov 64	I CAN'T STAND IT *Fontana TF 499*	47	3 wks
25 Feb 65	EVERY LITTLE BIT HURTS *Fontana TF 530*	43	2 wks
18 Mar 65	EVERY LITTLE BIT HURTS (re-entry) *Fontana TF 530*	41	1 wk
10 Jun 65	STRONG LOVE *Fontana TF 571*	50	1 wk
24 Jun 65	STRONG LOVE (re-entry) *Fontana TF 571*	44	3 wks
2 Dec 65 ★	KEEP ON RUNNING *Fontana TF 632*	1	14 wks
24 Mar 66 ★	SOMEBODY HELP ME *Fontana TF 679*	1	10 wks
1 Sep 66	WHEN I COME HOME *Fontana TF 739*	12	9 wks
3 Nov 66 ●	GIMME SOME LOVING *Fontana TF 762*	2	12 wks
26 Jan 67 ●	I'M A MAN *Fontana TF 785*	9	7 wks
9 Aug 67	TIME SELLER *Fontana TF 854*	30	5 wks
10 Jan 68	MR. SECOND CLASS *United Artists UP 1203*	35	4 wks

Doris DAY

US, female vocalist

Date	Title Label Number	Position	
12 Mar 64 ●	MOVE OVER DARLING *CBS AAG 183*	8	16 wks

DEAN — See *JAN and DEAN*

Jimmy DEAN

US, male vocalist

Date	Title Label Number	Position	
26 Oct 61 ●	BIG BAD JOHN *Philips PB 1187*	2	13 wks
8 Nov 62	LITTLE BLACK BOOK *CBS AAG 122*	33	4 wks

Dave DEE, DOZY, BEAKY, MICK and TICH

UK, male vocal/instrumental group

Date	Title Label Number	Position	
23 Dec 65	YOU MAKE IT MOVE *Fontana TF 630*	26	8 wks
3 Mar 66 ●	HOLD TIGHT *Fontana TF 671*	4	17 wks
9 Jun 66 ●	HIDEAWAY *Fontana TF 711*	10	11 wks
15 Sep 66 ●	BEND IT *Fontana TF 746*	2	12 wks
8 Dec 66 ●	SAVE ME *Fontana TF 775*	4	10 wks
9 Mar 67	TOUCH ME TOUCH ME *Fontana TF 798*	13	9 wks
18 May 67 ●	OKAY! *Fontana TF 830*	4	11 wks
11 Oct 67 ●	ZABADAK! *Fontana TF 873*	3	14 wks
14 Feb 68 ★	LEGEND OF XANADU *Fontana TF 903*	1	12 wks
3 Jul 68 ●	LAST NIGHT IN SOHO *Fontana TF 953*	8	11 wks
2 Oct 68	WRECK OF THE ANTOINETTE *Fontana TF 971*	14	9 wks
5 Mar 69	DON JUAN *Fontana TF 1000*	23	9 wks
14 May 69	SNAKE IN THE GRASS *Fontana TF 1020*	23	8 wks

Joey DEE and the STARLITERS

US, male vocal/instrumental group

Date	Title Label Number	Position	
8 Feb 62	PEPPERMINT TWIST *Columbia DB 4758*	33	8 wks

DEEDEE — See *DICK and DEEDEE*

Carol DEENE

UK, female vocalist

Date	Title Label Number	Position	
26 Oct 61	SAD MOVIES *HMV POP 922*	44	3 wks
25 Jan 62	NORMAN *HMV POP 973*	24	8 wks
5 Jul 62	JOHNNY GET ANGRY *HMV POP 1027*	32	4 wks
23 Aug 62	SOME PEOPLE *HMV POP 1058*	25	10 wks

Desmond DEKKER and the ACES

Jamaica, male vocal/instrumental group

Date	Title Label Number	Position	
12 Jul 67	007 *Pyramid PYR 6004*	14	11 wks
19 Mar 69 ★	ISRAELITES *Pyramid PYR 6058*	1	14 wks
25 Jun 69 ●	IT MIEK *Pyramid PYR 6068*	7	11 wks
2 Jul 69	ISRAELITES (re-entry) *Pyramid PYR 6058*	45	1 wk

DELANEY and BONNIE and FRIENDS featuring Eric CLAPTON

US male/female vocal/instrumental group

Date	Title Label Number	Position	
20 Dec 69	COMIN' HOME *Atlantic 584 308*	16	9 wks

DELLS

US, male vocal group

Date	Title Label Number	Position	
16 Jul 69	I CAN SING A RAINBOW - LOVE IS BLUE (MEDLEY) *Chess CRS 8099*	15	9 wks

DELRONS — See *REPARATA and the DELRONS*

DENNISONS

UK, male vocal/instrumental group

Date	Title Label Number	Position	
15 Aug 63	BE MY GIRL *Decca F 11691*	46	6 wks
7 May 64	WALKIN' THE DOG *Decca F 11880*	36	7 wks

Karl DENVER

UK, male vocalist

Date	Title Label Number	Position	
22 Jun 61 ●	MARCHETA *Decca F 11360*	8	20 wks
19 Oct 61 ●	MEXICALI ROSE *Decca F 11395*	8	11 wks
25 Jan 62 ●	WIMOWEH *Decca F 11420*	4	17 wks
22 Feb 62 ●	NEVER GOODBYE *Decca F 11431*	9	18 wks
7 Jun 62	A LITTLE LOVE A LITTLE KISS *Decca F 11470*	19	10 wks
20 Sep 62	BLUE WEEKEND *Decca F 11505*	33	5 wks
21 Mar 63	CAN YOU FORGIVE ME *Decca F 11608*	32	8 wks
13 Jun 63	INDIAN LOVE CALL *Decca F 11674*	32	8 wks
22 Aug 63	STILL *Decca F 11720*	13	15 wks
5 Mar 64	MY WORLD OF BLUE *Decca F 11828*	29	6 wks
4 Jun 64	LOVE ME WITH ALL YOUR HEART *Decca F 11905*	37	6 wks

DETROIT WHEELS — See *Mitch RYDER and the DETROIT WHEELS*

Date	Title Label Number	Position

DICK and DEEDEE

US, male/female vocal duo

26 Oct 61	THE MOUNTAIN'S HIGH *London HLG 9408*	37	3 wks

Charles DICKENS

UK, male vocalist

1 Jul 65	THAT'S THE WAY LOVE GOES *Pye 7N 15887*	37	8 wks

Neville DICKIE

UK, male instrumentalist, piano

25 Oct 69	ROBIN'S RETURN *Major Minor MM 644*	33	7 wks
20 Dec 69	ROBIN'S RETURN (re-entry) *Major Minor MM 644*	43	3 wks

Bo DIDDLEY

US, male vocalist/instrumentalist - guitar

10 Oct 63	PRETTY THING *Pye International 7N 25217*	34	6 wks
18 Mar 65	HEY GOOD LOOKIN' *Chess 8000*	39	4 wks

Mark DINNING

US, male vocalist

10 Mar 60	TEEN ANGEL *MGM 1053*	37	3 wks
7 Apr 60	TEEN ANGEL (re-entry) *MGM 1053*	42	1 wk

DION

US, male vocalist

19 Jan 61	LONELY TEENAGER *Top Rank JAR 521*	47	1 wk
2 Nov 61	RUNAROUND SUE *Top Rank JAR 586*	11	9 wks
15 Feb 62	● THE WANDERER *HMV POP 971*	10	12 wks

DIXIE CUPS

US, female vocal group

18 Jun 64	CHAPEL OF LOVE *Pye International 7N 25245*	22	8 wks
13 May 65	IKO IKO *Red Bird RB 10024*	23	8 wks

Carl DOBKINS Jr.

US, male vocalist

31 Mar 60	LUCKY DEVIL *Brunswick 05817*	44	1 wk

Date	Title Label Number	Position

Ken DODD

UK, male vocalist

7 Jul 60	● LOVE IS LIKE A VIOLIN *Decca F 11248*	8	18 wks
15 Jun 61	ONCE IN EVERY LIFETIME *Decca F 11355*	28	7 wks
10 Aug 61	ONCE IN EVERY LIFETIME (re-entry) *Decca F 11355*	47	1 wk
24 Aug 61	ONCE IN EVERY LIFETIME (2nd re-entry) *Decca F 11355*	31	10 wks
1 Feb 62	PIANISSIMO *Decca F 11422*	21	15 wks
29 Aug 63	STILL *Columbia DB 7094*	35	10 wks
6 Feb 64	EIGHT BY TEN *Columbia DB 7191*	22	11 wks
23 Jul 64	HAPPINESS *Columbia DB 7325*	31	13 wks
26 Nov 64	SO DEEP IS THE NIGHT *Columbia DB 7398*	31	7 wks
2 Sep 65	★ TEARS *Columbia DB 7659*	1	24 wks
18 Nov 65	● THE RIVER (LE COLLINE SONO IN FIORO) *Columbia DB 7750*	3	14 wks
12 May 66	● PROMISES *Columbia DB 7914*	6	14 wks
4 Aug 66	MORE THAN LOVE *Columbia DB 7976*	14	11 wks
27 Oct 66	IT'S LOVE *Columbia DB 8031*	36	7 wks
19 Jan 67	LET ME CRY ON YOUR SHOULDER *Columbia DB 8101*	11	10 wks
30 Jul 69	TEARS WON'T WASH AWAY MY HEARTACHE *Columbia DB 8600*	22	11 wks

Joe DOLAN

Ireland, male vocalist

25 Jun 69	● MAKE ME AN ISLAND *Pye 7N 17731*	3	18 wks
1 Nov 69	TERESA *Pye 7N 17833*	20	7 wks
8 Nov 69	MAKE ME AN ISLAND (re-entry) *Pye 7N 17731*	48	1 wk

Fats DOMINO

US, male vocalist/instrumentalist, piano

1 Jan 60	BE MY GUEST *London HLP 9005*	11	6 wks
19 Feb 60	BE MY GUEST (re-entry) *London HLP 9005*	19	4 wks
17 Mar 60	COUNTRY BOY *London HLP 9073*	19	11 wks
21 Jul 60	WALKING TO NEW ORLEANS *London HLP 9163*	19	10 wks
10 Nov 60	THREE NIGHTS A WEEK *London HLP 9198*	45	2 wks
5 Jan 61	MY GIRL JOSEPHINE *London HLP 9244*	32	4 wks
27 Jul 61	IT KEEPS RAININ' *London HLP 9374*	49	1 wk
30 Nov 61	WHAT A PARTY *London HLP 9456*	43	1 wk
29 Mar 62	JAMBALAYA *London HLP 9520*	41	1 wk
31 Oct 63	RED SAILS IN THE SUNSET *HMV POP 1219*	34	6 wks

Lonnie DONEGAN

UK, male vocalist

24 Mar 60	★ MY OLD MAN'S A DUSTMAN *Pye 7N 15256*	1	13 wks
26 May 60	● I WANNA GO HOME *Pye 7N 15267*	5	17 wks
25 Aug 60	● LORELEI *Pye 7N 15275*	10	8 wks
24 Nov 60	LIVELY *Pye 7N 15312*	13	9 wks
8 Dec 60	VIRGIN MARY *Pye 7N 15315*	27	5 wks
11 May 61	● HAVE A DRINK ON ME *Pye 7N 15354*	8	15 wks
31 Aug 61	● MICHAEL ROW THE BOAT/ LUMBERED *Pye 7N 15371*	6	11 wks
18 Jan 62	THE COMANCHEROS *Pye 7N 15410*	14	10 wks
5 Apr 62	● THE PARTY'S OVER *Pye 7N 15424*	9	12 wks
16 Aug 62	PICK A BALE OF COTTON *Pye 7N 15455*	11	10 wks

The DENNISONS *Far left* After just 13 weeks inside, Liverpool lads the Dennisons go 'over the wall!'

Lonnie DONEGAN *Left* The King of Skiffle's run of hits ended the very month that the Kings of Beat first entered the chart with 'Love Me Do!'

The DRIFTERS *Below* Now, how many of you want to go before the plane takes off?

Date	Title Label Number	Position	Date	Title Label Number	Position

Ral DONNER

US, male vocalist

| 21 Sep 61 | YOU DON'T KNOW WHAT YOU'VE GOT Parlophone R 4820 | 25 | 10 wks |

DONOVAN

UK, male vocalist

25 Mar 65	● CATCH THE WIND Pye 7N 15801	4	13 wks
3 Jun 65	● COLOURS Pye 7N 15866	4	12 wks
11 Nov 65	TURQUOISE Pye 7N 15984	30	6 wks
8 Dec 66	● SUNSHINE SUPERMAN Pye 7N 17241	3	11 wks
9 Feb 67	● MELLOW YELLOW Pye 7N 17267	8	8 wks
25 Oct 67	● THERE IS A MOUNTAIN Pye 7N 17403	8	11 wks
21 Feb 68	● JENNIFER JUNIPER Pye 7N 17457	5	11 wks
29 May 68	● HURDY GURDY MAN Pye 7N 17537	4	10 wks
4 Dec 68	ATLANTIS Pye 7N 17660	23	8 wks

See also Donovan with The Jeff Beck Group.

DONOVAN with the Jeff BECK GROUP

UK, male vocalist/instrumental group

| 9 Jul 69 | GOO GOO BARABAJAGAL (LOVE IS HOT) Pye 7N 17778 | 12 | 9 wks |

See also Donovan, Jeff Beck.

Val DOONICAN

Ireland, male vocalist

15 Oct 64	● WALK TALL Decca F 11982	3	21 wks
21 Jan 65	● THE SPECIAL YEARS Decca F 12049	7	12 wks
22 Apr 65	THE SPECIAL YEARS (re-entry) Decca F 12049	49	1 wk
8 Apr 65	I'M GONNA GET THERE SOMEHOW Decca F 12118	25	5 wks
17 Mar 66	● ELUSIVE BUTTERFLY Decca F 12358	5	12 wks
3 Nov 66	● WHAT WOULD I BE Decca F 12505	2	17 wks
23 Feb 67	MEMORIES ARE MADE OF THIS Decca F 12566	11	12 wks
25 May 67	TWO STREETS Decca F 12608	39	4 wks
18 Oct 67	● IF THE WHOLE WORLD STOPPED LOVING Pye 7N 17396	3	19 wks
21 Feb 68	YOU'RE THE ONLY ONE Pye 7N 17465	37	4 wks
12 Jun 68	NOW Pye 7N 17534	43	2 wks
23 Oct 68	IF I KNEW THEN WHAT I KNOW NOW Pye 7N 17616	14	13 wks
23 Apr 69	RING OF BRIGHT WATER Pye 7N 17713	48	1 wk

DOORS

US, male vocal/instrumental group

| 16 Aug 67 | LIGHT MY FIRE Elektra EKSN 45014 | 49 | 1 wk |
| 28 Aug 68 | HELLO I LOVE YOU Elektra EKSN 45037 | 15 | 12 wks |

Lee DORSEY

US, male vocalist

3 Feb 66	GET OUT OF MY LIFE WOMAN Stateside SS 485	22	7 wks
5 May 66	CONFUSION Stateside SS 506	38	6 wks
11 Aug 66	● WORKING IN THE COALMINE Stateside SS 528	8	11 wks
27 Oct 66	● HOLY COW Stateside SS 552	6	12 wks

Craig DOUGLAS

UK, male vocalist

22 Jan 60	● PRETTY BLUE EYES Top Rank JAR 268	4	14 wks
28 Apr 60	● THE HEART OF A TEENAGE GIRL Top Rank JAR 340	10	9 wks
11 Aug 60	OH! WHAT A DAY Top Rank JAR 406	43	1 wk
20 Apr 61	● A HUNDRED POUNDS OF CLAY Top Rank JAR 555	9	9 wks
29 Jun 61	● TIME Top Rank JAR 569	9	14 wks
22 Mar 62	● WHEN MY LITTLE GIRL IS SMILING Top Rank JAR 610	9	13 wks
28 Jun 62	● OUR FAVOURITE MELODIES Columbia DB 4854	9	10 wks
18 Oct 62	OH LONESOME ME Decca F 11523	15	12 wks
28 Feb 63	TOWN CRIER Decca F 11575	36	4 wks

DOWLANDS

UK, male vocal duo

| 9 Jan 64 | ALL MY LOVING Oriole CB 1897 | 33 | 7 wks |

DOZY — See *Dave DEE, DOZY, BEAKY, MICK and TICH*

Charlie DRAKE

UK, male vocalist

| 27 Oct 60 | MR. CUSTER Parlophone R 4699 | 12 | 12 wks |
| 5 Oct 61 | MY BOOMERANG WON'T COME BACK Parlophone R 4824 | 14 | 11 wks |

Rusty DRAPER

US, male vocalist

| 11 Aug 60 | MULE SKINNER BLUES Mercury AMT 1101 | 39 | 4 wks |

DREAMERS — See *FREDDIE and the DREAMERS*

Alan DREW

UK, male vocalist

| 26 Sep 63 | ALWAYS THE LONELY ONE Columbia DB 7090 | 48 | 2 wks |

Date	Title Label Number	Position		Date	Title Label Number	Position	

DRIFTERS

US, male vocal group

8 Jan 60	DANCE WITH ME London HLE 8988	17	4 wks
10 Mar 60	DANCE WITH ME (re-entry) London HLE 8988	35	1 wk
3 Nov 60	● SAVE THE LAST DANCE FOR ME London HLK 9201	2	18 wks
16 Mar 61	I COUNT THE TEARS London HLK 9287	28	6 wks
5 Apr 62	WHEN MY LITTLE GIRL IS SMILING London HLK 9522	31	3 wks
10 Oct 63	I'LL TAKE YOU HOME London HLK 9785	37	5 wks
24 Sep 64	UNDER THE BOARDWALK Atlantic AT 4001	45	4 wks
8 Apr 65	AT THE CLUB Atlantic AT 4019	35	7 wks
29 Apr 65	COME ON OVER TO MY PLACE Atlantic AT 4023	40	5 wks
2 Feb 67	BABY WHAT I MEAN Atlantic 584 065	49	1 wk

Julie DRISCOLL, Brian AUGER and the TRINITY

UK, female vocalist/male instrumental group

17 Apr 68	● THIS WHEEL'S ON FIRE Marmalade 598 006	5	16 wks

Frank D'RONE

US, male vocalist

22 Dec 60	STRAWBERRY BLONDE Mercury AMT 1123	24	6 wks

DUBLINERS

Ireland, male vocal/instrumental group

30 Mar 67	● SEVEN DRUNKEN NIGHTS Major Minor MM 506	7	17 wks
30 Aug 67	BLACK VELVET BAND Major Minor MM 530	15	15 wks
20 Dec 67	NEVER WED AN OLD MAN Major Minor MM 551	43	3 wks

Simon DUPREE and The BIG SOUND

UK, male vocal/instrumental group

22 Nov 67	● KITES Parlophone R 5646	9	13 wks
3 Apr 68	FOR WHOM THE BELL TOLLS Parlophone R 5670	43	3 wks

Judith DURHAM

Australia, female vocalist

15 Jun 67	OLIVE TREE Columbia DB 8207	33	5 wks

Bob DYLAN

US, male vocalist

25 Mar 65	● TIMES THEY ARE A-CHANGIN' CBS 201751	9	11 wks
29 Apr 65	● SUBTERRANEAN HOMESICK BLUES CBS 201753	9	9 wks
17 Jun 65	MAGGIE'S FARM CBS 201781	22	8 wks
19 Aug 65	● LIKE A ROLLING STONE CBS 201811	4	12 wks
28 Oct 65	● POSITIVELY FOURTH STREET CBS 201824	8	12 wks
27 Jan 66	CAN YOU PLEASE CRAWL OUT YOUR WINDOW CBS 201900	17	5 wks
14 Apr 66	ONE OF US MUST KNOW (SOONER OR LATER) CBS 202053	33	5 wks
12 May 66	● RAINY DAY WOMEN NOS. 12 & 35 CBS 202307	7	8 wks
21 Jul 66	I WANT YOU CBS 202258	16	9 wks
14 May 69	I THREW IT ALL AWAY CBS 4219	30	6 wks
13 Sep 69	● LAY LADY LAY CBS 4434	5	12 wks

E

EARL — See *BOB and EARL*

EASYBEATS

Australia, male vocal/instrumental group

27 Oct 66	● FRIDAY ON MY MIND United Artists UP 1157	6	15 wks
10 Apr 68	HELLO HOW ARE YOU United Artists UP 2209	20	9 wks

Billy ECKSTINE and Sarah VAUGHAN

US, male/female vocal duo

12 Mar 69	PASSING STRANGERS Mercury MF 1082	20	15 wks

See also Sarah Vaughan.

Duane EDDY

US, male instrumentalist, guitar

1 Jan 60	SOME KINDA EARTHQUAKE London HLW 9007	12	3 wks
19 Feb 60	BONNIE CAME BACK London HLW 9050	12	10 wks
28 Apr 60	● SHAZAM! London HLW 9104	4	13 wks
21 Jul 60	● BECAUSE THEY'RE YOUNG London HLW 9162	2	18 wks
10 Nov 60	KOMMOTION London HLW 9225	13	10 wks
12 Jan 61	PEPE London HLW 9257	2	14 wks
20 Apr 61	● THEME FROM DIXIE London HLW 9324	7	10 wks
22 Jun 61	RING OF FIRE London HLW 9370	17	10 wks
14 Sep 61	DRIVIN' HOME London HLW 9406	30	4 wks
5 Oct 61	CARAVAN Parlophone R 4826	42	3 wks
24 May 62	DEEP IN THE HEART OF TEXAS RCA 1288	19	8 wks
23 Aug 62	● BALLAD OF PALADIN RCA 1300	10	10 wks
8 Nov 62	● DANCE WITH THE GUITAR MAN RCA 1316	4	16 wks

Date	Title Label Number	Position	
14 Feb 63	**BOSS GUITAR** RCA 1329	**27**	8 wks
30 May 63	**LONELY BOY LONELY GUITAR** RCA 1344	**35**	4 wks
29 Aug 63	**YOUR BABY'S GONE SURFIN'** RCA 1357	**49**	1 wk

The London Hits featured Duane Eddy and the Rebels. Dance With The Guitar Man, Boss Guitar featured Duane Eddy and the Rebelettes.

ELECTRIC PRUNES

US, male vocal/instrumental group

Date	Title Label Number	Position	
9 Feb 67	**I HAD TOO MUCH TO DREAM LAST NIGHT** Reprise RS 20532	**49**	1 wk
11 May 67	**GET ME TO THE WORLD ON TIME** Reprise RS 20564	**42**	4 wks

Ray ELLINGTON

UK, orchestra

Date	Title Label Number	Position	
15 Nov 62	**THE MADISON** Ember S 102	**41**	2 wks
20 Dec 62	**THE MADISON** (re-entry) Ember S 102	**36**	2 wks

Bern ELLIOTT and the FENMEN

UK, male vocalist, male vocal/instrumental backing group

Date	Title Label Number	Position	
21 Nov 63	**MONEY** Decca F 11770	**14**	13 wks
19 Mar 64	**NEW ORLEANS** Decca F 11852	**24**	9 wks

Shirley ELLIS

US, female vocalist

Date	Title Label Number	Position	
6 May 65	● **THE CLAPPING SONG** London HLR 9961	**6**	13 wks

Dick EMERY

UK, male vocalist

Date	Title Label Number	Position	
26 Feb 69	**IF YOU LOVE HER** Pye 7N 17644	**32**	4 wks

ENGLAND SISTERS

UK, female vocal group

Date	Title Label Number	Position	
17 Mar 60	**HEARTBEAT** HMV POP 710	**33**	1 wk

EQUALS

UK, male vocal/instrumental group

Date	Title Label Number	Position	
21 Feb 68	**I GET SO EXCITED** President PT 180	**44**	4 wks
1 May 68	**BABY COME BACK** President PT 135	**50**	1 wk
15 May 68	★ **BABY COME BACK** (re-entry) President PT 135	**1**	17 wks
21 Aug 68	**LAUREL & HARDY** President PT 200	**35**	5 wks
27 Nov 68	**SOFTLY SOFTLY** President PT 222	**48**	3 wks
2 Apr 69	**MICHAEL & THE SLIPPER TREE** President PT 240	**24**	7 wks
30 Jul 69	● **VIVA BOBBY JOE** President PT 260	**6**	14 wks
27 Dec 69	**RUB A DUB DUB** President PT 275	**34**	7 wks

ESCORTS

UK, male vocal/instrumental group

Date	Title Label Number	Position	
2 Jul 64	**THE ONE TO CRY** Fontana TF 474	**49**	2 wks

ESSEX

US, male/female vocal group

Date	Title Label Number	Position	
8 Aug 63	**EASIER SAID THAN DONE** Columbia DB 7077	**41**	5 wks

ETHIOPIANS

Jamaica, male vocal/instrumental group

Date	Title Label Number	Position	
13 Sep 67	**TRAIN TO SKAVILLE** Rio RIO 130	**40**	6 wks

EVANS — See *ZAGER and EVANS*

Maureen EVANS

UK, female vocalist

Date	Title Label Number	Position	
22 Jan 60	**THE BIG HURT** Oriole CB 1533	**26**	2 wks
17 Mar 60	**LOVE KISSES & HEARTACHES** Oriole CB 1540	**44**	1 wk
2 Jun 60	**PAPER ROSES** Oriole CB 1550	**40**	5 wks
29 Nov 62	● **LIKE I DO** Oriole CB 1763	**3**	18 wks
27 Feb 64	**I LOVE HOW YOU LOVE ME** Oriole CB 1906	**34**	10 wks
14 May 64	**I LOVE HOW YOU LOVE ME** (re-entry) Oriole CB 1906	**50**	1 wk

Paul EVANS

US, male vocalist

Date	Title Label Number	Position	
31 Mar 60	**MIDNIGHT SPECIAL** London HLL 9045	**41**	1 wk

Betty EVERETT

US, female vocalist

Date	Title Label Number	Position	
14 Jan 65	**GETTING MIGHTY CROWDED** Fontana TF 520	**29**	7 wks
30 Oct 68	**IT'S IN HIS KISS** President PT 215	**34**	7 wks

EVERLY BROTHERS

US, male vocal duo

Date	Title Label Number	Position	
12 Feb 60	**LET IT BE ME** London HLA 9039	**13**	5 wks
31 Mar 60	**LET IT BE ME** (re-entry) London HLA 9039	**26**	4 wks
14 Apr 60	★ **CATHY'S CLOWN** Warner Bros. WB 1	**1**	18 wks
14 Jul 60	● **WHEN WILL I BE LOVED** London HLA 9157	**4**	16 wks
22 Sep 60	● **LUCILLE / SO SAD (TO WATCH GOOD LOVE GO BAD)** Warner Bros. WB 19	**4**	15 wks
15 Dec 60	**LIKE STRANGERS** London HLA 9250	**11**	10 wks
9 Feb 61	★ **WALK RIGHT BACK** Warner Bros. WB 33	**1**	16 wks
15 Jun 61	★ **TEMPTATION** Warner Bros. WB 42	**1**	15 wks
5 Oct 61	**MUSKRAT** Warner Bros. WB 50	**20**	6 wks
18 Jan 62	● **CRYIN' IN THE RAIN** Warner Bros. WB 56	**6**	15 wks

Date	Title Label Number	Position		Date	Title Label Number	Position	
17 May 62	HOW CAN I MEET HER *Warner Bros. WB 67*	12	10 wks	20 Jul 61	DON'T YOU KNOW IT *Parlophone R 4807*	12	10 wks
25 Oct 62	NO ONE CAN MAKE MY SUNSHINE SMILE *Warner Bros. WB 79*	11	11 wks	26 Oct 61	● THE TIME HAS COME *Parlophone R 4837*	4	14 wks
21 Mar 63	SO IT WILL ALWAYS BE *Warner Bros. WB 94*	23	11 wks	18 Jan 62	LONESOME *Parlophone R 4864*	12	9 wks
13 Jun 63	IT'S BEEN NICE *Warner Bros. WB 99*	26	5 wks	3 May 62	● AS YOU LIKE IT *Parlophone R 4896*	5	15 wks
17 Oct 63	THE GIRL SANG THE BLUES *Warner Bros. WB 109*	25	9 wks	30 Aug 62	● DON'T THAT BEAT ALL *Parlophone R 4930*	8	11 wks
16 Jul 64	FERRIS WHEEL *Warner Bros. WB 135*	22	10 wks	13 Dec 62	BABY TAKE A BOW *Parlophone R 4964*	22	6 wks
3 Dec 64	GONE GONE GONE *Warner Bros. WB 146*	36	7 wks	31 Jan 63	WHAT NOW *Parlophone R 4990*	31	5 wks
6 May 65	THAT'LL BE THE DAY *Warner Bros. WB 158*	30	4 wks	11 Jul 63	WALKIN' TALL *Parlophone R 5039*	23	6 wks
20 May 65	● THE PRICE OF LOVE *Warner Bros. WB 161*	2	14 wks	19 Sep 63	● THE FIRST TIME *Parlophone R 5061*	5	13 wks
26 Aug 65	I'LL NEVER GET OVER YOU *Warner Bros. WB 5639*	35	5 wks	12 Dec 63	WE ARE IN LOVE *Parlophone R 5091*	11	12 wks
21 Oct 65	LOVE IS STRANGE *Warner Bros. WB 5649*	11	9 wks	12 Mar 64	IF HE TELLS YOU *Parlophone R 5109*	25	9 wks
8 May 68	IT'S MY TIME *Warner Bros. WB 7192*	39	6 wks	28 May 64	I LOVE BEING IN LOVE WITH YOU *Parlophone R 5138*	33	6 wks
				26 Nov 64	MESSAGE TO MARTHA (KENTUCKY BLUEBIRD) *Parlophone R 5201*	12	11 wks
				11 Feb 65	STOP FEELING SORRY FOR YOURSELF *Parlophone R 5235*	23	6 wks
				17 Jun 65	SOMEONE'S TAKEN MARIA AWAY *Parlophone R 5289*	34	5 wks
				20 Oct 66	CHERYL'S GOIN' HOME *Parlophone R 5516*	46	2 wks

EXCITERS

US, male/female vocal group

Date	Title Label Number	Position	
21 Feb 63	TELL HIM *United Artists UP 1011*	46	1 wk

F

Shelley FABARES

US, female vocalist

Date	Title Label Number	Position	
26 Apr 62	JOHNNY ANGEL *Pye International 7N 25132*	41	4 wks

FABIAN

US, male vocalist

Date	Title Label Number	Position	
10 Mar 60	HOUND DOG MAN *HMV POP 695*	46	1 wk

FAIRPORT CONVENTION

UK, male/female vocal/instrumental group

Date	Title Label Number	Position	
23 Jul 69	SI TU DOIS PARTIR *Island WIP 6064*	21	8 wks
27 Sep 69	SI TU DOIS PARTIR (re-entry) *Island WIP 6064*	49	1 wk

Adam FAITH

UK, male vocalist

Date	Title Label Number	Position	
1 Jan 60	● WHAT DO YOU WANT *Parlophone R 4591*	2	9 wks
22 Jan 60	★ POOR ME *Parlophone R 4623*	1	17 wks
10 Mar 60	WHAT DO YOU WANT (re-entry) *Parlophone R 4591*	24	4 wks
14 Apr 60	● SOMEONE ELSE'S BABY *Parlophone R 4643*	2	13 wks
30 Jun 60	● WHEN JOHNNY COMES MARCHING HOME/ MADE YOU *Parlophone R 4665*	5	13 wks
15 Sep 60	● HOW ABOUT THAT *Parlophone R 4689*	4	14 wks
17 Nov 60	● LONELY PUP (IN A CHRISTMAS SHOP) *Parlophone R 4708*	4	11 wks
9 Feb 61	● THIS IS IT / WHO AM I *Parlophone R 4735*	5	14 wks
27 Apr 61	EASY GOING ME *Parlophone R 4766*	12	10 wks

The following hits featured the Roulettes, UK, male vocal/instrumental group, backing Adam Faith: The First Time, We Are In Love, If He Tells You, I Love Being In Love With You.

Percy FAITH

US, orchestra

Date	Title Label Number	Position	
10 Mar 60	● THEME FROM 'A SUMMER PLACE' *Philips PB 989*	2	30 wks

Marianne FAITHFULL

UK, female vocalist

Date	Title Label Number	Position	
13 Aug 64	● AS TEARS GO BY *Decca F 11923*	9	13 wks
18 Feb 65	● COME AND STAY WITH ME *Decca F 12075*	4	13 wks
6 May 65	● THIS LITTLE BIRD *Decca F 12162*	6	11 wks
22 Jul 65	● SUMMER NIGHTS *Decca F 12193*	10	10 wks
4 Nov 65	YESTERDAY *Decca F 12268*	36	4 wks
9 Mar 67	IS THIS WHAT I GET FOR LOVING YOU *Decca F 22524*	43	2 wks

Georgie FAME

UK, male vocalist

Date	Title Label Number	Position	
17 Dec 64	★ YEH YEH *Columbia DB 7428*	1	12 wks
4 Mar 65	IN THE MEANTIME *Columbia DB 7494*	22	8 wks
29 Jul 65	LIKE WE USED TO BE *Columbia DB 7633*	33	7 wks
28 Oct 65	SOMETHING *Columbia DB 7727*	23	7 wks
23 Jun 66	★ GET AWAY *Columbia DB 7946*	1	11 wks
22 Sep 66	SUNNY *Columbia DB 8015*	13	8 wks
22 Dec 66	SITTING IN THE PARK *Columbia DB 8096*	12	10 wks
23 Mar 67	BECAUSE I LOVE YOU *CBS 202587*	15	8 wks
13 Sep 67	TRY MY WORLD *CBS 2945*	37	5 wks
13 Dec 67	★ BALLAD OF BONNIE & CLYDE *CBS 3124*	1	13 wks
9 Jul 69	PEACEFUL *CBS 4295*	16	9 wks
13 Dec 69	SEVENTH SON *CBS 4659*	25	7 wks

All Columbia hits except Sunny credit The Blue Flames backing Georgie Fame.

FAMILY

UK, male vocal/instrumental group

Date	Title Label Number	Position	
1 Nov 69	NO MULE'S FOOL *Reprise RS 27001*	29	7 wks

FLEETWOOD MAC *Below* Long serving member Mick Fleetwood, son of an RAF Wing Commander, got his first ever set of drums in 1962. By the following year, at the age of sixteen, he had played dozens of clubs with Pete Bardens' group the Cheynes, including the famous Cavern Club in Liverpool. The first record he ever made was the Cheynes' 'It's Gonna Happen To Me', in November '63.

Georgie FAME *Top*
Aretha FRANKLIN *Middle*
and FABIAN *Above.*

FAMILY DOGG *Left* Leader
Steve Rowland anticipates
Adam Ant while the other
Doggs – look cool/wear
wigs/do Frank Zappa
impressions.

Date	Title Label Number	Position

FAMILY DOGG
UK, male/female vocal group

28 May 69 ● WAY OF LIFE *Bell 1055*	**6** 14 wks

FAMILY STONE — See *SLY and the FAMILY STONE*

FAMOUS FLAMES — See *James BROWN and the FAMOUS FLAMES*

Chris FARLOWE
UK, male vocalist

27 Jan 66	THINK *Immediate IM 023*	**49**	1 wk
10 Feb 66	THINK (re-entry) *Immediate IM 023*	**37**	2 wks
23 Jun 66 ★	OUT OF TIME *Immediate IM 035*	**1**	13 wks
27 Oct 66	RIDE ON BABY *Immediate IM 038*	**31**	7 wks
16 Feb 67	MY WAY OF GIVING IN *Immediate IM 041*	**48**	1 wk
29 Jun 67	MOANIN' *Immediate IM 056*	**46**	2 wks
13 Dec 67	HANDBAGS & GLADRAGS *Immediate IM 065*	**33**	6 wks

José FELICIANO
US, male vocalist/instrumentalist, guitar

18 Sep 68 ●	LIGHT MY FIRE *RCA 1715*	**6**	16 wks
18 Oct 69	AND THE SUN WILL SHINE *RCA 1871*	**25**	7 wks

FENDERMEN
US, male vocal/instrumental duo, guitars

18 Aug 60	MULE SKINNER BLUES *Top Rank JAR 395*	**50**	1 wk
1 Sep 60	MULE SKINNER BLUES (re-entry) *Top Rank JAR 395*	**37**	2 wks
29 Sep 60	MULE SKINNER BLUES (2nd re-entry) *Top Rank JAR 395*	**32**	6 wks

FENMEN — See *Bern ELLIOTT and the FENMEN*

Peter FENTON
UK, male vocalist

10 Nov 66	MARBLE BREAKS IRON BENDS *Fontana TF 748*	**46**	3 wks

Shane FENTON and the FENTONES
UK, male vocal/instrumental group

26 Oct 61	I'M A MOODY GUY *Parlophone R 4827*	**22**	8 wks
1 Feb 62	WALK AWAY *Parlophone R 4866*	**38**	5 wks
5 Apr 62	IT'S ALL OVER NOW *Parlophone R 4883*	**29**	7 wks
12 Jul 62	CINDY'S BIRTHDAY *Parlophone R 4921*	**19**	8 wks

See also Fentones.

FENTONES
UK, male instrumental group

19 Apr 62	THE MEXICAN *Parlophone R 4899*	**41**	3 wks
27 Sep 62	THE BREEZE & I *Parlophone R 4937*	**48**	1 wk

See also Shane Fenton and the Fentones.

FERRANTE and TEICHER
US, male instrumental duo, pianos

18 Aug 60	THEME FROM 'THE APPARTMENT' *London HLT 9164*	**44**	1 wk
9 Mar 61 ●	THEME FROM 'EXODUS' *London HLT 9298 and HMV POP 881*	**6**	17 wks

Theme From Exodus *available first on London, then on HMV when the American label, United Artists, changed its UK outlet.*

Ernie FIELDS
US, orchestra

1 Jan 60	IN THE MOOD *London HL 8985*	**13**	7 wks

FIFTH DIMENSION
US, male/female vocal group

23 Apr 69	AQUARIUS - LET THE SUNSHINE IN (MEDLEY) *Liberty LBF 15198*	**11**	11 wks

FIREBALLS
US, male instrumental group

27 Jul 61	QUITE A PARTY *Pye International 7N 25092*	**29**	9 wks

See also Jimmy Gilmer and the Fireballs.

FIRST EDITION — See *Kenny ROGERS and the FIRST EDITION*

Toni FISHER
US, female vocalist

12 Feb 60	THE BIG HURT *Top Rank JAR 261*	**30**	1 wk

Ella FITZGERALD
US, female vocalist

21 Apr 60	MACK THE KNIFE *HMV POP 736*	**19**	9 wks
6 Oct 60	HOW HIGH THE MOON *HMV POP 782*	**46**	1 wk
22 Nov 62	DESAFINADO *Verve VS 502*	**38**	4 wks
27 Dec 62	DESAFINADO (re-entry) *Verve VS 502*	**41**	2 wks
30 Apr 64	CAN'T BUY ME LOVE *Verve VS 519*	**34**	5 wks

FLAMINGOS
US, male vocal group

4 Jun 69	BOOGALOO PARTY *Philips BF 1786*	**26**	5 wks

Date	Title *Label Number*	Position		Date	Title *Label Number*	Position

Lester FLATT and Earl SCRUGGS

US, male instrumental duo, banjos

15 Nov 67	**FOGGY MOUNTAIN BREAKDOWN**	**39**	6 wks
	CBS 3038 and Mercury MF 1007		

The versions on the two labels were not the same cuts; CBS had a 1965 recording, Mercury a 1967. The chart did not differentiate and listed both together.

FLEE-REKKERS

UK, male instrumental group

19 May 60	**GREEN JEANS** *Triumph RGM 1008*	**23**	13 wks

FLEETWOOD MAC

UK, male vocal/instrumental group

10 Apr 68	**BLACK MAGIC WOMAN**	**37**	7 wks
	Blue Horizon 57 3138		
17 Jul 68	**NEED YOUR LOVE SO BAD**	**31**	13 wks
	Blue Horizon 57 3139		
4 Dec 68	★ **ALBATROSS** *Blue Horizon 57 3145*	**1**	20 wks
16 Apr 69	● **MAN OF THE WORLD** *Immediate IM 080*	**2**	14 wks
23 Jul 69	**NEED YOUR LOVE SO BAD** (re-issue)	**32**	6 wks
	Blue Horizon 57 3157		
13 Sep 69	**NEED YOUR LOVE SO BAD** (re-entry of re-issue) *Blue Horizon 57 3157*	**42**	3 wks
4 Oct 69	● **OH WELL** *Reprise RS 27000*	**2**	16 wks

FLOWERPOT MEN

UK, male vocal group

23 Aug 67	● **LET'S GO TO SAN FRANCISCO**	**4**	12 wks
	Deram DM 142		

Eddie FLOYD

US, male vocalist

2 Feb 67	**KNOCK ON WOOD** *Atlantic 584 041*	**50**	1 wk
2 Mar 67	**KNOCK ON WOOD** (re-entry)	**19**	17 wks
	Atlantic 584 041		
16 Mar 67	**RAISE YOUR HAND** *Stax 601 001*	**42**	3 wks
9 Aug 67	**THINGS GET BETTER** *Stax 601 016*	**31**	8 wks

Wayne FONTANA

UK, male vocalist

9 Dec 65	**IT WAS EASIER TO HURT HER**	**36**	6 wks
	Fontana TF 642		
21 Apr 66	**COME ON HOME** *Fontana TF 684*	**16**	12 wks
25 Aug 66	**GOODBYE BLUEBIRD** *Fontana TF 737*	**49**	1 wk
8 Dec 66	**PAMELA PAMELA** *Fontana TF 770*	**11**	12 wks

See also Wayne Fontana and the Mindbenders.

Wayne FONTANA and the MINDBENDERS

UK, male vocalist, male vocal/instrumental backing group

11 Jul 63	**HELLO JOSEPHINE** *Fontana TF 404*	**46**	2 wks
28 May 64	**STOP LOOK & LISTEN** *Fontana TF 451*	**37**	4 wks
8 Oct 64	● **UM UM UM UM UM UM** *Fontana TF 497*	**5**	15 wks
4 Feb 65	● **GAME OF LOVE** *Fontana TF 535*	**2**	11 wks
17 Jun 65	**JUST A LITTLE BIT TOO LATE**	**20**	7 wks
	Fontana TF 579		
30 Sep 65	**SHE NEEDS LOVE** *Fontana TF 611*	**32**	6 wks

See also Wayne Fontana, Mindbenders.

Bill FORBES

UK, male vocalist

15 Jan 60	**TOO YOUNG** *Columbia DB 4386*	**29**	1 wk

Clinton FORD

UK, male vocalist

17 Aug 61	**TOO MANY BEAUTIFUL GIRLS**	**48**	1 wk
	Oriole CB 1623		
8 Mar 62	**FANLIGHT FANNY** *Oriole CB 1706*	**22**	10 wks
5 Jan 67	**RUN TO THE DOOR** *Piccadilly 7N 35361*	**25**	13 wks

Emile FORD and the CHECKMATES

UK, male vocal/instrumental group

1 Jan 60	★ **WHAT DO YOU WANT TO MAKE THOSE EYES AT ME FOR** *Pye 7N 15225*	**1**	17 wks
5 Feb 60	● **ON A SLOW BOAT TO CHINA** *Pye 7N 15245*	**3**	14 wks
26 May 60	**YOU'LL NEVER KNOW WHAT YOU'RE MISSING** *Pye 7N 15268*	**12**	9 wks
1 Sep 60	**THEM THERE EYES** *Pye 7N 15282*	**18**	16 wks
8 Dec 60	● **COUNTING TEARDROPS** *Pye 7N 15314*	**4**	12 wks
2 Mar 61	**WHAT AM I GONNA DO** *Pye 7N 15331*	**33**	6 wks
18 May 61	**HALF OF MY HEART** *Piccadilly 7N 35003*	**50**	1 wk
22 Jun 61	**HALF OF MY HEART** (re-entry)	**42**	3 wks
	Piccadilly 7N 35003		
8 Mar 62	**I WONDER WHO'S KISSING HER NOW**	**43**	1 wk
	Piccadilly 7N 35033		

Checkmates not on Them There Eyes *or the two Piccadilly hits.*

George FORMBY

UK, male vocalist/instrumentalist, ukelele

21 Jul 60	**HAPPY GO LUCKY ME**/ **BANJO BOY**	**40**	3 wks
	Pye 7N 15269		

Lance FORTUNE

UK, male vocalist

19 Feb 60	● **BE MINE** *Pye 7N 15240*	**4**	12 wks
5 May 60	**THIS LOVE I HAVE FOR YOU** *Pye 7N 15260*	**26**	5 wks

Date	Title Label Number	Position

FORTUNES

UK, male vocal/instrumental group

Date	Title Label Number	Position	
8 Jul 65	● YOU'VE GOT YOUR TROUBLES Decca F 12173	2	14 wks
7 Oct 65	● HERE IT COMES AGAIN Decca F 12243	4	14 wks
3 Feb 66	THIS GOLDEN RING Decca F 12321	15	9 wks

FOUNDATIONS

UK, male vocal/instrumental group

Date	Title Label Number	Position	
27 Sep 67	★ BABY NOW THAT I'VE FOUND YOU Pye 7N 17366	1	16 wks
24 Jan 68	BACK ON MY FEET AGAIN Pye 7N 17417	18	10 wks
1 May 68	ANY OLD TIME Pye 7N 17503	48	1 wk
15 May 68	ANY OLD TIME (re-entry) Pye 7N 17503	50	1 wk
20 Nov 68	● BUILD ME UP BUTTERCUP Pye 7N 17638	2	15 wks
12 Mar 69	● IN THE BAD BAD OLD DAYS Pye 7N 17702	8	10 wks
13 Sep 69	BORN TO LIVE AND BORN TO DIE Pye 7N 17809	46	3 wks

FOUR LADS

US, male vocal group

Date	Title Label Number	Position	
28 Apr 60	STANDING ON THE CORNER Philips PB 1000	34	4 wks

FOUR PENNIES

UK, male vocal/instrumental group

Date	Title Label Number	Position	
16 Jan 64	DO YOU WANT ME TO Philips BF 1296	47	1 wk
6 Feb 64	DO YOU WANT ME TO (re-entry) Philips BF 1296	49	1 wk
2 Apr 64	★ JULIET Philips BF 1322	1	15 wks
16 Jul 64	I FOUND OUT THE HARD WAY Philips BF 1349	14	11 wks
29 Oct 64	BLACK GIRL Philips BF 1366	20	12 wks
7 Oct 65	UNTIL IT'S TIME FOR YOU TO GO Philips BF 1435	19	11 wks
17 Feb 66	TROUBLE IS MY MIDDLE NAME Philips BF 1469	32	5 wks

FOUR PREPS

US male vocal group

Date	Title Label Number	Position	
26 May 60	GOT A GIRL Capitol CL 15128	28	6 wks
14 Jul 60	GOT A GIRL (re-entry) Capitol CL 15128	47	1 wk
2 Nov 61	MORE MONEY FOR YOU AND ME (MEDLEY) Capitol CL 15217	39	2 wks

Tracks of medley: Mr. Blue/ Alley Oop/ Smoke Gets In Your Eyes/ In This Whole Wide World/ A Worried Man/ Tom Dooley/ A Teenager In Love, all with new lyrics.

FOUR SEASONS

US, male vocal group

Date	Title Label Number	Position	
4 Oct 62	● SHERRY Stateside SS 122	8	16 wks
17 Jan 63	BIG GIRLS DONT CRY Stateside SS 145	13	10 wks
28 Mar 63	WALK LIKE A MAN Stateside SS 169	12	12 wks
27 Jun 63	AIN'T THAT A SHAME Stateside SS 194	38	3 wks
27 Aug 64	● RAG DOLL Philips BF 1347	2	13 wks
18 Nov 65	● LET'S HANG ON Philips BF 1439	4	16 wks
31 Mar 66	WORKIN' MY WAY BACK TO YOU Philips BF 1474	50	3 wks
2 Jun 66	OPUS 17 (DON'T YOU WORRY 'BOUT ME) Philips BF 1493	20	9 wks
29 Sep 66	I'VE GOT YOU UNDER MY SKIN Philips BF 1511	12	11 wks
12 Jan 67	TELL IT TO THE RAIN Philips BF 1538	37	5 wks

First two Philips hits 'with the sound of Frankie Valli', last four Philips hits 'with Frankie Valli'.

FOUR TOPS

US, male vocal group

Date	Title Label Number	Position	
1 Jul 65	I CAN'T HELP MYSELF Tamla Motown TMG 515	23	9 wks
2 Sep 65	IT'S THE SAME OLD SONG Tamla Motown TMG 528	34	8 wks
21 Jul 66	LOVING YOU IS SWEETER THAN EVER Tamla Motown TMG 568	21	12 wks
13 Oct 66	★ REACH OUT I'LL BE THERE Tamla Motown TMG 579	1	16 wks
12 Jan 67	● STANDING IN THE SHADOWS OF LOVE Tamla Motown TMG 589	6	8 wks
30 Mar 67	● BERNADETTE Tamla Motown TMG 601	8	10 wks
15 Jun 67	SEVEN ROOMS OF GLOOM Tamla Motown TMG 612	12	9 wks
11 Oct 67	YOU KEEP RUNNING AWAY Tamla Motown TMG 623	26	7 wks
13 Dec 67	● WALK AWAY RENEE Tamla Motown TMG 634	3	11 wks
13 Mar 68	● IF I WERE A CARPENTER Tamla Motown TMG 647	7	11 wks
21 Aug 68	YESTERDAY'S DREAMS Tamla Motown TMG 665	23	15 wks
13 Nov 68	I'M IN A DIFFERENT WORLD Tamla Motown TMG 675	27	13 wks
28 May 69	WHAT IS A MAN Tamla Motown TMG 698	16	11 wks
27 Sep 69	DO WHAT YOU GOTTA DO Tamla Motown TMG 710	11	11 wks

FOURMOST

UK, male vocal/instrumental group

Date	Title Label Number	Position	
12 Sep 63	● HELLO LITTLE GIRL Parlophone R 5056	9	17 wks
26 Dec 63	I'M IN LOVE Parlophone R 5078	17	12 wks
23 Apr 64	● A LITTLE LOVING Parlophone R 5128	6	13 wks
13 Aug 64	HOW CAN I TELL HER Parlophone R 5157	33	4 wks
26 Nov 64	BABY I NEED YOUR LOVIN' Parlophone R 5194	24	12 wks
9 Dec 65	GIRLS GIRLS GIRLS Parlophone R 5379	33	7 wks

Inez FOXX

US, female vocalist

Date	Title Label Number	Position	
23 Jul 64	HURT BY LOVE Sue WI 323	40	3 wks

See also Inez and Charlie Foxx.

Date	Title *Label Number*	Position		Date	Title *Label Number*	Position

Inez and Charlie FOXX

US, female/male vocal/instrumental duo, Charlie Foxx

guitar

Date	Title *Label Number*	Position	
19 Feb 69	**MOCKINGBIRD** *United Artists UP 2269*	**36**	2 wks
19 Mar 69	**MOCKINGBIRD** (re-entry) *United Artists UP 2269*	**34**	3 wks

See also Inez Foxx.

Connie FRANCIS

US, female vocalist

Date	Title *Label Number*	Position	
1 Jan 60	**AMONG MY SOUVENIRS** *MGM 1046*	**11**	6 wks
17 Mar 60	**VALENTINO** *MGM 1060*	**27**	8 wks
19 May 60	● **MAMA/ ROBOT MAN** *MGM 1076*	**2**	19 wks
18 Aug 60	● **EVERYBODY'S SOMEBODY'S FOOL** *MGM 1086*	**5**	13 wks
3 Nov 60	● **MY HEART HAS A MIND OF ITS OWN** *MGM 1100*	**3**	15 wks
12 Jan 61	**MANY TEARS AGO** *MGM 1111*	**12**	9 wks
16 Mar 61	● **WHERE THE BOYS ARE/ BABY ROO** *MGM 1121*	**5**	14 wks
15 Jun 61	**BREAKIN' IN A BRAND NEW BROKEN HEART** *MGM 1136*	**12**	11 wks
14 Sep 61	● **TOGETHER** *MGM 1138*	**6**	11 wks
14 Dec 61	**BABY'S FIRST CHRISTMAS** *MGM 1145*	**30**	4 wks
26 Apr 62	**DON'T BREAK THE HEART THAT LOVES YOU** *MGM 1157*	**39**	3 wks
2 Aug 62	● **VACATION** *MGM 1165*	**10**	9 wks
20 Dec 62	**I'M GONNA BE WARM THIS WINTER** *MGM 1185*	**48**	1 wk
10 Jun 65	**MY CHILD** *MGM 1271*	**26**	6 wks
20 Jan 66	**JEALOUS HEART** *MGM 1293*	**44**	2 wks

Aretha FRANKLIN

US, female vocalist

Date	Title *Label Number*	Position	
8 Jun 67	● **RESPECT** *Atlantic 584 115*	**10**	14 wks
23 Aug 67	**BABY I LOVE YOU** *Atlantic 584 127*	**39**	4 wks
20 Dec 67	**CHAIN OF FOOLS/ SATISFACTION** *Atlantic 584 157*	**43**	2 wks
10 Jan 68	**SATISFACTION** (re-entry) *Atlantic 584 157*	**37**	5 wks
13 Mar 68	**SINCE YOU'VE BEEN GONE** *Atlantic 584 172*	**47**	1 wk
22 May 68	**THINK** *Atlantic 584 186*	**26**	9 wks
7 Aug 68	● **I SAY A LITTLE PRAYER** *Atlantic 584 206*	**4**	14 wks

John FRED and the PLAYBOY BAND

US, male vocal/instrumental group

Date	Title *Label Number*	Position	
3 Jan 68	● **JUDY IN DISGUISE (WITH GLASSES)** *Pye International 7N 25442*	**3**	12 wks

FREDDIE and the DREAMERS

UK, male vocal/instrumental group

Date	Title *Label Number*	Position	
9 May 63	● **IF YOU GOTTA MAKE A FOOL OF SOMEBODY** *Columbia DB 7032*	**3**	14 wks
8 Aug 63	● **I'M TELLING YOU NOW** *Columbia DB 7068*	**2**	11 wks
7 Nov 63	● **YOU WERE MADE FOR ME** *Columbia DB 7147*	**3**	15 wks
20 Feb 64	**OVER YOU** *Columbia DB 7214*	**13**	11 wks
14 May 64	**I LOVE YOU BABY** *Columbia DB 7286*	**16**	8 wks
16 Jul 64	**JUST FOR YOU** *Columbia DB 7322*	**41**	3 wks
5 Nov 64	● **I UNDERSTAND** *Columbia DB 7381*	**5**	15 wks
22 Apr 65	**A LITTLE YOU** *Columbia DB 7526*	**26**	5 wks
4 Nov 65	**THOU SHALT NOT STEAL** *Columbia DB 7720*	**44**	3 wks

FREDERICK — See *NINA and FREDERICK*

FRIENDS — See *DELANEY and BONNIE and FRIENDS featuring Eric CLAPTON*

Bobby FULLER FOUR

US, male vocal/instrumental group

Date	Title *Label Number*	Position	
14 Apr 66	**I FOUGHT THE LAW** *London HL 10030*	**33**	4 wks

Billy FURY

UK, male vocalist

Date	Title *Label Number*	Position	
10 Mar 60	● **COLETTE** *Decca F 11200*	**9**	10 wks
26 May 60	**THAT'S LOVE** *Decca F 11237*	**19**	11 wks
22 Sep 60	**WONDROUS PLACE** *Decca F 11267*	**25**	9 wks
19 Jan 61	**A THOUSAND STARS** *Decca F 11311*	**14**	10 wks
27 Apr 61	**DON'T WORRY** *Decca F 11334*	**40**	2 wks
11 May 61	● **HALFWAY TO PARADISE** *Decca F 11349*	**3**	23 wks
7 Sep 61	● **JEALOUSY** *Decca F 11384*	**2**	12 wks
14 Dec 61	● **I'D NEVER FIND ANOTHER YOU** *Decca F 11409*	**5**	15 wks
15 Mar 62	**LETTER FULL OF TEARS** *Decca F 11437*	**32**	6 wks
3 May 62	● **LAST NIGHT WAS MADE FOR LOVE** *Decca F 11458*	**4**	16 wks
19 Jul 62	● **ONCE UPON A DREAM** *Decca F 11485*	**7**	13 wks
25 Oct 62	**BECAUSE OF LOVE** *Decca F 11508*	**18**	14 wks
14 Feb 63	● **LIKE I'VE NEVER BEEN GONE** *Decca F11582*	**3**	15 wks
16 May 63	● **WHEN WILL YOU SAY I LOVE YOU** *Decca F 11655*	**3**	12 wks
25 Jul 63	● **IN SUMMER** *Decca F 11701*	**5**	11 wks
3 Oct 63	**SOMEBODY ELSE'S GIRL** *Decca F 11744*	**18**	7 wks
2 Jan 64	**DO YOU REALLY LOVE ME TOO** *Decca F 11792*	**13**	10 wks
30 Apr 64	**I WILL** *Decca F 118888*	**14**	12 wks
23 Jul 64	● **IT'S ONLY MAKE BELIEVE** *Decca F 11939*	**10**	10 wks
14 Jan 65	**I'M LOST WITHOUT YOU** *Decca F 12048*	**16**	10 wks
22 Jul 65	● **IN THOUGHTS OF YOU** *Decca F 12178*	**9**	11 wks
16 Sep 65	**RUN TO MY LOVIN' ARMS** *Decca F 12230*	**25**	7 wks
10 Feb 66	**I'LL NEVER QUITE GET OVER YOU** *Decca F 12325*	**35**	5 wks
4 Aug 66	**GIVE ME YOUR WORD** *Decca F 12459*	**27**	7 wks

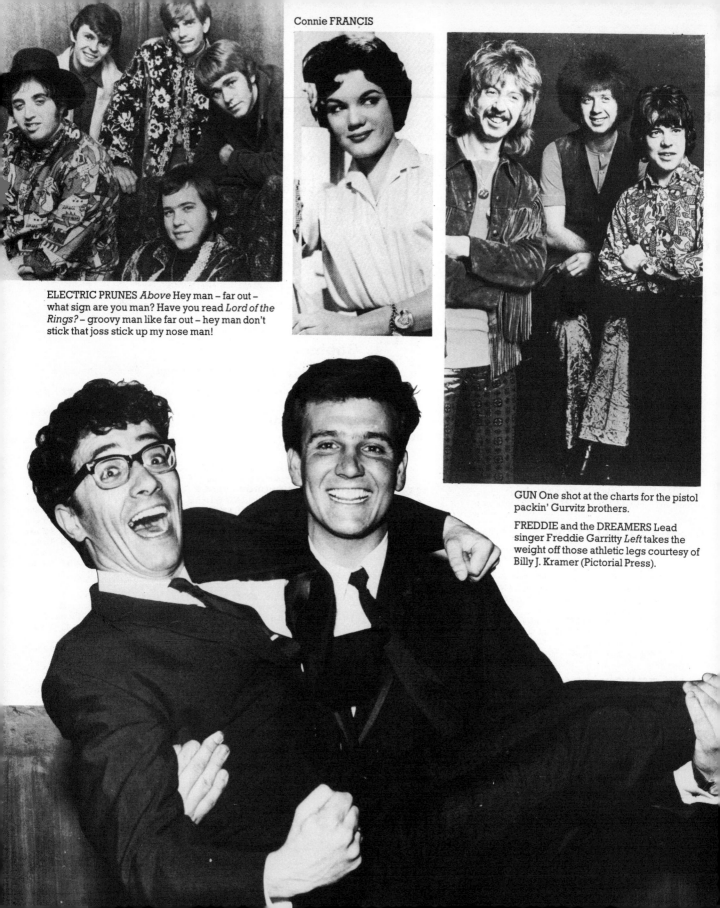

Connie FRANCIS

ELECTRIC PRUNES *Above* Hey man – far out – what sign are you man? Have you read *Lord of the Rings?* – groovy man like far out – hey man don't stick that joss stick up my nose man!

GUN One shot at the charts for the pistol packin' Gurvitz brothers.

FREDDIE and the DREAMERS Lead singer Freddie Garritty *Left* takes the weight off those athletic legs courtesy of Billy J. Kramer (Pictorial Press).

Date	Title *Label Number*	Position		Date	Title *Label Number*	Position

Serge GAINSBOURG — See *Jane BIRKIN and Serge GAINSBOURG*

David GARRICK

UK, male vocalist

| 9 Jun 66 | **LADY JANE** *Piccadilly 7N 35317* | **28** | 7 wks |
| 22 Sep 66 | **DEAR MRS. APPLEBEE** *Piccadilly 7N 35335* | **22** | 9 wks |

Marvin GAYE

US, male vocalist

10 Dec 64	**HOW SWEET IT IS** *Stateside SS 360*	**49**	1 wk
29 Sep 66	**LITTLE DARLIN'** *Tamla Motown TMG 574*	**50**	1 wk
12 Feb 69	★ **I HEARD IT THROUGH THE GRAPEVINE** *Tamla Motown TMG 686*	**1**	15 wks
23 Jul 69	● **TOO BUSY THINKING 'BOUT MY BABY** *Tamla Motown TMG 705*	**5**	16 wks

See also Marvin Gaye and Tammi Terrell; Marvin Gaye and Mary Wells; Marvin Gaye and Kim Weston.

Marvin GAYE and Tammi TERRELL

US, male/female vocal duo

17 Jan 68	**IF I COULD BUILD MY WHOLE WORLD AROUND YOU** *Tamla Motown TMG 635*	**41**	7 wks
12 Jun 68	**AIN'T NOTHIN' LIKE THE REAL THING** *Tamla Motown TMG 655*	**34**	7 wks
2 Oct 68	**YOU'RE ALL I NEED TO GET BY** *Tamla Motown TMG 668*	**19**	19 wks
22 Jan 69	**YOU AIN'T LIVIN' TILL YOU'RE LOVIN'** *Tamla Motown TMG 681*	**21**	8 wks
4 Jun 69	**GOOD LOVIN' AIN'T EASY TO COME BY** *Tamla Motown TMG 697*	**26**	7 wks
30 Jul 69	**GOOD LOVIN' AIN'T EASY TO COME BY** (re-entry) *Tamla Motown TMG 697*	**48**	1 wk
15 Nov 69	● **ONION SONG** *Tamla Motown TMG 715*	**9**	12 wks

See also Marvin Gaye; Marvin Gaye and Mary Wells; Marvin Gaye and Kim Weston.

Marvin GAYE and Mary WELLS

US, male/female vocal duo

| 30 Jul 64 | **ONCE UPON A TIME** *Stateside SS 316* | **50** | 1 wk |

See also Marvin Gaye; Mary Wells; Marvin Gaye and Tammi Terrell; Marvin Gaye and Kim Weston.

Marvin GAYE and Kim WESTON

US, male/female vocal duo

| 26 Jan 67 | **IT TAKES TWO** *Tamla Motown TMG 590* | **16** | 11 wks |

See also Marvin Gaye; Marvin Gaye and Tammi Terrell; Marvin Gaye and Mary Wells.

G-CLEFS

US, male vocal group

| 30 Nov 61 | **I UNDERSTAND** *London HLU 9433* | **17** | 12 wks |

GENEVIEVE

France, female vocalist

| 5 May 66 | **ONCE** *CBS 202061* | **43** | 1 wk |

Bobbie GENTRY

US, female vocalist

| 13 Sep 67 | **ODE TO BILLY JOE** *Capitol CL 15511* | **13** | 11 wks |
| 30 Aug 69 | ★ **I'LL NEVER FALL IN LOVE AGAIN** *Capitol CL 15606* | **1** | 19 wks |

See also Bobbie Gentry and Glen Campbell.

Bobbie GENTRY and Glen CAMPBELL

US, female/male vocal duo

| 6 Dec 69 | ● **ALL I HAVE TO DO IS DREAM** *Capitol CL 15619* | **3** | 14 wks |

See also Bobbie Gentry and Glen Campbell.

GERRY and the PACEMAKERS

UK, male vocal/instrumental group

14 Mar 63	★ **HOW DO YOU DO IT?** *Columbia DB 4987*	**1**	18 wks
30 May 63	★ **I LIKE IT** *Columbia DB 7041*	**1**	15 wks
10 Oct 63	★ **YOU'LL NEVER WALK ALONE** *Columbia DB 7126*	**1**	19 wks
16 Jan 64	● **I'M THE ONE** *Columbia DB 7189*	**2**	15 wks
16 Apr 64	● **DON'T LET THE SUN CATCH YOU CRYING** *Columbia DB 7268*	**6**	11 wks
3 Sep 64	**IT'S GONNA BE ALL RIGHT** *Columbia DB 7353*	**24**	7 wks
17 Dec 64	● **FERRY ACROSS THE MERSEY** *Columbia DB 7437*	**8**	13 wks
25 Mar 65	**I'LL BE THERE** *Columbia DB 7504*	**15**	9 wks
18 Nov 65	**WALK HAND IN HAND** *Columbia DB 7738*	**29**	7 wks

Stan GETZ and Charlie BYRD

US, male instrumental duo, sax and guitar

| 8 Nov 62 | **DESAFINADO** *HMV POP 1061* | **11** | 11 wks |

See also Stan Getz and Joao Gilberto.

Stan GETZ and Joao GILBERTO

US/Brazil, male instrumentalist, tenor sax/male vocalist

| 23 Jul 64 | **THE GIRL FROM IPANEMA (GAROTA DE IPANEMA)** *Verve VS 520* | **29** | 10 wks |

See also Stan Getz and Charlie Byrd. Joao Gilberto did not actually appear on this hit. The vocalist is in fact Astrud, his wife.

Date	Title *Label Number*	Position	Date	Title *Label Number*	Position

Robin GIBB

UK, male vocalist

| 9 Jul 69 | ● SAVED BY THE BELL *Polydor 56-337* | **2** 16 wks |
| 15 Nov 69 | SAVED BY THE BELL (re-entry) *Polydor 56-337* | **49** 1 wk |

Don GIBSON

US, male vocalist

| 31 Aug 61 | SEA OF HEARTBREAK *RCA 1243* | **14** 13 wks |
| 1 Feb 62 | LONESOME NUMBER ONE *RCA 1272* | **47** 3 wks |

Wayne GIBSON

UK, male vocalist

| 3 Sep 64 | KELLY *Pye 7N 15680* | **48** 2 wks |

Joao GILBERTO — See *Stan GETZ and Joao GILBERTO*

Jimmy GILMER and the FIREBALLS

US, male vocalist/instrumental backing group

| 14 Nov 63 | SUGAR SHACK *London HLD 9789* | **45** 4 wks |
| 19 Dec 63 | SUGAR SHACK (re-entry) *London HLD 9789* | **46** 4 wks |

See also Fireballs.

James GILREATH

US, male vocalist

| 2 May 63 | LITTLE BAND OF GOLD *Pye International 7N 25190* | **29** 10 wks |

GINGERBREADS — See *GOLDIE and the GINGERBREADS*

GLADIATORS — See *NERO and the GLADIATORS*

GOLDIE and the GINGERBREADS

US, female vocal/instrumental group

| 25 Feb 65 | CAN'T YOU HEAR MY HEART BEAT? *Decca F 12070* | **25** 5 wks |

Bobby GOLDSBORO

US, male vocalist

| 17 Apr 68 | ● HONEY *United Artists UP2215* | **2** 15 wks |

GORDON — See *PETER and GORDON*

Lesley GORE

US, female vocalist

| 20 Jun 63 | ● IT'S MY PARTY *Mercury AMT 1205* | **9** 12 wks |
| 24 Sep 64 | MAYBE I KNOW *Mercury MF 829* | **20** 8 wks |

Eydie GORME

US, female vocalist

| 21 Jun 62 | ● YES MY DARLING DAUGHTER *CBS AAG 105* | **10** 9 wks |
| 31 Jan 63 | BLAME IT ON THE BOSSA NOVA *CBS AAG 131* | **32** 6 wks |

See also Steve and Eydie.

GRACE — See *DALE and GRACE*

Boysie GRANT — See *Ezz RECO and the LAUNCHERS with Boysie GRANT*

Julie GRANT

UK, female vocalist

3 Jan 63	UP ON THE ROOF *Pye 7N 15483*	**33** 3 wks
28 Mar 63	COUNT ON ME *Pye 7N 15508*	**24** 9 wks
24 Sep 64	COME TO ME *Pye 7N 15684*	**31** 5 wks

GRAPEFRUIT

UK, male vocal/instrumental group

| 14 Feb 68 | DEAR DELILAH *RCA 1656* | **21** 9 wks |
| 14 Aug 68 | C'MON MARIANNE *RCA 1716* | **31** 10 wks |

Dobie GRAY

US, male vocalist

| 25 Feb 65 | THE IN CROWD *London HL 9953* | **25** 7 wks |

Dorian GRAY

UK, male vocalist

| 27 Mar 68 | I'VE GOT YOU ON MY MIND *Parlophone R 5667* | **36** 7 wks |

Buddy GRECO

US, male vocalist

| 7 Jul 60 | LADY IS A TRAMP *Fontana H 225* | **26** 8 wks |

GREEK SERENADERS — See *MAKADOPOULOS and his GREEK SERENADERS*

HEINZ *Left* Heinz the ex-Tornado snapped in March 1965 by a pop magazine which described him as looking like a 'searchlight on a foggy night!'

Jet HARRIS *Below* Seven hits with the Shadows, three with Tony Meehan, two as a solo artist.

Noel HARRISON Son of actor Rex.

HARMONY GRASS Led by ex-Castaway Tony Rivers, (being attacked below by a large moth), who now arranges for Cliff Richard as well as singing in his backing trio.

Date	Title Label Number	Position

Lorne GREENE
US, male vocalist

17 Dec 64   **RINGO** *RCA 1428*   **22**   8 wks

Iain GREGORY
UK, male vocalist

4 Jan 62   **CAN'T YOU HEAR THE BEAT OF A BROKEN HEART** *Pye 7N 15397*   **39**   2 wks

Johnny GREGORY — See *CHAQUITO*

GUESS WHO
Canada, male vocal/instrumental group

16 Feb 67   **HIS GIRL** *King KG 1044*   **45**   1 wk

GUN
UK, male vocal/instrumental group

20 Nov 68 ● **RACE WITH THE DEVIL** *CBS 3764*   **8**   11 wks

H

Bill HALEY and his COMETS
US, male vocalist/guitarist, male vocal/instrumental backing group

3 Apr 68   **ROCK AROUND THE CLOCK** *MCA MU 1013*   **20**   11 wks

HAPPENINGS
US, male vocal group

18 May 67   **I GOT RHYTHM** *Stateside SS 2013*   **28**   9 wks
16 Aug 67   **MY MAMMY** *Pye International 7N 25501 and B. T. Puppy BTS 45530*   **34**   5 wks

Pye gave the American B. T. Puppy label its own identification halfway through the success of My Mammy.

Tim HARDIN
US, male vocalist

5 Jan 67   **HANG ON TO A DREAM** *Verve VS 1504*   **50**   1 wk

Francoise HARDY
France, female vocalist

25 Jun 64   **TOUS LES GARCONS ET LES FILLES** *Pye 7N 15653*   **36**   7 wks
7 Jan 65   **ET MÊME** *Pye 7N 15740*   **31**   4 wks
25 Mar 65   **ALL OVER THE WORLD** *Pye 7N 15802*   **16**   15 wks

HARMONY GRASS
UK, male vocal/instrumental group

29 Jan 69   **MOVE IN A LITTLE CLOSER** *RCA 1772*   **24**   7 wks

HARPERS BIZARRE
US, male vocal group

30 Mar 67   **59TH STREET BRIDGE SONG (FEELING GROOVY)** *Warner Bros. WB 5890*   **34**   7 wks
4 Oct 67   **ANYTHING GOES** *Warner Bros. WB 7063*   **33**   6 wks

Anita HARRIS
UK, female vocalist

29 Jun 67 ● **JUST LOVING YOU** *CBS 2724*   **6**   30 wks
11 Oct 67   **PLAYGROUND** *CBS 2991*   **46**   3 wks
24 Jan 68   **ANNIVERSARY WALTZ** *CBS 3211*   **21**   9 wks
14 Aug 68   **DREAM A LITTLE DREAM OF ME** *CBS 3637*   **33**   8 wks

Jet HARRIS
UK, male instrumentalist, bass guitar

24 May 62   **BESAME MUCHO** *Decca F 11466*   **22**   7 wks
16 Aug 62   **MAIN TITLE THEME FROM 'MAN WITH THE GOLDEN ARM'** *Decca F 11488*   **12**   11 wks
See also Jet Harris and Tony Meehan.

Jet HARRIS and Tony MEEHAN
UK, male instrumental duo, bass guitar and drums

10 Jan 63 ★ **DIAMONDS** *Decca F 11563*   **1**   12 wks
25 Apr 63 ● **SCARLETT O'HARA** *Decca F 11644*   **2**   13 wks
5 Sep 63 ● **APPLEJACK** *Decca F 11710*   **4**   13 wks
See also Jet Harris, Tony Meehan Combo.

Max HARRIS
UK, orchestra

1 Dec 60   **GURNEY SLADE** *Fontana H 282*   **11**   10 wks

Richard HARRIS
Ireland, male vocalist

26 Jun 68 ● **MACARTHUR PARK** *RCA 1699*   **4**   12 wks

Date	Title *Label Number*	Position

Rolf HARRIS

Australia, male vocalist

21 Jul 60	● TIE ME KANGAROO DOWN SPORT *Columbia DB 4483*	9	13 wks
25 Oct 62	● SUN ARISE *Columbia DB 4888*	3	16 wks
28 Feb 63	JOHNNY DAY *Columbia DB 4979*	44	2 wks
16 Apr 69	BLUER THAN BLUE *Columbia DB 8553*	30	8 wks
22 Nov 69	★ TWO LITTLE BOYS *Columbia DB 8630*	1	24 wks

Noel HARRISON

UK, male vocalist

26 Feb 69	● WINDMILLS OF YOUR MIND *Reprise RS 20758*	8	14 wks

HARRY J. ALL STARS

Jamaica, male instrumental group

25 Oct 69	● LIQUIDATOR *Trojan TR 675*	9	20 wks

Tony HATCH

UK, orchestra

4 Oct 62	OUT OF THIS WORLD *Pye 7N 15460*	50	1 wk

Edwin HAWKINS SINGERS

US, male/female vocal group

21 May 69	● OH HAPPY DAY *Buddah 201 048*	2	12 wks
23 Aug 69	OH HAPPY DAY (re-entry) *Buddah 201 048*	43	1 wk

Hit credits soloist : Dorothy Combs Morrison

Lee HAZLEWOOD — See *Nancy SINATRA and Lee HAZLEWOOD*

Roy HEAD

US, male vocalist

4 Nov 65	TREAT HER RIGHT *Vocalion V-P 9248*	30	5 wks

Ted HEATH

UK, orchestra

5 Oct 61	SUCU SUCU *Decca F 11392*	36	4 wks
9 Nov 61	SUCU SUCU (re-entry) *Decca F 11392*	47	1 wk

Bobby HEBB

US, male vocalist

8 Sep 66	SUNNY *Philips BF 1503*	12	9 wks

HEDGEHOPPERS ANONYMOUS

UK, male vocal/instrumental group

30 Sep 65	● IT'S GOOD NEWS WEEK *Decca F 12241*	5	12 wks

HEINZ

UK, male vocalist

8 Aug 63	● JUST LIKE EDDIE *Decca F 11693*	5	15 wks
28 Nov 63	COUNTRY BOY *Decca F 11768*	26	9 wks
27 Feb 64	YOU WERE THERE *Decca F 11831*	26	8 wks
15 Oct 64	QUESTIONS I CAN'T ANSWER *Columbia DB 7374*	39	2 wks
18 Mar 65	DIGGIN' MY POTATOES *Columbia DB 7482*	49	1 wk

Joe 'Mr. Piano' HENDERSON

UK, male instrumentalist, piano

24 Mar 60	OOH LA LA *Pye 7N 15257*	46	1 wk

Jimi HENDRIX EXPERIENCE

US/UK, male vocal/instrumental group, Jimi Hendrix, vocals and guitar

5 Jan 67	● HEY JOE *Polydor 56 139*	6	10 wks
23 Mar 67	● PURPLE HAZE *Track 604 001*	3	14 wks
11 May 67	● THE WIND CRIES MARY *Track 604 004*	6	11 wks
30 Aug 67	BURNING OF THE MIDNIGHT LAMP *Track 604 007*	18	9 wks
23 Oct 68	● ALL ALONG THE WATCHTOWER *Track 604 025*	5	11 wks
16 Apr 69	CROSSTOWN TRAFFIC *Track 604 029*	37	3 wks

On Polydor the act is simply billed as Jimi Hendrix.

Clarence 'Frogman' HENRY

US, male vocalist

4 May 61	● BUT I DO *Pye international 7N 25078*	3	19 wks
13 Jul 61	● YOU ALWAYS HURT THE ONE YOU LOVE *Pye International 7N 25089*	6	12 wks
21 Sep 61	LONELY STREET/ WHY CAN'T YOU *Pye International 7N 25108*	42	2 wks

HERD

UK, male vocal/instrumental group

13 Sep 67	● FROM THE UNDERWORLD *Fontana TF 856*	6	13 wks
20 Dec 67	PARADISE LOST *Fontana TF 887*	15	9 wks
10 Apr 68	● I DON'T WANT OUR LOVING TO DIE *Fontana TF 925*	5	13 wks

Mary HOPKIN *Left* Originally spotted performing on Hughie Green's television show *Opportunity Knocks* by Twiggy who sang Mary's praises to Paul McCartney. He helped the Welsh girl to a number one with her first single.

JAN and DEAN *Far left* Only two British chart hits for Jan and Dean but check out classics like 'Dead Man's Curve', 'I Found A Girl', 'Honolulu Lulu' and 'New Girl In School' at your friendly oldies shop.

Horst JANKOWSKI *Above* 'I've been through the forest on a Horst with no mane . . !'

HERD *Right* First heard in 1967.

Date	Title Label Number	Position		Date	Title Label Number	Position	

HERMAN'S HERMITS

UK, male vocal/instrumental group

Date	Title Label Number	Position	
20 Aug 64	★ I'M INTO SOMETHING GOOD	1	15 wks
	Columbia DB 7338		
19 Nov 64	SHOW ME GIRL Columbia DB 7408	19	9 wks
18 Feb 65	● SILHOUETTES Columbia DB 7475	3	12 wks
29 Apr 65	● WONDERFUL WORLD Columbia DB 7546	7	9 wks
2 Sep 65	JUST A LITTLE BIT BETTER	15	9 wks
	Columbia DB 7670		
23 Dec 65	● A MUST TO AVOID Columbia DB 7791	6	11 wks
24 Mar 66	YOU WON'T BE LEAVING Columbia DB 7861	20	7 wks
23 Jun 66	THIS DOOR SWINGS BOTH WAYS	18	7 wks
	Columbia DB 7947		
6 Oct 66	● NO MILK TODAY Columbia DB 8012	7	11 wks
1 Dec 66	EAST WEST Columbia DB 8076	37	7 wks
9 Feb 67	● THERE'S A KIND OF HUSH	7	11 wks
	Columbia DB 8123		
17 Jan 68	I CAN TAKE OR LEAVE YOUR LOVING	11	9 wks
	Columbia DB 8327		
1 May 68	SLEEPY JOE Columbia DB 8404	12	10 wks
17 Jul 68	● SUNSHINE GIRL Columbia DB 8446	8	14 wks
18 Dec 68	● SOMETHING'S HAPPENING	6	15 wks
	Columbia DB 8504		
23 Apr 69	● MY SENTIMENTAL FRIEND	2	12 wks
	Columbia DB 8563		
8 Nov 69	HERE COMES THE STAR Columbia DB 8626	33	9 wks

HIGHWAYMEN

US, male vocal group

Date	Title Label Number	Position	
7 Sep 61	★ MICHAEL HMV POP 910	1	14 wks
7 Dec 61	GYPSY ROVER HMV POP 948	41	3 wks
11 Jan 62	GYPSY ROVER (re-entry) HMV POP 948	43	1 wk

Benny HILL

UK, male vocalist

Date	Title Label Number	Position	
16 Feb 61	GATHER IN THE MUSHROOMS	12	8 wks
	Pye 7N 15327		
1 Jun 61	TRANSISTOR RADIO Pye 7N 15359	24	6 wks
16 May 63	HARVEST OF LOVE Pye 7N 15520	20	8 wks

Vince HILL

UK, male vocalist

Date	Title Label Number	Position	
7 Jun 62	THE RIVER'S RUN DRY Piccadilly 7N 35043	49	1 wk
28 Jun 62	THE RIVER'S RUN DRY (re-entry)	41	1 wk
	Piccadilly 7N 35043		
6 Jan 66	TAKE ME TO YOUR HEART AGAIN	13	11 wks
	Columbia DB 7781		
17 Mar 66	HEARTACHES Columbia DB 7852	28	5 wks
2 Jun 66	MERCI CHERI Columbia DB 7924	36	6 wks
9 Feb 67	● EDELWEISS Columbia DB 8127	2	17 wks
11 May 67	ROSES OF PICARDY Columbia DB 8185	13	11 wks
27 Sep 67	LOVE LETTERS IN THE SAND	23	9 wks
	Columbia DB 8268		

Date	Title Label Number	Position	
26 Jun 68	IMPORTANCE OF YOUR LOVE	32	12 wks
	Columbia DB 8414		
12 Feb 69	DOESN'T ANYBODY KNOW MY NAME?	50	1 wk
	Columbia DB 8515		
25 Oct 69	LITTLE BLUE BIRD Columbia DB 8616	42	1 wk

Ronnie HILTON

UK, male vocalist

Date	Title Label Number	Position	
21 May 64	DON'T LET THE RAIN COME DOWN	21	10 wks
	HMV POP 1291		
11 Feb 65	A WINDMILL IN OLD AMSTERDAM	23	13 wks
	HMV POP 1378		

Eddie HODGES

US, male vocalist

Date	Title Label Number	Position	
28 Sep 61	I'M GONNA KNOCK ON YOUR DOOR	37	6 wks
	London HLA 9369		
9 Aug 62	MADE TO LOVE (GIRLS GIRLS GIRLS)	37	4 wks
	London HLA 9576		

Michael HOLLIDAY

UK, male vocalist

Date	Title Label Number	Position	
1 Jan 60	★ STARRY EYED Columbia DB 4378	1	12 wks
14 Apr 60	SKYLARK Columbia DB 4437	39	3 wks
1 Sep 60	LITTLE BOY LOST Columbia DB 4475	50	1 wk

HOLLIES

UK, male vocal/instrumental group

Date	Title Label Number	Position	
30 May 63	JUST LIKE ME Parlophone R 5030	25	10 wks
29 Aug 63	SEARCHIN' Parlophone R 5052	12	14 wks
21 Nov 63	● STAY Parlophone R 5077	8	16 wks
27 Feb 64	● JUST ONE LOOK Parlophone R 5104	2	13 wks
21 May 64	● HERE I GO AGAIN Parlophone R 5137	4	12 wks
17 Sep 64	● WE'RE THROUGH Parlophone R 5178	7	11 wks
28 Jan 65	● YES I WILL Parlophone R 5232	9	13 wks
27 May 65	★ I'M ALIVE Parlophone R 5287	1	14 wks
2 Sep 65	● LOOK THROUGH ANY WINDOW	4	11 wks
	Parlophone R 5322		
9 Dec 65	IF I NEEDED SOMEONE Parlophone R 5392	20	9 wks
24 Feb 66	● I CAN'T LET GO Parlophone R 5409	2	10 wks
23 Jun 66	● BUS STOP Parlophone R 5469	5	9 wks
13 Oct 66	● STOP STOP STOP Parlophone R 5508	2	12 wks
16 Feb 67	● ON A CAROUSEL Parlophone R 5562	4	11 wks
1 Jun 67	● CARRIE-ANNE Parlophone R 5602	3	11 wks
27 Sep 67	KING MIDAS IN REVERSE	18	8 wks
	Parlophone R 5637		
27 Mar 68	● JENNIFER ECCLES Parlophone R 5680	7	11 wks
2 Oct 68	LISTEN TO ME Parlophone R 5733	11	11 wks
5 Mar 69	● SORRY SUZANNE Parlophone R 5765	3	12 wks
4 Oct 69	● HE AIN'T HEAVY HE'S MY BROTHER	3	15 wks
	Parlophone R 5806		

Date	Title *Label Number*	Position

Buddy HOLLY

US, male vocalist

28 Apr 60	**HEARTBEAT** *Coral Q 72392*	**30**	3 wks
26 May 60	**TRUE LOVE WAYS** *Coral Q 72397*	**25**	7 wks
20 Oct 60	**LEARNIN' THE GAME** *Coral Q 72411*	**36**	3 wks
26 Jan 61	**WHAT TO DO** *Coral Q 72419*	**34**	6 wks
6 Jul 61	**BABY I DON'T CARE/ VALLEY OF TEARS** *Coral Q 72432*	**12**	14 wks
15 Mar 62	**LISTEN TO ME** *Coral Q 72449*	**48**	1 wk
13 Sep 62	**REMINISCING** *Coral Q 72455*	**17**	11 wks
14 Mar 63	● **BROWN-EYED HANDSOME MAN** *Coral Q 72459*	**3**	17 wks
6 Jun 63	● **BO DIDDLEY** *Coral Q 72463*	**4**	12 wks
5 Sep 63	● **WISHING** *Coral Q 72466*	**10**	11 wks
19 Dec 63	**WHAT TO DO** *Coral Q 72469*	**27**	8 wks
14 May 64	**YOU'VE GOT LOVE** *Coral Q 72472*	**40**	6 wks
10 Sep 64	**LOVE'S MADE A FOOL OF YOU** *Coral Q 72475*	**39**	6 wks
3 Apr 68	**PEGGY SUE/ RAVE ON** *MCA MU 1012*	**32**	9 wks

You've Got Love was released with credit to Buddy Holly and The Crickets. Valley Of Tears was not listed together with Baby I Don't Care until 13 Jul 61. See also Crickets.

HOLLYWOOD ARGYLES

US, male vocal group

21 Jul 60	**ALLEY OOP** *London HLU 9146*	**24**	10 wks

HONEYBUS

UK, male vocal/instrumental group

20 Mar 68	● **I CAN'T LET MAGGIE GO** *Deram DM 182*	**8**	12 wks

HONEYCOMBS

UK, male/female vocal/instrumental group

23 Jul 64	★ **HAVE I THE RIGHT** *Pye 7N 15664*	**1**	15 wks
22 Oct 64	**IS IT BECAUSE** *Pye 7N 15705*	**38**	6 wks
29 Apr 65	**SOMETHING BETTER BEGINNING** *Pye 7N 15827*	**39**	4 wks
5 Aug 65	**THAT'S THE WAY** *Pye 7N 15890*	**12**	14 wks

John Lee HOOKER

US, male vocalist

11 Jun 64	**DIMPLES** *Stateside SS 297*	**23**	10 wks

Mary HOPKIN

UK, female vocalist

4 Sep 68	★ **THOSE WERE THE DAYS** *Apple 2*	**1**	21 wks
2 Apr 69	● **GOODBYE** *Apple 10*	**2**	14 wks

Johnny HORTON

US, male vocalist

19 Jan 61	**NORTH TO ALASKA** *Philips PB 1062*	**23**	11 wks

HOWLIN' WOLF

US, male vocalist

4 Jun 64	**SMOKESTACK LIGHTNIN'** *Pye International 7N 25244*	**42**	5 wks

HUMBLE PIE

UK, male vocal/instrumental group

23 Aug 69	● **NATURAL BORN BUGIE** *Immediate IM 082*	**4**	10 wks

Engelbert HUMPERDINCK

UK, male vocalist

26 Jan 67	★ **RELEASE ME** *Decca F 12541*	**1**	56 wks
25 May 67	● **THERE GOES MY EVERYTHING** *Decca F 12610*	**2**	29 wks
23 Aug 67	★ **THE LAST WALTZ** *Decca F 12655*	**1**	27 wks
10 Jan 68	● **AM I THAT EASY TO FORGET** *Decca F 12722*	**3**	13 wks
24 Apr 68	● **A MAN WITHOUT LOVE** *Decca F 12770*	**2**	15 wks
25 Sep 68	● **LES BICYCLETTES DE BELSIZE** *Decca F 12834*	**5**	15 wks
5 Feb 69	● **THE WAY IT USED TO BE** *Decca F 12879*	**3**	14 wks
9 Aug 69	**I'M A BETTER MAN** *Decca F 12957*	**15**	13 wks
15 Nov 69	● **WINTER WORLD OF LOVE** *Decca F 12980*	**7**	13 wks

Marsha HUNT

US, female vocalist

21 May 69	**WALK ON GILDED SPLINTERS** *Track 604 030*	**46**	2 wks

HURRICANES — See *JOHNNY and the HURRICANES*

Brian HYLAND

US, male vocalist

7 Jul 60	● **ITSY BITSY TEENY WEENY YELLOW POLKA DOT BIKINI** *London HLR 9161*	**8**	13 wks
20 Oct 60	**FOUR LITTLE HEELS** *London HLR 9203*	**29**	6 wks
10 May 62	● **GINNY COME LATELY** *HMV POP 1013*	**5**	15 wks
2 Aug 62	● **SEALED WITH A KISS** *HMV POP 1051*	**3**	15 wks
8 Nov 62	**WARMED OVER KISSES** *HMV POP 1079*	**28**	6 wks

Date	Title Label Number	Position

I

Frank IFIELD
UK, male vocalist

19 Feb 60	LUCKY DEVIL *Columbia DB 4399*	22	2 wks
7 Apr 60	LUCKY DEVIL (re-entry) *Columbia DB 4399*	33	2 wks
29 Sep 60	GOTTA GET A DATE *Columbia DB 4496*	49	1 wk
5 Jul 62 ★	I REMEMBER YOU *Columbia DB 4856*	1	28 wks
25 Oct 62 ★	LOVESICK BLUES *Columbia DB 4913*	1	17 wks
24 Jan 63 ★	WAYWARD WIND *Columbia DB 4960*	1	13 wks
11 Apr 63 ●	NOBODY'S DARLIN' BUT MINE *Columbia DB 7007*	4	16 wks
27 Jun 63 ★	CONFESSIN' *Columbia DB 7062*	1	16 wks
17 Oct 63	MULE TRAIN *Columbia DB 7131*	22	6 wks
9 Jan 64 ●	DON'T BLAME ME *Columbia DB 7184*	8	13 wks
23 Apr 64	ANGRY AT THE BIG OAK TREE *Columbia DB 7263*	25	8 wks
23 Jul 64	I SHOULD CARE *Columbia DB 7319*	33	3 wks
1 Oct 64	SUMMER IS OVER *Columbia DB 7355*	25	6 wks
19 Aug 65	PARADISE *Columbia DB 7655*	26	9 wks
23 Jun 66	NO ONE WILL EVER KNOW *Columbia DB 7940*	25	4 wks
8 Dec 66	CALL HER YOUR SWEETHEART *Columbia DB 8078*	24	11 wks

IN CROWD
UK, male vocal/instrumental group

| 20 May 65 | THAT'S HOW STRONG MY LOVE IS *Parlophone R 5276* | 48 | 1 wk |

Los INDIOS TABAJARAS
Brazil, male instrumental duo, guitars

| 31 Oct 63 ● | MARIA ELENA *RCA 1365* | 5 | 17 wks |

Big Dee IRWIN
US, male vocalist

| 21 Nov 63 ● | SWINGING ON A STAR *Colpix PX 11010* | 7 | 17 wks |

This hit was in fact a vocal duet by Big Dee Irwin and Little Eva, though Little Eva was not credited. See also Little Eva.

ISLEY BROTHERS
US, male vocal/instrumental group

25 Jul 63	TWIST AND SHOUT *Stateside SS 112*	42	1 wk
28 Apr 66	THIS OLD HEART OF MINE *Tamla Motown TMG 555*	47	1 wk
1 Sep 66	I GUESS I'LL ALWAYS LOVE YOU *Tamla Motown TMG 572*	45	2 wks
23 Oct 68 ●	THIS OLD HEART OF MINE (re-entry) *Tamla Motown TMG 555*	3	16 wks

15 Jan 69	I GUESS I'LL ALWAYS LOVE YOU (re-issue) *Tamla Motown TMG 683*	11	9 wks
16 Apr 69 ●	BEHIND A PAINTED SMILE *Tamla Motown TMG 693*	5	12 wks
25 Jun 69	IT'S YOUR THING *Major Minor MM 621*	30	5 wks
30 Aug 69	PUT YOURSELF IN MY PLACE *Tamla Motown TMG 708*	13	11 wks

Burl IVES
US, male vocalist

| 25 Jan 62 ● | A LITTLE BITTY TEAR *Brunswick 05863* | 9 | 15 wks |
| 17 May 62 | FUNNY WAY OF LAUGHIN' *Brunswick 05868* | 29 | 10 wks |

IVY LEAGUE
UK, male vocal group

4 Feb 65 ●	FUNNY HOW LOVE CAN BE *Piccadilly 7N 35222*	8	9 wks
6 May 65	THAT'S WHY I'M CRYING *Piccadilly 7N 35228*	22	8 wks
24 Jun 65 ●	TOSSING AND TURNING *Piccadilly 7N 35251*	3	13 wks
14 Jul 66	WILLOW TREE *Piccadilly 7N 35326*	50	1 wk

J

Tony JACKSON and the VIBRATIONS
UK, male vocal/instrumental group

| 8 Oct 64 | BYE BYE BABY *Pye 7N 15685* | 38 | 3 wks |

Wanda JACKSON
US, female vocalist

1 Sep 60	LET'S HAVE A PARTY *Capitol CL 15147*	32	8 wks
26 Jan 61	MEAN MEAN MAN *Capitol CL 15176*	46	1 wk
9 Feb 61	MEAN MEAN MAN (re-entry) *Capitol CL 15176*	40	2 wks

JACKY
UK, female vocalist

| 10 Apr 68 ● | WHITE HORSES *Philips BF 1674* | 10 | 14 wks |

Jimmy JAMES and the VAGABONDS
UK, male vocal/instrumental group

| 11 Sep 68 | RED RED WINE *Pye 7N 17579* | 36 | 8 wks |

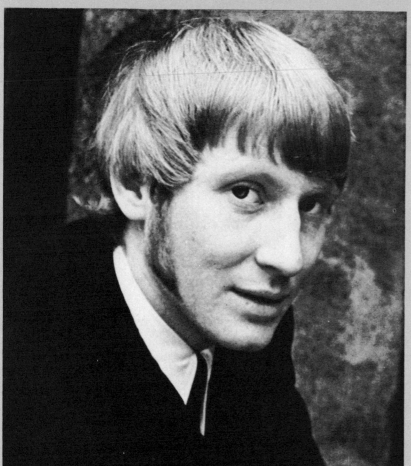

JEFFERSON *Left* Ex-Rockin' Berry Geoff Turton (he sang falsetto) left the group to go solo as Jefferson.

Tommy JAMES *Below* His first British hit, a cover of the Raindrops 'Hanky Panky', prevented him from becoming a one-hit wonder in 1968, and balding hippies on park benches discuss to this day the surprising lack of success of 'I Think We're Alone Now' and 'Crimson and Clover'.

Jimmy JONES *Below* Prior to his falsetto-laced hits he'd recorded with the 'Sparks of Rhythm', 'The Pretenders' and the 'Savoys'.

KINKS *Right* Ray Davies, Mick Avory, Pete Quaife and Dave Davies bash out the classic 'Waterloo Sunset' live on stage.

Bob LIND *Above* A failed lepidopterist.

Brenda LEE *Left* Discovered by Red Foley, her TV début came at the age of 9 on 31 March, 1956, when she sang her way into a long term recording contract with her version of Hank Williams' 'Jambalaya'.

John LEYTON *Below* Shot to fame as 'Ginger' in Granada TV series *Biggles*. His 1961 fact file reveals that he drives an MGA sports car and occasionally flies an Auster from Fairoak aerodrome – oh and girls – he's 5ft 10½" with gold hair and blue eyes.

Date	Title Label Number	Position

Tommy JAMES and the SHONDELLS

US, male vocal/instrumental group

21 Jul 66	HANKY PANKY *Roulette RK 7000*	38	7 wks
5 Jun 68 ★	MONY MONY *Major Minor MM 567*	1	18 wks

JAN and DEAN

US, male vocal duo

24 Aug 61	HEART AND SOUL *London HLH 9395*	24	8 wks
15 Aug 63	SURF CITY *Liberty LIB 55580*	26	10 wks

JAN and KJELD

Denmark, male vocal duo

21 Jul 60	BANJO BOY *Ember S 101*	36	4 wks

Horst JANKOWSKI

Germany, male instrumentalist, piano

29 Jul 65	● A WALK IN THE BLACK FOREST *Mercury MF 861*	3	18 wks

Peter JAY and the JAYWALKERS

UK, male instrumental group, Peter Jay, drums

8 Nov 62	CAN CAN 62 *Decca F 11531*	31	11 wks

JAYWALKERS — See *Peter JAY and the JAYWALKERS*

JEFFERSON

UK, male vocalist

9 Apr 69	COLOUR OF MY LOVE *Pye 7N 17706*	22	8 wks

JETHRO TULL

UK, male vocal/instrumental group

1 Jan 69	LOVE STORY *Island WIP 6048*	29	8 wks
14 May 69	● LIVING IN THE PAST *Island WIP 6056*	3	14 wks
1 Nov 69	● SWEET DREAM *Chrysalis WIP 6070*	7	11 wks

Robert JOHN

US, male vocalist

17 Jul 68	IF YOU DON'T WANT MY LOVE *CBS 3436*	42	5 wks

JOHNNY — See *SANTO and JOHNNY*

JOHNNY and CHARLEY

Spain, male vocal duo

14 Oct 65	LA YENKA *Pye International 7N 25326*	49	1 wk

JOHNNY and the HURRICANES

US, male instrumental group

1 Jan 60	● RED RIVER ROCK *London HL 8948*	10	4 wks
1 Jan 60	REVEILLE ROCK *London HL 9017*	14	4 wks
17 Mar 60	● BEATNIK FLY *London HLI 9072*	8	19 wks
16 Jun 60	● DOWN YONDER *London HLX 9134*	8	11 wks
29 Sep 60	● ROCKING GOOSE *London HLX 9190*	3	20 wks
2 Mar 61	JA-DA *London HLX 9289*	14	9 wks
6 Jul 61	OLD SMOKEY/ HIGH VOLTAGE *London HLX 9378*	24	8 wks

Bryan JOHNSON

UK, male vocalist

10 Mar 60	LOOKING HIGH HIGH HIGH *Decca F 11213*	20	11 wks

Laurie JOHNSON

UK, orchestra

28 Sep 61	● SUCU SUCU *Pye 7N 15383*	9	12 wks

Lou JOHNSON

US, male vocalist

26 Nov 64	MESSAGE TO MARTHA *London HL 9929*	36	2 wks

Marv JOHNSON

US, male vocalist

12 Feb 60	● YOU GOT WHAT IT TAKES *London HLT 9013*	5	16 wks
5 May 60	I LOVE THE WAY YOU LOVE *London HLT 9109*	35	3 wks
11 Aug 60	AIN'T GONNA BE THAT WAY *London HLT 9156*	50	1 wk
22 Jan 69	● I'LL PICK A ROSE FOR MY ROSE *Tamla Motown TMG 680*	10	11 wks
25 Oct 69	I MISS YOU BABY *Tamla Motown TMG 713*	25	8 wks

Teddy JOHNSON — See *Pearl CARR and Teddy JOHNSON*

JONATHAN — See *DAVID and JONATHAN*

Janie JONES

UK, female vocalist

27 Jan 66	WITCHES' BREW *HMV POP 1495*	46	3 wks

Date	Title *Label Number*	Position	Date	Title *Label Number*	Position

Jimmy JONES

US, male vocalist

17 Mar 60	● HANDY MAN *MGM 1051*	**3**	21 wks
16 Jun 60	★ GOOD TIMIN' *MGM 1078*	**1**	15 wks
18 Aug 60	HANDY MAN (re-entry) *MGM 1051*	**32**	3 wks
8 Sep 60	I JUST GO FOR YOU *MGM 1091*	**35**	4 wks
17 Nov 60	READY FOR LOVE *MGM 1103*	**46**	1 wk
30 Mar 61	I TOLD YOU SO *MGM 1123*	**33**	3 wks

Paul JONES

UK, male vocalist

6 Oct 66	● HIGH TIME *HMV POP 1554*	**4**	15 wks
19 Jan 67	● I'VE BEEN A BAD BAD BOY *HMV POP 1576*	**5**	9 wks
23 Aug 67	THINKIN' AIN'T FOR ME *HMV POP 1602*	**47**	1 wk
13 Sep 67	THINKIN' AIN'T FOR ME (re-entry) *HMV POP 1602*	**32**	7 wks
5 Feb 69	AQUARIUS *Columbia DB 8514*	**45**	2 wks

See also Manfred Mann.

Tom JONES

UK, male vocalist

11 Feb 65	★ IT'S NOT UNUSUAL *Decca F 12062*	**1**	14 wks
6 May 65	ONCE UPON A TIME *Decca F 12121*	**32**	4 wks
8 Jul 65	WITH THESE HANDS *Decca F 12191*	**13**	11 wks
12 Aug 65	WHAT'S NEW PUSSYCAT *Decca F 12203*	**11**	10 wks
13 Jan 66	THUNDERBALL *Decca F 12292*	**35**	4 wks
19 May 66	ONCE THERE WAS A TIME/ NOT RESPONSIBLE *Decca F 12390*	**18**	9 wks
18 Aug 66	THIS AND THAT *Decca F 12461*	**44**	3 wks
10 Nov 66	★ GREEN GREEN GRASS OF HOME *Decca F 22511*	**1**	22 wks
16 Feb 67	● DETROIT CITY *Decca F 22555*	**8**	10 wks
13 Apr 67	● FUNNY FAMILIAR FORGOTTEN FEELINGS *Decca F 12599*	**7**	15 wks
26 Jul 67	● I'LL NEVER FALL IN LOVE AGAIN *Decca F 12639*	**2**	25 wks
22 Nov 67	● I'M COMING HOME *Decca F 12693*	**2**	16 wks
28 Feb 68	● DELILAH *Decca F 12747*	**2**	17 wks
17 Jul 68	● HELP YOURSELF *Decca F 12812*	**5**	26 wks
27 Nov 68	A MINUTE OF YOUR TIME *Decca F 12854*	**14**	15 wks
14 May 69	● LOVE ME TONIGHT *Decca F 12924*	**9**	12 wks
13 Dec 69	● WITHOUT LOVE *Decca F 12990*	**10**	11 wks

Dick JORDAN

UK, male vocalist

17 Mar 60	HALLELUJAH I LOVE HER SO *Oriole CB 1534*	**47**	1 wk
9 Jun 60	LITTLE CHRISTINE *Oriole CB 1548*	**39**	3 wks

JOY STRINGS

UK, male/female vocal/instrumental group

27 Feb 64	IT'S AN OPEN SECRET *Regal-Zonophone RZ 501*	**32**	7 wks
17 Dec 64	A STARRY NIGHT *Regal-Zonophone RZ 504*	**35**	4 wks

JUMPING JACKS — See *Danny PEPPERMINT and the JUMPING JACKS*

Jimmy JUSTICE

UK, male vocalist

29 Mar 62	● WHEN MY LITTLE GIRL IS SMILING *Pye 7N 15421*	**9**	13 wks
14 Jun 62	● AIN'T THAT FUNNY *Pye 7N 15443*	**8**	10 wks
23 Aug 62	SPANISH HARLEM *Pye 7N 15457*	**20**	11 wks

K

Bert KAEMPFERT

Germany, orchestra

23 Dec 65	BYE BYE BLUES *Polydor BM 56 504*	**24**	10 wks

Gunther KALLMAN CHOIR

Germany, male/female vocal group

24 Dec 64	ELISABETH SERENADE *Polydor NH 24678*	**45**	3 wks

Eden KANE

UK, male vocalist

1 Jun 61	★ WELL I ASK YOU *Decca F 11353*	**1**	21 wks
14 Sep 61	● GET LOST *Decca F 11381*	**10**	11 wks
18 Jan 62	● FORGET ME NOT *Decca F 11418*	**3**	14 wks
10 May 62	● I DON'T KNOW WHY *Decca F 11460*	**7**	14 wks
30 Jan 64	● BOYS CRY *Fontana TF 438*	**8**	14 wks

KASENETZ-KATZ SINGING ORCHESTRAL CIRCUS

US, male vocal/instrumental group

20 Nov 68	QUICK JOEY SMALL (RUN JOEY RUN) *Buddah 201 022*	**19**	15 wks

KAYE SISTERS

UK, female vocal group

7 Jul 60	● PAPER ROSES *Philips PB 1024*	**7**	19 wks

Ernie K-DOE

US, male vocalist

11 May 61	MOTHER-IN-LAW *London HLU 9330*	**29**	7 wks

John LENNON *Right*
John's "tuned to a natural E" – 'Baby You're A Rich Man.'

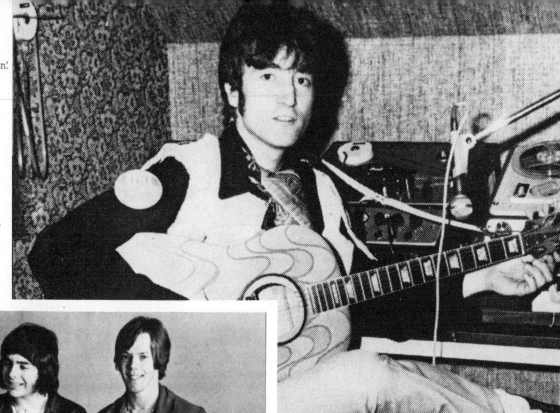

LOVE AFFAIR *Below*
Their first success was a cover of Robert Knight's American hit. Lead singer Steve Ellis, the only one who could afford the 6d for a deck chair, went on to make some strong but relatively unsuccessful solo singles.

Joe LOSS *Left* His Carl-Alan award winning 'Wheels Cha-Cha!' was Joe's first chart entry since his first release in 1934!

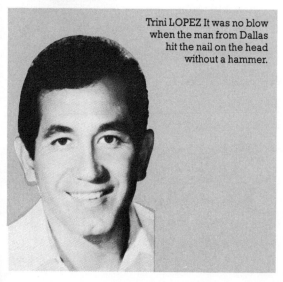

Trini LOPEZ It was no blow when the man from Dallas hit the nail on the head without a hammer.

Date	Title *Label Number*	Position

Johnny KEATING

UK, orchestra

1 Mar 62	● THEME FROM Z CARS *Piccadilly 7N 35032*	8	14 wks

Nelson KEENE

UK, male vocalist

25 Aug 60	IMAGE OF A GIRL *HMV POP 771*	37	4 wks
29 Sep 60	IMAGE OF A GIRL (re-entry) *HMV POP 771*	45	1 wk

KEITH

US, male vocalist

26 Jan 67	98.6 *Mercury MF 955*	24	7 wks
16 Mar 67	TELL ME TO MY FACE *Mercury MF 968*	50	1 wk

Keith KELLY

UK, male vocalist

5 May 60	TEASE ME *Parlophone R 4640*	46	1 wk
19 May 60	TEASE ME (re-entry) *Parlophone R 4640*	27	3 wks
18 Aug 60	LISTEN LITTLE GIRL *Parlophone R 4676*	47	1 wk

Johnny KIDD and the PIRATES

UK, male vocal/instrumental group

12 Feb 60	YOU GOT WHAT IT TAKES *HMV POP 698*	25	3 wks
16 Jun 60	★ SHAKIN' ALL OVER *HMV POP 753*	1	19 wks
6 Oct 60	RESTLESS *HMV POP 790*	22	7 wks
13 Apr 61	LINDA LU *HMV POP 853*	47	1 wk
10 Jan 63	SHOT OF RHYTHM & BLUES *HMV POP 1088*	48	1 wk
25 Jul 63	● I'LL NEVER GET OVER YOU *HMV POP 1173*	4	15 wks
28 Nov 63	HUNGRY FOR LOVE *HMV POP 1228*	20	10 wks
30 Apr 64	ALWAYS AND EVER *HMV POP 1269*	46	1 wk

Ben E. KING

US, male vocalist

2 Feb 61	FIRST TASTE OF LOVE *London HLK 9258*	27	11 wks
22 Jun 61	STAND BY ME *London HLK 9358*	50	1 wk
6 Jul 61	STAND BY ME (re-entry) *London HLK 9358*	27	6 wks
5 Oct 61	AMOR AMOR *London HLK 9416*	38	4 wks

Carole KING

US, female vocalist

20 Sep 62	● IT MIGHT AS WELL RAIN UNTIL SEPTEMBER *London HLU 9591*	3	13 wks

Jonathan KING

UK, male vocalist

29 Jul 65	● EVERYONE'S GONE TO THE MOON *Decca F 12187*	4	11 wks

Solomon KING

US, male vocalist

3 Jan 68	● SHE WEARS MY RING *Columbia DB 8325*	3	18 wks
1 May 68	WHEN WE WERE YOUNG *Columbia DB 8402*	21	10 wks

KING BROTHERS

UK, male vocal/instrumental group

14 Apr 60	● STANDING ON THE CORNER *Parlophone R 4639*	4	11 wks
28 Jul 60	MAIS OUI *Parlophone R 4672*	16	10 wks
12 Jan 61	DOLL HOUSE *Parlophone R 4715*	21	8 wks
2 Mar 61	76 TROMBONES *Parlophone R 4737*	19	11 wks

KINGSMEN

US, male vocal/instrumental group

30 Jan 64	LOUIE LOUIE *Pye International 7N 25231*	26	7 wks

KINKS

UK, male vocal/instrumental group

13 Aug 64	★ YOU REALLY GOT ME *Pye 7N 15673*	1	12 wks
29 Oct 64	● ALL DAY AND ALL OF THE NIGHT *Pye 7N 15714*	2	14 wks
21 Jan 65	★ TIRED OF WAITING FOR YOU *Pye 7N 15759*	1	10 wks
25 Mar 65	EVERYBODY'S GONNA BE HAPPY *Pye 7N 15813*	17	8 wks
27 May 65	● SET ME FREE *Pye 7N 15854*	9	11 wks
5 Aug 65	● SEE MY FRIEND *Pye 7N 15919*	10	9 wks
2 Dec 65	● TILL THE END OF THE DAY *Pye 7N 15981*	8	12 wks
3 Mar 66	● DEDICATED FOLLOWER OF FASHION *Pye 7N 17064*	4	11 wks
9 Jun 66	★ SUNNY AFTERNOON *Pye 7N 17125*	1	13 wks
24 Nov 66	● DEAD END STREET *Pye 7N 17222*	5	11 wks
11 May 67	● WATERLOO SUNSET *Pye 7N 17321*	2	11 wks
18 Oct 67	● AUTUMN ALMANAC *Pye 7N 17400*	3	11 wks
17 Apr 68	WONDERBOY *Pye 7N 17468*	36	5 wks
17 Jul 68	DAYS *Pye 7N 17573*	12	10 wks
16 Apr 69	PLASTIC MAN *Pye 7N 17724*	31	4 wks

Kathy KIRBY

UK, female vocalist

15 Aug 63	DANCE ON *Decca F 11682*	11	13 wks
7 Nov 63	● SECRET LOVE *Decca F 11759*	4	18 wks
20 Feb 64	● LET ME GO LOVER *Decca F 11832*	10	11 wks
7 May 64	YOU'RE THE ONE *Decca F 11892*	17	9 wks
4 Mar 65	I BELONG *Decca F 12087*	36	3 wks

KJELD — See *JAN and KJELD*

Date	Title *Label Number*	Position	Date	Title *Label Number*	Position

Gladys KNIGHT and the PIPS

US, female vocalist/male vocal backing group

Date	Title *Label Number*	Position	
8 Jun 67	TAKE ME IN YOUR ARMS & LOVE ME Tamla Motown TMG 604	13	15 wks
27 Dec 67	I HEARD IT THROUGH THE GRAPEVINE Tamla Motown TMG 629	47	1 wk

Buddy KNOX

US, male vocalist

Date	Title *Label Number*	Position	
6 Aug 62	SHE'S GONE *Liberty LIB 55473*	45	2 wks

KOKOMO

US, male instrumentalist, pianist

Date	Title *Label Number*	Position	
13 Apr 61	ASIA MINOR *London HLU 9305*	35	7 wks

Billy J. KRAMER and the DAKOTAS

UK, male vocalist/male instrumental backing group

Date	Title *Label Number*	Position	
2 May 63	● DO YOU WANT TO KNOW A SECRET? Parlophone R 5023	2	15 wks
1 Aug 63	★ BAD TO ME *Parlophone R 5049*	1	14 wks
7 Nov 63	● I'LL KEEP YOU SATISFIED Parlophone R 5073	4	13 wks
27 Feb 64	★ LITTLE CHILDREN *Parlophone R 5105*	1	13 wks
23 Jul 64	● FROM A WINDOW *Parlophone R 5156*	10	8 wks
20 May 65	TRAINS AND BOATS AND PLANES Parlophone R 5285	12	8 wks

See also Dakotas.

KREW-KATS

UK, male instrumental group

Date	Title *Label Number*	Position	
9 Mar 61	TRAMBONE *HMV POP 840*	33	9 wks
18 May 61	TRAMBONE (re-entry) *HMV POP 840*	49	1 wk

L

Danny LA RUE

UK, male vocalist

Date	Title *Label Number*	Position	
18 Dec 68	ON MOTHER KELLY'S DOORSTEP Page One POF 108	33	9 wks

Cleo LAINE

UK, female vocalist

Date	Title *Label Number*	Position	
29 Dec 60	LET'S SLIP AWAY *Fontana H 269*	42	1 wk
14 Sep 61	● YOU'LL ANSWER TO ME *Fontana H 326*	5	13 wks

Frankie LAINE

US, male vocalist

Date	Title *Label Number*	Position	
1 Jan 60	● RAWHIDE *Philips PB 965*	6	10 wks
31 Mar 60	RAWHIDE (re-entry) *Philips PB 965*	41	2 wks
11 May 61	GUNSLINGER *Philips PB 1135*	50	1 wk

LANCASTRIANS

UK, male vocal/instrumental group

Date	Title *Label Number*	Position	
24 Dec 64	WE'LL SING IN THE SUNSHINE Pye 7N 15732	47	2 wks

Major LANCE

US, male vocalist

Date	Title *Label Number*	Position	
13 Feb 64	UM UM UM UM UM UM *Columbia DB 7205*	40	2 wks

Don LANG

UK, male vocalist

Date	Title *Label Number*	Position	
10 Mar 60	SINK THE BISMARCK *HMV POP 714*	43	1 wk

LAUNCHERS — See Ezz RECO and the LAUNCHERS with Boysie GRANT

Steve LAWRENCE

US, male vocalist

Date	Title *Label Number*	Position	
21 Apr 60	● FOOTSTEPS *HMV POP 726*	4	13 wks
18 Aug 60	GIRLS GIRLS GIRLS *London HLT 9166*	49	1 wk

See also Steve and Eydie.

Brenda LEE

US, female vocalist

Date	Title *Label Number*	Position	
17 Mar 60	SWEET NUTHINS *Brunswick 05819*	45	1 wk
7 Apr 60	● SWEET NUTHINS (re-entry) *Brunswick 05819*	4	18 wks
30 Jun 60	I'M SORRY *Brunswick 05833*	12	16 wks
20 Oct 60	I WANT TO BE WANTED *Brunswick 05839*	31	6 wks
19 Jan 61	LET'S JUMP THE BROOMSTICK Brunswick 05823	12	15 wks
6 Apr 61	EMOTIONS *Brunswick 05847*	45	1 wk
20 Jul 61	DUM DUM *Brunswick 05854*	22	8 wks
16 Nov 61	FOOL NUMBER ONE *Brunswick 05860*	38	3 wks
8 Feb 62	BREAK IT TO ME GENTLY *Brunswick 05864*	46	2 wks
5 Apr 62	● SPEAK TO ME PRETTY *Brunswick 05867*	3	12 wks
21 Jun 62	● HERE COMES THAT FEELING Brunswick 05871	5	12 wks
13 Sep 62	IT STARTED ALL OVER AGAIN Brunswick 05876	15	11 wks
29 Nov 62	● ROCKIN' AROUND THE CHRISTMAS TREE Brunswick 05880	6	7 wks
17 Jan 63	● ALL ALONE AM I *Brunswick 05882*	7	17 wks
28 Mar 63	● LOSING YOU *Brunswick 05886*	10	16 wks
18 Jul 63	I WONDER *Brunswick 05891*	14	9 wks
31 Oct 63	SWEET IMPOSSIBLE YOU *Brunswick 05896*	28	6 wks
9 Jan 64	● AS USUAL *Brunswick 05899*	5	15 wks
9 Apr 64	THINK *Brunswick 05903*	26	8 wks

MERSEYS Aaron Banks and Tony Crane of the MERSEYBEATS perform in Liverpool's Cavern Club (*Main picture*). Following the demise of this group, Crane and fellow member Billy Kinsley formed a duo, the MERSEYS (*Inset*) and had a hit with the McCoys' 'Sorrow'.

Scott McKENZIE *Left* His song became the most successful Flower Power anthem but the follow up 'Like An Old Time Movie' was true to its title and maintained silence.

LULU *Far left* Lulu just about to press button 'B' and retrieve her fourpence.

Date	Title Label Number	Position		Date	Title Label Number	Position	
10 Sep 64	IS IT TRUE Brunswick 05915	17	8 wks				
10 Dec 64	CHRISTMAS WILL BE JUST ANOTHER LONELY DAY Brunswick 05921	29	5 wks				
4 Feb 65	THANKS A LOT Brunswick 05927	41	2 wks				
29 Jul 65	TOO MANY RIVERS Brunswick 05936	22	12 wks				

Curtis LEE

US, male vocalist

Date	Title Label Number	Position	
31 Aug 61	PRETTY LITTLE ANGEL EYES London HLX 9397	47	1 wk
14 Sep 61	PRETTY LITTLE ANGEL EYES (re-entry) London HLX 9397	48	1 wk

Leapy LEE

UK, male vocalist

Date	Title Label Number	Position	
21 Aug 68	● LITTLE ARROWS MCA MU 1028	2	21 wks
20 Dec 69	GOOD MORNING MCA MK 5021	47	1 wk

Peggy LEE

US, female vocalist

Date	Title Label Number	Position	
23 Mar 61	TILL THERE WAS YOU Capitol CL 15184	40	1 wk
6 Apr 61	TILL THERE WAS YOU (re-entry) Capitol CL 15184	30	3 wks

Raymond LEFEVRE

France, orchestra

Date	Title Label Number	Position	
15 May 68	SOUL COAXING Major Minor MM 559	46	2 wks

LEMON PIPERS

US, male vocal/instrumental group

Date	Title Label Number	Position	
7 Feb 68	● GREEN TAMBOURINE Pye International 7N 25444	7	11 wks
1 May 68	RICE IS NICE Pye International 7N 25454	41	5 wks

Ketty LESTER

US, female vocalist

Date	Title Label Number	Position	
19 Apr 62	● LOVE LETTERS London HLN 9527	4	12 wks
19 Jul 62	BUT NOT FOR ME London HLN 9574	45	4 wks

LETTERMEN

US, male vocal group

Date	Title Label Number	Position	
23 Nov 61	THE WAY YOU LOOK TONIGHT Capitol CL 15222	36	3 wks

Hank LEVINE

US, orchestra

Date	Title Label Number	Position	
21 Dec 61	IMAGE HMV POP 947	45	4 wks

Jerry Lee LEWIS

US, male vocalist/instrumentalist, piano

Date	Title Label Number	Position	
9 Jun 60	BABY BABY BYE BYE London HLS 9131	47	1 wk
4 May 61	● WHAT'D I SAY London HLS 9335	10	12 wks
3 Aug 61	WHAT'D I SAY (re-entry) London HLS 9335	49	2 wks
6 Sep 62	SWEET LITTLE SIXTEEN London HLS 9584	38	5 wks
14 Mar 63	GOOD GOLLY MISS MOLLY London HLS 9688	31	6 wks

John LEYTON

UK, male vocalist

Date	Title Label Number	Position	
3 Aug 61	★ JOHNNY REMEMBER ME Top Rank JAR 577	1	15 wks
5 Oct 61	● WILD WIND Top Rank JAR 585	2	10 wks
28 Dec 61	SON THIS IS SHE HMV POP 956	15	10 wks
15 Mar 62	LONE RIDER HMV POP 992	40	5 wks
3 May 62	LONELY CITY HMV POP 1014	14	11 wks
23 Aug 62	DOWN THE RIVER NILE HMV POP 1054	42	3 wks
21 Feb 63	CUPBOARD LOVE HMV POP 1122	22	12 wks
18 Jul 63	I'LL CUT YOUR TAIL OFF HMV POP 1175	50	1 wk
8 Aug 63	I'LL CUT YOUR TAIL OFF (re-entry) HMV POP 1175	36	2 wks
20 Feb 64	MAKE LOVE TO ME HMV POP 1264	49	1 wk

Terry LIGHTFOOT and his NEW ORLEANS JAZZMEN

UK, male vocal/instrumental group, Terry Lightfoot clarinet and vocals

Date	Title Label Number	Position	
7 Sep 61	TRUE LOVE Columbia DB 4696	33	4 wks
23 Nov 61	KING KONG Columbia SCD 2165	29	12 wks
3 May 62	TAVERN IN THE TOWN Columbia DB 4822	49	1 wk

Bob LIND

US, male vocalist

Date	Title Label Number	Position	
10 Mar 66	● ELUSIVE BUTTERFLY Fontana TF 670	5	9 wks
26 May 66	REMEMBER THE RAIN Fontana TF 702	46	1 wk

LITTLE EVA

US, female vocalist

Date	Title Label Number	Position	
6 Sep 62	● THE LOCO-MOTION London HL 9581	2	17 wks
3 Jan 63	KEEP YOUR HANDS OFF MY BABY London HLU 9633	30	4 wks
7 Mar 63	LET'S TURKEY TROT London HLU 9687	13	12 wks

See also Big Dee Irwin.

Date	Title Label Number	Position	Date	Title Label Number	Position

LITTLE RICHARD

US, male vocalist

11 Oct 62	**HE GOT WHAT HE WANTED** *Mercury AMT 1189*	**38**	4 wks
4 Jun 64	**BAMA LAMA BAMA LOO** *London HL 9896*	**20**	7 wks

LITTLE TONY

Italy, male vocalist

15 Jan 60	**TOO GOOD** *Decca F 11190*	**19**	3 wks

Hank LOCKLIN

US, male vocalist

11 Aug 60	● **PLEASE HELP ME I'M FALLING** *RCA 1188*	**9**	19 wks
15 Feb 62	**FROM HERE TO THERE TO YOU** *RCA 1273*	**44**	3 wks
15 Nov 62	**WE'RE GONNA GO FISHIN'** *RCA 1305*	**18**	11 wks
5 May 66	**I FEEL A CRY COMING ON** *RCA 1510*	**28**	8 wks

LOCOMOTIVE

UK, male vocal/instrumental group

16 Oct 68	**RUDI'S IN LOVE** *Parlophone R 5718*	**25**	8 wks

Shorty LONG

US, male vocalist

17 Jul 68	**HERE COMES THE JUDGE** *Tamla Motown TMG 663*	**30**	7 wks

LONG AND THE SHORT

UK, male vocal/instrumental group

10 Sep 64	**LETTER** *Decca F 11959*	**30**	5 wks
24 Dec 64	**CHOC ICE** *Decca F 12043*	**49**	3 wks

Trini LOPEZ

US, male vocalist

12 Sep 63	● **IF I HAD A HAMMER** *Reprise R 20198*	**4**	17 wks
12 Dec 63	**KANSAS CITY** *Reprise R 20236*	**35**	5 wks
12 May 66	**I'M COMING HOME CINDY** *Reprise R 20455*	**28**	5 wks
6 Apr 67	**GONNA GET ALONG WITHOUT YA NOW** *Reprise R 20547*	**41**	5 wks

Jerry LORDAN

UK, male vocalist

8 Jan 60	**I'LL STAY SINGLE** *Parlophone R 4588*	**26**	2 wks
26 Feb 60	**WHO COULD BE BLUER** *Parlophone R 4627*	**17**	9 wks
10 Mar 60	**I'LL STAY SINGLE** (re-entry) *Parlophone R 4588*	**41**	1 wk
19 May 60	**WHO COULD BE BLUER** (re-entry) *Parlophone R 4627*	**45**	1 wk
2 Jun 60	**SING LIKE AN ANGEL** *Parlophone R 4653*	**36**	2 wks

Sophia LOREN — See *Peter SELLERS and Sophia LOREN*

Joe LOSS

UK, orchestra

29 Jun 61	**WHEELS CHA CHA** *HMV POP 880*	**21**	21 wks
19 Oct 61	**SUCU SUCU** *HMV POP 937*	**48**	1 wk
29 Mar 62	**THE MAIGRET THEME** *HMV POP 995*	**20**	10 wks
1 Nov 62	**MUST BE MADISON** *HMV POP 1075*	**20**	13 wks
5 Nov 64	**MARCH OF THE MODS** *HMV POP 1351*	**35**	4 wks
24 Dec 64	**MARCH OF THE MODS** (re-entry) *HMV POP 1351*	**31**	4 wks

John D. LOUDERMILK

US, male vocalist

4 Jan 62	**THE LANGUAGE OF LOVE** *RCA 1269*	**13**	10 wks

Geoff LOVE — See *MANUEL and his MUSIC OF THE MOUNTAINS*

LOVE AFFAIR

UK, male vocal/instrumental group

3 Jan 68	★ **EVERLASTING LOVE** *CBS 3125*	**1**	12 wks
17 Apr 68	● **RAINBOW VALLEY** *CBS 3366*	**5**	13 wks
11 Sep 68	● **A DAY WITHOUT LOVE** *CBS 3674*	**6**	12 wks
19 Feb 69	**ONE ROAD** *CBS 3994*	**16**	9 wks
16 Jul 69	● **BRINGING ON BACK THE GOOD TIMES** *CBS 4300*	**9**	10 wks

LOVE SCULPTURE

UK, instrumental group

27 Nov 68	● **SABRE DANCE** *Parlophone R 5744*	**5**	14 wks

LOVIN' SPOONFUL

Canada, male vocal/instrumental group

14 Apr 66	● **DAYDREAM** *Pye International 7N 25361*	**2**	13 wks
14 Jul 66	● **SUMMER IN THE CITY** *Kama Sutra KAS 200*	**8**	11 wks
5 Jan 67	**NASHVILLE CATS** *Kama Sutra KAS 204*	**26**	7 wks
9 Mar 67	**DARLING BE HOME SOON** *Kama Sutra KAS 207*	**44**	2 wks

Date	Title Label Number	Position		Date	Title Label Number	Position	

LULU

UK, female vocalist

14 May 64	● SHOUT *Decca F 11884*	**7**	13 wks
12 Nov 64	HERE COMES THE NIGHT *Decca F 12017*	**50**	1 wk
17 Jun 65	● LEAVE A LITTLE LOVE *Decca F 12169*	**8**	11 wks
2 Sep 65	TRY TO UNDERSTAND *Decca F 12214*	**25**	8 wks
13 Apr 67	● THE BOAT THAT I ROW *Columbia DB 8169*	**6**	11 wks
29 Jun 67	LET'S PRETEND *Columbia DB 8221*	**11**	11 wks
8 Nov 67	LOVE LOVES TO LOVE LOVE *Columbia DB 8295*	**32**	6 wks
28 Feb 68	● ME THE PEACEFUL HEART *Columbia DB 8358*	**9**	9 wks
5 Jun 68	BOY *Columbia DB 8425*	**15**	7 wks
6 Nov 68	● I'M A TIGER *Columbia DB 8500*	**9**	13 wks
12 Mar 69	● BOOM BANG-A-BANG *Columbia DB 8550*	**2**	13 wks
22 Nov 69	OH ME OH MY (I'M A FOOL FOR YOU BABY) *Atco 226 008*	**47**	2 wks

Shout *credited to Lulu and The Luvvers.*

Bob LUMAN

US, male vocalist

8 Sep 60	● LET'S THINK ABOUT LIVING *Warner Bros. WB 18*	**6**	18 wks
15 Dec 60	WHY WHY BYE BYE *Warner Bros. WB 28*	**46**	1 wk
4 May 61	THE GREAT SNOWMAN *Warner Bros. WB 37*	**49**	2 wks

LUVVERS — See *LULU*

Kenny LYNCH

UK, male vocalist

30 Jun 60	MOUNTAIN OF LOVE *HMV POP 751*	**33**	3 wks
13 Sep 62	PUFF *HMV POP 1057*	**33**	5 wks
25 Oct 62	PUFF (re-entry) *HMV POP 1057*	**46**	1 wk
6 Dec 62	● UP ON THE ROOF *HMV POP 1090*	**10**	12 wks
20 Jun 63	● YOU CAN NEVER STOP ME LOVING YOU *HMV POP 1165*	**10**	14 wks
16 Apr 64	STAND BY ME *HMV POP 1280*	**39**	7 wks
27 Aug 64	WHAT AM I TO DO *HMV POP 1321*	**37**	4 wks
1 Oct 64	WHAT AM I TO DO (re-entry) *HMV POP 1321*	**44**	2 wks
17 Jun 65	I'LL STAY BY YOU *HMV POP 1430*	**29**	7 wks

Patti LYNN

UK, female vocalist

| 10 May 62 | JOHNNY ANGEL *Fontana H 391* | **37** | 5 wks |

M

Lorin MAAZEL — See *PHILHARMONIA ORCHESTRA, conductor Lorin MAAZEL*

Neil MacARTHUR

UK, male vocalist

| 5 Feb 69 | SHE'S NOT THERE *Deram DM 225* | **34** | 5 wks |

Frankie McBRIDE

Ireland, male vocalist

| 9 Aug 67 | FIVE LITTLE FINGERS *Emerald MD 1081* | **19** | 15 wks |

David McCALLUM

UK, male vocalist

| 14 Apr 66 | COMMUNICATION *Capitol CL 15439* | **32** | 4 wks |

McCOYS

US, male vocal/instrumental group

| 2 Sep 65 | ● HANG ON SLOOPY *Immediate IM 001* | **5** | 13 wks |
| 16 Dec 65 | FEVER *Immediate IM 021* | **44** | 4 wks |

Gene McDANIELS

US, male vocalist

| 16 Nov 61 | TOWER OF STRENGTH *London HLG 9448* | **49** | 1 wk |
| 30 Nov 61 | TOWER OF STRENGTH (re-entry) *London HLG 9448* | **49** | 1 wk |

Barry McGUIRE

US, male vocalist

| 9 Sep 65 | ● EVE OF DESTRUCTION *RCA 1469* | **3** | 12 wks |

Kenneth McKELLAR

UK, male vocalist

| 10 Mar 66 | A MAN WITHOUT LOVE *Decca F 12341* | **30** | 4 wks |

Scott McKENZIE

US, male vocalist

| 12 Jul 67 | ★ SAN FRANCISCO (BE SURE TO WEAR FLOWERS IN YOUR HAIR) *CBS 2816* | **1** | 17 wks |
| 1 Nov 67 | LIKE AN OLD TIME MOVIE *CBS 3009* | **50** | 1 wk |

Second hit credited to The Voice Of Scott McKenzie

Ken MACKINTOSH

UK, orchestra

| 10 Mar 60 | NO HIDING PLACE *HMV POP 713* | **45** | 1 wk |

Date	Title Label Number	Position

Tommy McLAIN

US, male vocalist

8 Sep 66	**SWEET DREAMS** *London HL 10065*	**49** 1 wk

Phil McLEAN

US, male vocalist

18 Jan 62	**SMALL SAD SAM** *Top Rank JAR 597*	**34** 4 wks

Carmen McRAE — See *Sammy DAVIS Jr. and Carmen McRAE*

MAGIC LANTERNS

UK, male vocal/instrumental group

7 Jul 66	**EXCUSE ME BABY** *CBS 202094*	**46** 1 wk
28 Jul 66	**EXCUSE ME BABY** (re-entry) *CBS 202094*	**44** 1 wk
11 Aug 66	**EXCUSE ME BABY** (2nd re-entry) *CBS 202094*	**46** 1 wk

MAKADOPULOS and his GREEK SERENADERS

Greece, male vocal/instrumental group

20 Oct 60	**NEVER ON SUNDAY** *Palette PG 9005*	**36** 14 wks

MAMAS and the PAPAS

US, female/male vocal group

28 Apr 66	**CALIFORNIA DREAMIN'** *RCA 1503*	**23** 9 wks
12 May 66	● **MONDAY MONDAY** *RCA 1516*	**3** 13 wks
28 Jul 66	**I SAW HER AGAIN** *RCA 1533*	**11** 11 wks
9 Feb 67	**WORDS OF LOVE** *RCA 1564*	**47** 3 wks
6 Apr 67	● **DEDICATED TO THE ONE I LOVE** *RCA 1576*	**2** 17 wks
26 Jul 67	● **CREEQUE ALLEY** *RCA 1613*	**9** 11 wks

See also Mama Cass

Henry MANCINI

US, orchestra/chorus

7 Dec 61	**MOON RIVER** *RCA 1256*	**46** 2 wks
28 Dec 61	**MOON RIVER** (re-entry) *RCA 1256*	**44** 1 wk
24 Sep 64	● **HOW SOON** *RCA 1414*	**10** 12 wks

MANFRED MANN

South Africa/UK, male vocal/instrumental group

23 Jan 64	● **5-4-3-2-1** *HMV POP 1252*	**5** 13 wks
16 Apr 64	**HUBBLE BUBBLE TOIL AND TROUBLE** *HMV POP 1282*	**11** 8 wks
16 Jul 64	★ **DO WAH DIDDY DIDDY** *HMV POP 1320*	**1** 14 wks
15 Oct 64	● **SHA LA LA** *HMV POP 1346*	**3** 12 wks
14 Jan 65	● **COME TOMORROW** *HMV POP 1381*	**4** 9 wks
15 Apr 65	**OH NO NOT MY BABY** *HMV POP 1413*	**11** 10 wks
16 Sep 65	● **IF YOU GOTTA GO GO NOW** *HMV POP 1466*	**2** 12 wks

21 Apr 66	★ **PRETTY FLAMINGO** *HMV POP 1523*	**1** 12 wks
7 Jul 66	**YOU GAVE ME SOMEBODY TO LOVE** *HMV POP 1541*	**36** 4 wks
4 Aug 66	● **JUST LIKE A WOMAN** *Fontana TF 730*	**10** 10 wks
27 Oct 66	● **SEMI-DETACHED SUBURBAN MR. JAMES** *Fontana TF 757*	**2** 12 wks
30 Mar 67	● **HA HA SAID THE CLOWN** *Fontana TF 812*	**4** 11 wks
25 May 67	**SWEET PEA** *Fontana TF 828*	**36** 4 wks
24 Jan 68	★ **MIGHTY QUINN** *Fontana TF 897*	**1** 11 wks
12 Jun 68	● **MY NAME IS JACK** *Fontana TF 943*	**8** 11 wks
18 Dec 68	● **FOX ON THE RUN** *Fontana TF 985*	**5** 12 wks
30 Apr 69	● **RAGAMUFFIN MAN** *Fontana TF 1013*	**8** 11 wks

The HMV hits featured Paul Jones as lead vocalist and the Fontana hits Mike d'Abo, except for *Sweet Pea,* an instrumental disc. See also Paul Jones.

Johnny MANN SINGERS

US, male/female vocal group

12 Jul 67	● **UP, UP AND AWAY** *Liberty LIB 55972*	**6** 13 wks

MANUEL and his MUSIC OF THE MOUNTAINS

UK, orchestra, leader Geoff Love

13 Oct 60	**NEVER ON SUNDAY** *Columbia DB 4515*	**29** 10 wks
13 Oct 66	**SOMEWHERE MY LOVE** *Columbia DB 7969*	**42** 2 wks

MARAUDERS

UK, male vocal/instrumental group

8 Aug 63	**THAT'S WHAT I WANT** *Decca F 11695*	**48** 1 wk
22 Aug 63	**THAT'S WHAT I WANT** (re-entry) *Decca F 11695*	**43** 3 wks

MARBLES

UK, male vocal duo

25 Sep 68	● **ONLY ONE WOMAN** *Polydor 56 272*	**5** 12 wks
26 Mar 69	**THE WALLS FELL DOWN** *Polydor 56 310*	**28** 6 wks

MARCELS

US, male vocal group

13 Apr 61	★ **BLUE MOON** *Pye International 7N 25073*	**1** 13 wks
8 Jun 61	**SUMMERTIME** *Pye International 7N 25083*	**46** 4 wks

Little Peggy MARCH

US, female vocalist

12 Sep 63	**HELLO HEARTACHE GOODBYE LOVE** *RCA 1362*	**29** 7 wks

MIKI and GRIFF Championed by Lonnie Donegan, Miki (the one in the dress) and Griff (the one with the moustache) had their greatest success with covers of Burl Ives and Steve Lawrence and Eydie Gorme tunes.

MILLIE Thoroughly modern Millie.

MOVE Watching the support act.

MOJOS Unarmed and cornered . . . things look grim for the Mojos . . . how will they escape? . . . and can they ever hope to find their collars again . . . don't miss episode two 'Everything's Alright' next week at the same time.

Date	Title Label Number	Position		Date	Title Label Number	Position

Pigmeat MARKHAM
US, male vocalist

17 Jul 68   **HERE COMES THE JUDGE** *Chess CRS 8077*   **19**   8 wks

MARMALADE
UK, male vocal group

22 May 68 ● **LOVIN' THINGS** *CBS 3412*   **6** 13 wks
23 Oct 68   **WAIT FOR ME MARIANNE** *CBS 3708*   **30** 5 wks
4 Dec 68 ★ **OB-LA-DI OB-LA-DA** *CBS 3892*   **1** 20 wks
11 Jun 69 ● **BABY MAKE IT SOON** *CBS 4287*   **9** 13 wks
20 Dec 69 ● **REFLECTIONS OF MY LIFE** *Decca F 12982*   **3** 12 wks

Stevie MARSH
UK, female vocalist

1 Jan 60   **THE ONLY BOY IN THE WORLD**   **37** 2 wks
Decca F 11181

Joy MARSHALL
UK, female vocalist

23 Jun 66   **THE MORE I SEE YOU** *Decca F 12422*   **34** 2 wks

MARTHA and the VANDELLAS — See *Martha REEVES and the VANDELLAS*

Dean MARTIN
US, male vocalist

27 Aug 64   **EVERYBODY LOVES SOMEBODY**   **11** 13 wks
Reprise R 20281
12 Nov 64   **THE DOOR IS STILL OPEN TO MY HEART**   **42** 4 wks
Reprise R 20307
5 Feb 69 ● **GENTLE ON MY MIND** *Reprise RS 23343*   **2** 23 wks
30 Aug 69   **GENTLE ON MY MIND** (re-entry)   **49** 1 wk
Reprise RS 23343

Wink MARTINDALE
US, male vocalist

1 Jan 60   **DECK OF CARDS** *London HLD 8962*   **23** 1 wk
15 Jan 60   **DECK OF CARDS** (re-entry) *London HLD 8962* **28** 2 wks
31 Mar 60   **DECK OF CARDS** (2nd re-entry)   **45** 1 wk
London HLD 8962
18 Apr 63 ● **DECK OF CARDS** (3rd re-entry)   **5** 21 wks
London HLD 8962

Al MARTINO
US, male vocalist

31 Mar 60   **SUMMERTIME** *Top Rank JAR 312*   **49** 1 wk
29 Aug 63   **I LOVE YOU BECAUSE** *Capitol CL 15300*   **48** 1 wk

MARVELETTES
US, female vocal group

15 Jun 67   **WHEN YOU'RE YOUNG AND IN LOVE**   **13** 10 wks
Tamla Motown TMG 609

MARY — See *PETER, PAUL and MARY*

MASSIEL
Spain, female vocalist

24 Apr 68   **LA LA LA** *Philips BF 1667*   **35** 4 wks

MASTER SINGERS
UK, male vocal group

14 Apr 66   **HIGHWAY CODE** *Parlophone R 5428*   **25** 6 wks
17 Nov 66   **WEATHER FORECAST** *Parlophone R 5523*   **50** 1 wk

Sammy MASTERS
US, male vocalist

9 Jun 60   **ROCKIN' RED WING** *Warner Bros. WB 10*   **36** 5 wks

Mireille MATHIEU
France, female vocalist

13 Dec 67   **LA DERNIERE VALSE** *Columbia DB 8323*   **26** 7 wks

Johnny MATHIS
US, male vocalist

29 Jan 60   **MISTY** *Fontana H 219*   **12** 13 wks
24 Mar 60   **YOU ARE BEAUTIFUL** *Fontana H 234*   **38** 8 wks
26 May 60   **YOU ARE BEAUTIFUL** (re-entry)   **46** 1 wk
Fontana H 234
28 Jul 60   **STARBRIGHT** *Fontana H 254*   **47** 2 wks
6 Oct 60 ● **MY LOVE FOR YOU** *Fontana H 267*   **9** 18 wks
4 Apr 63   **WHAT WILL MY MARY SAY** *CBS AAG 127*   **49** 1 wk

Susan MAUGHAN
UK, female vocalist

11 Oct 62 ● **BOBBY'S GIRL** *Philips 326544 BF*   **3** 19 wks
14 Feb 63   **HAND A HANDKERCHIEF TO HELEN**   **41** 3 wks
Philips 326562 BF
9 May 63   **SHE'S NEW TO YOU** *Philips 326586 BF*   **45** 3 wks

Paul MAURIAT
France, orchestra

21 Feb 68   **LOVE IS BLUE (L'AMOUR EST BLEU)**   **12** 14 wks
Philips BF 1637

Date	Title Label Number	Position

Mary MAY

UK, female vocalist

| 27 Feb 64 | **ANYONE WHO HAD A HEART** Fontana TF 440 | **49** | 1 wk |

Carmen McRAE — See *Sammy DAVIS Jr. and Carmen McRAE*

Tony MEEHAN COMBO

UK, male instrumentalist, drums

| 16 Jan 64 | **SONG OF MEXICO** Decca F 11801 | **39** | 4 wks |

See also *Jet Harris and Tony Meehan.*

Tony MERRICK

UK, male vocalist

| 2 Jun 66 | **LADY JANE** Columbia DB 7913 | **49** | 1 wk |

MERSEYBEATS

UK, male vocal/instrumental group

12 Sep 63	**IT'S LOVE THAT REALLY COUNTS** Fontana TF 412	**24**	12 wks
16 Jan 64	● **I THINK OF YOU** Fontana TF 431	**5**	17 wks
16 Apr 64	**DON'T TURN AROUND** Fontana TF 459	**13**	11 wks
9 Jul 64	**WISHIN' AND HOPIN'** Fontana TF 482	**13**	10 wks
5 Nov 64	**LAST NIGHT** Fontana TF 504	**40**	3 wks
14 Oct 65	**I LOVE YOU, YES I DO** Fontana TF 607	**22**	8 wks
20 Jan 66	**I STAND ACCUSED** Fontana TF 645	**38**	3 wks

MERSEYS

UK, male vocal duo

| 28 Apr 66 | ● **SORROW** Fontana TF 694 | **4** | 13 wks |

M.G.'S — See *BOOKER T. and the M.G.'s*

MICK — See *Dave DEE, DOZY, BEAKY, MICK and TICH*

MICROBE

UK, male vocalist

| 14 May 69 | **GROOVY BABY** CBS 4158 | **29** | 7 wks |

MIGHTY AVENGERS

UK, male vocal/instrumental group

| 26 Nov 64 | **SO MUCH IN LOVE** Decca F 11962 | **46** | 2 wks |

MIGHTY AVONS — See *Larry CUNNINGHAM and the MIGHTY AVONS*

MIGIL FIVE

UK, male vocal/instrumental group

| 19 Mar 64 | ● **MOCKINGBIRD HILL** Pye 7N 15597 | **10** | 13 wks |
| 4 Jun 64 | **NEAR YOU** Pye 7N 15645 | **31** | 7 wks |

MIKI and GRIFF

UK, male/female vocal duo

13 Oct 60	**ROCKIN' ALONE** Pye 7N 15296	**44**	3 wks
1 Feb 62	**LITTLE BITTY TEAR** Pye 7N 15412	**16**	13 wks
22 Aug 63	**I WANNA STAY HERE** Pye 7N 15555	**23**	7 wks

Gary MILLER

UK, male vocalist

| 21 Dec 61 | **THERE GOES THAT SONG AGAIN/ THE NIGHT IS YOUNG** Pye 7N 15404 | **29** | 9 wks |
| 1 Mar 62 | **THERE GOES THAT SONG AGAIN** (re-entry) Pye 7N 15404 | **48** | 1 wk |

The Night Is Young only listed with There Goes That Song Again for weeks 21 and 28 Dec 61 and 4 Jan 62.

Jody MILLER

US, female vocalist

| 21 Oct 65 | **HOME OF THE BRAVE** Capitol CL 15415 | **49** | 1 wk |

Ned MILLER

US, male vocalist

| 14 Feb 63 | ● **FROM A JACK TO A KING** London HL 9648 | **2** | 21 wks |
| 18 Feb 65 | **DO WHAT YOU DO DO WELL** London HL 9937 | **48** | 1 wk |

Roger MILLER

US, male vocalist

18 Mar 65	★ **KING OF THE ROAD** Philips BF 1397	**1**	15 wks
3 Jun 65	**ENGINE ENGINE NO. 9** Philips BF 1416	**33**	5 wks
21 Oct 65	**KANSAS CITY STAR** Philips BF 1437	**48**	1 wk
16 Dec 65	**ENGLAND SWINGS** Philips BF 1456	**45**	1 wk
6 Jan 66	**ENGLAND SWINGS** (re-entry) Philips BF 1456	**13**	7 wks
27 Mar 68	**LITTLE GREEN APPLES** Mercury MF 1021	**19**	10 wks
2 Apr 69	**LITTLE GREEN APPLES** (re-entry) Mercury MF 1021	**48**	1 wk
7 May 69	**LITTLE GREEN APPLES** (2nd re-entry) Mercury MF 1021	**39**	2 wks

MILLIE

Jamaica, female vocalist

12 Mar 64	● **MY BOY LOLLIPOP** Fontana TF 449	**2**	18 wks
25 Jun 64	**SWEET WILLIAM** Fontana TF 479	**30**	9 wks
11 Nov 65	**BLOODSHOT EYES** Fontana TF 617	**48**	1 wk

Date	Title Label Number	Position

Garry MILLS
UK, male vocalist

7 Jul 60	● LOOK FOR A STAR *Top Rank JAR 336*	**7**	14 wks
20 Oct 60	TOP TEEN BABY *Top Rank JAR 500*	**24**	12 wks
22 Jun 61	I'LL STEP DOWN *Decca F 11358*	**39**	5 wks

Hayley MILLS
UK, female vocalist

19 Oct 61	LET'S GET TOGETHER *Decca F 21396*	**17**	11 wks

Mrs. MILLS
UK, female instrumentalist, piano

14 Dec 61	MRS MILLS' MEDLEY *Parlophone R 4856*	**18**	5 wks

Mrs Mills' Medley *consisted of the following tunes: I Want To Be Happy/ Sheik Of Araby/ Baby Face/ Somebody Stole My Gal/ Ma (He's Making Eyes At Me)/ Swanee/ Ain't She Sweet/ California Here I Come.*

MINDBENDERS
UK, male vocal/instrumental group

13 Jan 66	● A GROOVY KIND OF LOVE *Fontana TF 644*	**2**	14 wks
5 May 66	CAN'T LIVE WITH YOU (CAN'T LIVE WITHOUT YOU) *Fontana TF 697*	**28**	7 wks
25 Aug 66	ASHES TO ASHES *Fontana TF 731*	**14**	9 wks
20 Sep 67	THE LETTER *Fontana TF 869*	**42**	4 wks

See also Wayne Fontana and The Mindbenders.

Marcello MINERBI
Italy, orchestra

22 Jul 65	● ZORBA'S DANCE *Durium DRS 54001*	**6**	16 wks

MIRACLES — See *Smokey ROBINSON and the MIRACLES*

Guy MITCHELL
US, male vocalist

1 Jan 60	● HEARTACHES BY THE NUMBER *Philips PB 964*	**5**	13 wks

Willie MITCHELL
US, male instrumentalist, guitar

24 Apr 68	SOUL SERENADE *London HLU 10186*	**43**	1 wk

MOJOS
UK, male vocal/instrumental group

26 Mar 64	● EVERYTHING'S ALRIGHT *Decca F 11853*	**9**	11 wks
11 Jun 64	WHY NOT TONIGHT *Decca F 11918*	**25**	10 wks
10 Sep 64	SEVEN DAFFODILS *Decca F 11959*	**30**	5 wks

Zoot MONEY and the BIG ROLL BAND
UK, male vocalist/instrumentalist - keyboards, male instrumental backing group

18 Aug 66	BIG TIME OPERATOR *Columbia DB 7975*	**25**	8 wks

MONKEES
US/UK, male vocal/instrumental group

5 Jan 67	★ I'M A BELIEVER *RCA 1560*	**1**	17 wks
26 Jan 67	LAST TRAIN TO CLARKSVILLE *RCA 1547*	**23**	7 wks
6 Apr 67	● A LITTLE BIT ME A LITTLE BIT YOU *RCA 1580*	**3**	12 wks
22 Jun 67	● ALTERNATE TITLE *RCA 1604*	**2**	12 wks
16 Aug 67	PLEASANT VALLEY SUNDAY *RCA 1620*	**11**	8 wks
15 Nov 67	● DAYDREAM BELIEVER *RCA 1645*	**5**	17 wks
27 Mar 68	VALLERI *RCA 1679*	**12**	8 wks
26 Jun 68	D. W. WASHBURN *RCA 1706*	**17**	6 wks
26 Mar 69	TEARDROP CITY *RCA 1802*	**46**	1 wk
25 Jun 69	SOMEDAY MAN *RCA 1824*	**47**	1 wk

Matt MONRO
UK, male vocalist

15 Dec 60	● PORTRAIT OF MY LOVE *Parlophone R 4714*	**3**	16 wks
9 Mar 61	● MY KIND OF GIRL *Parlophone R 4755*	**5**	12 wks
18 May 61	WHY NOT NOW/ CAN THIS BE LOVE *Parlophone R 4775*	**24**	9 wks
28 Sep 61	GONNA BUILD A MOUNTAIN *Parlophone R 4819*	**44**	3 wks
8 Feb 62	● SOFTLY AS I LEAVE YOU *Parlophone R 4868*	**10**	18 wks
14 Jun 62	WHEN LOVE COMES ALONG *Parlophone R 4911*	**46**	3 wks
8 Nov 62	MY LOVE AND DEVOTION *Parlophone R 4954*	**29**	5 wks
14 Nov 63	FROM RUSSIA WITH LOVE *Parlophone R 5068*	**20**	13 wks
17 Sep 64	● WALK AWAY *Parlophone R 5171*	**4**	20 wks
24 Dec 64	FOR MAMA *Parlophone R 5215*	**36**	4 wks
25 Mar 65	WITHOUT YOU *Parlophone R 5251*	**37**	4 wks
21 Oct 65	● YESTERDAY *Parlophone R 5348*	**8**	12 wks

Hugo MONTENEGRO
US, orchestra

11 Sep 68	★ THE GOOD THE BAD & THE UGLY *RCA 1727*	**1**	24 wks
8 Jan 69	HANG 'EM HIGH *RCA 1771*	**50**	1 wk
19 Mar 69	THE GOOD THE BAD & THE UGLY (re-entry) *RCA 1727*	**48**	1 wk

Chris MONTEZ
US, male vocalist

4 Oct 62	● LET'S DANCE *London HLU 9596*	**2**	18 wks
17 Jan 63	● SOME KINDA FUN *London HLU 9650*	**10**	9 wks
30 Jun 66	● THE MORE I SEE YOU *Pye International 7N 25369*	**3**	13 wks
22 Sep 66	THERE WILL NEVER BE ANOTHER YOU *Pye International 7N 25381*	**37**	4 wks

Date	Title Label Number	Position

MOODY BLUES

UK, male vocal/instrumental group

Date	Title Label Number	Position	
10 Dec 64	★ GO NOW *Decca F 12022*	1	14 wks
4 Mar 65	I DON'T WANT TO GO ON WITHOUT YOU *Decca F 12095*	33	9 wks
10 Jun 65	FROM THE BOTTOM OF MY HEART *Decca F 12166*	22	9 wks
18 Nov 65	EVERYDAY *Decca F 12266*	44	2 wks
27 Dec 67	NIGHTS IN WHITE SATIN *Deram DM 161*	19	11 wks
7 Aug 68	VOICES IN THE SKY *Deram DM 196*	27	10 wks
4 Dec 68	RIDE MY SEE-SAW *Deram DM 213*	42	1 wk

MOONTREKKERS

UK, male instrumental group

Date	Title Label Number	Position	
2 Nov 61	NIGHT OF THE VAMPIRE *Parlophone R 4814*	50	1 wk

Dudley MOORE — See *Peter COOK and Dudley MOORE*

Jane MORGAN

US, female vocalist

Date	Title Label Number	Position	
21 Jul 60	ROMANTICA *London HLR 9120*	39	5 wks

Dorothy Combs MORRISON — See *Edwin HAWKINS SINGERS*

Mickie MOST

UK, male vocalist

Date	Title Label Number	Position	
25 Jul 63	MISTER PORTER *Decca F 11664*	45	1 wk

MOVE

UK, male vocal/instrumental group

Date	Title Label Number	Position	
5 Jan 67	● NIGHT OF FEAR *Deram DM 109*	2	10 wks
6 Apr 67	● I CAN HEAR THE GRASS GROW *Deram DM 117*	5	10 wks
6 Sep 67	● FLOWERS IN THE RAIN *Regal Zonophone RZ3001*	2	13 wks
7 Feb 68	● FIRE BRIGADE *Regal Zonophone RZ3005*	3	11 wks
25 Dec 68	★ BLACKBERRY WAY *Regal Zonophone RZ3015*	1	12 wks
23 Jul 69	CURLY *Regal Zonophone RZ3021*	12	12 wks

MUSTAFAS — See *STAIFFI and his MUSTAFAS*

Tim MYCROFT — See *SOUNDS NICE*

MYSTERIANS — See *?(QUESTION MARK) and the MYSTERIANS*

N

NAPOLEON XIV

US, male vocalist

Date	Title Label Number	Position	
4 Aug 66	● THEY'RE COMING TO TAKE ME AWAY HA-HAAA! *Warner Bros. WB 5831*	4	10 wks

NASH — See *CROSBY, STILLS and NASH*

Johnny NASH

US, male vocalist

Date	Title Label Number	Position	
7 Aug 68	● HOLD ME TIGHT *Regal Zonophone RZ 3010*	5	16 wks
8 Jan 69	● YOU GOT SOUL *Major Minor MM 586*	6	12 wks
2 Apr 69	● CUPID *Major Minor MM 603*	6	11 wks
25 Jun 69	CUPID (re-entry) *Major Minor MM 603*	50	1 wk

NASHVILLE TEENS

UK, male vocal/instrumental group

Date	Title Label Number	Position	
9 Jul 64	● TOBACCO ROAD *Decca F 11930*	6	13 wks
22 Oct 64	● GOOGLE EYE *Decca F 12000*	10	11 wks
4 Mar 65	FIND MY WAY BACK HOME *Decca F 12089*	34	6 wks
20 May 65	THIS LITTLE BIRD *Decca F 12143*	38	4 wks
3 Feb 66	THE HARD WAY *Decca F 12316*	45	2 wks
24 Feb 66	THE HARD WAY (re-entry) *Decca F 12316*	48	1 wk

NATURALS

UK, male vocal/instrumental group

Date	Title Label Number	Position	
20 Aug 64	I SHOULD HAVE KNOWN BETTER *Parlophone R 5165*	24	9 wks

Rick NELSON

US, male vocalist

Date	Title Label Number	Position	
15 Jan 60	I WANNA BE LOVED *London HLP 9021*	30	1 wk
7 Jul 60	YOUNG EMOTIONS *London HLP 9121*	48	1 wk
1 Jun 61	● HELLO MARY LOU/ TRAVELLIN' MAN *London HLP 9347*	2	18 wks
16 Nov 61	EVERLOVIN' *London HLP 9440*	23	5 wks
29 Mar 62	YOUNG WORLD *London HLP 9524*	19	13 wks
30 Aug 62	TEENAGE IDOL *London HLP 9583*	39	4 wks
17 Jan 63	IT'S UP TO YOU *London HLP 9648*	22	9 wks
17 Oct 63	FOOLS RUSH IN *Brunswick 05895*	12	9 wks
30 Jan 64	FOR YOU *Brunswick 05900*	14	10 wks

Billed as Ricky Nelson on the first three hits.

Date	Title Label Number	Position	Date	Title Label Number	Position

Sandy NELSON

US, male instrumentalist, drums

1 Jan 60	**TEEN BEAT** *Top Rank JAR 197*	**18**	3 wks
5 Feb 60	**TEEN BEAT** (re-entry) *Top Rank JAR 197*	**25**	1 wk
14 Dec 61	● **LET THERE BE DRUMS** *London HLP 9466*	**3**	16 wks
22 Mar 62	**DRUMS ARE MY BEAT** *London HLP 9521*	**30**	6 wks
7 Jun 62	**DRUMMIN' UP A STORM** *London HLP 9558*	**39**	8 wks

NERO and the GLADIATORS

UK, male instrumental group

23 Mar 61	**ENTRY OF THE GLADIATORS** *Decca F 11329*	**50**	1 wk
6 Apr 61	**ENTRY OF THE GLADIATORS** (re-entry) *Decca F 11329*	**37**	4 wks
27 Jul 61	**IN THE HALL OF THE MOUNTAIN KING** *Decca F 11367*	**48**	1 wk

NEW GENERATION

UK, male vocal/instrumental group

26 Jun 68	**SMOKEY BLUES AWAY** *Spark SRL 1007*	**38**	5 wks

NEW ORLEANS JAZZMEN — See *Terry LIGHTFOOT and his NEW ORLEANS JAZZMEN*

NEW VAUDEVILLE BAND

UK, male vocal/instrumental group

8 Sep 66	● **WINCHESTER CATHEDRAL** *Fontana TF 741*	**4**	19 wks
26 Jan 67	● **PEEK-A-BOO** *Fontana TF 784*	**7**	11 wks
11 May 67	**FINCHLEY CENTRAL** *Fontana TF 824*	**11**	9 wks
2 Aug 67	**GREEN STREET GREEN** *Fontana TF 853*	**37**	4 wks

Peek-A-Boo has credit: Featuring Tristram.

NEWBEATS

US, male vocal group

10 Sep 64	**BREAD AND BUTTER** *Hickory 1269*	**15**	9 wks

Anthony NEWLEY

UK, male vocalist

15 Jan 60	★ **WHY** *Decca F 11194*	**1**	17 wks
24 Mar 60	★ **DO YOU MIND** *Decca F 11220*	**1**	15 wks
14 Jul 60	● **IF SHE SHOULD COME TO YOU** *Decca F 11254*	**6**	15 wks
24 Nov 60	● **STRAWBERRY FAIR** *Decca F 11295*	**3**	11 wks
16 Mar 61	● **AND THE HEAVENS CRIED** *Decca F 11331*	**6**	12 wks
15 Jun 61	**POP GOES THE WEASEL/ BEE BOM** *Decca F 11362*	**12**	9 wks
3 Aug 61	**WHAT KIND OF FOOL AM I?** *Decca F 11376*	**36**	8 wks
25 Jan 62	**D-DARLING** *Decca F 11419*	**25**	6 wks
26 Jul 62	**THAT NOISE** *Decca F 11486*	**34**	4 wks

Brad NEWMAN

UK, male vocalist

22 Feb 62	**SOMEBODY TO LOVE** *Fontana H 357*	**47**	1 wk

NICE

UK, male instrumental group

10 Jul 68	**AMERICA** *Immediate IM 068*	**21**	15 wks

Sue NICHOLS

UK, female vocalist

3 Jul 68	**WHERE WILL YOU BE** *Pye 7N 17565*	**17**	8 wks

NILSSON

US, male vocalist

27 Sep 69	**EVERYBODY'S TALKIN'** *RCA 1876*	**50**	1 wk
11 Oct 69	**EVERYBODY'S TALKIN'** (re-entry) *RCA 1876*	**23**	9 wks

NINA and FREDERICK

Denmark, female/male vocal duo

10 Mar 60	**LISTEN TO THE OCEAN** *Columbia DB 4332*	**47**	1 wk
7 Apr 60	**LISTEN TO THE OCEAN** (re-entry) *Columbia DB 4332*	**46**	1 wk
17 Nov 60	● **LITTLE DONKEY** *Columbia DB 4536*	**3**	10 wks
28 Sep 61	**LONGTIME BOY** *Columbia DB 4703*	**43**	3 wks
5 Oct 61	**SUCU SUCU** *Columbia DB 4632*	**23**	13 wks

1910 FRUITGUM CO.

US, male vocal/instrumental group

20 Mar 68	● **SIMON SAYS** *Pye International 7N 25447*	**2**	16 wks

NIRVANA

UK, male vocal/instrumental duo

15 May 68	**RAINBOW CHASER** *Island WIP 6029*	**34**	6 wks

Dermot O'BRIEN

Ireland, male vocalist

20 Oct 66	**THE MERRY PLOUGHBOY** *Envoy ENV 016*	**46**	1 wk
3 Nov 66	**THE MERRY PLOUGHBOY** (re-entry) *Envoy ENV 016*	**50**	1 wk

Date	Title Label Number	Position

Des O'CONNOR

UK, male vocalist

1 Nov 67	● CARELESS HANDS *Columbia DB 8275*	6	15 wks
8 May 68	★ I PRETEND *Columbia DB 8397*	1	36 wks
20 Nov 68	● 1-2-3 O'LEARY *Columbia DB 8492*	4	11 wks
7 May 69	DICK-A-DUM-DUM (KING'S ROAD) *Columbia DB 8566*	14	10 wks
29 Nov 69	LONELINESS *Columbia DB 8632*	18	11 wks

ODETTA — See *Harry BELAFONTE and ODETTA*

Esther and Abi OFARIM

Israel, female/male vocal duo

14 Feb 68	★ CINDERELLA ROCKEFELLA *Philips BF 1640*	1	13 wks
19 Jun 68	ONE MORE DANCE *Philips BF 1678*	13	9 wks

OHIO EXPRESS

US, male vocal/instrumental group

5 Jun 68	● YUMMY YUMMY YUMMY *Pye International 7N 25459*	5	15 wks

OLIVER

US, male vocalist

9 Aug 69	● GOOD MORNING STARSHINE *CBS 4435*	6	16 wks
27 Dec 69	GOOD MORNING STARSHINE (re-entry) *CBS 4435*	39	2 wks

OLYMPICS

US, male vocal group

19 Jan 61	I WISH I COULD SHIMMY LIKE MY SISTER KATE *Vogue V 9174*	45	1 wk

Roy ORBISON

US, male vocalist

28 Jul 60	ONLY THE LONELY *London HLU 9149*	36	1 wk
11 Aug 60	★ ONLY THE LONELY (re-entry) *London HLU 9149*	1	23 wks
27 Oct 60	BLUE ANGEL *London HLU 9207*	11	16 wks
25 May 61	● RUNNING SCARED *London HLU 9342*	9	15 wks
21 Sep 61	CRYIN' *London HLU 9405*	25	9 wks
8 Mar 62	● DREAM BABY *London HLU 9511*	2	14 wks
28 Jun 62	THE CROWD *London HLU 9561*	40	4 wks
8 Nov 62	WORKIN' FOR THE MAN *London HLU 9607*	50	1 wk
28 Feb 63	● IN DREAMS *London HLU 9676*	6	23 wks
30 May 63	● FALLING *London HLU 9727*	9	11 wks
19 Sep 63	● BLUE BAYOU/ MEAN WOMAN BLUES *London HLU 9777*	3	19 wks
20 Feb 64	BORNE ON THE WIND *London HLU 9845*	15	10 wks
30 Apr 64	★ IT'S OVER *London HLU 9882*	1	18 wks
10 Sep 64	★ OH PRETTY WOMAN *London HLU 9919*	1	18 wks
19 Nov 64	● PRETTY PAPER *London HLU 9930*	6	11 wks
11 Feb 65	GOODNIGHT *London HLU 9951*	14	9 wks

22 Jul 65	(SAY) YOU'RE MY GIRL *London HLU 9978*	23	8 wks
9 Sep 65	RIDE AWAY *London HLU 9986*	34	6 wks
4 Nov 65	CRAWLIN' BACK *London HLU 10000*	19	9 wks
27 Jan 66	BREAKIN' UP IS BREAKIN' MY HEART *London HL 10015*	22	6 wks
7 Apr 66	TWINKLE TOES *London HLU 10034*	29	5 wks
16 Jun 66	LANA *London HL 10051*	15	9 wks
18 Aug 66	● TOO SOON TO KNOW *London HLU 10067*	3	17 wks
1 Dec 66	THERE WON'T BE MANY COMING HOME *London HL 10096*	18	9 wks
23 Feb 67	SO GOOD *London HL 10113*	32	6 wks
24 Jul 68	WALK ON *London HLU 10206*	39	10 wks
25 Sep 68	HEARTACHE *London HLU 10222*	44	4 wks
30 Apr 69	MY FRIEND *London HL 10261*	35	4 wks
13 Sep 69	PENNY ARCADE *London HL 10285*	40	3 wks
11 Oct 69	PENNY ARCADE (re-entry) *London HL 10285*	27	11 wks

Tony ORLANDO

US, male vocalist

5 Oct 61	● BLESS YOU *Fontana H 330*	5	11 wks

ORLONS

US, female/male vocal group

27 Dec 62	DON'T HANG UP *Cameo Parkway C 231*	50	1 wk
10 Jan 63	DON'T HANG UP (re-entry) *Cameo Parkway C 231*	39	2 wks

Tony OSBORNE SOUND

UK, orchestra

23 Feb 61	MAN FROM MADRID *HMV POP 827*	50	1 wk

Hit has credit featuring Joanne Brown, UK female vocalist.

OUTLAWS

UK, male instrumental group

13 Apr 61	SWINGIN' LOW *HMV POP 844*	46	2 wks
8 Jun 61	AMBUSH *HMV POP 877*	43	2 wks

See also Mike Berry with the Outlaws.

OVERLANDERS

UK, male vocal/instrumental group

13 Jan 66	★ MICHELLE *Pye 7N 17034*	1	10 wks

UK, orchestra

27 Oct 60	OBSESSION *Palette PG 9004*	43	2 wks

Wilson PICKETT 'The Wicked Pickett'.

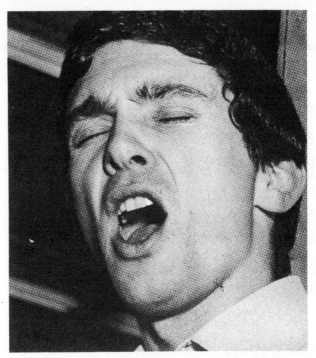

Gene PITNEY Gene practices for a forthcoming dental examination.

Cliff RICHARD 'Bongo Herbert' as he appears singing "The Shrine On The Second Floor" in the film *Expresso Bongo*.

Elvis PRESLEY His 60s record: 15 number one singles, five number one albums, four number one EPs.

Date	Title *Label Number*	Position	Date	Title *Label Number*	Position

P

PACEMAKERS — See *GERRY and the PACEMAKERS*

PACKABEATS
UK, male instrumental group

23 Feb 61	**GYPSY BEAT** *Parlophone R 4729*	**49** 1 wk

Hal PAGE and the WHALERS
US, male vocal/instrumental group

25 Aug 60	**GOING BACK TO MY HOME TOWN** *Melodisc MEL 1553*	**50** 1 wk

PAPER DOLLS
UK, female vocal group

13 Mar 68	**SOMETHING HERE IN MY HEART (KEEPS A-TELLIN' ME NO)** *Pye 7N 17456*	**11** 13 wks

Norrie PARAMOR
UK, orchestra

17 Mar 60	**THEME FROM 'A SUMMER PLACE'** *Columbia*	**36** 2 wks
22 Mar 62	**THEME FROM 'Z CARS'** *Columbia*	**33** 6 wks

PARAMOUNT JAZZ BAND — See *Mr. Acker BILK*

PARAMOUNTS
UK, male vocal/instrumental group

16 Jan 64	**POISON IVY** *Parlophone R 5093*	**35** 7 wks

Robert PARKER
US, male vocalist

4 Aug 66	**BAREFOOTIN'** *Island WI 286*	**24** 8 wks

Don PARTRIDGE
UK, male vocalist

7 Feb 68	● **ROSIE** *Columbia DB 8330*	**4** 12 wks
29 May 68	● **BLUE EYES** *Columbia DB 8416*	**3** 13 wks
19 Feb 69	**BREAKFAST ON PLUTO** *Columbia DB 8538*	**26** 7 wks

PAUL — See *PETER, PAUL and MARY*

PAUL and PAULA
US, male/female vocal duo

14 Feb 63	● **HEY PAULA** *Philips 304012 BF*	**8** 12 wks
18 Apr 63	● **YOUNG LOVERS** *Philips 304016 BF*	**9** 14 wks
16 May 63	**HEY PAULA** (re-entry) *Philips 304012 BF*	**37** 5 wks

PAULA — See *PAUL and PAULA*

Rita PAVONE
Italy, female vocalist

1 Dec 66	**HEART** *RCA 1553*	**27** 12 wks
19 Jan 67	**YOU ONLY YOU** *RCA 1561*	**21** 7 wks

PEDDLERS
UK, male vocal/instrumental group

7 Jan 65	**LET THE SUNSHINE IN** *Philips BF 1375*	**50** 1 wk
23 Aug 69	**BIRTH** *CBS 4449*	**17** 9 wks

Donald PEERS
UK, male vocalist

18 Dec 68	● **PLEASE DON'T GO** *Columbia DB 8502*	**3** 18 wks
30 Apr 69	**PLEASE DON'T GO** (re-entry) *Columbia DB 8502*	**38** 3 wks

PENTANGLE
UK, male/female vocal/instrumental group

28 May 69	**ONCE I HAD A SWEETHEART** *Big T BIG 124*	**46** 1 wk

Danny PEPPERMINT and the JUMPING JACKS
US, male vocal/instrumental group

18 Jan 62	**PEPPERMINT TWIST** *London HLL 9478*	**26** 8 wks

Lance PERCIVAL
UK, male vocalist

28 Oct 65	**SHAME AND SCANDAL IN THE FAMILY** *Parlophone R 5335*	**37** 3 wks

Emilio PERICOLI
Italy, male vocalist

28 Jun 62	**AL DI LA** *Warner Bros. WB 69*	**30** 14 wks

Steve PERRY
UK, male vocalist

4 Aug 60	**STEP BY STEP** *HMV POP 745*	**41** 1 wk

Date	Title Label Number	Position

PETER and GORDON

UK, male vocal duo

12 Mar 64	★ **A WORLD WITHOUT LOVE** Columbia DB 7225	**1**	14 wks
4 Jun 64	● **NOBODY I KNOW** Columbia DB 7292	**10**	11 wks
8 Apr 65	● **TRUE LOVE WAYS** Columbia DB 7524	**2**	15 wks
24 Jun 65	● **TO KNOW YOU IS TO LOVE YOU** Columbia DB 7617	**5**	10 wks
21 Oct 65	**BABY I'M YOURS** Columbia DB 7729	**19**	9 wks
24 Feb 66	**WOMAN** Columbia DB 7834	**28**	7 wks
22 Sep 66	**LADY GODIVA** Columbia DB 8003	**16**	11 wks

PETER, PAUL and MARY

US, male/female vocal/instrumental group

10 Oct 63	**BLOWING IN THE WIND** Warner Bros. WB 104	**13**	16 wks
16 Apr 64	**TELL IT ON THE MOUNTAIN** Warner Bros. WB 127	**33**	4 wks
15 Oct 64	**THE TIMES THEY ARE A-CHANGIN'** Warner Bros. WB 142	**44**	2 wks

Ray PETERSON

US, male vocalist

24 Mar 60	**ANSWER ME** RCA 1175	**47**	1 wk
19 Jan 61	**CORRINE, CORRINA** London HLX 9246	**48**	1 wk
2 Feb 61	**CORRINE, CORRINA** (re-entry) London HLX 9246	**41**	6 wks

PHARAOHS — See *SAM THE SHAM and the PHARAOHS*

PHILHARMONIA ORCHESTRA, conductor Lorin MAAZEL

UK, orchestra, US, male conductor

30 Jul 69	**THUS SPAKE ZARATHUSTRA** Columbia DB 8607	**33**	7 wks

Edith PIAF

France, female vocalist

12 May 60	**MILORD** Columbia DC 754	**41**	4 wks
3 Nov 60	**MILORD** (re-entry) Columbia DC 754	**24**	11 wks

Wilson PICKETT

US, male vocalist

23 Sep 65	**IN THE MIDNIGHT HOUR** Atlantic AT 4036	**12**	11 wks
25 Nov 65	**DON'T FIGHT IT** Atlantic AT 4052	**29**	8 wks
10 Mar 66	**634-5789** Atlantic AT 4072	**36**	5 wks
1 Sep 66	**LAND OF 1000 DANCES** Atlantic 584-039	**22**	9 wks
15 Dec 66	**MUSTANG SALLY** Atlantic 584-066	**28**	7 wks

27 Sep 67	**FUNKY BROADWAY** Atlantic 584-130	**43**	3 wks
11 Sep 68	**IN THE MIDNIGHT HOUR** (re-issue) Atlantic 584-203	**38**	6 wks
8 Jan 69	**HEY JUDE** Atlantic 584-236	**16**	9 wks

PILTDOWN MEN

US, male instrumental group

8 Sep 60	**MACDONALD'S CAVE** Capitol CL 15149	**14**	18 wks
12 Jan 61	**PILTDOWN RIDES AGAIN** Capitol CL 15175	**14**	10 wks
9 Mar 61	**GOODNIGHT MRS. FLINTSTONE** Capitol CL 15186	**18**	8 wks

PING PING and AI VERLAINE

Belgium, male vocal duo

28 Sep 61	**SUCU SUCU** Oriole CB 1589	**41**	4 wks

PINK FLOYD

UK, male vocal/instrumental group

30 Mar 67	**ARNOLD LAYNE** Columbia DB 8156	**20**	8 wks
22 Jun 67	● **SEE EMILY PLAY** Columbia DB 8214	**6**	12 wks

PINKERTON'S ASSORTED COLOURS

UK, male vocal/instrumental group

13 Jan 66	● **MIRROR MIRROR** Decca F 12307	**9**	11 wks
21 Apr 66	**DON'T STOP LOVIN' ME BABY** Decca F 12377	**50**	1 wk

PIONEERS

Jamaica, male vocal/instrumental group

18 Oct 69	**LONG SHOT KICK DE BUCKET** Trojan TR 672	**21**	10 wks

PIPS — See *Gladys KNIGHT and the PIPS*

PIRATES — See *Johnny KIDD and the PIRATES*

Gene PITNEY

US, male vocalist

23 Mar 61	**I WANNA LOVE MY LIFE AWAY** London HL 9270	**26**	11 wks
8 Mar 62	**TOWN WITHOUT PITY** HMV POP 952	**32**	6 wks
5 Dec 63	● **TWENTY FOUR HOURS FROM TULSA** United Artists UP 1035	**5**	19 wks
5 Mar 64	● **THAT GIRL BELONGS TO YESTERDAY** United Artists UP 1045	**7**	12 wks
15 Oct 64	**IT HURTS TO BE IN LOVE** United Artists UP 1063	**36**	4 wks
12 Nov 64	● **I'M GONNA BE STRONG** Stateside SS 358	**2**	14 wks
18 Feb 65	● **I MUST BE SEEING THINGS** Stateside SS 390	**6**	10 wks
10 Jun 65	● **LOOKING THROUGH THE EYES OF LOVE** Stateside SS 420	**3**	12 wks
4 Nov 65	● **PRINCESS IN RAGS** Stateside SS 471	**9**	12 wks

Date	Title *Label Number*	Position
17 Feb 66	● **BACKSTAGE** *Stateside SS 490*	**4** 10 wks
9 Jun 66	● **NOBODY NEEDS YOUR LOVE** *Stateside SS 518*	**2** 13 wks
10 Nov 66	● **JUST ONE SMILE** *Stateside SS 558*	**8** 12 wks
23 Feb 67	**COLD LIGHT OF DAY** *Stateside SS 597*	**38** 6 wks
15 Nov 67	**SOMETHING'S GOTTEN HOLD OF MY HEART** *Stateside SS 2060*	**5** 13 wks
3 Apr 68	**SOMEWHERE IN THE COUNTRY** *Stateside SS 2013*	**19** 9 wks
27 Nov 68	**YOURS UNTIL TOMORROW** *Stateside SS 2131*	**34** 7 wks
5 Mar 69	**MARIA ELENA** *Stateside SS 2142*	**25** 6 wks

PLASTIC ONO BAND

UK, male vocalist

Date	Title *Label Number*	Position
9 Jul 69	● **GIVE PEACE A CHANCE** *Apple 13*	**2** 13 wks
1 Nov 69	**COLD TURKEY** *Apple APPLES 1001*	**14** 8 wks

PLASTIC PENNY

UK, male vocal/instrumental group

Date	Title *Label Number*	Position
3 Jan 68	● **EVERYTHING I AM** *Page One POF 051*	**6** 10 wks

PLATTERS

US, male/female vocal group

Date	Title *Label Number*	Position
29 Jan 60	**HARBOUR LIGHTS** *Mercury AMT 1081*	**11** 11 wks

PLAYBOY BAND — See *John FRED and the PLAYBOY BAND*

POETS

UK, male vocal/instrumental group

Date	Title *Label Number*	Position
29 Oct 64	**NOW WE'RE THRU** *Decca F 11995*	**31** 5 wks

Brian POOLE and the TREMELOES

UK, male vocalist, male vocal/instrumental backing group

Date	Title *Label Number*	Position
4 Jul 63	● **TWIST AND SHOUT** *Decca F 11694*	**4** 14 wks
12 Sep 63	★ **DO YOU LOVE ME** *Decca F 11739*	**1** 14 wks
28 Nov 63	**I CAN DANCE** *Decca F 11771*	**31** 8 wks
30 Jan 64	● **CANDY MAN** *Decca F 11823*	**6** 13 wks
7 May 64	● **SOMEONE SOMEONE** *Decca F 11893*	**2** 17 wks
20 Aug 64	**TWELVE STEPS TO LOVE** *Decca F 11951*	**32** 7 wks
7 Jan 65	**THREE BELLS** *Decca F 12037*	**17** 9 wks
22 Jul 65	**I WANT CANDY** *Decca F 12197*	**25** 8 wks

See also Tremeloes.

Sandy POSEY

US, female vocalist

Date	Title *Label Number*	Position
15 Sep 66	**BORN A WOMAN** *MGM 1321*	**24** 11 wks
5 Jan 67	**SINGLE GIRL** *MGM 1330*	**15** 13 wks
13 Apr 67	**WHAT A WOMAN IN LOVE WON'T DO** *MGM 1335*	**48** 3 wks

Elvis PRESLEY

US, male vocalist

Date	Title *Label Number*	Position
12 Feb 60	**STRICTLY ELVIS** (EP) *RCA RCX 175*	**26** 1 wk
7 Apr 60	● **STUCK ON YOU** *RCA 1187*	**3** 14 wks
28 Jul 60	● **A MESS OF BLUES** *RCA 1194*	**2** 18 wks
3 Nov 60	★ **IT'S NOW OR NEVER** *RCA 1207*	**1** 19 wks
19 Jan 61	★ **ARE YOU LONESOME TONIGHT** *RCA 1216*	**1** 15 wks
9 Mar 61	★ **WOODEN HEART** *RCA 1226*	**1** 27 wks
25 May 61	★ **SURRENDER** *RCA 1227*	**1** 15 wks
7 Sep 61	● **WILD IN THE COUNTRY/ I FEEL SO BAD** *RCA 1244*	**4** 12 wks
2 Nov 61	★ **HIS LATEST FLAME/ LITTLE SISTER** *RCA 1258*	**1** 13 wks
1 Feb 62	★ **ROCK A HULA BABY/ CAN'T HELP FALLING IN LOVE** *RCA 1270*	**1** 20 wks
10 May 62	★ **GOOD LUCK CHARM** *RCA 1280*	**1** 17 wks
21 Jun 62	★ **FOLLOW THAT DREAM** (EP) *RCA RCX 211*	**34** 2 wks
30 Aug 62	★ **SHE'S NOT YOU** *RCA 1303*	**1** 14 wks
29 Nov 62	★ **RETURN TO SENDER** *RCA 1320*	**1** 14 wks
28 Feb 63	**ONE BROKEN HEART FOR SALE** *RCA 1337*	**12** 9 wks
4 Jul 63	★ **DEVIL IN DISGUISE** *RCA 1355*	**1** 12 wks
24 Oct 63	**BOSSA NOVA BABY** *RCA 1374*	**13** 8 wks
19 Dec 63	**KISS ME QUICK** *RCA 1375*	**14** 10 wks
12 Mar 64	**VIVA LAS VEGAS** *RCA 1390*	**17** 12 wks
25 Jun 64	● **KISSIN' COUSINS** *RCA 1404*	**10** 11 wks
20 Aug 64	**SUCH A NIGHT** *RCA 1411*	**13** 10 wks
29 Oct 64	**AIN'T THAT LOVIN' YOU BABY** *RCA 1422*	**15** 8 wks
3 Dec 64	**BLUE CHRISTMAS** *RCA 1430*	**11** 7 wks
11 Mar 65	**DO THE CLAM** *RCA 1443*	**19** 8 wks
27 May 65	★ **CRYING IN THE CHAPEL** *RCA 1455*	**1** 15 wks
11 Nov 65	**TELL ME WHY** *RCA 1489*	**15** 10 wks
24 Feb 66	**BLUE RIVER** *RCA 1504*	**22** 7 wks
7 Apr 66	**FRANKIE AND JOHNNY** *RCA 1509*	**21** 9 wks
7 Jul 66	● **LOVE LETTERS** *RCA 1526*	**6** 10 wks
13 Oct 66	**ALL THAT I AM** *RCA 1545*	**18** 8 wks
1 Dec 66	**IF EVERY DAY WAS LIKE CHRISTMAS** *RCA 1557*	**13** 7 wks
9 Feb 67	**INDESCRIBABLY BLUE** *RCA 1565*	**21** 5 wks
11 May 67	**YOU GOTTA STOP/ LOVE MACHINE** *RCA 1593*	**38** 5 wks
16 Aug 67	**LONG LEGGED GIRL** *RCA Victor RCA 1616*	**49** 2 wks
21 Feb 68	**GUITAR MAN** *RCA 1663*	**19** 9 wks
15 May 68	**U. S. MALE** *RCA 1673*	**15** 8 wks
17 Jul 68	**YOUR TIME HASN'T COME YET BABY** *RCA 1714*	**22** 11 wks
16 Oct 68	**YOU'LL NEVER WALK ALONE** *RCA 1747*	**44** 3 wks
26 Feb 69	**IF I CAN DREAM** *RCA 1795*	**11** 10 wks
11 Jun 69	● **IN THE GHETTO** *RCA 1831*	**2** 16 wks
6 Sep 69	● **CLEAN UP YOUR OWN BACK YARD** *RCA 1869*	**2** 7 wks
18 Oct 69	**IN THE GHETTO** (re-entry) *RCA 1831*	**50** 1 wk
29 Nov 69	● **SUSPICIOUS MINDS** *RCA 1900*	**2** 14 wks

Tracks on Strictly Elvis EP: *Old Shep/ Any Place Is Paradise/ Paralysed/ Is It So Strange.* Follow That Dream EP: *Follow That Dream/ Angel/ What A Wonderful Life/ I'm Not The Marrying Kind. On 5 July 62 a note on the Top 50 for that week stated "Due to difficulties in assessing returns of* Follow That Dream EP, *it has been decided not to include it in Britain's Top 50. It is of course No. 1 in the EP charts". Therefore this EP only had a 2 week run on the chart when its sales would certainly have justified a much longer one. Can't Help Falling In Love listed from 1 March 1962.*

Date	Title Label Number	Position

Billy PRESTON

US, male vocalist/instrumentalist, keyboards

2 Jul 69	THAT'S THE WAY GOD PLANNED IT	11	10 wks
	Apple 12		

See also Beatles.

Johnny PRESTON

US, male vocalist

12 Feb 60	★ RUNNING BEAR *Mercury AMT 1079*	1	14 wks
21 Apr 60	● CRADLE OF LOVE *Mercury AMT 1092*	2	16 wks
2 Jun 60	RUNNING BEAR (re-entry) *Mercury AMT 1079*	41	1 wk
28 Jul 60	I'M STARTING TO GO STEADY	49	1 wk
	Mercury AMT 1104		
11 Aug 60	FEEL SO FINE *Mercury AMT 1104*	18	10 wks
8 Dec 60	CHARMING BILLY *Mercury AMT 1114*	34	1 wk
22 Dec 60	CHARMING BILLY (re-entry)	42	2 wks
	Mercury AMT 1114		

Mike PRESTON

UK, male vocalist

25 Aug 60	I'D DO ANYTHING *Decca F 11255*	23	10 wks
22 Dec 60	TOGETHERNESS *Decca F 11287*	41	5 wks
9 Mar 61	MARRY ME *Decca F 11335*	14	10 wks

PRETTY THINGS

UK, male vocal/instrumental group

18 Jun 64	ROSALYN *Fontana TF 469*	41	5 wks
22 Oct 64	● DON'T BRING ME DOWN *Fontana TF 503*	10	11 wks
25 Feb 65	HONEY I NEED *Fontana TF 537*	13	10 wks
15 Jul 65	CRY TO ME *Fontana TF 585*	28	7 wks
20 Jan 66	MIDNIGHT TO SIX MAN *Fontana TF 647*	46	1 wk
5 May 66	COME SEE ME *Fontana TF 688*	43	5 wks
21 Jul 66	A HOUSE IN THE COUNTRY *Fontana TF 722*	50	1 wk
4 Aug 66	A HOUSE IN THE COUNTRY (re-entry)	50	1 wk
	Fontana TF 722		

Lloyd PRICE

US, male vocalist

21 Apr 60	LADY LUCK *HMV POP 712*	45	1 wk

Alan PRICE SET

UK, male vocal/instrumental group

31 Mar 66	● I PUT A SPELL ON YOU *Decca F 12367*	9	10 wks
14 Jul 66	HI LILI HI LO *Decca F 12442*	11	12 wks
2 Mar 67	● SIMON SMITH & HIS AMAZING DANCING BEAR *Decca F 12570*	4	12 wks
2 Aug 67	● THE HOUSE THAT JACK BUILT *Decca F 12641*	4	10 wks
15 Nov 67	SHAME *Decca F 12691*	45	2 wks
31 Jan 68	DON'T STOP THE CARNIVAL *Decca F 12731*	13	8 wks

P. J. PROBY

US, male vocalist

28 May 64	● HOLD ME *Decca F 11904*	3	15 wks
3 Sep 64	● TOGETHER *Decca F 11967*	8	11 wks
10 Dec 64	● SOMEWHERE *Liberty LIB 10182*	6	12 wks
25 Feb 65	I APOLOGISE *Liberty LIB 10188*	11	8 wks
8 Jul 65	LET THE WATER RUN DOWN	19	8 wks
	Liberty LIB 10206		
30 Sep 65	THAT MEANS A LOT *Liberty LIB 10215*	30	6 wks
25 Nov 65	● MARIA *Liberty LIB 10218*	8	9 wks
10 Feb 66	YOU'VE COME BACK *Liberty LIB 10223*	25	7 wks
16 Jun 66	TO MAKE A BIG MAN CRY *Liberty LIB 10236*	34	3 wks
27 Oct 66	I CAN'T MAKE IT ALONE *Liberty LIB 10250*	37	5 wks
6 Mar 68	IT'S YOUR DAY TODAY *Liberty LBF 15046*	32	5 wks

PROCOL HARUM

UK, male vocal/instrumental group

25 May 67	★ A WHITER SHADE OF PALE *Deram DM 126*	1	15 wks
4 Oct 67	● HOMBURG *Regal Zonophone RZ 3003*	6	10 wks
24 Apr 68	QUITE RIGHTLY SO	50	1 wk
	Regal Zonophone RZ 3007		
18 Jun 69	SALTY DOG *Regal Zonophone RZ 3019*	44	1 wk
2 Jul 69	SALTY DOG (re-entry)	44	1 wk
	Regal Zonophone RZ 3019		
16 Jul 69	SALTY DOG (2nd re-entry)	44	1 wk
	Regal Zonophone RZ 3019		

Dorothy PROVINE

US, female vocalist

7 Dec 61	DON'T BRING LULU *Warner Bros. WB 53*	17	12 wks
28 Jun 62	CRAZY WORDS CRAZY TUNE	45	3 wks
	Warner Bros. WB 70		

Gary PUCKETT and the UNION GAP

US, male vocalist, male vocal/instrumental backing group

17 Apr 68	★ YOUNG GIRL *CBS 3365*	1	17 wks
7 Aug 68	● LADY WILLPOWER *CBS 3551*	5	16 wks
28 Aug 68	WOMAN WOMAN *CBS 3100*	48	1 wk

Billed as The Union Gap featuring Gary Puckett on Young Girl and Lady Willpower.

PYRAMIDS

Jamaica, male vocal/instrumental group

22 Nov 67	TRAIN TOUR TO RAINBOW CITY	35	4 wks
	President PT 161		

Bobby RYDELL (*Above*) found solo success after leaving Rocco and the Saints.

RIGHTEOUS BROTHERS *Top right* Sammy Davis Jr. sells the Righteous Brothers a gold disc.

Kenny ROGERS and the FIRST EDITION *Right* His tale of a crippled Vietnam war hero was held at bay in the number two position for 5 weeks by first the Archies and then Rolf Harris.

Mitch RYDER *Far right* The microphone was apparently returned to the museum directly after the performance.

RONETTES *Bottom right* Began as the Dolly Sisters, appeared in 'Twist Around The Clock' and had five unsuccessful singles before a successful marriage (in Veronica Bennett's case literally) with Phil Spector.

Date	Title Label Number	Position
27 Nov 68	DON'T FORGET TO CATCH ME Columbia DB 8503	21 10 wks
26 Feb 69	GOOD TIMES (BETTER TIMES) Columbia DB 8548	12 11 wks
28 May 69	● BIG SHIP Columbia DB 8581	8 10 wks
13 Sep 69	● THROW DOWN A LINE Columbia DB 8615	7 9 wks
6 Dec 69	WITH THE EYES OF A CHILD Columbia DB 8641	20 11 wks

The Shadows appear on all Cliff's hits from Living Doll to A Girl Like You. After that they are on the following hits. The Young Ones, Do You Wanna Dance, It'll Be Me, The Next Time, Bachelor Boy, Summer Holiday, Lucky Lips, Don't Talk To Him', I'm The Lonely One, On The Beach, I Could Easily Fall, The Time In Between, Blue Turns To Grey, Time Drags By, In The Country and Don't Forget To Catch Me. Throw Down A Line is credited to 'Cliff and Hank', Hank being Hank B. Marvin of the Shadows, who played guitar and sang on this hit. The tracks on the Expresso Bongo EP: Love/ A Voice In The Wilderness/ The Shrine On The Second Floor/ Bongo Blues. Bongo Blues features only the Shadows. See also Shadows.

Wendy RICHARD — See Mike SARNE

RIGHTEOUS BROTHERS

US, male vocal duo

14 Jan 65	★ YOU'VE LOST THAT LOVIN' FEELIN' London HLU 9943	1 10 wks
12 Aug 65	UNCHAINED MELODY London HL 9975	14 12 wks
13 Jan 66	EBB TIDE London HL 10011	48 2 wks
14 Apr 66	(YOU'RE MY) SOUL AND INSPIRATION Verve VS 535	15 10 wks
10 Nov 66	WHITE CLIFFS OF DOVER London HL 10086	21 9 wks
22 Dec 66	ISLAND IN THE SUN Verve VS 547	36 5 wks
12 Feb 69	● YOU'VE LOST THAT LOVIN' FEELIN' (re-issue) London HL 10241	10 11 wks

Jeannie C. RILEY

US, female vocalist

16 Oct 68	HARPER VALLEY P. T. A. Polydor 56 148	12 15 wks

Danny RIVERS

UK, male vocalist

12 Jan 61	CAN'T YOU HEAR MY HEART Decca F 11294	36 3 wks

Marty ROBBINS

US, male vocalist

29 Jan 60	EL PASO Fontana H 233	19 7 wks
7 Apr 60	EL PASO (re-entry) Fontana H 233	44 1 wk
26 May 60	BIG IRON Fontana H 229	48 1 wk
27 Sep 62	● DEVIL WOMAN CBS AAG 114	5 17 wks
17 Jan 63	RUBY ANN CBS AAG 128	24 6 wks

Malcolm ROBERTS

UK, male vocalist

11 May 67	TIME ALONE WILL TELL RCA 1578	45 2 wks
30 Oct 68	● MAY I HAVE THE NEXT DREAM WITH YOU Major Minor MM 581	8 14 wks
12 Feb 69	MAY I HAVE THE NEXT DREAM WITH YOU (re-entry) Major Minor MM 581	45 1 wk
22 Nov 69	LOVE IS ALL Major Minor MM 637	12 12 wks

Smokey ROBINSON and the MIRACLES

US, male vocal group

24 Feb 66	GOING TO A GO-GO Tamla Motown TMG 547	44 5 wks
22 Dec 66	(COME 'ROUND HERE) I'M THE ONE YOU NEED Tamla Motown TMG 584	45 2 wks
27 Dec 67	I SECOND THAT EMOTION Tamla Motown TMG 631	27 11 wks
3 Apr 68	IF YOU CAN WANT Tamla Motown TMG 648	50 1 wk
7 May 69	● TRACKS OF MY TEARS Tamla Motown TMG 696	9 13 wks

ROCKIN' BERRIES

UK, male vocal/instrumental group

1 Oct 64	I DIDN'T MEAN TO HURT YOU Piccadilly 7N 35197	43 1 wk
15 Oct 64	● HE'S IN TOWN Piccadilly 7N 35203	3 13 wks
21 Jan 65	WHAT IN THE WORLD'S COME OVER YOU Piccadilly 7N 35217	23 7 wks
13 May 65	● POOR MAN'S SON Piccadilly 7N 35236	5 11 wks
26 Aug 65	YOU'RE MY GIRL Piccadilly 7N 35254	40 7 wks
6 Jan 66	THE WATER IS OVER MY HEAD Piccadilly 7N 35270	43 1 wk
20 Jan 66	THE WATER IS OVER MY HEAD (re-entry) Piccadilly 7N 35270	50 1 wk

Clodagh RODGERS

Ireland, female vocalist

26 Mar 69	● COME BACK AND SHAKE ME RCA 1792	3 14 wks
9 Jul 69	● GOODNIGHT MIDNIGHT RCA 1852	4 11 wks
4 Oct 69	GOODNIGHT MIDNIGHT (re-entry) RCA 1852	48 1 wk
8 Nov 69	BILJO RCA 1891	22 9 wks

Jimmie RODGERS

US, male vocalist

14 Jun 62	● ENGLISH COUNTRY GARDEN Columbia DB 4847	5 13 wks

Date	Title Label Number	Position

Tommy ROE

US, male vocalist

6 Sep 62	● SHEILA *HMV POP 1060*	**3**	14 wks
6 Dec 62	SUSIE DARLIN' *HMV POP 1092*	**37**	5 wks
21 Mar 63	● THE FOLK SINGER *HMV POP 1138*	**4**	13 wks
26 Sep 63	● EVERYBODY *HMV POP 1207*	**9**	11 wks
19 Dec 63	EVERYBODY (re-entry) *HMV POP 1207*	**49**	3 wks
16 Apr 69	★ DIZZY *Stateside SS 2143*	**1**	19 wks
23 Jul 69	HEATHER HONEY *Stateside SS 2152*	**24**	9 wks

Julie ROGERS

UK, female vocalist

13 Aug 64	● THE WEDDING *Mercury MF 820*	**3**	23 wks
10 Dec 64	LIKE A CHILD *Mercury MF 838*	**21**	9 wks
25 Mar 65	HAWAIIAN WEDDING SONG *Mercury MF 849*	**31**	6 wks

Kenny ROGERS and the FIRST EDITION

US, male vocalist and male/female vocal/instrumental group

18 Oct 69	● RUBY DON'T TAKE YOUR LOVE TO TOWN *Reprise RS 20829*	**2**	23 wks

ROLLING STONES

UK, male vocal/instrumental group

25 Jul 63	COME ON *Decca F 11675*	**21**	14 wks
14 Nov 63	I WANNA BE YOUR MAN *Decca F 11764*	**12**	16 wks
27 Feb 64	● NOT FADE AWAY *Decca F 11845*	**3**	15 wks
2 Jul 64	★ IT'S ALL OVER NOW *Decca F 11934*	**1**	15 wks
19 Nov 64	★ LITTLE RED ROOSTER *Decca F 12014*	**1**	12 wks
4 Mar 65	★ THE LAST TIME *Decca F 12104*	**1**	13 wks
26 Aug 65	★ (I CAN'T GET NO) SATISFACTION *Decca F 12220*	**1**	12 wks
28 Oct 65	★ GET OFF OF MY CLOUD *Decca F 12263*	**1**	12 wks
10 Feb 66	● NINETEENTH NERVOUS BREAKDOWN *Decca F 12331*	**2**	8 wks
19 May 66	★ PAINT IT BLACK *Decca F 12395*	**1**	10 wks
29 Sep 66	● HAVE YOU SEEN YOUR MOTHER BABY STANDING IN THE SHADOW *Decca F 12497*	**5**	8 wks
19 Jan 67	● LET'S SPEND THE NIGHT TOGETHER/ RUBY TUESDAY *Decca F 12546*	**3**	10 wks
23 Aug 67	● WE LOVE YOU/ DANDELION *Decca F 12654*	**8**	8 wks
29 May 68	★ JUMPING JACK FLASH *Decca F 12782*	**1**	11 wks
9 Jul 69	★ HONKY TONK WOMEN *Decca F 12952*	**1**	17 wks

ROMANTICS — See *RUBY and the ROMANTICS*

Max ROMEO

Jamaica, male vocalist

28 May 69	● WET DREAM *Unity UN 503*	**10**	24 wks
29 Nov 69	WET DREAM (re-entry) *Unity UN 503*	**50**	1 wk

RONETTES

US, female vocal group

17 Oct 63	● BE MY BABY *London HLU 9793*	**4**	13 wks
9 Jan 64	BABY I LOVE YOU *London HLU 9826*	**11**	14 wks
27 Aug 64	BEST PART OF BREAKING UP *London HLU 9905*	**43**	3 wks
8 Oct 64	DO I LOVE YOU *London HLU 9922*	**35**	4 wks

ROOFTOP SINGERS

US, male/female vocal group

31 Jan 63	● WALK RIGHT IN *Fontana TF 271700*	**10**	12 wks

Diana ROSS and the SUPREMES and the TEMPTATIONS

US, female and male vocal groups

29 Jan 69	● I'M GONNA MAKE YOU LOVE ME *Tamla Motown TMG 685*	**3**	11 wks
23 Apr 69	I'M GONNA MAKE YOU LOVE ME (re-entry) *Tamla Motown TMG 685*	**49**	1 wk
20 Sep 69	I SECOND THAT EMOTION *Tamla Motown TMG 709*	**18**	8 wks

See also Supremes; Temptations.

Nini ROSSO

Italy, male instrumentalist, trumpet

26 Aug 65	● IL SILENZIO *Durium DRS 54000*	**8**	14 wks

ROULETTES — See *Adam FAITH*

ROUTERS

US, male instrumental group

27 Dec 62	LET'S GO *Warner Bros. WB 77*	**32**	7 wks

John ROWLES

New Zealand, male vocalist

13 Mar 68	● IF I ONLY HAD TIME *MCA MU 1000*	**3**	18 wks
19 Jun 68	HUSH NOT A WORD TO MARY *MCA MU 1023*	**12**	10 wks

Date	Title *Label Number*	Position	Date	Title *Label Number*	Position

Billy Joe ROYAL

US, male vocalist

7 Oct 65	**DOWN IN THE BOONDOCKS** *CBS 201802*	**38**	4 wks

ROYAL GUARDSMEN

US, male vocal/instrumental group

19 Jan 67	● **SNOOPY VS. THE RED BARON** *Stateside SS 574*	**8**	13 wks
6 Apr 67	**RETURN OF THE RED BARON** *Stateside SS 2010*	**37**	4 wks

RUBY and the ROMANTICS

US, female vocalist, male vocal backing group

28 Mar 63	**OUR DAY WILL COME** *London HLR 9679*	**38**	6 wks

Jimmy RUFFIN

US, male vocalist

27 Oct 66	● **WHAT BECOMES OF THE BROKEN HEARTED** *Tamla Motown TMG 577*	**10**	15 wks
9 Feb 67	**I'VE PASSED THIS WAY BEFORE** *Tamla Motown TMG 593*	**29**	7 wks
20 Apr 67	**GONNA GIVE HER ALL THE LOVE I'VE GOT** *Tamla Motown TMG 603*	**26**	6 wks
9 Aug 69	**I'VE PASSED THIS WAY BEFORE** (re-issue) *Tamla Motown TMG 703*	**33**	6 wks

Barry RYAN

UK, male vocalist

23 Oct 68	● **ELOISE** *MGM 1442*	**2**	12 wks
19 Feb 69	**LOVE IS LOVE** *MGM 1464*	**25**	4 wks
4 Oct 69	**HUNT** *Polydor 56 348*	**34**	5 wks

See also Paul and Barry Ryan.

Paul and Barry RYAN

UK, male vocal duo

11 Nov 65	**DON'T BRING ME YOUR HEARTACHES** *Decca F 12260*	**13**	9 wks
3 Feb 66	**HAVE PITY ON THE BOY** *Decca F 12319*	**18**	6 wks
12 May 66	**I LOVE HER** *Decca F 12391*	**17**	8 wks
14 Jul 66	**I LOVE HOW YOU LOVE ME** *Decca F 12445*	**21**	7 wks
29 Sep 66	**HAVE YOU EVER LOVED SOMEBODY** *Decca F 12494*	**49**	1 wk
8 Dec 66	**MISSY MISSY** *Decca F 12520*	**43**	4 wks
2 Mar 67	**KEEP IT OUT OF SIGHT** *Decca F 12567*	**30**	6 wks
29 Jun 67	**CLAIRE** *Decca F 12633*	**47**	2 wks

See also Barry Ryan.

Bobby RYDELL

US, male vocalist

10 Mar 60	● **WILD ONE** *Columbia DB 4429*	**7**	14 wks
30 Jun 60	**SWINGING SCHOOL** *Columbia DB 4471*	**44**	1 wk
1 Sep 60	**VOLARE** *Columbia DB 4495*	**46**	1 wk
15 Sep 60	**VOLARE** (re-entry) *Columbia DB 4495*	**22**	5 wks
15 Dec 60	**SWAY** *Columbia DB 4545*	**12**	13 wks
23 Mar 61	**GOOD TIME BABY** *Columbia DB 4600*	**42**	7 wks
23 May 63	**FORGET HIM** *Cameo Parkway C 108*	**13**	14 wks

See also Chubby Checker and Bobby Rydell.

Mitch RYDER and the DETROIT WHEELS

US, male vocalist, male vocal/instrumental backing group

10 Feb 66	**JENNY TAKE A RIDE** *Stateside SS 481*	**44**	1 wk
24 Feb 66	**JENNY TAKE A RIDE** (re-entry) *Stateside SS 481*	**33**	4 wks

SABRES — See *Denny SEYTON and the SABRES*

Staff Sergeant Barry SADLER

US, male vocalist

24 Mar 66	**BALLAD OF THE GREEN BERETS** *RCA 1506*	**24**	8 wks

Mike SAGAR

UK, male vocalist

8 Dec 60	**DEEP FEELING** *HMV POP 819*	**44**	5 wks

Barry ST. JOHN

UK, female vocalist

9 Dec 65	**COME AWAY MELINDA** *Columbia DB 7783*	**47**	1 wk

ST. LOUIS UNION

UK, male vocal/instrumental group

13 Jan 66	**GIRL** *Decca F 12318*	**11**	10 wks

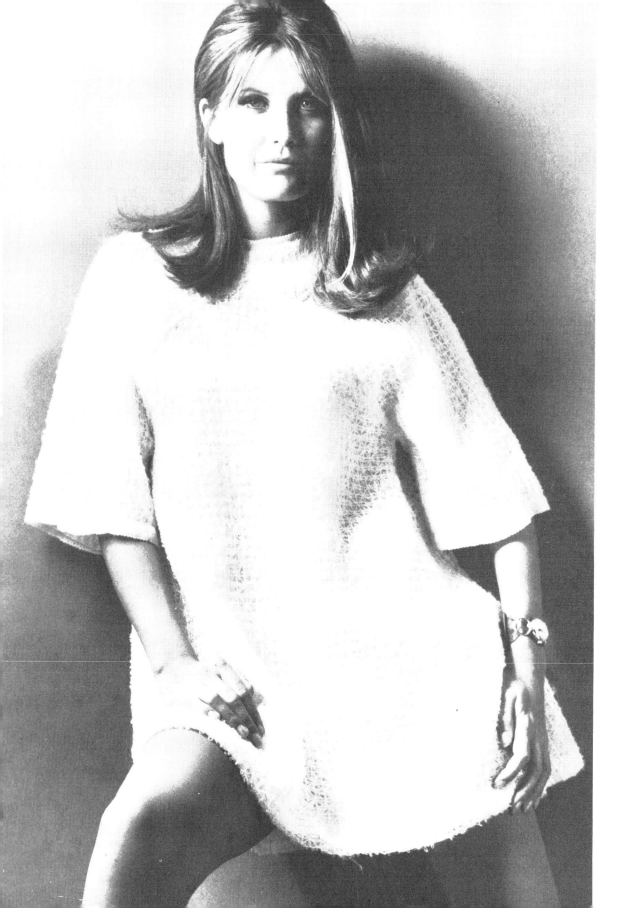

Sandie SHAW
Models her own
design of the mini
skirt, although the
famous feet are
not pictured here.
From '64 to '69
she amassed a
remarkable 17 hit
singles with three
number ones
(Pictorial Press).

Crispian ST PETERS *Right* His Top Ten hits were covers of American successes for 'We Five' and 'Changin' Times' respectively.

SPOTNICKS *Right* The Spotnicks fly in from Sweden.

SPRINGFIELDS *Below* The Swinging Blue Jeans join two Springfields, Tom and Dusty, in the changing room before the match.

Date	Title *Label Number*	Position		Date	Title *Label Number*	Position	

Crispian ST. PETERS

UK, male vocalist

6 Jan 66	● YOU WERE ON MY MIND *Decca F 12287*	2	14 wks
31 Mar 66	● PIED PIPER *Decca F 12359*	5	13 wks
15 Sep 66	CHANGES *Decca F 12480*	49	1 wk
29 Sep 66	CHANGES (re-entry) *Decca F 12480*	47	3 wks

Kyu SAKAMOTO

Japan, male vocalist

| 27 Jun 63 | ● SUKIYAKI *HMV POP 1171* | 6 | 13 wks |

SAM and DAVE

US, male vocal duo

16 Mar 67	SOOTHE ME *Stax 601 004*	48	2 wks
1 Nov 67	SOUL MAN *Stax 601 023*	24	14 wks
13 Mar 68	I THANK YOU *Stax 601 030*	34	9 wks
29 Jan 69	SOUL SISTER BROWN SUGAR *Atlantic 584 237*	15	8 wks

SAM THE SHAM and the PHARAOHS

US, male vocal/instrumental group

24 Jun 65	WOOLY BULLY *MGM 1269*	11	15 wks
4 Aug 66	LIL' RED RIDING HOOD *MGM 1315*	48	1 wk
18 Aug 66	LIL' RED RIDING HOOD (re-entry) *MGM 1315*	46	2 wks

Mike SAMMES SINGERS

UK, male/female vocal group

| 15 Sep 66 | SOMEWHERE MY LOVE *HMV POP 1546* | 22 | 19 wks |
| 12 Jul 67 | SOMEWHERE MY LOVE (re-entry) *HMV POP 1546* | 14 | 19 wks |

Dave SAMPSON

UK, male vocalist

| 19 May 60 | SWEET DREAMS *Columbia DB 4449* | 48 | 1 wk |
| 2 Jun 60 | SWEET DREAMS (re-entry) *Columbia DB 4449* | 29 | 5 wks |

Chris SANDFORD

UK, male vocalist

| 12 Dec 63 | NOT TOO LITTLE NOT TOO MUCH *Decca F 11778* | 17 | 9 wks |

SANDPIPERS

US, male vocal group

15 Sep 66	● GUANTANAMERA *Pye International 7N 25380*	7	17 wks
5 Jun 68	QUANDO M'INNAMORO (A MAN WITHOUT LOVE) *A & M AMS 723*	33	6 wks
26 Mar 69	KUMBAYA *A & M AMS 744*	39	1 wk
9 Apr 69	KUMBAYA (re-entry) *A & M AMS 744*	49	1 wk

Tommy SANDS

US, male vocalist

| 4 Aug 60 | OLD OAKEN BUCKET *Capitol CL 15143* | 25 | 7 wks |

SANTO and JOHNNY

US, male instrumental duo, steel and electric guitars

| 31 Mar 60 | TEARDROP *Parlophone R 4619* | 50 | 1 wk |

Mike SARNE

UK, male vocalist

10 May 62	COME OUTSIDE *Parlophone R 4902*	1	19 wks
30 Aug 62	WILL I WHAT *Parlophone R 4932*	18	10 wks
10 Jan 63	JUST FOR KICKS *Parlophone R 4974*	22	7 wks
28 Mar 63	CODE OF LOVE *Parlophone R 5010*	29	7 wks

Come Outside - *with Wendy Richard;* Will I What *with Billie Davis. See also Billie Davis.*

Peter SARSTEDT

UK, male vocalist

| 5 Feb 69 | WHERE DO YOU GO TO MY LOVELY *United Artists UP 2262* | 1 | 16 wks |
| 4 Jun 69 | ● FROZEN ORANGE JUICE *United Artists UP 35021* | 10 | 9 wks |

Al SAXON

UK, male vocalist

| 22 Dec 60 | BLUE-EYED BOY *Fontana H 278* | 39 | 2 wks |
| 7 Sep 61 | THERE I'VE SAID IT AGAIN *Piccadilly 7N 35011* | 48 | 1 wk |

SCAFFOLD

UK, male vocal group

22 Nov 67	● THANK U VERY MUCH *Parlophone R 5643*	4	12 wks
27 Mar 68	DO YOU REMEMBER *Parlophone R 5679*	34	5 wks
6 Nov 68	LILY THE PINK *Parlophone R 5734*	1	24 wks
1 Nov 69	GIN GAN GOOLIE *Parlophone R 5812*	38	11 wks

Date	Title *Label Number*	Position		Date	Title *Label Number*	Position	

Jack SCOTT

Canada, male vocalist

10 Mar 60	**WHAT IN THE WORLD'S COME OVER YOU**	**11**	15 wks
	Top Rank JAR 280		
2 Jun 60	**BURNING BRIDGES** *Top Rank JAR 375*	**32**	2 wks

Linda SCOTT

US, female vocalist

18 May 61	● **I'VE TOLD EVERY LITTLE STAR**	**7**	13 wks
	Columbia DB 4638		
14 Sep 61	**DON'T BET MONEY HONEY**	**50**	1 wk
	Columbia DB 4692		

Simon SCOTT

UK, male vocalist

13 Aug 64	**MOVE IT BABY** *Parlophone R 5164*	**37**	8 wks

Earl SCRUGGS — See *Lester FLATT and Earl SCRUGGS*

SEARCHERS

UK, male vocal/instrumental group

27 Jun 63	★ **SWEETS FOR MY SWEET** *Pye 7N 15533*	**1**	16 wks
10 Oct 63	**SWEET NOTHINS** *Philips BF 1274*	**48**	2 wks
24 Oct 63	● **SUGAR AND SPICE** *Pye 7N 15566*	**2**	13 wks
16 Jan 64	★ **NEEDLES AND PINS** *Pye 7N 15594*	**1**	15 wks
16 Apr 64	★ **DON'T THROW YOUR LOVE AWAY**	**1**	11 wks
	Pye 7N 15630		
16 Jul 64	**SOMEDAY WE'RE GONNA LOVE AGAIN**	**11**	8 wks
	Pye 7N 15670		
17 Sep 64	● **WHEN YOU WALK IN THE ROOM**	**3**	12 wks
	Pye 7N 15694		
3 Dec 64	**WHAT HAVE THEY DONE TO THE RAIN**	**13**	11 wks
	Pye 7N 15739		
4 Mar 65	● **GOODBYE MY LOVE** *Pye 7N 15794*	**4**	11 wks
8 Jul 65	**HE'S GOT NO LOVE** *Pye 7N 15878*	**12**	10 wks
14 Oct 65	**WHEN I GET HOME** *Pye 7N 15950*	**35**	3 wks
16 Dec 65	**TAKE ME FOR WHAT I'M WORTH**	**20**	8 wks
	Pye 7N 15992		
21 Apr 66	**TAKE IT OR LEAVE IT** *Pye 7N 17094*	**31**	6 wks
13 Oct 66	**HAVE YOU EVER LOVED SOMEBODY**	**48**	2 wks
	Pye 7N 17170		

Harry SECOMBE

UK, male vocalist

3 Oct 63	**IF I RULED THE WORLD** *Philips BF 1261*	**44**	2 wks
21 Nov 63	**IF I RULED THE WORLD** (re-entry)	**18**	15 wks
	Philips BF 1261		
23 Feb 67	● **THIS IS MY SONG** *Philips BF 1539*	**2**	15 wks

SECOND CITY SOUND

UK, instrumental group

20 Jan 66	**TCHAIKOVSKY ONE** *Decca F 12310*	**22**	7 wks
2 Apr 69	**DREAM OF OLWEN** *Major Minor MM 600*	**43**	1 wk

Neil SEDAKA

US, male vocalist

1 Jan 60	● **OH CAROL** *RCA 1152*	**3**	10 wks
14 Apr 60	● **STAIRWAY TO HEAVEN** *RCA 1178*	**8**	15 wks
1 Sep 60	**YOU MEAN EVERYTHING TO ME** *RCA 1198*	**45**	3 wks
2 Feb 61	● **CALENDAR GIRL** *RCA 1220*	**8**	14 wks
18 May 61	● **LITTLE DEVIL** *RCA 1236*	**9**	12 wks
21 Dec 61	● **HAPPY BIRTHDAY SWEET SIXTEEN**	**3**	18 wks
	RCA 1266		
19 Apr 62	**KING OF CLOWNS** *RCA 1282*	**23**	10 wks
19 Jul 62	● **BREAKING UP IS HARD TO DO** *RCA 1298*	**7**	16 wks
22 Nov 62	**NEXT DOOR TO AN ANGEL** *RCA 1319*	**29**	4 wks
30 May 63	**LET'S GO STEADY AGAIN** *RCA 1343*	**42**	1 wk
13 Jun 63	**LET'S GO STEADY AGAIN** (re-entry)	**43**	2 wks
	RCA 1343		

SEEKERS

Australia, male/female vocal group

7 Jan 65	★ **I'LL NEVER FIND ANOTHER YOU**	**1**	23 wks
	Columbia DB 7431		
15 Apr 65	● **A WORLD OF OUR OWN** *Columbia DB 7532*	**3**	18 wks
28 Oct 65	★ **THE CARNIVAL IS OVER** *Columbia DB 7711*	**1**	17 wks
24 Mar 66	**SOMEDAY ONE DAY** *Columbia DB 7867*	**11**	11 wks
8 Sep 66	● **WALK WITH ME** *Columbia DB 8000*	**10**	12 wks
24 Nov 66	● **MORNINGTOWN RIDE** *Columbia DB 8060*	**2**	15 wks
23 Feb 67	● **GEORGY GIRL** *Columbia DB 8134*	**3**	11 wks
20 Sep 67	**WHEN WILL THE GOOD APPLES FALL**	**11**	12 wks
	Columbia DB 8273		
13 Dec 67	**EMERALD CITY** *Columbia DB 8313*	**50**	1 wk

Peter SELLERS

UK, male vocalist

23 Dec 65	**A HARD DAY'S NIGHT** *Parlophone R 5393*	**14**	7 wks

See also *Peter Sellers And Sophia Loren.*

Peter SELLERS and Sophia LOREN

UK/Italy, male/female vocal duo

10 Nov 60	● **GOODNESS GRACIOUS ME**	**4**	14 wks
	Parlophone R 4702		
12 Jan 61	**BANGERS AND MASH** *Parlophone R 4724*	**22**	4 wks

See also *Peter Sellers.*

SEMPRINI

UK, orchestra

16 Mar 61	**THEME FROM 'EXODUS'** *HMV POP 842*	**25**	8 wks

Date	Title *Label Number*	Position

Denny SEYTON and the SABRES

UK, male vocal/instrumental group

| 17 Sep 64 | **THE WAY YOU LOOK TONIGHT** *Mercury MF 824* | **48** 1 wk |

SHADOWS

UK, male instrumental/vocal group

21 Jul 60	★ **APACHE** *Columbia DB 4484*	**1** 21 wks
10 Nov 60	● **MAN OF MYSTERY/ THE STRANGER** *Columbia DB 4530*	**5** 15 wks
9 Feb 61	● **F. B. I.** *Columbia DB 4580*	**6** 19 wks
11 May 61	● **FRIGHTENED CITY** *Columbia DB 4637*	**3** 20 wks
7 Sep 61	★ **KON-TIKI** *Columbia DB 4698*	**1** 10 wks
23 Nov 61	**KON-TIKI** (re-entry) *Columbia DB 4698*	**37** 2 wks
16 Nov 61	● **THE SAVAGE** *Columbia DB 4726*	**10** 8 wks
1 Mar 62	★ **WONDERFUL LAND** *Columbia DB 4790*	**1** 19 wks
2 Aug 62	● **GUITAR TANGO** *Columbia DB 4870*	**4** 15 wks
13 Dec 62	★ **DANCE ON!** *Columbia DB 4948*	**1** 15 wks
7 Mar 63	★ **FOOT TAPPER** *Columbia DB 4984*	**1** 16 wks
6 Jun 63	● **ATLANTIS** *Columbia DB 7047*	**2** 17 wks
19 Sep 63	● **SHINDIG** *Columbia DB 7106*	**6** 12 wks
5 Dec 63	**GERONIMO** *Columbia DB 7163*	**11** 12 wks
5 Mar 64	**THEME FOR YOUNG LOVERS** *Columbia DB 7231*	**12** 10 wks
7 May 64	● **THE RISE & FALL OF FLINGEL BUNT** *Columbia DB 7261*	**5** 14 wks
3 Sep 64	**RHYTHM & GREENS** *Columbia DB 7342*	**22** 7 wks
3 Dec 64	**GENIE WITH THE LIGHT BROWN LAMP** *Columbia DB 7416*	**17** 10 wks
11 Feb 65	**MARY ANNE** *Columbia DB 7476*	**17** 10 wks
10 Jun 65	**STINGRAY** *Columbia DB 7588*	**19** 7 wks
5 Aug 65	● **DON'T MAKE MY BABY BLUE** *Columbia DB 7650*	**10** 10 wks
25 Nov 65	**WAR LORD** *Columbia DB 7769*	**18** 9 wks
17 Mar 66	**I MET A GIRL** *Columbia DB 7853*	**22** 5 wks
7 Jul 66	**A PLACE IN THE SUN** *Columbia DB 7952*	**24** 6 wks
3 Nov 66	**THE DREAMS I DREAM** *Columbia DB 8034*	**42** 6 wks
13 Apr 67	**MAROC 7** *Columbia DB 8170*	**24** 8 wks

See also Cliff Richard. All the above hits were instrumentals except for Mary Anne, Don't Make My Baby Blue, I Met A Girl, The Dreams I Dream.

SHANGRI-LAS

US, female vocal group

| 8 Oct 64 | **REMEMBER (WALKIN' IN THE SAND)** *Red Bird RB 10008* | **14** 13 wks |
| 14 Jan 65 | **LEADER OF THE PACK** *Red Bird RB 10014* | **11** 9 wks |

Del SHANNON

US, male vocalist

27 Apr 61	★ **RUNAWAY** *London HLX 9317*	**1** 22 wks
14 Sep 61	● **HATS OFF TO LARRY** *London HLX 9402*	**6** 12 wks
7 Dec 61	● **SO LONG BABY** *London HLX 9462*	**10** 11 wks
15 Mar 62	● **HEY LITTLE GIRL** *London HLX 9515*	**2** 15 wks
6 Sep 62	● **CRY MYSELF TO SLEEP** *London HLX 9587*	**29** 6 wks
11 Oct 62	● **SWISS MAID** *London HLX 9609*	**2** 17 wks
17 Jan 63	● **LITTLE TOWN FLIRT** *London HLX 9653*	**4** 13 wks
25 Apr 63	● **TWO KINDS OF TEARDROPS** *London HLX 9710*	**5** 13 wks

Date	Title *Label Number*	Position

22 Aug 63	**TWO SILHOUETTES** *London HLX 9761*	**23** 8 wks
24 Oct 63	**SUE'S GONNA BE MINE** *London HLU 9800*	**21** 8 wks
12 Mar 64	**MARY JANE** *Stateside SS 269*	**35** 5 wks
30 Jul 64	**HANDY MAN** *Stateside SS 317*	**36** 4 wks
14 Jan 65	● **KEEP SEARCHIN' (WE'LL FOLLOW THE SUN)** *Stateside SS 368*	**3** 11 wks
18 Mar 65	**STRANGER IN TOWN** *Stateside SS 395*	**40** 2 wks

Helen SHAPIRO

UK, female vocalist

23 Mar 61	● **DON'T TREAT ME LIKE A CHILD** *Columbia DB 4589*	**3** 20 wks
29 Jun 61	★ **YOU DON'T KNOW** *Columbia DB 4670*	**1** 23 wks
28 Sep 61	★ **WALKIN' BACK TO HAPPINESS** *Columbia DB 4715*	**1** 19 wks
15 Feb 62	● **TELL ME WHAT HE SAID** *Columbia DB 4782*	**2** 15 wks
3 May 62	**LET'S TALK ABOUT LOVE** *Columbia DB 4824*	**23** 7 wks
12 Jul 62	● **LITTLE MISS LONELY** *Columbia DB 4869*	**8** 11 wks
18 Oct 62	**KEEP AWAY FROM OTHER GIRLS** *Columbia DB 4908*	**40** 6 wks
7 Feb 63	**QUEEN FOR TONIGHT** *Columbia DB 4966*	**33** 5 wks
25 Apr 63	**WOE IS ME** *Columbia DB 7026*	**35** 6 wks
24 Oct 63	**LOOK WHO IT IS** *Columbia DB 7130*	**47** 3 wks
23 Jan 64	**FEVER** *Columbia DB 7190*	**38** 4 wks

Dee Dee SHARP

US, female vocalist

| 25 Apr 63 | **DO THE BIRD** *Cameo Parkway C 244* | **46** 2 wks |

Sandie SHAW

UK, female vocalist

8 Oct 64	★ **(THERE'S) ALWAYS SOMETHING THERE TO REMIND ME** *Pye 7N 15704*	**1** 11 wks
10 Dec 64	● **GIRL DON'T COME** *Pye 7N 15743*	**3** 12 wks
18 Feb 65	● **I'LL STOP AT NOTHING** *Pye 7N 15783*	**4** 11 wks
13 May 65	★ **LONG LIVE LOVE** *Pye 7N 15841*	**1** 14 wks
23 Sep 65	● **MESSAGE UNDERSTOOD** *Pye 7N 15940*	**6** 10 wks
18 Nov 65	**HOW CAN YOU TELL** *Pye 7N 15987*	**21** 9 wks
27 Jan 66	● **TOMORROW** *Pye 7N 17036*	**9** 9 wks
19 May 66	**NOTHING COMES EASY** *Pye 7N 17086*	**14** 9 wks
8 Sep 66	**RUN** *Pye 7N 17163*	**32** 5 wks
24 Nov 66	**THINK SOMETIMES ABOUT ME** *Pye 7N 17212*	**32** 4 wks
19 Jan 67	**I DON'T NEED ANYTHING** *Pye 7N 17239*	**50** 1 wk
16 Mar 67	★ **PUPPET ON A STRING** *Pye 7N 17272*	**1** 18 wks
12 Jul 67	**TONIGHT IN TOKYO** *Pye 7N 17346*	**21** 6 wks
4 Oct 67	**YOU'VE NOT CHANGED** *Pye 7N 17378*	**18** 12 wks
7 Feb 68	**TODAY** *Pye 7N 17441*	**27** 7 wks
12 Feb 69	● **MONSIEUR DUPONT** *Pye 7N 17615*	**6** 15 wks
14 May 69	**THINK IT ALL OVER** *Pye 7N 17726*	**42** 4 wks

George SHEARING

UK, male instrumentalist, piano

| 4 Oct 62 | **BAUBLES BANGLES & BEADS** *Capitol CL 15269* | **49** 1 wk |

See also Nat King Cole.

Date	Title Label Number	Position

Doug SHELDON

UK, male vocalist

9 Nov 61	**RUNAROUND SUE** Decca F 11398	36	3 wks
4 Jan 62	**YOUR MA SAID YOU CRIED IN YOUR SLEEP LAST NIGHT** Decca F 11416	29	6 wks
7 Feb 63	**I SAW LINDA YESTERDAY** Decca F 11564	36	6 wks

Anne SHELTON

UK, female vocalist

26 Jan 61	● **SAILOR** Philips PB 1096	10	8 wks

Tony SHERIDAN and the BEATLES

UK, male vocalist, male instrumental backing group

6 Jun 63	**MY BONNIE** Polydor NH 66833	48	1 wk

See also Beatles.

Allan SHERMAN

US, male vocalist

12 Sep 63	**HELLO MUDDAH HELLO FADDAH** Warner Bros. WB 106	14	10 wks

Tony SHEVETON

UK, male vocalist

13 Feb 64	**MILLION DRUMS** Oriole CB 1895	49	1 wk

SHIRELLES

US, female vocal group

9 Feb 61	● **WILL YOU LOVE ME TOMORROW** Top Rank JAR 540	4	15 wks
31 May 62	**SOLDIER BOY** HMV POP 1019	23	9 wks
23 May 63	**FOOLISH LITTLE GIRL** Stateside SS 181	38	5 wks

Troy SHONDELL

US, male vocalist

2 Nov 61	**THIS TIME** London HLG 9432	22	11 wks

SHONDELLS — See Tommy JAMES and the SHONDELLS

SHOWSTOPPERS

US, male vocal group

13 Mar 68	**AIN'T NOTHING BUT A HOUSEPARTY** Beacon 3-100	11	15 wks
13 Nov 68	**EENY MEENY** MGM 1346	33	7 wks

SILKIE

UK, male/female vocal/instrumental group

23 Sep 65	**YOU'VE GOT TO HIDE YOUR LOVE AWAY** Fontana TF 603	28	6 wks

Harry SIMEONE CHORALE

US, choir

22 Dec 60	**ONWARD CHRISTIAN SOLDIERS** Ember EMBS 118	35	1 wk
5 Jan 61	**ONWARD CHRISTIAN SOLDIERS** (re-entry) Ember EMBS 118	38	1 wk
21 Dec 61	**ONWARD CHRISTIAN SOLDIERS** (2nd re-entry) Ember EMBS 118	36	3 wks
20 Dec 62	**ONWARD CHRISTIAN SOLDIERS** (re-issue) Ember EMBS 144	38	2 wks

SIMON and GARFUNKEL

US, male vocal duo

24 Mar 66	● **HOMEWARD BOUND** CBS 202045	9	12 wks
16 Jun 66	**I AM A ROCK** CBS 202303	17	10 wks
10 Jul 68	● **MRS. ROBINSON** CBS 3443	4	12 wks
8 Jan 69	● **MRS. ROBINSON** (EP) CBS EP 6400	9	5 wks
30 Apr 69	● **THE BOXER** CBS 4162	6	14 wks

Titles on Mrs. Robinson EP: Mrs. Robinson/ Scarborough Fair-Canticle/ Sounds Of Silence/ April Come She Will. This EP would have stayed more than 5 weeks on chart had a decision to exclude EP's from the chart not been taken in February 1969.

Nina SIMONE

US, female vocalist

5 Aug 65	**I PUT A SPELL ON YOU** Philips BF 1415	49	1 wk
16 Oct 68	● **AIN'T GOT NO - I GOT LIFE/ DO WHAT YOU GOTTA DO** RCA 1743	2	18 wks
15 Jan 69	● **TO LOVE SOMEBODY** RCA 1779	5	9 wks
15 Jan 69	**I PUT A SPELL ON YOU** (re-issue) Philips BF 1736	28	4 wks

Do What You Gotta Do was only credited on the charts for 8 weeks of the 18, its highest position being 7.

Frank SINATRA

US, male vocalist

10 Mar 60	**HIGH HOPES** Capitol CL 15052	42	1 2 wks
7 Apr 60	**IT'S NICE TO GO TRAV'LING** Capitol CL 15116	48	2 wks
16 Jun 60	**RIVER STAY 'WAY FROM MY DOOR** Capitol CL 15135	18	9 wks
8 Sep 60	**NICE 'N EASY** Capitol CL 15150	15	12 wks
24 Nov 60	**OL' MACDONALD** Capitol CL 15168	11	8 wks
20 Apr 61	**MY BLUE HEAVEN** Capitol CL 15193	33	7 wks
28 Sep 61	**GRANADA** Reprise R 20010	15	8 wks
23 Nov 61	**THE COFFEE SONG** Reprise R 20035	39	3 wks
5 Apr 62	**EVERYBODY'S TWISTING** Reprise R 20063	22	12 wks
7 Mar 63	**MY KIND OF GIRL** Reprise R 20148	35	6 wks
24 Sep 64	**HELLO DOLLY** Reprise R 20351	47	1 wk
12 May 66	★ **STRANGERS IN THE NIGHT** Reprise R 23052	1	20 wks
29 Sep 66	**SUMMER WIND** Reprise RS 20509	36	5 wks

STATUS QUO *Above*
Once upon a time, long ago in a land not so far away, before faded denims were ever invented . . .

SWINGING BLUE JEANS
Four severe cases of the 'Hippy Hippy Flake'.

Date	Title Label Number	Position		Date	Title Label Number	Position

Date	Title Label Number	Position
15 Dec 66	THAT'S LIFE Reprise RS 20531	46 5 wks
23 Aug 67	THE WORLD WE KNEW Reprise RS 20610	33 11 wks
2 Apr 69	● MY WAY Reprise RS 20817	5 42 wks
4 Oct 69	● LOVE'S BEEN GOOD TO ME Reprise RS 20852	8 18 wks

See also Frank Sinatra and Sammy Davis Jr; Nancy Sinatra and Frank Sinatra. My Kind Of Girl and Hello Dolly with Count Basie

Frank SINATRA and Sammy DAVIS JR.

US, male vocal duo

Date	Title Label Number	Position
13 Dec 62	ME AND MY SHADOW Reprise R 20128	20 7 wks
7 Feb 63	ME AND MY SHADOW (re-entry) Reprise R 20128	47 2 wks

See also Frank Sinatra; Sammy Davis Jr; Nancy Sinatra and Frank Sinatra; Sammy Davis Jr. and Carmen McRae.

Nancy SINATRA

US, female vocalist

Date	Title Label Number	Position
27 Jan 66	★ THESE BOOTS ARE MADE FOR WALKIN' Reprise R 20432	1 14 wks
28 Apr 66	HOW DOES THAT GRAB YOU DARLIN' Reprise R 20461	19 8 wks
19 Jan 67	● SUGAR TOWN Reprise RS 20527	8 10 wks
5 Jul 67	YOU ONLY LIVE TWICE/ JACKSON Reprise RS 20595	11 19 wks
29 Nov 69	HIGHWAY SONG Reprise RS 20869	21 10 wks

See also Nancy Sinatra and Frank Sinatra; Nancy Sinatra and Lee Hazlewood. Jackson was billed together with You Only Live Twice; from 12 Jul 67. Jackson is by Nancy Sinatra and Lee Hazlewood.

Nancy SINATRA and Lee HAZLEWOOD

US, female/male vocal duo

Date	Title Label Number	Position
8 Nov 67	LADYBIRD Reprise RS 20629	47 1 wk

See also Nancy Sinatra, Nancy Sinatra and Frank Sinatra.

Nancy SINATRA and Frank SINATRA

US, female/male vocal duo

Date	Title Label Number	Position
23 Mar 67	★ SOMETHIN' STUPID Reprise RS 23166	1 18 wks

See also Nancy Sinatra; Nancy Sinatra and Lee Hazlewood. Frank Sinatra; Frank Sinatra and Sammy Davis Jr.

SINGING NUN (Soeur Sourire)

Belgium, female vocalist

Date	Title Label Number	Position
5 Dec 63	● DOMINIQUE Philips BF 1293	7 13 wks

SIR DOUGLAS QUINTET

US, male vocal/instrumental group

Date	Title Label Number	Position
17 Jun 65	SHE'S ABOUT A MOVER London HLU 9964	15 10 wks

SKATALITES

Jamaica, male instrumental group

Date	Title Label Number	Position
20 Apr 67	GUNS OF NAVARONE Island WI 168	36 6 wks

Percy SLEDGE

US, male vocalist

Date	Title Label Number	Position
12 May 66	● WHEN A MAN LOVES A WOMAN Atlantic 584 001	4 17 wks
4 Aug 66	WARM & TENDER LOVE Atlantic 584 034	34 7 wks

P. F. SLOAN

US, male vocalist

Date	Title Label Number	Position
4 Nov 65	SINS OF THE FAMILY RCA 1482	38 3 wks

SLY and the FAMILY STONE

US, male/female vocal/instrumental group. Sly Stone, vocals and keyboards

Date	Title Label Number	Position
10 Jul 68	● DANCE TO THE MUSIC Direction 58 3568	7 14 wks
2 Oct 68	M'LADY Direction 58 3707	32 7 wks
19 Mar 69	EVERYDAY PEOPLE Direction 58 3938	36 1 wk
9 Apr 69	EVERYDAY PEOPLE (re-entry) Direction 58 3938	37 4 wks

SMALL FACES

UK, male vocal/instrumental group

Date	Title Label Number	Position
2 Sep 65	WHATCHA GONNA DO ABOUT IT? Decca F 12208	14 12 wks
10 Feb 66	● SHA LA LA LA LEE Decca F 12317	3 11 wks
12 May 66	● HEY GIRL Decca F 12393	10 9 wks
11 Aug 66	★ ALL OR NOTHING Decca F 12470	1 12 wks
17 Nov 66	● MY MIND'S EYE Decca F 12500	4 11 wks
9 Mar 67	I CAN'T MAKE IT Decca F 12565	26 7 wks
8 Jun 67	HERE COMES THE NICE Immediate IM 050	12 10 wks
9 Aug 67	● ITCHYCOO PARK Immediate IM 057	3 14 wks
6 Dec 67	● TIN SOLDIER Immediate IM 062	9 12 wks
17 Apr 68	● LAZY SUNDAY Immediate IM 064	2 11 wks
10 Jul 68	UNIVERSAL Immediate IM 069	16 11 wks
19 Mar 69	AFTERGLOW OF YOUR LOVE Immediate IM 077	36 1 wk

Jimmy SMITH

US, male instrumentalist, organ

Date	Title Label Number	Position
28 Apr 66	GOT MY MOJO WORKING Verve VS 536	48 2 wks
19 May 66	GOT MY MOJO WORKING (re-entry) Verve VS 536	48 1 wk

Date	Title *Label Number*	Position	Date	Title *Label Number*	Position

Keely SMITH

US, female vocalist

| 18 Mar 65 | **YOU'RE BREAKIN' MY HEART** *Reprise R 20346* | **14** 10 wks |

O. C. SMITH

US, male vocalist

| 29 May 68 | ● **SON OF HICKORY HOLLER'S TRAMP** *CBS 3343* | **2** 15 wks |

Whistling Jack SMITH

UK, male whistler

| 2 Mar 67 | ● **I WAS KAISER BILL'S BATMAN** *Deram DM 112* | **5** 12 wks |

SMOKE

UK, male vocal/instrumental group

| 9 Mar 67 | **MY FRIEND JACK** *Columbia DB 8115* | **45** 3 wks |

SONNY

US, male vocalist

| 19 Aug 65 | ● **LAUGH AT ME** *Atlantic AT 4038* | **9** 11 wks |

See also Sonny and Cher.

SONNY and CHER

US, male/female vocal duo

12 Aug 65	★ **I GOT YOU BABE** *Atlantic AT 4035*	**1** 12 wks
16 Sep 65	**BABY DON'T GO** *Reprise R 20309*	**11** 9 wks
21 Oct 65	**BUT YOU'RE MINE** *Atlantic AT 4047*	**17** 8 wks
17 Feb 66	**WHAT NOW MY LOVE** *Atlantic AT 4069*	**13** 11 wks
30 Jun 66	**HAVE I STAYED TOO LONG** *Atlantic 584 018*	**42** 3 wks
8 Sep 66	● **LITTLE MAN** *Atlantic 584 040*	**4** 10 wks
17 Nov 66	**LIVING FOR YOU** *Atlantic 584 057*	**44** 4 wks
2 Feb 67	**THE BEAT GOES ON** *Atlantic 584 078*	**29** 8 wks

See also Sonny; Cher.

SORROWS

UK, male vocal/instrumental group

| 16 Sep 65 | **TAKE A HEART** *Piccadilly 7N 35260* | **21** 8 wks |

Jimmy SOUL

US, male vocalist

| 11 Jul 63 | **IF YOU WANNA BE HAPPY** *Stateside SS 178* | **39** 2 wks |

SOUL BROTHERS

UK, male vocal/instrumental group

| 22 Apr 65 | **I KEEP RINGING MY BABY** *Decca F 12116* | **42** 3 wks |

SOUNDS INCORPORATED

UK, male instrumental group

| 23 Apr 64 | **THE SPARTANS** *Columbia DB 7239* | **30** 6 wks |
| 30 Jul 64 | **SPANISH HARLEM** *Columbia DB 7321* | **35** 5 wks |

SOUNDS NICE

UK, male instrumental group

| 6 Sep 69 | **LOVE AT FIRST SIGHT (JE T'AIME ... MOI NON PLUS)** *Parlophone R 5797* | **18** 11 wks |

Has credit: Tim Mycroft on organ.

SOUNDS ORCHESTRAL

UK, orchestra

| 3 Dec 64 | ● **CAST YOUR FATE TO THE WIND** *Piccadilly 7N 35206* | **5** 16 wks |
| 8 Jul 65 | **MOONGLOW** *Piccadilly 7N 35248* | **43** 2 wks |

Joe SOUTH

US, male vocalist

| 5 Mar 69 | ● **GAMES PEOPLE PLAY** *Capitol CL 15579* | **6** 11 wks |

Bob B SOXX and the BLUE JEANS

US, male/female vocal group

| 31 Jan 63 | **ZIP-A-DEE-DOO-DAH** *London HLU 9646* | **45** 2 wks |

Johnny SPENCE

UK, orchestra

| 1 Mar 62 | **THEME FROM DR. KILDARE** *Parlophone R 4872* | **15** 15 wks |

Don SPENCER

UK, male vocalist

| 21 Mar 63 | **FIREBALL** *HMV POP 1087* | **32** 11 wks |
| 13 Jun 63 | **FIREBALL** (re-entry) *HMV POP 1087* | **49** 1 wk |

Date	Title Label Number	Position

SPOTNICKS

Sweden, male instrumental group

14 Jun 62	**ORANGE BLOSSOM SPECIAL**	**29**	10 wks
	Oriole CB 1724		
6 Sep 62	**ROCKET MAN** Oriole CB 1755	**38**	9 wks
31 Jan 63	**HAVA NAGILA** Oriole CB 1790	**13**	12 wks
25 Apr 63	**JUST LISTEN TO MY HEART** Oriole CB 1818	**36**	6 wks

Dusty SPRINGFIELD

UK, female vocalist

21 Nov 63	● **I ONLY WANT TO BE WITH YOU**	**4**	18 wks
	Philips BF 1292		
20 Feb 64	**STAY AWHILE** Philips BF 1311	**13**	10 wks
2 Jul 64	● **I JUST DON'T KNOW WHAT TO DO WITH**	**3**	12 wks
	MYSELF Philips BF 1348		
22 Oct 64	● **LOSING YOU** Philips BF 1369	**9**	13 wks
18 Feb 65	**YOUR HURTIN' KIND OF LOVE**	**37**	4 wks
	Philips BF 1396		
1 Jul 65	● **IN THE MIDDLE OF NOWHERE**	**8**	10 wks
	Philips BF 1418		
16 Sep 65	● **SOME OF YOUR LOVIN'** Philips BF 1430	**8**	12 wks
27 Jan 66	**LITTLE BY LITTLE** Philips BF 1466	**17**	9 wks
31 Mar 66	★ **YOU DON'T HAVE TO SAY YOU LOVE ME**	**1**	13 wks
	Philips BF 1482		
7 Jul 66	● **GOING BACK** Philips BF 1502	**10**	10 wks
15 Sep 66	● **ALL I SEE IS YOU** Philips BF 1510	**9**	12 wks
23 Feb 67	**I'LL TRY ANYTHING** Philips BF 1553	**13**	9 wks
25 May 67	**GIVE ME TIME** Philips BF 1577	**24**	6 wks
10 Jul 68	● **I CLOSE MY EYES AND COUNT TO TEN**	**4**	12 wks
	Philips BF 1682		
4 Dec 68	● **SON OF A PREACHER MAN** Philips BF 1730	**9**	9 wks
20 Sep 69	**AM I THE SAME GIRL** Philips BF 1811	**43**	3 wks
18 Oct 69	**AM I THE SAME GIRL** (re-entry)	**46**	1 wk
	Philips BF 1811		

See also Springfields.

SPRINGFIELDS

UK, male/female vocal/instrumental group

31 Aug 61	**BREAKAWAY** Philips BF 1168	**31**	8 wks
16 Nov 61	**BAMBINO** Philips BF 1178	**16**	11 wks
13 Dec 62	● **ISLAND OF DREAMS** Philips 326557 BF	**5**	26 wks
28 Mar 63	● **SAY I WON'T BE THERE** Philips 326577 BF	**5**	15 wks
25 Jul 63	**COME ON HOME** Philips BF 1263	**31**	6 wks

See also Dusty Springfield.

Dorothy SQUIRES

UK, female vocalist

20 Sep 69	**FOR ONCE IN MY LIFE** President PT 267	**24**	10 wks
20 Dec 69	**FOR ONCE IN MY LIFE** (re-entry)	**48**	1 wk
	President PT 267		

See also Dorothy Squires and Russ Conway.

Dorothy SQUIRES and Russ CONWAY

UK, female vocalist, male instrumentalist, piano

24 Aug 61	**SAY IT WITH FLOWERS** Columbia DB 4665	**23**	10 wks

See also Dorothy Squires; Russ Conway.

Terry STAFFORD

US, male vocalist

7 May 64	**SUSPICION** London HLU 9871	**31**	9 wks

STAIFFI and his MUSTAFAS

France, male vocal/instrumental group

28 Jul 60	**MUSTAFA** Pye International 7N 25057	**43**	1 wk

STARLITERS — See *Joey DEE and the STARLITERS*

Edwin STARR

US, male vocalist

12 May 66	**STOP HER ON SIGHT (SOS)**	**35**	8 wks
	Polydor BM 56 702		
18 Aug 66	**HEADLINE NEWS** Polydor 56 717	**39**	3 wks
11 Dec 68	**STOP HER ON SIGHT (SOS)/ HEADLINE**	**11**	11 wks
	NEWS (re-issue) Polydor 56 153		
13 Sep 69	**25 MILES** Tamla Motown TMG 672	**36**	6 wks

Headline News *not listed with* SOS *from 22 Jan 69 to 19 Feb 69.*

STATLER BROTHERS

US, male vocal group

24 Feb 66	**FLOWERS ON THE WALL** CBS 201976	**38**	4 wks

STATUS QUO

UK, male vocal/instrumental group

24 Jan 68	● **PICTURES OF MATCHSTICK MEN**	**7**	12 wks
	Pye 7N 17449		
21 Aug 68	● **ICE IN THE SUN** Pye 7N 17581	**8**	12 wks
28 May 69	**ARE YOU GROWING TIRED OF MY LOVE**	**46**	2 wks
	Pye 7N 17728		
18 Jun 69	**ARE YOU GROWING TIRED OF MY LOVE**	**50**	1 wk
	(re-entry) Pye 7N 17728		

Tommy STEELE

UK, male vocalist

1 Jan 60	● **LITTLE WHITE BULL** Decca F 11177	**6**	8 wks
10 Mar 60	**LITTLE WHITE BULL** (re-entry)	**30**	5 wks
	Decca F 11177		
23 Jun 60	● **WHAT A MOUTH** Decca F 11245	**5**	11 wks
29 Dec 60	**MUST BE SANTA** Decca F 11299	**40**	1 wk
17 Aug 61	**WRITING ON THE WALL** Decca F 11372	**30**	5 wks

Date	Title Label Number	Position	Date	Title Label Number	Position

STEPPENWOLF

US, male vocal/instrumental group

| 11 Jun 69 | **BORN TO BE WILD** *Stateside SS 8017* | **30** 7 wks |
| 9 Aug 69 | **BORN TO BE WILD** (re-entry) *Stateside SS 8017* | **50** 2 wks |

STEVE and EYDIE

US, male/female vocal duo

| 22 Aug 63 | ● **I WANT TO STAY HERE** *CBS AAG 163* | **3** 13 wks |

See also Steve Lawrence, Eydie Gorme.

April STEVENS — See *Nino TEMPO and April STEVENS*

Cat STEVENS

UK, male vocalist

20 Oct 66	**I LOVE MY DOG** *Deram DM 102*	**28** 7 wks
12 Jan 67	● **MATTHEW AND SON** *Deram DM 110*	**2** 10 wks
30 Mar 67	● **I'M GONNA GET ME A GUN** *Deram DM 118*	**6** 10 wks
2 Aug 67	**A BAD NIGHT** *Deram DM 140*	**20** 8 wks
20 Dec 67	**KITTY** *Deram DM 156*	**47** 1 wk

Connie STEVENS

US, female vocalist

| 5 May 60 | ● **SIXTEEN REASONS** *Warner Bros. WB 3* | **9** 11 wks |
| 4 Aug 60 | **SIXTEEN REASONS** (re-entry) *Warner Bros. WB 3* | **45** 1 wk |

See also Edward Byrnes and Connie Stevens.

Ricky STEVENS

UK, male vocalist

| 14 Dec 61 | **I CRIED FOR YOU** *Columbia DB 4739* | **34** 7 wks |

Andy STEWART

UK, male vocalist

15 Dec 60	**DONALD WHERE'S YOUR TROOSERS** *Top Rank JAR 427*	**37** 1 wk
12 Jan 61	**A SCOTTISH SOLDIER** *Top Rank JAR 512*	**19** 38 wks
1 Jun 61	**THE BATTLE'S O'ER** *Top Rank JAR 565*	**28** 13 wks
12 Oct 61	**A SCOTTISH SOLDIER** (re-entry) *Top Rank JAR 512*	**43** 2 wks
12 Aug 65	**DR. FINLAY** *HMV POP 1454*	**50** 1 wk
26 Aug 65	**DR. FINLAY** (re-entry) *HMV POP 1454*	**43** 4 wks

Billy STEWART

US, male vocalist

| 8 Sep 66 | **SUMMERTIME** *Chess CRS 8040* | **39** 2 wks |

STINGERS — See *B. BUMBLE and the STINGERS*

Rhet STOLLER

UK, male instrumentalist - guitar

| 12 Jan 61 | **CHARIOT** *Decca F 11302* | **26** 8 wks |

Danny STORM

UK, male vocalist

| 12 Apr 62 | **HONEST I DO** *Piccadilly 7N 35025* | **42** 4 wks |

STORYVILLE JAZZ BAND — See *Bob WALLIS and his STORYVILLE JAZZ BAND*

Barbra STREISAND

US, female vocalist

| 20 Jan 66 | **SECOND HAND ROSE** *CBS 202025* | **14** 13 wks |

STRING-A-LONGS

US, male instrumental group

| 23 Feb 61 | ● **WHEELS** *London HLU 9278* | **8** 16 wks |

Chad STUART and Jeremy CLYDE

UK, male vocal duo

| 28 Nov 63 | **YESTERDAY'S GONE** *Ember EMB S 180* | **37** 7 wks |

SUNDRAGON

UK, male vocal/instrumental duo

| 21 Feb 68 | **GREEN TAMBOURINE** *MGM 1380* | **50** 1 wk |

SUPREMES

US, female vocal group

3 Sep 64	● **WHERE DID OUR LOVE GO** *Stateside SS 327*	**3** 14 wks
22 Oct 64	★ **BABY LOVE** *Stateside SS 350*	**1** 15 wks
21 Jan 65	**COME SEE ABOUT ME** *Stateside SS 376*	**27** 6 wks
25 Mar 65	● **STOP IN THE NAME OF LOVE** *Tamla Motown TMG 501*	**7** 12 wks
10 Jun 65	**BACK IN MY ARMS AGAIN** *Tamla Motown TMG 516*	**40** 5 wks
9 Dec 65	**I HEAR A SYMPHONY** *Tamla Motown TMG 543*	**50** 1 wk
23 Dec 65	**I HEAR A SYMPHONY** (re-entry) *Tamla Motown TMG 543*	**39** 4 wks
8 Sep 66	● **YOU CAN'T HURRY LOVE** *Tamla Motown TMG 575*	**3** 12 wks
1 Dec 66	● **YOU KEEP ME HANGIN' ON** *Tamla Motown TMG 585*	**8** 10 wks
2 Mar 67	**LOVE IS HERE AND NOW YOU'RE GONE** *Tamla Motown TMG 597*	**17** 10 wks
11 May 67	● **THE HAPPENING** *Tamla Motown TMG 607*	**6** 12 wks
30 Aug 67	● **REFLECTIONS** *Tamla Motown TMG 616*	**5** 14 wks

TREMELOES *Above* and *Right* With and without
Brian Poole in their various arrangements, they
collectively hit the charts first in 1963
('Twist And Shout') and ended on a high note in 1969
with ('Call Me) Number One'.

TIMEBOX Ollie Halsall, Mike Patto, Chris Holmes, Clive Griffiths and John Halsy formed
Timebox in 1966 and had a hit with a cover of a Four Seasons' classic in '68 before evolving
into Patto just over a year later.

Ike and Tina TURNER Tina points out the
importance of brushing your teeth regularly.

Date	Title *Label Number*	Position		Date	Title *Label Number*	Position
29 Nov 67	**IN AND OUT OF LOVE** *Tamla Motown TMG 632*	**13** 13 wks			**Felice TAYLOR**	
10 Apr 68	**FOREVER CAME TODAY** *Tamla Motown TMG 650*	**28** 8 wks			*US, female vocalist*	
3 Jul 68	**SOME THINGS YOU NEVER GET USED TO** *Tamla Motown TMG 662*	**34** 6 wks		25 Oct 67	**I FEEL LOVE COMIN' ON** *President PT 155*	**11** 13 wks
20 Nov 68	**LOVE CHILD** *Tamla Motown TMG 677*	**15** 14 wks			**R. Dean TAYLOR**	
23 Apr 69	**I'M LIVING IN SHAME** *Tamla Motown TMG 695*	**14** 9 wks			*US, male vocalist*	
2 Jul 69	**I'M LIVING IN SHAME** (re-entry) *Tamla Motown TMG 695*	**50** 1 wk		19 Jun 68	**GOTTA SEE JANE** *Tamla Motown TMG 656*	**17** 12 wks
16 Jul 69	**NO MATTER WHAT SIGN YOU ARE** *Tamla Motown TMG 704*	**37** 7 wks		**TEICHER** — See *FERRANTE and TEICHER*	
13 Dec 69	**SOMEDAY WE'LL BE TOGETHER** *Tamla Motown TMG 721*	**13** 13 wks			**TEMPERANCE SEVEN**	

From Reflections *onwards the group is billed as Diana Ross and the Supremes. See also Diana Ross and the Supremes and the Temptations.*

SURFARIS

US, male instrumental group

25 Jul 63	● **WIPE OUT** *London HLD 9751*	**5** 14 wks

Pat SUZUKI

US, female vocalist

14 Apr 60	**I ENJOY BEING A GIRL** *RCA 1171*	**49** 1 wk

SWINGING BLUE JEANS

UK, male vocal/instrumental group

20 Jun 63	**IT'S TOO LATE NOW** *HMV POP 1170*	**30** 6 wks
8 Aug 63	**IT'S TOO LATE NOW** (re-entry) *HMV POP 1170*	**46** 3 wks
12 Dec 63	● **HIPPY HIPPY SHAKE** *HMV POP 1242*	**2** 17 wks
19 Mar 64	**GOOD GOLLY MISS MOLLY** *HMV POP 1273*	**11** 10 wks
4 Jun 64	● **YOU'RE NO GOOD** *HMV POP 1304*	**3** 13 wks
20 Jan 66	**DON'T MAKE ME OVER** *HMV POP 1501*	**31** 8 wks

SYMBOLS

UK, male vocal/instrumental group

2 Aug 67	**BYE BYE BABY** *President PT 144*	**44** 3 wks
3 Jan 68	**BEST PART OF BREAKING UP** *President PT 173*	**25** 12 wks

T

Norma TANEGA

US, female vocalist

7 Apr 66	**WALKING MY CAT NAMED DOG** *Stateside SS 496*	**22** 8 wks

TEMPERANCE SEVEN

UK, male vocal/instrumental band

30 Mar 61	⋆ **YOU'RE DRIVING ME CRAZY** *Parlophone R 4757*	**1** 16 wks
15 Jun 61	● **PASADENA** *Parlophone R 4781*	**4** 17 wks
28 Sep 61	**HARD HEARTED HANNAH/ CHILI BOM BOM** *Parlophone R 4823*	**28** 4 wks
7 Dec 61	**CHARLESTON** *Parlophone R 4851*	**22** 8 wks

Chili Bom Bom *only listed with* Hard Hearted Hannah *for the weeks of 12 and 19 Oct 61.*

Nino TEMPO and April STEVENS

US, male/female vocal duo

7 Nov 63	**DEEP PURPLE** *London HLK 9785*	**17** 11 wks
16 Jan 64	**WHISPERING** *London HLK 9829*	**20** 8 wks

TEMPTATIONS

US, male vocal group

18 Mar 65	**MY GIRL** *Stateside SS 395*	**43** 1 wk
1 Apr 65	**IT'S GROWING** *Tamla Motown TMG 504*	**49** 1 wk
15 Apr 65	**IT'S GROWING** (re-entry) *Tamla Motown TMG 504*	**45** 1 wk
14 Jul 66	**AIN'T TOO PROUD TO BEG** *Tamla Motown TMG 565*	**21** 11 wks
6 Oct 66	**BEAUTY IS ONLY SKIN DEEP** *Tamla Motown TMG 578*	**18** 10 wks
15 Dec 66	**(I KNOW) I'M LOSING YOU** *Tamla Motown TMG 587*	**19** 9 wks
6 Sep 67	**YOU'RE MY EVERYTHING** *Tamla Motown TMG 620*	**26** 15 wks
6 Mar 68	**I WISH IT WOULD RAIN** *Tamla Motown TMG 641*	**45** 1 wk
12 Jun 68	**I COULD NEVER LOVE ANOTHER** *Tamla Motown TMG 658*	**47** 1 wk
5 Mar 69	● **GET READY** *Tamla Motown TMG 688*	**10** 9 wks
23 Aug 69	**CLOUD NINE** *Tamla Motown TMG 707*	**15** 10 wks

See also Diana Ross and the Supremes and the Temptations.

Tammi TERRELL — See *Marvin GAYE and Tammi TERRELL*

Date	Title *Label Number*	Position

THEM
UK male vocal/instrumental group

7 Jan 65	● BABY PLEASE DON'T GO *Decca F 12018*	10	9 wks
25 Mar 65	● HERE COMES THE NIGHT *Decca F 12094*	2	12 wks

Carla THOMAS — See *Otis REDDING and Carla THOMAS*

Jamo THOMAS
US, male vocalist

26 Feb 69	I SPY FOR THE FBI *Polydor 56755*	48	1 wk
12 Mar 69	I SPY FOR THE FBI (re-entry) *Polydor 56755*	44	1 wk

Sue THOMPSON
US, female vocalist

2 Nov 61	SAD MOVIES *Polydor NH 66967*	46	1 wk
16 Nov 61	SAD MOVIES (re-entry) *Polydor NH 66967*	48	1 wk
21 Jan 65	PAPER TIGER *Hickory 1284*	50	1 wk
11 Feb 65	PAPER TIGER (re-entry) *Hickory 1284*	30	6 wks

David THORNE
US, male vocalist

24 Jan 63	ALLEY CAT SONG *Stateside SS 141*	21	8 wks

Ken THORNE
UK, orchestra

18 Jul 63	● THEME FROM THE FILM 'THE LEGION'S LAST PATROL' *HMV POP 1176*	4	15 wks

THREE GOOD REASONS
UK, male vocal/instrumental group

10 Mar 66	NOWHERE MAN *Mercury MF 899*	47	3 wks

THUNDERCLAP NEWMAN
UK, male vocal/instrumental group

11 Jun 69	★ SOMETHING IN THE AIR *Track 604-031*	1	12 wks

TICH — See *Dave DEE, DOZY, BEAKY, MICK and TICH*

TIJUANA BRASS — See *Herb ALPERT and the TIJUANA BRASS*

Johnny TILLOTSON
US, male vocalist

1 Dec 60	★ POETRY IN MOTION *London HLA 9231*	1	15 wks
2 Feb 61	JIMMY'S GIRL *London HLA 9275*	50	1 wk
16 Feb 61	JIMMY'S GIRL (re-entry) *London HLA 9275*	43	1 wk

12 Jul 62	IT KEEPS RIGHT ON A HURTIN' *London HLA 9550*	31	10 wks
4 Oct 62	SEND ME THE PILLOW YOU DREAM ON *London HLA 9598*	21	10 wks
27 Dec 62	I CAN'T HELP IT *London HLA 9642*	42	1 wk
10 Jan 63	I CAN'T HELP IT (re-entry) *London HLA 9642*	47	1 wk
24 Jan 63	I CAN'T HELP IT (2nd re-entry) *London HLA 9642*	41	4 wks
9 May 63	OUT OF MY MIND *London HLA 9695*	34	5 wks

TIMEBOX
UK, male vocal/instrumental group

24 Jul 68	BEGGIN' *Deram DM 194*	38	4 wks

TINY TIM
US, male vocalist

5 Feb 69	GREAT BALLS OF FIRE *Reprise RS 20802*	45	1 wk

TOKENS
US, male vocal group

21 Dec 61	THE LION SLEEPS TONIGHT *RCA 1263*	11	12 wks

TOPOL
Israel, male vocalist

20 Apr 67	● IF I WERE A RICH MAN *CBS 202651*	9	20 wks

Mel TORME
US, male vocalist

3 Jan 63	COMING HOME BABY *London HLK 9643*	13	8 wks

TORNADOS
UK, male instrumental group

30 Aug 62	★ TELSTAR *Decca F 11494*	1	25 wks
10 Jan 63	● GLOBETROTTER *Decca F 11562*	5	11 wks
21 Mar 63	ROBOT *Decca F 11606*	17	12 wks
6 Jun 63	THE ICE CREAM MAN *Decca F 11662*	18	9 wks
10 Oct 63	DRAGONFLY *Decca F 11745*	41	2 wks

TOYS
US, female vocal group

4 Nov 65	● A LOVER'S CONCERTO *Stateside SS 460*	5	13 wks
27 Jan 66	ATTACK *Stateside SS 483*	36	4 wks

YOUNG RASCALS *Left* It's competition time - spot the
Dave Lee Travis impersonator.

Date	Title Label Number	Position

TRAFFIC

UK, male vocal/instrumental group

1 Jun 67	● PAPER SUN *Island WIP 6002*	5	10 wks
6 Sep 67	● HOLE IN MY SHOE *Island WIP 6017*	2	14 wks
29 Nov 67	● HERE WE GO ROUND THE MULBERRY BUSH *Island WIP 6025*	8	12 wks
6 Mar 68	NO FACE, NO NAME, NO NUMBER *Island WIP 6030*	40	4 wks

TRASH

UK, male vocal/instrumental group

25 Oct 69	GOLDEN SLUMBERS - CARRY THAT WEIGHT (MEDLEY) *Apple 17*	35	3 wks

TREMELOES

UK, male vocal/instrumental group

2 Feb 67	● HERE COMES MY BABY *CBS 202519*	4	11 wks
27 Apr 67	★ SILENCE IS GOLDEN *CBS 2723*	1	15 wks
2 Aug 67	● EVEN THE BAD TIMES ARE GOOD *CBS 2930*	4	13 wks
8 Nov 67	BE MINE *CBS 3043*	39	2 wks
17 Jan 68	● SUDDENLY YOU LOVE ME *CBS 3234*	6	11 wks
8 May 68	HELULE HELULE *CBS 2889*	14	9 wks
18 Sep 68	● MY LITTLE LADY *CBS 3443*	6	12 wks
11 Dec 68	I SHALL BE RELEASED *CBS 3873*	29	5 wks
19 Mar 69	HELLO WORLD *CBS 4065*	14	8 wks
1 Nov 69	● (CALL ME) NUMBER ONE *CBS 4582*	2	14 wks

See also Brian Poole and the Tremeloes.

Jackie TRENT

UK, female vocalist

22 Apr 65	★ WHERE ARE YOU NOW (MY LOVE) *Pye 7N 15776*	1	11 wks
1 Jul 65	WHEN THE SUMMERTIME IS OVER *Pye 7N 15865*	39	2 wks
2 Apr 69	I'LL BE THERE *Pye 7N 17693*	38	4 wks

Tony TRIBE

Jamaica, male vocalist

16 Jul 69	RED RED WINE *Downtown DT 419*	50	1 wk
9 Aug 69	RED RED WINE (re-entry) *Downtown DT 419*	46	1 wk

TRINITY — See *Julie DRISCOLL, Brian AUGER and the TRINITY*

TRISTRAM — See *NEW VAUDEVILLE BAND*

TROGGS

UK, male vocal/instrumental group

5 May 66	● WILD THING *Fontana TF 689*	2	12 wks
14 Jul 66	★ WITH A GIRL LIKE YOU *Fontana TF 717*	1	12 wks
29 Sep 66	● I CAN'T CONTROL MYSELF *Page One POF 001*	2	14 wks
15 Dec 66	● ANY WAY THAT YOU WANT ME *Page One POF 010*	8	10 wks
16 Feb 67	GIVE IT TO ME *Page One POF 015*	12	10 wks
1 Jun 67	NIGHT OF THE LONG GRASS *Page One POF 022*	17	6 wks
26 Jul 67	HI HI HAZEL *Page One POF 030*	42	3 wks
18 Oct 67	● LOVE IS ALL AROUND *Page One POF 040*	5	14 wks
28 Feb 68	LITTLE GIRL *Page One POF 056*	37	4 wks

TROUBADOURS DU ROI BAUDOUIN

Zaire, male/female vocal group

19 Mar 69	SANCTUS (MISSA LUBA) *Philips BF 1732*	28	6 wks
7 May 69	SANCTUS (MISSA LUBA) (re-entry) *Philips BF 1732*	37	5 wks

Doris TROY

US, female vocalist

19 Nov 64	WHATCHA GONNA DO ABOUT IT *Atlantic AT 4011*	37	7 wks
21 Jan 65	WHATCHA GONNA DO ABOUT IT (re-entry) *Atlantic AT 4011*	38	5 wks

TRUTH

UK, male vocal duo

3 Feb 66	GIRL *Pye 7N 17035*	27	6 wks

Tommy TUCKER

US, male vocalist

26 Mar 64	HI-HEEL SNEAKERS *Pye 7N 25238*	23	10 wks

Ike and Tina TURNER

US, male instrumentalist - guitar, and female vocalist

9 Jun 66	● RIVER DEEP MOUNTAIN HIGH *London HL 10046*	3	13 wks
28 Jul 66	TELL HER I'M NOT HOME *Warner Bros. WB 5753*	48	1 wk
27 Oct 66	A LOVE LIKE YOURS *London HL 10083*	16	10 wks
12 Feb 69	RIVER DEEP MOUNTAIN HIGH (re-issue) *London HLU 10242*	33	7 wks

Date	Title Label Number	Position		Date	Title Label Number	Position

TURTLES

US, male vocal/instrumental group

23 Mar 67	HAPPY TOGETHER *London HL 10115*	**12** 12 wks
15 Jun 67	● SHE'D RATHER BE WITH ME *London HLU 10135*	**4** 15 wks
30 Oct 68	● ELENORE *London HL 10223*	**7** 12 wks

TUXEDOS — See *Bobby ANGELO and the TUXEDOS*

TWICE AS MUCH

UK, male vocal duo

| 16 Jun 66 | SITTIN' ON A FENCE *Immediate IM 033* | **25** 9 wks |

TWINKLE

UK, female vocalist

| 26 Nov 64 | ● TERRY *Decca F 12013* | **4** 15 wks |
| 25 Feb 65 | GOLDEN LIGHTS *Decca F 12076* | **21** 5 wks |

Conway TWITTY

US, male vocalist

| 21 Jul 60 | IS A BLUE BIRD BLUE *MGM 1082* | **43** 3 wks |
| 23 Feb 61 | C'EST SI BON *MGM 1118* | **40** 3 wks |

TYMES

US, male vocal group

| 25 Jul 63 | SO MUCH IN LOVE *Cameo Parkway P 871* | **21** 8 wks |
| 15 Jan 69 | PEOPLE *Direction 58 3903* | **16** 10 wks |

TYRANNOSAURUS REX

UK, male vocal/instrumental duo

8 May 68	DEBORA *Regal Zonophone RZ 3008*	**34** 7 wks
4 Sep 68	ONE INCH ROCK *Regal Zonophone RZ 3011*	**28** 7 wks
9 Aug 69	KING OF THE RUMBLING SPIRES *Regal Zonophone RZ 3022*	**44** 1 wk

U

UNDERTAKERS

UK, male vocal/instrumental group

| 9 Apr 64 | JUST A LITTLE BIT *Pye 7N 15607* | **49** 1 wk |

UNION GAP — See *Gary PUCKETT and the UNION GAP*

UNIT FOUR PLUS TWO

UK, male vocal/instrumental group

13 Feb 64	GREEN FIELDS *Decca F 11821*	**48** 2 wks
25 Feb 65	CONCRETE AND CLAY *Decca F 12071*	**1** 15 wks
13 May 65	YOU'VE NEVER BEEN IN LOVE LIKE THIS BEFORE *Decca F 12144*	**14** 11 wks
17 Mar 66	BABY NEVER SAY GOODBYE *Decca F 12333*	**49** 1 wk

Phil UPCHURCH COMBO

US, male instrumental group, Phil Upchurch bass guitar

| 5 May 66 | YOU CAN'T SIT DOWN *Sue WI 4005* | **39** 2 wks |

UPSETTERS

Jamaica, male instrumental group

| 4 Oct 69 | ● RETURN OF DJANGO/ DOLLAR IN THE TEETH *Upsetter US 301* | **5** 15 wks |

U.S. BONDS

US, male vocalist

| 19 Jan 61 | NEW ORLEANS *Top Rank JAR 527* | **16** 11 wks |
| 20 Jul 61 | ● QUARTER TO THREE *Top Rank JAR 575* | **7** 13 wks |

V

VAGABONDS — See *Jimmy JAMES and the VAGABONDS*

Ricky VALANCE

UK, male vocalist

| 25 Aug 60 | TELL LAURA I LOVE HER *Columbia DB 4493* | **1** 16 wks |

Frankie VALLI — See *FOUR SEASONS*

Leroy VAN DYKE

US, male vocalist

| 4 Jan 62 | ● WALK ON BY *Mercury AMT 1166* | **5** 17 wks |
| 26 Apr 62 | BIG MAN IN A BIG HOUSE *Mercury AMT 1173* | **34** 3 wks |

VANDELLAS — See *Martha REEVES and the VANDELLAS*

VANILLA FUDGE

US, male vocal/instrumental group

| 9 Aug 67 | YOU KEEP ME HANGIN' ON *Atlantic 584 123* | **18** 11 wks |

YARDBIRDS *Above* Before deciding on the name Yardbirds other possibilities they'd considered included Roll-ups, Thames, Backyard, Hobo, Motivator and Leather.

THE ZOMBIES Lead singer Colin Blunstone sandwiched between two Zombie guitarists on a 1964 edition of Top of the Pops.

Date	Title *Label Number*	Position		Date	Title *Label Number*	Position	

VANITY FARE

UK, male vocal/instrumental group

28 Aug 68	I LIVE FOR THE SUN *Page One POF 075*	20	9 wks
23 Jul 69	● EARLY IN THE MORNING *Page One POF 142*	8	12 wks
27 Dec 69	HITCHIN' A RIDE *Page One POF 158*	16	13 wks

Frankie VAUGHAN

UK, male vocalist

29 Jan 60	WHAT MORE DO YOU WANT *Philips PB 985*	25	2 wks
22 Sep 60	KOOKIE LITTLE PARADISE *Philips PB 1054*	31	5 wks
27 Oct 60	MILORD *Philips PB 1066*	34	6 wks
9 Nov 61	★ TOWER OF STRENGTH *Philips PB 1195*	1	13 wks
1 Feb 62	DON'T STOP TWIST *Philips 1219*	22	7 wks
27 Sep 62	HERCULES *Philips 326542 BF*	42	4 wks
24 Jan 63	● LOOP-DE-LOOP *Philips 326566 BF*	5	12 wks
20 Jun 63	HEY MAMA *Philips BF 1254*	21	9 wks
4 Jun 64	HELLO DOLLY *Philips BF 1339*	18	11 wks
11 Mar 65	SOMEONE MUST HAVE HURT YOU A LOT *Philips BF 1394*	46	1 wk
23 Aug 67	● THERE MUST BE A WAY *Columbia DB 8248*	7	21 wks
15 Nov 67	SO TIRED *Columbia DB 8298*	21	9 wks
28 Feb 68	NEVERTHELESS *Columbia DB 8354*	29	5 wks

Norman VAUGHAN

UK, male vocalist

| 17 May 62 | SWINGING IN THE RAIN *Pye 7N 15438* | 34 | 5 wks |

Sarah VAUGHAN

US, female vocalist

| 29 Dec 60 | LET'S/ SERENATA *Columbia DB 4542* | 37 | 3 wks |
| 2 Feb 61 | LET'S/ SERENATA (re-entry) *Columbia DB 4542* | 47 | 1 wk |

See also Billy Eckstine and Sarah Vaughan.

Bobby VEE

US, male vocalist

19 Jan 61	● RUBBER BALL *London HLG 9255*	4	11 wks
13 Apr 61	● MORE THAN I CAN SAY *London HLG 9316*	4	16 wks
3 Aug 61	● HOW MANY TEARS *London HLG 9389*	10	13 wks
26 Oct 61	● TAKE GOOD CARE OF MY BABY *London HLG 9438*	3	16 wks
21 Dec 61	● RUN TO HIM *London HLG 9470*	6	15 wks
8 Mar 62	PLEASE DON'T ASK ABOUT BARBARA *Liberty LIB 55419*	29	9 wks
7 Jun 62	● SHARING YOU *Liberty LIB 55451*	10	13 wks
27 Sep 62	A FOREVER KIND OF LOVE *Liberty LIB 10046*	13	19 wks
7 Feb 63	● THE NIGHT HAS A THOUSAND EYES *Liberty LIB 10069*	3	12 wks
20 Jun 63	BOBBY TOMORROW *Liberty LIB 55530*	21	10 wks

VELVETS

US, male vocal group

| 11 May 61 | THAT LUCKY OLD SUN *London HLU 9328* | 46 | 1 wk |
| 17 Aug 61 | TONIGHT (COULD BE THE NIGHT) *London HLU 9372* | 50 | 1 wk |

VENTURES

US, male instrumental group

8 Sep 60	● WALK DON'T RUN *Top Rank JAR 417*	8	13 wks
1 Dec 60	● PERFIDIA *London HLG 9232*	4	13 wks
9 Mar 61	RAM-BUNK-SHUSH *London HLG 9292*	45	1 wk
11 May 61	LULLABY OF THE LEAVES *London HLG 9344*	43	4 wks

Al VERLANE — See *PING PING and Al VERLANE*

VERNONS GIRLS

UK, female vocal group

17 May 62	LOVER PLEASE *Decca F 11450*	16	9 wks
23 Aug 62	LOVER PLEASE/ YOU KNOW WHAT I MEAN (re-entry) *Decca F 11450*	39	7 wks
6 Sep 62	LOCO-MOTION *Decca F 11495*	47	1 wk
18 Oct 62	YOU KNOW WHAT I MEAN (2nd re-entry) *Decca F 11450*	37	3 wks
15 Nov 62	YOU KNOW WHAT I MEAN (3rd re-entry) *Decca F 11450*	50	1 wk
3 Jan 63	FUNNY ALL OVER *Decca F 11549*	31	8 wks
18 Apr 63	DO THE BIRD *Decca F 11629*	50	1 wk
2 May 63	DO THE BIRD (re-entry) *Decca F 11629*	44	1 wk

You Know What I Mean *was not coupled with* Lover Please *on the chart of 23 Aug 62, but both sides of this record were listed for the following 6 weeks.*

VIBRATIONS — See *Tony JACKSON and the VIBRATIONS*

Gene VINCENT

US, male vocalist

8 Jan 60	WILD CAT *Capitol CL 15099*	21	3 wks
10 Mar 60	WILD CAT (re-entry) *Capitol CL 15099*	39	3 wks
10 Mar 60	MY HEART *Capitol CL 15115*	16	6 wks
28 Apr 60	MY HEART (re-entry) *Capitol CL 15115*	47	1 wk
16 Jun 60	PISTOL PACKIN' MAMA *Capitol CL 15136*	15	9 wks
1 Jun 61	SHE SHE LITTLE SHEILA *Capitol CL 15202*	22	10 wks
17 Aug 61	SHE SHE LITTLE SHEILA (re-entry) *Capitol CL 15202*	44	1 wk
31 Aug 61	I'M GOING HOME *Capitol CL 15215*	36	4 wks

Bobby VINTON

US, male vocalist

| 2 Aug 62 | ROSES ARE RED *Columbia DB 4878* | 15 | 8 wks |
| 19 Dec 63 | THERE I'VE SAID IT AGAIN *Columbia DB 7179* | 34 | 10 wks |

Date	Title Label Number	Position

VISCOUNTS

UK, male vocal group

13 Oct 60	SHORT'NIN' BREAD *Pye 7N 15287*	16	8 wks
14 Sep 61	WHO PUT THE BOMP *Pye 7N 15379*	21	10 wks

W

Adam WADE

US, male vocalist

8 Jun 61	TAKE GOOD CARE OF HER *HMV POP 843*	38	1 wk
22 Jun 61	TAKE GOOD CARE OF HER (re-entry) *HMV POP 843*	38	5 wks

WAIKIKIS

US, male instrumental group

11 Mar 65	HAWAIIAN TATTOO *Palette PG 9025*	41	2 wks

Gary WALKER

US, male vocalist

24 Feb 66	YOU DON'T LOVE ME *CBS 202036*	26	6 wks
26 May 66	TWINKIE LEE *CBS 202081*	26	6 wks

See also Walker Brothers.

John WALKER

US, male vocalist

5 Jul 67	ANNABELLA *Philips BF 1593*	48	1 wk
19 Jul 67	ANNABELLA (re-entry) *Philips BF 1593*	24	5 wks

See also Walker Brothers.

Junior WALKER and the ALL-STARS

US, male instrumental/vocal group, Junior Walker tenor sax

18 Aug 66	HOW SWEET IT IS *Tamla Motown TMG 571*	22	10 wks
2 Apr 69	(I'M A) ROAD RUNNER *Tamla Motown TMG 691*	12	12 wks
18 Oct 69	WHAT DOES IT TAKE (TO WIN YOUR LOVE) *Tamla Motown TMG 712*	13	12 wks

Scott WALKER

US, male vocalist

8 Dec 67	JACKIE *Philips BF 1628*	22	9 wks
1 May 68	● JOANNA *Philips BF 1662*	7	11 wks
11 Jun 69	LIGHTS OF CINCINATTI *Philips BF 1793*	13	10 wks

See also Walker Brothers.

WALKER BROTHERS

US, male vocal group

29 Apr 65	LOVE HER *Philips BF 1409*	20	13 wks
19 Aug 65	★ MAKE IT EASY ON YOURSELF *Philips BF 1428*	1	14 wks
2 Dec 65	● MY SHIP IS COMING IN *Philips BF 1454*	3	12 wks
3 Mar 66	★ THE SUN AIN'T GONNA SHINE ANYMORE *Philips BF 1473*	1	11 wks
14 Jul 66	(BABY) YOU DON'T HAVE TO TELL ME *Philips BF 1497*	13	8 wks
22 Sep 66	ANOTHER TEAR FALLS *Philips BF 1514*	12	8 wks
15 Dec 66	DEADLIER THAN THE MALE *Philips BF 1537*	34	6 wks
9 Feb 67	STAY WITH ME BABY *Philips BF 1548*	26	6 wks
18 May 67	WALKING IN THE RAIN *Philips BF 1576*	26	6 wks

See also Gary Walker; John Walker; Scott Walker.

Jerry WALLACE

US, male vocalist

23 Jun 60	YOU'RE SINGING OUR LOVE SONG TO SOMEBODY ELSE *London HLH 9110*	46	1 wk

Bob WALLIS and his STORYVILLE JAZZ BAND

UK, male jazz band, Bob Wallis trumpet

6 Jul 61	I'M SHY MARY ELLEN I'M SHY *Pye Jazz 7NJ 2043*	44	2 wks
4 Jan 62	COME ALONG PLEASE *Pye Jazz 7NJ 2048*	33	5 wks

WARM SOUNDS

UK, male vocal duo

4 May 67	BIRDS AND BEES *Deram DM 120*	27	6 wks

Dionne WARWICK

US, female vocalist

13 Feb 64	ANYONE WHO HAD A HEART *Pye International 7N 25234*	42	3 wks
16 Apr 64	● WALK ON BY *Pye International 7N 25241*	9	14 wks
30 Jul 64	YOU'LL NEVER GET TO HEAVEN *Pye International 7N 25256*	20	8 wks
8 Oct 64	REACH OUT FOR ME *Pye International 7N 25265*	23	7 wks

Date	Title Label Number	Position
1 Apr 65	**YOU CAN HAVE HIM** Pye International 7N 25290	37 5 wks
13 Mar 68	**VALLEY OF THE DOLLS** Pye International 7N 25445	28 8 wks
15 May 68	● **DO YOU KNOW THE WAY TO SAN JOSE** Pye International 7N 25457	8 10 wks

US, female vocalist

30 Nov 61	**SEPTEMBER IN THE RAIN** Mercury AMT 1162	35 3 wks
18 Jan 62	**SEPTEMBER IN THE RAIN** (re-entry) Mercury AMT 1162	49 1 wk

JAM BAND

UK, male vocalist, male instrumental backing group

19 May 66	**WATER** Piccadilly 7N 35312	39 8 wks
21 Jul 66	**HI HI HAZEL** Piccadilly 7N 35329	45 3 wks
25 Aug 66	**HI HI HAZEL** (re-entry) Piccadilly 7N 35329	48 1 wk
6 Oct 66	**QUE SERA SERA** Piccadilly 7N 35346	43 3 wks
2 Feb 67	**MICHAEL** Piccadilly 7N 35359	39 5 wks

UK, male instrumentalist, guitar

10 Mar 60	**BIG BEAT BOOGIE** Top Rank JAR 300	37 3 wks
7 Apr 60	**BIG BEAT BOOGIE** (re-entry) Top Rank JAR 300	49 1 wk
9 Jun 60	**TWELFTH STREET RAG** Top Rank JAR 360	47 2 wks
28 Jul 60	**APACHE** Top Rank JAR 415	44 1 wk
11 Aug 60	**APACHE** (re-entry) Top Rank JAR 415	24 3 wks
27 Oct 60	**SORRY ROBBIE** Top Rank JAR 517	28 11 wks
2 Feb 61	**GINCHY** Top Rank JAR 537	35 5 wks
4 May 61	**MR. GUITAR** Top Rank JAR 559	47 1 wk

UK, orchestra

15 Sep 60	**CARIBBEAN HONEYMOON** Oriole CB 1559	42 4 wks

UK, male vocalist

1 Aug 63	**ONLY THE HEARTACHES** Parlophone R 5031	22 10 wks

US, female vocalist

21 May 64	● **MY GUY** Stateside SS 288	5 14 wks

See also Marvin Gaye and Mary Wells.

Date	Title Label Number	Position
	UK, male instrumentalist, trumpet	
10 Aug 61	**TANSY** Columbia DB 4686	45 4 wks

UK, female vocalist

14 Jan 65	**GOING OUT OF MY HEAD** Decca F 12046	39 4 wks

UK, male vocalist

9 Aug 67	● **EXCERPT FROM A TEENAGE OPERA** Parlophone R 5623	2 15 wks
22 Nov 67	**SAM** Parlophone R 5651	38 3 wks

Kim WESTON — See *Marvin GAYE and Kim WESTON*

WHALERS — See *Hal PAGE and the WHALERS*

UK, male vocalist

24 Nov 60	**I BELIEVE** Decca F 11289	49 1 wk

South Africa, male vocalist

8 Nov 69	**DURHAM TOWN (THE LEAVIN')** Columbia DB 8613	12 18 wks

UK, male vocal/instrumental group

18 Feb 65	● **I CAN'T EXPLAIN** Brunswick 05926	8 13 wks
27 May 65	● **ANYWAY ANYHOW ANYWHERE** Brunswick 05935	10 12 wks
4 Nov 65	● **MY GENERATION** Brunswick 05944	2 13 wks
10 Mar 66	● **SUBSTITUTE** Reaction 591 001	5 13 wks
24 Mar 66	**A LEGAL MATTER** Brunswick 05956	32 6 wks
1 Sep 66	● **I'M A BOY** Reaction 591 004	2 13 wks
1 Sep 66	**THE KIDS ARE ALRIGHT** Brunswick 05965	41 2 wks
22 Sep 66	**THE KIDS ARE ALRIGHT** (re-entry) Brunswick 05965	48 1 wk
15 Dec 66	● **HAPPY JACK** Reaction 591 010	3 11 wks
27 Apr 67	● **PICTURES OF LILY** Track 604 002	4 10 wks
26 Jul 67	**THE LAST TIME/ UNDER MY THUMB** Track 604 006	44 3 wks
18 Oct 67	● **I CAN SEE FOR MILES** Track 604 011	10 12 wks
19 Jun 68	**DOGS** Track 604 023	25 5 wks
23 Oct 68	**MAGIC BUS** Track 604 024	26 6 wks
19 Mar 69	● **PINBALL WIZARD** Track 604 027	4 13 wks

Date	Title Label Number	Position		Date	Title Label Number	Position

Marty WILDE

UK, male vocalist

1 Jan 60	● BAD BOY *Philips PB 972*	**7**	5 wks
10 Mar 60	JOHNNY ROCCO *Philips PB 1002*	**30**	4 wks
19 May 60	THE FIGHT *Philips PB 1022*	**47**	1 wk
22 Dec 60	LITTLE GIRL *Philips PB 1078*	**16**	9 wks
26 Jan 61	● RUBBER BALL *Philips PB 1101*	**9**	9 wks
27 Jul 61	HIDE AND SEEK *Philips PB 1161*	**47**	2 wks
9 Nov 61	TOMORROW'S CLOWN *Philips PB 1191*	**33**	5 wks
24 May 62	JEZEBEL *Philips PB 1240*	**19**	12 wks
25 Oct 62	EVER SINCE YOU SAID GOODBYE *Philips 326546 BF*	**31**	7 wks

Andy WILLIAMS

US, male vocalist

14 Jun 62	STRANGER ON THE SHORE *CBS AAG 103*	**30**	10 wks
21 Mar 63	● CAN'T GET USED TO LOSING YOU *CBS AAG 138*	**2**	18 wks
27 Feb 64	A FOOL NEVER LEARNS *CBS AAG 182*	**40**	4 wks
16 Sep 65	● ALMOST THERE *CBS 201813*	**2**	17 wks
24 Feb 66	MAY EACH DAY *CBS 202042*	**19**	8 wks
22 Sep 66	IN THE ARMS OF LOVE *CBS 202300*	**33**	7 wks
4 May 67	MUSIC TO WATCH GIRLS BY *CBS 2675*	**33**	6 wks
2 Aug 67	MORE AND MORE *CBS 2886*	**45**	1 wk
13 Mar 68	● CAN'T TAKE MY EYES OFF YOU *CBS 3928*	**5**	18 wks
7 May 69	HAPPY HEART *CBS 4062*	**47**	1 wk
21 May 69	HAPPY HEART (re-entry) *CBS 4062*	**19**	9 wks

Danny WILLIAMS

UK, male vocalist

25 May 61	WE WILL NEVER BE AS YOUNG AS THIS AGAIN *HMV POP 839*	**44**	3 wks
6 Jul 61	THE MIRACLE OF YOU *HMV POP 885*	**41**	8 wks
2 Nov 61	★ MOON RIVER *HMV POP 932*	**1**	19 wks
18 Jan 62	JEANNIE *HMV POP 968*	**14**	14 wks
12 Apr 62	● WONDERFUL WORLD OF THE YOUNG *HMV POP 1002*	**8**	13 wks
5 Jul 62	TEARS *HMV POP 1035*	**22**	7 wks
28 Feb 63	MY OWN TRUE LOVE *HMV POP 1112*	**45**	3 wks

Mason WILLIAMS

US, male instrumentalist, guitar

28 Aug 68	● CLASSICAL GAS *Warner Bros. WB 7190*	**9**	13 wks

Maurice WILLIAMS and the ZODIACS

US, male vocal group

5 Jan 61	STAY *Top Rank JAR 526*	**14**	9 wks

Jackie WILSON

US, male vocalist

15 Sep 60	ALL MY LOVE *Coral Q 72407*	**33**	6 wks
3 Nov 60	ALL MY LOVE (re-entry) *Coral Q 72407*	**47**	1 wk
22 Dec 60	ALONE AT LAST *Coral Q 72412*	**50**	1 wk
14 May 69	(YOUR LOVE KEEPS LIFTING ME) HIGHER AND HIGHER *MCA BAG 2*	**11**	11 wks

Stevie WONDER

US, male vocalist/instrumentalist, mainly keyboards & harmonica

3 Feb 66	UPTIGHT *Tamla Motown TMG 545*	**14**	10 wks
18 Aug 66	BLOWIN' IN THE WIND *Tamla Motown TMG 570*	**36**	5 wks
5 Jan 67	A PLACE IN THE SUN *Tamla Motown TMG 588*	**20**	5 wks
26 Jul 67	● I WAS MADE TO LOVE HER *Tamla Motown TMG 613*	**5**	15 wks
25 Oct 67	I'M WONDERING *Tamla Motown TMG 626*	**22**	8 wks
8 May 68	SHOO BE DOO BE DOO DA DAY *Tamla Motown TMG 653*	**46**	4 wks
18 Dec 68	● FOR ONCE IN MY LIFE *Tamla Motown TMG 679*	**3**	13 wks
19 Mar 69	I DON'T KNOW WHY *Tamla Motown TMG 690*	**14**	10 wks
9 Jul 69	I DON'T KNOW WHY (re-entry) *Tamla Motown TMG 690*	**43**	1 wk
16 Jul 69	● MY CHERIE AMOUR *Tamla Motown TMG 690*	**4**	16 wks
15 Nov 69	● YESTER-ME YESTER-YOU YESTERDAY *Tamla Motown TMG 717*	**2**	13 wks

Brenton WOOD

US, male vocalist

27 Dec 67	● GIMME LITTLE SIGN *Liberty LBF 15021*	**8**	14 wks

Mark WYNTER

UK, male vocalist

25 Aug 60	IMAGE OF A GIRL *Decca F 11263*	**11**	10 wks
10 Nov 60	KICKING UP THE LEAVES *Decca F 11279*	**24**	10 wks
9 Mar 61	DREAM GIRL *Decca F 11323*	**27**	5 wks
8 Jun 61	EXCLUSIVELY YOURS *Decca F 11354*	**32**	7 wks
4 Oct 62	● VENUS IN BLUE JEANS *Pye 7N 15466*	**4**	15 wks
13 Dec 62	● GO AWAY LITTLE GIRL *Pye 7N 15482*	**6**	11 wks
6 Jun 63	SHY GIRL *Pye 7N 15525*	**28**	6 wks
14 Nov 63	IT'S ALMOST TOMORROW *Pye 7N 15577*	**12**	12 wks
9 Apr 64	ONLY YOU *Pye 7N 15626*	**38**	4 wks

Date	Title Label Number	Position	Date	Title Label Number	Position

X

UK, female vocalist

1 Aug 63	**CHRISTINE** *Ember S 175*	**37**	6 wks

Miss X was Joyce Blair.

Y

Germany, orchestra

29 Oct 64	● **TOKYO MELODY** *Polydor YNH 52341*	**9**	11 wks

US, male vocal duo

9 Aug 69	**IN THE YEAR 2525 (EXORDIUM AND TERMINUS)** *RCA 1860*	**1**	13 wks

YARDBIRDS

UK, male vocal/instrumental group

12 Nov 64	**GOOD MORNING LITTLE SCHOOLGIRL** *Columbia DB 7391*	**44**	4 wks
18 Mar 65	● **FOR YOUR LOVE** *Columbia DB 7499*	**3**	12 wks
17 Jun 65	● **HEART FULL OF SOUL** *Columbia DB 7594*	**2**	13 wks
14 Oct 65	● **EVIL HEARTED YOU/ STILL I'M SAD** *Columbia DB 7706*	**3**	10 wks
3 Mar 66	● **SHAPES OF THINGS** *Columbia DB 7848*	**3**	9 wks
2 Jun 66	● **OVER UNDER SIDEWAYS DOWN** *Columbia DB 7928*	**10**	9 wks
27 Oct 66	**HAPPENINGS TEN YEARS TIME AGO** *Columbia DB 8024*	**43**	5 wks

US, male vocalist

16 Feb 61	**HEY GOOD LOOKING** *Polydor NH 66957*	**45**	1 wk

UK, male vocal/instrumental group

18 Mar 65	**SHE'S LOST YOU** *Columbia DB 7481*	**48**	1 wk

ZODIACS — See *Maurice WILLIAMS and the ZODIACS*

Jimmy YOUNG

UK, male vocalist

10 Oct 63	**MISS YOU** *Columbia DB 7119*	**15**	13 wks
26 Mar 64	**UNCHAINED MELODY** *Columbia DB 7234*	**43**	3 wks

UK, male vocal/instrumental group

13 Aug 64	**SHE'S NOT THERE** *Decca F 11940*	**12**	11 wks
11 Feb 65	**TELL HER NO** *Decca F 12072*	**42**	5 wks

Karen YOUNG

UK, female vocalist

6 Sep 69	● **NOBODY'S CHILD** *Major Minor MM 625*	**6**	21 wks

YOUNG IDEA

UK, male vocal duo

29 Jun 67	● **WITH A LITTLE HELP FROM MY FRIENDS** *Columbia DB 8205*	**10**	6 wks

YOUNG RASCALS

US, male vocal/instrumental group

25 May 67	● **GROOVIN'** *Atlantic 584 111*	**8**	13 wks
16 Aug 67	**A GIRL LIKE YOU** *Atlantic 584 128*	**37**	4 wks

Leon YOUNG STRING CHORALE — See *Mr Acker BILK*

Hit singles alphabetically by title

133

Title — Act (Position)	Year of Chart Entry
DELTA LADY — Joe **Cocker** (10)	69
LA DERNIERE VALSE — Mireille **Mathieu** (26)	67
DESAFINADO — Ella **Fitzgerald** (38)	62
DESAFINADO — Stan **Getz** and Charlie **Byrd** (11)	62
DETROIT CITY — Tom **Jones** (8)	67
DEVIL IN DISGUISE — Elvis **Presley** (1)	63
DEVIL WOMAN — Marty **Robbins** (5)	62
DIAMONDS — Jet **Harris** and Tony **Meehan** (1)	63
DIANE — **Bachelors** (1)	64
DICK-A-DUM-DUM (KING'S ROAD) — Des **O'Connor** (14)	69
DIGGIN' MY POTATOES — **Heinz** (49)	65
DIMPLES — John Lee **Hooker** (23)	64
DISTANT DRUMS — Jim **Reeves** (1)	66
DIZZY — Tommy **Roe** (1)	69
DO I LOVE YOU — **Ronettes** (35)	64
DO IT AGAIN — **Beach Boys** (1)	68
DO THE BIRD — Dee Dee **Sharp** (46)	63
DO THE BIRD — **Vernons Girls** (44)	63
DO THE CLAM — Elvis **Presley** (19)	65
DO WAH DIDDY DIDDY — **Manfred Mann** (1)	64
DO WHAT YOU DO DO WELL — Ned **Miller** (48)	65
DO WHAT YOU GOTTA DO — **Four Tops** (11)	69
DO WHAT YOU GOTTA DO — Nina **Simone** (2)	68
DO YOU KNOW THE WAY TO SAN JOSE — Dionne **Warwick** (8)	68
DO YOU LOVE ME — Dave **Clark Five** (30)	63
DO YOU LOVE ME — Brian **Poole** and the Tremeloes (1)	63
DO YOU MIND — Anthony **Newley** (1)	60
DO YOU REALLY LOVE ME TOO — Billy **Fury** (13)	64
DO YOU REMEMBER — **Scaffold** (34)	68
DO YOU WANNA DANCE — Cliff **Richard** (2)	62
DO YOU WANT ME TO — **Four Pennies** (47)	64
DO YOU WANT TO KNOW A SECRET? — Billy J. **Kramer** and the Dakotas (2)	63
DR. FINLAY — Andy **Stewart** (43)	65
THEME FROM DR. KILDARE — Johnny **Spence** (15)	62
DR. KILDARE (THREE STARS WILL SHINE TONIGHT), THEME FROM — Richard **Chamberlain** (12)	62
DOESN'T ANYBODY KNOW MY NAME? — Vince **Hill** (50)	69
DOGS — **Who** (25)	68
DOLL HOUSE — **King Brothers** (21)	61
DOLLAR IN THE TEETH — **Upsetters** (5)	69
DOMINIQUE — **Singing Nun (Soeur Sourire)** (7)	63
DON JUAN — Dave **Dee, Dozy, Beaky, Mick and Tich** (23)	69
DONALD WHERE'S YOUR TROOSERS — Andy **Stewart** (37)	60
DON'T ANSWER ME — Cilla **Black** (6)	66
DON'T BE CRUEL — Bill **Black's Combo** (32)	60
DON'T BET MONEY HONEY — Linda **Scott** (50)	61
DON'T BLAME ME — Frank **Ifield** (8)	64
DON'T BREAK THE HEART THAT LOVES YOU — Connie **Francis** (39)	62
DON'T BRING LULU — Dorothy **Provine** (17)	61
DON'T BRING ME DOWN [A] — **Pretty Things** (10)	64
DON'T BRING ME DOWN [B] — **Animals** (6)	66
DON'T BRING ME YOUR HEARTACHES — Paul and Barry **Ryan** (13)	65
DON'T EVER CHANGE — **Crickets** (5)	62
DON'T FIGHT IT — Wilson **Pickett** (29)	65
DON'T FORGET TO CATCH ME — Cliff **Richard** (21)	68
DON'T FORGET TO REMEMBER — **Bee Gees** (2)	69
DON'T HANG UP — **Orlons** (39)	62
DON'T JUMP OFF THE ROOF DAD — Tommy **Cooper** (40)	61
DON'T LET ME BE MISUNDERSTOOD — **Animals** (3)	65
DON'T LET THE RAIN COME DOWN — Ronnie **Hilton** (21)	64
DON'T LET THE SUN CATCH YOU CRYING — **Gerry and the Pacemakers** (6)	64
DON'T MAKE ME — Babbity **Blue** (48)	65
DON'T MAKE ME OVER — **Swinging Blue Jeans** (31)	66
DON'T MAKE MY BABY BLUE — **Shadows** (10)	65
DON'T SET ME FREE — Ray **Charles** (37)	63
DON'T SLEEP IN THE SUBWAY — Petula **Clark** (12)	67
DON'T STOP LOVIN' ME BABY — **Pinkerton's Assorted Colours** (50)	66
DON'T STOP THE CARNIVAL — Alan **Price Set** (13)	68
DON'T STOP TWIST — Frankie **Vaughan** (22)	62
DON'T TALK TO HIM — Cliff **Richard** (2)	63
DON'T THAT BEAT ALL — Adam **Faith** (8)	62

Title — Act (Position)	Year of Chart Entry
DON'T THROW AWAY ALL THOSE TEARDROPS — Frankie **Avalon** (37)	60
DON'T THROW YOUR LOVE AWAY — **Searchers** (1)	64
DON'T TREAT ME LIKE A CHILD — Helen **Shapiro** (3)	61
DON'T TRY TO CHANGE ME — **Crickets** (37)	63
DON'T TURN AROUND — **Merseybeats** (13)	64
DON'T WORRY — Billy **Fury** (40)	61
DON'T YOU KNOW IT — Adam **Faith** (12)	61
DON'T YOU THINK IT'S TIME — Mike **Berry** with the Outlaws (6)	63
DOOR IS STILL OPEN TO MY HEART, THE — Dean **Martin** (42)	64
DOWN IN THE BOONDOCKS — Billy Joe **Royal** (38)	65
DOWN THE RIVER NILE — John **Leyton** (42)	62
DOWN YONDER — **Johnny and the Hurricanes** (8)	60
DOWNTOWN — Petula **Clark** (2)	64
DRAGONFLY — **Tornados** (41)	63
DREAM A LITTLE DREAM OF ME — Mama **Cass** (11)	68
DREAM A LITTLE DREAM OF ME — Anita **Harris** (33)	68
DREAM BABY — Roy **Orbison** (2)	62
DREAM GIRL — Mark **Wynter** (27)	61
DREAM OF OLWEN — **Second City Sound** (43)	69
DREAMIN' — Johnny **Burnette** (5)	60
DREAMS I DREAM, THE — **Shadows** (42)	66
DRINK UP THY ZIDER — Adge **Cutler and the Wurzels** (45)	67
DRIVIN' HOME — Duane **Eddy** (30)	61
DRUMMIN' UP A STORM — Sandy **Nelson** (39)	62
DRUMS ARE MY BEAT — Sandy **Nelson** (30)	62
DUM DUM — Brenda **Lee** (22)	61
DURHAM TOWN (THE LEAVIN') — Roger **Whittaker** (12)	69
EARLY IN THE MORNING — **Vanity Fare** (8)	69
EASIER SAID THAN DONE — **Essex** (41)	63
EAST WEST — **Herman's Hermits** (37)	66
EASY GOING ME — Adam **Faith** (12)	61
EBB TIDE — **Righteous Brothers** (48)	66
EDELWEISS — Vince **Hill** (2)	67
EENY MEENY — **Showstoppers** (33)	68
EIGHT BY TEN — Ken **Dodd** (22)	64
EIGHT MILES HIGH — **Byrds** (24)	66
EIGHTEEN YELLOW ROSES — Bobby **Darin** (37)	63
EL PASO — Marty **Robbins** (19)	60
ELEANOR RIGBY — **Beatles** (1)	66
ELEANOR RIGBY — Ray **Charles** (36)	68
ELENORE — **Turtles** (7)	68
ELISABETH SERENADE — Gunther **Kallman Choir** (45)	64
ELOISE — Barry **Ryan** (2)	68
ELUSIVE BUTTERFLY — Val **Doonican** (5)	66
ELUSIVE BUTTERFLY — Bob **Lind** (5)	66
EMERALD CITY — **Seekers** (50)	67
EMOTIONS — Brenda **Lee** (45)	61
END OF THE WORLD — Skeeter **Davis** (18)	63
ENGINE ENGINE NO. 9 — Roger **Miller** (33)	65
ENGLAND SWINGS — Roger **Miller** (13)	65
ENGLISH COUNTRY GARDEN — Jimmie **Rodgers** (5)	62
ENTRY OF THE GLADIATORS — **Nero and the Gladiators** (37)	61
ET MÊME — Francoise **Hardy** (31)	65
EVE OF DESTRUCTION — Barry **McGuire** (3)	65
EVEN MORE PARTY POPS — Russ **Conway** (27)	60
EVEN THE BAD TIMES ARE GOOD — **Tremeloes** (4)	67
EVER SINCE YOU SAID GOODBYE — Marty **Wilde** (31)	62
EVERLASTING LOVE — **Love Affair** (1)	68
EVERLOVIN' — Rick **Nelson** (23)	61
EVERY LITTLE BIT HURTS — **Spencer Davis Group** (41)	65
EVERYBODY — Tommy **Roe** (9)	63
EVERYBODY KNOWS [A] — Dave **Clark Five** (37)	65
EVERYBODY KNOWS [B] — Dave **Clark Five** (2)	67
EVERYBODY LOVES SOMEBODY — Dean **Martin** (11)	64
EVERYBODY'S GONNA BE HAPPY — **Kinks** (17)	65
EVERYBODY'S SOMEBODY'S FOOL — Connie **Francis** (5)	60
EVERYBODY'S TALKIN' — **Nilsson** (23)	69
EVERYBODY'S TWISTING — Frank **Sinatra** (22)	62
EVERYDAY — **Moody Blues** (44)	65

Title — Act (Position)	Year of Chart Entry
EVERYDAY PEOPLE — **Sly and the Family Stone** (36)	69
EVERYONE'S GONE TO THE MOON — Jonathan **King** (4)	65
EVERYTHING I AM — **Plastic Penny** (6)	68
EVERYTHING'S ALRIGHT — **Mojos** (9)	64
EVIL HEARTED YOU — **Yardbirds** (3)	65
EXCLUSIVELY YOURS — Mark **Wynter** (32)	61
EXCUSE ME BABY — **Magic Lanterns** (44)	66
'EXODUS', THEME FROM — **Ferrante and Teicher** (6)	61
'EXODUS', THEME FROM — **Semprini** (25)	61
EXPRESSO BONGO (EP) — Cliff **Richard** (14)	60
F. B. I. — **Shadows** (6)	61
FA FA FA FA FA (SAD SONG) — Otis **Redding** (23)	66
FALL IN LOVE WITH YOU — Cliff **Richard** (2)	60
FALLING — Roy **Orbison** (9)	63
FANLIGHT FANNY — Clinton **Ford** (22)	62
FAR AWAY — Shirley **Bassey** (24)	62
FARAWAY PLACES — **Bachelors** (36)	63
FAREWELL ANGELINA — Joan **Baez** (35)	65
FEEL SO FINE — Johnny **Preston** (18)	60
FERRIS WHEEL — **Everly Brothers** (22)	64
FERRY ACROSS THE MERSEY — **Gerry and the Pacemakers** (8)	64
FEVER — **McCoys** (44)	65
FEVER — Helen **Shapiro** (38)	64
59TH STREET BRIDGE SONG (FEELING GROOVY) — **Harpers Bizarre** (34)	67
FIGHT, THE — Marty **Wilde** (47)	60
FINCHLEY CENTRAL — **New Vaudeville Band** (11)	67
FIND MY WAY BACK HOME — **Nashville Teens** (34)	65
FINGS AIN'T WOT THEY USED T'BE — Max **Bygraves** (5)	60
FINGS AIN'T WOT THEY USED T'BE — Russ **Conway** (47)	60
FIRE — **Crazy World of Arthur Brown** (1)	68
FIRE BRIGADE — **Move** (3)	68
FIREBALL — Don **Spencer** (32)	63
FIRST CUT IS THE DEEPEST — P. P. **Arnold** (18)	67
FIRST OF MAY — **Bee Gees** (6)	69
FIRST TASTE OF LOVE — Ben E. **King** (27)	61
FIRST TIME, THE — Adam **Faith** (5)	63
5-4-3-2-1 — **Manfred Mann** (5)	64
FIVE LITTLE FINGERS — Frankie **McBride** (19)	67
FLOWERS IN THE RAIN — **Move** (2)	67
FLOWERS ON THE WALL — **Statler Brothers** (38)	66
FOGGY MOUNTAIN BREAKDOWN — Lester **Flatt and Earl Scruggs** (39)	67
FOLK SINGER, THE — Tommy **Roe** (4)	63
FOLLOW THAT DREAM (EP) — Elvis **Presley** (34)	62
FOOL AM I, A — Cilla **Black** (13)	66
FOOL NEVER LEARNS, A — Andy **Williams** (40)	64
FOOL NUMBER ONE — Brenda **Lee** (38)	61
FOOLISH LITTLE GIRL — **Shirelles** (38)	63
FOOLS RUSH IN — Brook **Benton** (50)	61
FOOLS RUSH IN — Rick **Nelson** (12)	63
FOOT TAPPER — **Shadows** (1)	63
FOOTSTEPS — Ronnie **Carroll** (36)	60
FOOTSTEPS — Steve **Lawrence** (4)	60
FOR MAMA — Matt **Monro** (36)	64
FOR ONCE IN MY LIFE — Dorothy **Squires** (24)	69
FOR ONCE IN MY LIFE — Stevie **Wonder** (3)	68
FOR WHOM THE BELL TOLLS — Simon **Dupree and The Big Sound** (43)	68
FOR YOU — Rick **Nelson** (14)	64
FOR YOUR LOVE — **Yardbirds** (3)	65
FOREVER CAME TODAY — **Supremes** (28)	68
FOREVER KIND OF LOVE, A — Bobby **Vee** (13)	62
FORGET HIM — Bobby **Rydell** (13)	63
FORGET ME NOT — Eden **Kane** (3)	62
FOUR LITTLE HEELS — **Avons** (45)	60
FOUR LITTLE HEELS — Brian **Hyland** (29)	60
FOX ON THE RUN — **Manfred Mann** (5)	68
FRANKIE AND JOHNNY — Sam **Cooke** (30)	63
FRANKIE AND JOHNNY — Elvis **Presley** (21)	66
FRIDAY ON MY MIND — **Easybeats** (6)	66
FRIENDS — **Beach Boys** (25)	68
FRIGHTENED CITY — **Shadows** (3)	61
FROM A JACK TO A KING — Ned **Miller** (2)	63
FROM A WINDOW — Billy J. **Kramer and the Dakotas** (10)	64
FROM HERE TO THERE TO YOU — Hank **Locklin** (44)	62

Title — Act (Position)	Year of Chart Entry

Title — Act (Position)	Year of Chart Entry

HELULE HELULE — **Tremeloes** (14) — 68
HER ROYAL MAJESTY — James **Darren** (36) — 62
HERCULES — Frankie **Vaughan** (42) — 62
HERE COMES MY BABY — **Tremeloes** (4) — 67
HERE COMES THAT FEELING — Brenda **Lee** (5) — 62
HERE COMES THE JUDGE [A] — Shorty **Long** (30) — 68
HERE COMES THE JUDGE [B] — Pigmeat **Markham** (19) — 68
HERE COMES THE NICE — **Small Faces** (12) — 67
HERE COMES THE NIGHT — **Lulu** (50) — 64
HERE COMES THE NIGHT — **Them** (2) — 65
HERE COMES THE STAR — **Herman's Hermits** (33) — 69
HERE I GO AGAIN — **Hollies** (4) — 64
HERE IT COMES AGAIN — **Fortunes** (4) — 65
HERE WE GO AGAIN — Ray **Charles** (38) — 67
HERE WE GO ROUND THE MULBERRY BUSH — **Traffic** (8) — 67
HEROES AND VILLAINS — **Beach Boys** (8) — 67
HE'S A REBEL — **Crystals** (19) — 62
HE'S GOT NO LOVE — **Searchers** (12) — 65
HE'S IN TOWN — **Rockin' Berries** (3) — 64
HE'S OLD ENOUGH TO KNOW BETTER — **Brook Brothers** (37) — 62
HE'S SO FINE — **Chiffons** (16) — 63
HE'S THE ONE — Billie **Davis** (40) — 63
HEY! BABY — Bruce **Channel** (2) — 62
HEY GIRL — **Small Faces** (10) — 66
HEY GOOD LOOKIN' — Bo **Diddley** (39) — 65
HEY GOOD LOOKING — Tommy **Zang** (45) — 61
HEY JOE — Jimi **Hendrix Experience** (6) — 67
HEY JUDE — **Beatles** (1) — 68
HEY JUDE — Wilson **Pickett** (16) — 69
HEY LITTLE GIRL — Del **Shannon** (2) — 62
HEY MAMA — Frankie **Vaughan** (21) — 63
HEY PAULA — **Paul and Paula** (8) — 63
HI HI HAZEL — **Troggs** (42) — 67
HI HI HAZEL — Geno **Washington and the Ram Jam Band** (45) — 66
HI LILI HI LO — Alan **Price Set** (11) — 66
HIDE AND SEEK — Marty **Wilde** (47) — 61
HIDEAWAY — Dave **Dee, Dozy, Beaky, Mick and Tich** (10) — 66
HIGH HOPES — Frank **Sinatra** (42) — 60
HIGH IN THE SKY — **Amen Corner** (6) — 68
HIGH TIME — Paul **Jones** (4) — 66
HIGH VOLTAGE — **Johnny and the Hurricanes** (24) — 61
HIGHWAY CODE — **Master Singers** (25) — 66
HIGHWAY SONG — Nancy **Sinatra** (21) — 69
HI-HEEL SNEAKERS — Tommy **Tucker** (23) — 64
HI-HO SILVER LINING — Jeff **Beck** (14) — 67
HI-LILI HI-LO — Richard **Chamberlain** (20) — 63
HIPPY HIPPY SHAKE — **Swinging Blue Jeans** (2) — 63
HIS GIRL — **Guess Who** (45) — 67
HIS LATEST FLAME — Elvis **Presley** (1) — 61
HIT AND MISS — John **Barry** (10) — 60
HIT THE ROAD JACK — Ray **Charles** (6) — 61
HITCHIN' A RIDE — **Vanity Fare** (16) — 69
HOLD ME — P. J. **Proby** (3) — 64
HOLD ME TIGHT — Johnny **Nash** (5) — 68
HOLD TIGHT — Dave **Dee, Dozy, Beaky, Mick and Tich** (4) — 66
HOLE IN MY SHOE — **Traffic** (2) — 67
HOLE IN THE BUCKET — Harry **Belafonte** and Odetta (32) — 61
HOLE IN THE GROUND — Bernard **Cribbins** (9) — 62
HOLY CITY — Moira **Anderson** (43) — 69
HOLY COW — Lee **Dorsey** (6) — 67
HOMBURG — **Procol Harum** (6) — 67
HOME OF THE BRAVE — Jody **Miller** (49) — 65
HOMEWARD BOUND — Quiet **Five** (44) — 66
HOMEWARD BOUND — **Simon and Garfunkel** (9) — 66
HONEST I DO — Danny **Storm** (42) — 62
HONEY — Bobby **Goldsboro** (2) — 68
HONEY CHILE — Martha **Reeves and the Vandellas** (30) — 68
HONEY I NEED — **Pretty Things** (13) — 65
HONKY TONK WOMEN — **Rolling Stones** (1) — 69
HOT PEPPER — Floyd **Cramer** (46) — 62
HOUND DOG MAN — **Fabian** (46) — 60
HOUSE IN THE COUNTRY, A — **Pretty Things** (50) — 66
HOUSE OF THE RISING SUN — **Animals** (1) — 64
HOUSE THAT JACK BUILT, THE — Alan **Price Set** (4) — 67
HOW ABOUT THAT — Adam **Faith** (4) — 60
HOW CAN I MEET HER — **Everly Brothers** (12) — 62
HOW CAN I TELL HER — **Fourmost** (33) — 64

HOW CAN YOU TELL — Sandie **Shaw** (21) — 65
HOW DO YOU DO IT? — **Gerry and the Pacemakers** (1) — 63
HOW DO YOU KNOW IT'S LOVE — Teresa **Brewer** (21) — 60
HOW DOES THAT GRAB YOU DARLIN' — Nancy **Sinatra** (19) — 66
HOW HIGH THE MOON — Ella **Fitzgerald** (46) — 60
HOW LONG HAS IT BEEN — Jim **Reeves** (45) — 65
HOW MANY TEARS — Bobby **Vee** (10) — 61
HOW SOON — Henry **Mancini** (10) — 64
HOW SWEET IT IS — Marvin **Gaye** (49) — 64
HOW SWEET IT IS — Junior **Walker and the All-Stars** (22) — 66
HOW WONDERFUL TO KNOW — Pearl **Carr** and Teddy **Johnson** (23) — 61
HUBBLE BUBBLE TOIL AND TROUBLE — **Manfred Mann** (11) — 64
HUNDRED POUNDS OF CLAY, A — Craig **Douglas** (9) — 61
HUNGRY FOR LOVE — Johnny **Kidd and the Pirates** (20) — 63
HUNT — Barry **Ryan** (34) — 69
HURDY GURDY MAN — **Donovan** (4) — 68
HURT BY LOVE — Inez **Foxx** (40) — 64
HUSH NOT A WORD TO MARY — John **Rowles** (12) — 68
I AM A ROCK — **Simon and Garfunkel** (17) — 66
I APOLOGISE — P. J. **Proby** (11) — 65
I BELIEVE — **Bachelors** (2) — 64
I BELIEVE — David **Whitfield** (49) — 60
I BELONG — Kathy **Kirby** (36) — 65
I CAN DANCE — Brian **Poole and the Tremeloes** (31) — 63
I CAN HEAR MUSIC — **Beach Boys** (10) — 69
I CAN HEAR THE GRASS GROW — **Move** (5) — 67
I CAN SEE FOR MILES — **Who** (10) — 67
I CAN SING A RAINBOW - LOVE IS BLUE (MEDLEY) — **Dells** (15) — 69
I CAN TAKE OR LEAVE YOUR LOVING — **Herman's Hermits** (11) — 68
I CAN'T CONTROL MYSELF — **Troggs** (2) — 66
I CAN'T EXPLAIN — **Who** (8) — 65
(I CAN'T GET NO) SATISFACTION — **Rolling Stones** (1) — 65
I CAN'T HELP IT — Johnny **Tillotson** (41) — 63,62
I CAN'T HELP MYSELF — **Four Tops** (23) — 65
I CAN'T LET GO — **Hollies** (2) — 66
I CAN'T LET MAGGIE GO — **Honeybus** (8) — 68
I CAN'T MAKE IT — **Small Faces** (26) — 67
I CAN'T MAKE IT ALONE — P. J. **Proby** (37) — 66
I CAN'T STAND IT — Spencer **Davis Group** (47) — 64
I CAN'T STOP LOVING YOU — Ray **Charles** (1) — 62
I CAN'T TURN YOU LOOSE — Otis **Redding** (29) — 66
I CLOSE MY EYES AND COUNT TO TEN — Dusty **Springfield** (4) — 68
I COULD EASILY FALL — Cliff **Richard** (9) — 64
I COULD NEVER LOVE ANOTHER — **Temptations** (47) — 68
I COULDN'T LIVE WITHOUT YOUR LOVE — Petula **Clark** (6) — 66
I COUNT THE TEARS — **Drifters** (28) — 61
I CRIED FOR YOU — Ricky **Stevens** (34) — 61
I DIDN'T MEAN TO HURT YOU — **Rockin' Berries** (43) — 64
I DON'T CARE — Los **Bravos** (16) — 66
I DON'T KNOW WHY — Stevie **Wonder** (43) — 69
I DON'T KNOW WHY [A] — Eden **Kane** (7) — 62
I DON'T KNOW WHY [B] — Stevie **Wonder** (14) — 69
I DON'T NEED ANYTHING — Sandie **Shaw** (50) — 69
I DON'T WANT OUR LOVING TO DIE — **Herd** (5) — 68
I DON'T WANT TO GO ON WITHOUT YOU — **Moody Blues** (33) — 65
I ENJOY BEING A GIRL — Pat **Suzuki** (49) — 60
I FEEL A CRY COMING ON — Hank **Locklin** (28) — 66
I FEEL FINE — **Beatles** (1) — 64
I FEEL FREE — **Cream** (11) — 66
I FEEL LOVE COMIN' ON — Felice **Taylor** (11) — 67
I FEEL SO BAD — Elvis **Presley** (4) — 61
I FEEL SOMETHING IN THE AIR — **Cher** (43) — 66
I FOUGHT THE LAW — Bobby **Fuller Four** (33) — 66
I FOUND OUT THE HARD WAY — Four **Pennies** (14) — 64
I GET AROUND — **Beach Boys** (7) — 64
I GET SO EXCITED — **Equals** (44) — 68

I GOT RHYTHM — **Happenings** (28) — 67
I GOT YOU — James **Brown and the Famous Flames** (29) — 66
I GOT YOU BABE — **Sonny and Cher** (1) — 65
I GUESS I'LL ALWAYS LOVE YOU — **Isley Brothers** (11) — 66,69
I HAD TOO MUCH TO DREAM LAST NIGHT — Electric **Prunes** (49) — 67
I HEAR A SYMPHONY — **Supremes** (39) — 65
I HEARD A HEART BREAK LAST NIGHT — Jim **Reeves** (38) — 67
I HEARD IT THROUGH THE GRAPEVINE — Marvin **Gaye** (1) — 69
I HEARD IT THROUGH THE GRAPEVINE — Gladys **Knight and the Pips** (47) — 67
I JUST DON'T KNOW WHAT TO DO WITH MYSELF — Dusty **Springfield** (3) — 64
I JUST GO FOR YOU — Jimmy **Jones** (35) — 60
I KEEP RINGING MY BABY — **Soul Brothers** (42) — 65
I KNOW A PLACE — Petula **Clark** (17) — 65
(I KNOW) I'M LOSING YOU — **Temptations** (19) — 66
I KNOW WHERE I'M GOING — **Countrymen** (45) — 62
I LEFT MY HEART IN SAN FRANCISCO — Tony **Bennett** (25) — 65
I LIKE IT — **Gerry and the Pacemakers** (1) — 63
I LIVE FOR THE SUN — **Vanity Fare** (20) — 68
I LOVE BEING IN LOVE WITH YOU — Adam **Faith** (33) — 64
I LOVE HER — Paul and Barry **Ryan** (17) — 66
I LOVE HOW YOU LOVE ME — Jimmy **Crawford** (18) — 61
I LOVE HOW YOU LOVE ME — Maureen **Evans** (34) — 64
I LOVE HOW YOU LOVE ME — Paul and Barry **Ryan** (21) — 66
I LOVE MY DOG — Cat **Stevens** (28) — 66
I LOVE THE WAY YOU LOVE — Marv **Johnson** (35) — 60
I LOVE YOU — Cliff **Richard** (1) — 60
I LOVE YOU BABY — **Freddie and the Dreamers** (16) — 64
I LOVE YOU BECAUSE — Al **Martino** (48) — 63
I LOVE YOU BECAUSE — Jim **Reeves** (5) — 64
I LOVE YOU, YES I DO — **Merseybeats** (22) — 65
I MET A GIRL — **Shadows** (22) — 66
I MISS YOU BABY — Marv **Johnson** (25) — 69
I MUST BE SEEING THINGS — Gene **Pitney** (6) — 65
I ONLY LIVE TO LOVE YOU — Cilla **Black** (26) — 67
I ONLY WANT TO BE WITH YOU — Dusty **Springfield** (4) — 63
I PRETEND — Des **O'Connor** (1) — 68
I PUT A SPELL ON YOU — Alan **Price Set** (9) — 66
I PUT A SPELL ON YOU — Nina **Simone** (28) — 65,69
I REMEMBER YOU — Frank **Ifield** (1) — 62
I SAW HER AGAIN — **Mamas and the Papas** (11) — 66
I SAW LINDA YESTERDAY — Doug **Sheldon** (36) — 63
I SAY A LITTLE PRAYER — Aretha **Franklin** (4) — 68
I SECOND THAT EMOTION — Smokey **Robinson and the Miracles** (27) — 67
I SECOND THAT EMOTION — Diana **Ross and the Supremes Temptations** (18) — 69
I SHALL BE RELEASED — **Tremeloes** (29) — 68
I SHOULD CARE — Frank **Ifield** (33) — 64
I SHOULD HAVE KNOWN BETTER — **Naturals** (24) — 64
I SPY FOR THE FBI — Jamo **Thomas** (44) — 69
I STAND ACCUSED — **Merseybeats** (38) — 66
I STILL LOVE YOU ALL — Kenny **Ball and his Jazzmen** (24) — 61
I THANK YOU — **Sam and Dave** (34) — 68
I THINK OF YOU — **Merseybeats** (5) — 64
I THREW IT ALL AWAY — Bob **Dylan** (30) — 69
I TOLD YOU SO — Jimmy **Jones** (33) — 61
I UNDERSTAND — **Freddie and the Dreamers** (5) — 64
I UNDERSTAND — **G-Clefs** (17) — 61
I WANNA BE LOVED — Ricky **Nelson** (30) — 60
I WANNA BE YOUR MAN — **Rolling Stones** (12) — 63
I WANNA GO HOME — Lonnie **Donegan** (5) — 60
I WANNA LOVE MY LIFE AWAY — Gene **Pitney** (26) — 61
I WANNA STAY HERE — **Miki and Griff** (23) — 63
I WANT CANDY — Brian **Poole and the Tremeloes** (25) — 65
I WANT TO BE WANTED — Brenda **Lee** (31) — 60
I WANT TO GO WITH YOU — Eddy **Arnold** (46) — 66
I WANT TO HOLD YOUR HAND — **Beatles** (1) — 63
I WANT TO STAY HERE — Steve and **Eydie** (3) — 63
I WANT YOU — Bob **Dylan** (16) — 66
I WANT YOU TO BE MY BABY — Billie **Davis** (33) — 68

Title — Act (Position)	Year of Chart Entry

Title — Act (Position)	Year of Chart Entry
MY OWN TRUE LOVE — Danny **Williams** (45)	63
MY SENTIMENTAL FRIEND — **Herman's Hermits** (2)	69
MY SHIP IS COMING IN — **Walker Brothers** (3)	65
MY SPECIAL DREAM — Shirley **Bassey** (32)	64
MY SUNDAY BABY — Dale **Sisters** (36)	61
MY WAY [A] — Eddie **Cochran** (23)	63
MY WAY [B] — Frank **Sinatra** (5)	69
MY WAY OF GIVING IN — Chris **Farlowe** (48)	67
MY WORLD — **Cupid's Inspiration** (33)	68
MY WORLD OF BLUE — Karl **Denver** (29)	64
MYSTERY GIRL — Jess **Conrad** (18)	61
NADINE (IS IT YOU) — Chuck **Berry** (27)	64
NASHVILLE CATS — **Lovin' Spoonful** (26)	67
NATURAL BORN BUGIE — **Humble Pie** (4)	69
NATURE BOY — Bobby **Darin** (24)	61
NATURE'S TIME FOR LOVE — Joe **Brown** (26)	63
NEAR YOU — **Migil Five** (31)	64
NEED YOUR LOVE SO BAD — **Fleetwood Mac** (31)	68,69
NEEDLES AND PINS — **Searchers** (1)	64
NEVER GOODBYE — Karl **Denver** (9)	62
NEVER LET GO — John **Barry** (49)	60
NEVER ON SUNDAY — **Chaquito** (50)	60
NEVER ON SUNDAY — Lynn **Cornell** (30)	60
NEVER ON SUNDAY — Don **Costa** (27)	60
NEVER ON SUNDAY — **Makadopulos and his Greek Serenaders** (36)	60
NEVER ON SUNDAY — **Manuel and his Music Of The Mountains** (29)	60
NEVER WED AN OLD MAN — **Dubliners** (43)	67
NEVERTHELESS — Frankie **Vaughan** (29)	68
NEW ORLEANS — **Bern Elliott and the Fenmen** (24)	64
NEW ORLEANS — 'U.S.' **Bonds** (16)	61
NEW YORK MINING DISASTER 1941 — **Bee Gees** (12)	67
NEXT DOOR TO AN ANGEL — Neil **Sedaka** (29)	62
NEXT TIME, THE — Cliff **Richard** (1)	62
NICE 'N EASY — Frank **Sinatra** (15)	60
NIGHT HAS A THOUSAND EYES, THE — Bobby **Vee** (3)	63
NIGHT IS YOUNG, THE — Gary **Miller** (29)	61
NIGHT OF FEAR — **Move** (2)	67
NIGHT OF THE LONG GRASS — **Troggs** (17)	67
NIGHT OF THE VAMPIRE — **Moontrekkers** (50)	61
NIGHTS IN WHITE SATIN — **Moody Blues** (19)	67
NINE TIMES OUT OF TEN — Cliff **Richard** (3)	60
NINETEENTH NERVOUS BREAKDOWN — **Rolling Stones** (2)	66
96 TEARS — **? (Question Mark) and the Mysterians** (37)	66
98.6 — **Bystanders** (45)	67
98.6 — **Keith** (24)	67
NO ARMS CAN EVER HOLD YOU — **Bachelors** (7)	64
NO FACE, NO NAME, NO NUMBER — **Traffic** (40)	68
NO HIDING PLACE — Ken **Mackintosh** (45)	60
NO MATTER WHAT SIGN YOU ARE — **Supremes** (37)	69
NO MILK TODAY — **Herman's Hermits** (7)	66
NO MULE'S FOOL — **Family** (29)	69
NO ONE — Ray **Charles** (35)	63
NO ONE CAN BREAK A HEART LIKE YOU — **Dave Clark Five** (28)	68
NO ONE CAN MAKE MY SUNSHINE SMILE — **Everly Brothers** (11)	62
NO ONE WILL EVER KNOW — Frank **Ifield** (25)	66
NO PARTICULAR PLACE TO GO — Chuck **Berry** (3)	64
NO REGRETS — Shirley **Bassey** (39)	65
NOBODY I KNOW — **Peter and Gordon** (10)	64
NOBODY NEEDS YOUR LOVE — Gene **Pitney** (2)	66
NOBODY'S CHILD — Karen **Young** (6)	69
NOBODY'S DARLIN' BUT MINE — Frank **Ifield** (4)	63
NON HO L'ETA PER AMARTI — Gigliola **Cinquetti** (17)	64
NO-ONE TO CRY TO — Ray **Charles** (38)	64
NORMAN — Carol **Deene** (24)	62
NORTH TO ALASKA — Johnny **Horton** (23)	61
NOT FADE AWAY — **Rolling Stones** (3)	64
NOT RESPONSIBLE — Tom **Jones** (18)	66
NOT TOO LITTLE NOT TOO MUCH — Chris **Sandford** (17)	63
NOT UNTIL THE NEXT TIME — Jim **Reeves** (13)	65
NOTHING CAN STOP ME — Gene **Chandler** (41)	68
NOTHING COMES EASY — Sandie **Shaw** (14)	66
NOW — Val **Doonican** (43)	68

Title — Act (Position)	Year of Chart Entry
NOW WE'RE THRU — **Poets** (31)	64
NOWHERE MAN — **Three Good Reasons** (47)	66
NOWHERE TO RUN — Martha Reeves and the **Vandellas** (26)	65,69
NUT ROCKER — **B. Bumble and the Stingers** (1)	62
007 — Desmond **Dekker and the Aces** (14)	67
OB-LA-DI OB-LA-DA — **Bedrocks** (20)	68
OB-LA-DI OB-LA-DA — **Marmalade** (1)	68
OBSESSION — Reg **Owen** (43)	60
ODE TO BILLY JOE — Bobbie **Gentry** (13)	67
OH CAROL — Neil **Sedaka** (3)	60
OH HAPPY DAY — Edwin **Hawkins Singers** (2)	69
OH HOW I MISS YOU — **Bachelors** (30)	67
OH LONESOME ME — Craig **Douglas** (15)	62
OH ME OH MY (I'M A FOOL FOR YOU BABY) — **Lulu** (47)	69
OH NO NOT MY BABY — **Manfred Mann** (11)	65
OH PRETTY WOMAN — Roy **Orbison** (1)	64
OH WELL — **Fleetwood Mac** (2)	69
OH! WHAT A DAY — Craig **Douglas** (43)	60
OKAY! — **Dave Dee, Dozy, Beaky, Mick and Tich** (4)	67
OL' MACDONALD — Frank **Sinatra** (11)	60
OLD OAKEN BUCKET — Tommy **Sands** (25)	60
OLD RIVERS — Walter **Brennan** (38)	62
OLD SMOKEY — **Johnny and the Hurricanes** (24)	61
OLIVE TREE — Judith **Durham** (33)	67
OLYMPIC RECORD, AN — **Barron Knights** (35)	68
ON A CAROUSEL — **Hollies** (4)	67
ON A SLOW BOAT TO CHINA — Emile **Ford and the Checkmates** (3)	60
ON MOTHER KELLY'S DOORSTEP — Danny **La Rue** (33)	68
ON MY WORD — Cliff **Richard** (12)	65
ON THE BEACH — Cliff **Richard** (7)	64
ON THE REBOUND — Floyd **Cramer** (1)	61
ON THE ROAD AGAIN — **Canned Heat** (8)	68
ONCE — **Genevieve** (43)	66
ONCE I HAD A SWEETHEART — **Pentangle** (46)	69
ONCE IN EVERY LIFETIME — Ken **Dodd** (28)	61
ONCE THERE WAS A TIME — Tom **Jones** (18)	66
ONCE UPON A DREAM — Billy **Fury** (7)	62
ONCE UPON A TIME [A] — Marvin **Gaye and Mary Wells** (50)	64
ONCE UPON A TIME [B] — Tom **Jones** (32)	65
ONE BROKEN HEART FOR SALE — Elvis **Presley** (12)	63
ONE FINE DAY — **Chiffons** (29)	63
ONE HEART BETWEEN TWO — Dave **Berry** (41)	64
ONE INCH ROCK — **Tyrannosaurus Rex** (28)	68
ONE MORE DANCE — Esther and Abi **Ofarim** (13)	68
ONE OF THE LUCKY ONES — Joan **Regan** (47)	60
ONE OF US MUST KNOW (SOONER OR LATER) — Bob **Dylan** (33)	66
ONE ROAD — **Love Affair** (16)	69
ONE TO CRY, THE — **Escorts** (49)	64
1-2-3 — Len **Barry** (3)	65
1-2-3 O'LEARY — Des O'**Connor** (4)	68
ONE WAY LOVE — Cliff **Bennett and the Rebel Rousers** (9)	64
ONION SONG — Marvin **Gaye and Tammi Terrell** (9)	69
ONLY BOY IN THE WORLD, THE — Stevie **Marsh** (37)	60
ONLY ONE WOMAN — **Marbles** (5)	68
ONLY THE HEARTACHES — Houston **Wells** (22)	63
ONLY THE LONELY — Roy **Orbison** (1)	60
ONLY YOU — Mark **Wynter** (38)	64
ONWARD CHRISTIAN SOLDIERS — Harry **Simeone Chorale** (35)	60,61,62
OOH LA LA — Joe 'Mr. Piano' **Henderson** (46)	60
OPUS 17 (DON'T YOU WORRY 'BOUT ME) — **Four Seasons** (20)	66
ORANGE BLOSSOM SPECIAL — **Spotnicks** (29)	62
OTHER MAN'S GRASS, THE — Petula **Clark** (20)	67
OUR DAY WILL COME — **Ruby and the Romantics** (38)	63
OUR FAVOURITE MELODIES — Craig **Douglas** (9)	62
OUT OF MY MIND — Johnny **Tillotson** (34)	63
OUT OF THIS WORLD — Tony **Hatch** (50)	62
OUT OF TIME — Chris **Farlowe** (1)	66
OVER AND OVER — Dave **Clark Five** (45)	65
OVER UNDER SIDEWAYS DOWN — **Yardbirds** (10)	66
OVER YOU — **Freddie and the Dreamers** (13)	64
PABLO — Russ **Conway** (45)	61

Title — Act (Position)	Year of Chart Entry
PACK UP YOUR SORROWS — Joan **Baez** (50)	66
PAINT IT BLACK — **Rolling Stones** (1)	66
PAINTER MAN — **Creation** (36)	66
PALISADES PARK — Freddy **Cannon** (20)	62
PAMELA PAMELA — Wayne **Fontana** (11)	66
PAPA LOVES MAMA — Joan **Regan** (29)	60
PAPA'S GOT A BRAND NEW BAG — James **Brown and the Famous Flames** (25)	65
PAPER ROSES — Anita **Bryant** (24)	60
PAPER ROSES — Maureen **Evans** (40)	60
PAPER ROSES — Kaye **Sisters** (7)	60
PAPER SUN — **Traffic** (5)	67
PAPER TIGER — Sue **Thompson** (30)	65
PAPERBACK WRITER — **Beatles** (1)	66
PARADISE — Frank **Ifield** (26)	65
PARADISE LOST — **Herd** (15)	67
PARTY'S OVER, THE — Lonnie **Donegan** (9)	62
PASADENA — **Temperance Seven** (4)	61
PASSING BREEZE — Russ **Conway** (16)	60
PASSING STRANGERS — Billy **Eckstine and Sarah Vaughan** (20)	69
PAY OFF, THE — Kenny **Ball and his Jazzmen** (23)	62
PEACEFUL — Georgie **Fame** (16)	69
PEEK-A-BOO — **New Vaudeville Band** (7)	67
PEGGY SUE — Buddy **Holly** (32)	68
PENNY ARCADE — Roy **Orbison** (27)	69
PENNY LANE — **Beatles** (2)	67
PEOPLE — **Tymes** (16)	69
PEPE — Russ **Conway** (19)	61
PEPE — Duane **Eddy** (2)	61
PEPPERMINT TWIST [A] — Joey **Dee and the Starliters** (33)	62
PEPPERMINT TWIST [B] — Danny **Peppermint and the Jumping Jacks** (26)	62
PERFIDIA — **Ventures** (4)	60
PETER AND THE WOLF — **Clyde Valley Stompers** (25)	62
PIANISSIMO — Ken **Dodd** (21)	62
PIANO PARTY — Winifred **Atwell** (15)	60
PICK A BALE OF COTTON — Lonnie **Donegan** (11)	62
PICTURE OF YOU, A — Joe **Brown** (2)	62
PICTURES OF LILY — **Who** (4)	67
PICTURES OF MATCHSTICK MEN — **Status Quo** (7)	68
PIED PIPER — Crispian **St. Peters** (5)	66
PIED PIPER (THE BEEJE) — Steve **Race** (29)	63
PILTDOWN RIDES AGAIN — **Piltdown Men** (14)	61
PINBALL WIZARD — **Who** (4)	69
PIPELINE — **Chantays** (16)	63
PISTOL PACKIN' MAMA — Gene **Vincent** (15)	60
PLACE IN THE SUN [A] — **Shadows** (24)	66
PLACE IN THE SUN [B] — Stevie **Wonder** (20)	67
PLASTIC MAN — **Kinks** (31)	69
PLAYGROUND — Anita **Harris** (46)	67
PLEASANT VALLEY SUNDAY — **Monkees** (11)	67
PLEASE DON'T ASK ABOUT BARBARA — Bobby **Vee** (29)	62
PLEASE DON'T GO — Donald **Peers** (3)	68
PLEASE DON'T TEASE — Cliff **Richard** (1)	60
PLEASE HELP ME I'M FALLING — Hank **Locklin** (9)	60
PLEASE PLEASE ME — **Beatles** (2)	63
PLEASE STAY — **Cryin' Shames** (26)	66
POETRY IN MOTION — Johnny **Tillotson** (1)	60
POISON IVY — **Paramounts** (35)	64
PONY TIME — Chubby **Checker** (27)	61
POOR MAN'S SON — **Rockin' Berries** (5)	65
POOR ME — Adam **Faith** (1)	60
POP GO THE WORKERS — **Barron Knights** (5)	65
POP GOES THE WEASEL — Anthony **Newley** (12)	61
PORTRAIT OF MY LOVE — Matt **Monro** (3)	60
POSITIVELY FOURTH STREET — Bob **Dylan** (8)	65
PRETTY BLUE EYES — Craig **Douglas** (4)	60
PRETTY BROWN EYES — Jim **Reeves** (33)	68
PRETTY FLAMINGO — **Manfred Mann** (1)	66
PRETTY JENNY — Jess **Conrad** (50)	62
PRETTY LITTLE ANGEL EYES — Curtis **Lee** (47)	61
PRETTY PAPER — Roy **Orbison** (6)	64
PRETTY THING — Bo **Diddley** (34)	63
PRICE OF LOVE, THE — **Everly Brothers** (2)	65
PRINCESS IN RAGS — Gene **Pitney** (9)	65
PRIVATE NUMBER — Judy **Clay and William Bell** (8)	68
PROMISED LAND — Chuck **Berry** (26)	65
PROMISES — Ken **Dodd** (6)	66
PROUD MARY — **Checkmates Ltd.** (30)	69
PROUD MARY — **Creedence Clearwater Revival** (8)	69
PUFF — Kenny **Lynch** (33)	62

Title — Act (Position)	Year of Chart Entry
PUPPET ON A STRING — Sandie **Shaw** (1)	67
PUPPY LOVE — Paul **Anka** (33)	60
PURPLE HAZE — Jimi **Hendrix** Experience (3)	67
PUT A LITTLE LOVE IN YOUR HEART — Dave **Clark** Five (31)	69
PUT YOUR HEAD ON MY SHOULDER — Paul **Anka** (17)	60
PUT YOURSELF IN MY PLACE — **Isley** Brothers (13)	69
QUANDO M'INNAMORO (A MAN WITHOUT LOVE) — **Sandpipers** (33)	68
QUANDO QUANDO QUANDO — Pat **Boone** (41)	62
QUARTER TO THREE — **'U.S.' Bonds** (7)	61
QUE SERA SERA — Geno **Washington** and the Ram Jam Band (43)	66
QUEEN FOR TONIGHT — Helen **Shapiro** (33)	63
QUESTIONS I CAN'T ANSWER — **Heinz** (39)	64
QUICK JOEY SMALL (RUN JOEY RUN) — **Kasenetz-Katz** Singing Orchestral Circus (19)	68
QUITE A PARTY — **Fireballs** (29)	61
QUITE RIGHTLY SO — **Procol Harum** (50)	68
RACE WITH THE DEVIL — **Gun** (8)	68
RAG DOLL — **Four Seasons** (2)	64
RAGAMUFFIN MAN — **Manfred Mann** (8)	69
RAIN AND TEARS — **Aphrodite's** Child (30)	68
RAINBOW CHASER — **Nirvana** (34)	68
RAINBOW VALLEY — **Love Affair** (5)	68
RAINY DAY WOMEN NOS. 12 & 35 — Bob **Dylan** (7)	66
RAISE YOUR HAND — Eddie **Floyd** (42)	67
RAMBLIN' ROSE — Nat 'King' **Cole** (5)	62
RAM-BUNK-SHUSH — **Ventures** (45)	61
RAMONA — **Bachelors** (4)	64
RAVE ON — Buddy **Holly** (32)	68
RAWHIDE — Frankie **Laine** (6)	60
REACH FOR THE STARS — Shirley **Bassey** (1)	61
REACH OUT FOR ME — Dionne **Warwick** (23)	64
REACH OUT I'LL BE THERE — **Four Tops** (1)	66
READY FOR LOVE — Jimmy **Jones** (46)	60
RECOVERY — Fontella **Bass** (32)	66
RED BALLOON — Dave **Clark** Five (7)	68
RED RED WINE — Jimmy **James** and the Vagabonds (36)	68
RED RED WINE — Tony **Tribe** (46)	69
RED RIVER ROCK — **Johnny** and the Hurricanes (10)	60
RED SAILS IN THE SUNSET — Fats **Domino** (34)	63
REELIN' AND ROCKIN' — Dave **Clark** Five (24)	65
REFLECTIONS — **Supremes** (5)	67
REFLECTIONS OF MY LIFE — **Marmalade** (3)	69
RELEASE ME — Engelbert **Humperdinck** (1)	67
REMEMBER THE RAIN — Bob **Lind** (46)	66
REMEMBER (WALKIN' IN THE SAND) — **Shangri-Las** (14)	64
REMINISCING — Buddy **Holly** (17)	62
RESCUE ME — Fontella **Bass** (11)	65
RESPECT — Aretha **Franklin** (10)	67
RESTLESS — Johnny **Kidd** and the Pirates (22)	60
RETURN OF DJANGO — **Upsetters** (5)	69
RETURN OF THE RED BARON — Royal **Guardsmen** (37)	67
RETURN TO SENDER — Elvis **Presley** (1)	62
REVEILLE ROCK — **Johnny** and the Hurricanes (14)	60
REVIVAL — Chris **Barber's** Jazz Band (43)	62
RHAPSODY IN THE RAIN — Lou **Christie** (37)	66
RHYTHM & GREENS — **Shadows** (22)	64
RHYTHM OF THE RAIN — **Cascades** (5)	63
RICE IS NICE — **Lemon Pipers** (41)	68
RIDE AWAY — Roy **Orbison** (34)	65
RIDE MY SEE-SAW — **Moody Blues** (42)	68
RIDE ON BABY — Chris **Farlowe** (31)	66
RIDERS IN THE SKY — **Ramrods** (8)	61
RIGHT SAID FRED — Bernard **Cribbins** (10)	62
RIGHT THING TO SAY, THE — Nat 'King' **Cole** (42)	62
RING A DING GIRL — Ronnie **Carroll** (46)	62
RING OF BRIGHT WATER — Val **Doonican** (48)	69
RING OF FIRE [A] — Eric **Burdon** (35)	69
RING OF FIRE [B] — Duane **Eddy** (17)	61
RINGO — Lorne **Greene** (22)	64
RISE & FALL OF FLINGEL BUNT, THE — **Shadows** (5)	64
RIVER DEEP MOUNTAIN HIGH — Ike and Tina **Turner** (3)	66,69
RIVER (LE COLLINE SONO IN FIORO), THE — Ken **Dodd** (3)	65
RIVER STAY 'WAY FROM MY DOOR — Frank **Sinatra** (18)	60
RIVER'S RUN DRY, THE — Vince **Hill** (41)	62
ROBIN'S RETURN — Neville **Dickie** (33)	69
ROBOT — **Tornados** (17)	63
ROBOT MAN — Connie **Francis** (2)	60
ROCK A HULA BABY — Elvis **Presley** (1)	62
ROCK AROUND THE CLOCK — Bill **Haley** and his Comets (20)	68
ROCKET MAN — **Spotnicks** (38)	62
ROCKIN' ALONE — **Miki** and Griff (44)	60
ROCKIN' AROUND THE CHRISTMAS TREE — Brenda **Lee** (6)	62
ROCKIN' RED WING — Sammy **Masters** (36)	60
ROCKING GOOSE — **Johnny** and the Hurricanes (3)	60
ROMANTICA — Jane **Morgan** (39)	60
ROMEO — Petula **Clark** (3)	61
RONDO — Kenny **Ball** and his Jazzmen (24)	63
ROSALYN — **Pretty Things** (41)	64
ROSES ARE RED — Ronnie **Carroll** (3)	62
ROSES ARE RED — Bobby **Vinton** (15)	62
ROSES OF PICARDY — Vince **Hill** (13)	67
ROSIE — Don **Partridge** (4)	68
ROUND EVERY CORNER — Petula **Clark** (43)	65
ROYAL EVENT — Russ **Conway** (15)	60
RUB A DUB DUB — **Equals** (34)	69
RUBBER BALL — **Avons** (30)	61
RUBBER BALL — Bobby **Vee** (4)	61
RUBBER BALL — Marty **Wilde** (9)	61
RUBY ANN — Marty **Robbins** (24)	63
RUBY DON'T TAKE YOUR LOVE TO TOWN — Kenny **Rogers** and the First Edition (2)	69
RUBY TUESDAY — **Rolling Stones** (3)	67
RUDI'S IN LOVE — **Locomotive** (25)	68
RUN — Sandie **Shaw** (32)	66
RUN RUDOLPH RUN — Chuck **Berry** (36)	63
RUN TO HIM — Bobby **Vee** (6)	61
RUN TO MY LOVIN' ARMS — Billy **Fury** (25)	65
RUN TO THE DOOR — Clinton **Ford** (25)	67
RUNAROUND SUE — **Dion** (11)	61
RUNAROUND SUE — Doug **Sheldon** (36)	61
RUNAWAY — Del **Shannon** (1)	61
RUNNING BEAR — Johnny **Preston** (1)	60
RUNNING SCARED — Roy **Orbison** (9)	61
SABRE DANCE — **Love Sculpture** (5)	68
SAD MOVIES — Carol **Deene** (44)	61
SAD MOVIES — Sue **Thompson** (46)	61
SAILOR — Petula **Clark** (1)	61
SAILOR — Anne **Shelton** (10)	61
SALLY ANN — Joe **Brown** (28)	63
SALTY DOG — **Procol Harum** (44)	69
SAM — Keith **West** (38)	67
SAMANTHA — Kenny **Ball** and his Jazzmen (13)	61
SAN ANTONIO ROSE — Floyd **Cramer** (36)	61
SAN FRANCISCAN NIGHTS — Eric **Burdon** (7)	67
SAN FRANCISCO (BE SURE TO WEAR FLOWERS IN YOUR HAIR) — Scott **McKenzie** (1)	67
SANCTUS (MISSA LUBA) — **Troubadours Du Roi Baudouin** (28)	69
SATISFACTION — Aretha **Franklin** (37)	67
SATISFACTION — Otis **Redding** (33)	66
SATURDAY NITE AT THE DUCK POND — **Cougars** (33)	63
SAVAGE, THE — **Shadows** (10)	61
SAVE ME — Dave **Dee, Dozy, Beaky, Mick and Tich** (4)	66
SAVE THE LAST DANCE FOR ME — **Drifters** (2)	60
SAVED BY THE BELL — Robin **Gibb** (2)	69
SAY I WON'T BE THERE — **Springfields** (5)	63
SAY IT WITH FLOWERS — Dorothy **Squires** and Russ Conway (23)	61
SAY WONDERFUL THINGS — Ronnie **Carroll** (6)	63
(SAY) YOU'RE MY GIRL — Roy **Orbison** (23)	65
SCARLETT O'HARA — Jet **Harris** and Tony Meehan (2)	63
SCOTTISH SOLDIER, A — Andy **Stewart** (19)	61
SEA OF HEARTBREAK — Don **Gibson** (14)	61
SEALED WITH A KISS — Brian **Hyland** (3)	62
SEARCHIN' — **Hollies** (12)	63
SECOND HAND ROSE — Barbra **Streisand** (14)	66
SECRET LOVE — Kathy **Kirby** (4)	63
SEE EMILY PLAY — **Pink Floyd** (6)	67
SEE MY FRIEND — **Kinks** (10)	65
SEMI-DETACHED SUBURBAN MR. JAMES — **Manfred Mann** (2)	66
SEND ME THE PILLOW YOU DREAM ON — Johnny **Tillotson** (21)	62
SEPTEMBER IN THE RAIN — Dinah **Washington** (35)	61
SERENATA — Tony **Bennett** (35)	61
SERENATA — Sarah **Vaughan** (37)	60
SET ME FREE — **Kinks** (9)	65
SEVEN DAFFODILS — **Cherokees** (33)	64
SEVEN DAFFODILS — **Mojos** (30)	64
SEVEN DRUNKEN NIGHTS — **Dubliners** (7)	67
SEVEN LITTLE GIRLS SITTING IN THE BACK SEAT — **Avons** (3)	60
SEVEN ROOMS OF GLOOM — **Four Tops** (12)	67
SEVENTH SON — Georgie **Fame** (25)	69
76 TROMBONES — **King** Brothers (19)	61
SHA LA LA — **Manfred Mann** (3)	64
SHA LA LA LA LEE — **Small Faces** (3)	66
SHAKE — Otis **Redding** (28)	67
SHAKIN' ALL OVER — Johnny **Kidd** and the Pirates (1)	60
SHAME — Alan **Price** Set (45)	67
SHAME AND SCANDAL IN THE FAMILY — Lance **Percival** (37)	65
SHAME SHAME SHAME — Jimmy **Reed** (45)	64
SHAPES OF THINGS — **Yardbirds** (3)	66
SHARING YOU — Bobby **Vee** (10)	62
SHAZAM! — Duane **Eddy** (4)	60
SHE LOVES YOU — **Beatles** (1)	63
SHE NEEDS LOVE — Wayne **Fontana** and the Mindbenders (32)	65
SHE SHE LITTLE SHEILA — Gene **Vincent** (22)	61
SHE SOLD ME MAGIC — Lou **Christie** (25)	69
SHE WEARS MY RING — Solomon **King** (3)	68
SHE'D RATHER BE WITH ME — **Turtles** (4)	67
SHEILA — Tommy **Roe** (3)	62
SHERRY — **Four Seasons** (8)	62
SHE'S ABOUT A MOVER — **Sir Douglas Quintet** (15)	65
SHE'S GONE — Buddy **Knox** (45)	62
SHE'S GOT YOU — Patsy **Cline** (43)	62
SHE'S LOST YOU — **Zephyrs** (48)	65
SHE'S NEW TO YOU — Susan **Maughan** (45)	63
SHE'S NOT THERE — Neil **MacArthur** (34)	69
SHE'S NOT THERE — **Zombies** (12)	64
SHE'S NOT YOU — Elvis **Presley** (1)	62
SHINDIG — **Shadows** (6)	63
SHINE — Joe **Brown** (33)	61
SHOO BE DOO BE DOO DA DAY — Stevie **Wonder** (46)	68
SHORT'NIN' BREAD — **Viscounts** (16)	60
SHOT OF RHYTHM & BLUES — Johnny **Kidd** and the Pirates (48)	63
SHOTGUN WEDDING — Roy **'C'** (6)	66
SHOUT — **Lulu** (7)	64
SHOW ME GIRL — **Herman's Hermits** (19)	64
SHY GIRL — Mark **Wynter** (28)	63
SI TU DOIS PARTIR — **Fairport Convention** (21)	69
SIGN OF THE TIMES, A — Petula **Clark** (49)	66
SILENCE IS GOLDEN — **Tremeloes** (1)	67
SILHOUETTES — **Herman's Hermits** (3)	65
SIMON SAYS — **1910 Fruitgum Co.** (2)	68
SIMON SMITH & HIS AMAZING DANCING BEAR — Alan **Price** Set (4)	67
SINCE YOU'VE BEEN GONE — Aretha **Franklin** (47)	68
SING LIKE AN ANGEL — Jerry **Lordan** (36)	60
SINGER SANG HIS SONG, THE — **Bee Gees** (25)	68
SINGLE GIRL — Sandy **Posey** (15)	67
SINK THE BISMARCK — Don **Lang** (43)	60
SINS OF THE FAMILY — P. F. **Sloan** (38)	65
SITTIN' ON A FENCE — **Twice As Much** (25)	66
(SITTIN' ON) THE DOCK OF THE BAY — Otis **Redding** (3)	68
SITTING IN THE PARK — Georgie **Fame** (12)	66
634-5789 — Wilson **Pickett** (36)	66
SIXTEEN REASONS — Connie **Stevens** (9)	60
SKY PILOT — Eric **Burdon** (40)	68
SKYLARK — Michael **Holliday** (39)	60
SLEEPY JOE — **Herman's Hermits** (12)	68
SLOOP JOHN B — **Beach Boys** (2)	66
SLOW TWISTIN' — Chubby **Checker** (23)	62
SMALL SAD SAM — Phil **McLean** (34)	62
SMOKESTACK LIGHTNIN' — Howlin' **Wolf** (42)	66
SMOKEY BLUES AWAY — **New Generation** (38)	68

Title — Act (Position)	Year of Chart Entry
SNAKE IN THE GRASS — Dave **Dee, Dozy, Beaky, Mick and Tich** (23)	69
SNOOPY VS. THE RED BARON — **Royal Guardsmen** (8)	67
SNOW COACH — Russ **Conway** (8)	60
SO DEEP IS THE NIGHT — Ken **Dodd** (31)	64
SO DO I — Kenny **Ball and his Jazzmen** (14)	62
SO GOOD — Roy **Orbison** (32)	67
SO IT WILL ALWAYS BE — **Everly Brothers** (23)	63
SO LONG BABY — Del **Shannon** (10)	61
SO MUCH IN LOVE [A] — **Mighty Avengers** (46)	64
SO MUCH IN LOVE [B] — **Tymes** (21)	63
SO MUCH LOVE — Tony **Blackburn** (31)	68
SO SAD (TO WATCH GOOD LOVE GO BAD) — **Everly Brothers** (4)	60
SO TIRED — Frankie **Vaughan** (21)	67
SOFTLY AS I LEAVE YOU — Matt **Monro** (10)	62
SOFTLY SOFTLY — **Equals** (48)	68
SOLDIER BOY — **Cheetahs** (39)	65
SOLDIER BOY — **Shirelles** (23)	62
SOME KINDA EARTHQUAKE — Duane **Eddy** (12)	60
SOME KINDA FUN — Chris **Montez** (10)	63
SOME OF YOUR LOVIN' — Dusty **Springfield** (8)	65
SOME OTHER GUY — **Big Three** (37)	63
SOME PEOPLE — Carol **Deene** (25)	62
SOME THINGS YOU NEVER GET USED TO — **Supremes** (34)	68
SOMEBODY ELSE'S GIRL — Billy **Fury** (18)	63
SOMEBODY HELP ME — Spencer **Davis Group** (1)	66
SOMEBODY TO LOVE — Brad **Newman** (47)	62
SOMEDAY — Kenny **Ball and his Jazzmen** (28)	61
SOMEDAY MAN — **Monkees** (47)	69
SOMEDAY ONE DAY — **Seekers** (11)	66
SOMEDAY WE'LL BE TOGETHER — **Supremes** (13)	69
SOMEDAY WE'RE GONNA LOVE AGAIN — **Searchers** (11)	64
SOMEONE ELSE'S BABY — Adam **Faith** (2)	60
SOMEONE MUST HAVE HURT YOU A LOT — Frankie **Vaughan** (46)	65
SOMEONE SOMEONE — Brian **Poole and the Tremeloes** (2)	64
SOMEONE'S TAKEN MARIA AWAY — Adam **Faith** (34)	65
SOMETHIN' STUPID — Nancy **Sinatra and Frank Sinatra** (1)	67
SOMETHING [A] — **Beatles** (4)	69
SOMETHING [B] — Georgie **Fame** (23)	65
SOMETHING BETTER BEGINNING — **Honeycombs** (39)	65
SOMETHING HERE IN MY HEART (KEEPS A-TELLIN' ME NO) — **Paper Dolls** (11)	68
SOMETHING IN THE AIR — **Thunderclap Newman** (1)	69
SOMETHING MISSING — Petula **Clark** (44)	61
SOMETHING ON MY MIND — Chris **Andrews** (41)	65
SOMETHING'S GOTTEN HOLD OF MY HEART — Gene **Pitney** (5)	67
SOMETHING'S HAPPENING — **Herman's Hermits** (6)	68
SOMEWHERE — P. J. **Proby** (6)	64
SOMEWHERE IN THE COUNTRY — Gene **Pitney** (19)	68
SOMEWHERE MY LOVE — **Manuel and his Music Of The Mountains** (42)	66
SOMEWHERE MY LOVE — Mike **Sammes Singers** (14)	66,67
SON OF A PREACHER MAN — Dusty **Springfield** (9)	68
SON OF HICKORY HOLLER'S TRAMP — O. C. **Smith** (2)	68
SON THIS IS SHE — John **Leyton** (15)	61
SONG OF MEXICO — Tony **Meehan Combo** (39)	64
SOOTHE ME — **Sam and Dave** (48)	67
SORROW — **Merseys** (4)	66
SORRY ROBBIE — Bert **Weedon** (28)	60
SORRY SUZANNE — **Hollies** (3)	69
SOUL CLAP '69 — **Booker T. & The M. G.'s** (35)	69
SOUL COAXING — Raymond **Lefevre** (46)	68
SOUL DEEP — **Box Tops** (22)	69
SOUL FINGER — **Bar-Kays** (33)	67
SOUL LIMBO — **Booker T. & The M. G.'s** (30)	68
SOUL MAN — **Sam and Dave** (24)	67
SOUL SERENADE — Willie **Mitchell** (43)	68
SOUL SISTER BROWN SUGAR — **Sam and Dave** (15)	69
SOUND OF SILENCE, THE — **Bachelors** (3)	66
SPACE ODDITY — David **Bowie** (5)	69

Title — Act (Position)	Year of Chart Entry
SPANISH FLEA — Herb **Alpert** (3)	65
SPANISH HARLEM — Jimmy **Justice** (20)	62
SPANISH HARLEM — **Sounds Incorporated** (35)	64
SPARTANS, THE — **Sounds Incorporated** (30)	64
SPEAK TO ME PRETTY — Brenda **Lee** (3)	62
SPECIAL YEARS, THE — Val **Doonican** (7)	65
SPEEDY GONZALES — Pat **Boone** (2)	62
SPOOKY — **Classics IV** (46)	68
STACCATO'S THEME — Elmer **Bernstein** (4)	60
STAIRWAY TO HEAVEN — Neil **Sedaka** (8)	60
STAND BY ME — Ben E. **King** (27)	61
STAND BY ME — Kenny **Lynch** (39)	64
STANDING IN THE SHADOWS OF LOVE — **Four Tops** (6)	67
STANDING ON THE CORNER — **Four Lads** (34)	60
STANDING ON THE CORNER — **King Brothers** (4)	60
STARBRIGHT — Johnny **Mathis** (47)	60
STARRY EYED — Michael **Holliday** (1)	60
STARRY NIGHT, A — **Joy Strings** (35)	64
STARS AND STRIPES FOREVER — Mr. Acker **Bilk** (22)	61
STAY — **Hollies** (8)	63
STAY — Maurice **Williams and the Zodiacs** (14)	61
STAY AWHILE — Dusty **Springfield** (13)	64
STAY WITH ME BABY — **Walker Brothers** (26)	67
STEEL GUITAR AND A GLASS OF WINE, A — Paul **Anka** (41)	62
STEP BY STEP — Steve **Perry** (41)	60
STEP INSIDE LOVE — Cilla **Black** (8)	68
STILL — Karl **Denver** (13)	63
STILL — Ken **Dodd** (35)	63
STILL I'M SAD — **Yardbirds** (3)	65
STINGRAY — **Shadows** (19)	65
STOP FEELING SORRY FOR YOURSELF — Adam **Faith** (23)	65
STOP HER ON SIGHT (SOS) — Edwin **Starr** (11)	66,68
STOP IN THE NAME OF LOVE — **Supremes** (7)	65
STOP LOOK & LISTEN — Wayne **Fontana and the Mindbenders** (37)	64
STOP STOP STOP — **Hollies** (2)	66
STOP THAT GIRL — Chris **Andrews** (36)	66
STRANGE BREW — **Cream** (17)	67
STRANGER IN TOWN — Del **Shannon** (40)	65
STRANGER ON THE SHORE — Mr. Acker **Bilk** (2)	61
STRANGER ON THE SHORE — Andy **Williams** (30)	62
STRANGER, THE — **Shadows** (5)	60
STRANGERS IN THE NIGHT — Frank **Sinatra** (1)	66
STRAWBERRY BLONDE — Frank **D'rone** (24)	60
STRAWBERRY FAIR — Anthony **Newley** (3)	60
STRAWBERRY FIELDS FOREVER — **Beatles** (2)	67
STRICTLY ELVIS (EP) — Elvis **Presley** (26)	60
STRONG LOVE — Spencer **Davis Group** (44)	65
STUCK ON YOU — Elvis **Presley** (3)	60
SUBSTITUTE — **Who** (5)	66
SUBTERRANEAN HOMESICK BLUES — Bob **Dylan** (9)	65
SUCH A NIGHT — Elvis **Presley** (13)	64
SUCU SUCU — Ted **Heath** (36)	61
SUCU SUCU — Laurie **Johnson** (9)	61
SUCU SUCU — Joe **Loss** (48)	61
SUCU SUCU — **Nina and Frederick** (23)	61
SUCU SUCU — **Ping Ping and Al Verlaine** (41)	61
SUDDENLY YOU LOVE ME — **Tremeloes** (6)	68
SUE'S GONNA BE MINE — Del **Shannon** (21)	63
SUGAR AND SPICE — **Searchers** (2)	63
SUGAR SHACK — Jimmy **Gilmer and the Fireballs** (45)	63
SUGAR SUGAR — **Archies** (1)	69
SUGAR TOWN — Nancy **Sinatra** (8)	67
SUKIYAKI — Kenny **Ball and his Jazzmen** (10)	63
SUKIYAKI — Kyu **Sakamoto** (6)	63
SUMMER HOLIDAY — Cliff **Richard** (1)	63
SUMMER IN THE CITY — **Lovin' Spoonful** (8)	66
SUMMER IS OVER — Frank **Ifield** (25)	64
SUMMER NIGHTS — Marianne **Faithfull** (10)	65
'SUMMER PLACE', THEME FROM A — Percy **Faith**	60
'SUMMER PLACE', THEME FROM A — Norrie **Paramor** (36)	60
SUMMER SET — Mr. Acker **Bilk** (5)	60
SUMMER WIND — Frank **Sinatra** (36)	66
SUMMERTIME — **Marcels** (46)	61
SUMMERTIME — Al **Martino** (49)	60
SUMMERTIME — Billy **Stewart** (39)	66
SUMMERTIME BLUES — Eddie **Cochran** (34)	68

Title — Act (Position)	Year of Chart Entry
SUN AIN'T GONNA SHINE ANYMORE, THE — **Walker Brothers** (1)	66
SUN ARISE — Rolf **Harris** (3)	62
SUNNY — **Cher** (32)	66
SUNNY — Georgie **Fame** (13)	66
SUNNY — Bobby **Hebb** (12)	66
SUNNY AFTERNOON — **Kinks** (1)	66
SUNSHINE GIRL — **Herman's Hermits** (8)	68
SUNSHINE OF LOVE — Louis **Armstrong** (41)	68
SUNSHINE OF YOUR LOVE — **Cream** (25)	68
SUNSHINE SUPERMAN — **Donovan** (3)	66
SUPERGIRL — Graham **Bonney** (19)	66
SURF CITY — Jan and Dean (26)	63
SURFIN' USA — **Beach Boys** (34)	63
SURRENDER — Elvis **Presley** (1)	61
SURROUND YOURSELF WITH SORROW — Cilla **Black** (3)	69
SUSANNAH'S STILL ALIVE — Dave **Davies** (20)	67
SUSIE DARLIN' — Tommy **Roe** (37)	62
SUSPICION — Terry **Stafford** (31)	64
SUSPICIOUS MINDS — Elvis **Presley** (2)	69
SWAN LAKE — **Cats** (48)	69
SWAY — Bobby **Rydell** (12)	60
SWEET DREAM — **Jethro Tull** (7)	69
SWEET DREAMS [A] — Dave **Sampson** (29)	60
SWEET DREAMS [B] — Tommy **McLain** (49)	66
SWEET IMPOSSIBLE YOU — Brenda **Lee** (28)	63
SWEET LITTLE SIXTEEN — Jerry Lee **Lewis** (38)	62
SWEET NOTHINS — **Searchers** (48)	63
SWEET NOTHINS — Brenda **Lee** (4)	60
SWEET PEA — **Manfred Mann** (36)	67
SWEET SOUL MUSIC — Arthur **Conley** (7)	67
SWEET TALKIN' GUY — **Chiffons** (31)	66
SWEET WILLIAM — **Millie** (30)	64
SWEETIE PIE — Eddie **Cochran** (38)	60
SWEETS FOR MY SWEET — **Searchers** (1)	63
SWING THAT HAMMER — Mike **Cotton's Jazzmen** (36)	63
SWINGIN' LOW — **Outlaws** (46)	61
SWINGING IN THE RAIN — Norman **Vaughan** (34)	62
SWINGING ON A STAR — Big Dee **Irwin** (7)	63
SWINGING SCHOOL — Bobby **Rydell** (44)	60
SWISS MAID — Del **Shannon** (2)	62
TAKE A HEART — **Sorrows** (21)	65
TAKE FIVE — Dave **Brubeck Quartet** (6)	61
TAKE GOOD CARE OF HER — Adam **Wade** (38)	61
TAKE GOOD CARE OF MY BABY — Bobby **Vee** (3)	61
TAKE IT OR LEAVE IT — **Searchers** (31)	66
TAKE ME FOR WHAT I'M WORTH — **Searchers** (20)	65
TAKE ME IN YOUR ARMS & LOVE ME — Gladys **Knight and the Pips** (13)	67
TAKE ME TO YOUR HEART AGAIN — Vince **Hill** (13)	66
TAKE THESE CHAINS FROM MY HEART — Ray **Charles** (5)	63
TALL DARK STRANGER — Rose **Brennan** (31)	61
TALLYMAN — Jeff **Beck** (30)	67
TANSY — Alex **Welsh** (45)	61
TASTE OF HONEY, A — Mr. Acker **Bilk** (16)	63
TAVERN IN THE TOWN — Terry **Lightfoot and his New Orleans Jazzmen** (49)	62
TCHAIKOVSKY ONE — **Second City Sound** (22)	66
TEACH ME TO TWIST — Chubby **Checker and Bobby Rydell** (45)	62
TEARDROP — **Santo and Johnny** (50)	60
TEARDROP CITY — **Monkees** (46)	69
TEARS [A] — Ken **Dodd** (1)	65
TEARS [B] — Danny **Williams** (22)	62
TEARS IN THE WIND — **Chicken Shack** (29)	69
TEARS WON'T WASH AWAY MY HEARTACHE — Ken **Dodd** (22)	69
TEASE ME — Keith **Kelly** (27)	60
TEEN ANGEL — Mark **Dinning** (37)	60
TEEN BEAT — Sandy **Nelson** (18)	60
TEENAGE IDOL — Rick **Nelson** (39)	62
TEENAGE OPERA, EXCERPT FROM A — Keith **West** (2)	67
TEENSVILLE — Chet **Atkins** (46)	60
TELL HER I'M NOT HOME — Ike and Tina **Turner** (48)	66
TELL HER NO — **Zombies** (42)	65
TELL HIM — Billie **Davis** (10)	63
TELL HIM — **Exciters** (46)	63
TELL IT ON THE MOUNTAIN — Peter, **Paul and Mary** (33)	64

Title — Act (Position)	Year of Chart Entry
VIRGIN MARY — Lonnie **Donegan** (27)	60
VISIONS — Cliff **Richard** (7)	66
VIVA BOBBY JOE — **Equals** (6)	69
VIVA LAS VEGAS — Elvis **Presley** (17)	64
VOICE IN THE WILDERNESS — Cliff **Richard** (2)	60
VOICES IN THE SKY — **Moody Blues** (27)	68
VOLARE — Bobby **Rydell** (22)	60
WAIT FOR ME MARIANNE — **Marmalade** (30)	68
WALK AWAY [A] — Shane **Fenton** and the Fentones (38)	62
WALK AWAY [B] — Matt **Monro** (4)	64
WALK AWAY RENEE — **Four Tops** (3)	67
WALK DON'T RUN — John **Barry** (11)	60
WALK DON'T RUN — **Ventures** (8)	60
WALK HAND IN HAND — **Gerry and the Pacemakers** (29)	65
WALK IN THE BLACK FOREST, A — Horst **Jankowski** (3)	65
WALK LIKE A MAN — **Four Seasons** (12)	63
WALK ON — Roy **Orbison** (39)	68
WALK ON BY [A] — Leroy **Van Dyke** (5)	62
WALK ON BY [B] — Dionne **Warwick** (9)	64
WALK ON GILDED SPLINTERS — Marsha **Hunt** (46)	69
WALK RIGHT BACK — **Everly Brothers** (1)	61
WALK RIGHT IN — **Rooftop Singers** (10)	63
WALK TALL — Val **Doonican** (3)	64
WALK WITH FAITH IN YOUR HEART — **Bachelors** (22)	66
WALK WITH ME — **Seekers** (10)	66
WALK WITH ME MY ANGEL — Don **Charles** (39)	62
WALKIN' BACK TO HAPPINESS — Helen **Shapiro** (1)	61
WALKIN' TALL — Adam **Faith** (23)	63
WALKIN' THE DOG — **Dennisons** (36)	64
WALKING ALONE — Richard **Anthony** (37)	63
WALKING IN THE RAIN — **Walker Brothers** (26)	67
WALKING MY CAT NAMED DOG — Norma **Tanega** (22)	66
WALKING THE FLOOR OVER YOU — Pat **Boone** (39)	60
WALKING TO NEW ORLEANS — Fats **Domino** (19)	60
WALLS FELL DOWN, THE — **Marbles** (28)	69
WANDERER, THE — **Dion** (10)	62
WAR LORD — **Shadows** (18)	65
WARM & TENDER LOVE — Percy **Sledge** (34)	66
WARMED OVER KISSES — Brian **Hyland** (28)	62
WARPAINT — **Brook Brothers** (5)	61
WATER — Geno **Washington** and the Ram Jam Band (39)	66
WATER IS OVER MY HEAD, THE — **Rockin' Berries** (43)	66
WATERLOO SUNSET — **Kinks** (2)	67
WAY DOWN YONDER IN NEW ORLEANS — Freddy **Cannon** (3)	60
WAY IT USED TO BE, THE — Engelbert **Humperdinck** (3)	69
WAY OF LIFE — **Family Dogg** (6)	69
WAY YOU LOOK TONIGHT, THE — **Lettermen** (36)	61
WAY YOU LOOK TONIGHT, THE — Denny **Seyton** and the Sabres (48)	64
WAYWARD WIND — Frank **Ifield** (1)	63
WE ARE IN LOVE — Adam **Faith** (11)	63
WE CAN WORK IT OUT — **Beatles** (1)	65
WE GOT LOVE — Alma **Cogan** (26)	60
WE LOVE YOU — **Rolling Stones** (8)	67
WE SHALL OVERCOME — Joan **Baez** (26)	65
WE WILL NEVER BE AS YOUNG AS THIS AGAIN — Danny **Williams** (44)	61
WEATHER FORECAST — **Master Singers** (50)	66
WEDDING, THE — Julie **Rogers** (3)	64
WEEKEND — Eddie **Cochran** (15)	61
WEIGHT, THE — **Band** (21)	68
WELCOME HOME BABY — **Brook Brothers** (33)	62
WELCOME TO MY WORLD — Jim **Reeves** (6)	63
WELL I ASK YOU — Eden **Kane** (1)	61
WE'LL SING IN THE SUNSHINE — **Lancastrians** (47)	64
WE'RE GONNA GO FISHIN' — Hank **Locklin** (18)	62
WE'RE ONLY YOUNG ONCE — **Avons** (45)	60
WE'RE THROUGH — **Hollies** (7)	64
WET DREAM — Max **Romeo** (10)	69
WE'VE GOTTA GET OUT OF THIS PLACE — **Animals** (2)	65
WHAT A CRAZY WORLD WE'RE LIVING IN — Joe **Brown** (37)	62
WHAT A MOUTH — Tommy **Steele** (5)	60
WHAT A PARTY — Fats **Domino** (43)	61
WHAT A WOMAN IN LOVE WON'T DO — Sandy **Posey** (48)	67
WHAT A WONDERFUL WORLD — Louis **Armstrong** (1)	68
WHAT AM I GONNA DO — Emile **Ford** and the Checkmates (33)	61
WHAT AM I TO DO — Kenny **Lynch** (37)	64
WHAT BECOMES OF THE BROKEN HEARTED — Jimmy **Ruffin** (10)	66
WHAT DO YA SAY — Chubby **Checker** (37)	63
WHAT DO YOU WANT — Adam **Faith** (2)	60
WHAT DO YOU WANT TO MAKE THOSE EYES AT ME FOR — Emile **Ford** and the Checkmates (1)	60
WHAT DOES IT TAKE (TO WIN YOUR LOVE) — Junior **Walker** and the All-Stars (13)	69
WHAT GOOD AM I — Cilla **Black** (24)	67
WHAT HAVE THEY DONE TO THE RAIN — **Searchers** (13)	64
WHAT IN THE WORLD'S COME OVER YOU [A] — Jack **Scott** (11)	60
WHAT IN THE WORLD'S COME OVER YOU [B] — **Rockin' Berries** (23)	65
WHAT IS A MAN — **Four Tops** (16)	69
WHAT KIND OF FOOL AM I? — Shirley **Bassey** (47)	63
WHAT KIND OF FOOL AM I? — Sammy **Davis** Jr. (26)	62
WHAT KIND OF FOOL AM I? — Anthony **Newley** (36)	61
WHAT MORE DO YOU WANT — Frankie **Vaughan** (25)	60
WHAT NOW — Adam **Faith** (31)	63
WHAT NOW MY LOVE — Shirley **Bassey** (5)	62
WHAT NOW MY LOVE — **Sonny and Cher** (13)	66
WHAT TO DO — Buddy **Holly** (27)	61,63
WHAT WILL MY MARY SAY — Johnny **Mathis** (49)	63
WHAT WOULD I BE — Val **Doonican** (2)	66
WHATCHA GONNA DO ABOUT IT? — **Small Faces** (14)	65
WHATCHA GONNA DO ABOUT IT — Doris **Troy** (37)	64
WHATCHA GONNA DO NOW — Chris **Andrews** (40)	66
WHAT'D I SAY — Jerry Lee **Lewis** (10)	61
WHAT'S NEW PUSSYCAT — Tom **Jones** (11)	65
WHEELS — **String-A-Longs** (8)	61
WHEELS CHA CHA — Joe **Loss** (21)	61
WHEN A MAN LOVES A WOMAN — Percy **Sledge** (4)	66
WHEN I COME HOME — Spencer **Davis Group** (12)	66
WHEN I GET HOME — **Searchers** (35)	65
WHEN I GROW UP (TO BE A MAN) — **Beach Boys** (27)	64
WHEN I WAS YOUNG — Eric **Burdon** (45)	67
WHEN I'M 64 — Kenny **Ball** and his Jazzmen (43)	67
WHEN JOHNNY COMES MARCHING HOME — Adam **Faith** (5)	60
WHEN LOVE COMES ALONG — Matt **Monro** (46)	62
WHEN MY LITTLE GIRL IS SMILING — Craig **Douglas** (9)	62
WHEN MY LITTLE GIRL IS SMILING — **Drifters** (31)	62
WHEN MY LITTLE GIRL IS SMILING — Jimmy **Justice** (9)	62
WHEN THE GIRL IN YOUR ARMS IS THE GIRL IN YOUR HEART — Cliff **Richard** (3)	61
WHEN THE MORNING SUN DRIES THE DEW — **Quiet Five** (45)	65
WHEN THE SUMMERTIME IS OVER — Jackie **Trent** (39)	65
WHEN THE SUN COMES SHININ' THRU — Long John **Baldry** (29)	68
WHEN TWO WORLDS COLLIDE — Jim **Reeves** (17)	69
WHEN WE WERE YOUNG — Solomon **King** (21)	68
WHEN WILL I BE LOVED — **Everly Brothers** (4)	60
WHEN WILL THE GOOD APPLES FALL — **Seekers** (11)	67
WHEN WILL YOU SAY I LOVE YOU — Billy **Fury** (3)	63
WHEN YOU ASK ABOUT LOVE — **Crickets** (27)	60
WHEN YOU WALK IN THE ROOM — **Searchers** (3)	64
WHEN YOU'RE YOUNG AND IN LOVE — **Marvelettes** (13)	67
WHERE ARE YOU NOW (MY LOVE) — Jackie **Trent** (1)	65
WHERE DID OUR LOVE GO — **Supremes** (3)	64
WHERE DO YOU GO TO MY LOVELY — Peter **Sarstedt** (1)	69
WHERE IS TOMORROW — Cilla **Black** (40)	68
WHERE THE BOYS ARE — Connie **Francis** (5)	61
WHERE WILL YOU BE — Sue **Nichols** (17)	68
WHILE I LIVE — Kenny **Damon** (48)	66
WHISPERING — **Bachelors** (18)	63
WHISPERING — Nino **Tempo** and April Stevens (20)	64
WHISPERING HOPE — Jim **Reeves** (50)	61
WHITE CLIFFS OF DOVER — Mr. Acker **Bilk** (30)	60
WHITE CLIFFS OF DOVER — **Righteous Brothers** (21)	66
WHITE HORSES — **Jacky** (10)	68
WHITE ROOM — **Cream** (28)	69
WHITE SILVER SANDS — Bill **Black's** Combo (50)	60
WHITER SHADE OF PALE, A — **Procol Harum** (1)	67
WHO AM I — Adam **Faith** (5)	61
WHO COULD BE BLUER — Jerry **Lordan** (17)	60
WHO PUT THE BOMP — **Viscounts** (21)	61
WHY — Frankie **Avalon** (20)	60
WHY — Anthony **Newley** (1)	60
WHY CAN'T YOU — Clarence 'Frogman' **Henry** (42)	61
WHY NOT NOW — Matt **Monro** (24)	61
WHY NOT TONIGHT — **Mojos** (25)	64
WHY WHY BYE BYE — Bob **Luman** (46)	60
WICHITA LINEMAN — Glen **Campbell** (7)	69
WILD CAT — Gene **Vincent** (21)	60
WILD HONEY — **Beach Boys** (29)	67
WILD IN THE COUNTRY — Elvis **Presley** (4)	61
WILD ONE — Bobby **Rydell** (7)	60
WILD SIDE OF LIFE — Tommy **Quickly** (33)	64
WILD THING — **Troggs** (2)	66
WILD WIND — John **Leyton** (2)	61
WILL I WHAT — Mike **Sarne** (18)	62
WILL YOU LOVE ME TOMORROW — **Shirelles** (4)	61
WILLOW TREE — **Ivy League** (50)	66
WIMOWEH — Karl **Denver** (4)	62
WINCHESTER CATHEDRAL — **New Vaudeville Band** (4)	66
WIND CRIES MARY, THE — Jimi **Hendrix Experience** (6)	67
WIND ME UP (LET ME GO) — Cliff **Richard** (2)	65
WINDMILL IN OLD AMSTERDAM, A — Ronnie **Hilton** (23)	65
WINDMILLS OF YOUR MIND — Noel **Harrison** (8)	69
WINTER WORLD OF LOVE — Engelbert **Humperdinck** (7)	69
WIPE OUT — **Surfaris** (5)	63
WISHIN' AND HOPIN' — **Merseybeats** (13)	64
WISHING — Buddy **Holly** (10)	63
WITCHES' BREW — Janie **Jones** (46)	66
WITH A GIRL LIKE YOU — **Troggs** (1)	66
WITH A LITTLE HELP FROM MY FRIENDS — Joe **Brown** (32)	67
WITH A LITTLE HELP FROM MY FRIENDS — Joe **Cocker** (1)	68
WITH A LITTLE HELP FROM MY FRIENDS — **Young Idea** (10)	67
WITH PEN IN HAND — Vikki **Carr** (40)	69
WITH THESE HANDS — Shirley **Bassey** (31)	60
WITH THESE HANDS — Tom **Jones** (13)	65
WITHOUT HER — Herb **Alpert** (36)	69
WITHOUT LOVE — Tom **Jones** (10)	69
WITHOUT YOU — Matt **Monro** (37)	65
WOE IS ME — Helen **Shapiro** (35)	63
WOMAN — **Peter and Gordon** (28)	66
WOMAN WOMAN — Gary **Puckett** and the Union Gap (48)	68
WONDERBOY — **Kinks** (36)	68
WONDERFUL LAND — **Shadows** (1)	62
WONDERFUL WORLD — Sam **Cooke** (27)	60
WONDERFUL WORLD — **Herman's Hermits** (7)	65
WONDERFUL WORLD BEAUTIFUL PEOPLE — Jimmy **Cliff** (6)	69
WONDERFUL WORLD OF THE YOUNG — Danny **Williams** (8)	62
WONDROUS PLACE — Billy **Fury** (25)	60
WOODEN HEART — Elvis **Presley** (1)	61
WOOLY BULLY — **Sam The Sham and the Pharaohs** (11)	65
WORDS [A] — **Allisons** (34)	61
WORDS [B] — **Bee Gees** (8)	68
WORDS OF LOVE — **Mamas and the Papas** (47)	67
WORKIN' FOR THE MAN — Roy **Orbison** (50)	62

Title — Act (Position)	Year of Chart Entry	Title — Act (Position)	Year of Chart Entry
WORKIN' MY WAY BACK TO YOU — Four Seasons (50)	66	YOU'LL NEVER WALK ALONE — Gerry and the Pacemakers (1)	63
WORKING IN THE COALMINE — Lee Dorsey (8)	66	YOU'LL NEVER WALK ALONE — Elvis Presley (44)	68
WORLD — Bee Gees (9)	67	YOUNG EMOTIONS — Ricky Nelson (48)	60
WORLD IN MY ARMS, THE — Nat 'King' Cole (36)	61	YOUNG GIRL — Gary Puckett and the Union Gap (1)	68
WORLD OF BROKEN HEARTS — Amen Corner (26)	67	YOUNG LOVERS — Paul and Paula (9)	63
WORLD OF OUR OWN, A — Seekers (3)	65	YOUNG ONES, THE — Cliff Richard (1)	62
WORLD WE KNEW, THE — Frank Sinatra (33)	67	YOUNG WORLD — Rick Nelson (19)	62
WORLD WITHOUT LOVE, A — Peter and Gordon (1)	64	YOUNGER GIRL — Critters (38)	66
WRAPPING PAPER — Cream (34)	66	YOUR BABY'S GONE SURFIN' — Duane Eddy (49)	63
WRECK OF THE ANTOINETTE — Dave Dee, Dozy, Beaky, Mick and Tich (14)	68	YOUR CHEATING HEART — Ray Charles (13)	62
WRITING ON THE WALL — Tommy Steele (30)	61	YOUR HURTIN' KIND OF LOVE — Dusty Springfield (37)	65
YA YA TWIST — Petula Clark (14)	62	(YOUR LOVE KEEPS LIFTING ME) HIGHER AND HIGHER — Jackie Wilson (11)	69
YEH YEH — Georgie Fame (1)	64	YOUR MA SAID YOU CRIED IN YOUR SLEEP LAST NIGHT — Doug Sheldon (29)	62
YELLOW SUBMARINE — Beatles (1)	66	YOUR TENDER LOOK — Joe Brown (31)	62
YES I WILL — Hollies (9)	65	YOUR TIME HASN'T COME YET BABY — Elvis Presley (22)	68
YES MY DARLING DAUGHTER — Eydie Gorme (10)	62	YOU'RE ALL I NEED TO GET BY — Marvin Gaye and Tammi Terrell (19)	68
YESTERDAY — Ray Charles (44)	67	YOU'RE BREAKIN' MY HEART — Keely Smith (14)	65
YESTERDAY — Marianne Faithfull (36)	65	YOU'RE DRIVING ME CRAZY — Temperance Seven (1)	61
YESTERDAY — Matt Monro (8)	65	YOU'RE MY EVERYTHING [A] — Max Bygraves (34)	69
YESTERDAY HAS GONE — Cupid's Inspiration (4)	68	YOU'RE MY EVERYTHING [B] — Temptations (26)	67
YESTERDAY MAN — Chris Andrews (3)	65	YOU'RE MY GIRL — Rockin' Berries (40)	65
YESTERDAY'S DREAMS — Four Tops (23)	68	(YOU'RE MY) SOUL AND INSPIRATION — Righteous Brothers (15)	66
YESTERDAY'S GONE — Chad Stuart and Jeremy Clyde (37)	63	YOU'RE MY WORLD — Cilla Black (1)	64
YESTER-ME YESTER-YOU YESTERDAY — Stevie Wonder (2)	69	YOU'RE NO GOOD — Swinging Blue Jeans (3)	64
YOU — Bandwagon (34)	69	YOU'RE SINGING OUR LOVE SONG TO SOMEBODY ELSE — Jerry Wallace (46)	60
YOU AIN'T GOIN' NOWHERE — Byrds (45)	68	YOU'RE SIXTEEN — Johnny Burnette (3)	61
YOU AIN'T LIVIN' TILL YOU'RE LOVIN' — Marvin Gaye and Tammi Terrell (21)	69	YOU'RE THE ONE [A] — Petula Clark (23)	65
YOU ALWAYS HURT THE ONE YOU LOVE — Clarence 'Frogman' Henry (6)	61	YOU'RE THE ONE [B] — Kathy Kirby (17)	64
YOU ARE BEAUTIFUL — Johnny Mathis (38)	60	YOU'RE THE ONLY GOOD THING — Jim Reeves (17)	61
YOU BETTER COME HOME — Petula Clark (44)	65	YOU'RE THE ONLY ONE — Val Doonican (37)	68
YOU CAN HAVE HIM — Dionne Warwick (37)	65	YOURS UNTIL TOMORROW — Gene Pitney (34)	68
YOU CAN NEVER STOP ME LOVING YOU — Kenny Lynch (10)	63	YOU'VE COME BACK — P. J. Proby (25)	66
YOU CAN'T HURRY LOVE — Supremes (3)	66	YOU'VE GOT LOVE — Buddy Holly (40)	64
YOU CAN'T SIT DOWN — Phil Upchurch Combo (39)	66	YOU'VE GOT TO HIDE YOUR LOVE AWAY — Silkie (28)	65
YOU DON'T HAVE TO BE A BABY TO CRY — Caravelles (6)	63	YOU'VE GOT YOUR TROUBLES — Fortunes (2)	65
YOU DON'T HAVE TO SAY YOU LOVE ME — Dusty Springfield (1)	66	YOU'VE LOST THAT LOVIN' FEELIN' — Cilla Black (2)	65
YOU DON'T KNOW — Helen Shapiro (1)	61	YOU'VE LOST THAT LOVIN' FEELIN' — Righteous Brothers (1)	65,69
YOU DON'T KNOW ME — Ray Charles (9)	62	YOU'VE MADE ME SO VERY HAPPY — Blood Sweat And Tears (35)	69
YOU DON'T KNOW WHAT YOU'VE GOT — Ral Donner (25)	61	YOU'VE NEVER BEEN IN LOVE LIKE THIS BEFORE — Unit Four Plus Two (14)	65
YOU DON'T LOVE ME — Gary Walker (26)	66	YOU'VE NOT CHANGED — Sandie Shaw (18)	67
YOU GAVE ME SOMEBODY TO LOVE — Manfred Mann (36)	66	YUMMY YUMMY YUMMY — Ohio Express (5)	68
YOU GOT SOUL — Johnny Nash (6)	69	'Z CARS', THEME FROM — Johnny Keating (8)	62
YOU GOT WHAT IT TAKES — Dave Clark Five (28)	67	'Z CARS', THEME FROM — Norrie Paramor (33)	62
YOU GOT WHAT IT TAKES — Marv Johnson (5)	60	ZABADAK! — Dave Dee, Dozy, Beaky, Mick and Tich (3)	67
YOU GOT WHAT IT TAKES — Johnny Kidd and the Pirates (25)	60	ZIP-A-DEE-DOO-DAH — Bob B Soxx and the Blue Jeans (45)	63
YOU GOTTA STOP — Elvis Presley (38)	67	ZORBA'S DANCE — Marcello Minerbi (6)	65
YOU KEEP ME HANGIN' ON — Supremes (8)	66		
YOU KEEP ME HANGIN' ON — Vanilla Fudge (18)	67		
YOU KEEP RUNNING AWAY — Four Tops (26)	67		
YOU KNOW WHAT I MEAN — Vernons Girls (37)	62		
YOU MAKE IT MOVE — Dave Dee, Dozy, Beaky, Mick and Tich (26)	65		
YOU MEAN EVERYTHING TO ME — Neil Sedaka (45)	60		
YOU MUST HAVE BEEN A BEAUTIFUL BABY — Bobby Darin (10)	61		
YOU NEVER CAN TELL — Chuck Berry (23)	64		
YOU ONLY LIVE TWICE — Nancy Sinatra (11)	67		
YOU ONLY YOU — Rita Pavone (21)	67		
YOU REALLY GOT ME — Kinks (1)	64		
YOU WERE MADE FOR ME — Freddie and the Dreamers (3)	63		
YOU WERE ON MY MIND — Crispian St. Peters (2)	66		
YOU WERE THERE — Heinz (26)	64		
YOU WON'T BE LEAVING — Herman's Hermits (20)	66		
YOU'LL ANSWER TO ME — Cleo Laine (5)	61		
YOU'LL NEVER GET TO HEAVEN — Dionne Warwick (20)	64		
YOU'LL NEVER KNOW — Shirley Bassey (6)	61		
YOU'LL NEVER KNOW WHAT YOU'RE MISSING — Emile Ford and the Checkmates (12)	60		

SINGLES CHARTS FACTS AND FEATS

Most weeks on chart: by artist

The following table lists all the recording acts that spent 100 weeks or more on the British singles chart from 1 January 1960 up to and including the chart for 27 December 1969. It is of course possible for an act to be credited with 2 or more chart weeks in the same week from simultaneous hits, which is why Cliff Richard's total exceeds the total number of weeks in the decade. Double-sided hits, EPs, LPs and double singles only count as one week each week.

	Weeks
Cliff Richard	537
Elvis Presley	444
Beatles	333
(plus 1 week backing Tony Sheridan)	
Roy Orbison	309
Shadows	303
(plus 328 weeks backing Cliff Richard)	
Jim Reeves	292
Billy Fury	258
Adam Faith	245
Hollies	231
Everly Brothers	221
Tom Jones	216
Brenda Lee	210
Beach Boys	193
Engelbert Humperdinck	189
Bachelors	187
Ken Dodd	183
Shirley Bassey	182
Rolling Stones	181
Herman's Hermits	176
Manfred Mann	176
Gene Pitney	176
Supremes	176
Cilla Black	166
Dusty Springfield	163
(plus 66 weeks with Springfields)	
Frank Sinatra	162
(plus 18 weeks with Nancy Sinatra, 9 weeks with Sammy Davis Jr)	

Six faces of Cliff RICHARD, the most successful artist of the decade with 537 weeks on the chart beating his nearest rival by almost 100 weeks.

Petula Clark	160
Mr Acker Bilk	158
Frank Ifield	158
Sandie Shaw	157
Kinks	152
Four Tops	151
Del Shannon	147
Dave Clark Five	146
Duane Eddy	142
Dave Dee, Dozy, Beaky, Mick and Tich	141
Kenny Ball	136
Bobby Vee	134
Who	133
Connie Francis	131
Searchers	128
Karl Denver	124
Ray Charles	123
Val Doonican	123
Small Faces	121
Seekers	120
Matt Monro	119
Helen Shapiro	119
Bobby Darin	118
Bee Gees	114
Gerry and the Pacemakers	114
Buddy Holly	114
Lonnie Donegan	110
Otis Redding (plus 16 weeks with Carla Thomas)	108
Lulu	105
Neil Sedaka	105
Frankie Vaughan	105
Georgie Fame	101

303 weeks for the SHADOWS. More weeks on the chart than any other group except the Beatles.

In terms of total weeks on the chart as a member of any chart act, the champion of the 1960s is Hank B Marvin, who recorded 303 weeks as a Shadow, 328 more weeks on Cliff Richard and the Shadows hits, and a final 9 weeks on 'Throw Down A Line,' a hit at the very end of 1969 for 'Cliff and Hank.' This gives him a total of 640 weeks on the singles charts of the 1960s.

Only four acts hit the charts in every year of the sixties. They were Cliff Richard (the only act to achieve a Top Ten hit in every year of the sixties), Elvis Presley (who missed the Top Ten only in 1967 and 1968), Roy Orbison (whose entire chart career has been confined to the sixties), and Jim Reeves.

ROLLING STONES relax with a drink in the company of Gene Pitney.

Most weeks on chart: year by year

The Top Ten chart acts for each year of the 1960s are as follows:

1960 Weeks
1. Cliff Richard — 78
2. Adam Faith — 77

3. Everly Brothers — 61
4. Emile Ford — 60
5. Connie Francis — 55
6. Anthony Newley — 53
7. Johnny and the Hurricanes — 52
   Duane Eddy — 52
9. Lonnie Donegan — 48
10. Johnny Preston — 45

1961 Weeks
1. Elvis Presley — 88

1962	Weeks
2 Shadows	65
3 Cliff Richard	64
4 Helen Shapiro	57
5 Connie Francis	54
6 Andy Stewart	53
7 Bobby Vee	52
8 Billy Fury	50
9 Shirley Bassey	49
10 Adam Faith	48

1962 Weeks
1. Mr Acker Bilk — 71
2. Chubby Checker — 70
3. Elvis Presley — 62
4. Cliff Richard — 58
5. Billy Fury — 57
6. Bobby Vee — 55
7. Kenny Ball — 54
8. Karl Denver — 50
9. Pat Boone — 48
10. Neil Sedaka — 46

Note: Chubby Checker 3 more weeks with Bobby Rydell

1963 Weeks
1. Beatles — 67
   Cliff Richard — 67
3. Shadows — 61
4. Frank Ifield — 60
5. Brenda Lee — 50
6. Billy Fury — 49
   Roy Orbison — 49
8. Del Shannon — 47
9. Gerry and the Pacemakers — 45
10. Springfields — 44

Note: Beatles 1 more week with Tony Sheridan

1964 Weeks
1. Jim Reeves — 73
2. Beatles — 72
3. Bachelors — 70
4. Cliff Richard — 57
5. Roy Orbison — 56
6. Elvis Presley — 54
   Searchers — 54
8. Manfred Mann — 47
9. Hollies — 46
   Rolling Stones — 46

1965 Weeks
1. Seekers — 51
2. Bob Dylan — 50
   Sandie Shaw — 50
4. Jim Reeves — 49
5. Cliff Richard — 48
6. Kinks — 47

Top Bob DYLAN and *Above* SONNY and CHER.

7. Animals — 42
   Hollies — 42
9. Rolling Stones — 40
10. Beatles — 39
    Tom Jones — 39

Note: Sonny and Cher chalked up 29 weeks in 1965, Sonny 11 more solo and Cher 10 more solo.

1966 Weeks
1. Dave Dee, Dozy, Beaky Mick and Tich — 50
2. Beach Boys — 48
3. Ken Dodd — 45
4. Dusty Springfield — 44
5. Cliff Richard — 43

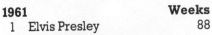

6	Cilla Black	42
	Roy Orbison	42
	Who	42
9	Elvis Presley	41
	Troggs	41

Note: Sonny and Cher managed 28 weeks in 1966 and Cher a further 19 solo.

1967   **Weeks**

1	Engelbert Humperdinck	97

2	Tom Jones	68
3	Monkees	63
4	Cliff Richard	46
	Supremes	46
6	Jimi Hendrix Experience	44

7	Four Tops	41
	Tremeloes	41
9	Small Faces	39
10	Vince Hill	37
	Sandie Shaw	37
	Troggs	37

Note: Kinks 27 weeks, Dave Davies a further 17 weeks solo.
Nancy Sinatra 29 weeks, plus 18 with Frank Sinatra and 1 with Lee Hazelwood
Otis Redding 24 solo plus 16 with Carla Thomas

1968   **Weeks**

1	Tom Jones	58
2	Engelbert Humperdinck	57
3	Des O'Connor	46
4	Bee Gees	42
5	Four Tops	41
	Otis Redding	41
7	Beatles	40
8	Beach Boys	37
	Love Affair	37
	Cliff Richard	37

1969   **Weeks**

1	Fleetwood Mac	52
	Frank Sinatra	52

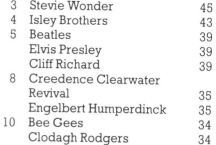

3	Stevie Wonder	45
4	Isley Brothers	43
5	Beatles	39
	Elvis Presley	39
	Cliff Richard	39
8	Creedence Clearwater Revival	35
	Engelbert Humperdinck	35
10	Bee Gees	34
	Clodagh Rodgers	34

Note: Marvin Gaye 31 weeks, plus 29 with Tammi Terrell,
Supremes 28, Temptations 19,
Supremes and Temptations 20

The annual chart champions of the sixties are therefore:

1960	Cliff Richard
1961	Elvis Presley
1962	Mr Acker Bilk
1963	Beatles
	Cliff Richard
1964	Jim Reeves
1965	Seekers
1966	Dave Dee, Dozy, Beaky, Mick and Tich
1967	Engelbert Humperdinck

1968	Tom Jones
1969	Fleetwood Mac
	Frank Sinatra

60 weeks or more in one year was achieved in the sixties as follows:

97 weeks	Engelbert Humperdinck	1967
88 weeks	Elvis Presley	1961
78 weeks	Cliff Richard	1960
77 weeks	Adam Faith	1960
73 weeks	Jim Reeves	1964
72 weeks	Beatles	1964
71 weeks	Mr Acker Bilk	1962
70 weeks	Bachelors	1964
	Chubby Checker	1962
68 weeks	Tom Jones	1967
67 weeks	Beatles	1963
	Cliff Richard	1963
65 weeks	Shadows	1961
64 weeks	Cliff Richard	1961
63 weeks	Monkees	1967
62 weeks	Elvis Presley	1962
61 weeks	Everly Brothers	1960
	Shadows	1963
60 weeks	Emile Ford	1960
	Frank Ifield	1963

Most weeks on chart by disc: consecutively

Weeks		
56	*Release Me	Engelbert Humperdinck
55	Stranger On The Shore	Mr Acker Bilk
39	My Way	Frank Sinatra
39	I Love You Because	Jim Reeves
38	A Scottish Soldier	Andy Stewart
36	*I Pretend	Des O'Connor
31	*She Loves You	The Beatles
30	As Long As He Needs Me	Shirley Bassey
30	Theme From "A Summer Place"	Percy Faith
30	Just Loving You	Anita Harris
30	He'll Have To Go	Jim Reeves
29	*What A Wonderful World/Cabaret	Louis Armstrong
29	There Goes My Everything	Engelbert Humperdinck
28	*I Remember You	Frank Ifield
27	Let's Twist Again	Chubby Checker
27	*The Last Waltz	Engelbert Humperdinck
27	*Wooden Heart	Elvis Presley
26	Help Yourself	Tom Jones
26	Island Of Dreams	Springfields
25	I'll Never Fall In Love Again	Tom Jones
25	*Distant Drums	Jim Reeves
25	I Won't Forget You	Jim Reeves
25	*Telstar	The Tornados

The Archies' 'Sugar Sugar' spent the first 12 of its total of 26 weeks on the chart during the sixties. It dropped off the chart after 14 weeks of chart life in 1970.

*Indicates record was a number one hit.

Most weeks on chart by disc: in total

TOTAL WEEKS irrespective of the number of re-issues or re-entries

Weeks	Separate chart runs		
56	1	*Release Me	Engelbert Humperdinck
55	1	Stranger On The Shore	Mr Acker Bilk
40	2	A Scottish Soldier	Andy Stewart
39	1	My Way	Frank Sinatra
39	1	I Love You Because	Jim Reeves
38	2	Somewhere My Love	Mike Sammes Singers
36	1	*I Pretend	Des O'Connor
34	4	Let's Twist Again	Chubby Checker
33	2	*She Loves You	The Beatles
31	2	He'll Have To Go	Jim Reeves
30	1	As Long As He Needs Me	Shirley Bassey
30	1	Theme From "A Summer Place"	Percy Faith
30	1	Just Loving You	Anita Harris

*Indicates record was a number one hit. It is remarkable that only three of the thirteen records that enjoyed a total chart life of over thirty weeks in the sixties hit number one.

All these songs, apart from 'She Loves You' and 'Let's Twist Again' were romantic ballads very far away in style from the dominant beat of the sixties.

Most hits by artist

Double-sided hits, EPs and LPs only count as one hit each time. Re-issues and re-entries do not count as new hits, but re-recordings of the same song by the same act do count as two hits. A record is a hit if it made the singles chart, even if only for 1 week at number 50.

45 Cliff Richard
42 Elvis Presley
28 Roy Orbison
25 Shadows
(plus 25 backing Cliff Richard)
24 Adam Faith
24 Billy Fury
23 Beatles
(plus one backing Tony Sheridan)
22 Brenda Lee
22 Jim Reeves
21 Everly Brothers
20 Hollies
19 Beach Boys
19 Petula Clark
19 Dave Clark Five
18 Supremes
(plus one with Temptations)
17 Bachelors
17 Cilla Black
17 Herman's Hermits
17 Tom Jones
17 Manfred Mann
17 Gene Pitney
17 Sandie Shaw
17 Frank Sinatra
(plus one with Sammy Davis Jr,
one with Nancy Sinatra)
16 Shirley Bassey
16 Ray Charles
16 Duane Eddy
16 Dusty Springfield
(plus five with Springfields)
15 Connie Francis
15 Frank Ifield
15 Kinks
15 Rolling Stones
14 Bobby Darin
14 Ken Dodd
14 Four Tops
14 Otis Redding
(plus two with Carla Thomas)
14 Searchers
14 Del Shannon
14 Who
13 Dave Dee, Dozy, Beaky,
   Mick and Tich
13 Buddy Holly

13 Frankie Vaughan
12 Russ Conway
(plus one with Dorothy Squires)
12 Val Doonican
12 Georgie Fame
12 Lulu
12 Matt Monro
12 Small Faces
11 Karl Denver
11 Bob Dylan
11 P J Proby
11 Helen Shapiro
10 Bee Gees
10 Mr Acker Bilk
10 Joe Brown
10 Nat 'King' Cole
10 Spencer Davis Group
10 Lonnie Donegan
10 Four Seasons
10 Vince Hill
10 Monkees
10 Neil Sedaka
10 Temptations
(plus one with Diana Ross and the Supremes)
10 Tremeloes
(plus eight backing Brian Poole)
10 Bobby Vee
10 Andy Williams

Mention should also be made of the Animals who had nine hits plus four as the reconstituted Eric Burdon and the Animals. Eric Burdon also had two more solo hits, bringing to 15 the number of hits featuring his lead vocals. Donovan had nine solo hits plus one more with the Jeff Beck Group. Wayne Fontana had four solo hits and six earlier when backed by the Mindbenders. They went on to have four hits without Wayne Fontana. Marvin Gaye had four solo hits in the sixties, plus eight more in partnership with four different female singers. Sonny and Cher had eight hits, and Cher had four more on her own. The Walker Brothers had nine hits, and then Scott Walker had three solo hits, Gary Walker two on his own and John Walker one.

Most Top Ten hits by artist

The same rules apply as for the 'Most Hits' list, except that a disc must have made the Top Ten for at least one week between 1 Jan. 60 and 31 Dec. 69 to qualify.

34 Cliff Richard
(includes one hit as 'Cliff and Hank')
21 Beatles
(includes one hit as
'Beatles with Billy Preston')
19 Elvis Presley
15 Hollies
14 Shadows
(plus 21 backing Cliff Richard)
13 Manfred Mann
13 Rolling Stones
11 Adam Faith
11 Billy Fury
11 Kinks
10 Beach Boys
10 Cilla Black
10 Tom Jones
10 Roy Orbison
10 Gene Pitney
10 Dusty Springfield
(plus two with Springfields)
9 Herman's Hermits
9 Who
8 Bachelors
8 Dave Dee, Dozy, Beaky,
  Mick and Tich
8 Engelbert Humperdinck
8 Del Shannon
8 Sandie Shaw
7 Animals
7 Petula Clark
7 Bobby Darin
7 Donovan
7 Everly Brothers
7 Brenda Lee
7 Small Faces
7 Supremes
(plus one with Temptations)
7 Bobby Vee
6 Shirley Bassey
6 Bee Gees
6 Dave Clark Five
6 Lonnie Donegan
6 Craig Douglas
6 Bob Dylan
6 Duane Eddy
6 Connie Francis
6 Gerry and the Pacemakers
6 Frank Ifield
6 Lulu
6 Jim Reeves
6 Searchers
6 Neil Sedaka
6 Seekers
6 Tremeloes
(plus four with Brian Poole)
5 Val Doonican

5 Four Tops
5 Eden Kane
5 Billy J Kramer and the Dakotas
5 Matt Monro
5 Move
5 Anthony Newley
5 Helen Shapiro
5 Troggs
5 Yardbirds

Most hits without a number one hit

24 Billy Fury
(who had one number two hit)
22 Brenda Lee
(who had one number three hit)
17 Gene Pitney
(who had two number two hits)
16 Duane Eddy
(who had two number two hits)
15 Connie Francis
(who had one number two hit)
14 Bobby Darin
(who had two number two hits)
14 Otis Redding
(whose only Top Ten hit reached number 3)
14 Who
(who had two number two hits)
13 Buddy Holly
(who had one number three hit)
12 Russ Conway
(who had one number seven hit)
12 Val Doonican
(who had one number two hit)
12 Lulu
(who had one number two hit)
12 Matt Monroe
(who had one number three hit)

Connie Francis, Bobby Darin, Buddy Holly and Russ Conway all had number one hits in the Fifties.

Most Top Ten hits without a number one hit

11 Billy Fury
10 Gene Pitney
9 Who
7 Bobby Darin, Donovan, Brenda Lee, Bobby Vee

Most hits without a Top Ten hit

None of these acts had a Top Ten hit during the sixties, despite having at least five hit singles.

9 Fats Domino
(highest sixties chart placing: 11)
8 Wilson Pickett
(highest sixties chart placing: 12)
8 Paul and Barry Ryan
(highest sixties chart placing: 13)
7 Cream
(highest sixties chart placing: 11)
6 Paul Anka
(highest sixties chart placing: 17)
6 Bert Weedon
(highest sixties chart placing: 24)
5 Tony Bennett
(highest sixties chart placing: 21)
5 Joe Loss
(highest sixties chart placing: 21)
5 Gene Vincent
(highest sixties chart placing: 15)

Andy Stewart was on the chart for 53 weeks in 1961 without ever climbing higher than number 19.

Paul Anka, Tony Bennett, Fats Domino and Bert Weedon all had Top Ten hits in the fifties.

Least successful chart acts

The following acts managed a total chart career in the sixties which consisted of 1 week at number 50.

31 Mar 60	Santo and Johnny	Teardrop
21 Jul 60	Jimmy Clanton	Another Sleepless Night
25 Aug 60	Hal Page and the Whalers	Going Back To My Home Town
27 Oct 60	Chaquito	Never On Sunday
23 Feb 61	Tony Osborne Sound	The Man From Madrid
2 Nov 61	Moontrekkers	Night Of The Vampire
4 Oct 62	Tony Hatch	Out Of This World
10 Jan 63	Cookies	Chains
3 Oct 63	Angels	My Boyfriend's Back
30 Jul 64	Marvin Gaye and Mary Wells	Once Upon A Time
22 May 66	Keith Relf	Mr Zero
5 Jun 67	Tim Hardin	Hang On To A Dream
21 Feb 68	Sundragon	Green Tambourine

Santo and Johnny had a hit in the fifties, while Tony Osborne had a hit in the seventies. Marvin Gaye and Mary Wells had solo hits in the sixties, and Keith Relf was the lead singer of the highly successful Yardbirds.

Before the chart was extended from a 30 to a 50 (from 10 Mar 60) Toni Fisher managed to make her only chart appearance at number 30 – on 12 Feb 60 with her American number three hit, 'The Big Hurt.'

Number one hits by artist

There were 187 number ones in the 1960s, by 113 different acts.

17 Beatles
(including one with Billy Preston)
11 Elvis Presley
8 Rolling Stones
7 Cliff Richard
5 Shadows
(plus five backing Cliff Richard)
4 Frank Ifield
3 Everly Brothers
3 Georgie Fame
3 Gerry and the Pacemakers
3 Kinks
3 Manfred Mann
3 Roy Orbison
3 Sandie Shaw
3 Searchers
2 Beach Boys
2 Bee Gees
2 Cilla Black
2 Petula Clark
2 Spencer Davis Group
2 Engelbert Humperdinck

Five leather jackets comprising three full-time BEATLES joined by Pete Best and Gene Vincent doing his Nelson impression. *Below* The Beatles joined by Ringo displaying a more outlandish style towards the end of the decade fronted on this occasion by George Harrison.

2   Tom Jones
2   Billy J Kramer and the Dakotas
2   Anthony Newley
2   Seekers
2   Helen Shapiro
2   Walker Brothers

The Tremeloes had one chart topper, and one more backing Brian Poole. Frank and Nancy Sinatra both had one solo number one, and one more as a duet. The following acts had number one hits in both the fifties and the sixties: Shirley Bassey, Lonnie Donegan, Everly Brothers, Adam Faith, Michael Holliday, Elvis Presley, Cliff Richard, Frank Sinatra and Frankie Vaughan.

Of the sixties chart toppers, only Elvis Presley, Cliff Richard and the Bee Gees had further number one hits in the seventies. Elvis and Cliff thus share the distinction of being the only acts to top the charts in each of three decades.

Most weeks at number one by artist

69   Beatles
44   Elvis Presley
20   Cliff Richard
18   Rolling Stones
17   Frank Ifield
16   Shadows
     (plus 17 weeks backing Cliff Richard)
12   Everly Brothers
11   Gerry and the Pacemakers
11   Engelbert Humperdinck

Most weeks at number one by one record

8	It's Now Or Never	Elvis Presley	(1960)
8	Wonderful Land	The Shadows	(1962)
8	Sugar Sugar	Archies	(1969)
7	Cathy's Clown	Everly Brothers	(1960)
7	I Remember You	Frank Ifield	(1962)
7	From Me To You	Beatles	(1963)
7	Green Green Grass Of Home	Tom Jones	(1966-7)
7	Hello Goodbye	Beatles	(1967-8)
6	Wooden Heart	Elvis Presley	(1961)
6	The Young Ones	Cliff Richard and the Shadows	(1962)
6	She Loves You	Beatles	(1963)
6	Release Me	Engelbert Humperdinck	(1967)
6	A Whiter Shade Of Pale	Procol Harum	(1967)
6	Those Were The Days	Mary Hopkin	(1968)
6	Get Back	Beatles with Billy Preston	(1969)

All these records had only one spell at the top of the charts, with the exception of 'She Loves You,' which spent 4 weeks at the top, then slipped down for a total of 7 weeks before returning to the top for a further 2 weeks at number one. 'What Do You Want To Make Those Eyes At Me For?' by Emile Ford and the Checkmates was at number one for 6 weeks, of which only 4 weeks were in the sixties. 'Two Little Boys' by Rolf Harris was also at number one for 6 weeks, of which only 2 weeks were in the sixties.

First two hits at number one

In the sixties, only one act hit number one with each of its first two hits, and they went on to complete the hat-trick of chart-toppers with their first three hits, which were also their first three releases. They were **Gerry and the Pacemakers,** who thereby set a record which is unlikely ever to be equalled.

Number one on first chart of the sixties – Emile FORD seen here without his Checkmates. *Pictorial Press.*

First chart of the sixties

1	What Do You Want To Make Those Eyes At Me For? Emile Ford and the Checkmates
2	What Do You Want? Adam Faith
3	Seven Little Girls Sitting In The Back Seat Avons
4	Oh Carol Neil Sedaka
5	Travellin' Light Cliff Richard
6	Rawhide Frankie Laine
7	Jingle Bell Rock Max Bygraves
8	Staccato's Theme Elmer Bernstein
8	Snow Coach Russ Conway
10	Little White Bull Tommy Steele
11	More And More Party Pops Russ Conway
12	Among My Souvenirs Connie Francis
13	Some Kinda Earthquake Duane Eddy
14	Bad Boy Marty Wilde
15	Piano Party Winifred Atwell
16	Little Donkey Beverly Sisters
17	Put Your Head On My Shoulder Paul Anka
17	Heartaches By The Number Guy Mitchell
19	Reveille Rock Johnny and the Hurricanes
19	Red River Rock Johnny and the Hurricanes
19	Mack The Knife Bobby Darin
22	Teenbeat Sandy Nelson
23	Deck Of Cards Wink Martindale
24	Way Down Yonder In New Orleans Freddy Cannon
25	Be My Guest Fats Domino

26 We Got Love
    Alma Cogan
27 Only Boy In The World
    Stevie Marsh
28 In The Mood
    Ernie Fields
28 Starry Eyed
    Michael Holliday
28 Living Doll
    Cliff Richard

Last chart of the sixties

1   Two Little Boys
    Rolf Harris
2   Ruby Don't Take Your Love
    To Town
    Kenny Rogers and the First Edition
3   Sugar Sugar
    Archies
4   Suspicious Minds
    Elvis Presley
5   Melting Pot
    Blue Mink
6   Yester-Me, Yester-You, Yester-Day
    Stevie Wonder
7   All I Have To Do Is Dream
    Bobbie Gentry and Glen Campbell
8   Winter World Of Love
    Engelbert Humperdinck

9   Tracy
    Cuff Links
10 Without Love
    Tom Jones
11 The Onion Song
    Marvin Gaye and Tammi Terrell
12 Good Old Rock 'n' Roll
    Dave Clark Five
13 The Leavin' (Durham Town)
    Roger Whittaker
14 (Call Me) Number One
    Tremeloes
15 Love Is All
    Malcolm Roberts
16 The Liquidator
    Harry J and the All Stars
17 But You Love Me Daddy
    Jim Reeves
18 Loneliness
    Des O'Connor
19 Green River
    Creedence Clearwater Revival
20 Nobody's Child
    Karen Young
21 Something/Come Together
    Beatles
22 With The Eyes Of A Child
    Cliff Richard
23 Sweet Dream
    Jethro Tull
24 Wonderful World
    Beautiful People
    Jimmy Cliff

25 Love's Been Good To Me
    Frank Sinatra
26 Highway Song
    Nancy Sinatra
27 Someday We'll Be Together
    Diana Ross and the Supremes
28 Return Of Django
    Upsetters
29 If I Thought You'd Ever Change
    Your Mind
    Cilla Black
30 Reflections Of My Life
    Marmalade
31 Oh Well
    Fleetwood Mac
32 She Sold Me Magic
    Lou Christie
33 Biljo
    Clodagh Rodgers
34 I'm Gonna Make You Mine
    Lou Christie
35 Seventh Son
    Georgie Fame
36 Boy Named Sue
    Johnny Cash
37 Hitchin' A Ride
    Vanity Fare
38 Gin Gan Goolie
    Scaffold
39 Good Morning Starshine
    Oliver
40 I'll Never Fall In Love Again
    Bobbie Gentry
41 Rub A Dub Dub
    Equals
42 My Way
    Frank Sinatra
43 Holy City
    Moira Anderson
44 He Ain't Heavy, He's My Brother
    Hollies
45 Here Comes The Star
    Herman's Hermits
46 Proud Mary
    Checkmates Ltd
47 Comin' Home
    Delaney and Bonnie and Friends
    featuring Eric Clapton
48 Robin's Return
    Neville Dickie
49 Je T'Aime . . . Moi Non Plus
    Jane Birkin and Serge Gainsbourg
50 What Does It Take
    Junior Walker and the All Stars

The last number one single of the sixties – Rolf HARRIS. *Pictorial Press.*

One Hit wonders

THUNDERCLAP NEWMAN. *Pictorial Press.*

Qualification: One number one hit in the sixties, and no other singles chart placing during that decade.

Archies	Sugar Sugar	(1969)
Jane Birkin and Serge Gainsbourg	Je T'Aime...Moi Non Plus	(1969)
Crazy World Of Arthur Brown	Fire	(1968)
B Bumble and the Stingers	Nut Rocker	(1962)
Overlanders	Michelle	(1966)
Nancy Sinatra and Frank Sinatra	Something Stupid	(1967)
Thunderclap Newman	Something In The Air	(1969)
Ricky Valance	Tell Laura I Love Her	(1960)
Zager and Evans	In The Year 2525	(1969)

Four of the nine acts to qualify for this list did so in the final year of the decade. Only Thunderclap Newman, who enjoyed one further week on the chart in 1970, have had hits either before or after the sixties.

Nancy Sinatra and Frank Sinatra have of course had hits as solo singers. The most successful of these one hit wonders are the Archies, who enjoyed 8 weeks at number one. The Overlanders' at the other end of the spectrum, had only 10 weeks of chart life, of which 3 weeks were spent at the very top.

Straight in at Number One

Nancy and Frank SINATRA, a one hit wonder, father and daughter partnership. *Pictorial Press.*

Only three records came into the chart at number one in the sixties.

3 Nov 60	It's Now Or Never	Elvis Presley
11 Jan 62	The Young Ones	Cliff Richard and the Shadows
23 Apr 69	Get Back	The Beatles with Billy Preston

'Get Back' was Billy Preston's first chart record, so he became the only person since Al Martino (in the first British singles chart of all on 14 Nov 52) to spend his first week on the singles chart at number one.

Highest new entries

Apart from the three records listed above that came straight into the singles chart at number one, the following records came straight into the Top Ten in their first week.

Straight in at number two:

Day Tripper/We Can Work It Out	The Beatles	9 Dec 65
Paperback Writer	The Beatles	16 Jun 66
All You Need Is Love	The Beatles	12 Jul 67

Straight in at number three:

A Hard Day's Night	The Beatles	16 Jul 64

Straight in at number four:

Little Sister/His Latest Flame	Elvis Presley	2 Nov 61
The Ballad Of John And Yoko	The Beatles	4 Jun 69

Straight in at number five:

My Old Man's A Dustman	Lonnie Donegan	24 Mar 60
Help!	The Beatles	29 Jul 65
Paint It Black	The Rolling Stones	19 May 66
Penny Lane/Strawberry Fields Forever	The Beatles	23 Feb 67

Straight in at number six:

Fall In Love With You	Cliff Richard	24 Mar 60
I Feel Fine	The Beatles	3 Dec 64

Straight in at number eight:

When Johnny Comes Marching Home	Adam Faith	30 Jun 60
Can't Buy Me Love	The Beatles	26 Mar 64
Yellow Submarine/Eleanor Rigby	The Beatles	11 Aug 66

Straight in at number nine:

Hello Goodbye	The Beatles	29 Nov 67
Honky Tonk Women	The Rolling Stones	9 Jul 69

Straight in at number ten:

A Voice In The Wilderness	Cliff Richard	22 Jan 60
Stuck On You	Elvis Presley	7 Apr 60
I Want To Hold Your Hand	The Beatles	5 Dec 63

The ROLLING STONES came straight in at number five with 'Paint It Black' in 1966. *Pictorial Press.*

All these records hit number one except 'Penny Lane/Strawberry Fields Forever,' 'Fall In Love With You,' 'When Johnny Comes Marching Home' and 'A Voice In The Wilderness.' This list shows the rapid and massive sales regularly achieved by the Beatles in the mid-sixties. From the beginning of 1962, when Cliff Richard's 'The Young Ones' crashed in at number one, until the end of the decade, no record by any act except the Beatles (13 times) and the Rolling Stones (twice) came into the chart in the Top Ten. In 1968, no record came in first week into the Top Ten. The highest new entry that year was at number 11 – by the Beatles with 'Lady Madonna' on 20 March. Of the Beatles' 17 number ones in the sixties, one came straight in at number one, and 14 others hit number one in their second week on the chart. Eleven of those 14 spent their first week on the charts in the Top Ten.

Most consecutive number ones

11 in a row:	Beatles	(From Me To You through to Yellow Submarine/Eleanor Rigby, 1963 to 1966)
6 in a row:	Beatles	(All You Need Is Love through to Ballad Of John and Yoko, 1967 to 1969)
5 in a row:	Elvis Presley	(His Latest Flame through to Return To Sender, 1961 to 1962)
5 in a row:	Rolling Stones	(It's All Over Now through to Get Off Of My Cloud, 1964 to 1965)
4 in a row:	Elvis Presley	(It's Now Or Never through to Surrender, 1960 to 1961). When the third of these four, Wooden Heart, hit the top on 23 March 1961, Elvis completed the first number one hat-trick in British chart history.
3 in a row:	Frank Ifield	(I Remember You, Lovesick Blues and Wayward Wind, 1962 to 1963). The first number one hat-trick by a British artist.
3 in a row:	Gerry and the Pacemakers	(How Do You Do It, I Like It and You'll Never Walk Alone, 1963). The first and only instance of an act hitting number one with each of their first three releases.

Gerry without his Pacemakers. *Pictorial Press.*

Successive releases for the purposes of this table are successive official single releases. The Beatles' two runs of number ones were each interrupted by irregular releases. An old single with Tony Sheridan reached number 29 in the midst of their 11 number ones, and their double EP 'Magical Mystery Tour' made number two while 'Hello Goodbye' was becoming the second of their six chart-toppers on the trot. An EP by Elvis, 'Follow That Dream,' pottered about the lower reaches of the charts during Elvis' run of five consecutive number ones.

The number one singles

Date disc hit the top	Title/Artist/Label	Number of weeks at number one

1960

1 Jan	**What Do You Want To Make Those Eyes At Me For?** Emile Ford and the Checkmates (Pye)	4 (plus 2 in 1959)
29 Jan	**Starry Eyed** Michael Holliday (Columbia)	1
5 Feb	**Why** Anthony Newley (Decca)	4

Record Retailer, now *Music Week,* began publication of a Top Fifty in their issue dated 10 Mar 60. From this date onwards, their charts are used. The final *New Musical Express* chart used is that of 26 Feb 60, as the chart published in *Record Retailer* on 10 Mar 60 was dated 5 Mar 60 and clearly corresponded with the *New Musical Express* chart of 4 Mar 60.

10 Mar	**Poor Me** Adam Faith (Parlophone)	1
17 Mar	**Running Bear** Johnny Preston (Mercury)	2
31 Mar	**My Old Man's A Dustman** Lonnie Donegan (Pye)	4
28 Apr	**Do You Mind** Anthony Newley (Decca)	1
5 May	**Cathy's Clown** Everly Brothers (Warner Brothers)	7
23 Jun	**Three Steps To Heaven** Eddie Cochran (London)	2
7 Jul	**Good Timin'** Jimmy Jones (MGM)	3
28 Jul	**Please Don't Tease** Cliff Richard and the Shadows (Columbia)	1
4 Aug	**Shakin' All Over** Johnny Kidd and the Pirates (HMV)	1
11 Aug	**Please Don't Tease** Cliff Richard and the Shadows (Columbia)	2
25 Aug	**Apache** Shadows (Columbia)	5
29 Sep	**Tell Laura I Love Her** Ricky Valance (Columbia)	3
20 Oct	**Only The Lonely** Roy Orbison (London)	2
3 Nov	**It's Now Or Never** Elvis Presley (RCA)	8
29 Dec	**I Love You** Cliff Richard and the Shadows (Columbia)	2

1961

12 Jan	**Poetry In Motion** Johnny Tillotson (London)	2
26 Jan	**Are You Lonesome Tonight?** Elvis Presley (RCA)	4
23 Feb	**Sailor** Petula Clark (Pye)	1
2 Mar	**Walk Right Back** Everly Brothers (Warner Brothers)	3
23 Mar	**Wooden Heart** Elvis Presley (RCA)	6
4 May	**Blue Moon** Marcels (Pye International)	2
18 May	**On The Rebound** Floyd Cramer (RCA)	1
25 May	**You're Driving Me Crazy** Temperance Seven (Parlophone)	1
1 Jun	**Surrender** Elvis Presley (RCA)	4
29 Jun	**Runaway** Del Shannon (London)	3
20 Jul	**Temptation** Everly Brothers (Warner Brothers)	2
3 Aug	**Well I Ask You** Eden Kane (Decca)	1
10 Aug	**You Don't Know** Helen Shapiro (Columbia)	3
31 Aug	**Johnny Remember Me** John Leyton (Top Rank)	3
21 Sep	**Reach For The Stars/Climb Ev'ry Mountain** Shirley Bassey (Columbia)	1
28 Sep	**Johnny Remember Me** John Leyton (Top Rank)	1
5 Oct	**Kon-Tiki** Shadows (Columbia)	1
12 Oct	**Michael** Highwaymen (HMV)	1

19 Oct	**Walkin' Back To Happiness**	
	Helen Shapiro (Columbia)	3
9 Nov	**Little Sister/His Latest Flame**	
	Elvis Presley (RCA)	4
7 Dec	**Tower Of Strength** Frankie Vaughan (Philips)	3
28 Dec	**Moon River** Danny Williams (HMV)	2

1962

11 Jan	**The Young Ones**	
	Cliff Richard and the Shadows (Columbia)	6
22 Feb	**Rock-A-Hula Baby/Can't Help Falling In Love**	
	Elvis Presley (RCA)	4
22 Mar	**Wonderful Land** Shadows (Columbia)	8
17 May	**Nut Rocker** B. Bumble and the Stingers (Top Rank)	1
24 May	**Good Luck Charm** Elvis Presley (RCA)	5
28 Jun	**Come Outside**	
	Mike Sarne with Wendy Richard (Parlophone)	2
12 Jul	**I Can't Stop Loving You** Ray Charles (HMV)	2
26 Jul	**I Remember You** Frank Ifield (Columbia)	7
13 Sep	**She's Not You** Elvis Presley (RCA)	3
4 Oct	**Telstar** Tornados (Decca)	5
8 Nov	**Lovesick Blues** Frank Ifield (Columbia)	5
13 Dec	**Return To Sender** Elvis Presley (RCA)	3

1963

3 Jan	**The Next Time/Bachelor Boy**	
	Cliff Richard and the Shadows (Columbia)	3
24 Jan	**Dance On** Shadows (Columbia)	1
31 Jan	**Diamonds** Jet Harris and Tony Meehan (Decca)	3
21 Feb	**Wayward Wind** Frank Ifield (Columbia)	3
14 Mar	**Summer Holiday**	
	Cliff Richard and the Shadows (Columbia)	2
28 Mar	**Foot Tapper** Shadows (Columbia)	1
4 Apr	**Summer Holiday**	
	Cliff Richard and the Shadows (Columbia)	1
11 Apr	**How Do You Do It?**	
	Gerry and the Pacemakers (Columbia)	3
2 May	**From Me To You** Beatles (Parlophone)	7
20 Jun	**I Like It** Gerry and the Pacemakers (Columbia)	4
18 Jul	**Confessin'** Frank Ifield (Columbia)	2
1 Aug	**(You're The) Devil In Disguise**	
	Elvis Presley (RCA)	1
8 Aug	**Sweets For My Sweet** Searchers (Pye)	2
22 Aug	**Bad To Me**	
	Billy J Kramer and the Dakotas (Parlophone)	3
12 Sep	**She Loves You** Beatles (Parlophone)	4
10 Oct	**Do You Love Me**	
	Brian Poole and the Tremeloes (Decca)	3
31 Oct	**You'll Never Walk Alone**	
	Gerry and the Pacemakers (Columbia)	4
28 Nov	**She Loves You** Beatles (Parlophone)	2
12 Dec	**I Want To Hold Your Hand** Beatles (Parlophone)	5

1964

16 Jan	**Glad All Over** Dave Clark Five (Columbia)	2
30 Jan	**Needles And Pins** Searchers (Pye)	3
20 Feb	**Diane** Bachelors (Decca)	1
27 Feb	**Anyone Who Had A Heart** Cilla Black (Parlophone)	3

Date	Title	Weeks
19 Mar	**Little Children** Billy J Kramer and the Dakotas (Parlophone)	2
2 Apr	**Can't Buy Me Love** Beatles (Parlophone)	3
23 Apr	**World Without Love** Peter and Gordon (Columbia)	2
7 May	**Don't Throw Your Love Away** Searchers (Pye)	2
21 May	**Juliet** Four Pennies (Philips)	1
28 May	**You're My World** Cilla Black (Parlophone)	4
25 Jun	**It's Over** Roy Orbison (London)	2
9 Jul	**House Of The Rising Sun** Animals (Columbia)	1
16 Jul	**It's All Over Now** Rolling Stones (Decca)	1
23 Jul	**A Hard Day's Night** Beatles (Parlophone)	3
13 Aug	**Do Wah Diddy Diddy** Manfred Mann (HMV)	2
27 Aug	**Have I The Right** Honeycombs (Pye)	2
10 Sep	**You Really Got Me** Kinks (Pye)	2
24 Sep	**I'm Into Something Good** Herman's Hermits (Columbia)	2
8 Oct	**Oh Pretty Woman** Roy Orbison (London)	2
22 Oct	**(There's) Always Something There To Remind Me** Sandie Shaw (Pye)	3
12 Nov	**Oh Pretty Woman** Roy Orbison (London)	1
19 Nov	**Baby Love** Supremes (Stateside)	2
3 Dec	**Little Red Rooster** Rolling Stones (Decca)	1
10 Dec	**I Feel Fine** Beatles (Parlophone)	5

1965

Date	Title	Weeks
14 Jan	**Yeh Yeh** Georgie Fame with the Blue Flames (Columbia)	2
28 Jan	**Go Now** Moody Blues (Decca)	1
4 Feb	**You've Lost That Lovin' Feelin'** Righteous Brothers (London)	2
18 Feb	**Tired Of Waiting For You** Kinks (Pye)	1
25 Feb	**I'll Never Find Another You** Seekers (Columbia)	2
11 Mar	**It's Not Unusual** Tom Jones (Decca)	1
18 Mar	**The Last Time** Rolling Stones (Decca)	3
8 Apr	**Concrete And Clay** Unit Four Plus Two (Decca)	1
15 Apr	**The Minute You're Gone** Cliff Richard (Columbia)	1
22 Apr	**Ticket To Ride** Beatles (Parlophone)	3
13 May	**King Of The Road** Roger Miller (Philips)	1
20 May	**Where Are You Now (My Love)** Jackie Trent (Pye)	1
27 May	**Long Live Love** Sandie Shaw (Pye)	3
17 Jun	**Crying In The Chapel** Elvis Presley (RCA)	1
24 Jun	**I'm Alive** Hollies (Parlophone)	1
1 Jul	**Crying In The Chapel** Elvis Presley (RCA)	1
8 Jul	**I'm Alive** Hollies (Parlophone)	2
22 Jul	**Mr Tambourine Man** Byrds (CBS)	2
5 Aug	**Help!** Beatles (Parlophone)	3
26 Aug	**I Got You Babe** Sonny and Cher (Atlantic)	2
9 Sep	**(I Can't Get No) Satisfaction** Rolling Stones (Decca)	2
23 Sep	**Make It Easy On Yourself** Walker Brothers (Philips)	1
30 Sep	**Tears** Ken Dodd (Columbia)	5
4 Nov	**Get Off Of My Cloud** Rolling Stones (Decca)	3
25 Nov	**The Carnival Is Over** Seekers (Columbia)	3
16 Dec	**Day Tripper/We Can Work It Out** Beatles (Parlophone)	5

1966	20 Jan	**Keep On Running**	
		Spencer Davis Group (Fontana)	1
	27 Jan	**Michelle** Overlanders (Pye)	3
	17 Feb	**These Boots Are Made For Walkin'**	
		Nancy Sinatra (Reprise)	4
	17 Mar	**The Sun Ain't Gonna Shine Anymore**	
		Walker Brothers (Philips)	4
	14 Apr	**Somebody Help Me**	
		Spencer Davis Group (Fontana)	2
	28 Apr	**You Don't Have To Say You Love Me**	
		Dusty Springfield (Philips)	1
	5 May	**Pretty Flamingo** Manfred Mann (HMV)	3
	26 May	**Paint It Black** Rolling Stones (Decca)	1
	2 Jun	**Strangers In The Night** Frank Sinatra (Reprise)	3
	23 Jun	**Paperback Writer** Beatles (Parlophone)	2
	7 Jul	**Sunny Afternoon** Kinks (Pye)	2
	21 Jul	**Get Away**	
		Georgie Fame with the Blue Flames (Columbia)	1
	28 Jul	**Out Of Time**	
		Chris Farlowe and the Thunderbirds (Immediate)	1
	4 Aug	**With A Girl Like You** Troggs (Fontana)	2
	18 Aug	**Yellow Submarine/Eleanor Rigby**	
		Beatles (Parlophone)	4
	15 Sep	**All Or Nothing** Small Faces (Decca)	1
	22 Sep	**Distant Drums** Jim Reeves (RCA)·	5
	27 Oct	**Reach Out I'll Be There**	
		Four Tops (Tamla Motown)	3
	17 Nov	**Good Vibrations** Beach Boys (Capitol)	2
	1 Dec	**Green Green Grass Of Home** Tom Jones (Decca)	7
1967	19 Jan	**I'm A Believer** Monkees (RCA)	4
	16 Feb	**This Is My Song** Petula Clark (Pye)	2
	2 Mar	**Release Me** Engelbert Humperdinck (Decca)	6
	13 Apr	**Something Stupid**	
		Nancy Sinatra and Frank Sinatra (Reprise)	2
	27 Apr	**Puppet On A String** Sandie Shaw (Pye)	3
	18 May	**Silence Is Golden** Tremeloes (CBS)	3
	8 Jun	**A Whiter Shade Of Pale** Procol Harum (Deram)	6
	19 Jul	**All You Need Is Love** Beatles (Parlophone)	3
	9 Aug	**San Francisco (Be Sure To Wear Some Flowers**	
		In Your Hair) Scott McKenzie (CBS)	4
	6 Sep	**The Last Waltz** Engelbert Humperdinck (Decca)	5
	11 Oct	**Massachusetts** Bee Gees (Polydor)	4
	8 Nov	**Baby Now That I've Found You** Foundations (Pye)	2
	22 Nov	**Let The Heartaches Begin** Long John Baldry (Pye)	2
	6 Dec	**Hello Goodbye** Beatles (Parlophone)	7
1968	24 Jan	**The Ballad Of Bonnie And Clyde**	
		Georgie Fame (CBS)	1
	31 Jan	**Everlasting Love** Love Affair (CBS)	2
	14 Feb	**Mighty Quinn** Manfred Mann (Fontana)	2
	28 Feb	**Cinderella Rockefella**	
		Esther and Abi Ofarim (Philips)	3
	20 Mar	**The Legend Of Xanadu**	
		Dave Dee, Dozy, Beaky, Mick and Tich (Fontana)	1

Date	Title / Artist	Weeks
27 Mar	**Lady Madonna** Beatles (Parlophone)	2
10 Apr	**Congratulations** Cliff Richard (Columbia)	2
24 Apr	**What A Wonderful World/Cabaret** Louis Armstrong (HMV)	4
22 May	**Young Girl** Union Gap featuring Gary Puckett (CBS)	4
19 Jun	**Jumping Jack Flash** Rolling Stones (Decca)	2
3 Jul	**Baby Come Back** Equals (President)	3
24 Jul	**I Pretend** Des O'Connor (Columbia)	1
31 Jul	**Mony Mony** Tommy James and the Shondells (Major Minor)	2
14 Aug	**Fire** Crazy World Of Arthur Brown (Track)	1
21 Aug	**Mony Mony** Tommy James and the Shondells (Major Minor)	1
28 Aug	**Do It Again** Beach Boys (Capitol)	1
4 Sep	**I've Gotta Get A Message To You** Bee Gees (Polydor)	1
11 Sep	**Hey Jude** Beatles (Apple)	2
25 Sep	**Those Were The Days** Mary Hopkin (Apple)	6
6 Nov	**With A Little Help From My Friends** Joe Cocker (Regal-Zonophone)	1
13 Nov	**The Good The Bad And The Ugly** Hugo Montenegro and his Orchestra and Chorus (RCA)	4
11 Dec	**Lily The Pink** Scaffold (Parlophone)	3

1969

Date	Title / Artist	Weeks
1 Jan	**Ob-La-Di Ob-La-Da** Marmalade (CBS)	1
8 Jan	**Lily The Pink** Scaffold (Parlophone)	1
15 Jan	**Ob-La-Di Ob-La-Da** Marmalade (CBS)	2
29 Jan	**Albatross** Fleetwood Mac (Blue Horizon)	1
5 Feb	**Blackberry Way** Move (Regal-Zonophone)	1
12 Feb	**(If Paradise Is) Half As Nice** Amen Corner (Immediate)	2
26 Feb	**Where Do You Go To My Lovely** Peter Sarstedt (United Artists)	4
26 Mar	**I Heard It Through The Grapevine** Marvin Gaye (Tamla Motown)	3
16 Apr	**The Israelites** Desmond Dekker and the Aces (Pyramid)	1
23 Apr	**Get Back** Beatles with Billy Preston (Apple)	6
4 Jun	**Dizzy** Tommy Roe (Stateside)	1
11 Jun	**The Ballad Of John And Yoko** Beatles (Apple)	3
2 Apr	**Something In The Air** Thunderclap Newman (Track)	3
23 Jul	**Honky Tonk Women** Rolling Stones (Decca)	5
30 Aug	**In The Year 2525 (Exordium And Terminus)** Zager and Evans (RCA)	3
20 Sep	**Bad Moon Rising** Creedence Clearwater Revival (Liberty)	3
11 Oct	**Je T'Aime Moi Non Plus** Jane Birkin and Serge Gainsbourg (Major Minor)	1
18 Oct	**I'll Never Fall In Love Again** Bobby Gentry (Capitol)	1
25 Oct	**Sugar Sugar** Archies (RCA)	8
20 Dec	**Two Little Boys** Rolf Harris (Columbia)	2

(plus 4 in 1970)

THE BEATLES

The act that dominated the sixties both reflected and inspired many of the decade's fashion trends. At the Cavern in Liverpool in 1961 (top left, with American singer Davy Jones) they were wearing the leather of their rock 'n' roll days. The following year manager Brian Epstein put them in suits (bottom left) that helped make them acceptable to a mass audience. "Beatle jackets" became world famous. By a 1966 appearance on **Top of the Pops** (adjacent) their influential mop top haircuts had inched closer to their eyes and they had mostly dispensed with ties. By 1969 (below, on the set of Ringo's film **The Magic Christian)** their last full year together, they were in a fashion free-for-all.

ALMOST THERE

TYRANNOSAURUS REX: Although major chart success didn't come until the seventies, Marc Bolan's sixties releases included three solo singles, two more with John's Children and four with Steve Peregrin-Took (pictured here with Bolan) as Tyrannosaurus Rex. They just about scraped the charts with their songs about Wizards and magic but were popular at such festivals as Woburn and Kempton. Steve Peregrin-Took was replaced by Mickey Finn in 1969 and as T. Rex the success that had eluded Bolan in the sixties was reached in the seventies.

Madeline BELL: Although she appeared as a session singer on dozens and dozens of hits Madeline never had a solo success.

Below: CHAUSSETTES NOIR: Tribe of early sixties Frenchmen, 'the black socks', who failed to score in Britain despite 'la popularité en Francais'.

The EPs

This is the first time in these books we have ventured into the realms of the Extended Play charts. It is a suitable book in which to feature them as they were very much a sixties phenomenon. Although EPs still appear in the charts of today, they are generally special releases, in place of a single. In the sixties they were released alongside singles and, in fact, often featured a collection of the artists previous hits.

EP sales peaked during the height of the Mersey explosion but by the time **Record Retailer** stopped publishing the chart in November 1967 there were very few new discs entering the chart.

The following list shows the changes in structure of the EP chart during the 7 years it was published.

10 Mar 1960	First separate EP chart published in **Record Retailer** featuring 10 discs
17 Mar 1960	Increases to Top 15
24 Mar 1960	Increases to Top 20
14 Apr 1966	Reduces to Top 10
21 Sep 1967	Reduces to Top 9
30 Nov 1967	**Record Retailer** publishes last separate EP chart

As in the other books in this series, if ever a week went by without a chart being published the previous week's chart is repeated for all the statistics.

There were other occasional hiccups in the chart: for instance in two cases the same EP was placed at two different positions in the same chart. We hope we have managed to straighten out these discrepancies.

★ Number one EP
● Top Ten EP

Contents

Hit EPs alphabetically by artist

Date	Title *Label Number*	Position	

ALEXANDER BROTHERS

UK, male vocal duo

3 Mar 66	**NOBODY'S CHILD** *Pye NEP 24231*	**20**	1 wk

AMERICANS — See *JAY and the AMERICANS*

ANIMALS *UK, male vocal/instrumental group*

7 Jan 65	●**THE ANIMALS IS HERE** *Columbia SEG 8374*	**3**	37 wks
21 Oct 65	●**THE ANIMALS ARE BACK** *Columbia SEG 8452*	**8**	14 wks
15 Sep 66	●**ANIMAL TRACKS** *Columbia SEG 8499*	**7**	4 wks

ANONYMOUS COVER VERSIONS — See *VARIOUS ARTISTS SECTION*

Richard ANTHONY *France, male vocalist*

30 Apr 64	**RICHARD ANTHONY** *Columbia SEG 8298*	**18**	1 wk
9 Jul 64	●**WALKIN' ALONE** *Columbia SEG 8319*	**6**	10 wks

Chet ATKINS *US, male instrumentalist - guitar*

19 Dec 63	**GUITAR GENIUS** *RCA RCX 7118*	**19**	1 wk

Date	Title *Label Number*	Position	

BACHELORS *Ireland, male vocal group*

12 Mar 64	**BACHELORS Vol 2** *Decca DFE 8564*	**14**	2 wks
19 Mar 64	●**BACHELORS** *Decca DFE 8529*	**5**	21 wks
23 Apr 64	●**BACHELORS Vol 2** (re-entry) *Decca DFE 8564*	**10**	7 wks
18 Jun 64	●**BACHELORS Vol 2** (2nd re-entry) *Decca DFE 8564*	**7**	21 wks
5 Nov 64	**BACHELORS** (re-entry) *Decca DFE 8529*	**18**	1 wk
3 Dec 64	★**BACHELORS' HITS** *Decca DFE 8595*	**1**	32 wks
6 Jan 66	●**BACHELORS' HITS Vol 2** *Decca DFE 8637*	**9**	14 wks

Joan BAEZ *US, female vocalist*

15 Apr 65	**DON'T THINK TWICE, IT'S ALRIGHT** *Fontana TF 564*	**13**	8 wks
15 Apr 65	●**SILVER DAGGER AND OTHER THINGS** *Philips TFL 6002*	**3**	33 wks
24 Jun 65	●**DON'T THINK TWICE, IT'S ALRIGHT** (re-entry) *Fontana TF564*	**10**	15 wks
24 Mar 66	★**WITH GOD ON OUR SIDE** *Fontana TFE 18012*	**1**	36 wks
30 Jun 66	●**A HARD RAIN'S GONNA FALL** *Fontana TFE 18013*	**7**	2 wks
28 Jul 66	●**A HARD RAIN'S GONNA FALL** (re-entry) *Fontana TFE 18013*	**7**	3 wks

Kenny BALL and his JAZZMEN

UK, male jazz band, Kenny Ball vocals and trumpet

30 Nov 61	●**KENNY'S BIG FOUR** *Pye NJE 1080*	**3**	24 wks
1 Mar 62	●**KENNY BALL'S HIT PARADE** *Pye 1082*	**5**	34 wks
17 Jan 63	**KENNY BALL'S HIT PARADE** (re-entry) *Pye NJE 1082*	**16**	4 wks
24 Feb 63	**KENNY BALL'S HIT PARADE** (2nd re-entry) *Pye NJE 1082*	**15**	5 wks

Chris BARBER'S JAZZBAND

UK, male Jazzband, Chris Barber vocals and trombone

23 Jun 60	**BARBER'S BEST Vol 1** *Decca DFE 6382*	**11**	1 wk

BAROCK AND ROLL ENSEMBLE

Germany, orchestra

27 May 65	●**EINE KLEINE BEATLE MUSIK** *HMV 7EG 8887*	**4**	12 wks

John BARRY 7+4 *UK, male instrumental group*

23 Feb 61	●**JOHN BARRY SOUND** *Columbia SEG 8069*	**4**	21 wks
27 Jul 61	**JOHN BARRY SOUND** (re-entry) *Columbia SEG 8069*	**14**	4 wks

BEATLES Their 60s record
17 number one Singles, ten number
one LPs, eight number one EPs.

ANIMALS Top ten Nine singles,
four albums, three LPs for the
two-legged Animals

Wilfred BRAMBELL and
Harry H CORBETT Left Harry H
Corbett and Wilfred Brambell, and
Hercules the horse.

Date	Title *Label Number*	Position			Date	Title *Label Number*	Position	
					22 Oct 64	**TWIST AND SHOUT** (2nd re-entry) *Parlophone GEP 8882*	17	5 wks
Lionel BART *UK, male vocalist*					12 Nov 64	★**A HARD DAY'S NIGHT** *Parlophone GEP 8920*	1	30 wks
24 Mar 60	**BART FOR BART'S SAKE** *Decca DFE 6619*	20	1 wk		7 Jan 65	●**A HARD DAY'S NIGHT Vol 2** *Parlophone GEP 8921*	8	9 wks
Shirley BASSEY *UK, female vocalist*					8 Apr 65	★**BEATLES FOR SALE** *Parlophone GEP 8931*	1	26 wks
20 Oct 60	●**FABULOUS MISS BASSEY** *Columbia SEG 8027*	5	8 wks		15 Apr 65	**A HARD DAY'S NIGHT Vol 2** (re-entry) *Parlophone GEP 8921*	15	2 wks
22 Dec 60	**FABULOUS MISS BASSEY** (re-entry) *Columbia SEG 8027*	14	2 wks		6 May 65	**LONG TALL SALLY** (re-entry) *Parlophone GEP 8913*	16	1 wk
19 Jan 61	●**AS LONG AS HE NEEDS ME** *Columbia SEG 8063*	3	15 wks		20 May 65	**A HARD DAY'S NIGHT Vol 2** (2nd re-entry) *Parlophone GEP 8921*	17	2 wks
16 Feb 61	**FABULOUS SHIRLEY BASSEY No 2** *Columbia SEG 8068*	15	2 wks		10 Jun 65	●**BEATLES FOR SALE No 2** *Parlophone GEP 8938*	5	19 wks
25 May 61	**FABULOUS MISS BASSEY** (2nd re-entry) *Columbia SEG 8027*	13	5 wks		29 Jul 65	**A HARD DAY'S NIGHT Vol 2** (3rd re-entry) *Parlophone GEP 8921*	14	4 wks
1 Jun 61	●**AS LONG AS HE NEEDS ME** (re-entry) *Columbia SEG 8063*	6	31 wks		28 Oct 65	**BEATLES FOR SALE** (re-entry) *Parlophone GEP 8931*	17	1 wk
30 Nov 61	**SHIRLEY No 2** *Columbia SEG 8116*	18	1 wk		11 Nov 65	●**BEATLES FOR SALE** (2nd re-entry) *Parlophone GEP 8931*	10	20 wks
4 Jan 62	●**AS LONG AS HE NEEDS ME** (2nd re-entry) *Columbia SEG 8063*	7	11 wks		2 Dec 65	**BEATLES FOR SALE No 2** (re-entry) *Parlophone GEP 8938*	14	2 wks
11 Jan 62	**SHIRLEY No 2** (re-entry) *Columbia SEG 8116*	15	2 wks		9 Dec 65	★**BEATLES' MILLION SELLERS** *Parlophone GEP 8946*	1	26 wks
26 Nov 64	**DYNAMIC SHIRLEY BASSEY** *Columbia SEG 8369*	15	1 wk		23 Dec 65	**BEATLES FOR SALE No 2** (2nd re-entry) *Parlophone GEP 8938*	18	3 wks
					10 Mar 66	★**YESTERDAY** *Parlophone GEP 8948*	1	13 wks
BBC SYMPHONY ORCHESTRA					14 Jul 66	●**NOWHERE MAN** *Parlophone GEP 8952*	4	18 wks
UK, orchestra					**Harry BELAFONTE** *US, male vocalist*			
24 Mar 60	**PLANET SUITE - MARS AND JUPITER** *HMV 7ER 5122*	14	1 wk		14 Apr 60	**SCARLET RIBBONS** *RCA RCX 1049*	18	1 wk
					7 Dec 61	**BELAFONTE AT CHRISTMAS TIME** *RCA RCX 163*	18	1 wk
BEACH BOYS *US, male vocal/instrumental group*					**Tony BENNETT** *US, male vocalist*			
27 Aug 64	**FUN, FUN, FUN** *Capitol EAP 1-20603*	19	1 wk		2 Dec 65	●**TONY BENNETT** *CBS EP 6066*	5	19 wks
12 Nov 64	**FOUR BY THE BEACH BOYS** *Capitol EAP 1-5267*	11	8 wks		19 May 66	●**TILL** *CBS EP 6071*	7	5 wks
12 May 66	★**BEACH BOY HITS** *Capitol EAP 1-20781*	1	82 wks		30 Jun 66	●**TILL** (re-entry) *CBS EP 6071*	9	1 wk
10 Nov 66	●**GOD ONLY KNOWS** *Capitol EAP 6-2458*	3	17 wks		5 Jan 67	●**BEST OF BENNETT** *CBS EP 6151*	3	17 wks
					11 May 67	●**BEST OF BENNETT** (re-entry) *CBS EP 6151*	2	30 wks
BEAKY — See *Dave DEE, DOZY, BEAKY, MICK and TITCH*					**Elmer BERNSTEIN** *US, orchestra*			
BEATLES *UK, male vocal/instrumental group*					10 Mar 60	●**JOHNNY STACCATO** *Capitol EAP 1-1287*	6	1 wk
18 Jul 63	★**TWIST AND SHOUT** *Parlophone GEP 8882*	1	57 wks		**Chuck BERRY**			
19 Sep 63	★**THE BEATLES' HITS** *Parlophone GEP 8880*	1	33 wks		*US, male vocalist/instrumentalist - guitar*			
7 Nov 63	●**THE BEATLES No 1** *Parlophone GEP 8883*	2	26 wks		3 Oct 63	●**CHUCK BERRY** *Pye NEP 44011*	7	10 wks
6 Feb 64	★**ALL MY LOVING** *Parlophone GEP 8891*	1	44 wks		19 Dec 63	**CHUCK BERRY** (re-entry) *Pye NEP 44011*	15	3 wks
4 Jun 64	**THE BEATLES' HITS** (re-entry) *Parlophone GEP 8880*	17	3 wks		16 Jan 64	**CHUCK BERRY** (2nd re-entry) *Pye NEP 44011*	20	1 wk
2 Jul 64	★**LONG TALL SALLY** *Parlophone GEP 8913*	1	36 wks		6 Feb 64	●**THE BEST OF CHUCK BERRY** *Pye NEP 44018*	10	6 wks
16 Jul 64	**THE BEATLES' HITS** (2nd re-entry) *Parlophone GEP 8880*	16	1 wk		26 Mar 64	**THE BEST OF CHUCK BERRY** (re-entry) *Pye NEP 44018*	15	3 wks
23 Jul 64	**THE BEATLES No 1** (re-entry) *Parlophone GEP 8883*	17	3 wks		21 May 64	●**THE BEST OF CHUCK BERRY** (2nd re-entry) *Pye NEP 44018*	5	12 wks
13 Aug 64	**THE BEATLES' HITS** (3rd re-entry) *Parlophone GEP 8880*	15	2 wks		27 Aug 64	**THE BEST OF CHUCK BERRY** (3rd re-entry) *Pye NEP 44018*	13	4 wks
3 Sep 64	**THE BEATLES' HITS** (4th re-entry) *Parlophone GEP 8880*	19	1 wk		*See also Chuck Berry and Bo Diddley.*			
17 Sep 64	**TWIST AND SHOUT** (re-entry) *Parlophone GEP 8882*	17	2 wks					
24 Sep 64	**THE BEATLES' HITS** (5th re-entry) *Parlophone GEP 8880*	13	1 wk					
8 Oct 64	**THE BEATLES' HITS** (6th re-entry) *Parlophone GEP 8880*	13	2 wks					

Date	Title Label Number	Position		Date	Title Label Number	Position	

Chuck BERRY and Bo DIDDLEY

US, male vocal/instrumental duo-guitars

Date	Title Label Number	Pos	wks
3 Oct 63	●CHUCK AND BO *Pye NEP 44009*	6	15 wks
28 Nov 63	CHUCK AND BO Vol 2 *Pye NEP 44012*	15	2 wks
23 Jan 64	CHUCK AND BO (re-entry) *Pye NEP 44009*	17	4 wks
13 Feb 64	CHUCK AND BO Vol 3 *Pye NEP 44017*	12	5 wks
30 April 64	CHUCK AND BO (2nd re-entry) *Pye NEP 44009*	18	3 wks

See also Chuck Berry

Dave BERRY *UK, male vocalist*

Date	Title Label Number	Pos	wks
8 Jul 65	CAN I GET IT FROM YOU *Decca DFE 8625*	12	6 wks

Mike BERRY with the OUTLAWS

UK, male vocalist and male instrumental backing group

Date	Title Label Number	Pos	wks
29 Aug 63	TRIBUTE TO BUDDY HOLLY *HMV 7EG 8808*	17	3 wks
31 Oct 63	TRIBUTE TO BUDDY HOLLY (re-entry) *HMV 7EG 8808*	20	1 wk

BEVERLEY SISTERS *UK, female vocal trio*

Date	Title Label Number	Pos	wks
22 Dec 60	THE BEVS FOR CHRISTMAS *Decca DFE 6611*	11	2 wks

BIG THREE *UK, male vocal/instrumental group*

Date	Title Label Number	Pos	wks
12 Dec 63	AT THE CAVERN *Decca DFE 8552*	17	1 wk
2 Jan 64	●AT THE CAVERN (re-entry) *Decca DFE 8552*	6	16 wks

Mr. Acker BILK

UK, male vocalist/instrumentalist - clarinet

Date	Title Label Number	Pos	wks
24 Mar 60	ACKER'S AWAY *Columbia SEG 7940*	17	1 wk
31 Mar 60	MR ACKER BILK REQUESTS Vol 2 *Pye NJE 1070*	12	2 wks
21 Apr 60	MR ACKER BILK REQUESTS Vol 2 (re-entry) *Pye NJE 1070*	11	1 wk
5 May 60	MR ACKER BILK MARCHES ON *Pye NJE 1061*	12	1 wk
19 May 60	MR ACKER BILK REQUESTS Vol 2 (2nd re-entry) *Pye NJE 1070*	12	3 wks
9 Jun 60	MR ACKER BILK SINGS *Pye NJE 1067*	15	1 wk
23 Jun 60	ACKER'S AWAY (re-entry) *Columbia SEG 7940*	16	1 wk
7 Jul 60	MR ACKER BILK MARCHES ON (re-entry) *Pye NJE 1061*	15	1 wk
1 Sep 60	MR ACKER BILK REQUESTS Vol 2 (3rd re-entry) *Pye NJE 1070*	15	2 wks
3 Nov 60	SEVEN AGES OF ACKER *Columbia SEG 8029*	11	7 wks
5 Jan 61	●SEVEN AGES OF ACKER (re-entry) *Columbia SEG 8029*	6	11 wks
16 Mar 61	●SEVEN AGES OF ACKER Vol 2 *Columbia SEG 8076*	9	12 wks
18 May 61	SEVEN AGES OF ACKER (2nd re-entry) *Columbia SEG 8029*	11	1 wk
27 Jul 61	SEVEN AGES OF ACKER (3rd re-entry) *Columbia SEG 8029*	19	1 wk
24 Aug 61	SEVEN AGES OF ACKER (4th re-entry) *Columbia SEG 8029*	20	1 wk
24 Aug 61	●ACKER No 1 *Columbia SEG 8089*	6	5 wks
11 Jan 62	ACKER Vol 2 *Columbia SEG 8102*	11	7 wks
1 Feb 62	SEVEN AGES OF ACKER (5th re-entry) *Columbia SEG 8029*	20	2 wks
12 Apr 62	●FOUR HITS AND A MISTER *Columbia SEG 8156*	2	34 wks
27 Sep 62	●BAND OF THIEVES *Columbia SEG 8178*	6	17 wks
10 Jan 63	●FOUR HITS AND A MISTER (re-entry) *Columbia SEG 8156*	6	22 wks

Band of Thieves credited to Acker Bilk and His Paramount Jazz Band. See also Mr. Acker Bilk and Terry Lightfoot.

Mr. Acker BILK and Terry LIGHTFOOT

UK, male vocal/instrumental duo-clarinets

Date	Title Label Number	Pos	wks
2 Mar 61	CLARINET JAMBOREE *Columbia SEG 8053*	19	1 wk

See also Mr. Acker Bilk.

Cilla BLACK *UK, female vocalist*

Date	Title Label Number	Pos	wks
23 Apr 64	●ANYONE WHO HAD A HEART *Parlophone GEP 8901*	5	17 wks
15 Oct 64	IT'S FOR YOU *Parlophone GEP 8916*	12	8 wks
15 Sep 66	●CILLA'S HITS *Parlophone GEP 8954*	6	4 wks

BO DIDDLEY—See *Chuck BERRY and Bo DIDDLEY*

BOOKER T. and the M.G.'s

US, male instrumental group

Date	Title Label Number	Pos	wks
25 Feb 65	R & B WITH BOOKER T *Atlantic AET 6002*	19	1 wk

Pat BOONE *US, male vocalist*

Date	Title Label Number	Pos	wks
10 Mar 60	●JOURNEY TO THE CENTRE OF THE EARTH (film soundtrack) *London RE 1244*	8	3 wks
7 Apr 60	●JOURNEY TO THE CENTRE OF THE EARTH (film soundtrack) (re-entry) *London RE 1244*	8	2 wks

Victor BORGE

Denmark, male comedian/instrumentalist - piano

Date	Title Label Number	Pos	wks
5 Jan 61	PHONETIC PUNCTUATION *Philips BBE 12154*	15	2 wks

Wilfred BRAMBELL and Harry H. CORBETT *UK, male comic duo*

Date	Title Label Number	Pos	wks
6 Jun 63	●FACTS OF LIFE FROM STEPTOE AND SON *Pye NEP 24169*	4	19 wks
7 Nov 63	FACTS OF LIFE FROM STEPTOE AND SON (re-entry) *Pye NEP 24169*	15	4 wks
12 Dec 63	FACTS OF LIFE FROM STEPTOE AND SON (2nd re-entry) *Pye NEP 24169*	20	1 wk
19 Dec 63	●WAGES OF SIN *Pye NEP 24180*	10	8 wks
26 Dec 63	FACTS OF LIFE FROM STEPTOE AND SON (3rd re-entry) *Pye NEP 24169*	14	3 wks
23 Jan 64	FACTS OF LIFE FROM STEPTOE AND SON (4th re-entry) *Pye NEP 24169*	16	1 wk

Date	Title Label Number	Position

Joe BROWN

UK, male vocalist/instrumentalist -guitar

26 Sep 63	**JOE BROWN HIT PARADE** *Pye NEP 34025*	**20** 1 wk

Dave BRUBECK

US, male jazz group leader/instrumentalist - piano

24 Mar 60	**BRUBECK IN EUROPE** *Fontana TFE 17196*	**15** 1 wk
28 Sep 61	●**TAKE FIVE** *Fontana TFE 17307*	**4** 7 wks
23 Nov 61	●**TAKE FIVE** (re-entry) *Fontana TFE 17307*	**7** 16 wks
31 May 62	**TAKE FIVE** (2nd re-entry) *Fontana TFE 17307*	**13** 17 wks

BYRDS *US, male vocal/instrumental group*

17 Feb 66	**TIMES THEY ARE A CHANGIN'** *CBS EP 6069*	**15** 4 wks
13 Oct 66	●**EIGHT MILES HIGH** *CBS EP 6077*	**8** 1 wk

Ed BYRNES *US, male vocalist*

23 Mar 61	**KOOKIE** *Warner Bros. WEP 6010*	**20** 1 wk

C

Ian CARMICHAEL *UK, male storyteller*

21 Dec 61	●**HOUSE AT POOH CORNER** *HMV 7EG 117*	**10** 3 wks

Johnny CASH *US, male vocalist*

2 Jun 66	●**MEAN AS HELL** *CBS EP 6073*	**8** 2 wks

Ray CHARLES

US, male vocalist/instrumentalist - piano

10 Jan 63	●**I CAN'T STOP LOVING YOU** *HMV 7EG 8781*	**10** 36 wks
19 Sep 63	**TAKE THESE CHAINS FROM MY HEART** *HMV 7EG 8812*	**17** 3 wks
24 Oct 63	**TAKE THESE CHAINS FROM MY HEART** (re-entry) *HMV 7EG 8812*	**16** 2 wks

Chubby CHECKER *US, male vocalist*

15 Mar 62	●**KING OF TWIST** *Columbia SEG 8155*	**3** 12 wks
14 Jun 62	●**KING OF TWIST** (re-entry) *Columbia SEG 8155*	**6** 31 wks
31 Jan 63	**DANCING PARTY** *Cameo Parkway CPE 550*	**17** 3 wks

CHECKMATES — See *Emile FORD and the CHECKMATES*

CHER *US, female vocalist*

20 Oct 66	●**CHER** *Liberty LEP 4047*	**10** 1 wk

Maurice CHEVALIER and Hayley MILLS

France/UK, male/female vocal duo

7 Feb 63	**IN SEARCH OF THE CASTAWAYS** (film soundtrack) *Decca DFE 8512*	**18** 1 wk

Dave CLARK FIVE

UK, male vocal/instrumental group

16 Jan 64	●**THE DAVE CLARK FIVE** *Columbia SEG 8289*	**3** 24 wks
21 Jan 65	**HITS OF THE DAVE CLARK FIVE** *Columbia SEG 8381*	**20** 1 wk
23 Sep 65	●**WILD WEEKEND** *Columbia SEG 8447*	**10** 10 wks

Petula CLARK *UK, female vocalist*

18 Feb 65	**DOWNTOWN** *Pye NEP 24206*	**15** 3 wks
15 Apr 65	**DOWNTOWN** (re-entry) *Pye NEP 24206*	**12** 3 wks
27 Apr 67	●**THIS IS MY SONG** *Pye NEP 24279*	**6** 6 wks

Eddie COCHRAN

US, male vocalist/instrumentalist - guitar

5 May 60	**SOMETHING ELSE** *London REU 1239*	**10** 1 wk
19 May 60	●**SOMETHING ELSE** (re-entry) *London REU 1239*	**6** 10 wks
16 Jun 60	●**C'MON EVERYBODY** *London REU 1214*	**2** 15 wks
13 Oct 60	**C'MON EVERYBODY** (re-entry) *London REU 1214*	**15** 6 wks
1 Dec 60	**C'MON EVERYBODY** (2nd re-entry) *London REU 1214*	**14** 3 wks
5 Jan 61	**C'MON EVERYBODY** (3rd re-entry) *London REU 1214*	**11** 2 wks
2 Feb 61	**C'MON EVERYBODY** (4th re-entry) *London REU 1214*	**20** 1 wk
14 Feb 63	**NEVER TO BE FORGOTTEN** *Liberty LEP 2052*	**18** 2 wks
19 Sep 63	●**C'MON EVERYBODY** (re-issue)	**9** 11 wks

Nat "King" COLE *US, male vocalist*

26 May 60	**LOVE IS THE THING** *Capitol EAP 1 824*	**14** 1 wk
9 Jun 60	●**LOVE IS THE THING** (re-entry) *Capitol EAP 1 824*	**2** 19 wks
13 Oct 60	●**UNFORGETTABLE** *Capitol EAP 20053*	**2** 60 wks
15 Dec 60	**LOVE IS THE THING** (2nd re-entry) *Capitol EAP 1 824*	**12** 3 wks
20 Apr 61	**TENDERLY** *Capitol EAP 1 20108*	**20** 1 wk
4 May 61	●**TENDERLY** (re-entry) *Capitol EAP 1 20108*	**9** 5 wks
27 Jul 61	**TENDERLY** (2nd re-entry) *Capitol EAP 1 20108*	**16** 3 wks
8 Mar 62	**UNFORGETTABLE** (re-entry) *Capitol EAP 20053*	**19** 1 wk
11 Mar 65	**UNFORGETTABLE** (2nd re-entry) *Capitol EAP 20053*	**20** 1 wk

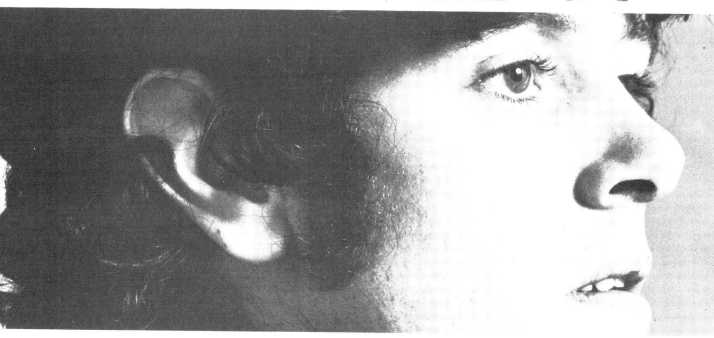

Dave DEE, DOZY, BEAKY, MICK and TICH. *Top* Dave 'Mr Sandeman' Dee with two cloaked cut-throats attempting to shoot a couple of caped waiters offering postprandial cigars. *Above* DONOVAN 'When sundown pales the sky I want to hide a while behind your smile'... *Below* DAVE CLARK FIVE Rick Huxley and Lenny Davidson – guitar, Dave Clark – drums, Dennis Payton – saxophone, bass, Mike Smith – keyboards, vocals.

Date	Title *Label Number*	Position		Date	Title *Label Number*	Position	

Perry COMO *US, male vocalist*

16 Jun 60   **YOU'LL NEVER WALK ALONE**   **20**   1 wk
          RCA RCX 1018

Russ CONWAY *UK, male instrumentalist - piano*

7 Apr 60	**TIME TO CELEBRATE** *Columbia 33SX 1197*	**18**	1 wk
21 Apr 60	**TIME TO CELEBRATE** (re-entry) *Columbia 33SX 1197*	**18**	1 wk
7 Jul 60	**TIME TO CELEBRATE** (2nd re-entry) *Columbia 33SX 1197*	**17**	1 wk
11 Aug 60	**ANOTHER SIX** *Columbia SEG 7905*	**12**	3 wks
27 Oct 60	**ROCKING HORSE COWBOY** *Columbia SEG 8028*	**12**	3 wks
22 Dec 60	●**MORE PARTY POPS** *Columbia SEG 7957*	**7**	4 wks
26 Jan 61	**MORE PARTY POPS** (re-entry) *Columbia SEG 7957*	**14**	2 wks
9 Feb 61	**ANOTHER SIX** (re-entry) *Columbia SEG 7905*	**20**	2 wks
27 Apr 61	**MY CONCERTO FOR YOU No 2** *Columbia SEG 8079*	**11**	6 wks
21 Dec 61	**MORE PARTY POPS** (2nd re-entry) *Columbia SEG 7957*	**17**	2 wks

Peter COOK and Dudley MOORE

UK, male comic duo

27 Jan 66   **BY APPOINTMENT** *Decca DFE 8644*   **18**   3 wks

HARRY H. CORBETT — See *Wilfred BRAMBELL and Harry H. CORBETT*

CRICKETS *US, male vocal/instrumental group*

16 Jun 60	●**FOUR MORE** *Coral FET 2000*	**7**	1 wk
30 Jun 60	**FOUR MORE** (re-entry) *Coral FET 2000*	**14**	1 wk
14 Jul 60	**FOUR MORE** (2nd re-entry) *Coral FET 2000*	**17**	2 wks
18 Aug 60	**FOUR MORE** (3rd re-entry) *Coral FET 2000*	**19**	1 wk
18 Jan 62	**IT'S SO EASY** *Coral FEP 2014*	**18**	1 wk

See also *Bobby Vee and the Crickets*

Bing CROSBY *US, male vocalist*

1 Dec 60   ●**MERRY CHRISTMAS Part 1**   **9**   6 wks
          Columbia OE 9069

CRYSTALS *US, female vocal group*

30 Jan 64   **DA DOO RON RON** *London REU 1381*   **18**   1 wk

D

DAKOTAS *UK, male instrumental group*

12 Dec 63   **MEET THE DAKOTAS** *Parlophone GEP 8588*   **19**   1 wk
See also *Billy J Kramer and the Dakotas.*

Bobby DARIN *US, male vocalist*

17 Mar 60	●**THAT'S ALL** *London RE 1243*	**10**	2 wks
7 Apr 60	●**THAT'S ALL** (re-entry) *London RE 1243*	**6**	1 wk
21 Apr 60	**THAT'S ALL** (2nd re-entry) *London RE 1243*	**15**	1 wk
5 May 60	**THAT'S ALL** (3rd re-entry) *London RE 1243*	**15**	3 wks
28 Jul 60	**THAT'S ALL** (4th re-entry) *London RE 1243*	**19**	1 wk
11 Aug 60	**THAT'S ALL** (5th re-entry) *London RE 1243*	**14**	1 wk

Sammy DAVIS JR. *US, male vocalist*

| 28 Jul 60 | **STARRING SAMMY DAVIS Vol 1** *Brunswick OE 9146* | **20** | 1 wk |
| 29 Aug 63 | **SAMMY DAVIS JR. IMPERSONATING** *Pye R 30004* | **18** | 2 wks |

Doris DAY *US, female vocalist*

17 Mar 60	**PILLOW TALK** *Philips BBE 12339*	**11**	1 wk
31 Mar 60	**PILLOW TALK** (re-entry) *Philips BBE 12339*	**12**	4 wks
12 May 60	**PILLOW TALK** (2nd re-entry) *Philips BBE 12339*	**18**	1 wk

Dave DEE, DOZY, BEAKY, MICK and TICH *UK, male vocal/instrumental group*

2 Mar 67   ●**THE LOOS OF ENGLAND** *Fontana TE 17488*   **8**   3 wks

Karl DENVER *UK, male vocalist*

13 Sep 62	●**BY A SLEEPY LAGOON** *Decca DFE 8501*	**2**	20 wks
22 Nov 62	●**KARL DENVER HITS** *Decca DFE 8504*	**7**	5 wks
3 Jan 63	**KARL DENVER HITS** (re-entry) *Decca DFE 8504*	**18**	4 wks

Ken DODD *UK, male vocalist*

20 Feb 64	**STILL** *Columbia SEG 8297*	**18**	1 wk
23 Dec 65	●**DODDY AND THE DIDDY MEN** *Columbia SEG 8466*	**4**	16 wks
26 May 66	●**DODDY AND THE DIDDY MEN** (re-entry) *Columbia SEG 8466*	**10**	1 wk
5 Jan 67	●**DIDDYNESS** *Columbia SEG 8524*	**8**	1 wk

Lonnie DONEGAN *UK, male vocalist*

29 Sep 60   ●**YANKEE DOODLE DONEGAN**   **8**   8 wks
          Pye NEP 24127

Date	Title *Label Number*	Position	

DONOVAN *UK, male vocalist*

19 Aug 65	**UNIVERSAL SOLDIER** *Pye NEP 24219*	**1**	28 wks
3 Mar 66	**DONOVAN Vol 1** *Pye NEP 24239*	**12**	6 wks
10 Mar 66	**UNIVERSAL SOLDIER** (re-entry) *Pye NEP 24219*	**16**	2 wks

Val DOONICAN *Ireland, male vocalist*

18 Feb 65	**GREEN SHADES OF VAL DOONICAN** *Decca DFE 8608*	**1**	20 wks
7 Apr 66	●**GREEN SHADES OF VAL DOONICAN** (re-entry) *Decca DFE 8608*	**9**	2 wks
5 May 66	●**GREEN SHADES OF VAL DOONICAN** (2nd re-entry) *Decca DFE 8608*	**6**	2 wks
26 May 66	●**DOONICAN'S IRISH STEW** *Decca DFE 8656*	**4**	5 wks
12 Jan 67	●**GREEN SHADES OF VAL DOONICAN** (3rd re-entry) *Decca DFE 8608*	**6**	15 wks

Lee DORSEY *US, male vocalist*

| 1 Sep 66 | ●**YOU'RE BREAKIN' ME UP** *Stateside SE 1043* | **7** | 4 wks |

DOZY — See *Dave DEE, DOZY, BEAKY, MICK and TICH*

DREAMERS — See *FREDDIE and the DREAMERS*

Bob DYLAN *US, male vocalist*

1 Jul 65	●**DYLAN** *CBS EP 6051*	**3**	41 wks
17 Feb 66	●**ONE TOO MANY MORNINGS** *CBS EP 6070*	**8**	8 wks
13 Oct 66	●**MR. TAMBOURINE MAN** *CBS EP 6078*	**4**	8 wks

E

Duane EDDY *US, male instrumentalist - guitar*

28 Jul 60	**YEP** *London REW 1217*	**16**	1 wk
11 Aug 60	**YEP** (re-entry) *London REW 1217*	**19**	1 wk
8 Dec 60	●**TWANGY** *London REW 1257*	**4**	22 wks
16 Feb 61	**BECAUSE THEY'RE YOUNG** *London REW 1252*	**17**	1 wk
18 May 61	**THE LONELY ONE** *London REW 1216*	**16**	1 wk
29 Jun 61	●**PEPE** *London REW 1287*	**10**	3 wks
29 Jun 61	●**TWANGY** (re-entry) *London REW 1257*	**10**	8 wks

Nelson EDDY *US, male vocalist*

| 21 Apr 60 | **INDIAN LOVE CALL** *RCA RCX 1051* | **12** | 1 wk |

Tommy EDWARDS *US, male vocalist*

| 14 Apr 60 | **THE WAYS OF LOVE** *MGM EP 712* | **15** | 1 wk |

Bern ELLIOT and the FENMEN

UK, male vocal/instrumental group

| 16 Jan 64 | ●**BERN ELLIOT AND THE FENMEN** *Decca DFE 8561* | **10** | 5 wks |

Ivor EMMANUEL *UK, male vocalist*

19 Jan 61	**LAND OF SONG** *Delyse EDP 209/210*	**15**	1 wk
2 Feb 61	**LAND OF SONG** (re-entry) *Delyse EDP 209/210*	**19**	1 wk
16 Feb 61	**LAND OF SONG** (2nd re-entry) *Delyse EDP 209/210*	**13**	3 wks

EVERLY BROTHERS *US, male vocal duo*

5 May 60	**EVERLY BROTHERS No 5** *London REA 1229*	**13**	1 wk
23 Jun 60	**EVERLY BROTHERS No 5** (re-entry) *London REA 1229*	**13**	1 wk
7 Jul 60	●**EVERLY BROTHERS No 5** (2nd re-entry) *London REA 1229*	**7**	3 wks
21 Jul 60	●**EVERLY BROTHERS No 4** *London RE 1174*	**8**	3 wks
21 Jul 60	●**EVERLY BROTHERS No 1** *London RE 1113*	**15**	1 wk
18 Aug 60	●**EVERLY BROTHERS No 5** (3rd re-entry) *London REA 1229*	**8**	1 wk
22 Dec 60	**EVERLY BROTHERS No 4** (re-entry) *London RE 1174*	**17**	1 wk
7 Jun 62	**EVERLY BROTHERS No 6** *London REA 1311*	**20**	1 wk
3 May 64	**EVERLY BROTHERS No 4** (2nd re-entry) *London RE 16065*	**15**	1 wk

F

Adam FAITH *UK, male vocalist*

15 Sep 60	**ADAM'S HIT PARADE** *Parlophone GEP 8811*	**1**	76 wks
9 Mar 61	●**ADAM No 1** *Parlophone GEP 8824*	**4**	11 wks
22 Jun 61	**ADAM No 1** (re-entry) *Parlophone GEP 8824*	**16**	1 wk
12 Oct 61	**ADAM No 1** (2nd re-entry) *Parlophone GEP 8824*	**19**	1 wk
15 Mar 62	**ADAM FAITH No 1** *Parlophone GEP 8851*	**12**	4 wks
15 Mar 62	**ADAM'S HIT PARADE** (re-entry) *Parlophone GEP 8811*	**17**	1 wk
11 Mar 65	**A MESSAGE TO MARTHA FROM ADAM** *Parlophone GEP 8929*	**17**	1 wk

Marianne FAITHFULL *UK, female vocalist*

17 Jun 65	●**GO AWAY FROM MY WORLD** *Decca DFE 8624*	**4**	14 wks
30 Sep 65	**GO AWAY FROM MY WORLD** (re-entry) *Decca DFE 8624*	**11**	4 wks
4 Nov 65	**GO AWAY FROM MY WORLD** (2nd re-entry) *Decca DFE 8624*	**17**	1 wk

Date	Title Label Number	Position		Date	Title Label Number	Position	

Georgie FAME
UK, male vocalist/instrumentalist - guitar

14 Jan 65	●RHYTHM & BLUES AT THE FLAMINGO Columbia SEG 8382	8	11 wks
6 May 65	RHYTHM & BLUES AT THE FLAMINGO (re-entry) Columbia SEG 8382	19	2 wks
3 Jun 65	FATS FOR FAME Columbia SEG 8406	15	1 wk
24 Jun 65	FATS FOR FAME (re-entry) Columbia SEG 8406	20	1 wk
8 Dec 66	●GETAWAY Columbia SEG 8518	7	4 wks
19 Jan 67	●GETAWAY (re-entry) Columbia SEG 8518	7	3 wks
8 Jun 67	●GEORGIE FAME CBS EP 6363	2	26 wks

Chris FARLOWE *UK, male vocalist*

| 13 Jan 66 | ●FARLOWE IN THE MIDNIGHT HOUR Immediate IMEP 001 | 6 | 13 wks |

Julie FELIX *US, female vocalist*

| 11 Aug 66 | ●SONGS FROM THE FROST REPORT Fontana TE 17474 | 5 | 4 wks |
| 15 Sep 66 | ●SONGS FROM THE FROST REPORT (re-entry) Fontana TE 17474 | 8 | 2 wks |

FENMEN — See *Bern ELLIOT and the FENMEN*

Gracie FIELDS *UK, female vocalist*

| 24 Nov 60 | OUR GRACIE SINGS COMEDY SONGS HMV 7EG 8299 | 16 | 1 wk |

FILM SOUNDTRACKS — See *VARIOUS ARTISTS SECTION*

Ella FITZGERALD *US, female vocalist*

9 Jun 60	●WITH A SONG IN MY HEART HMV 7EG 8503	10	1 wk
11 Aug 60	MOODS OF ELLA HMV 7EG 8392	17	1 wk
25 Aug 60	ELLA SINGS IRVING BERLIN HMV 7EG 8563	18	1 wk
5 Jan 61	ELLA SINGS IRVING BERLIN (re-entry) HMV 7EG 8563	17	2 wks
13 Apr 61	WITH A SONG IN MY HEART (re-entry) HMV 7EG 8503	17	2 wks

Wayne FONTANA and the MINDBENDERS
UK, male vocalist and male instrumental backing group

10 Dec 64	●UM UM UM UM UM UM Fontana TE 17435	7	17 wks
22 Apr 65	UM UM UM UM UM UM (re-entry) Fontana TE 17435	12	2 wks
13 May 65	GAME OF LOVE Fontana TE 17449	19	1 wk

Emile FORD and the CHECKMATES
UK, male vocalist and male instrumental backing group

| 7 Apr 60 | ★EMILE Pye NEP 24119 | 1 | 13 wks |
| 14 Jul 60 | ●EMILE (re-entry) Pye NEP 24119 | 5 | 10 wks |

FOURMOST *UK, male vocal/instrumental group*

| 27 Feb 64 | FOURMOST SOUND Parlophone GEP 24184 | 15 | 3 wks |
| 4 Jun 64 | FOURMOST SOUND (re-entry) Parlophone GEP 24184 | 15 | 2 wks |

FOUR PENNIES *UK, male vocal/instrumental group*

| 30 Jul 64 | ●SPIN WITH THE PENNIES Philips BE 12562 | 6 | 15 wks |

FOUR TOPS *US, male vocal group*

| 27 Oct 66 | ●FOUR TOPS Tamla Motown TME 2012 | 2 | 58 wks |
| 9 Mar 67 | ★FOUR TOPS' HITS Tamla Motown TME 2018 | 1 | 39 wks |

Connie FRANCIS *US, female vocalist*

5 Jan 61	HEARTACHES MGM EP 677	14	2 wks
19 Jan 61	FIRST LADY OF RECORD MGM EP 742	12	1 wk
9 Feb 61	FIRST LADY OF RECORD (re-entry) MGM EP 742	16	1 wk
2 Mar 61	●FIRST LADY OF RECORD (2nd re-entry) MGM EP 742	7	9 wks
11 May 61	●FIRST LADY OF RECORD (3rd re-entry) MGM EP 742	10	4 wks

FREDDIE and the DREAMERS
UK, male vocalist and male instrumental backing group

17 Oct 63	●IF YOU GOTTA MAKE A FOOL OF SOMEBODY Columbia SEG 8257	8	8 wks
26 Dec 63	IF YOU GOTTA MAKE A FOOL OF SOMEBODY(re-entry) Columbia SEG 8257	17	1 wk
9 Jan 64	IF YOU GOTTA MAKE A FOOL OF SOMEBODY(2nd re-entry) Columbia SEG 8257	15	2 wks
6 Feb 64	WHAT A CRAZY WORLD Columbia SEG 8287	15	2 wks
2 Jul 64	OVER YOU Columbia SEG 8321	17	1 wk

FREDERICK — See *NINA and FREDERICK*

Billy FURY *UK, male vocalist*

7 Jun 62	●PLAY IT COOL Decca DFE 6708	2	45 wks
8 Nov 62	●BILLY FURY HITS No 2 Decca DFE 8505	8	6 wks
27 Dec 62	●BILLY FURY HITS No 2 (re-entry) Decca DFE 8505	9	5 wks
14 Feb 63	●BILLY FURY HITS No 2 (2nd re-entry) Decca DFE 8505	10	18 wks
4 Aug 63	BILLY FURY HITS No 2 (3rd re-entry) Decca DFE 8505	18	1 wk

See also *Billy Fury and the Tornados.*

Date	Title Label Number	Position	Date	Title Label Number	Position

Billy FURY and the TORNADOS

UK, male vocalist and male instrumental backing group

23 May 63	●**BILLY FURY AND THE TORNADOS** *Decca DFE 8510*	**2** 16 wks

See also the Tornados; Billy Fury

G

GARFUNKEL — See *SIMON and GARFUNKEL*

Judy GARLAND *US, female vocalist*

3 Dec 64	**MAGGIE MAY** *Capitol EAP 1 20630*	**18** 3 wks

Marvin GAYE *US, male vocalist*

13 Apr 67	●**ORIGINALS FROM MARVIN GAYE** *Tamla Motown TME 2019*	**3** 8 wks

GERRY and the PACEMAKERS

UK, male vocalist and male instrumental backing group

11 Jul 63	●**HOW DO YOU DO IT?** *Columbia SEG 8257*	**2** 35 wks
20 Feb 64	●**YOU'LL NEVER WALK ALONE** *Columbia SEG 8295*	**8** 7 wks
16 Apr 64	**I'M THE ONE** *Columbia SEG 8311*	**17** 2 wks
7 May 64	**I'M THE ONE** (re-entry) *Columbia SEG 8311*	**11** 3 wks
28 May 64	**YOU'LL NEVER WALK ALONE** (re-entry) *Columbia SEG 8295*	**20** 1 wk
8 Oct 64	**DON'T LET THE SUN CATCH YOU CRYING** *Columbia SEG 8356*	**15** 1 wk

GORDON — See *PETER and GORDON*

Ron GRAINER *UK, composer and orchestra leader*

18 Jan 62	**MAIGRET THEME MUSIC** *Warner Bros. WEP 6012*	**13** 1 wk

GRIFF — See *MIKI and GRIFF*

H

Tony HANCOCK *UK, male comedian*

10 May 62	●**LITTLE PIECES OF HANCOCK** *Pye NEP 24146*	**6** 33 wks
3 Jan 63	**LITTLE PIECES OF HANCOCK** (re-entry) *Pye NEP 24146*	**13** 6 wks

Françoise HARDY *France, female vocalist*

2 Jul 64	●**C'EST FAB** *Pye NEP 24188*	**5** 21 wks
8 Oct 64	**C'EST FRANCOISE** *Pye NEP 24193*	**20** 1 wk
12 Nov 64	**C'EST FRANCOISE** (re-entry) *Pye NEP 24193*	**18** 1 wk

Rolf HARRIS *Australia, male vocalist*

20 Oct 66	●**ROLF HARRIS AND SHAMUS O'SHEAN THE LEPRACHAUN** *Columbia SEG 8508*	**9** 2 wks

Jet HARRIS and Tony MEEHAN

UK, male instrumental duo-bass and drums

27 Jun 63	●**JET AND TONY** *Decca DFE 8528*	**3** 21 wks

HEINZ *UK, male vocalist*

30 Jan 64	**LIVE IT UP** *Decca DFE 8559*	**12** 9 wks

HERMAN'S HERMITS

UK, male vocal/instrumental group

28 Jan 65	**HERMANIA** *Columbia SEG 8380*	**19** 1 wk
10 Jun 65	●**MRS BROWN YOU'VE GOT A LOVELY DAUGHTER** *Columbia SEG 8440*	**3** 20 wks
23 Sep 65	**HERMAN'S HERMITS' HITS** *Columbia SEG 8442*	**10** 10 wks
4 Nov 65	**MRS BROWN YOU'VE GOT A LOVELY DAUGHTER** (re-entry) *Columbia SEG 8440*	**19** 1 wk
25 Aug 66	●**HOLD ON** *Columbia SEG 8503*	**4** 10 wks

Edmund HOCKRIDGE *Canada, male vocalist*

19 May 60	●**MOST HAPPY FELLA** *Pye NEP 24122*	**10** 1 wk
2 Jun 60	●**MOST HAPPY FELLA** (re-entry) *Pye NEP 24122*	**8** 2 wks
7 Jul 60	**MOST HAPPY FELLA** (2nd re-entry) *Pye NEP 24122*	**18** 1 wk
6 Apr 61	**THE MUSIC MAN** *Pye NEP 24135*	**20** 1 wk

Chris FARLOWE *Above*
Six places higher for the EP
'Farlowe In The Midnight Hour'
than Wilson Pickett's single
version in the singles chart.

Paul JONES *Right* The
bluesman, thespian and
film star looks pensive in
low-slung cable-knit pullover.

KINKS *Above* The Kinks
Klimbed to the Koveted
number one spot with
'Kinksize Session' and
'Kwyet Kinks'.

Date	Title *Label Number*	Position		Date	Title *Label Number*	Position	

HOLLIES *UK, male vocal/instrumental group*

4 Jun 64	●HOLLIES *Parlophone GEP 8909*	**6**	8 wks
25 Jun 64	●JUST ONE LOOK *Parlophone GEP 8911*	**10**	4 wks
30 Jul 64	JUST ONE LOOK (re-entry) *Parlophone GEP 8911*	**11**	4 wks
23 Sep 65	●I'M ALIVE *Parlophone GEP 8142*	**5**	15 wks
7 Jul 66	●I CAN'T LET GO *Parlophone GEP 8951*	**9**	2 wks

Buddy HOLLY *US, male vocalist*

17 Mar 60	●THE LATE GREAT BUDDY HOLLY *Coral FEP 2044*	**4**	32 wks
3 Nov 60	THE LATE GREAT BUDDY HOLLY (re-entry) *Coral FEP 2044*	**20**	1 wk
1 Dec 60	THE LATE GREAT BUDDY HOLLY (2nd re-entry) *Coral FEP 2044*	**17**	1 wk
20 Jul 61	●RAVE ON *Coral FE 2005*	**9**	15 wks
24 Aug 61	BUDDY HOLLY No 1 *Brunswick OE 9456*	**18**	2 wks
31 Aug 61	HEARTBEAT *Coral FE 2015*	**13**	3 wks
19 Oct 61	●THE LATE GREAT BUDDY HOLLY (3rd re-entry) *Coral FEP 2044*	**9**	8 wks
4 Jan 62	THE LATE GREAT BUDDY HOLLY (4th re-entry) *Coral FEP 2044*	**19**	1 wk
15 Mar 62	LISTEN TO ME *Coral SEP 2002*	**12**	12 wks
9 Aug 62	LISTEN TO ME (re-entry) *Coral SEP 2002*	**19**	2 wks
15 Nov 62	LISTEN TO ME (2nd re-entry) *Coral SEP 2002*	**14**	3 wks
13 Jun 63	●RAVE ON (re-entry) *Coral FEP 2005*	**10**	7 wks
3 Oct 63	HEARTBEAT (re-entry) *Coral FEP 2015*	**18**	3 wks

Robert HORTON *US, male vocalist*

10 Mar 60	●SUNDAY NIGHT AT THE LONDON PALLADIUM *Pye NEP 24118*	**7**	6 wks
28 Apr 60	●SUNDAY NIGHT AT THE LONDON PALLADIUM (re-entry) *Pye NEP 24118*	**8**	2 wks

HOWLIN' WOLF *US, male vocalist*

8 Oct 64	TELL ME *Pye NEP 44032*	**18**	1 wk
22 Oct 64	TELL ME (re-entry) *Pye NEP 44032*	**16**	3 wks

Frank IFIELD *UK, male vocalist*

6 Dec 62	FRANK IFIELD'S HITS *Columbia SEG 8210*	**1**	50 wks
23 Jan 63	PLEASE *Columbia SEG 8288*	**18**	3 wks
20 Jun 63	●MORE OF FRANK IFIELD'S HITS *Colombia SEG 8254*	**4**	15 wks
19 Sep 63	●JUST ONE MORE CHANCE *Columbia SEG 8262*	**5**	13 wks
10 Oct 63	VIVA IFIELD *Columbia SEG 8270*	**11**	11 wks
5 Dec 63	●FRANK IFIELD'S HITS (re-entry) *Columbia SEG 8210*	**10**	9 wks
16 Apr 64	DON'T BLAME ME *Columbia SEG 8300*	**19**	2 wks

J

JAY and the AMERICANS

US, male vocalist and male instrumental backing group

29 Sep 66	●LIVIN' *United Artists UEP 1017*	**10**	1 wk

Paul JONES *UK, male vocalist*

4 May 67	PRIVILEGE *HMV 7EG 8975*	**1**	31 wks

Tom JONES *UK, male vocalist*

8 Apr 65	●TOM JONES ON STAGE *Decca DFE 8617*	**3**	28 wks

K

Eden KANE *UK, male vocalist*

27 Sep 62	EDEN KANE HITS *Decca DFE 8502*	**12**	8 wks

Johnny KIDD and the PIRATES

UK, male vocalist and male instrumental backing group

12 Jan 61	SHAKIN' ALL OVER *HMV 7EG 8628*	**11**	7 wks

KINKS *UK, male vocal/instrumental group*

10 Dec 64	KINKSIZE SESSION *Pye NEP 24200*	**1**	21 wks
28 Jan 65	●KINKSIZE HITS *Pye NEP 20403*	**3**	21 wks
15 Jul 65	KINKSIZE SESSION (re-entry) *Pye NEP 24200*	**18**	1 wk
23 Sep 65	KWYET KINKS *Pye NEP 24221*	**1**	32 wks
21 Jul 66	●DEDICATED KINKS *Pye NEP 24258*	**7**	4 wks

Kathy KIRBY *UK, female vocalist*

26 Nov 64	KATHY KIRBY Vol 2 *Decca DFE 8596*	**20**	1 wk
4 Mar 65	●A SONG FOR EUROPE *Decca DFE 8611*	**9**	9 wks

Eartha KITT *US, female vocalist*

29 Nov 62	EARTHA KITT REVISITED *London RER 1266*	**18**	1 wk

Date	Title *Label Number*	Position	Date	Title *Label Number*	Position

Billy J KRAMER and the DAKOTAS

UK, male vocalist and male instrumental backing group

24 Oct 63	●THE BILLY J KRAMER HITS *Parlophone GEP 8885*	8	10 wks
9 Jan 64	THE BILLY J KRAMER HITS (re-entry) *Parlophone GEP 8885*	11	2 wks
30 Jan 64	THE BILLY J KRAMER HITS (2nd re-entry) *Parlophone GEP 8885*	17	1 wk

See also Dakotas.

L

US, male vocalist

20 Jul 61	WESTERN FAVOURITES *Philips BBE 12447*	17	1 wk
7 Sep 61	●WESTERN FAVOURITES (re-entry) *Philips BBE 12447*	7	10 wks
14 Dec 61	WESTERN FAVOURITES (2nd re-entry) *Philips BBE 12447*	15	1 wk

Mario LANZA *US, male vocalist*

14 Apr 60	THE GREAT CARUSO *RCA RCX 1046*	16	1 wk
21 Apr 60	●STUDENT PRINCE *Camden RCX 133*	8	5 wks
2 Jun 60	STUDENT PRINCE (re-entry) *Camden RCX 133*	11	1 wk
11 Aug 60	●STUDENT PRINCE (2nd re-entry) *Camden RCX 133*	8	17 wks
4 Dec 60	●SINGS CHRISTMAS CAROLS *RCA RCX 162*	10	2 wks
4 May 61	●STUDENT PRINCE (3rd re-entry) *Camden RCX 133*	15	2 wks
26 Apr 62	STUDENT PRINCE (4th re-entry) *Camden RCX 133*	17	2 wks

LEE — See *SHIRLEY and LEE*

Brenda LEE *US, female vocalist*

8 Nov 62	SPEAK TO ME PRETTY *Brunswick OE 9488*	18	3 wks
1 Aug 63	●ALL ALONE AM I *Brunswick OE 9492*	8	8 wks

Jerry LEE LEWIS

US, male vocalist/instrumentalist - piano

4 Oct 62	JERRY LEE LEWIS No 4 *London RES 1296*	13	5 wks
25 Oct 62	JERRY LEE LEWIS No 5 *London RES 1336*	14	6 wks

John LEYTON *UK, male vocalist*

8 Mar 62	JOHN LEYTON *Top Rank JKP 3016*	11	13 wks

TERRY LIGHTFOOT — See *Mr. Acker BILK and Terry LIGHTFOOT*

Trini LOPEZ *US, male vocalist*

5 Dec 63	TRINI LOPEZ AT PJ's *Reprise R 30013*	15	2 wks
26 Dec 63	TRINI LOPEZ AT PJ's (re-entry) *Reprise R 30013*	11	5 wks
17 Sep 64	AMERICA *Reprise R 30014*	16	1 wk
19 Nov 64	AMERICA (re-entry) *Reprise R 30014*	17	2 wks
28 Jan 65	AMERICA (2nd re-entry) *Reprise R 30014*	20	1 wk

Joe LOSS *UK, orchestra leader*

14 Dec 61	DANCING TIME FOR LATINS *HMV 7EG 8587*	19	1 wk
29 Mar 62	DANCING TIME FOR LATINS (re-entry) *HMV 7EG 8587*	17	2 wks
25 Jan 62	LATIN STYLE *HMV 7EG 8725*	19	1 wk

LOVIN' SPOONFUL

US, male vocal/instrumental group

23 Jun 66	●DID YOU EVER HAVE TO MAKE UP YOUR MIND? *Kama Sutra KEP 300*	3	11 wks
25 Aug 66	●JUG BAND MUSIC *Kama Sutra KEP 301*	8	2 wks

M

Kenneth McKELLAR *UK, male vocalist*

24 Mar 60	KENNETH McKELLAR SINGS HANDEL *Decca DFE 6663*	12	2 wks
14 Apr 60	KENNETH McKELLAR SINGS HANDEL (re-entry) *Decca DFE 6663*	19	1 wk
1 Sep 60	●HANDEL'S ARIAS *Decca DFE 6623*	9	1 wk
22 Sep 60	KENNETH McKELLAR No 2 *Decca DFE 6394*	13	1 wk
22 Dec 60	●ROAD TO THE ISLES *Decca DFE 6575*	8	2 wks

Henry MANCINI and his ORCHESTRA

US, orchestra

16 Apr 64	PINK PANTHER *RCA RCX 7136*	14	3 wks
14 May 64	PINK PANTHER (re-entry) *RCA RCX 7136*	14	3 wks
11 Jun 64	PINK PANTHER (2nd re-entry) *RCA RCX 7136*	20	1 wk
25 Jun 64	PINK PANTHER (3rd re-entry) *RCA RCX 7136*	16	3 wks

MANFRED MANN

South Africa/UK, male vocal/instrumental group

19 Nov 64	●GROOVIN' WITH MANFRED MANN *HMV 7EG 8876*	3	18 wks
10 Jun 65	★THE ONE IN THE MIDDLE *HMV 7EG 8908*	1	38 wks
25 Nov 65	★NO LIVING WITHOUT YOUR LOVING *HMV 7EG 8922*	1	24 wks
14 Apr 66	★MACHINES *HMV 7EG 8942*	1	13 wks
9 Jun 66	●INSTRUMENTAL ASYLUM *HMV 7EG 8949*	3	9 wks
13 Oct 66	●ASWAS *HMV 7EG 8962*	4	9 wks

Date	Title Label Number	Position	Date	Title Label Number	Position

MANTOVANI *UK, orchestra leader*

10 Mar 60	●MANTOVANI'S BIG FOUR *Decca DFE 6148*	**6**	1 wk
31 Mar 60	DREAMS OF OLWEN *Decca DFE 6618*	**20**	1 wk
12 May 60	MANTOVANI'S BIG FOUR (re-entry) *Decca DFE 6148*	**20**	1 wk
26 May 60	●MANTOVANI'S BIG FOUR (2nd re-entry) *Decca DFE 6148*	**7**	4 wks
30 Jun 60	MANTOVANI'S BIG FOUR (3rd re-entry) *Decca DFE 6148*	**19**	1 wk
14 Jul 60	MANTOVANI'S BIG FOUR (4th re-entry) *Decca DFE 6148*	**18**	2 wks
18 Aug 60	DREAMS OF OLWEN (re-entry) *Decca DFE 6618*	**17**	2 wks
8 Dec 60	●MANTOVANI'S BIG FOUR (5th re-entry) *Decca DFE 6148*	**6**	9 wks
23 Feb 61	MANTOVANI'S BIG FOUR (6th re-entry) *Decca DFE 6148*	**11**	11 wks
30 Mar 61	●EXODUS AND OTHER THEMES *Decca DFE 6671*	**3**	34 wks
25 May 61	MANTOVANI'S BIG FOUR (7th re-entry) *Decca DFE 6148*	**20**	1 wk
15 Jun 61	MANTOVANI'S BIG FOUR (8th re-entry) *Decca DFE 6418*	**19**	1 wk
29 Mar 62	EXODUS AND OTHER THEMES (re-entry) *Decca DFE 6671*	**20**	1 wk
27 Sep 62	DREAMS OF OLWEN (2nd re-entry) *Decca DFE 6618*	**20**	1 wk

Mary MARTIN *US, female vocalist*

7 Apr 60	SOUTH PACIFIC *Philips BBE 12261*	**20**	1 wk
21 Apr 60	SOUTH PACIFIC (re-entry)	**20**	1 wk

Wink MARTINDALE *US, male vocalist*

11 Jul 63	DECK OF CARDS *London RED 1370*	**11**	12 wks

MARY — See *PETER, PAUL and MARY*

Mireille MATHIEU *France, female vocalist*

10 Aug 67	●MIRIELLE MATHIEU *Fontana TE 17492*	**9**	6 wks

Johnny MATHIS *US, male vocalist*

5 May 60	MEET MR MATHIS *Fontana TFE 17177*	**18**	1 wk
13 Apr 61	IT'S LOVE *Fontana TFE 17319*	**20**	1 wk
24 Aug 61	FOUR HITS *Fontana TFE 17275*	**17**	1 wk
5 Oct 61	FOUR SHOW HITS *Fontana TFE 17317*	**17**	1 wk

Tony MEEHAN — See *Jet HARRIS and Tony MEEHAN*

MERSEYBEATS *UK, male vocal/instrumental group*

9 Mar 64	●I THINK OF YOU *Fontana TE 17423*	**10**	4 wks
9 Apr 64	●ON STAGE *Fontana TE 17422*	**2**	23 wks
23 Apr 64	●I THINK OF YOU (re-entry) *Fontana TE 17423*	**8**	6 wks
11 Jun 64	I THINK OF YOU (2nd re-entry) *Fontana TE 17423*	**16**	2 wks
1 Oct 64	ON STAGE (re-entry) *Fontana TE 17422*	**12**	2 wks

M.G.s — See *BOOKER T. and the M.G.s*

MICK — See *Dave DEE, DOZY, BEAKY, MICK and TICH*

MIKI and GRIFF *UK, male/female vocal duo*

1 Sep 60	●MIKI AND GRIFF *Pye NEP 24116*	**2**	18 wks
12 Jan 61	MIKI AND GRIFF (re-entry) *Pye NEP 24116*	**19**	1 wk
26 Jan 61	MIKI AND GRIFF (2nd re-entry) *Pye NEP 24116*	**16**	2 wks
17 Aug 61	MIKI AND GRIFF (3rd re-entry) *Pye NEP 24116*	**16**	1 wk

Hayley MILLS — See *Maurice CHEVALIER and Hayley MILLS*

MINDBENDERS — See *Wayne FONTANA and the MINDBENDERS*

George MITCHELL *UK, male/female vocal group*

7 Dec 61	●CHRISTMAS WITH THE MINSTRELS *HMV 7EG 8714*	**4**	6 wks
21 Jun 62	BLACK AND WHITE MINSTREL SHOW *HMV 7EG 8724*	**1**	53 wks
6 Dec 62	●CHRISTMAS WITH THE MINSTRELS (re-entry) *HMV 7EG 8714*	**8**	4 wks
28 Feb 63	BLACK AND WHITE MINSTREL SHOW No 2 *HMV 7EG 8782*	**20**	1 wk
2 Jan 64	●BLACK AND WHITE MINSTREL SHOW (re-entry) *HMV 7EG 8724*	**18**	2 wks

MOJOS *UK, male vocal/instrumental group*

15 Oct 64	MOJOS *Decca DFE 8591*	**12**	3 wks

Matt MONRO *UK, male vocalist*

27 Feb 64	SONG FOR EUROPE *Parlophone GEP 8898*	**16**	6 wks
20 May 65	SOMEWHERE *Parlophone GEP 8932*	**19**	1 wk

MOODY BLUES *UK, male vocal/instrumental group*

10 Jun 65	MOODY BLUES *Decca DE 8622*	**12**	8 wks
12 Aug 65	MOODY BLUES (re-entry) *Decca DE 8622*	**15**	6 wks

Dudley MOORE — See *Peter COOK and Dudley MOORE*

N

NEW CHRISTY MINSTRELS *US, male vocal/instrumental group*

17 Mar 66	●THREE WHEELS ON MY WAGON *CBS EP 6057*	**5**	10 wks

THE MERSEYBEATS

ON STAGE

fontana

MERSEYBEATS *Above left* The mini-skirted fans on the cover were screaming for 'Long Tall Sally,' 'I'm Gonna Sit Right Down and Cry' 'Shame' and 'You Can't Judge A Book By It's Cover.'

Elvis PRESLEY *Above* As handyman Charlie Main in 'Roustabout.'

MANFRED MANN *Left* Paul Jones in trousers kindly loaned by Rubert Bear for a Marquee gig.

PETER, PAUL and MARY *Left* Peter Yarrow, Mary Travis and Paul Stookey sing lustily despite their worried accountant (right with spectacles) wondering how they can afford to pay the 49 strong backing group.

Date	Title *Label Number*	Position		Date	Title *Label Number*	Position

Bob NEWHART *US, male comedian*

Date	Title *Label Number*	Position	
8 Jun 61	●BUTTON DOWN MIND OF BOB NEWHART Vol 1 *Warner Bros. WEP 6031*	**2**	62 wks
6 Sep 62	BUTTON DOWN MIND OF BOB NEWHART Vol 1 (re-entry) *Warner Bros. WEP 6031*	**20**	1 wk
27 Sep 62	BUTTON DOWN MIND OF BOB NEWHART Vol 1 (2nd re-entry) *Warner Bros. WEP 6031*	**18**	1 wk
18 Oct 62	THE BUTTON DOWN MOON STRIKES BACK *Warner Bros. WEP 6042*	**20**	1 wk

Anthony NEWLEY *UK, male vocalist*

Date	Title *Label Number*	Position	
14 Apr 60	TONY'S HITS *Decca DFE 6629*	**14**	1 wk
28 Apr 60	●TONY'S HITS (re-entry) *Decca DFE 6629*	**6**	6 wk
9 Jun 60	TONY'S HITS (2nd re-entry) *Decca DFE 6629*	**16**	1 wk
30 Jun 60	TONY'S HITS (3rd re-entry) *Decca DFE 6629*	**20**	1 wk

NINA and FREDERICK

Denmark, female/male vocal duo

Date	Title *Label Number*	Position	
10 Mar 60	●NINA AND FREDERICK Vol 1 *Columbia SEG 7926*	**2**	115 wks
31 Mar 60	NINA AND FREDERICK No 1 *Nixe NEP 44002*	**13**	2 wks
21 Apr 60	●NINA AND FREDERICK No 2 *Pye NEP 44003*	**10**	3 wks
19 May 60	●NINA AND FREDERICK No 2 (re-entry) *Pye NEP 44003*	**9**	2 wks
9 Jun 60	●NINA AND FREDERICK Vol 2 *Columbia SEG 7997*	**5**	3 wks
30 Jun 60	●NINA AND FREDERICK No 2 (2nd re-entry) *Pye NEP 44003*	**8**	2 wks
7 Jul 60	●NINA AND FREDERICK Vol 2 (re-entry) *Columbia SEG 7997*	**3**	10 wks
6 Oct 60	●NINA AND FREDERICK Vol 2 (2nd re-entry) *Columbia SEG 7997*	**8**	13 wks
24 Nov 60	●NINA AND FREDERICK Vol 3 *Columbia SEG 8049*	**8**	7 wks
16 Nov 61	●CHRISTMAS AT HOME WITH NINA AND FREDERICK *Columbia SEG 8111*	**2**	9 wks
13 Dec 62	WHITE CHRISTMAS *Columbia SEG 8215*	**11**	3 wks

Roy ORBISON *US, male vocalist*

Date	Title *Label Number*	Position	
30 May 63	ONLY THE LONELY *London REU 1274*	**15**	11 wks
8 Aug 63	●IN DREAMS *London REU 1373*	**6**	36 wks
4 Jun 64	IN DREAMS (re-entry) *London REU 1373*	**20**	1 wk
30 Jul 64	IN DREAMS (2nd re-entry) *London REU 1373*	**17**	5 wks
27 Aug 64	●IT'S OVER *London REU 1435*	**3**	22 wks
10 Sep 64	IN DREAMS (3rd re-entry) *London REU 1373*	**15**	2 wks
7 Jan 65	●OH PRETTY WOMAN *London REU 1437*	**9**	15 wks
4 Feb 65	IT'S OVER (re-entry) *London REU 1435*	**18**	1 wk
25 Mar 65	●STAGE SHOW HITS *London REU 1439*	**10**	8 wks

OUTLAWS — See *Mike BERRY and the OUTLAWS*

P

PACEMAKERS — See *GERRY and the PACEMAKERS*

PAUL— See *PETER, PAUL and MARY*

PERKY — See *PINKY and PERKY*

PETER, PAUL and MARY

US, male/female vocal instrumental group

Date	Title *Label Number*	Position	
28 Nov 63	●PETER, PAUL AND MARY *Warner Bros. WEP 6114*	**3**	79 wks
16 Apr 64	MOVING *Warner Bros. WEP 6119*	**18**	1 wk
23 Jul 64	MOVING (re-entry) *Warner Bros. WEP 6119*	**16**	1 wk
26 Nov 64	BLOWIN' IN THE WIND *Warner Bros. WB 104*	**13**	6 wks
11 Feb 65	BLOWIN' IN THE WIND (re-entry) *Warner Bros. WB 104*	**18**	1 wk
11 Mar 65	BLOWIN' IN THE WIND (2nd re-entry) *Warner Bros. WB 104*	**14**	5 wks
6 May 65	IN THE WIND Vol 1 *Warner Bros. WEP 6135*	**12**	6 wks

PETER and GORDON *UK, male vocal duo*

Date	Title *Label Number*	Position	
20 Aug 64	JUST FOR YOU *Columbia SEG 8337*	**20**	1 wk

PINKY and PERKY *UK, male pig vocal duo*

Date	Title *Label Number*	Position	
21 Dec 61	CHRISTMAS WITH PINKY AND PERKY *Columbia SEG 8122*	**16**	2 wks
20 Dec 62	CHRISTMAS WITH PINKY AND PERKY (re-entry) *Columbia SEG 8122*	**17**	2 wks

PIRATES — See *Johnny KIDD and the PIRATES*

Gene PITNEY *US, male vocalist*

Date	Title *Label Number*	Position	
27 Feb 64	●TWENTY FOUR HOURS FROM TULSA *United Artists UEP 1001*	**7**	16 wks
25 Feb 65	THAT GIRL BELONGS TO YESTERDAY *Stateside SE 1028*	**13**	7 wks
7 Jul 66	●BACKSTAGE *Stateside SE 1040*	**6**	2 wks
18 Aug 66	●BACKSTAGE (re-entry) *Stateside SE 1040*	**9**	1 wk

Elvis PRESLEY *US, male vocalist*

Date	Title *Label Number*	Position	
10 Mar 60	STRICTLY ELVIS *RCA RCX 175*	**1**	37 wks
17 Mar 60	●TOUCH OF GOLD Vol 1 *RCA RCX 1045*	**8**	3 wks
7 Apr 60	TOUCH OF GOLD Vol 2 *RCA RCX 1048*	**12**	3 wks
5 May 60	TOUCH OF GOLD Vol 1 (re-entry) *RCA RCX 1045*	**11**	2 wks
12 May 60	STRICTLY ELVIS (re-entry) *RCA RCX 175*	**19**	1 wk
12 May 60	TOUCH OF GOLD Vol 2 (re-entry) *RCA RCX 1048*	**11**	3 wks
2 Jun 60	TOUCH OF GOLD Vol 1 (2nd re-entry) *RCA RCX 1045*	**16**	2 wks
16 Jun 60	●TOUCH OF GOLD Vol 2 (2nd re-entry) *RCA RCX 1048*	**10**	2 wks

Date	Title *Label Number*	Position	
30 Jun 60	**TOUCH OF GOLD Vol 1** (3rd re-entry) *RCA RCX 1045*	12	4 wks
28 Jul 60	**TOUCH OF GOLD Vol 2** (3rd re-entry) *RCA RCX 1048*	18	1 wk
15 Sep 60	**TOUCH OF GOLD Vol 2** (4th re-entry) *RCA RCX 1048*	15	3 wks
3 Nov 60	**SUCH A NIGHT** *RCA RCX 190*	16	2 wks
17 Nov 60	**TOUCH OF GOLD Vol 2** (5th re-entry) *RCA RCX 1048*	20	1 wk
24 Nov 60	**ELVIS SINGS CHRISTMAS SONGS** *RCA RCX 121*	17	1 wk
1 Dec 60	●**STRICTLY ELVIS** (2nd re-entry) *RCA RCX 175*	4	18 wks
5 Jan 61	●**SUCH A NIGHT** (re-entry) *RCA RCX 190*	4	41 wks
6 Jul 61	**STRICTLY ELVIS** (3rd re-entry) *RCA RCX 175*	13	6 wks
24 Aug 61	**JAILHOUSE ROCK** (film soundtrack) *RCA RCX 106*	14	7 wks
14 Sep 61	**PEACE IN THE VALLEY** *RCA RCX 101*	19	2 wks
26 Oct 61	●**SUCH A NIGHT** (2nd re-entry) *RCA RCX 190*	8	15 wks
2 Nov 61	**PEACE IN THE VALLEY** (re-entry) *RCA RCX 101*	12	4 wks
23 Nov 61	**ELVIS SINGS CHRISTMAS SONGS** (re-entry) *RCA RCX 121*	16	2 wks
7 Dec 61	**PEACE IN THE VALLEY** (2nd re-entry) *RCA RCX 101*	19	1 wk
21 Dec 61	**ELVIS SINGS CHRISTMAS SONGS** (2nd re-entry) *RCA RCX 121*	18	2 wks
4 Jan 62	**PEACE IN THE VALLEY** (3rd re-entry) *RCA RCX 101*	18	1 wk
15 Feb 62	**SUCH A NIGHT** (3rd re-entry) *RCA RCX 190*	16	2 wks
1 Mar 62	**PEACE IN THE VALLEY** (4th re-entry) *RCA RCX 101*	18	1 wk
1 Mar 62	**STRICTLY ELVIS** (4th re-entry) *RCA RCX 175*	19	2 wks
24 May 62	**SUCH A NIGHT** (4th re-entry) *RCA RCX 190*	16	2 wks
7 Jun 62	★**FOLLOW THAT DREAM** (film soundtrack) *RCA RCX 211*	1	51 wks
1 Nov 62	★**KID GALAHAD** (film soundtrack) *RCA RCX 7106*	1	44 wks
5 Dec 63	**PEACE IN THE VALLEY** (5th re-entry) *RCA RCX 101*	20	1 wk
16 Apr 64	●**LOVE IN LAS VEGAS** *RCA RCX 7141*	3	19 wks
21 May 64	**ELVIS FOR YOU Vol 1** *RCA RCX 7142*	16	1 wk
4 Jun 64	**ELVIS FOR YOU Vol 1** (re-entry) *RCA RCX 7142*	11	5 wks
18 Jun 64	**ELVIS FOR YOU Vol 2** *RCA RCX 7143*	18	1 wk
3 Sep 64	●**LOVE IN LAS VEGAS** (film soundtrack) (re-entry) *RCA RCX 7141*	9	6 wks
8 Jul 65	●**TICKLE ME Vol 1** (film soundtrack) *RCA RCX 7173*	3	19 wks
2 Sep 65	●**TICKLE ME Vol 2** (film soundtrack) *RCA RCX 7174*	8	18 wks
25 Nov 65	●**TICKLE ME** (film soundtrack) (re-entry) *RCA RCX 7173*	10	7 wks
26 Jun 67	★**EASY COME EASY GO** (film soundtrack) *RCA RCX 7187*	1	23 wks

PRETTY THINGS

UK, male vocal/instrumental group

Date	Title *Label Number*	Position	
10 Dec 64	●**PRETTY THINGS** *Fontana TE 17434*	6	25 wks
17 Jun 65	**PRETTY THINGS** (re-entry) *Fontana TE 17434*	19	1 wk
8 Jul 65	**PRETTY THINGS** (2nd re-entry) *Fontana TE 17434*	19	1 wk
29 Jul 65	**PRETTY THINGS** (3rd re-entry) *Fontana TE 17434*	15	1 wk
21 Oct 65	**RAINING IN MY HEART** *Fontana TE 17442*	12	9 wks

Louis PRIMA *US, male vocalist*

Date	Title *Label Number*	Position	
23 Jun 60	**STRICTLY PRIMA** *Capitol EAP 1 1132*	19	1 wk
29 Sep 60	**STRICTLY PRIMA** (re-entry) *Capitol EAP 1 1132*	12	1 wk

P J PROBY *US, male vocalist*

Date	Title *Label Number*	Position	
7 Jan 65	**P J PROBY** *Liberty LEP 2192*	13	6 wks
7 Oct 65	**SOMEWHERE** *Liberty LEP 2229*	20	2 wks
28 Oct 65	**SOMEWHERE** (re-entry) *Liberty LEP 2229*	20	1 wk
11 Nov 65	**SOMEWHERE** (2nd re-entry) *Liberty LEP 2229*	19	2 wks

R

RAM JAM BAND — See *Geno WASHINGTON and the RAM JAM BAND*

Jim REEVES *US, male vocalist*

Date	Title *Label Number*	Position	
29 Nov 62	**SONGS TO WARM THE HEART** *RCA RCX 173*	19	1 wk
2 Apr 64	**WELCOME TO MY WORLD** *RCA RCX 7119*	20	2 wks
13 Aug 64	●**FROM THE HEART** *RCA RCX 7131*	4	22 wks
3 Sep 64	●**WELCOME TO MY WORLD** (re-entry) *RCA RCX 7119*	6	15 wks
10 Sep 64	●**SONGS TO WARM THE HEART Vol 2** *RCA RCX 215*	9	3 wks
24 Sep 64	**FROM THE HEART Vol 2** *RCA RCX 7145*	14	1 wk
1 Oct 64	**SONGS TO WARM THE HEART** (re-entry) *RCA RCX 173*	12	1 wk
17 Dec 64	**SONGS TO WARM THE HEART** (2nd re-entry) *RCA RCX 173*	12	3 wks
24 Dec 64	**WELCOME TO MY WORLD** (2nd re-entry) *RCA RCX 7119*	14	4 wks
14 Jan 65	**SONGS TO WARM THE HEART** (3rd re-entry) *RCA RCX 173*	18	2 wks
4 Feb 65	**SONGS TO WARM THE HEART** (4th re-entry)	15	5 wks
18 Mar 65	**WELCOME TO MY WORLD** (3rd re-entry) *RCA RCX 7119*	16	4 wks
8 Apr 65	**FROM THE HEART** (re-entry) *RCA RCX 7131*	15	1 wk
27 May 65	**FROM THE HEART** (2nd re-entry) *RCA RCX 7131*	20	1 wk
8 Oct 65	**SONGS TO WARM THE HEART Vol 2** (4th re-entry) *RCA RCX 215*	17	2 wks
15 Oct 65	**SONGS TO WARM THE HEART Vol 2** (re-entry) *RCA RCX 215*	13	1 wk
29 Oct 65	**SONGS TO WARM THE HEART Vol 2** (2nd re-entry) *RCA RCX 215*	16	3 wks
3 Dec 65	**SONGS TO WARM THE HEART Vol 2** (3rd re-entry) *RCA RCX 215*	16	1 wk
6 Oct 66	●**FROM THE HEART** (3rd re-entry) *RCA RCX 7131*	6	2 wks
1 Dec 66	●**CHRISTMAS CARD FROM JIM REEVES** *RCA RCX 7185*	3	5 wks

Cliff RICHARD. The many faces of Cliff Richard. EP hits in each of the first five years of the decade for the Lucknow born singer.

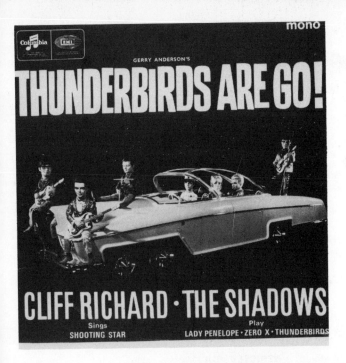

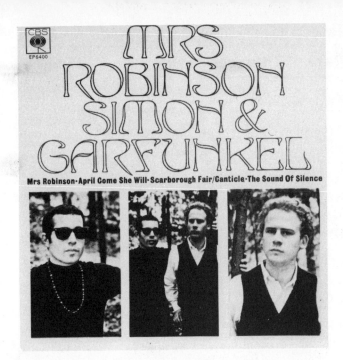

Cliff RICHARD and the SHADOWS *(above left)* became film stars as puppet characters in Gerry Anderson's *Thunderbirds Are Go!* Here the Shadows ride the pink Rolls Royce FAB 1 on the cover of the EP from the film.

SIMON and GARFUNKEL *Above right* Their 'Mrs. Robinson' EP spent 5 weeks on the singles chart before it's run was ended by a decision to exclude EPs from the listings in February '69.

ROLLING STONES *Left* Charlie Watts does a fry up for the other lads. *Right* Brian Jones gets to grip with the Hit Parader crossword while waiting for replacement light bulbs. Of the Stones' six EP hits, three were number ones.

Date	Title *Label Number*	Position

Cliff RICHARD *UK, male vocalist*

Date	Title *Label Number*	Position	
10 Mar 60	●CLIFF SINGS No 1 *Columbia SEG 7979*	**4**	13 wks
10 Mar 60	EXPRESSO BONGO *Columbia COL 7971*	**1**	22 wks
17 Mar 60	●CLIFF SINGS No 2 *Columbia SEG 7987*	**3**	14 wks
2 Jun 60	●CLIFF SINGS No 3 *Columbia SEG 8005*	**2**	10 wks
16 Jun 60	●CLIFF SINGS No 1 (re-entry) *Columbia SEG 7979*	**10**	1 wk
30 Jun 60	●CLIFF SINGS No 1 (2nd re-entry) *Columbia SEG 7979*	**10**	1 wk
14 Jul 60	CLIFF SINGS No 1 (3rd re-entry) *Columbia SEG 7979*	**19**	1 wk
21 Jul 60	●CLIFF SINGS No 2 (re-entry) *Columbia SEG 7987*	**3**	21 wks
4 Aug 60	CLIFF SINGS No 1 (4th re-entry) *Columbia SEG 7979*	**13**	1 wk
18 Aug 60	●EXPRESSO BONGO (re-entry) *Columbia COL 7971*	**7**	6 wks
25 Aug 60	CLIFF SINGS No 3 (re-entry) *Columbia SEG 8005*	**20**	1 wk
22 Sep 60	CLIFF SINGS No 3 (2nd re-entry) *Columbia SEG 8005*	**15**	4 wks
10 Nov 60	CLIFF SINGS No 1 (5th re-entry) *Columbia SEG 7979*	**19**	1 wk
8 Dec 60	CLIFF'S SILVER DISCS *Columbia SEG 8050*	**1**	52 wks
9 Feb 61	CLIFF SINGS No 2 (2nd re-entry) *Columbia SEG 7987*	**17**	1 wk
9 Feb 61	●ME AND MY SHADOWS No 1 *Columbia SEG 8065*	**6**	4 wks
16 Mar 61	●ME AND MY SHADOWS No 1 (re-entry) *Columbia SEG 8065*	**5**	8 wks
27 Apr 61	●ME AND MY SHADOWS No 2 *Columbia SEG 8071*	**8**	3 wks
27 Apr 61	●ME AND MY SHADOWS No 3 *Columbia SEG 8078*	**6**	11 wks
18 May 61	ME AND MY SHADOWS No 1 (2nd re-entry) *Columbia SEG 8065*	**18**	1 wk
25 May 61	ME AND MY SHADOWS No 2 (re-entry) *Columbia SEG 8071*	**16**	1 wk
29 Jun 61	ME AND MY SHADOWS No 1 (3rd re-entry) *Columbia SEG 8065*	**15**	8 wks
31 Aug 61	ME AND MY SHADOWS No 1 (4th re-entry) *Columbia SEG 8065*	**19**	2 wks
2 Nov 61	LISTEN TO CLIFF *Columbia SEG 8105*	**17**	2 wks
16 Nov 61	●DREAM *Columbia SEG 8119*	**3**	49 wks
25 Jan 62	●CLIFF'S SILVER DISCS (re-entry) *Columbia SEG 8050*	**9**	5 wks
8 Feb 62	●CLIFF'S HIT PARADE *Columbia SEG 8133*	**4**	25 wks
12 Apr 62	HITS FROM THE FILM 'THE YOUNG ONES' *Columbia SEG 8159*	**14**	2 wks
10 May 62	HITS FROM THE FILM 'THE YOUNG ONES' (re-entry) *Columbia SEG 8159*	**11**	29 wks
21 Jun 62	CLIFF RICHARD No 2 *Columbia SEG 8168*	**20**	1 wk
19 Jul 62	CLIFF RICHARD No 2 (re-entry) *Columbia SEG 8168*	**19**	1 wk
6 Sep 62	CLIFF'S HIT PARADE (re-entry) *Columbia SEG 8133*	**17**	3 wks
6 Dec 62	CLIFF'S HIT PARADE (2nd re-entry) *Columbia SEG 8133*	**20**	1 wk
17 Jan 63	DREAM (re-entry) *Columbia SEG 8119*	**20**	2 wks
31 Jan 63	HITS FROM THE FILM 'THE YOUNG ONES' (2nd re-entry) *Columbia SEG 8159*	**15**	8 wks
14 Feb 63	CLIFF'S HIT PARADE (3rd re-entry) *Columbia SEG 8133*	**13**	13 wks
4 Apr 63	HITS FROM THE FILM 'THE YOUNG ONES' (3rd re-entry) *Columbia SEG 8159*	**20**	1 wk

Date	Title *Label Number*	Position	
16 May 63	HOLIDAY CARNIVAL *Columbia SEG 8246*	**1**	22 wks
13 Jun 63	●HITS FROM THE FILM SUMMER HOLIDAY *Columbia SEG 8250*	**4**	20 wks
17 Oct 63	LUCKY LIPS *Columbia SEG 8269*	**18**	3 wks
7 Nov 63	HITS FROM THE FILM SUMMER HOLIDAY (re-entry) *Columbia SEG 8250*	**18**	1 wk
14 Nov 63	LUCKY LIPS (re-entry) *Columbia 8269*	**17**	2 wks
14 Nov 63	●LOVE SONGS *Columbia SEG 8272*	**4**	15 wks
28 May 64	DON'T TALK TO HIM *Columbia SEG 8299*	**15**	1 wk
13 Aug 64	●WONDERFUL LIFE *Columbia SEG 8338*	**3**	21 wks
20 May 65	ALADDIN *Columbia SEG 8395*	**20**	1 wk
22 Jul 65	LOOK IN MY EYES MARIA *Columbia SEG 8405*	**15**	1 wk
30 Sep 65	●TAKE FOUR *Columbia SEG 8450*	**4**	16 wks

The Shadows feature on all of Cliff's hits except Cliff Sings No 3, Love Songs *and* Look In My Eyes Maria. *See also the Shadows.*

Tex RITTER *US, male vocalist*

Date	Title *Label Number*	Position	
6 Dec 62	DECK OF CARDS *Capitol EAP 1323*	**19**	1 wk

Paddy ROBERTS *South Africa, male vocalist*

Date	Title *Label Number*	Position	
10 Mar 60	STRICTLY FOR GROWN UPS *Decca DFE 6584*	**1**	61 wks
28 Jul 60	PADDY ROBERTS STRIKES AGAIN *Decca DFE 6641*	**1**	20 wks
5 Jan 61	PADDY ROBERTS STRIKES AGAIN (re-entry) *Decca DFE 6641*	**14**	3 wks
23 Feb 61	PADDY ROBERTS STRIKES AGAIN (2nd re-entry) *Decca DFE 6641*	**19**	1 wk
25 May 61	STRICTLY FOR GROWN UPS (re-entry) *Decca DFE 6584*	**12**	5 wks

ROLLING STONES

UK, male vocal/instrumental group

Date	Title *Label Number*	Position	
16 Jan 64	THE ROLLING STONES *Decca DFE 8560*	**1**	52 wks
20 Aug 64	FIVE BY FIVE *Decca DFE 8590*	**1**	47 wks
28 Jan 65	THE ROLLING STONES (re-entry) *Decca DFE 8560*	**13**	4 wks
15 Apr 65	THE ROLLING STONES (2nd re-entry) *Decca DFE 8560*	**13**	2 wks
17 Jun 65	GOT LIVE IF YOU WANT IT *Decca DFE 8620*	**1**	42 wks
5 Aug 65	FIVE BY FIVE (re-entry) *Decca DFE 8590*	**12**	7 wks

Date	Title *Label Number*	Position		Date	Title *Label Number*	Position	

S

SEARCHERS *UK, male vocal/instrumental group*

Date	Title *Label Number*	Position	
19 Sep 63	★**AIN'T GONNA KISS YA** *Pye NEP 24177*	**1**	23 wks
12 Dec 63	●**SWEETS FOR MY SWEET** *Pye NEP 24183*	**5**	18 wks
27 Feb 64	●**HUNGRY FOR LOVE** *Pye NEP 24184*	**4**	18 wks
28 May 64	**AIN'T GONNA KISS YA** (re-entry) *Pye NEP 24177*	**18**	1 wk
9 Jul 64	**HUNGRY FOR LOVE** (re-entry) *Pye NEP 24184*	**17**	1 wk
10 Dec 64	●**SEARCHERS PLAY THE SYSTEM** *Pye NEP 24184*	**4**	18 wks
25 Mar 65	**WHEN YOU WALK IN THE ROOM** *Pye NEP 24204*	**12**	2 wks
6 May 65	★**BUMBLE BEE** *Pye NEP 24218*	**1**	17 wks
23 Sep 65	**SEARCHERS '65** *Pye NEP 24222*	**18**	1 wk
7 Oct 65	**SEARCHERS '65** (re-entry) *Pye NEP 24222*	**15**	4 wks
11 Nov 65	**SEARCHERS '65** (re-entry) *Pye NEP 24222*	**16**	3 wks

Harry SECOMBE *UK, male vocalist*

Date	Title *Label Number*	Position	
31 Mar 60	●**SACRED SONGS** *Philips BBE 12300*	**9**	2 wks
21 Apr 60	●**SACRED SONGS** (re-entry) *Philips BBE 12300*	**9**	23 wks
12 May 60	●**LAND OF MY FATHERS** *Philips BBE 12207*	**8**	1 wk
26 May 60	**LAND OF MY FATHERS** (re-entry) *Philips BBE 12207*	**19**	1 wk
9 Jun 60	**LAND OF MY FATHERS** (2nd re-entry) *Philips BBE 12207*	**19**	1 wk
23 Jun 60	**LAND OF MY FATHERS** (3rd re-entry) *Philips BBE 12207*	**12**	9 wks
28 Jul 60	**AT YOUR REQUEST Vol 2** *Philips BBE 12237*	**17**	1 wk
1 Sep 60	**LAND OF MY FATHERS** (4th re-entry) *Philips BBE 12207*	**11**	7 wks
6 Oct 60	**SACRED SONGS** (2nd re-entry) *Philips BBE 12300*	**18**	1 wk
20 Oct 60	**SACRED SONGS** (3rd re-entry) *Philips BBE 12300*	**18**	2 wks
27 Oct 60	**LAND OF MY FATHERS** (5th re-entry) *Philips BBE 12207*	**20**	1 wk
10 Nov 60	**SACRED SONGS** (4th re-entry) *Philips BBE 12300*	**11**	5 wks
22 Dec 60	**SACRED SONGS VOL 2** *Philips BBE 12393*	**15**	4 wks
19 Jan 61	**LAND OF MY FATHERS** (6th re-entry) *Philips BBE 12207*	**17**	1 wk
2 Mar 61	**LAND OF MY FATHERS** (7th re-entry) *Philips BBE 12207*	**20**	1 wk
3 May 62	**TAUBER FAVOURITES** *Philips BBE 12131*	**18**	1 wk
26 Jul 62	**SHOW SOUVENIRS** *Philips BBE 12513*	**18**	2 wks
2 Aug 62	**SACRED SONGS** (5th re-entry) *Philips BBE 12300*	**15**	5 wks

Pete SEEGER *US, male vocalist*

Date	Title *Label Number*	Position	
1 Oct 64	**PETE SEEGER IN CONCERT** *CBS AGG 20055*	**18**	1 wk

SEEKERS *Australia, male/female vocal group*

Date	Title *Label Number*	Position	
22 Jul 65	★**SEEKERS** *Columbia SEG 8425*	**1**	49 wks
14 Jul 66	★**HITS FROM THE SEEKERS** *Columbia SEG 8496*	**1**	73 wks
18 Aug 66	●**SEEKERS** (re-entry) *Columbia SEG 8425*	**10**	1 wk
9 Feb 67	★**MORNINGTOWN RIDE** *Columbia SEG 8522*	**1**	43 wks

Peter SELLERS *UK, male vocalist*

Date	Title *Label Number*	Position	
26 May 60	**BEST OF SELLERS** *Parlophone GEP 8770*	**15**	1 wk
25 Aug 60	●**BEST OF SELLERS No 2** *Parlophone GEP 8784*	**8**	1 wk
15 Sep 60	**BEST OF SELLERS No 2** (re-entry) *Parlophone GEP 8784*	**18**	1 wk
6 Apr 61	**BEST OF SELLERS** (re-entry) *Parlophone GEP 8770*	**19**	1 wk

SHADOWS *UK, male instrumental group*

Date	Title *Label Number*	Position	
19 Jan 61	★**SHADOWS** *Columbia SEG 8061*	**1**	47 wks
8 Jun 61	★**SHADOWS TO THE FORE** *Columbia SEG 8094*	**1**	81 wks
21 Dec 61	●**SHADOWS** (re-entry) *Columbia SEG 8061*	**3**	39 wks
8 Feb 62	★**SPOTLIGHT ON THE SHADOWS** *Columbia SEG 8135*	**1**	34 wks
7 Jun 62	**SHADOWS No 2** *Columbia SEG 8148*	**15**	9 wks
9 Aug 62	**SHADOWS No 3** *Columbia SEG 8166*	**13**	4 wks
16 Aug 62	**SHADOWS No 2** (re-entry) *Columbia SEG 8148*	**12**	7 wks
20 Sep 62	●**WONDERFUL LAND OF THE SHADOWS** *Columbia SEG 8171*	**6**	29 wks
11 Oct 62	★**THE BOYS** *Columbia SEG 8193*	**1**	46 wks
25 Oct 62	**SPOTLIGHT ON THE SHADOWS** (re-entry) *Columbia SEG 8135*	**14**	5 wks
29 Nov 62	**SHADOWS TO THE FORE** (re-entry) *Columbia SEG 8094*	**20**	1 wk
6 Dec 62	●**SPOTLIGHT ON THE SHADOWS** (2nd re-entry) *Columbia SEG 8135*	**7**	20 wks
3 Jan 63	●**SHADOWS TO THE FORE** (2nd re-entry) *Columbia SEG 8094*	**4**	24 wks
21 Feb 63	●**OUT OF THE SHADOWS** *Columbia SEG 8218*	**3**	15 wks
7 Mar 63	**DANCE ON WITH THE SHADOWS** *Columbia SEG 8233*	**31**	3 wks
13 Jun 63	●**OUT OF THE SHADOWS** (re-entry) *Columbia SEG 8218*	**9**	3 wks
20 Jun 63	**OUT OF THE SHADOWS No 2** *Columbia SEG 8249*	**20**	1 wk
27 Jun 63	**SHADOWS TO THE FORE** (3rd re-entry) *Columbia SEG 8094*	**16**	2 wks
11 Jul 63	**OUT OF THE SHADOWS** (2nd re-entry) *Columbia SEG 8218*	**16**	1 wk
18 Jul 63	**SHADOWS TO THE FORE** (4th re-entry) *Columbia SEG 8094*	**17**	5 wks
5 Sep 63	**OUT OF THE SHADOWS** (3rd re-entry) *Columbia SEG 8218*	**15**	2 wks
12 Sep 63	**SHADOWS TO THE FORE** (5th re-entry) *Columbia SEG 8094*	**16**	3 wks
19 Sep 63	●**LOS SHADOWS** *Columbia SEG 8278*	**4**	18 wks
10 Oct 63	●**FOOT TAPPING WITH THE SHADOWS** *Columbia SEG 8268*	**7**	9 wks
12 Dec 63	●**SHINDIG WITH THE SHADOWS** *Columbia SEG 8286*	**9**	4 wks
19 Dec 63	**FOOT TAPPING WITH THE SHADOWS** (re-entry) *Columbia SEG 8268*	**18**	1 wk

Date	Title Label Number	Position			Date	Title Label Number	Position		

Date	Title *Label Number*		Position		Date	Title *Label Number*		Position	
26 Dec 63	**DANCE ON WITH THE SHADOWS** (re-entry) *Columbia SEG 8233*		**16**	1 wk		**SIMON and GARFUNKEL** *US, male vocal duo*			
18 Jun 64	●**THOSE BRILLIANT SHADOWS** *Columbia SEG 8321*		**6**	13 wks	16 Jun 66	●**I AM A ROCK** *CBS EP 6074*		**4**	11 wks
25 Jun 64	**WONDERFUL LAND OF THE SHADOWS** (re-entry) *Columbia SEG 8171*		**19**	5 wks		**Frank SINATRA** *US, male vocalist*			
24 Sep 64	**THOSE BRILLIANT SHADOWS** (re-entry) *Columbia SEG 8321*		**20**	1 wk	24 Mar 60	**COME DANCE WITH ME** *Capitol EAP 1 1609*		**11**	1 wk
1 Oct 64	**DANCE ON WITH THE SHADOWS** (2nd re-entry) *Columbia SEG 8233*		**20**	1 wk	31 Mar 60	**THE SONG IS YOU** *Fontana TFE 17253*		**19**	1 wk
22 Oct 64	●**RHYTHM AND GREENS** (Film Soundtrack) *Columbia SEG 8362*		**8**	14 wks	14 Apr 60	**SONGS FOR SWINGING LOVERS Pt 1** *Capitol EAP 1 653*		**20**	1 wk
25 Mar 65	**THEME FOR ALADDIN** *Columbia SEG 8396*		**14**	2 wks	21 Apr 60	**THE LADY IS A TRAMP** *Capitol EAP 1013*		**13**	1 wk
3 Jun 65	**DANCE WITH THE SHADOWS No 3** *Columbia SEG 8408*		**16**	2 wks	7 Jul 60	**I'VE GOT A CRUSH ON YOU** *Fontana TFE 17254*		**14**	1 wk
29 Sep 66	●**THOSE TALENTED SHADOWS** *Columbia SEG 8500*		**9**	2 wks	7 Jul 60	●**THE LADY IS A TRAMP** (re-entry) *Capitol EAP 1013*		**8**	1 wk
17 Nov 66	●**THUNDERBIRDS ARE GO** *Columbia SEG 8510*		**6**	7 wks	4 Aug 60	●**THE LADY IS A TRAMP** (2nd re-entry) *Capitol EAP 1013*		**7**	17 wks

Thunderbirds Are Go *features one track performed by Cliff Richard. See also Cliff Richard.*

					24 Nov 60	**COME DANCE WITH ME Vol 2** *Capitol EAP 21069*		**18**	1 wk

Jimmy SHAND *UK, dance band leader*

Date	Title *Label Number*		Position		Date	Title *Label Number*		Position	
					12 Jan 61	●**ALL THE WAY** *Capitol EAP 20062*		**6**	15 wks
4 Jan 62	**DANCE WITH JIMMY SHAND No 2** *Parlophone GEP 8823*		**15**	3 wks	26 Jan 61	**COME DANCE WITH ME Vol 2** (re-entry) *Capitol EAP 21069*		**13**	4 wks
					16 Mar 61	**COME DANCE WITH ME Vol 2** (2nd re-entry) *Capitol EAP 21069*		**18**	3 wks

Del SHANNON *US, male vocalist*

					1 Jun 61	**COME DANCE WITH ME Vol 2** (3rd re-entry) *Capitol EAP 21069*		**17**	1 wk
25 Jan 62	**HATS OFF TO LARRY** *London RCX 1332*		**14**	2 wks	15 Jun 61	**COME DANCE WITH ME** (re-entry) *Capitol EAP 1 1609*		**14**	1 wk
9 May 63	●**DEL SHANNON No 2** *London RCX 1346*		**9**	19 wks	29 Jun 61	**COME DANCE WITH ME Vol 2** (4th re-entry) *Capitol EAP 21069*		**17**	1 wk

Helen SHAPIRO *UK, female vocalist*

SINGING POSTMAN — See *Allan SMETHURST*

Date	Title *Label Number*		Position	
23 Nov 61	**HELEN** *Columbia SEG 8128*		**1**	30 wks
8 Feb 62	**HELEN'S HIT PARADE** *Columbia SEG 8136*		**1**	36 wks
28 Jun 62	**HELEN** (re-entry) *Columbia SEG 8128*		**13**	13 wks

Allan SMETHURST *UK, male vocalist*

4 Oct 62	**MORE HITS FROM HELEN** *Columbia SEG 8174*		**12**	5 wks	3 Jun 65	**THE SINGING POSTMAN** *Ralph TUCK 152/3*		**20**	2 wks
11 Oct 62	**HELEN'S HIT PARADE** (re-entry) *Columbia SEG 8136*		**15**	5 wks	8 Dec 66	●**FIRST DELIVERY** *Parlophone GEP 8956*		**7**	10 wks
6 Dec 62	**MORE HITS FROM HELEN** (re-entry) *Columbia SEG 8174*		**16**	2 wks					

Jimmy SMITH *US, male instrumentalist - organ*

27 Dec 62	**MORE HITS FROM HELEN** (2nd re-entry) *Columbia SEG 8174*		**16**	1 wk	21 Jul 66	**SWINGIN' WITH THE INCREDIBLE JIMMY SMITH** *Verve VEP 5022*		**10**	1 wk

Sandie SHAW *UK, female vocalist*

SPENCER DAVIS GROUP

UK, male vocal/instrumental group

28 Jan 65	●**THERE'S ALWAYS SOMETHING HERE TO REMIND ME** *Pye NEP 24208*		**9**	12 wks	21 Oct 65	**YOU PUT THE HURT ON ME** *Fontana TE 1744*		**18**	1 wk
20 Apr 67	●**TELL THE BOYS** *Pye NEP 24281*		**4**	13 wks	4 Nov 65	**YOU PUT THE HURT ON ME** (re-entry) *Fontana TE 1744*		**20**	1 wk
27 Jul 67	●**TELL THE BOYS** (re entry) *Pye NEP 24281*		**9**	1 wk	18 Nov 65	**YOU PUT THE HURT ON ME** (2nd re-entry) *Fontana TE 1744*		**17**	1 wk

SHIRLEY and LEE *US, female/male vocal duo*

					2 Dec 65	●**YOU PUT THE HURT ON ME** (3rd re-entry) *Fontana TE 1744*		**4**	19 wks
23 Jun 60	**SHIRLEY AND LEE** *Vogue VE 170145*		**17**	1 wk	21 Apr 66	●**YOU PUT THE HURT ON ME** (4th re-entry) *Fontana TE 1744*		**6**	5 wks
29 Sep 60	**SHIRLEY AND LEE** (re-entry) *Vogue VE 170145*		**16**	4 wks	19 May 66	●**SITTING AND THINKING** *Fontana TE 17463*		**3**	7 wks

Harry SIMEONE CHORALE *US, choir*

SPOTNICKS *Sweden, male instrumental group*

7 Dec 61	●**GOLDEN HITS OF THE HARRY SIMEONE CHORALE** *Ember EP 4504*		**8**	6 wks	28 Mar 63	●**ON THE AIR** *Oriole EP 7075*		**2**	25 wks
27 Dec 62	**GOLDEN HITS OF THE HARRY SIMEONE CHORALE** (re-entry) *Ember EP 4504*		**13**	1 wk	17 Oct 63	**ON THE AIR** (re-entry) *Oriole EP 7075*		**17**	1 wk
					21 Nov 63	**ON THE AIR** (2nd re-entry) *Oriole EP 7075*		**20**	1 wk

Date	Title *Label Number*	Position	

Dusty SPRINGFIELD *UK, female vocalist*

26 Mar 64	●I ONLY WANT TO BE WITH YOU *Philips BF 1292*	8	6 wks
14 May 64	I ONLY WANT TO BE WITH YOU (re-entry) *Philips BF 1292*	12	6 wks
16 Jul 64	I ONLY WANT TO BE WITH YOU (2nd re-entry) *Philips BF 1292*	12	4 wks
20 Aug 64	I ONLY WANT TO BE WITH YOU (3rd re-entry) *Philips BF 1292*	12	3 wks
17 Sep 64	●DUSTY *Philips BE 12564*	3	19 wks
18 Mar 65	DUSTY (re-entry) *Philips BE 12564*	17	1 wk
6 May 65	DUSTY IN NEW YORK *Philips BF 12572*	13	5 wks
8 Jul 65	DUSTY IN NEW YORK (re-entry) *Philips BF 12572*	15	4 wks
5 Aug 65	MADMOISELLE DUSTY *Philips BE 12579*	20	1 wk
19 Aug 65	MADMOISELLE DUSTY (re-entry) *Philips BE 12579*	17	2 wks

STAGE CAST RECORDINGS — See *VARIOUS ARTISTS SECTION*

Tommy STEELE *UK, male vocalist*

10 Mar 60	●TOMMY THE TOREADOR (film soundtrack) *Decca DFE 6607*	4	9 wks
26 May 60	TOMMY THE TOREADOR (film soundtrack) (re-entry) *Decca DFE 6607*	15	2 wks
30 Jun 60	TOMMY THE TOREADOR (film soundtrack) (2nd re-entry) *Decca DFE 6607*	17	1 wk
14 Jul 60	TOMMY THE TOREADOR (film soundtrack) (3rd re-entry) *Decca DFE 6607*	13	1 wk
11 Aug 60	TOMMY THE TOREADOR (film soundtrack) (4th re-entry) *Decca DFE 6607*	15	1 wk

Connie STEVENS — See *Ed BYRNES*

Andy STEWART *UK, male vocalist*

15 Jun 61	●ANDY SINGS *Top Rank JKP 3009*	5	6 wks
3 Aug 61	●ANDY SINGS (re-entry) *Top Rank JKP 3009*	10	3 wks
31 Aug 61	●ANDY SINGS (2nd re-entry) *Top Rank JKP 3009*	3	11 wks
14 Dec 61	ANDY SINGS (3rd re-entry) *Top Rank JKP 3009*	14	1 wk
11 Jan 62	●ANDY SINGS (4th re-entry) *Top Rank JKP 3009*	7	27 wks
25 Jan 62	ANDY STEWART SINGS *Top Rank JKP 3004*	12	2 wks
5 Apr 62	ANDY STEWART SINGS (re-entry) *Top Rank JKP 3004*	19	1 wk
17 May 62	ANDY STEWART SINGS (2nd re-entry) *Top Rank JKP 3004*	14	3 wks

Barbra STREISAND *US, female vocalist*

13 Jan 66	●BARBRA STREISAND *CBS EP 6068*	10	8 wks
31 Mar 66	BARBRA STREISAND (re-entry) *CBS EP 6068*	14	2 wks
28 Apr 66	●BARBRA STREISAND (2nd re-entry) *CBS EP 6068*	8	3 wks
9 Jun 66	●BARBRA STREISAND EN FRANCAIS *CBS EP 6048*	10	1 wk

SUPREMES *US, female vocal group*

29 Apr 65	●SUPREMES' HITS *Tamla Motown TME 2008*	6	10 wks
15 Jul 65	SUPREMES' HITS (re-entry) *Tamla Motown TME 2008*	16	2 wks

SWINGING BLUE JEANS

UK, male vocal/instrumental group

16 Apr 64	SHAKE WITH THE SWINGING BLUE JEANS *HMV 7EG 8850*	15	6 wks
18 Jun 64	SHAKE WITH THE SWINGING BLUE JEANS (re-entry) *HMV 7EG 8850*	13	2 wks

SWINGLE SINGERS

US/France, male/female vocal group

14 May 64	JAZZ SEBASTIAN BACH *Philips BE 12557*	18	2 wks
4 Jun 64	JAZZ SEBASTIAN BACH (re-entry) *Philips BE 12557*	15	2 wks
25 Jun 64	JAZZ SEBASTIAN BACH (2nd re-entry) *Philips BE 12557*	11	4 wks
27 Aug 64	JAZZ SEBASTIAN BACH (3rd re-entry) *Philips BE 12557*	18	1 wk
15 Oct 64	JAZZ SEBASTIAN BACH (4th re-entry) *Philips BE 12557*	14	2 wks
12 Nov 64	JAZZ SEBASTIAN BACH (5th re-entry) *Philips BE 12557*	18	2 wks
29 Apr 65	JAZZ SEBASTIAN BACH (6th re-entry) *Philips BE 12558*	18	1 wk

T

TEMPERANCE SEVEN

UK, male vocal/instrumental group

11 May 61	●THE MUSICK *Argo EAF 14*	2	21 wks
21 Sep 61	●TEMPERANCE SEVEN *Parlophone GEP 8840*	3	36 wks

TEMPTATIONS *US, male vocal group*

1 Apr 65	TEMPTATIONS *Tamla Motown TME 2004*	18	1 wk
16 Feb 67	●IT'S THE TEMPTATIONS *Tamla Motown TME 2010*	8	2 wks

THEM *UK, male vocal/instrumental group*

18 Mar 65	THEM *Decca DFE 8612*	16	1 wk
8 Apr 65	●THEM (re-entry) *Deca DFE 8612*	5	13 wks
15 Jul 65	THEM (2nd re-entry) *Decca DFE 8612*	17	1 wk
2 Sep 65	THEM (3rd re-entry) *Decca DFE 8612*	16	3 wks

TICH — See *Dave DEE, DOZY, BEAKY, MICK and TICH*

Date	Title Label Number	Position		Date	Title Label Number	Position	

TORNADOS UK, male instrumental group

Date	Title Label Number	Position	
13 Dec 62	●THE SOUND OF THE TORNADOS *Decca DFE 8510*	**2**	25 wks
31 Jan 63	**TELSTAR** *Decca DFE 8511*	**4**	22 wks
13 Jun 63	THE SOUND OF THE TORNADOS (re-entry) *Decca DFE 8510*	**16**	1 wk
11 Apr 63	●MORE SOUNDS OF THE TORNADOS *Decca DFE 8521*	**8**	9 wks
20 Jun 63	MORE SOUNDS OF THE TORNADOS (re-entry) *Decca DFE 8521*	**18**	1 wk
4 Jul 63	MORE SOUNDS OF THE TORNADOS (2nd re-entry) *Decca DFE 8521*	**20**	1 wk
15 Aug 63	●TORNADO ROCK *Decca DFE 8533*	**7**	13 wks

See also Billy Fury and the Tornados.

TROGGS UK, male vocal/instrumental group

Date	Title Label Number	Position	
23 Mar 67	●TROGGS No 1 *Page One POE 001*	**8**	4 wks

TOTTENHAM HOTSPUR FA CUP SQUAD UK, male football team vocalists

Date	Title Label Number	Position	
8 Jun 67	●SPURS GO MARCHING ON *Columbia SEG 8532*	**6**	3 wks

U

UNIT FOUR PLUS TWO

UK, male vocal/instrumental group

Date	Title Label Number	Position	
3 Jun 65	**Unit 4+2** *Decca DFE 8619*	**11**	5 wks

V

Paul VAN KEMPEN Holland, male conductor

Date	Title Label Number	Position	
17 Mar 60	**1812 OVERTURE** *Philips ABE 10054*	**14**	1 wk
31 Mar 60	**1812 OVERTURE** (re-entry) *Philips ABE 10054*	**15**	1 wk
12 May 60	**1812 OVERTURE** (2nd re-entry) *Philips ABE 10054*	**11**	18 wks

Sarah VAUGHAN US, female vocalist

Date	Title Label Number	Position	
24 Mar 60	**SMOOTH SARAH** *Mercury ZEP 10054*	**11**	2 wks

Bobby VEE US, male vocalist

Date	Title Label Number	Position	
24 Aug 61	**HITS BY BOBBY VEE** *London REG 1278*	**19**	1 wk
20 Dec 62	●SINCERELY *Liberty LEP 2053*	**8**	23 wks
6 Jun 63	**SINCERELY** (re-entry) *Liberty LEP 2053*	**18**	1 wk
27 Jun 63	**FOREVER KIND OF LOVE** *Liberty LEP 2089*	**14**	4 wks
3 Oct 63	**BOBBY VEE'S BIGGEST HITS** *Stateside LEP 2102*	**16**	2 wks

See also Bobby Vee and the Crickets.

Bobby VEE and the CRICKETS

US, male vocalist and US, male vocal/instrumental group

Date	Title Label Number	Position	
18 Apr 63	**JUST FOR FUN** *Liberty LEP 2084*	**1**	13 wks
25 Jul 63	**JUST FOR FUN** (re-entry) *Liberty LEP 2084*	**14**	2 wks
22 Aug 63	**JUST FOR FUN** (2nd re-entry) *Liberty LEP 2084*	**20**	1 wk

See also the Crickets; and Bobby Vee.

VENTURES US, male instrumental group

Date	Title Label Number	Position	
11 May 61	**VENTURES** *London REG 1279*	**20**	1 wk

Gene VINCENT US, male vocalist

Date	Title Label Number	Position	
4 Oct 62	**RACE WITH THE DEVIL** *Capitol EAP 1 20354*	**19**	1 wk

W

WALKER BROTHERS US, male vocal group

Date	Title Label Number	Position	
16 Jun 66	**I NEED YOU** *Philips BE 12596*	**1**	25 wks
8 Dec 66	●SOLO JOHN — SOLO SCOTT *Philips BE12597*	**4**	7 wks

Second hit was without Gary Leeds.

Fats WALLER

US, male vocalist/instrumentalist - piano

Date	Title Label Number	Position	
1 Sep 60	**FATS WALLER** *RCA RCX 1053*	**14**	2 wks

Dionne WARWICK US, female vocalist

Date	Title Label Number	Position	
13 Aug 64	**IT'S LOVE THAT REALLY COUNTS** *Pye NEP 44024*	**18**	1 wk
1 Oct 64	**DON'T MAKE ME OVER** *Pye NEP 44026*	**15**	1 wk
15 Oct 64	**DON'T MAKE ME OVER** (re-entry) *Pye NEP 44026*	**13**	8 wks

Geno WASHINGTON and the RAM JAM BAND

US, male vocalist and male instrumental backing group

Date	Title Label Number	Position	
2 Feb 67	●HI! *Pye NEP 34054*	**10**	1 wk
20 Jul 67	●HI! (re-entry) *Pye NEP 34054*	**9**	1 wk
3 Aug 67	●HI! (2nd re-entry) *Pye NEP 34054*	**7**	1 wk

Geoffrey WEBB UK, male vocalist

Date	Title Label Number	Position	
2 Jun 60	**FOLLOW THAT GIRL** *Oriole EP 7030*	**19**	1 wk

Date	Title Label Number	Position		Date	Title Label Number	Position	

David WHITFIELD *UK, male vocalist*

22 Jun 61	**ROSE MARIE (SELECTION)** *Decca DFE 6669*	19	1 wk
17 Aug 61	**ROSE MARIE (SELECTION)** (re-entry) *Decca DFE 6669*	15	1 wk
26 Apr 62	**EXCERPTS FROM THE DESERT SONG** *Decca DFE 6707*	16	1 wk

WHO *UK, male vocal/instrumental group*

24 Nov 66	★**READY STEADY WHO** *Reaction 592–001*	1	20 wks

Arthur WILKINSON ORCHESTRA

UK, Orchestra

6 Jan 66	●**BEATLE CRACKER MUSIC** *HMV 7EG 8919*	7	14 wks

Andy WILLIAMS *US, male vocalist*

5 Aug 65	●**ANDY WILLIAMS FAVOURITES** *CBS EP 6054*	3	38 wks
2 Dec 65	**ANDY WILLIAMS FAVOURITES Vol 2** *CBS EP 6055*	17	1 wk
16 Dec 65	**ANDY WILLIAMS FAVOURITES Vol 2** (re-entry) *CBS EP 6055*	20	1 wk
12 Jan 67	●**ANDY'S NEWEST HITS** *CBS EP 6152*	10	1 wk
26 Jan 67	●**ANDY'S NEWEST HITS** (re-entry) *CBS EP 6152*	8	1 wk
9 Feb 67	●**ANDY'S NEWEST HITS** (2nd re-entry) *CBS EP 6152*	6	13 wks

Y

YARDBIRDS *UK, male vocal/instrumental group*

26 Aug 65	●**FIVE YARDBIRDS** *Columbia SEG 8421*	5	33 wks

VARIOUS ARTISTS

ANONYMOUS COVER VERSIONS

25 Apr 63	**TOP TEN RECORD** *Aral TPS 503*	15	4 wks
30 May 63	**TOP TEN RECORD** (re-entry) *Aral TPS 503*	17	2 wks
21 Nov 63	**TOP TEN RECORD** *Aral TPS 507*	16	2 wks
12 Dec 63	**TOP TEN RECORD** (re-entry) *Aral TPS 507*	16	1 wk
13 Feb 64	**TOP TEN RECORD** *Aral TPS 509*	17	2 wks
20 Feb 64	**TOP SIX** *Top Six SIX 1*	10	4 wks
19 Mar 64	**TOP SIX Vol 2** *Top Six SIX 2*	10	4 wks
19 Mar 64	**TOP TEN RECORD CLUB** *Aral TPS 510*	17	1 wk
9 Apr 64	**TOP SIX Vol 3** *Top Six SIX 3*	16	2 wks

The first three EPs, although identically named, are different.

FILM SOUNDTRACKS

12 May 60	**CAROUSEL No 1** *Capitol EAP 1 694*	12	6 wks
30 Jun 60	**CAROUSEL No 1** (re-entry) *Capitol EAP 1 694*	15	1 wk
14 Jul 60	**CAROUSEL No 1** (2nd re-entry) *Capitol EAP 1 694*	15	1 wk
4 Aug 60	**CAROUSEL No 1** (3rd re-entry) *Capitol EAP 1 694*	18	1 wk
4 Aug 60	**SEVEN BRIDES FOR SEVEN BROTHERS** *MGM EP 513*	19	1 wk
4 Aug 60	★**SOUTH PACIFIC No 1** *RCA RCX 181*	1	44 wks
15 Sep 60	**CAROUSEL No 1** (4th re-entry) *Capitol EAP 1 694*	16	1 wk
15 Sep 60	●**SEVEN BRIDES FOR SEVEN BROTHERS** (re-entry) *MGM EP 513*	9	12 wks
29 Sep 60	**KING AND I** *Capitol EAP 11740*	12	5 wks
15 Dec 60	**SEVEN BRIDES FOR SEVEN BROTHERS** (2nd re-entry) *MGM EP 513*	20	1 wk
19 Jan 61	**SEVEN BRIDES FOR SEVEN BROTHERS** (3rd re-entry) *MGM EP 513*	13	1 wk
9 Feb 61	**CAROUSEL No 1** (5th re-entry) *Capitol EAP 1 694*	19	1 wk
29 Jun 61	**SEVEN BRIDES FOR SEVEN BROTHERS Vol 2** *MGM EP 514*	18	1 wk
15 Jun 61	**NEVER ON SUNDAY** *London RET 1280*	17	2 wks
15 Jun 61	●**SOUTH PACIFIC No 1** (re-entry) *RCA RCX 181*	5	26 wks
20 Jul 61	**MUSIC MAN** *Pye NEP 24135*	20	1 wk
28 Sep 61	●**NEVER ON SUNDAY** (re-entry) *London RET 1280*	8	9 wks
18 Jan 62	●**SOUTH PACIFIC No 1** (2nd re-entry) *RCA RCX 181*	9	16 wks
23 Aug 62	●**SOME PEOPLE** *Pye NEP 24158*	2	21 wks
7 May 64	**LAWRENCE OF ARABIA** *Colpix PXE 3000*	16	2 wks
28 May 64	**LAWRENCE OF ARABIA** (re-entry) *Colpix PXE 3000*	16	1 wk
23 Jul 64	**LAWRENCE OF ARABIA** (2nd re-entry) *Colpix PXE 3000*	13	11 wks
11 Mar 65	**LAWRENCE OF ARABIA** (3rd re-entry) *Colpix PXE 3000*	18	1 wk

STAGE CAST RECORDINGS

19 May 60	**SALAD DAYS** (London) *Oriole EP 7028*	19	1 wk
8 Sep 60	**MY FAIR LADY No 4** (Broadway) *Philips BBE 12254*	20	1 wk
12 Oct 61	**SOUND OF MUSIC** (Broadway) *Philips BBE 12463*	13	3 wks
19 Oct 61	**MY FAIR LADY No 4** (re-entry) *Philips BBE 12254*	20	1 wk
16 Nov 61	●**OLIVER** (London) *Decca DFE 6680*	5	17 wks
16 Nov 61	**SOUND OF MUSIC** (re-entry) *Philips BBE 12463*	18	1 wk
22 Mar 62	**OLIVER** (London) (re-entry) *Decca DFE 6680*	19	1 wk
12 Apr 62	**OLIVER** (London) (2nd re-entry) *Decca DFE 6680*	18	1 wk
19 Apr 62	**SOUND OF MUSIC** (London) *HMV 7EG 8733*	19	1 wk
17 May 62	●**WEST SIDE STORY** (Original Broadway) *Philips BBE 12243*	5	21 wks
7 Jun 62	**OLIVER** (London) (3rd re-entry) *Decca DFE 6680*	18	2 wks
22 Nov 62	**WEST SIDE STORY** (re-entry) *Philips BBE 12243*	16	1 wk
24 Jan 63	**WEST SIDE STORY** (Broadway) *CBS APG 20020*	15	4 wks
11 Apr 63	**WEST SIDE STORY** (Original Broadway) (2nd re-entry) *Philips BBE 12243*	14	4 wks
12 Sep 63	**WEST SIDE STORY** (re-entry) *CBS APG 20020*	20	1 wk

On 10 March 1960 **Record Retailer** started to print a separate EP chart for the first time ever. The first chart consisted of the following ten discs.

1 Expresso Bongo – Cliff Richard
2 Strictly Elvis – Elvis Presley
3 Strictly For Grown Ups –
  Paddy Roberts
4 Cliff Sings No. 1 – Cliff Richard
5 Nina and Frederick –
  Nina and Frederick
6 Johnny Staccato – Elmer Bernstein
7 Charmaine – Mantovani
8 Journey To The Centre
  Of The Earth – Pat Boone
9 Tommy The Toreador –
  Tommy Steele
10 Sunday Night At The
  London Palladium – Robert Horton

Joan BAEZ had more weeks on the chart than any other female solo artist.
Below The BEACH BOYS Number one on the last chart of all-time.
Pictorial Press.

On 30 November 1967 **Record Retailer** printed the last EP chart. EPs were being produced in lesser quantities than before and a separate chart seemed pointless. By now the chart was reduced to feature just nine discs. Elvis Presley has the unique distinction of appearing in both the first and last chart.

1 Beach Boy Hits – Beach Boys
2 Four Top's Hits – Four Tops
3 Four Tops – Four Tops
4 Best Of Bennett – Tony Bennett
5 Hits From The Seekers – Seekers
6 Morningtown Ride – Seekers
7 Privilege – Paul Jones
8 Easy Come Easy Go–Elvis Presley
9 Georgie Fame – Georgie Fame

Most weeks on chart: by artist

The following list is of all artists who spent 50 or more weeks in the EP charts. It is of course possible to be credited with 2 or more chart weeks in the same week owing to simultaneous hits.

	Weeks
Shadows	461
Cliff Richard	432
Beatles	392
Elvis Presley	366
Nina and Frederick	169
Seekers	166
Rolling Stones	154
Acker Bilk	133
Manfred Mann	111
Beach Boys	108
Searchers	106
Frank Ifield	103
Roy Orbison	101
Bachelors	99
Peter, Paul and Mary	99
Joan Baez	97
Four Tops	97
Adam Faith	95
Nat King Cole	94
Helen Shapiro	92
Paddy Roberts	90
Buddy Holly	90
Kinks	79
Jim Reeves	79
Shirley Bassey	78
Billy Fury	75
(plus 6 weeks with the Tornados)	
Mantovani	75
Tony Bennett	72
Tornados	72
(plus 6 weeks with Billy Fury)	
Harry Secombe	68
Kenny Ball	67
George Mitchell Minstrels	66
Bob Newhart	65
Bob Dylan	57
Temperance Seven	57
Animals	55
Andy Williams	55
Andy Stewart	54
Eddie Cochran	51
Gerry and the Pacemakers	51
Frank Sinatra	51
Dusty Springfield	51

Most weeks on chart: Year by Year

1960
	Weeks
1 Cliff Richard	100
2 Nina and Frederick	84
3 Elvis Presley	70
4 Paddy Roberts	63
5 Harry Secombe	56
6 Eddie Cochran	35
Nat 'King' Cole	35
7 Buddy Holly	34
8 Buddy Holly	34
9 Mario Lanza	26
10 Frank Sinatra	24

1961
	Weeks
1 Cliff Richard	96
2 Elvis Presley	88
3 Shadows	79
4 Adam Faith	65
5 Nina and Frederick	60
6 Nat 'King' Cole	57
7 Shirley Bassey	54
8 Mantovani	52
9 Temperance Seven	36
10 Acker Bilk	31
Duane Eddy	31

Note: Acker Bilk 1 more week with Terry Lightfoot. The soundtrack EP from **South Pacific** clocked up 48 weeks in 1961.

1962
	Weeks
1 Shadows	179
2 Cliff Richard	109
3 Helen Shapiro	86
4 Acker Bilk	57
5 Kenny Ball	53
6 Elvis Presley	52
7 Chubby Checker	41
8 Billy Fury	37
9 Bob Newhart	35
10 George Mitchell Minstrels	34

1963
	Weeks
1 Shadows	152
2 Frank Ifield	89
3 Cliff Richard	79
4 Tornados	69
5 Elvis Presley	57
6 Beatles	47
7 Ray Charles	41
8 Billy Fury	38
9 Roy Orbison	32
10 Bobby Vee	28

Note: Tornados 16 more with Billy Fury, Billy Fury 16 more with Tornados. Bobby Vee 16 more with Crickets.

1964
	Weeks
1 Beatles	168
2 Rolling Stones	70
3 Peter, Paul and Mary	60
4 Bachelors	58
5 Jim Reeves	48
6 Searchers	47
7 Roy Orbison	42
8 Merseybeats	37
9 Shadows	35
Dusty Springfield	35

1965
	Weeks
1 Beatles	111
2 Rolling Stones	71
3 Joan Baez	56
4 Kinks	54
5 Animals	48
6 Manfred Mann	47
7 Elvis Presley	44
8 Searchers	41
9 Peter, Paul and Mary	34
10 Pretty Things	33

1966
	Weeks
1 Beatles	66
2 Manfred Mann	57
3 Seekers	51
4 Beach Boys	42
5 Joan Baez	41
6 Bob Dylan	30
7 Walker Brothers	29
8 Spencer Davis Group	26
9 Kinks	21
10 Donovan	16
Andy Williams	16

Note: Walker Brothers score includes 4 weeks for 'Solo Scott – Solo John' which did not include Gary Walker.

1967
	Weeks
1 Seekers	91
2 Four Tops	87
3 Beach Boys	57
4 Tony Bennett	47
5 Paul Jones	31
6 Georgie Fame	29
7 Elvis Presley	23
8 Val Doonican	15
Andy Williams	15
10 Who	14

1968, 1969: EP chart discontinued.

Weeks

Weeks	Title	Artist
115	Nina and Frederick	Nina and Frederick
82	Beach Boy Hits	Beach Boys
81	Shadows To The Fore	Shadows
79	Peter, Paul and Mary	Peter, Paul and Mary
76	Adam's Hit Parade	Adam Faith
73	Hits From The Seekers	Seekers
62	Button Down Mind Of Bob Newhart	Bob Newhart
61	Strictly For Grown Ups	Paddy Roberts
60	Unforgettable	Nat 'King' Cole
58	Four Tops	Four Tops
57	Twist And Shout	Beatles
53	Black And White Minstrel Show	George Mitchell Minstrels
52	Cliff's Silver Discs	Cliff Richard
52	Rolling Stones	Rolling Stones
51	Follow That Dream	Elvis Presley
50	Frank Ifield's Hits	Frank Ifield

NINA and FREDERICK. *Pictorial Press.*

Title	Artist	Weeks	Runs
Shadows To The Fore	Shadows	116	6
Nina and Frederick	Nina and Frederick	115	1
The Shadows	Shadows	86	2
South Pacific No. 1	Film Soundtrack	86	3
Beach Boy Hits	Beach Boys	82	1
Peter, Paul and Mary	Peter, Paul and Mary	79	1
Adam's Hit Parade	Adam Faith	77	2
Hits From The Seekers	Seekers	73	1
Strictly For Grown Ups	Paddy Roberts	66	2
Twist And Shout	Beatles	64	3
Button Down Mind Of Bob Newhart	Bob Newhart	64	3
Strictly Elvis	Elvis Presley	64	5
Unforgettable	Nat 'King' Cole	62	3
Such A Night	Elvis Presley	62	5
Frank Ifield's Hits	Frank Ifield	59	2
Spotlight On The Shadows	Shadows	59	3
Rolling Stones	Rolling Stones	58	3
Cliff's Silver Discs	Cliff Richard	57	2
As Long As He Needs Me	Shirley Bassey	57	3
Four Hits And A Mister	Acker Bilk	56	2
Black And White Minstrel Show	George Mitchell Minstrels	55	2
Five By Five	Rolling Stones	54	2
The Late-Great Buddy Holly	Buddy Holly	53	5
Follow That Dream	Elvis Presley	51	1
Dream	Cliff Richard	51	2
Seekers	Seekers	50	2

Bob NEWHART. *Pictorial Press.*

Most hits by artist

The following list is of all artists who have had five or more hits. Re-entries and re-issues do not count as a new hit.

23 Cliff Richard
19 Shadows
15 Elvis Presley
12 Beatles
10 Acker Bilk
 7 Nina and Frederick
 7 Searchers
 7 Frank Sinatra
 6 Frank Ifield
 6 Manfred Mann
 6 Jim Reeves
 6 Harry Secombe
 5 Shirley Bassey
 5 Russ Conway
 5 Duane Eddy
 5 Gerry and the Pacemakers
 5 Buddy Holly
 5 Roy Orbison

Brian Jones of ROLLING STONES (*Left*) and Peter Noone of HERMAN'S HERMITS, photographed watching Jonathan King on *Top of the Pops*.

Most Top Ten hits by artist

The following list is of all artists who have had three or more top ten hits. Rules as for most hits but the EP must have made the top ten for at least 1 week

17 Cliff Richard
13 Shadows
12 Beatles
10 Elvis Presley
 6 Manfred Mann
 5 Acker Bilk
 5 Nina and Frederick
 5 Searchers
 4 Bachelors
 4 Joan Baez
 4 Hollies
 4 Kinks
 4 Roy Orbison
 4 Jim Reeves
 4 Tornados
 3 Animals
 3 Nat 'King' Cole
 3 Bob Dylan
 3 Georgie Fame
 3 Herman's Hermits

3 Frank Ifield
3 Mantovani
3 Rolling Stones
3 Seekers

4 Johnny Mathis
4 Peter, Paul and Mary
4 Dusty Springfield
4 Tornados
4 Bobby Vee

Most hits without a Number One hit

10 Acker Bilk
 7 Nina and Frederick
 7 Frank Sinatra
 6 Jim Reeves
 5 Shirley Bassey
 5 Russ Conway
 5 Duane Eddy
 5 Gerry and the Pacemakers
 5 Buddy Holly
 5 Roy Orbison
 4 Everly Brothers
 4 Georgie Fame
 4 Herman's Hermits
 4 Hollies
 4 Kenneth McKellar
 4 Mantovani

Bobby VEE. *Pictorial Press.*

3 Animals
3 Tony Bennett
3 Chuck Berry and Bo Diddley
3 Cilla Black
3 Dave Clark Five
3 Eddie Cochran
3 Nat 'King' Cole
3 Ken Dodd
3 Bob Dylan
3 Ella Fitzgerald
3 Freddie and the Dreamers
3 Mario Lanzo
3 Gene Pitney

2 Searchers
2 Seekers
2 Helen Shapiro

The following all had one number one EP; Bachelors, Joan Baez, Beach Boys, Donovan, Val Doonican, Adam Faith, Emile Ford, Four Tops, Frank Ifield, Paul Jones, George Mitchell Minstrels, Bobby Vee and Crickets, Walker Brothers, Who.

	Weeks
Shadows – Shadows	17
Five By Five – Rolling Stones	15
Kid Galahad – Elvis Presley	13
Strictly For Grown Ups – Paddy Roberts	12
Rolling Stones – Rolling Stones	11
Twist And Shout – Beatles	11
Four Tops' Hits – Four Tops	10
I Need You – Walker Brothers	10
Twist And Shout – Beatles	10

Most hits without a Top Ten

Only Johnny Mathis has had more than three hits without ever reaching the Top Ten. None of his four hits could climb higher than seventeen.

Most hits by label

111 Columbia
51 Decca
48 Pye
34 Parlophone
31 RCA
26 HMV
26 London
23 Philips
22 Fontana
19 Capitol
18 CBS
8 Liberty
8 Warner Brothers
6 Coral
6 Tamla Motown
5 MGM

	Weeks
Beatles	63
Shadows	59
Elvis Presley	46
Rolling Stones	37
Beach Boys	32
Four Tops	22
Paddy Roberts	21
Manfred Mann	17
Helen Shapiro	13
Walker Brothers	13
Frank Ifield	12
Cliff Richard	10
Donovan	8
Kinks	8
Searchers	6
Who	5
Val Doonican	4
Seekers	4
Adam Faith	3
Emile Ford	3
Paul Jones	3
Bachelors	2
Joan Baez	1
George Mitchell Minstrels	1
Bobby Vee and the Crickets	1

	Weeks
Beach Boys' Hits – Beach Boys	32
Shadows To The Fore – Shadows	28
Four Tops' Hits – Four Tops	22
Five By Five – Rolling Stones	21
Twist And Shout – Beatles	21
Follow That Dream – Elvis Presley	20
Shadows – Shadows	20
Strictly For Grown Ups – Paddy Roberts	19
Kid Galahad – Elvis Presley	18
Rolling Stones – Rolling Stones	14
I Need You – Walker Brothers	13
Frank Ifield's Hits – Frank Ifield	12
No Living Without Your Loving – Manfred Mann	11
South Pacific No. 1 – Film Soundtrack	10

Number ones by artist

8 Beatles
4 Elvis Presley
4 Cliff Richard
4 Shadows
3 Manfred Mann
3 Rolling Stones
2 Kinks
2 Paddy Roberts

	Weeks
Shadows To The Fore – Shadows	23
Follow That Dream – Elvis Presley	20

		Weeks
1960	Paddy Roberts	21
1961	Shadows	43
1962	Elvis Presley	25
1963	Beatles	19
1964	Rolling Stones	29
1965	Manfred Mann	12
1966	Beach Boys	15
1967	Four Tops	22

Most weeks at Number One in a Year: by Label

		Weeks
1960	Decca	21
1961	Columbia	50
1962	Columbia	26
1963	Parlophone	19
1964	Decca	31
1965	Pye	18
1966	Capitol	15
1967	Tamla Motown	22

Weeks at Number One by Label

	Weeks
Columbia	99
Parlophone	66
Decca	64
RCA	46
Capitol	32
Pye	25
Tamla Motown	22
HMV	21
Philips	13
Reaction	5
Fontana	1
Liberty	1

Most Number Ones by Label

	Weeks
Columbia	13
Parlophone	9
Decca	7
Pye	6
HMV	5
RCA	5
Capitol	1
Fontana	1
Liberty	1
Philips	1
Reaction	1
Tamla Motown	1

Highest New Entries

Excluding the first chart of all-time, only ten EPs entered the charts in the Top Five. Only Cliff Richard came straight in at number one with his 'Expresso Bongo' EP and that was in the first chart. The following is the list of the ten discs that made the Top Five in their first week on the chart.

Position entered at

5	Beach Boy Hits–Beach Boys
5	Mr Tambourine Man–Bob Dylan
5	Nina and Frederick Vol. 2–Nina and Frederick
5	Paddy Roberts Strikes Again–Paddy Roberts
4	Got Live If You Want It–Rolling Stones
4	Shadows–Shadows
3	Five By Five–Rolling Stones
3	Ain't Gonna Kiss Ya–Searchers
2	Long Tall Sally–Beatles
2	Four Tops' Hits–Four Tops

Top singer song-writer Paddy ROBERTS runs through a score with singing sisters Anne and Jo Shelton. *Popperfoto.*

Date (Magazine) Reached Top	Title/Artist/Label	Weeks at Top
1960		
10 Mar	**Expresso Bongo** Cliff Richard (Columbia)	1
17 Mar	**Strictly Elvis** Elvis Presley (RCA)	5
21 Apr	**Expresso Bongo** Cliff Richard (Columbia)	1
28 Apr	**Strictly For Grown Ups** Paddy Roberts (Decca)	1
5 May	**Emile** Emile Ford (Pye)	1
12 May	**Strictly For Grown Ups** Paddy Roberts (Decca)	1
19 May	**Emile** Emile Ford (Pye)	2
2 Jun	**Strictly For Grown Ups** Paddy Roberts (Decca)	12
25 Aug	**Paddy Roberts Strikes Again** Paddy Roberts (Decca)	2
8 Sep	**Strictly For Grown Ups** Paddy Roberts (Decca)	1
15 Sep	**South Pacific No. 1** Film Soundtrack (RCA)	1
22 Sep	**Strictly For Grown Ups** Paddy Roberts (Decca)	3
13 Oct	**South Pacific No. 1** Film Soundtrack (RCA)	3
3 Nov	**Strictly For Grown Ups** Paddy Roberts (Decca)	1
10 Nov	**South Pacific No. 1** Film Soundtrack (RCA)	5
15 Dec	**Adam's Hit Parade** Adam Faith (Parlophone)	1
22 Dec	**Cliff's Silver Discs** Cliff Richard (Columbia)	1
29 Dec	**South Pacific No. 1** Film Soundtrack (RCA)	1
1961		
5 Jan	**Cliff's Silver Discs** Cliff Richard (Columbia)	2
19 Jan	**Adam's Hit Parade** Adam Faith (Parlophone)	1
26 Jan	**The Shadows** Shadows (Columbia)	17
25 May	**Adam's Hit Parade** Adam Faith (Parlophone)	1
1 Jun	**The Shadows** Shadows (Columbia)	3
22 Jun	**Shadows To The Fore** Shadows (Columbia)	23
30 Nov	**Helen** Helen Shapiro (Columbia)	9
1962		
1 Feb	**Shadows To The Fore** Shadows (Columbia)	4
1 Mar	**Spotlight On The Shadows** Shadows (Columbia)	3
22 Mar	**Helen's Hit Parade** Helen Shapiro (Columbia)	3
12 Apr	**Spotlight On The Shadows** Shadows (Columbia)	5
17 May	**Shadows To The Fore** Shadows (Columbia)	1
24 May	**Helen's Hit Parade** Helen Shapiro (Columbia)	1
31 May	**Hits From The Film 'The Young Ones'** – Cliff Richard and the Shadows (Columbia)	2
14 Jun	**Follow That Dream** Elvis Presley (RCA)	20
1 Nov	**The Boys** Shadows (Columbia)	3
22 Nov	**Kid Galahad** Elvis Presley (RCA)	5
27 Dec	**Black And White Minstrel Show** George Mitchell Minstrels (HMV)	1
1963		
3 Jan	**Kid Galahad** Elvis Presley (RCA)	13
4 Apr	**Frank Ifield's Hits** Frank Ifield (Columbia)	8
30 May	**Just For Fun** Bobby Vee and the Crickets (Liberty)	1
6 Jun	**Holiday Carnival** Cliff Richard (Columbia)	1
13 Jun	**Frank Ifield's Hits** Frank Ifield (Columbia)	2
27 Jun	**Holiday Carnival** Cliff Richard (Columbia)	1
4 Jul	**Frank Ifield's Hits** Frank Ifield (Columbia)	2
18 Jul	**Holiday Carnival** Cliff Richard (Columbia)	1
25 Jul	**Twist And Shout** Beatles (Parlophone)	10
3 Oct	**Ain't Gonna Kiss You** Searchers (Pye)	4
31 Oct	**The Beatles' Hits** Beatles (Parlophone)	3
21 Nov	**Twist And Shout** Beatles (Parlophone)	11

1964	6 Feb	**The Rolling Stones** Rolling Stones (Decca)	3
	27 Feb	**All My Loving** Beatles (Parlophone)	8
	23 Apr	**The Rolling Stones** Rolling Stones (Decca)	11
	9 Jul	**Long Tall Sally** Beatles (Parlophone)	7
	27 Aug	**Five By Five** Rolling Stones (Decca)	15
	10 Dec	**A Hard Day's Night** Beatles (Parlophone)	2
	24 Dec	**Bachelors' Hits** Bachelors (Decca)	2
1965	7 Jan	**A Hard Day's Night** Beatles (Parlophone)	3
	28 Jan	**Five By Five** Rolling Stones (Decca)	1
	4 Feb	**A Hard Day's Night** Beatles (Parlophone)	1
	11 Feb	**Five By Five** Rolling Stones (Decca)	1
	18 Feb	**Kinksize Session** Kinks (Pye)	1
	25 Feb	**Five By Five** Rolling Stones (Decca)	1
	4 Mar	**Green Shades Of Val Doonican** Val Doonican (Decca)	3
	25 Mar	**Five By Five** Rolling Stones (Decca)	3
	15 Apr	**Green Shades Of Val Doonican** Val Doonican (Decca)	1
	22 Apr	**Beatles For Sale** Beatles (Parlophone)	5
	27 May	**Bumble Bee** Searchers (Pye)	2
	10 Jun	**Beatles For Sale** Beatles (Parlophone)	1
	17 Jun	**The One In The Middle** Manfred Mann (HMV)	1
	24 Jun	**Got Live If You Want It** Rolling Stones (Decca)	1
	1 Jul	**The One In The Middle** Manfred Mann (HMV)	4
	29 Jul	**Got Live If You Want It** Rolling Stones (Decca)	1
	5 Aug	**The One In The Middle** Manfred Mann (HMV)	4
	2 Sep	**Universal Soldier** Donovan (Pye)	8
	28 Oct	**Kwyet Kinks** Kinks (Pye)	7
	16 Dec	**No Living Without Your Love** Manfred Mann (HMV)	7
1966	3 Feb	**Beatles' Million Sellers** Beatles (Parlophone)	2
	17 Feb	**Seekers** Seekers (Columbia)	3
	10 Mar	**Beatles' Million Sellers** Beatles (Parlophone)	2
	24 Mar	**Yesterday** Beatles (Parlophone)	8
	19 May	**With God On Our Side** Joan Baez (Fontana)	1
	26 May	**Machines** Manfred Mann (HMV)	1
	2 Jun	**Beach Boys' Hits** Beach Boys (Capitol)	4
	30 Jun	**I Need You** Walker Brothers (Philips)	10
	8 Sep	**Beach Boys' Hits** Beach Boys (Capitol)	4
	6 Oct	**I Need You** Walker Brothers (Philips)	3
	27 Oct	**Beach Boys' Hits** Beach Boys (Capitol)	7
	15 Dec	**Ready Steady Who** Who (Reaction)	5
1967	19 Jan	**Beach Boys' Hits** Beach Boys (Capitol)	7
	9 Mar	**Morningtown Ride** Seekers (Columbia)	1
	16 Mar	**Four Tops' Hits** Four Tops (Tamla Motown)	10
	25 May	**Privilege** Paul Jones (HMV)	3
	15 Jun	**Four Tops' Hits** Four Tops (Tamla Motown)	5
	20 Jul	**Easy Come, Easy Go** Elvis Presley (RCA)	3
	10 Aug	**Beach Boys' Hits** Beach Boys (Capitol)	6
	21 Sep	**Four Tops' Hits** Four Tops (Tamla Motown)	1
	28 Sep	**Beach Boys' Hits** Beach Boys (Capitol)	1
	5 Oct	**Four Tops' Hits** Four Tops (Tamla Motown)	1
	12 Oct	**Beach Boys' Hits** Beach Boys (Capitol)	1
	19 Oct	**Four Tops' Hits** Four Tops (Tamla Motown)	5
	23 Nov	**Beach Boys' Hits** Beach Boys (Capitol)	2

THE ROLLING STONES

The Rolling Stones' initial impact was, in part, a triumph of image, manager Andrew Loog Oldham making the most of what was considered an unkempt appearance. In 1964, the year of their first number one, they defiantly shook more hair than the Beatles, both on the key TV show **Ready Steady Go** (right) and posing in Hyde Park (below), where Keith Richard boldly brandished a cigarette. When they returned to Hyde Park on 5 July, 1969, performing a free concert before a quarter of a million fans, their hair was even longer, in fine flower power fashion, and Mick Jagger's flowing outfit was neither Savile Row nor Carnaby Street. The occasion was marred by Brian Jones' tragic death only two days before.

ALMOST THERE

BUFFALO SPRINGFIELD: Founder members included Richie Furay, who went on to join Poco, as well as Stephen Stills and Neil Young, who later became half of Crosby, Stills, Nash and Young. Despite five British singles and supporting the Byrds, the final gig came in 1966 for the group who christened themselves from the nameplate which appeared on the side of steamrollers working on Hollywood roads.

COUNT FIVE: Psychotic single which got little reaction in Britain for the sixties American punk outfit.

Johnny HALLYDAY: Billed as the 'Pope of Twist and Rock', Parisian Jean Philippe Smet was earning $1000 a night as Johnny Hallyday by the time he was 18.

SVENSK: So named because of their Scandinavian looks, Svensk got no nearer the land mass across the North Sea than extensive play on Radio Caroline.

The ALBUMS

The following begins with a section listing by artist all those acts who had hit albums during the period 1 January 1960 to 31 December 1969, and the albums with which they found success. Each album has the following information supplied: title, label and catalogue number, highest position reached and number of weeks spent on the chart. The albums are not indexed alphabetically by title because so many are called 'Greatest Hits' or are eponymously named.

This list below shows how the structure of the album chart changed during the period concerned:

Melody Maker
2 Jan 60   Ten records feature in the chart

Record Retailer
26 Mar 60   **Record Retailer** publish their own album chart for the first time, featuring Twenty discs
16 Apr 66   Chart increases to Top Thirty
10 Dec 66   Chart increases to Top Forty
15 Feb 69   Chart drops to Top Fifteen
14 Jun 69   Chart increases to Top Twenty
28 Jun 69   Chart increases to Top Forty
 9 Aug 69   Thirty two discs only in this week's chart
11 Oct 69   Chart drops to Top Twenty Five
 8 Nov 69 –
31 Dec 69   Chart varies between Twenty and Twenty Four discs each week

As in all the publications in this series, if ever a week went by without a chart being published, the previous week's chart is repeated for all the information and statistics used in this book.

When albums began to be issued in both mono and stereo form (around 1966) we list the stereo catalogue number only.

Special Note: On 8 Mar 69 the budget chart was combined with the full price chart for 1 week only. This caused a sudden influx of budget LPs for that week including the Four And Only Seekers at Number One.

The dates used correspond to the Saturday of the week in which the chart was published. This does not necessarily coincide with the date given on the chart, but we have tried to create a consistent dating over a period in which the dates of compilation of each week's charts tended to vary (see page 6). Unlike the first edition of **British Hit Albums** we have listed all re-entries separately.

    Number one album
● Top Ten album

Hit albums alphabetically by artist

Date	Title *Label Number*		Position	

ADAMS SINGERS *UK, male/female vocal group*

Date	Title *Label Number*		Position	
16 Apr 60	**SING SOMETHING SIMPLE** *Pye NPL 28013*		**18**	1 wk
18 Feb 61	**SING SOMETHING SIMPLE** (re-entry) *Pye NPL 28013*		**15**	3 wks
24 Nov 62	**SING SOMETHING SIMPLE** *Pye Golden Guinea GGL 0150*		**15**	1 wk
29 Dec 62	**SING SOMETHING SIMPLE** (re-entry) *Pye Golden Guinea GGL 0150*		**20**	1 wk

These two albums, although identically named, are different.

ALEXANDER BROTHERS *UK, male vocal duo*

Date	Title *Label Number*		Position	
10 Dec 66	**THESE ARE MY MOUNTAINS** *Pye GGL 0375*		**29**	1 wk

Mose ALLISON

US, male vocalist/instrumentalist - piano

Date	Title *Label Number*		Position	
4 Jun 66	**MOSE ALIVE** *Atlantic 587-007*		**30**	1 wk

Herb ALPERT and his TIJUANA BRASS

US, male instrumentalist-trumpet and male instrumentalists

Date	Title *Label Number*		Position	
29 Jan 66	●**GOING PLACES** *Pye NPL 28065*		**5**	22 wks
23 Apr 66	●**WHIPPED CREAM AND OTHER DELIGHTS** *Pye NPL 28058*		**2**	22 wks
28 May 66	**WHAT NOW MY LOVE** *Pye NPL 28077*		**18**	4 wks
13 Aug 66	●**GOING PLACES** (re-entry) *Pye NPL 28065*		**4**	91 wks
10 Sep 66	**WHAT NOW MY LOVE** (re-entry) *Pye NPL 28077*		**23**	6 wks
15 Oct 66	**WHIPPED CREAM AND OTHER DELIGHTS** (re-entry) *Pye NPL 28058*		**21**	20 wks
3 Dec 66	**WHAT NOW MY LOVE** (2nd re-entry) *Pye NPL 28077*		**25**	2 wks
11 Feb 67	●**S.R.O.** *Pye NSPL 28088*		**5**	26 wks
15 Jul 67	**SOUNDS LIKE** *A & M AMLS 900*		**21**	10 wks

Date	Title *Label Number*		Position	
15 Jul 67	**WHAT NOW MY LOVE** (re-issue) *A & M AMLS 977*		**19**	5 wks
3 Feb 68	**NINTH** *A & M AMLS 905*		**26**	19 wks
29 Jun 68	**BEAT OF THE BRASS** *A & M AMLS 916*		**17**	15 wks
11 Jan 69	**GOING PLACES** (2nd re-entry) *A & M AMLS 965*		**35**	1 wk
8 Mar 69	●**EARLY ALPERT** *Marble Arch AMLS 866*		**4**	1 wk
5 Apr 69	●**BEAT OF THE BRASS** (re-entry) *A & M AMLS 916*		**4**	3 wks
6 Apr 69	**GOING PLACES** (3rd re-entry) *A & M AMLS 965*		**14**	1 wk
9 Aug 69	**WARM** *A & M AMLS 937*		**30**	3 wks
6 Dec 69	**GOING PLACES** (4th re-entry) *A & M AMLS 965*		**12**	5 wks

*Going Places changed to the A & M Label **during** its 91 week run thus it was not strictly a re-issue.*

AMEN CORNER *UK, male vocal/instrumental group*

Date	Title *Label Number*		Position	
30 Mar 68	**ROUND AMEN CORNER** *Deram SML 1021*		**26**	7 wks
1 Nov 69	**EXPLOSIVE COMPANY** *Immediate IMSP 023*		**19**	1 wk

ANIMALS *UK, male vocal/instrumental group*

Date	Title *Label Number*		Position	
14 Nov 64	●**THE ANIMALS** *Columbia 33SX 1669*		**6**	19 wks
12 May 65	**THE ANIMALS** (re-entry) *Columbia 33SX 1669*		**18**	1 wk
22 May 65	●**ANIMAL TRACKS** *Columbia 33SX 1708*		**6**	18 wks
9 Nov 65	**ANIMAL TRACKS** (re-entry) *Columbia 33SX 1708*		**14**	8 wks
16 Apr 66	●**MOST OF THE ANIMALS** *Columbia 33SX 6035*		**4**	19 wks
10 Sep 66	**MOST OF THE ANIMALS** (re-entry) *Columbia 33SX 6035*		**24**	1 wk
28 May 66	●**ANIMALISMS** *Decca LK 4797*		**4**	17 wks

Louis ARMSTRONG

US, male vocalist/instrumentalist - trumpet

Date	Title *Label Number*		Position	
22 Oct 60	**SATCHMO PLAYS KING OLIVER** *Audio Fidelity AFLP 1930*		**20**	1 wk
28 Oct 61	**JAZZ CLASSICS** *Ace of Hearts AH 7*		**20**	1 wk
27 Jun 64	**HELLO DOLLY** *London HAR 8190*		**16**	2 wks
25 Jul 64	**HELLO DOLLY** (re-entry) *London HAR 8190*		**11**	4 wks
16 Nov 68	**WHAT A WONDERFUL WORLD** *Stateside SSL 10247*		**37**	3 wks

Chet ATKINS *US, male instrumentalist - guitar*

Date	Title *Label Number*		Position	
18 Mar 61	**THE OTHER CHET ATKINS** *RCA RD 27194*		**20**	1 wk
17 Jun 61	**CHET ATKINS WORKSHOP** *RCA RD 27214*		**19**	1 wk
30 Feb 63	**CARIBBEAN GUITAR** *RCA RD 7519*		**17**	3 wks

Brian AUGER TRINITY — See *Julie DRISCOLL and the Brian AUGER TRINITY*

Date	Title Label Number	Position	Date	Title Label Number	Position

B

BURT BACHARACH *US, orchestra leader*

Date	Title Label Number	Position	
22 May 65	●HIT MAKER-BURT BACHARACH *London HAR 8233*	**3**	14 wks
4 Sep 65	HIT MAKER-BURT BACHARACH (re-entry) *London HAR 8233*	**15**	4 wks

BACHELORS *Ireland, male vocal group*

Date	Title Label Number	Position	
27 Jun 64	●THE BACHELORS AND 16 GREAT SONGS *Decca LK 4614*	**2**	44 wks
9 Oct 65	MORE GREAT SONG HITS FROM THE BACHELORS *Decca LK 4721*	**19**	1 wk
30 Oct 65	MORE GREAT SONG HITS FROM THE BACHELORS (re-entry) *Decca LK 4721*	**15**	5 wks
9 Jul 66	HITS OF THE SIXTIES *Decca TXL 102*	**12**	9 wks
5 Nov 66	BACHELORS' GIRLS *Decca LK 4827*	**24**	4 wks
10 Dec 66	BACHELORS' GIRLS (re-entry) *Decca LK 4827*	**32**	4 wks
1 Jul 67	GOLDEN ALL TIME HITS *Decca SKL 4849*	**19**	7 wks
14 Jun 69	●WORLD OF THE BACHELORS *Decca SPA 2*	**8**	17 wks
23 Aug 69	WORLD OF THE BACHELORS Vol 2 *Decca SPA 22*	**11**	7 wks

JOAN BAEZ *US, female vocalist*

Date	Title Label Number	Position	
18 Jul 64	JOAN BAEZ IN CONCERT Vol 2 *Fontana TFL 6033*	**15**	2 wks
17 Apr 65	JOAN BAEZ IN CONCERT Vol 2 (re-entry) *Fontana TFL 6033*	**17**	1 wk
15 May 65	JOAN BAEZ IN CONCERT Vol 2 (2nd re-entry) *Fontana TFL 6033*	**17**	1 wk
15 May 65	JOAN BAEZ No 5 *Fontana TFL 6043*	**20**	1 wk
19 Jun 65	●JOAN BAEZ *Fontana TFL 6002*	**9**	13 wks
10 Jul 65	●JOAN BAEZ IN CONCERT Vol 2 (3rd re-entry) *Fontana TFL 6033*	**8**	13 wks
10 Jul 65	●JOAN BAEZ No 5 (re-entry) *Fontana TFL 6043*	**3**	21 wks
27 Nov 65	●FAREWELL ANGELINA *Fontana TFL 6058*	**5**	14 wks
12 Mar 66	FAREWELL ANGELINA (re-entry) *Fontana TFL 6058*	**12**	9 wks
16 Apr 66	JOAN BAEZ No 5 (2nd re-entry) *Fontana TFL 6043*	**23**	5 wks
9 Jul 66	JOAN BAEZ IN CONCERT Vol 2 (4th re-entry) *Fontana TFL 6033*	**27**	2 wks
19 Jul 69	JOAN BAEZ ON VANGUARD *Vanguard SVXL 100*	**15**	5 wks

KENNY BALL *UK, male vocalist/instrumentalist - trumpet*

Date	Title Label Number	Position	
7 Sep 63	●KENNY BALL'S GOLDEN HITS *Pye Golden Guinea GGL 0209*	**4**	26 wks

See also Kenny Ball, Chris Barber and Mr. Acker Bilk.

Kenny BALL, Chris BARBER and Mr. Acker BILK *UK, All That Jazz*

Date	Title Label Number	Position	
25 Aug 62	BEST OF BALL, BARBER AND BILK *Pye Golden Guinea GGL 0131*	**1**	22 wks
2 Feb 63	BEST OF BALL, BARBER AND BILK (re-entry) *Pye Golden Guinea GGL 0131*	**20**	1 wk
23 Mar 63	BEST OF BALL, BARBER AND BILK (2nd re-entry) *Pye Golden Guinea GGL 0131*	**19**	1 wk

See also Kenny Ball; Chris Barber; Chris Barber and Mr. Acker Bilk; Mr Acker Bilk.

Chris BARBER *UK, male vocalist/instrumentalist - trombone*

Date	Title Label Number	Position	
24 Sep 60	CHRIS BARBER BAND BOX No 2 *Columbia 33SX 3277*	**17**	1 wk
5 Nov 60	ELITE SYNCOPATIONS *Columbia 33SX 1245*	**18**	1 wk
12 Nov 60	BEST OF CHRIS BARBER *Ace of Clubs ACL 1037*	**17**	1 wk

See also Kenny Ball, Chris Barber and Mr. Acker Bilk; Chris Barber and Mr. Acker Bilk.

Chris BARBER and Mr. Acker BILK *UK, Jazzmen*

Date	Title Label Number	Position	
7 May 61	●BEST OF BARBER AND BILK Vol 1 *Pye GGL 0075*	**4**	27 wks
11 Nov 61	●BEST OF BARBER AND BILK Vol 2 *Pye Golden Guinea GGL 0096*	**8**	10 wks
23 Dec 61	●BEST OF BARBER AND BILK Vol 1 (re-entry) *Pye Golden Guinea GGL 0075*	**7**	9 wks
31 Mar 62	BEST OF BARBER AND BILK Vol 2 (re-entry) *Pye Golden Guinea GGL 0096*	**13**	8 wks
21 Apr 62	BEST OF BARBER AND BILK Vol 1 (2nd re-entry) *Pye Golden Guinea GGL 0075*	**12**	7 wks

See also Kenny Ball, Chris Barber and Mr. Acker Bilk; Chris Barber; Mr Acker Bilk.

JOHN BARRY — See *Adam FAITH*

Count BASIE *US, male orchestra leader and instrumentalist - piano*

Date	Title Label Number	Position	
16 Apr 60	CHAIRMAN OF THE BOARD *Columbia 33SX 1209*	**17**	1 wk

See also Frank Sinatra and Count Basie.

Shirley BASSEY *UK, female vocalist*

Date	Title Label Number	Position	
28 Jan 61	FABULOUS SHIRLEY BASSEY *Columbia 33SX 1178*	**12**	2 wks
23 Feb 61	●SHIRLEY *Columbia 33SX 1286*	**9**	5 wks
27 Jan 62	SHIRLEY (re-entry) *Columbia 33SX 1286*	**12**	5 wks
17 Feb 62	SHIRLEY BASSEY *Columbia 33SX 1382*	**16**	2 wks
17 Mar 62	SHIRLEY BASSEY (re-entry) *Columbia 33SX 1382*	**14**	6 wks
9 Jun 62	SHIRLEY BASSEY (2nd re-entry) *Columbia 33SX 1382*	**14**	3 wks
15 Dec 62	LET'S FACE THE MUSIC *Columbia 33SX 1454*	**12**	2 wks
12 Jan 63	LET'S FACE THE MUSIC (re-entry) *Columbia 33SX 1454*	**14**	5 wks
4 Dec 65	SHIRLEY BASSEY AT THE PIGALLE *Columbia 33SX 1787*	**16**	1 wk

BEACH BOYS
Bruce Johnston
perfects his Geronimo
impersonation while
the other Beach Boys
enjoy a joke with the
photographer.

BEATLES
"You say yes,
I say no.
You say stop,
I say go, go, go . . ."

Date	Title Label Number	Position		
18 Dec 65	SHIRLEY BASSEY AT THE PIGALLE (re-entry) Columbia 33SX 1787	20	1	wk
15 Jan 66	SHIRLEY BASSEY AT THE PIGALLE (2nd re-entry) Columbia 33SX 1787	15	5	wks
27 Aug 66	I'VE GOT A SONG FOR YOU United Artists ULP 1142	26	1	wk
17 Feb 68	TWELVE OF THOSE SONGS Columbia SCX 6204	40	1	wk
2 Mar 68	TWELVE OF THOSE SONGS (re-entry) Columbia SCX 6204	38	1	wk
23 Mar 68	TWELVE OF THOSE SONGS (2nd re-entry) Columbia SCX 6204	39	1	wk
7 Dec 68	GOLDEN HITS OF SHIRLEY BASSEY Columbia SCX 6294	29	7	wks

Let's Face the Music has credit 'with Nelson Riddle Orchestra'

BEACH BOYS US, male vocal/instrumental group

Date	Title	Position		
25 Sep 65	SURFIN' USA Capitol T 1890	17	1	wk
9 Oct 65	SURFIN' USA (re-entry) Capitol T 1890	19	4	wks
13 Nov 65	SURFIN' USA (2nd re-entry) Capitol T 1890	20	2	wks
19 Feb 66	●BEACH BOYS PARTY Capitol T 2398	3	14	wks
16 Apr 66	●BEACH BOYS TODAY Capitol T 2269	6	25	wks
9 Jul 66	●PET SOUNDS Capitol T 2458	2	39	wks
16 Jul 66	●SUMMER DAYS Capitol T 2354	4	22	wks
12 Nov 66	●BEST OF THE BEACH BOYS Capitol T 20865	2	118	wks
11 Mar 67	SURFER GIRL Capitol ST 1981	13	14	wks
21 Oct 67	●BEST OF THE BEACH BOYS Vol 2 Capitol ST 20956	3	39	wks
18 Nov 67	●SMILEY SMILE Capitol ST 9001	9	8	wks
16 Mar 68	●WILD HONEY Capitol ST 2859	7	15	wks
21 Sep 68	FRIENDS Capitol ST 2895	13	8	wks
23 Nov 68	●BEST OF THE BEACH BOYS Vol 3 Capitol ST 21142	8	12	wks
29 Mar 69	●20/20 Capitol EST 133	3	8	wks
31 May 69	20/20 (re-entry) Capitol EST 133	15	1	wk
5 Jul 69	20/20 (2nd re-entry) Capitol EST 133	35	1	wk
12 Jul 69	BEST OF THE BEACH BOYS (re-entry) Capitol T 20865	30	1	wk
26 Jul 69	BEST OF THE BEACH BOYS (2nd re-entry) Capitol T 20865	29	1	wk
16 Aug 69	BEST OF THE BEACH BOYS (3rd re-entry) Capitol T 20865	24	4	wks
27 Sep 69	BEST OF THE BEACH BOYS (4th re-entry) Capitol T 20865	28	1	wk

BEAKY — See Dave DEE, DOZY, BEAKY, MICK and TICH

BEATLES UK, male vocal/instrumental group

Date	Title	Position		
6 Apr 63	*PLEASE PLEASE ME Parlophone PMC 1202	1	67	wks
30 Nov 63	*WITH THE BEATLES Parlophone PMC 1206	1	50	wks
18 Jul 64	*A HARD DAY'S NIGHT Parlophone PMC 1230	1	35	wks
15 Aug 64	PLEASE PLEASE ME (re-entry) Parlophone PMC 1202	13	1	wk
3 Oct 64	PLEASE PLEASE ME (2nd re-entry) Parlophone PMC 1202	19	1	wk
14 Nov 64	PLEASE PLEASE ME (3rd re-entry) Parlophone PMC 1202	17	1	wk
14 Nov 64	WITH THE BEATLES (re-entry) Parlophone PMC 1206	19	1	wk
12 Dec 64	*BEATLES FOR SALE Parlophone PMC 1240	1	46	wks
1 May 65	A HARD DAY'S NIGHT (re-entry) Parlophone PMC 1230	18	2	wks
12 Jun 65	A HARD DAY'S NIGHT (2nd re-entry) Parlophone PMC 1230	18	1	wk
14 Aug 65	*HELP Parlophone PMC 1255	1	37	wks
11 Dec 65	*RUBBER SOUL Parlophone PMC 1267	1	42	wks

Date	Title Label Number	Position		
13 Aug 66	*REVOLVER Parlophone PMC 7009	1	34	wks
10 Dec 66	●A COLLECTION OF BEATLES' OLDIES Parlophone PMC 7016	7	18	wks
3 Jun 67	*SERGEANT PEPPER'S LONELY HEARTS CLUB BAND Parlophone PCS 7027	1	52	wks
13 Jan 68	MAGICAL MYSTERY TOUR (Import) Capitol SMAL 2835	31	2	wks
7 Dec 68	*THE BEATLES Apple PCS 7167/8	1	17	wks
19 Apr 69	YELLOW SUBMARINE (re-entry) Apple PCS 7070	14	1	wk
17 May 69	THE BEATLES (re-entry) Apple PCS 7167/8	13	1	wk
2 Aug 69	THE BEATLES (2nd re-entry) Apple PCS 7167/8	31	2	wks
30 Aug 69	SERGEANT PEPPER'S LONELY HEARTS CLUB BAND (re-entry) Parlophone PCS 7027	38	1	wk
6 Sep 69	THE BEATLES (3rd re-entry) Apple PCS 7167/8	37	1	wk
1 Sep 69	●YELLOW SUBMARINE Apple PCS 7070	4	9	wks
4 Oct 69	*ABBEY ROAD Apple PCS 7088	1	61	wks

The album Yellow Submarine featured several tracks by the George Martin Orchestra. The album The Beatles was often referred to as the 'White Album'.

Jeff BECK
UK, male vocalist/instrumentalist - guitar

Date	Title	Position		
13 Sep 69	COSA NOSTRA BECK — OLA Columbia SCX 6351	39	1	wk

BEE GEES
UK/Australia, male vocal/instrumental group

Date	Title	Position		
12 Aug 67	●BEE GEES FIRST Polydor 583-012	8	26	wks
24 Feb 68	HORIZONTAL Polydor 582-020	16	15	wks
28 Sep 68	●IDEA Polydor 583-036	4	18	wks
5 Apr 69	ODESSA Polydor 583-049/50	10	1	wk
8 Nov 69	●BEST OF THE BEE GEES Polydor 583-063	7	10	wks

Sir Thomas BEECHAM UK, conductor

Date	Title	Position		
26 Mar 60	CARMEN HMV ALP 1762/4	18	2	wks

Full credit on sleeve reads 'Orchestre de la Radio Diffusion Francais conducted by Sir Thomas Beecham'.

Captain BEEFHEART and his MAGIC BAND US, male vocal/instrumental group

Date	Title	Position		
6 Dec 69	TROUT MASK REPLICA Straight STS 1053	21	1	wk

Cliff BENNETT and the REBEL ROUSERS
UK, male vocalist and male instrumental backing group

Date	Title	Position		
22 Oct 66	DRIVIN' ME WILD MFP 1121	25	3	wks

Date	Title *Label Number*	Position	

Tony BENNETT *US, male vocalist*

29 May 65	**I LEFT MY HEART IN SAN FRANCISCO** *CBS BPG 62201*	**20**	1 wk
4 Dec 65	**I LEFT MY HEART IN SAN FRANCISCO** (re-entry) *CBS BPG 62201*	**13**	7 wks
5 Feb 66	**I LEFT MY HEART IN SAN FRANCISCO** (2nd re-entry) *CBS BPG 62201*	**15**	6 wks
19 Feb 66	●**A STRING OF TONY'S HITS** *CBS DP 66010*	**9**	12 wks
10 Jun 67	**TONY'S GREATEST HITS** *CBS SBPG 62821*	**14**	24 wks
23 Sep 67	**TONY MAKES IT HAPPEN** *CBS SBPG 63055*	**31**	3 wks
28 Oct 67	**A STRING OF TONY'S HITS** (re-entry) *CBS DP 66010*	**37**	1 wk
23 Mar 68	**FOR ONCE IN MY LIFE** *CBS SBPG 63166*	**29**	5 wks

Shelley BERMAN *US, male comedian*

19 Nov 60	**INSIDE SHELLEY BERMAN** *Capitol CLP 1300*	**19**	1 wk
3 Dec 60	**INSIDE SHELLEY BERMAN** (re-entry) *Capitol CLP 1300*	**12**	3 wks

Chuck BERRY

US, male vocalist/instrumentalist - guitar

25 May 63	**CHUCK BERRY** *Pye NPL 28024*	**17**	3 wks
29 June 63	**CHUCK BERRY** (re-entry) *Pye NPL 28024*	**18**	1 wk
27 Jul 63	**CHUCK BERRY** (2nd re-entry) *Pye NPL 28024*	**12**	7 wks
5 Oct 63	●**CHUCK BERRY ON STAGE** *Pye NPL 28027*	**6**	11 wks
19 Oct 63	**CHUCK BERRY** (3rd re-entry) *Pye NPL 28024*	**15**	5 wks
7 Dec 63	**MORE CHUCK BERRY** *Pye NPL 28028*	**16**	2 wks
4 Jan 64	●**MORE CHUCK BERRY** (re-entry) *Pye NPL 28028*	**9**	4 wks
8 Feb 64	**MORE CHUCK BERRY** (2nd re-entry) *Pye NPL 28028*	**19**	2 wks
30 May 64	●**HIS LATEST AND GREATEST** *Pye NPL 28037*	**8**	7 wks
3 Oct 64	**YOU NEVER CAN TELL** *Pye NPL 29039*	**18**	2 wks

BIG BEN BANJO BAND

UK, male instrumental group

17 Dec 60	**MORE MINSTREL MELODIES** *Columbia 33SX 1254*	**20**	1 wk

BIG ROLL BAND — See *Zoot MONEY and the BIG ROLL BAND*

BIG SOUND — See *Simon DUPREE and the BIG SOUND*

Mr. Acker BILK

UK, male vocalist/instrumentalist - clarinet

19 Mar 60	●**SEVEN AGES OF ACKER** *Columbia 33SX 1205*	**6**	3 wks
16 Apr 60	**SEVEN AGES OF ACKER** (re-entry) *Columbia 33SX 1205*	**13**	2 wks
8 Oct 60	**SEVEN AGES OF ACKER** (2nd re-entry) *Columbia 33SX 1205*	**20**	1 wk
9 Apr 60	**ACKER BILK'S OMNIBUS** *Pye NJL 22*	**16**	1 wk
23 Apr 60	**ACKER BILK'S OMNIBUS** (re-entry) *Pye NJL 22*	**20**	1 wk
7 May 60	**ACKER BILK'S OMNIBUS** (2nd re-entry) *Pye NJL 22*	**14**	1 wk
4 Mar 61	**ACKER** *Columbia 33SX 1248*	**17**	1 wk

Date	Title *Label Number*	Position	
1 Apr 61	**GOLDEN TREASURY OF BILK** *Columbia 33SX 1304*	**11**	6 wks
26 May 62	●**STRANGER ON THE SHORE** *Columbia 33SX 1407*	**6**	26 wks
8 Dec 62	**STRANGER ON THE SHORE** (re-entry) *Columbia 33SX 1407*	**15**	2 wks
4 May 63	**A TASTE OF HONEY** *Columbia 33SX 1493*	**17**	4 wks

See also Kenny Ball, Chris Barber and Mr. Acker Bilk; Chris Barber and Mr. Acker Bilk.

Cilla BLACK *UK, female vocalist*

13 Feb 65	●**CILLA** *Parlophone PMC 1243*	**5**	11 wks
14 May 66	●**CILLA SINGS A RAINBOW** *Parlophone PMC 7004*	**4**	15 wks
13 Apr 68	●**SHER-OO** *Parlophone PCS 7041*	**7**	11 wks
30 Nov 68	**BEST OF CILLA BLACK** *Parlophone PCS 7065*	**21**	6 wks
18 Jan 69	**BEST OF CILLA BLACK** (re-entry) *Parlophone PCS 7065*	**30**	4 wks
16 Aug 69	**BEST OF CILLA BLACK** (2nd re-entry) *Parlophone PCS 7065*	**38**	1 wk

BLIND FAITH *UK, male vocal/instrumental group*

13 Sep 69	★**BLIND FAITH** *Polydor 583-059*	**1**	10 wks

BLODWYN PIG *UK, male vocal/instrumental group*

16 Aug 69	●**AHEAD RINGS OUT** *Island ILPS 9101*	**9**	4 wks

BLOOD SWEAT AND TEARS

US, male vocal/instrumental group

13 Jul 68	**CHILD IS THE FATHER TO THE MAN** *CBS 63296*	**40**	1 wk
12 Apr 69	**BLOOD SWEAT AND TEARS** *CBS 63504*	**15**	1 wk
28 Jun 69	**BLOOD SWEAT AND TEARS** (re-entry) *CBS 63504*	**37**	1 wk
12 Jul 69	**BLOOD SWEAT AND TEARS** (2nd re-entry) *CBS 63504*	**23**	1 wk

BOOKER T and the M.G.s

US, male instrumental group

25 Jul 64	**GREEN ONIONS** *London HAK 8182*	**11**	3 wks
22 Aug 64	**GREEN ONIONS** (re-entry) *London HAK 8182*	**16**	1 wk

Pat BOONE *US, male vocalist*

28 May 60	**HYMNS WE HAVE LOVED** *London HAD 2228*	**18**	1 wk
11 Jun 60	**HYMNS WE HAVE LOVED** (re-entry) *London HAD 2228*	**12**	1 wk
25 Jun 60	**HYMNS WE LOVE** *London HAD 2092*	**14**	1 wk

Los BRAVOS

Spain/Germany, male vocal/instrumental group

8 Oct 66	**BLACK IS BLACK** *Decca LK 4822*	**29**	1 wk

Johnny CASH Old Golden Throat notched up six successful albums between '66 and '69 but only charted two singles, the first being a Bob Dylan classic

Date	Title *Label Number*	Position		Date	Title *Label Number*	Position	

June BRONHILL and Thomas ROUND

Australia/UK, female/male vocal duo

18 Jun 60	**LILAC TIME** *HMV CLP 1248*	17	1 wk

BONZO DOG DOO-DAH BAND

UK, male vocal/instrumental group

18 Jan 69	**DOUGHNUT IN GRANNY'S GREENHOUSE** *Liberty LBS 83158*	40	1 wk
30 Aug 69	**TADPOLES** *Liberty LBS 83257*	36	1 wk

Wilfred BRAMBELL and Harry H. CORBETT *UK, male comic duo*

11 Jan 63	**STEPTOE AND SON** *Pye NPL 18081*	13	9 wks
6 Jul 63	**STEPTOE AND SON** (re-entry) *Pye NPL 18081*	14	3 wks
31 Aug 63	●**STEPTOE AND SON** (2nd re-entry) *Pye NPL 18081*	4	13 wks
7 Dec 63	**STEPTOE AND SON** (3rd re-entry) *Pye NPL 18081*	20	1 wk
11 Jan 64	**STEPTOE & SON** *Pye GGL 0217*	14	3 wks
14 Mar 64	**STEPTOE & SON** (re-entry) *Pye GGL 0217*	15	2 wks
14 Mar 64	**MORE JUNK** *Pye NPL 18090*	19	1 wk
21 Aug 64	**STEPTOE AND SON** (4th re-entry) *Pye NPL 18081*	18	2 wks

Crazy World of Arthur BROWN

UK, male vocal/instrumental group

6 Jul 68	●**CRAZY WORLD OF ARTHUR BROWN** *Track 612005*	2	16 wks

Joe BROWN

UK, male vocalist/instrumentalist - guitar

1 Sep 62	●**A PICTURE OF YOU** *Pye Golden Guinea GGL 0146*	3	39 wks
25 May 63	**JOE BROWN — LIVE** *Piccadilly NPL 38006*	14	8 wks

Dave BRUBECK *US, male jazz group leader*

25 Jun 60	**TIME OUT** *Fontana TFL 5085*	11	1 wk
7 Apr 62	**TIME FURTHER OUT** *Fontana TFL 5161*	12	9 wks
16 Jun 62	**TIME FURTHER OUT** (re-entry) *Fontana TFL 5161*	12	7 wks

First album credited to Dave Brubeck Quartet.

Jack BRUCE *UK, male vocalist/instrumentalist - bass*

27 Sep 69	●**SONGS FOR A TAILOR** *Polydor 583-058*	6	7 wks

Max BYGRAVES *UK, male vocalist*

8 Mar 69	●**WORLD OF MAX BYGRAVES** *Decca SPA 9*	6	1 wk

Charlie BYRD — See *Stan GETZ and Charlie BYRD.*

BYRDS *US, male vocal/instrumental group*

28 Aug 65	●**MR TAMBOURINE MAN** *CBS BPG 62571*	7	12 wks
9 Apr 66	**TURN, TURN, TURN** *CBS BPG 62652*	11	5 wks
1 Oct 66	**5TH DIMENSION** *CBS BPG 62783*	28	1 wk
15 Oct 66	**5TH DIMENSION** (re-entry) *CBS BPG 62783*	27	1 wk
22 Apr 67	**YOUNGER THAN YESTERDAY** *CBS SBPG 62988*	37	4 wks
4 May 68	**THE NOTORIOUS BYRD BROTHERS** *CBS 63169*	12	11 wks
24 May 69	**DR BYRDS AND MR HYDE** *CBS 63545*	15	1 wk

C

CANNED HEAT *US, male vocal/instrumental group*

29 Jun 68	**BOOGIE WITH CANNED HEAT** *Liberty LBL 83103*	27	1 wk
13 Jul 68	●**BOOGIE WITH CANNED HEAT** (re-entry) *Liberty LBL 83103*	5	20 wks

Freddy CANNON *US, male vocalist*

27 Feb 60	★**THE EXPLOSIVE FREDDY CANNON** *Top Rank 25/108*	1	6 wks
16 Apr 60	●**THE EXPLOSIVE FREDDY CANNON** (re-entry) *Top Rank 25/108*	4	4 wks
23 Jul 60	**THE EXPLOSIVE FREDDY CANNON** (2nd re-entry) *Top Rank 25/108*	19	1 wk

Vicki CARR *US, female vocalist*

22 Jul 67	**WAY OF TODAY** *Liberty SLBY 1331*	31	1 wk
12 Aug 67	**IT MUST BE HIM** *Liberty LBS 83037*	12	10 wks
9 Sep 67	**WAY OF TODAY** (re-entry) *Liberty SLBY 1331*	40	1 wk

Johnny CASH *US, male vocalist*

23 Jul 66	**EVERYBODY LOVES A NUT** *CBS BPG 62717*	28	1 wk
4 May 68	**FROM SEA TO SHINING SEA** *CBS 62972*	40	1 wk
6 Jul 68	**OLD GOLDEN THROAT** *CBS 63316*	37	1 wk
24 Aug 68	●**FOLSOM PRISON** *CBS 63308*	8	21 wks
14 Sep 68	**OLD GOLDEN THROAT** (re-entry) *CBS 63316*	40	1 wk
23 Aug 69	●**JOHNNY CASH AT SAN QUENTIN** *CBS 63629*	2	85 wks
27 Sep 69	**FOLSOM PRISON** (re-entry) *CBS 63308*	31	1 wk
4 Oct 69	**GREATEST HITS Vol 1** *CBS 63062*	23	2 wks
25 Oct 69	**FOLSOM PRISON** (2nd re-entry) *CBS 63308*	22	1 wk
15 Nov 69	**FOLSOM PRISON** (3rd re-entry) *CBS 63308*	22	1 wk
22 Nov 69	**GREATEST HITS Vol 1** (re-entry) *CBS 63062*	23	1 wk
29 Nov 69	**FOLSOM PRISON** (4th re-entry) *CBS 63308*	21	1 wk

Date	Title Label Number	Position	Date	Title Label Number	Position

Frank CHACKSFIELD *UK, orchestra*

8 Mar 69 ●WORLD OF FRANK CHACKSFIELD **10** 1 wk
Decca SPA 5

Richard CHAMBERLAIN *US, male vocalist*

16 Mar 63 ●RICHARD CHAMBERLAIN SINGS **8** 8 wks
MGM C 923

CHAQUITO and QUEDO BRASS

UK, male arranger/conductor Johnny Gregory under a false name, and UK orchestra

24 Feb 68 THIS CHAQUITO *Fontana SFXL 50* **36** 1 wk

Ray CHARLES

US, male vocalist/instrumentalist - piano

28 Jul 62 ●MODERN SOUNDS IN COUNTRY AND **6** 16 wks
WESTERN MUSIC *HMV CLP 1580*
23 Feb 63 MODERN SOUNDS IN COUNTRY AND **15** 2 wks
WESTERN MUSIC Vol 2 *HMV CLP 1613*
16 Mar 63 MODERN SOUNDS IN COUNTRY AND **16** 3 wks
WESTERN MUSIC Vol 2 (re-entry)
HMV CLP 1613
20 Jul 63 GREATEST HITS *HMV CLP 1626* **16** 5 wks
5 Oct 68 GREATEST HITS Vol 2 *Stateside SSL 10241* **24** 7 wks
7 Dec 68 GREATEST HITS Vol 2 (re-entry) **36** 1 wk
Stateside SSL 10241

Chubby CHECKER *US, male vocalist*

27 Jan 62 TWIST WITH CHUBBY CHECKER **19** 1 wk
Columbia 33SX 1315
10 Feb 62 TWIST WITH CHUBBY CHECKER (re-entry) **13** 3 wks
Columbia 33SX 1315
3 Mar 62 FOR TWISTERS ONLY *Columbia 33SX 1341* **17** 3 wks

CHER *US, female vocalist*

2 Oct 65 ●ALL I REALLY WANT TO DO **7** 9 wks
Liberty LBY 3058
7 May 66 SONNY SIDE OF CHER *Liberty LBY 3072* **11** 11 wks
See also Sonny and Cher.

CHICAGO TRANSIT AUTHORITY

US, male vocal/instrumental group

27 Sep 69 CHICAGO TRANSIT AUTHORITY **37** 1 wk
CBS 66221

CHICKEN SHACK

UK, male/female vocal/instrumental group

22 Jun 68 FORTY BLUE FINGERS FRESHLY PACKED **12** 8 wks
Blue Horizon 7-63203
15 Feb 69 ●OK KEN? *Blue Horizon 7 63209* **9** 1 wk

Sir Winston CHURCHILL *UK, male statesman*

13 Feb 65 ●THE VOICE OF CHURCHILL *Decca LXT 6200* **6** 8 wks

CLANCY BROTHERS and Tommy MAKEM

Ireland, male vocal/instrumental group, male vocalist

16 Apr 66 ISN'T IT GRAND BOYS? *CBS BPG 62674* **22** 5 wks

ERIC CLAPTON — See *John MAYALL and Eric CLAPTON*

Petula CLARK *UK, female vocalist*

30 Jul 66 I COULDN'T LIVE WITHOUT YOUR LOVE **11** 10 wks
Pye NPL 18148
4 Feb 67 HIT PARADE *Pye NPL 18159* **18** 11 wks
18 Feb 67 COLOUR MY WORLD *Pye NSPL 18171* **16** 9 wks
7 Oct 67 THESE ARE MY SONGS *Pye NSPL 18197* **38** 3 wks
30 Mar 68 HIT PARADE (re-entry) *Pye NSPL 18159* **37** 2 wks
6 Apr 68 THE OTHER MAN'S GRASS IS **37** 1 wk
ALWAYS GREENER *Pye NSPL 18211*

Dave CLARK FIVE

UK, male vocal/instrumental group

18 Apr 64 ●A SESSION WITH THE DAVE CLARK FIVE **3** 8 wks
Columbia 33SX 1598
14 Aug 65 ●CATCH US IF YOU CAN *Columbia 33SX 1756* **8** 8 wks

Eddie COCHRAN

US, male vocalist/instrumentalist - guitar

30 Jul 60 SINGING TO MY BABY *London HAU 2093* **19** 1 wk
1 Oct 60 ●EDDIE COCHRAN MEMORIAL ALBUM **9** 9 wks
London HAU 2267
12 Jan 63 CHERISHED MEMORIES *Liberty LBY 1109* **15** 3 wks
20 Apr 63 EDDIE COCHRAN MEMORIAL ALBUM **11** 13 wks
(re-issue) *Liberty LBY 1127*
27 Jul 63 EDDIE COCHRAN MEMORIAL ALBUM **12** 5 wks
(re-entry of re-issue) *Liberty LBY 1127*
19 Oct 63 SINGING TO MY BABY (re-issue) **20** 1 wk
Liberty LBY 1158

Date	Title Label Number	Position	

Leonard COHEN *Canada, male vocalist*

Date	Title Label Number	Position	
31 Aug 68	SONGS OF LEONARD COHEN *CBS 63241*	39	1 wk
12 Oct 68	SONGS OF LEONARD COHEN (re-entry) *CBS 63241*	18	11 wks
26 Apr 69	SONGS OF LEONARD COHEN (2nd re-entry) *CBS 63241*	13	1 wk
3 May 69	●SONGS FROM A ROOM *CBS 63587*	2	6 wks
21 Jul 69	SONGS FROM A ROOM (re-entry) *CBS 63587*	19	4 wks
2 Aug 69	SONGS OF LEONARD COHEN (3rd re-entry) *CBS 63241*	22	1 wk
18 Oct 69	SONGS OF LEONARD COHEN (4th re-entry) *CBS 63241*	25	1 wk

Nat 'King' COLE *US, male vocalist*

Date	Title Label Number	Position	
19 Aug 61	STRING ALONG WITH NAT KING COLE *Encore ENC 102*	12	9 wks
27 Mar 65	UNFORGETTABLE NAT KING COLE *Capitol W 20664*	19	1 wk
17 Apr 65	UNFORGETTABLE NAT KING COLE (re-entry) *Capitol W 20664*	11	4 wks
22 May 65	UNFORGETTABLE NAT KING COLE (2nd re-entry) *Capitol W 20664*	15	3 wks
7 Dec 68	●BEST OF NAT KING COLE *Capitol ST 21139*	5	10 wks

See also Nat 'King' Cole and the George Shearing Quintet

Nat 'King' COLE and the George SHEARING QUINTET

US, male vocalist, male instrumental group

Date	Title Label Number	Position	
20 Oct 62	●NAT KING COLE SINGS AND THE GEORGE SHEARING QUINTET PLAYS *Capitol W 1675*	8	7 wks

See also Nat 'King' Cole; Peggy Lee and George Shearing.

Joan COLLINS — See *Anthony NEWLEY, Peter SELLERS and Joan COLLINS*

COLOSSEUM *UK, male vocal/instrumental group*

Date	Title Label Number	Position	
17 May 69	COLOSSEUM *Fontana S 5510*	15	1 wk
22 Nov 69	VALENTYNE SUITE *Vertigo VO 1*	15	2 wks
13 Dec 69	VALENTYNE SUITE (re-entry) *Vertigo VO 1*	16	1 wk

COMETS — See *Bill HALEY and his COMETS*

Ray CONNIFF *US, orchestra leader*

Date	Title Label Number	Position	
28 May 60	ITS THE TALK OF THE TOWN *Philips BBL 7354*	15	1 wk
25 Jun 60	'S AWFUL NICE *Philips BBL 7281*	13	1 wk
26 Nov 60	●HI-FI COMPANION ALBUM *Philips BET 101*	3	30 wks
20 May 61	MEMORIES ARE MADE OF THIS *Philips BBL 7439*	19	1 wk
10 Jun 61	MEMORIES ARE MADE OF THIS (re-entry) *Philips BBL 7439*	20	1 wk
24 Jun 61	MEMORIES ARE MADE OF THIS (2nd re-entry) *Philips BBL 7439*	14	2 wks
1 Jul 61	HI-FI COMPANION ALBUM (re-entry) *Philips BET 101*	11	12 wks
6 Jan 62	HI-FI COMPANION ALBUM (2nd re-entry) *Philips BET 101*	14	2 wks
29 Dec 62	WE WISH YOU A MERRY CHRISTMAS *CBS BPG 62092*	12	1 wk
29 Dec 62	'S WONDERFUL 'S MARVELLOUS *CBS DPG 66001*	18	3 wks
16 Apr 66	HI-FI COMPANION ALBUM (re-issue) *CBS DP 66011*	24	1 wk
28 May 66	HI-FI COMPANION ALBUM (re-entry of re-issue) *CBS DP 66011*	25	3 wks
9 Sep 67	SOMEWHERE MY LOVE *CBS SBPG 62740*	34	3 wks
21 Jun 69	★HIS ORCHESTRA, HIS CHORUS, HIS SINGERS, HIS SOUND *CBS SPR 27*	1	16 wks

Russ CONWAY *UK, male instrumentalist - piano*

Date	Title Label Number	Position	
2 Jan 60	●TIME TO CELEBRATE *Columbia 335X 1197*	3	5 wks
2 Jan 60	●FAMILY FAVOURITES *Columbia 335X 1169*	7	1 wk
2 Jan 60	●PACK UP YOUR TROUBLES *Columbia 33SX 1120*	10	1 wk
26 Mar 60	●MY CONCERTO FOR YOU *Columbia 33SX 1214*	5	5 wks
7 May 60	MY CONCERTO FOR YOU (re-entry) *Columbia 33SX 1214*	12	1 wk
18 Jun 60	MY CONCERTO FOR YOU (2nd re-entry) *Columbia 33SX 1214*	15	1 wk
2 Jul 60	MY CONCERTO FOR YOU (3rd re-entry) *Columbia 33SX 1214*	15	3 wks
30 Jul 60	●MY CONCERTO FOR YOU (4th re-entry) *Columbia 33SX 1214*	9	4 wks
3 Sep 60	MY CONCERTO FOR YOU (5th re-entry) *Columbia 33SX 1214*	19	1 wk
5 Nov 60	MY CONCERTO FOR YOU (6th re-entry) *Columbia 33SX 1214*	16	2 wks
17 Dec 60	●PARTY TIME *Columbia 33SX 1279*	7	11 wks

Peter COOK and Dudley MOORE

UK, male comic duo

Date	Title Label Number	Position	
21 May 66	ONCE MOORE WITH COOK *Decca LK 4785*	25	1 wk

See also Dudley Moore.

CREAM *UK, male vocal/instrumental group*

Date	Title Label Number	Position	
24 Dec 66	●FRESH CREAM *Reaction 593-001*	6	17 wks
18 Nov 67	●DISRAELI GEARS *Reaction 594-003*	5	24 wks
17 Aug 68	●WHEELS OF FIRE (Double; Live and Studio) *Polydor 583-031/2*	3	26 wks
17 Aug 68	●WHEELS OF FIRE (Single; Studio) *Polydor 583-033*	7	13 wks
25 Jan 69	●DISRAELI GEARS (re-entry) *Reaction 594-003*	25	3 wks
22 Feb 69	●DISRAELI GEARS (2nd re-entry) *Reaction 594-003*	7	1 wk
15 Mar 69	DISRAELI GEARS (3rd re-entry) *Reaction 594-003*	12	3 wks
15 Mar 69	★GOODBYE *Polydor 583-053*	1	22 wks
26 Mar 69	●DISRAELI GEARS (4th re-entry) *Reaction 594-003*	10	1 wk
10 May 69	DISRAELI GEARS (5th re-entry) *Reaction 594-003*	13	1 wk
7 Jun 69	DISRAELI GEARS (6th re-entry) *Reaction 594-003*	15	1 wk
5 Jul 69	DISRAELI GEARS (7th re-entry) *Reaction 594-003*	39	1 wk
19 Jul 69	DISRAELI GEARS (8th re-entry) *Reaction 594-003*	27	2 wks

CREAM *Below*
Ten re-entries in the
Album chart for
'Disraeli Gears' – a feat
only bettered by the
'King And I' (19
re-entries), 'The Buddy
Holly Story' (14) and
'Oklahoma' (11).

DOORS *Left*
No flashgear –
'Waiting For The Sun'.

Date	Title Label Number	Position		Date	Title Label Number	Position	
9 Aug 69	DISRAELI GEARS (9th re-entry) Reaction 594-003	24	3 wks				
6 Sep 69	GOODBYE (re-entry) Polydor 583-053	33	2 wks				
18 Oct 69	DISRAELI GEARS (10th re-entry) Reaction 594-003	19	1 wk				
18 Oct 69	GOODBYE (2nd re-entry) Polydor 583-053	21	2 wks				
8 Nov 69	●BEST OF CREAM Polydor 583-060	6	20 wks				

CRICKETS US, male vocal/instrumental group

25 Mar 61	IN STYLE WITH THE CRICKETS Coral LVA 9142	13	3 wks
22 Apr 61	IN STYLE WITH THE CRICKETS (re-entry) Coral LVA 9142	14	4 wks

See also Buddy Holly and the Crickets, and Bobby Vee and the Crickets.

Bing CROSBY US, male vocalist

8 Oct 60	●JOIN BING AND SING ALONG Warner Bros. WM 4021	9	8 wks
17 Dec 60	●JOIN BING AND SING ALONG (re-entry) Warner Bros. WM 4021	7	3 wks

CROSBY, STILLS and NASH

US/Canada/UK, male vocal/instrumental group

23 Aug 69	CROSBY, STILLS AND NASH Atlantic 588-189	25	5 wks

Adge CUTLER and the WURZELS

UK, male vocalist, male instrumental group

11 Mar 67	ADGE CUTLER AND THE WURZELS Columbia SX 6126	38	4 wks

D

DAKOTAS — See Billy J. KRAMER and the DAKOTAS

Bobby DARIN US, male vocalist

19 Mar 60	●THIS IS DARIN London HA 2235	4	6 wks
7 May 60	THIS IS DARIN (re-entry) London HA 2235	11	1 wk
11 Jun 60	THIS IS DARIN (2nd re-entry) London HA 2235	17	1 wk
9 Apr 60	THAT'S ALL London HAE 2172	15	1 wk

DAVE — See SAM and DAVE

Colin DAVIS/BBC SYMPHONY ORCHESTRA UK, conductor and orchestra

4 Oct 69	LAST NIGHT OF THE PROMS Philips SFM 23033	36	1 wk

Sammy DAVIS JR. US, male vocalist

13 Apr 63	SAMMY DAVIS JR. AT THE COCONUT GROVE Reprise R 6063/2	19	1 wk

Spencer DAVIS GROUP

8 Jan 66	●THEIR 1ST LP Fontana TL 5242	6	9 wks
22 Jan 66	●THE 2ND LP Fontana TL 5295	3	18 wks
11 Sep 66	●AUTUMN '66 Fontana TL 5359	4	20 wks

Manitas DE PLATA

Spanish, male instrumentalist - guitar

29 Jul 67	FLAMENCO GUITAR Philips SBL 7786	40	1 wk

Dave DEE, DOZY, BEAKY, MICK and TICH UK, male vocal/instrumental group

2 Jul 66	DAVE DEE, DOZY, BEAKY, MICK AND TICH Fontana STL 5350	11	10 wks
7 Jan 67	IF MUSIC BE THE FOOD OF LOVE . . . PREPARE FOR INDIGESTION Fontana STL 5388	27	5 wks

Desmond DEKKER Jamaica, male vocalist

5 Jul 69	THIS IS DESMOND DEKKER Trojan TTL 4	27	1 wk
19 Jul 69	THIS IS DESMOND DEKKER (re-entry) Trojan TTL 4	32	3 wks

Karl DENVER UK, male vocalist

23 Dec 61	●WIMOWEH Ace of Clubs ACL 1098	7	27 wks

Bo DIDDLEY

US, male vocalist/instrumentalist - guitar

5 Oct 63	BO DIDDLEY Pye NPL 28026	11	8 wks
9 Nov 63	BO DIDDLEY IS A GUNSLINGER Pye NJL 33	20	1 wk
30 Nov 63	BO DIDDLEY RIDES AGAIN Pye NPL 28029	19	1 wk
15 Feb 64	BO DIDDLEY'S BEACH PARTY Pye NPL 28032	13	6 wks

Richard DIMBLEBY UK, male broadcaster

4 Jun 66	VOICE OF RICHARD DIMBLEBY MFP 1087	14	5 wks

Ken DODD UK, male vocalist

25 Dec 65	●TEARS OF HAPPINESS Columbia 33SX 1793	6	10 wks
19 Mar 66	TEARS OF HAPPINESS (re-entry) Columbia 33SX 1793	20	2 wks
23 Jul 66	HITS FOR NOW AND ALWAYS Columbia SX 6060	14	11 wks
14 Jan 67	FOR SOMEONE SPECIAL Columbia SCX 6224	40	1 wk

Date	Title *Label Number*		Position		Date	Title *Label Number*		Position	

Lonnie DONEGAN *UK, male vocalist*

1 Sep 62	●GOLDEN AGE OF DONEGAN	**3**	23 wks
	Pye Golden Guinea GGL 0135		
9 Feb 63	GOLDEN AGE OF DONEGAN Vol 2	**15**	3 wks
	Pye Golden Guinea GGL 0135		

DONOVAN *UK, male vocalist*

5 Jun 65	●WHAT'S BIN DID AND WHAT'S BIN HID	**3**	16 wks
	Pye NPL 18117		
6 Nov 65	FAIRY TALE *Pye NPL 18128*	**20**	1 wk
11 Dec 65	FAIRY TALE (re-entry) *Pye NPL 18128*	**20**	1 wk
8 Jul 67	SUNSHINE SUPERMAN *Pye NPL 18181*	**25**	7 wks
14 Oct 67	●UNIVERSAL SOLDIER *Marble Arch MAL 718*	**5**	18 wks
11 May 68	A GIFT FROM A FLOWER TO A GARDEN	**13**	14 wks
	Pye NSPL 20000		
8 Mar 69	FAIRY TALE (re-issue) *Marble Arch MAL 869*	**27**	1 wk

Val DOONICAN *Ireland, male vocalist*

12 Dec 64	●LUCKY 13 SHADES OF VAL DOONICAN	**2**	25 wks
	Decca LK 4648		
19 Jun 65	LUCKY 13 SHADES OF VAL DOONICAN	**17**	2 wks
	(re-entry) *Decca LK 4648*		
3 Dec 66	●GENTLE SHADES OF VAL DOONICAN	**5**	24 wks
	Decca LK 4831		
2 Dec 67	☆ VAL DOONICAN ROCKS BUT GENTLY	**1**	23 wks
	Pye NSPL 18204		
19 Oct 68	GENTLE SHADES OF VAL DOONICAN	**23**	16 wks
	(re-entry) *Decca LK 4831*		
30 Nov 68	●VAL *Pye NSPL 18236*	**6**	11 wks
14 Jun 69	●WORLD OF VAL DOONICAN *Decca SPA 3*	**2**	17 wks
13 Dec 69	SOUNDS GENTLE *Pye NSPL 18321*	**22**	1 wk

DOORS *US, male vocal/instrumental group*

| 28 Sep 68 | WAITING FOR THE SUN *Elektra EKS 74024* | **16** | 10 wks |

Lee DORSEY *US, male vocalist*

| 17 Dec 66 | NEW LEE DORSEY *Stateside SSL 10192* | **34** | 4 wks |

Craig DOUGLAS *UK, male vocalist*

| 6 Aug 60 | CRAIG DOUGLAS *Top Rank BUY 049* | **17** | 2 wks |

DOZY — See *Dave DEE, DOZY, BEAKY, MICK and TICH*

DREAMERS — See *FREDDIE and the DREAMERS*

DRIFTERS *US, male vocal group*

| 18 May 68 | GOLDEN HITS *Atlantic 588-103* | **27** | 7 wks |

Julie DRISCOLL and the Brian AUGER TRINITY

UK, female vocalist, male vocal/instrumental group

| 8 Jun 68 | OPEN *Marmalade 608-002* | **12** | 13 wks |

DUBLINERS *Ireland, male vocal/instrumental group*

13 May 67	●A DROP OF THE HARD STUFF	**5**	41 wks
	Major Minor MMLP 3		
9 Sep 67	BEST OF THE DUBLINERS	**25**	11 wks
	Transatlantic TRA 158		
2 Mar 68	DRINKIN' AND COURTIN'	**31**	3 wks
	Major Minor SMLP 14		
7 Oct 68	●MORE OF THE HARD STUFF	**8**	23 wks
	Major Minor MMLP 5		

Simon DUPREE and the BIG SOUND

UK, male vocal/instrumental group

| 13 Aug 67 | WITHOUT RESERVATIONS | **39** | 1 wk |
| | *Parlophone PCS 7029* | | |

Bob DYLAN *US, male vocalist*

23 May 64	THE FREEWHEELIN' BOB DYLAN	**16**	3 wks
	CBS BPG 62193		
11 Jul 64	THE TIMES THEY ARE A-CHANGIN'	**20**	1 wk
	CBS BPG 62251		
8 Aug 64	THE FREEWHEELIN' BOB DYLAN (re-entry)	**16**	1 wk
	CBS BPG 62193		
26 Sep 64	THE FREEWHEELIN' BOB DYLAN	**20**	1 wk
	(2nd re-entry) *CBS BPG 62193*		
10 Oct 64	THE FREEWHEELIN' BOB DYLAN	**20**	1 wk
	(3rd re-entry) *CBS BPG 62193*		
17 Oct 64	THE TIMES THEY ARE A-CHANGIN'	**20**	1 wk
	(re-entry) *CBS BPG 62251*		
24 Oct 64	THE FREEWHEELIN' BOB DYLAN	**11**	7 wks
	(4th re-entry) *CBS BPG 62193*		
21 Nov 64	ANOTHER SIDE OF BOB DYLAN	**12**	4 wks
	CBS BPG 62429		
21 Nov 64	THE TIMES THEY ARE A-CHANGIN'	**15**	2 wks
	(2nd re-entry) *CBS BPG 62251*		
9 Jan 65	THE FREEWHEELIN' BOB DYLAN	**15**	4 wks
	(5th re-entry) *CBS BPG 62193*		
30 Jan 65	THE TIMES THEY ARE A-CHANGIN'	**16**	2 wks
	(3rd re-entry) *CBS BPG 62251*		
13 Feb 65	ANOTHER SIDE OF BOB DYLAN (re-entry)	**13**	4 wks
	CBS BPG 62429		
13 Mar 65	☆THE FREEWHEELIN' BOB DYLAN	**1**	15 wks
	(6th re-entry) *CBS BPG 62193*		
20 Mar 65	●ANOTHER SIDE OF BOB DYLAN	**8**	9 wks
	(2nd re-entry) *CBS BPG 62429*		
20 Mar 65	●THE TIMES THEY ARE A-CHANGIN'	**4**	14 wks
	(4th re-entry) *CBS BPG 62251*		
8 May 65	BOB DYLAN *CBS BPG 62022*	**13**	5 wks
15 May 65	☆ BRINGING IT ALL BACK HOME	**1**	29 wks
	CBS BPG 62515		
19 Jun 65	ANOTHER SIDE OF BOB DYLAN	**16**	2 wks
	(3rd re-entry) *CBS BPG 62429*		
24 Jun 65	BOB DYLAN (re-entry) *CBS BPG 62022*	**19**	1 wk
3 Jul 65	●THE FREEWHEELIN' BOB DYLAN	**9**	14 wks
	(7th re-entry) *CBS BPG 62193*		
9 Oct 65	●HIGHWAY 61 REVISITED *CBS BPG 62527*	**4**	15 wks
16 Oct 65	THE FREEWHEELIN' BOB DYLAN	**19**	1 wk
	(8th re-entry) *CBS BPG 62193*		
20 Aug 66	●BLONDE ON BLONDE *CBS DDP 66012*	**3**	15 wks
14 Jan 67	●GREATEST HITS *CBS SBPG 62847*	**6**	41 wks
2 Mar 68	☆ JOHN WESLEY HARDING *CBS SBPG 63252*	**1**	29 wks
17 May 69	☆ NASHVILLE SKYLINE *CBS 63601*	**1**	29 wks
13 Sep 69	GREATEST HITS (re-entry) *CBS SBPG 62847*	**17**	5 wks

Bob DYLAN *Right*
263 weeks on the album
chart, 57 weeks on the
EP chart and 133 weeks
on the Singles chart.

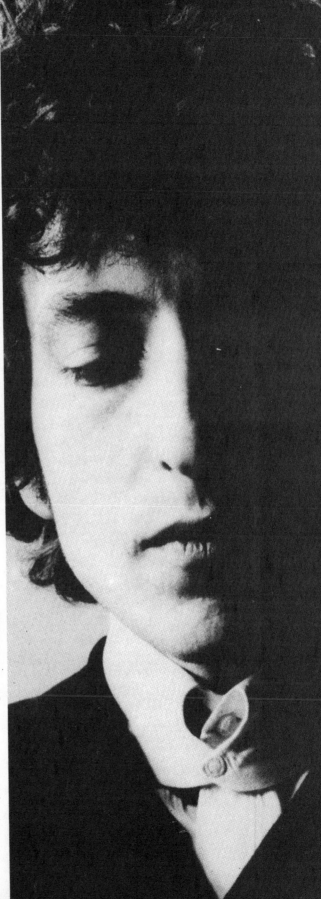

FLEETWOOD MAC *Top left to right* Mick Fleetwood and Jeremy Spencer *Above* Peter Green and John McVie.

Simon DUPREE and the BIG SOUND The Portsmouth group led by Derek Shulman first played as The Howlin' Wolves before becoming the Roadrunners, merging with the Classics and ending up as Simon Dupree and the Big Sound.

Date	Title Label Number	Position
1 Nov 69	**GREATEST HITS** (2nd re-entry) CBS SBPG 62847	**16** 2 wks
29 Nov 69	**GREATEST HITS** (3rd re-entry) CBS SBPG 62847	**18** 2 wks
20 Dec 69	**GREATEST HITS** (4th re-entry) CBS SBPG 62847	**23** 1 wk
20 Dec 69	**NASHVILLE SKYLINE** (re-entry) CBS 63601	**22** 1 wk

E

Duane EDDY *US, male instrumentalist - guitar*

Date	Title Label Number	Position
19 Mar 60	●**THE TWANG'S THE THANG** London HA 2236	**2** 14 wks
2 Jul 60	●**THE TWANG'S THE THANG** (re-entry) London HA 2236	**9** 11 wks
23 Jul 60	**ESPECIALLY FOR YOU** London HAW 2191	**14** 1 wk
11 Aug 60	**ESPECIALLY FOR YOU** (re-entry) London HAW 2191	**20** 1 wk
26 Nov 60	**SONGS OF OUR HERITAGE** London HAW 2285	**13** 5 wks
1 Apr 61	●**A MILLION DOLLARS' WORTH OF TWANG** London HAW 2325	**5** 18 wks
12 Aug 61	**A MILLION DOLLARS' WORTH OF TWANG** (re-entry) London HAW 2325	**17** 1 wk
9 Jun 62	**A MILLION DOLLARS' WORTH OF TWANG Vol 2** London HAW 2435	**18** 1 wk
21 Jul 62	●**TWISTIN' AND TWANGIN'** RCA RD 27264	**8** 12 wks
8 Dec 62	**TWANGY GUITAR-SILKY STRINGS** RCA RD 7510	**13** 8 wks
9 Feb 63	**TWANGY GUITAR-SILKY STRINGS** (re-entry) RCA RD 7510	**17** 2 wks
2 Mar 63	**TWANGY GUITAR-SILKY STRINGS** (2nd re-entry) RCA RD 7510	**20** 1 wk
16 Mar 63	**DANCE WITH THE GUITAR MAN** RCA RD 7545	**14** 4 wks

Duke ELLINGTON *US, orchestra leader*

Date	Title Label Number	Position
8 Apr 61	**NUT CRACKER SUITE** Philips BBL 7418	**11** 1 wk
22 Apr 61	**NUT CRACKER SUITE** (re-entry) Philips BBL 7418	**19** 1 wk

EQUALS *UK, male vocal/instrumental group*

Date	Title Label Number	Position
18 Nov 67	●**UNEQUALLED EQUALS** President PTL 1006	**10** 9 wks
9 Mar 68	**EQUALS EXPLOSION** President PTLS 1015	**32** 1 wk

EVERLY BROTHERS *US, male vocal duo*

Date	Title Label Number	Position
2 Jul 60	●**IT'S EVERLY TIME** Warner Bros. WM 4006	**2** 23 wks
15 Oct 60	●**FABULOUS STYLE OF THE EVERLY BROTHERS** London HAA 2266	**4** 7 wks
10 Dec 60	**FABULOUS STYLE OF THE EVERLY BROTHERS** (re-entry) London HAA 2266	**20** 1 wk
7 Jan 61	●**FABULOUS STYLE OF THE EVERLY BROTHERS** (2nd re-entry) London HAA 2266	**9** 2 wks
11 Feb 61	**FABULOUS STYLE OF THE EVERLY BROTHERS** (3rd re-entry) London HAA 2266	**19** 1 wk

Date	Title Label Number	Position
4 Mar 61	●**A DATE WITH THE EVERLY BROTHERS** Warner Bros. WM 4028	**3** 13 wks
10 Jun 61	**A DATE WITH THE EVERLY BROTHERS** (re-entry) Warner Bros. WM 4028	**19** 1 wk
21 Jun 62	**INSTANT PARTY** Warner Bros. WM 4061	**20** 1 wk

F

FAIRPORT CONVENTION *UK, male/female vocal/instrumental group*

Date	Title Label Number	Position
2 Aug 69	**UNHALFBRICKING** Island ILPS 9102	**12** 8 wks

Adam FAITH *UK, male vocalist*

Date	Title Label Number	Position
19 Nov 60	●**ADAM** Parlophone PMC 1128	**6** 33 wks
11 Feb 61	**BEAT GIRL** (Film Soundtrack) Columbia 33SX 1225	**11** 3 wks
27 Jan 62	**ADAM** (re-entry) Parlophone PMC 1128	**11** 3 wks
24 Mar 62	**ADAM FAITH** Parlophone PMC 1162	**20** 1 wk
25 Sep 65	**FAITH ALIVE** Parlophone PMC 1249	**19** 1 wk

The Beat Girl soundtrack also featured tracks by the John Barry Seven and the John Barry Orchestra.

Marianne FAITHFULL *UK, female vocalist*

Date	Title Label Number	Position
5 Jun 65	**COME MY WAY** Decca LK 4688	**12** 7 wks
5 Jun 65	**MARIANNE FAITHFULL** Decca LK 4689	**15** 2 wks

Georgie FAME *UK, male vocalist/instrumentalist - keyboards*

Date	Title Label Number	Position
17 Oct 64	**FAME AT LAST** Columbia 33SX 1638	**16** 2 wks
16 Jan 65	**FAME AT LAST** (re-entry) Columbia 33SX 1638	**15** 4 wks
13 Mar 65	**FAME AT LAST** (2nd re-entry) Columbia 33SX 1638	**19** 1 wk
3 Apr 65	**FAME AT LAST** (3rd re-entry) Columbia 33SX 1638	**19** 1 wk
14 May 66	●**SWEET THINGS** Columbia SX 6043	**6** 20 wks
8 Oct 66	**SWEET THINGS** (re-entry) Columbia SX 6043	**24** 2 wks
15 Oct 66	●**SOUND VENTURE** Columbia SX 6076	**9** 9 wks
11 Mar 67	**HALL OF FAME** Columbia SX 6120	**12** 16 wks
1 Jul 67	**TWO FACES OF FAME** CBS SBPG 63018	**22** 6 wks
19 Aug 67	**TWO FACES OF FAME** (re-entry) CBS SBPG 63018	**33** 4 wks
23 Sep 67	**HALL OF FAME** (re-entry) Columbia SX 6120	**37** 2 wks
27 Apr 68	**TWO FACES OF FAME** (2nd re-entry) CBS SBPG 63018	**31** 5 wks

FAMILY *UK, male vocal/instrumental group*

Date	Title Label Number	Position
10 Aug 68	**MUSIC IN THE DOLLS HOUSE** Reprise RLP 6312	**35** 3 wks
22 Mar 69	●**FAMILY ENTERTAINMENT** Reprise RSLP 6340	**6** 2 wks

Date	Title Label Number	Position		Date	Title Label Number	Position	

Chris FARLOWE *UK, male vocalist*

2 Apr 66	**14 THINGS TO THINK ABOUT**	**19**	1 wk
	Immediate IMPL 005		
10 Dec 66	**THE ART OF CHRIS FARLOWE**	**37**	2 wks
	Immediate IMPL 006		

Jose FELICIANO

US, male vocalist/instrumentalist - guitar

2 Nov 68	●**FELICIANO** *RCA Victor SF 7946*	**6**	17 wks
5 Apr 69	**FELICIANO** (re-entry) *RCA Victor SF 7946*	**15**	1 wk
26 Apr 69	**FELICIANO** (2nd re-entry) *RCA Victor SF 7946*	**14**	1 wk
5 Jul 69	**FELICIANO** (3rd re-entry) *RCA Victor SF 7946*	**40**	1 wk
27 Sep 69	**FELICIANO** (4th re-entry) *RCA Victor SF 7946*	**34**	1 wk
15 Nov 69	**FELICIANO** (5th re-entry) *RCA Victor SF 7946*	**22**	1 wk
29 Nov 69	**JOSE FELICIANO** *RCA Victor SF 8044*	**29**	1 wk
20 Dec 69	**FELICIANO** (6th re-entry) *RCA Victor SF 7946*	**21**	1 wk

Julie FELIX *US, female vocalist*

11 Sep 66	**CHANGES** *Fontana TL 5368*	**27**	3 wks
8 Oct 66	**CHANGES** (re-entry) *Fontana TL 5368*	**28**	1 wk
8 Mar 69	**WORLD OF JULIE FELIX** *Decca SPA 6*	**29**	1 wk

Ella FITZGERALD *US, female vocalist*

11 Jun 60	**ELLA SINGS GERSHWIN** *Brunswick LA 8648*	**19**	1 wk
18 Jun 60	**ELLA AT THE OPERA HOUSE**	**16**	1 wk
	Columbia 33SX 10126		
25 Jun 60	**ELLA SINGS GERSHWIN** (re-entry)	**18**	1 wk
	Brunswick LA 8648		
16 Jul 60	**ELLA SINGS GERSHWIN** (2nd re-entry)	**13**	1 wk
	Brunswick LA 8648		
23 Jul 60	**ELLA SINGS GERSHWIN Vol 5**	**18**	2 wks
	HMV CLP 1353		

FLEETWOOD MAC

UK, male vocal/instrumental group

2 Mar 68	●**FLEETWOOD MAC** *Blue Horizon BPG 7-63200*	**4**	37 wks
7 Sep 68	●**MR WONDERFUL** *Blue Horizon 7-63205*	**10**	11 wks
30 Aug 69	**PIOUS BIRD OF GOOD OMEN**	**18**	4 wks
	Blue Horizon 7-63215		
4 Oct 69	●**THEN PLAY ON** *Reprise RSLP 9000*	**6**	9 wks

First album credited to Peter Green's Fleetwood Mac.

Eddie FLOYD *US, male vocalist*

29 Apr 67	**KNOCK ON WOOD** *Stax 589-006*	**36**	5 wks

Wayne FONTANA and the MINDBENDERS

UK, male vocalist and male instrumental backing group

20 Feb 65	**WAYNE FONTANA AND THE**	**18**	1 wk
	MINDBENDERS *Fontana TL 5230*		

See also the Mindbenders.

Clinton FORD *UK, male vocalist*

26 May 62	**CLINTON FORD** *Oriole PS 40021*	**16**	4 wks

FOUR PENNIES *UK, male vocal/instrumental group*

7 Nov 64	**TWO SIDES OF FOUR PENNIES**	**13**	5 wks
	Philips BL 7642		

FOUR SEASONS *US, male vocal group*

6 Jul 63	**SHERRY** *Stateside SL 10033*	**20**	1 wk

FOUR TOPS *US, male vocal group*

19 Nov 66	●**FOUR TOPS ON TOP**	**9**	23 wks
	Tamla Motown TML 11037		
11 Feb 67	●**FOUR TOPS LIVE!**	**4**	72 wks
	Tamla Motown STML 11041		
25 Nov 67	●**REACH OUT** *Tamla Motown STML 11056*	**4**	34 wks
20 Jan 68	★**GREATEST HITS** *Tamla Motown STML 11061*	**1**	56 wks
8 Feb 69	**YESTERDAY'S DREAMS**	**37**	1 wk
	Tamla Motown STML 11087		

Connie FRANCIS *US, female vocalist*

26 Mar 60	**ROCK 'N ROLL MILLION SELLERS**	**12**	1 wk
	MGM C 804		
11 Feb 61	**CONNIE'S GREATEST HITS** *MGM C 831*	**16**	1 wk
8 Apr 61	**CONNIE'S GREATEST HITS** (re-entry)	**18**	2 wks
	MGM C 831		

Aretha FRANKLIN *US, female vocalist*

12 Aug 67	**I NEVER LOVED A MAN** *Atlantic 587-006*	**36**	2 wks
13 Apr 68	**LADY SOUL** *Atlantic 588-099*	**40**	1 wk
1 Jun 68	**LADY SOUL** (re-entry) *Atlantic 588-099*	**25**	5 wks
20 Jul 68	**LADY SOUL** (2nd re-entry) *Atlantic 588-099*	**25**	12 wks
14 Sep 68	●**ARETHA NOW** *Atlantic 588-114*	**6**	11 wks

FREDERICK— See *NINA and FREDERICK*

FREDDIE and the DREAMERS

UK, male vocalist and male instrumental group

9 Nov 63	●**FREDDIE AND THE DREAMERS**	**5**	26 wks
	Columbia 33SX 1577		

Billy FURY *UK, male vocalist*

4 Jun 60	**THE SOUND OF FURY** *Decca LF 1329*	**18**	1 wk
9 Jul 60	**THE SOUND OF FURY** (re-entry)	**20**	1 wk
	Decca LF 1329		
23 Sep 61	●**HALFWAY TO PARADISE**	**5**	9 wks
	Ace of Clubs ACL 1083		
11 May 63	●**BILLY** *Decca LK 4533*	**6**	21 wks
26 Oct 63	**WE WANT BILLY** *Decca LK 4548*	**14**	2 wks

Buddy HOLLY and the CRICKETS. Godfrey Evans and Dennis Compton give
some sound advice to the Crickets on Cricket! *Pictorial Press*.

Date	**Title** *Label Number*	**Position**	**Date**	**Title** *Label Number*	**Position**

GARFUNKEL — See *SIMON and GARFUNKEL*

Judy GARLAND *US, female vocalist*

| 3 Mar 62 | **JUDY AT CARNEGIE HALL** *Capitol W 1569* | **13** 3 wks |

Errol GARNER *US, male instrumentalist - piano*

| 14 Jul 62 | **CLOSE UP IN SWING** *Philips BBL 7579* | **20** 1 wk |

Marvin GAYE *US, male vocalist*

| 16 Mar 68 | **GREATEST HITS** *Tamla Motown STML 11065* | **40** 1 wk |

Bobbie GENTRY *US, female vocalist*

| 25 Oct 69 | **TOUCH 'EM WITH LOVE** *Capitol EST 155* | **21** 1 wk |

GERRY and the PACEMAKERS

UK, male vocalist and male instrumental backing group

26 Oct 63	●**HOW DO YOU LIKE IT?** *Columbia 33SX 1546*	**2** 28 wks
6 Feb 65	**FERRY ACROSS THE MERSEY**	**19** 1 wk
	Columbia 33SX 1676	

Stan GETZ and Charlie BYRD

US, male instrumental duo-saxophone and guitar

23 Feb 63	**JAZZ SAMBA** *Verve SULPH 9013*	**15** 1 wk
16 Mar 63	**JAZZ SAMBA** (re-entry) *Verve SULPH 9013*	**18** 1 wk
30 Mar 63	**JAZZ SAMBA** (2nd re-entry)	**16** 3 wks
	Verve SULPH 9013	
27 Apr 63	**JAZZ SAMBA** (3rd re-entry)	**19** 2 wks
	Verve SULPH 9013	

GOONS *UK, male vocal group*

2 Apr 60	**BEST OF THE GOON SHOWS**	**14** 2 wks
	Parlophone PMC 1108	
7 May 60	●**BEST OF THE GOON SHOWS** (re-entry)	**8** 4 wks
	Parlophone PMC 1108	
18 Jun 60	**BEST OF THE GOON SHOWS** (2nd re-entry)	**19** 1 wk
	Parlophone PMC 1108	
3 Dec 60	●**BEST OF THE GOON SHOWS** (3rd re-entry)	**8** 2 wks
	Parlophone PMC 1108	
17 Dec 60	**BEST OF THE GOON SHOWS Vol 2**	**11** 4 wks
	Parlophone PMC 1129	
21 Jan 61	**BEST OF THE GOON SHOWS Vol 2**	**18** 2 wks
	(re-entry) *Parlophone PMC 1129*	

GORDON – See *PETER and GORDON*

GUILDFORD CATHEDRAL CHOIR

UK, choir

| 10 Dec 66 | **CHRISTMAS CAROLS FROM GUILDFORD CATHEDRAL** *MFP 1104* | **24** 4 wks |

Record credits Barry Rose as conductor.

Bill HALEY and his COMETS

US, male vocalist and male instrumental backing group

| 18 May 68 | **ROCK AROUND THE CLOCK** | **34** 5 wks |
| | *Ace of Hearts AH 13* | |

HAMBURG STUDENTS CHOIR

Germany, choir

17 Dec 60	**HARK THE HERALD ANGELS SING**	**11** 3 wks
	Pye GGL 0023	
16 Dec 61	**HARK THE HERALD ANGELS SING**	**11** 3 wks
	(re-entry) *Pye GGL 0023*	

Tony HANCOCK *UK, male comedian*

9 Apr 60	**THIS IS HANCOCK** *Pye NPL 10845*	**2** 22 wks
12 Nov 60	**PIECES OF HANCOCK** *Pye NPL 18054*	**17** 2 wks
3 Mar 62	**HANCOCK** *Pye NPL 18068*	**12** 14 wks
30 Jun 62	**HANCOCK** (re-entry) *Pye NPL 18068*	**13** 4 wks
5 Aug 62	**HANCOCK** (2nd re-entry) *Pye NPL 18068*	**15** 4 wks
19 Jan 63	**HANCOCK** (3rd re-entry) *Pye NPL 18068*	**20** 1 wk
14 Sep 63	**THIS IS HANCOCK** (re-issue)	**16** 3 wks
	Pye Golden Guinea GGL 0206	
19 Oct 63	**THIS IS HANCOCK** (re-entry of re-issue)	**19** 1 wk
	Pye Golden Guinea GGL 0206	

John HANSON *UK, male vocalist*

23 Apr 60	**THE STUDENT PRINCE** *Pye NPL 18046*	**17** 1 wk
2 Sep 61	**THE STUDENT PRINCE/VAGABOND KING**	**9** 6 wks
	Pye GGL 0086	
2 Dec 61	**THE STUDENT PRINCE/VAGABOND KING**	**20** 1 wk
	(re-entry) *Pye GGL 0086*	

Anita HARRIS *UK, female vocalist*

| 27 Jan 68 | **JUST LOVING YOU** *CBS SBPG 63182* | **29** 5 wks |

Lee HAZLEWOOD — See *Nancy SINATRA and Lee HAZLEWOOD*

Ted HEATH and his MUSIC

UK, conductor and orchestra

| 21 Apr 62 | **BIG BAND PERCUSSION** *Decca PFM 24004* | **17** 5 wks |

Date	Title *Label Number*	Position

Jimi HENDRIX EXPERIENCE

US/UK, male vocal/instrumental trio

Date	Title *Label Number*	Position	
27 May 67	●ARE YOU EXPERIENCED *Track 612–001*	**2**	33 wks
16 Dec 67	●AXIS: BOLD AS LOVE *Track 613–003*	**5**	16 wks
27 Apr 68	●SMASH HITS *Track 613–004*	**4**	25 wks
16 Nov 68	●ELECTRIC LADYLAND *Track 613–008/9*	**6**	12 wks

See also Jimi Hendrix and Curtis Knight.

Jimi HENDRIX and Curtis KNIGHT

US, vocal/instrumental duo - guitars

Date	Title *Label Number*	Position	
18 May 68	GET THAT FEELING *London SH 8349*	**39**	2 wks

See also Jimi Hendrix Experience.

HERD, *UK, male vocal/instrumental group*

Date	Title *Label Number*	Position	
24 Feb 68	PARADISE LOST *Fontana STL 5458*	**38**	1 wk

HERMAN'S HERMITS

UK, male vocal/instrumental group

Date	Title *Label Number*	Position	
18 Sep 65	HERMAN'S HERMITS *Columbia 33SX 1727*	**20**	1 wk
9 Oct 65	HERMAN'S HERMITS (re-entry) *Columbia 33SX 1727*	**16**	1 wk

Vince HILL *UK, male vocalist*

Date	Title *Label Number*	Position	
20 May 67	EDELWEISS *Columbia SCX 6141*	**23**	9 wks

Ronnie HILTON *UK, male vocalist*

Date	Title *Label Number*	Position	
8 Mar 69	CHITTY CHITTY BANG BANG *MFP 1281*	**17**	1 wk

Gerard HOFFNUNG *UK, comedian*

Date	Title *Label Number*	Position	
3 Sep 60	●AT THE OXFORD UNION *Decca LF 1330*	**4**	15 wks
31 Dec 60	AT THE OXFORD UNION (re-entry) *Decca LF 1330*	**11**	3 wks
28 Jan 61	AT THE OXFORD UNION (2nd re-entry) *Decca LF 1330*	**20**	1 wk
3 Mar 62	AT THE OXFORD UNION (3rd re-entry) *Decca LF 1330*	**19**	1 wk

HOLLIES *UK, male vocal/instrumental group*

Date	Title *Label Number*	Position	
15 Feb 64	●STAY WITH THE HOLLIES *Parlophone PMC 1220*	**2**	25 wks
2 Oct 65	●HOLLIES *Parlophone PMC 1261*	**8**	14 wks
16 Jul 66	WOULD YOU BELIEVE *Parlophone PMC 7008*	**16**	8 wks
17 Dec 66	FOR CERTAIN BECAUSE *Parlophone PCS 17011*	**23**	7 wks
17 Jun 67	EVOLUTION *Parlophone PCS 7022*	**13**	10 wks
17 Aug 68	☆GREATEST HITS *Parlophone PCS 7057*	**1**	27 wks
17 May 69	●HOLLIES SING DYLAN *Parlophone PCS 7078*	**3**	7 wks

Buddy HOLLY and the CRICKETS

US, male vocalist and US, male vocal/instrumental group

Date	Title *Label Number*	Position	
2 Jan 60	●BUDDY HOLLY STORY *Coral LVA 9105*	**5**	6 wks
20 Feb 60	●BUDDY HOLLY STORY (re-entry) *Coral LVA 9105*	**9**	2 wks
9 Apr 60	BUDDY HOLLY STORY (2nd re-entry) *Coral LVA 9105*	**20**	1 wk
18 Jun 60	BUDDY HOLLY STORY (3rd re-entry) *Coral LVA 9105*	**18**	1 wk
30 Jul 60	●BUDDY HOLLY STORY (4th re-entry) *Coral LVA 9105*	**8**	8 wks
1 Oct 60	BUDDY HOLLY STORY (5th re-entry) *Coral LVA 9105*	**11**	4 wks
15 Oct 60	●BUDDY HOLLY STORY Vol 2 *Coral LVA 9127*	**7**	7 wks
7 Jan 61	BUDDY HOLLY STORY Vol 2 (re-entry) *Coral LVA 9127*	**14**	3 wks
21 Jan 61	●BUDDY HOLLY STORY (6th re-entry) *Coral LVA 9105*	**7**	11 wks
4 Feb 61	BUDDY HOLLY STORY Vol 2 (2nd re-entry) *Coral LVA 9127*	**20**	1 wk
1 Jul 61	BUDDY HOLLY STORY Vol 2 (5th re-entry) *Coral LVA 9127*	**19**	1 wk
8 Jul 61	●BUDDY HOLLY STORY (7th re-entry) *Coral LVA 9105*	**6**	23 wks
21 Oct 61	●THAT'LL BE THE DAY *Ace of Hearts AH 3*	**5**	14 wks
23 Dec 61	BUDDY HOLLY STORY (8th re-entry) *Coral LVA 9105*	**13**	3 wks
6 Jan 62	BUDDY HOLLY STORY Vol 2 (4th re-entry) *Coral LVA 9127*	**15**	1 wk
20 Jan 62	BUDDY HOLLY STORY (9th re-entry) *Coral LVA 9105*	**12**	1 wk
10 Feb 62	●BUDDY HOLLY STORY (10th re-entry) *Coral LVA 9105*	**10**	28 wks
15 Sep 62	BUDDY HOLLY STORY (11th re-entry) *Coral LVA 9105*	**11**	14 wks
2 Feb 63	●BUDDY HOLLY STORY (12th re-entry) *Coral LVA 9105*	**10**	14 wks
6 Apr 63	●REMINISCING *Coral LVA 9212*	**2**	31 wks
25 May 63	BUDDY HOLLY STORY (13th re-entry) *Coral LVA 9105*	**11**	20 wks
13 Jul 63	BUDDY HOLLY STORY Vol 2 (5th re-entry) *Coral LVA 9127*	**16**	1 wk
2 May 64	BUDDY HOLLY STORY (14th re-entry) *Coral LVA 9105*	**20**	1 wk
13 Jun 64	●BUDDY HOLLY SHOWCASE *Coral LVA 9222*	**3**	16 wks
26 Jun 65	HOLLY IN THE HILLS *Coral LVA 9227*	**13**	6 wks
15 Jul 67	●BUDDY HOLLY'S GREATEST HITS *Ace of Hearts AH 148*	**10**	21 wks
11 May 68	●BUDDY HOLLY'S GREATEST HITS (re-entry) *Ace of Hearts AH 148*	**9**	19 wks
12 Apr 69	GIANT *MCA MUPS 371*	**13**	1 wk

Most albums feature the Crickets on at least some tracks. See also the Crickets; Bobby Vee and the Crickets

John Lee HOOKER

US, male vocalist/instrumentalist - guitar

Date	Title *Label Number*	Position	
4 Feb 67	HOUSE OF THE BLUES *Marble Arch MAL 663*	**34**	2 wks

Date	Title Label Number	Position	

Mary HOPKIN *UK, female vocalist*

1 Mar 69	●POSTCARD *Apple SAPCOR 5*	**3**	4 wks
5 Apr 69	POSTCARD (re-entry) *Apple SAPCOR 5*	**11**	1 wk
19 Apr 69	●POSTCARD (2nd re-entry) *Apple SAPCOR 5*	**7**	4 wks

HUMBLE PIE *UK, male vocal/instrumental group*

| 6 Sep 69 | AS SAFE AS YESTERDAY IS | **32** | 1 wk |
| | *Immediate IMSP 025* | | |

Engelbert HUMPERDINCK *JK, male vocalist*

20 May 67	●RELEASE ME *Decca SKL 4868*	**6**	58 wks
25 Nov 67	●THE LAST WALTZ *Decca SKL 4901*	**3**	33 wks
3 Aug 68	●A MAN WITHOUT LOVE *Decca SKL 4939*	**3**	28 wks
1 Mar 69	●A MAN WITHOUT LOVE (re-entry) *Decca SKL 4939*	**10**	2 wks
1 Mar 69	●ENGELBERT *Decca SKL 4985*	**3**	7 wks
29 Mar 69	●A MAN WITHOUT LOVE (2nd re-entry) *Decca SKL 4939*	**9**	2 wks
3 May 69	ENGELBERT (re-entry) *Decca SKL 4985*	**14**	1 wk
4 Oct 69	A MAN WITHOUT LOVE (3rd re-entry) *Decca SKL 4939*	**21**	3 wks
6 Dec 69	●ENGELBERT HUMPERDINCK *Decca SKL 5030*	**5**	6 wks

HURRICANES—See *JOHNNY and the HURRICANES*

I

Frank IFIELD *UK, male vocalist*

16 Feb 63	●I'LL REMEMBER YOU *Columbia 33SX 1467*	**3**	36 wks
21 Sep 63	●BORN FREE *Columbia 33SX 1462*	**3**	32 wks
28 Mar 64	●BLUE SKIES *Columbia 33SX 1588*	**10**	12 wks
19 Dec 64	●GREATEST HITS *Columbia 33SX 1633*	**9**	3 wks

INCREDIBLE STRING BAND

UK, male/female vocal instrumental group

21 Oct 67	5,000 SPIRITS OR THE LAYERS OF AN ONION *Elektra EUKS 257*	**30**	2 wks
11 Nov 67	5,000 SPIRITS OR THE LAYERS OF AN ONION (re-entry) *Elektra EUKS 257*	**25**	3 wks
6 Apr 68	●HANGMAN'S BEAUTIFUL DAUGHTER *Elektra EVKS7 258*	**5**	21 wks
20 Jul 68	INCREDIBLE STRING BAND *Elektra EKL 254*	**34**	3 wks

ISLEY BROTHERS

US, male vocal/instrumental group

| 14 Dec 68 | THIS OLD HEART OF MINE *Tamla Motown STML 11034* | **23** | 6 wks |

J

JEFFERSON AIRPLANE

US, male/female vocal/instrumental group

| 28 Jun 69 | BLESS ITS POINTED LITTLE HEAD *RCA SF 8019* | **38** | 1 wk |

JETHRO TULL *UK, male vocal/instrumental group*

2 Nov 68	●THIS WAS *Island ILPS 9085*	**10**	14 wks
28 Jun 69	THIS WAS (re-entry) *Island ILPS 9085*	**21**	1 wk
12 Jul 69	THIS WAS (2nd re-entry) *Island ILPS 9085*	**35**	1 wk
26 Jul 69	THIS WAS (3rd re-entry) *Island ILPS 9085*	**40**	1 wk
9 Aug 69	★STAND UP *Island ILPS 9103*	**1**	19 wks
29 Nov 69	THIS WAS (4th re-entry) *Island ILPS 9085*	**14**	5 wks

JOHNNY and the HURRICANES

US, male instrumental group

3 Dec 60	STORMSVILLE *London HAI 2269*	**18**	1 wk
1 Apr 61	BIG SOUND OF JOHNNY AND THE HURRICANES *London HAK 2322*	**16**	1 wk
15 Apr 61	BIG SOUND OF JOHNNY AND THE HURRICANES (re-entry) *London HAK 2322*	**13**	1 wk
29 Apr 61	BIG SOUND OF JOHNNY AND THE HURRICANES (2nd re-entry) *London HAK 2322*	**14**	1 wk
3 Jun 61	BIG SOUND OF JOHNNY AND THE HURRICANES (3rd re-entry) *London HAK 2322*	**19**	1 wk

Tom JONES *UK, male vocalist*

5 Jun 65	ALONG CAME JONES *Decca LK 6693*	**11**	5 wks
8 Oct 66	FROM THE HEART *Decca LK 4814*	**30**	1 wk
7 Jan 67	FROM THE HEART (re-entry) *Decca LK 4814*	**23**	7 wks
8 Apr 67	●GREEN GREEN GRASS OF HOME *Decca SKL 4855*	**3**	49 wks
24 Jun 67	●LIVE AT THE TALK OF THE TOWN *Decca SKL 4874*	**6**	87 wks
30 Dec 67	●13 SMASH HITS *Decca SKL 4909*	**5**	49 wks
27 Jul 68	★DELILAH *Decca SKL 4946*	**1**	29 wks
21 Dec 68	●HELP YOURSELF *Decca SKL 4982*	**4**	9 wks
15 Mar 69	LIVE AT THE TALK OF THE TOWN (re-entry) *Decca SKL 4874*	**12**	1 wk
29 Mar 69	LIVE AT THE TALK OF THE TOWN (2nd re-entry) *Decca SKL 4874*	**14**	1 wk
28 Jun 69	●THIS IS TOM JONES *Decca SKL 5007*	**2**	13 wks
4 Oct 69	THIS IS TOM JONES (re-entry) *Decca SKL 5007*	**11**	4 wks
15 Nov 69	●TOM JONES LIVE IN LAS VEGAS *Decca SKL 5032*	**2**	28 wks

Date	Title Label Number	Position

K

Bert KAEMPFERT *Germany, orchestra leader*

Date	Title Label Number	Position	
5 Mar 66	●BYE BYE BLUES *Polydor BM 84086*	4	22 wks
16 Apr 66	BEST OF BERT KAEMPFERT *Polydor 84-012*	27	1 wk
28 May 66	SWINGING SAFARI *Polydor LPHM 46-384*	20	15 wks
30 Jul 66	STRANGERS IN THE NIGHT *Polydor 84-053*	13	21 wks
4 Feb 67	STRANGERS IN THE NIGHT (re-entry) *Polydor 84-053*	36	5 wks
4 Feb 67	RELAXING SOUND OF BERT KAEMPFERT *Polydor 583-501*	33	3 wks
18 Feb 67	BERT KAEMPFERT—BEST SELLER *Polydor 583-551*	25	18 wks
29 Apr 67	HOLD ME *Polydor 184-072*	36	5 wks
26 Aug 67	KAEMPFERT SPECIAL *Polydor 236-207*	24	5 wks

Ben E. KING *US, male vocalist*

1 Jul 67	SPANISH HARLEM *Atlantic 590-001*	30	3 wks

Solomon KING *US, male vocalist*

22 Jun 68	SHE WEARS MY RING *Columbia SCX 6250*	40	1 wk

KING CRIMSON

UK, male vocal/instrumental group

1 Nov 69	●IN THE COURT OF THE CRIMSON KING *Island ILPS 9111*	5	8 wks

KINKS *UK, male vocal/instrumental group*

17 Oct 64	●KINKS *Pye NPL 18069*	3	25 wks
13 Mar 65	●KINDA KINKS *Pye NPL 18112*	3	15 wks
4 Dec 65	●KINKS KONTROVERSY *Pye NPL 18131*	9	12 wks
11 Sep 66	●WELL RESPECTED KINKS *Marble Arch MAL 612*	5	31 wks
5 Nov 66	FACE TO FACE *Pye NPL 18149*	12	11 wks
14 Oct 67	SOMETHING ELSE *Pye NSPL 18193*	35	2 wks
2 Dec 67	●SUNNY AFTERNOON *Marble Arch MAL 716*	9	11 wks

Kathy KIRBY *UK, female vocalist*

4 Jan 64	16 HITS FROM 'STARS AND GARTERS' *Decca LK 4575*	11	8 wks

Eartha KITT *US, female vocalist*

11 Feb 61	REVISITED *London HA 2296*	17	1 wk

Curtis KNIGHT — See *Jimi HENDRIX and Curtis KNIGHT*

KNIGHTSBRIDGE STRINGS *UK, orchestra*

25 Jun 60	STRING AWAY *Top Rank BUY 017*	20	1 wk

Billy J. KRAMER and the DAKOTAS

UK, male vocalist and male instrumental backing group

Date	Title Label Number	Position	
16 Nov 63	LISTEN TO BILLY J. KRAMER *Parlophone PMC 1209*	11	9 wks
25 Jan 64	LISTEN TO BILLY J. KRAMER (re-entry) *Parlophone PMC 1209*	19	2 wks
7 Mar 64	LISTEN TO BILLY J. KRAMER (2nd re-entry) *Parlophone PMC 1209*	12	6 wks

Charlie KUNZ *US, male instrumentalist - piano*

14 Jun 69	●THE WORLD OF CHARLIE KUNZ *Decca SPA 15*	9	6 wks
2 Aug 69	THE WORLD OF CHARLIE KUNZ (re-entry) *Decca SPA 15*	24	1 wk
16 Aug 69	THE WORLD OF CHARLIE KUNZ (2nd re-entry) *Decca SPA 15*	29	2 wks
13 Sep 69	THE WORLD OF CHARLIE KUNZ (3rd re-entry) *Decca SPA 15*	23	1 wk
4 Oct 69	THE WORLD OF CHARLIE KUNZ (4th re-entry) *Decca SPA 15*	33	1 wk

L

Frankie LAINE *US, male vocalist*

24 Jun 61	HELL BENT FOR LEATHER *Philips BBL 7468*	16	1 wk
8 Jul 61	●HELL BENT FOR LEATHER (re-entry) *Philips BBL 7468*	7	19 wks
13 Jan 62	HELL BENT FOR LEATHER (2nd re-entry) *Philips BBL 7468*	19	2 wks
3 Feb 62	HELL BENT FOR LEATHER (3rd re-entry) *Philips BBL 7468*	12	1 wk

Mario LANZA *US, male vocalist*

9 Jan 60	●THE STUDENT PRINCE/ THE GREAT CARUSO *RCA RB 16113*	5	5 wks
20 Feb 60	●THE STUDENT PRINCE/ THE GREAT CARUSO (re-entry) *RCA RB 16113*	8	3 wks
2 Apr 60	THE STUDENT PRINCE/ THE GREAT CARUSO (2nd re-entry) *RCA RB 16113*	20	1 wk
23 Jul 60	●THE GREAT CARUSO *RCA RB 16112*	3	15 wks
29 Apr 61	THE STUDENT PRINCE/ THE GREAT CARUSO (3rd re-entry) *RCA RB 16113*	19	1 wk

The Great Caruso side of the first LP is a film soundtrack.

Date	Title Label Number	Position

James LAST *UK, orchestra leader*

Date	Title Label Number	Position	
15 Apr 67	●THIS IS JAMES LAST *Polydor 104-678*	**6**	46 wks
22 Jul 67	HAMMOND A-GO-GO *Polydor 249-043*	**27**	10 wks
26 Aug 67	NON-STOP DANCING *Polydor 236-203*	**35**	1 wk
26 Aug 67	LOVE THIS IS MY SONG *Polydor 583-553*	**32**	2 wks
22 Jun 68	JAMES LAST GOES POP *Polydor 249-160*	**32**	3 wks
8 Feb 69	DANCING '68 Vol 1 *Polydor 249-216*	**40**	1 wk
31 May 69	TRUMPET A-GO-GO *Polydor 249-239*	**13**	1 wk
5 Jul 69	THIS IS JAMES LAST (re-entry) *Polydor 104-678*	**34**	1 wk
19 Jul 69	THIS IS JAMES LAST (2nd re-entry) *Polydor 104-678*	**36**	1 wk
9 Aug 69	NON-STOP DANCING '69 *Polydor 249-294*	**26**	1 wk

LED ZEPPELIN *UK, male vocal/instrumental group*

Date	Title Label Number	Position	
12 Apr 69	●LED ZEPPELIN *Atlantic 588-171*	**9**	1 wk
26 Apr 69	●LED ZEPPELIN (re-entry) *Atlantic 588-171*	**6**	6 wks
28 Jun 69	LED ZEPPELIN (2nd re-entry) *Atlantic 588-171*	**11**	16 wks
25 Oct 69	LED ZEPPELIN (3rd re-entry) *Atlantic 588-171*	**24**	1 wk
8 Nov 69	★LED ZEPPELIN 2 *Atlantic 588-198*	**1**	97 wks

Brenda LEE *US, female vocalist*

Date	Title Label Number	Position	
24 Nov 62	ALL THE WAY *Brunswick LAT 8383*	**20**	2 wks
16 Feb 63	BRENDA—THAT'S ALL *Brunswick LAT 8516*	**17**	2 wks
30 Mar 63	BRENDA—THAT'S ALL (re-entry) *Brunswick LAT 8516*	**13**	7 wks
13 Apr 63	●ALL ALONE AM I *Brunswick LAT 8530*	**8**	16 wks
10 Aug 63	ALL ALONE AM I (re-entry) *Brunswick LAT 8530*	**14**	4 wks
16 Jul 66	BYE BYE BLUES *Brunswick LAT 8649*	**21**	2 wks

Peggy LEE *US, female vocalist*

Date	Title Label Number	Position	
4 Jun 60	●LATIN A LA LEE *Capitol T 1290*	**9**	2 wks
25 Jun 60	●LATIN A LA LEE (re-entry) *Capitol T 1290*	**8**	3 wks
23 Jul 60	●LATIN A LA LEE (2nd re-entry) *Capitol T 1290*	**8**	2 wks
13 Aug 60	LATIN A LA LEE (3rd re-entry) *Capitol T 1290*	**19**	1 wk
10 Sep 60	LATIN A LA LEE (4th re-entry) *Capitol T 1290*	**18**	4 wks
20 May 61	LATIN A LA LEE (5th re-entry) *Capitol T 1290*	**16**	2 wks
20 May 61	BEST OF PEGGY LEE Vol 2 *Brunswick LAT 8355*	**18**	1 wk
17 Jun 61	LATIN A LA LEE (6th re-entry) *Capitol T 1290*	**20**	1 wk
21 Oct 61	BLACK COFFEE *Ace of Hearts AH 5*	**20**	1 wk

See also Peggy Lee and George Shearing.

Peggy LEE and George SHEARING

US, female vocalist and UK, male band leader

Date	Title Label Number	Position	
11 Jun 60	BEAUTY AND THE BEAT *Capitol T 1219*	**18**	1 wk
20 Aug 60	BEAUTY AND THE BEAT (re-entry) *Capitol T 1219*	**18**	1 wk
1 Oct 60	BEAUTY AND THE BEAT (2nd re-entry) *Capitol T 1219*	**16**	1 wk
22 Apr 61	BEAUTY AND THE BEAT (3rd re-entry) *Capitol T 1219*	**18**	1 wk
26 Aug 61	BEAUTY AND THE BEAT (4th re-entry) *Capitol T 1219*	**20**	2 wks

See also Peggy Lee; Nat 'King' Cole and the George Shearing Quintet.

Raymond LEFEVRE *France, orchestra leader*

Date	Title Label Number	Position	
7 Oct 67	●RAYMOND LEFEVRE *Major Minor MMLP 4*	**10**	7 wks
17 Feb 68	RAYMOND LEFEVRE Vol 2 *Major Minor SMLP 13*	**37**	1 wk
2 Mar 68	RAYMOND LEFEVRE Vol 2 (re-entry) *Major Minor SMLP 13*	**37**	1 wk

Tom LEHRER *US, male vocalist*

Date	Title Label Number	Position	
25 Jun 60	●AN EVENING WASTED WITH TOM LEHRER *Decca LK 4332*	**7**	3 wks
25 Jun 60	SONGS BY TOM LEHRER *Decca LF 1311*	**17**	1 wk
30 Jul 60	AN EVENING WASTED WITH TOM LEHRER (re-entry) *Decca LK 4332*	**15**	1 wk
13 Aug 60	AN EVENING WASTED WITH TOM LEHRER (2nd re-entry) *Decca LK 4332*	**14**	3 wks
1 Oct 61	SONGS BY TOM LEHRER (re-entry) *Decca LF 1311*	**19**	2 wks

Jerry Lee LEWIS

US, male vocalist/instrumentalist - piano

Date	Title Label Number	Position	
2 Jun 62	JERRY LEE LEWIS Vol 2 *London HA 2440*	**14**	6 wks

Ramsey LEWIS TRIO

US, male vocal/instrumental group

Date	Title Label Number	Position	
21 May 66	HANG ON RAMSEY *Chess CRL 4520*	**20**	4 wks

Josef LOCKE

Date	Title Label Number	Position	
28 Jun 69	THE WORLD OF JOSEF LOCKE TODAY *Decca SPA 21*	**29**	1 wk

LONDON PHILHARMONIC CHOIR

UK, choir

Date	Title Label Number	Position	
3 Dec 60	●THE MESSIAH *Pye Golden Guinea GGL 0062*	**10**	7 wks

Full label credit reads 'London Philharmonic Choir with the London Orchestra conducted by Walter Suskind'.

LONDON PHILHARMONIC ORCHESTRA

UK, orchestra

Date	Title Label Number	Position	
23 Apr 60	RAVEL'S BOLERO *London HAU 2189*	**15**	1 wk
14 May 60	RAVEL'S BOLERO (re-entry) *London HAU 2189*	**18**	2 wks
11 Jun 60	RAVEL'S BOLERO (2nd re-entry) *London HAU 2189*	**16**	1 wk
8 Apr 61	VICTORY AT SEA *Pye GGL 0073*	**12**	1 wk

John MAYALL and the BLUESBREAKERS. The line-up of Mayall's Autumn '67 band. It stayed stable long enough for the picture to be taken. *Pictorial Press.*

Jose FELICIANO *Left* A Puerto Rican raised in Harlem, he was discovered singing at the Cafe Id in New York's Greenwich Village.

Jimi HENDRIX *Below*
James Marshall Hendrix,
27 November 1942 – 18 December 1970.

FOUR TOPS *Above* From Cleveland, Ohio, they first came to Britain in 1965, the year of their first hit here.

Date	Title *Label Number*	Position		Date	Title *Label Number*	Position

Trini LOPEZ *US, male vocalist*

26 Oct 63	●TRINI LOPEZ AT P.J.'S *Reprise R 6093*	**7**	25 wks
25 Mar 67	●TRINI LOPEZ IN LONDON	**6**	17 wks
	Reprise RSLP 6238		

Sophia LOREN — See *Peter SELLERS and Sophia LOREN*

LOVE *US, male vocal/instrumental group*

24 Feb 68	FOREVER CHANGES *Elektra EKS7 4013*	**24**	6 wks

LOVIN' SPOONFUL

US, male vocal/instrumental group

7 May 67	●DAYDREAM *Pye NPL 28078*	**8**	11 wks

Bob LUMAN *US, male vocalist*

14 Jan 61	LET'S THINK ABOUT LIVING	**18**	1 wk
	Warner Bros. WM 4025		

M

Frankie McBRIDE *Ireland, male vocalist*

17 Feb 68	FRANKIE McBRIDE *Emerald SLD 28*	**29**	1 wk
2 Mar 68	FRANKIE McBRIDE (re-entry)	**34**	2 wks
	Emerald SLD 28		

Kenneth McKELLAR *UK, male vocalist*

28 Jun 69	THE WORLD OF KENNETH McKELLAR	**33**	1 wk
	Decca SPA 11		
19 Jul 69	THE WORLD OF KENNETH McKELLAR	**29**	1 wk
	(re-entry) *Decca SPA 11*		
2 Aug 69	THE WORLD OF KENNETH McKELLAR	**27**	4 wks
	(2nd re-entry) *Decca SPA 11*		
20 Sep 69	THE WORLD OF KENNETH McKELLAR	**29**	1 wk
	(3rd re-entry) *Decca SPA 11*		

David McWILLIAMS *UK, male vocalist*

10 Jun 67	DAVID McWILLIAMS SINGS	**38**	1 wk
	Major Minor MMLP 2		
1 Jun 67	DAVID McWILLIAMS SINGS (re-entry)	**38**	1 wk
	Major Minor MMLP 2		
4 Nov 67	DAVID McWILLIAMS Vol 2	**23**	6 wks
	Major Minor MMLP 10		
9 Mar 68	DAVID McWILLIAMS Vol 3	**39**	1 wk
	Major Minor MMLP 11		

MAGIC BAND — See *Captain BEEFHEART and his MAGIC BAND*

Tommy MAKEM — See *CLANCY BROTHERS and Tommy MAKEM*

MAMAS and the PAPAS

US, male/female vocal group

25 Jun 66	●THE MAMAS AND THE PAPAS	**3**	18 wks
	RCA Victor RD 7803		
28 Jan 67	CASS, JOHN, MICHELLE, DENNY	**24**	6 wks
	RCA Victor SF 7639		
24 Jun 67	●MAMAS AND PAPAS DELIVER	**4**	22 wks
	RCA Victor SF 7880		
26 Apr 69	●HITS OF GOLD *Stateside S 5007*	**7**	1 wk
10 May 69	HITS OF GOLD (re-entry) *Stateside S 5007*	**14**	1 wk

MANFRED MANN

South Africa/UK, male vocal/instrumental group

19 Sep 64	●FIVE FACES OF MANFRED MANN	**3**	22 wks
	HMV CLP 1731		
27 Feb 65	FIVE FACES OF MANFRED MANN	**19**	2 wks
	(re-entry) *HMV CLP 1731*		
23 Oct 65	●MANN MADE *HMV CLP 1911*	**7**	11 wks
17 Sep 66	MANN MADE HITS *HMV CLP 3559*	**11**	18 wks
29 Oct 66	AS IS *Fontana TL 5377*	**22**	4 wks
21 Jan 67	SOUL OF MANN *HMV CSD 3594*	**40**	1 wk

Roberto MANN *UK, orchestra leader*

9 Dec 67	GREAT WALTZES *Deram SML 1010*	**19**	9 wks

Shelley MANN *US, male instrumentalist - drums*

18 Jun 60	MY FAIR LADY *Vogue LAC 12100*	**20**	1 wk

MANTOVANI *UK, orchestra leader*

9 Apr 60	●CONTINENTAL ENCORES *Decca LK 4298*	**10**	1 wk
18 Feb 61	CONTINENTAL SPECTACULAR	**16**	2 wks
	Decca LK 4377		
16 Apr 66	●MANTOVANI MAGIC *Decca LK 7949*	**3**	15 wks
15 Oct 66	MR MUSIC — MANTOVANI *Decca LK 4809*	**24**	3 wks
14 Jan 67	●MANTOVANI'S GOLDEN HITS	**10**	30 wks
	Decca SKL 4818		
30 Sep 67	HOLLYWOOD *Decca SKL 4887*	**37**	1 wk
8 Mar 69	●THE WORLD OF MANTOVANI *Decca SPA 1*	**6**	17 wks
4 Oct 69	●THE WORLD OF MANTOVANI Vol 2	**4**	1 wk
	Decca SPA 36		

MANUEL

UK, orchestra leader Geoff Love under pseudonym

10 Sep 60	MUSIC OF THE MOUNTAINS	**17**	1 wk
	Columbia 33SX 1212		

MOVE One of the great British songwriters, the moustachioed Roy Wood, attempts to surreptitiously remove somebody's hub cap.

MONKEES Davy, Peter and Micky do their Icarus impressions while Mike demonstrates the 1967 wooly bathing cap.

Jim REEVES *Left* Jim Reeves performs with his band on the Grand Ole Opry. *Pictorial Press*

Date	Title *Label Number*	Position

Dean MARTIN *US, male vocalist*

13 May 61	THIS TIME I'M SWINGING *Capitol T 1442*	18	1 wk
25 Feb 67	AT EASE WITH DEAN *Reprise RSLP 6322*	35	1 wk
4 Nov 67	WELCOME TO MY WORLD *Philips DBL 001*	39	1 wk
12 Oct 68	GREATEST HITS Vol 1 *Reprise RSLP 6301*	40	1 wk
22 Feb 69	●BEST OF DEAN MARTIN *Capitol ST 21194*	9	1 wk
22 Feb 69	GENTLE ON MY MIND *Reprise RSLP 6330*	11	1 wk
22 Mar 69	GENTLE ON MY MIND (re-entry) *Reprise RSLP 6330*	15	1 wk
12 Apr 69	●GENTLE ON MY MIND (2nd re-entry) *Reprise RSLP 6330*	9	4 wks
24 May 69	GENTLE ON MY MIND (3rd re-entry) *Reprise RSLP 6330*	13	1 wk
28 Jun 69	GENTLE ON MY MIND (4th re-entry) *Reprise RSLP 6330*	40	1 wk

George MARTIN — See *BEATLES*

Hank MARVIN
UK, male vocalist/instrumentalist - guitar

22 Nov 69	HANK MARVIN *Columbia SCX 6352*	14	2 wks

MARY — See *PETER, PAUL and MARY*

MASSED WELSH CHOIRS *UK, choir*

9 Aug 69	●CYMANSA GANN *BBC REC 53 M*	5	6 wks
27 Sep 69	CYMANSA GANN (re-entry) *BBC REC 53 M*	21	1 wk

Mirielle MATHIEU *France, female vocalist*

2 Mar 68	MIRIELLE MATHIEU *Columbia SCX 6210*	39	1 wk

Johnny MATHIS *US, male vocalist*

13 Feb 60	●RIDE ON A RAINBOW *Fontana TFL 5061*	10	1 wk
26 Mar 60	RIDE ON A RAINBOW (re-entry) *Fontana TFL 5061*	11	1 wk
10 Dec 60	●RHYTHMS AND BALLADS OF BROADWAY *Fontana SET 101*	6	10 wks
17 Jun 61	I'LL BUY YOU A STAR *Fontana TFL 5143*	18	1 wk

John MAYALL
UK, male vocalist/instrumentalist - keyboards

4 Mar 67	●A HARD ROAD *Decca SKL 4853*	10	19 wks
23 Sep 67	●CRUSADE *Decca SKL 4890*	8	14 wks
25 Nov 67	BLUES ALONE *Ace of Clubs SCL 1243*	24	5 wks
16 Mar 68	DIARY OF A BAND Vol 1 *Decca SKL 4918*	27	9 wks
16 Mar 68	DIARY OF A BAND Vol 2 *Decca SKL 4919*	28	5 wks
20 Jul 68	●BARE WIRES *Decca SKL 4945*	3	17 wks
18 Jan 69	BLUES FROM LAUREL CANYON *Decca SKL 4972*	33	3 wks
23 Aug 69	LOOKING BACK *Decca SKL 5010*	14	6 wks
18 Oct 69	LOOKING BACK (re-entry) *Decca SKL 5010*	23	1 wk
15 Nov 69	TURNING POINT *Polydor 583-571*	11	3 wks

A Hard Road *credited to John Mayall and the Bluesbreakers;* Crusade *to John Mayall and his Bluesbreakers;* Diary of a Band Vols 1 & 2 *to John Mayall's Bluesbreakers;* Bare Wire *to John Mayall Bluesbreakers. See also John Mayall and Eric Clapton.*

John MAYALL and Eric CLAPTON
UK, male vocal/instrumental duo - keyboards and guitar

30 Jul 66	●BLUES BREAKERS *Decca LK 4804*	6	17 wks

See also John Mayall.

Vaughn MEADER *US, comedian*

29 Dec 62	THE FIRST FAMILY *London HAA 8048*	12	7 wks
9 Mar 3	THE FIRST FAMILY (re-entry) *London HAA 8048*	16	1 wk

MERSEYBEATS *UK, male vocal/instrumental group*

20 Jun 64	THE MERSEYBEATS *Fontana TL 5210*	12	8 wks
22 Aug 64	THE MERSEYBEATS (re-entry) *Fontana TL 5210*	17	1 wk

M.G.s — See *Booker T and the M.G.s.*

MICK — See *Dave Dee, Dozy, Beaky, Mick and Tich.*

Glenn MILLER *US, orchestra leader*

28 Jan 61	●GLENN MILLER PLAYS SELECTIONS FROM 'THE GLENN MILLER STORY' AND OTHER HITS *RCA RD 27068*	10	5 wks
11 Mar 61	GLENN MILLER PLAYS SELECTIONS FROM 'THE GLENN MILLER STORY' AND OTHER HITS (re-entry) *RCA RD 27068*	19	2 wks
5 Jul 69	●BEST OF GLENN MILLER *RCA International INTS 1002*	5	14 wks
19 Jul 69	GLENN MILLER PLAYS SELECTIONS FROM 'THE GLENN MILLER STORY' AND OTHER HITS (2nd re-entry) *RCA RD 27068*	30	1 wk
2 Aug 69	GLENN MILLER PLAYS SELECTIONS FROM 'THE GLENN MILLER STORY' AND OTHER HITS (3rd re-entry) *RCA RD 27068*	40	1 wk
16 Aug 69	GLENN MILLER PLAYS SELECTIONS FROM 'THE GLENN MILLER STORY' AND OTHER HITS (4th re-entry) *RCA RD 27068*	28	1 wk
6 Sep 69	NEARNESS OF YOU *RCA International INTS 1019*	30	2 wks

Spike MILLIGAN *UK, comedian*

25 Nov 61	MILLIGAN PRESERVED *Parlophone PMC 1152*	11	4 wks

See also Harry Secombe, Peter Sellers and Spike Milligan.

Mrs. MILLS *UK, female instrumentalist - piano*

10 Dec 66	COME TO MY PARTY *Parlophone PMC 7010*	17	7 wks
28 Dec 68	MRS MILLS' PARTY PIECES *Parlophone PCS 7066*	32	3 wks
3 Dec 69	LET'S HAVE ANOTHER PARTY *Parlophone PCS 7035*	23	2 wks

Diana ROSS and the SUPREMES
The Supremes let their chart success go to their calves
Pictorial Press

Date	Title Label Number	Position		Date	Title Label Number	Position	

MINDBENDERS UK, male vocal/instrumental group

25 Jun 66	**THE MINDBENDERS** Fontana TL 5324	28	4 wks

See also Wayne Fontana and the Mindbenders.

George MITCHELL MINSTRELS

UK, male/female vocal group

26 Nov 60	★**THE BLACK AND WHITE MINSTREL SHOW** HMV CLP 1399	1	125 wks
21 Oct 61	★**ANOTHER BLACK AND WHITE MINSTREL SHOW** HMV CLP 1460	1	47 wks
22 Sep 62	**ANOTHER BLACK AND WHITE MINSTREL SHOW** (re-entry) HMV CLP 1460	14	4 wks
20 Oct 62	★**ON STAGE WITH THE GEORGE MITCHELL MINSTRELS** HMV CLP 1599	1	25 wks
29 Oct 62	**ANOTHER BLACK AND WHITE MINSTREL SHOW** (2nd re-entry) HMV CLP 1460	19	1 wk
1 Dec 62	●**ANOTHER BLACK AND WHITE MINSTREL SHOW** (3rd re-entry) HMV CLP 1460	5	10 wks
16 Feb 63	**ANOTHER BLACK AND WHITE MINSTREL SHOW** (4th re-entry) HMV CLP 1460	17	1 wk
27 Apr 63	**THE BLACK AND WHITE MINSTREL SHOW** (re-entry) HMV CLP 1399	13	7 wks
22 Jun 63	**THE BLACK AND WHITE MINSTREL SHOW** (2nd re-entry) HMV CLP 1399	19	1 wk
20 Jul 63	**THE BLACK AND WHITE MINSTREL SHOW** (3rd re-entry) HMV CLP 1399	11	4 wks
12 Oct 63	**ON STAGE WITH THE GEORGE MITCHELL MINSTRELS** (re-entry) HMV CLP 1599	20	1 wk
2 Nov 63	**ON TOUR WITH THE GEORGE MITCHELL MINSTRELS** HMV CLP 1667	20	1 wk
16 Nov 63	●**ON TOUR WITH THE GEORGE MITCHELL MINSTRELS** (re-entry) HMV CLP 1667	6	17 wks
7 Dec 63	**THE BLACK AND WHITE MINSTREL SHOW** (4th re-entry) HMV CLP 1399	11	5 wks
21 Dec 63	**ANOTHER BLACK AND WHITE MINSTREL SHOW** (5th re-entry) HMV CLP 1460	15	1 wk
12 Dec 64	●**SPOTLIGHT ON THE GEORGE MITCHELL MINSTRELS** HMV CLP 1803	6	7 wks
4 Dec 65	●**MAGIC OF THE MINSTRELS** HMV CLP 1917	9	7 wks
26 Nov 66	**HERE COME THE MINSTRELS** HMV CLP 3579	11	11 wks
16 Dec 67	**SHOWTIME** HMV CSD 3642	26	2 wks
14 Dec 68	**SING THE IRVING BERLIN SHOWBOOK** Columbia SCX 6267	33	1 wk

Zoot MONEY and the BIG ROLL BAND

UK, male vocalist/instrumentalist - keyboards and male vocal/instrumental group

15 Oct 66	**ZOOT** Columbia SX 6075	23	2 wks
5 Nov 66	**ZOOT** (re-entry) Columbia SX 6075	30	1 wk

MONKEES US/UK, male vocal/instrumental group

28 Jan 67	★**THE MONKEES** RCA Victor SF 7844	1	36 wks
15 Apr 67	★**MORE OF THE MONKEES** RCA Victor SF 7868	1	25 wks
8 Jul 67	●**HEADQUARTERS** RCA Victor SF 7886	2	19 wks
13 Jan 68	●**PISCES, AQUARIUS, CAPRICORN & JONES LTD.** RCA Victor SF 7912	5	11 wks

Matt MONRO UK, male vocalist

7 Aug 65	**I HAVE DREAMED** Parlophone PMC 1250	20	1 wk
17 Sep 66	**THIS IS MY LIFE** Capitol T 2540	25	2 wks
26 Aug 67	**INVITATION TO THE MOVIES** Capitol ST 2730	30	1 wk

MOODY BLUES UK, male vocal/instrumental group

27 Jan 68	**DAYS OF FUTURE PASSED** Deram SML 707	27	7 wks
3 Aug 68	●**IN SEARCH OF THE LOST CHORD** Deram SML 711	5	21 wks
3 May 69	★**ON THE THRESHOLD OF A DREAM** Deram SML 1035	1	26 wks
8 Nov 69	**ON THE THRESHOLD OF A DREAM** (re-entry) Deram SML 1035	21	2 wks
6 Dec 69	●**TO OUR CHILDREN'S CHILDREN'S CHILDREN** Threshold THS 1	2	21 wks

Dudley MOORE

UK, male vocalist/instrumentalist - piano

4 Dec 65	**THE OTHER SIDE OF DUDLEY MOORE** Decca LK 4732	11	9 wks
11 Jun 66	**GENUINE DUD** Decca LK 4788	13	10 wks

Second album credited to The Dudley Moore Trio. See also Peter Cook and Dudley Moore.

MOTHERS OF INVENTION

US, male vocal/instrumental group

29 Jun 68	**WE'RE ONLY IN IT FOR THE MONEY** Verve SVLP 9199	32	5 wks

Nana MOUSKOURI Greece, female vocalist

7 Jun 69	**OVER AND OVER** Fontana S 5511	14	2 wks
5 Jul 69	**OVER AND OVER** (re-entry) Fontana S 5511	22	5 wks

MOVE UK, male vocal/instrumental group

13 Apr 68	**MOVE** Regal Zonophone SLPZ 1002	15	9 wks

Gerry MULLIGAN and Ben WEBSTER

US, male instrumental duo - baritone and tenor sax

24 Sep 60	**GERRY MULLIGAN MEETS BEN WEBSTER** HMV CLP 1373	15	1 wk

Date	Title *Label Number*	Position	Date	Title *Label Number*	Position

N

NASH — See *CROSBY, STILLS and NASH.*

NEW WORLD THEATRE ORCHESTRA

UK, orchestra

24 Dec 60	**LET'S DANCE TO THE HITS OF THE 30's AND 40's** *Pye Golden Guinea GGL 0026*	**20**	1 wk

Bob NEWHART *US, male comedian*

1 Oct 60	●**BUTTON DOWN MIND OF BOB NEWHART** *Warner Bros. WM 4010*	**2**	24 wks
29 Apr 61	**BUTTON DOWN MIND OF BOB NEWHART** (re-entry) *Warner Bros. WM 4010*	**12**	3 wks
27 May 61	**BUTTON DOWN MIND OF BOB NEWHART** (2nd re-entry) *Warner Bros. WM 4010*	**14**	5 wks
27 May 61	●**BUTTON DOWN MIND OF BOB NEWHART** (3rd re-entry) *Warner Bros. WM 4010*	**2**	3 wks

Anthony NEWLEY *UK, male vocalist*

14 May 60	**LOVE IS A NOW AND THEN THING** *Decca LK 4343*	**19**	2 wks
8 Jul 61	●**TONY** *Decca LK 4406*	**5**	12 wks

See also Anthony Newley, Peter Sellers, Joan Collins.

Anthony NEWLEY, Peter SELLERS, Joan COLLINS

UK, male/female comic trio

28 Sep 63	●**FOOL BRITANNIA** *Ember CEL 902*	**10**	10 wks

See also Anthony Newley; Harry Secombe, Peter Sellers and Spike Milligan; Peter Sellers; Peter Sellers and Sophia Loren.

NICE *UK, male instrumental group*

13 Sep 69	●**NICE** *Immediate IMSP 026*	**3**	5 wks
1 Nov 69	**NICE** (re-entry) *Immediate IMSP 026*	**22**	1 wk

NINA and FREDERICK

Denmark, male/female vocal duo

13 Feb 60	●**NINA AND FREDERICK** *Pye NPT 19023*	**9**	1 wk
16 Apr 60	**NINA AND FREDERICK** (re-entry) *Pye NPT 19023*	**20**	1 wk
29 Apr 61	**NINA AND FREDERICK** *Columbia 33SX 1214*	**11**	4 wks

These two albums, although identically named, are different.

O

Des O'CONNOR *UK, male vocalist*

7 Dec 68	●**I PRETEND** *Columbia SCX 6295*	**8**	10 wks

Esther and Abi OFARIM

Israel, male/female vocal duo

24 Feb 68	●**2 IN 3** *Philips SBL 7825*	**6**	20 wks
12 Jul 69	**OFARIM CONCERT-LIVE '69** *Philips XL 4*	**29**	1 wk
26 Jul 69	**OFARIM CONCERT-LIVE '69** (re-entry) *Philips XL 4*	**35**	2 wks
30 Aug 69	**OFARIM CONCERT-LIVE '69** (2nd re-entry) *Philips XL 4*	**37**	1 wk

101 STRINGS *Germany, orchestra*

19 Mar 60	●**GYPSY CAMP FIRES** *Pye GGL 0009*	**10**	3 wks
26 Mar 60	**SOUL OF SPAIN** *Pye GGL 0017*	**17**	1 wk
16 Apr 60	**GRAND CANYON SUITE** *Pye GGL 0048*	**10**	1 wk
16 Apr 60	**GYPSY CAMP FIRES** (re-entry) *Pye GGL 0009*	**16**	1 wk
27 Aug 60	**DOWN DRURY LANE TO MEMORY LANE** *Pye GGL 0061*	**1**	21 wks

Roy ORBISON *US, male vocalist*

8 Jun 63	**LONELY AND BLUE** *London HAU 2342*	**15**	8 wks
29 Jun 63	**CRYING** *London HAU 2437*	**17**	2 wks
30 Nov 63	●**IN DREAMS** *London HAU 8108*	**6**	58 wks
4 Jul 64	**CRYING** (re-entry) *London HAU 2437*	**19**	1 wk
25 Jul 64	**EXCITING SOUNDS OF ROY ORBISON** *Ember NR 5013*	**17**	2 wks
5 Dec 64	●**OH PRETTY WOMAN** *London HAU 8207*	**4**	16 wks
25 Sep 65	●**THERE IS ONLY ONE ROY ORBISON** *London HAU 8252*	**10**	12 wks
26 Feb 66	**THE ORBISON WAY** *London HAU 8279*	**11**	10 wks
24 Sep 66	**THE CLASSIC ROY ORBISON** *London HAU 8297*	**12**	8 wks
22 Jul 67	**ORBISONGS** *Monument SMO 5004*	**40**	1 wk
30 Sep 67	**ROY ORBISON'S GREATEST HITS** *Monument SMO 5007*	**40**	1 wk

P

PACEMAKERS — See *GERRY and the PACEMAKERS*

PAPAS — See *MAMAS and the PAPAS*

PAUL — See *PETER, PAUL and MARY*

Date	Title *Label Number*	Position

PEDDLERS *UK, male vocal/instrumental group*

Date	Title *Label Number*	Position	
16 Mar 68	FREE WHEELERS *CBS SBPG 63183*	37	2 wks
6 Apr 68	FREE WHEELERS (re-entry) *CBS SBPG 63183*	27	11 wks

PENTANGLE

UK, male/female vocal instrumental group

15 Jun 68	THE PENTANGLE *Transatlantic TRA 162*	21	9 wks
1 Nov 69	BASKET OF LIGHT *Transatlantic TRA 205*	16	4 wks
20 Dec 69	BASKET OF LIGHT (re-entry) *Transatlantic TRA 205*	20	1 wk

PERKY — See *PINKY and PERKY*

PETER and GORDON *UK, male vocal duo*

20 Jun 64	PETER AND GORDON *Columbia 33SX 1630*	18	1 wk

PETER, PAUL and MARY

US, male/female vocal instrumental group

4 Jan 64	PETER, PAUL AND MARY *Warner Bros. WM 4064*	18	1 wk
21 Mar 64	IN THE WIND *Warner Bros. WM 8142*	11	15 wks
11 Jul 64	IN THE WIND (re-entry) *Warner Bros. WM 8142*	15	2 wks
8 Aug 64	IN THE WIND (2nd re-entry) *Warner Bros. WM 8142*	13	1 wk
19 Sep 64	IN THE WIND (3rd re-entry) *Warner Bros. WM 8142*	19	1 wk
13 Feb 65	IN CONCERT Vol 1 *Warner Bros. WM 8142*	20	2 wks

PINK FLOYD *UK, male vocal/instrumental group*

19 Aug 67	●PIPER AT THE GATES OF DAWN *Columbia SCX 6157*	6	14 wks
13 Jul 68	●SAUCERFUL OF SECRETS *Columbia SCX 6258*	9	11 wks
28 Jun 69	●MORE (film soundtrack) *Columbia SCX 6346*	9	4 wks
2 Aug 69	MORE (film soundtrack) (re-entry) *Columbia SCX 6346*	37	1 wk
15 Nov 69	●UMMAGUMMA *Harvest SHGW 1/2*	5	5 wks

PINKY and PERKY *UK, male pig vocal duo*

8 Mar 69	PINKY AND PERKY'S HIT PARADE *MFP 1282*	30	1 wk

Gene PITNEY *US, male vocalist*

11 Apr 64	●BLUE GENE *United Artists ULP 1061*	7	11 wks
6 Feb 65	GENE PITNEY'S BIG 16 *Stateside SL 10118*	12	6 wks
20 Mar 65	I'M GONNA BE STRONG *Stateside SL 10120*	15	2 wks
20 Nov 65	LOOKIN' THROUGH THE EYES OF LOVE *Stateside SL 10148*	15	5 wks
17 Sep 66	NOBODY NEEDS YOUR LOVE *Stateside SL 10183*	13	17 wks

Date	Title *Label Number*	Position	
4 Mar 67	YOUNG WARM AND WONDERFUL *Stateside SSL 10194*	39	1 wk
22 Apr 67	GENE PITNEY'S BIG 16 (re-issue) *Stateside SSL 10199*	40	1 wk
20 Sep 69	●BEST OF GENE PITNEY *Stateside SSL 10286*	8	8 wks

Sandy POSEY *US, female vocalist*

11 Mar 67	BORN A WOMAN *MGM MGMCS 8035*	39	1 wk

Elvis PRESLEY *US, male vocalist*

16 Jan 60	●A DATE WITH ELVIS *RCA RD 27128*	8	1 wk
12 Mar 60	●ELVIS' GOLDEN RECORDS *RCA RB 16069*	7	1 wk
26 Mar 60	●ELVIS' GOLDEN RECORDS (re-entry) *RCA RB 16069*	10	3 wks
23 Apr 60	ELVIS' GOLDEN RECORDS (2nd re-entry) *RCA RB 16069*	11	3 wks
18 Jun 60	●ELVIS' GOLDEN RECORDS Vol 2 *RCA RD 27159*	4	16 wks
23 Jul 60	★ELVIS IS BACK *RCA RD 27171*	1	22 wks
15 Oct 60	ELVIS' GOLDEN RECORDS Vol 2 (re-entry) *RCA RD 27159*	16	1 wk
10 Dec 60	★GI BLUES (film soundtrack) *RCA RD 29192*	1	51 wks
7 Jan 61	ELVIS IS BACK (re-entry) *RCA RD 27171*	16	3 wks
4 Feb 61	ELVIS IS BACK (2nd re-entry) *RCA RD 27171*	18	1 wk
4 Mar 61	ELVIS IS BACK (3rd re-entry) *RCA RD 27171*	16	1 wk
20 May 61	●HIS HAND IN MINE *RCA RD 27211*	3	25 wks
4 Nov 61	●SOMETHING FOR EVERYBODY *RCA RD 27224*	2	13 wks
9 Dec 61	★BLUE HAWAII (film soundtrack) *RCA RD 27238*	1	65 wks
9 Dec 61	GI BLUES (re-entry) *RCA RD 29192*	12	1 wk
20 Jan 62	GI BLUES (2nd re-entry) *RCA RD 29192*	15	3 wks
17 Feb 62	SOMETHING FOR EVERYBODY (re-entry) *RCA RD 27224*	14	4 wks
31 Mar 62	ELVIS' GOLDEN RECORDS Vol 2 (2nd re-entry) *RCA RD 27159*	18	1 wk
14 Apr 62	SOMETHING FOR EVERYBODY (2nd re-entry) *RCA RD 27224*	18	1 wk
7 Jul 62	★POT LUCK *RCA RD 27265*	1	25 wks
13 Oct 62	ELVIS' GOLDEN RECORDS Vol 2 (3rd re-entry) *RCA RD 27159*	17	2 wks
8 Dec 62	●ROCK 'N' ROLL No 2 *RCA RD 7528*	3	17 wks
5 Jan 63	ELVIS' GOLDEN RECORDS (3rd re-entry) *RCA RB 16069*	16	1 wk
26 Jan 63	●GIRLS GIRLS GIRLS (film soundtrack) *RCA RD 7534*	2	21 wks
11 May 63	●IT HAPPENED AT THE WORLD'S FAIR (film soundtrack) *RCA RD 7565*	4	20 wks
12 Oct 63	IT HAPPENED AT THE WORLD'S FAIR (re-entry) *RCA RD 7565*	17	1 wk
28 Dec 63	FUN IN ACAPULCO (film soundtrack) *RCA RD 7069*	15	1 wk
11 Jan 64	●FUN IN ACAPULCO (re-entry) *RCA RD 7069*	9	13 wks
11 Apr 64	●ELVIS' GOLDEN RECORDS Vol 3 *RCA RD 7630*	6	13 wks
9 May 64	ELVIS' GOLDEN RECORDS (4th re-entry) *RCA RB 16069*	16	1 wk
4 Jul 64	●KISSIN COUSINS (film soundtrack) *RCA RD 7645*	5	17 wks
9 Jan 65	ROUSTABOUT (film soundtrack) *RCA RD 7678*	12	4 wks
1 May 65	●GIRL HAPPY (film soundtrack) *RCA RD 7714*	8	18 wks
25 Sep 65	FLAMING STAR AND SUMMER KISSES *RCA RD 7723*	11	4 wks
4 Dec 65	●ELVIS FOR EVERYBODY *RCA RD 7782*	8	8 wks

Date	Title *Label Number*	Position	
15 Jan 66	**HAREM HOLIDAY** (film soundtrack) *RCA RD 7767*	**11**	5 wks
30 Apr 66	**FRANKIE AND JOHNNY** (film soundtrack) *RCA RD 7793*	**11**	5 wks
6 Aug 66	●**PARADISE HAWAIIAN STYLE** (film soundtrack) *RCA Victor RD 7810*	**7**	9 wks
26 Nov 66	**CALIFORNIA HOLIDAY** *RCA Victor RD 7820*	**17**	6 wks
8 Apr 67	**HOW GREAT THOU ART** *RCA Victor SF 7867*	**11**	14 wks
2 Sep 67	**DOUBLE TROUBLE** (film soundtrack) *RCA Victor SF 7892*	**34**	1 wk
20 Apr 68	**CLAMBAKE** (film soundtrack) *RCA Victor SF 7917*	**39**	1 wk
3 May 69	●**ELVIS NBC TV SPECIAL** *RCA RD 8011*	**2**	7 wks
28 Jun 69	**ELVIS NBC TV SPECIAL** (re-entry) *RCA RD 8011*	**13**	5 wks
5 Jul 69	●**FLAMING STAR** *RCA International INTS 1012*	**2**	14 wks
16 Aug 69	**ELVIS NBC TV SPECIAL** (2nd re-entry) *RCA RD 8011*	**39**	1 wk
23 Aug 69	☆**FROM ELVIS IN MEMPHIS** *RCA SF 8029*	**1**	9 wks
30 Aug 69	**ELVIS NBC TV SPECIAL** (3rd re-entry) *RCA RD 8011*	**21**	1 wk
1 Nov 69	**FROM ELVIS IN MEMPHIS** (re-entry) *RCA SF 8029*	**20**	2 wks

Most of Elvis's film soundtracks included bonus tracks not featured in film.

PRETTY THINGS

UK, male vocal/instrumental group

27 Mar 65	●**PRETTY THINGS** *Fontana TL 5239*	**6**	10 wks

P. J. PROBY *US, male vocalist*

27 Feb 65	**I'M P. J. PROBY** *Liberty LBY 1235*	**16**	3 wks

PROCOL HARUM

UK, male vocal/instrumental group,

19 Jul 69	**A SALTY DOG** *Regal Zonophone SLRZ 1009*	**27**	2 wks

DOROTHY PROVINE *US, female vocalist*

2 Dec 61	●**THE ROARING TWENTIES—SONGS FROM THE TV SERIES** *Warner Bros. WM 4035*	**3**	42 wks
10 Feb 62	●**VAMP OF THE ROARING TWENTIES** *Warner Bros. WM 4053*	**9**	7 wks

Gary PUCKETT and the UNION GAP

US, male vocalist and male instrumental group

29 Jun 68	**UNION GAP** *CBS 63342*	**24**	4 wks

QUEDO BRASS — See *CHAQUITO and QUEDO BRASS*

R

REBEL ROUSERS — See *Cliff BENNETT and the REBEL ROUSERS*

RAM JAM BAND — See *Geno WASHINGTON and the RAM JAM BAND*

Otis REDDING *US, male vocalist*

19 Feb 66	●**OTIS BLUE** *Atlantic ATL 5041*	**6**	21 wks
23 Apr 66	**SOUL BALLADS** *Atlantic ATL 5029*	**30**	1 wk
23 Jul 66	**SOUL ALBUM** *Atlantic 587 011*	**25**	3 wks
20 Aug 66	**SOUL ALBUM** (re-entry) *Atlantic 587 011*	**22**	3 wks
1 Oct 66	**SOUL ALBUM** (2nd re-entry) *Atlantic 587 011*	**24**	3 wks
21 Jan 67	**OTIS REDDING'S DICTIONARY OF SOUL** *Atlantic 588 050*	**23**	16 wks
21 Jan 67	**OTIS BLUE** (re-issue) *Atlantic 587 036*	**34**	3 wks
29 Apr 67	**PAIN IN MY HEART** *Atlantic 587 042*	**28**	9 wks
5 Aug 67	**OTIS BLUE** (re-entry of re-issue) *Atlantic 587 036*	**29**	11 wks
30 Dec 67	●**OTIS BLUE** (2nd re-entry of re-issue) *Atlantic 587 036*	**7**	40 wks
10 Feb 68	●**HISTORY OF OTIS REDDING** *Volt S 418*	**2**	43 wks
30 Mar 68	**OTIS REDDING IN EUROPE** *Stax 589 016*	**14**	16 wks
1 Jun 68	**DOCK OF THE BAY** *Stax 231 001*	**1**	15 wks
12 Oct 68	**IMMORTAL OTIS REDDING** *Atlantic 588 113*	**19**	8 wks

See also Otis Redding and Carla Thomas.

Otis REDDING and Carla THOMAS

US, male and female vocal duo

1 Jul 67	**KING AND QUEEN** *Atlantic 589 007*	**35**	1 wk
19 Aug 67	**KING AND QUEEN** (re-entry) *Atlantic 589 007*	**26**	1 wk
2 Sep 67	**KING AND QUEEN** (2nd re-entry) *Atlantic 589 007*	**18**	15 wks

See also Otis Redding.

Jim REEVES *US, male vocalist*

28 Mar 64	**GOOD 'N' COUNTRY** *RCA Camden CDN 5114*	**11**	5 wks
9 May 64	**GENTLEMAN JIM** *RCA RD 7541*	**18**	2 wks
15 Aug 64	●**GENTLEMAN JIM** (re-entry) *RCA RD 7541*	**3**	21 wks
15 Aug 64	●**GOOD 'N' COUNTRY** (re-entry) *RCA Camden CDN 5114*	**10**	15 wks
15 Aug 64	●**A TOUCH OF VELVET** *RCA RD 7521*	**8**	9 wks
15 Aug 64	**INTERNATIONAL JIM REEVES** *RCA RD 7577*	**14**	4 wks
22 Aug 64	**HE'LL HAVE TO GO** *RCA RD 27176*	**16**	4 wks
29 Aug 64	**THE INTIMATE JIM REEVES** *RCA RD 27193*	**17**	1 wk
29 Aug 64	●**GOD BE WITH YOU** *RCA RD 7636*	**10**	10 wks
5 Sep 64	●**MOONLIGHT AND ROSES** *RCA RD 7639*	**2**	25 wks
19 Sep 64	**COUNTRY SIDE OF JIM REEVES** *RCA Camden CDN 5100*	**12**	3 wks
26 Sep 64	**INTERNATIONAL JIM REEVES** (re-entry) *RCA RD 7577*	**11**	7 wks
26 Sep 64	**WE THANK THEE** *RCA RD 7637*	**18**	1 wk
10 Oct 64	**WE THANK THEE** (re-entry) *RCA RD 7637*	**17**	2 wks
24 Oct 64	**THE INTIMATE JIM REEVES** (re-entry) *RCA RD 27193*	**12**	3 wks

SAM and DAVE *Above*
Soul hommes Sam et Dave on
stage in Paris.

SEEKERS *Above Right* Beginning
– 1965 with a number one single.
End – 1968 with a number one LP.

SIMON and GARFUNKEL *Below*
324 weeks on the Album chart,
53 weeks on the Singles chart
and 11 weeks on the EP chart.

Dusty SPRINGFIELD In the *NME* polls
voted Top World Female Singer '65, '66,
'67, '69; Top UK Female Singer '64, '65,
'66; and as one third of the Springfields
voted Top UK Vocal Group '61 and '62.

Date	Title *Label Number*	Position
7 Nov 64	**COUNTRY SIDE OF JIM REEVES** (re-entry) *RCA Camden CDN 5100*	17 2 wks
21 Nov 64	**INTERNATIONAL JIM REEVES** (2nd re-entry) *RCA RD 7577*	13 3 wks
28 Nov 64	●**TWELVE SONGS OF CHRISTMAS** *RCA RD7663*	4 9 wks
19 Dec 64	**INTERNATIONAL JIM REEVES** (3rd re-entry) *RCA RD 7577*	20 3 wks
30 Jan 65	●**BEST OF JIM REEVES** *RCA RD 7666*	3 20 wks
10 Apr 65	**HAVE I TOLD YOU LATELY THAT I LOVE YOU** *Camden CDN 5122*	19 1 wk
24 Apr 65	**HAVE I TOLD YOU LATELY THAT I LOVE YOU** (re-entry) *Camden CDN 5122*	12 4 wks
22 May 65	**THE JIM REEVES WAY** *RCA RD 7694*	16 4 wks
4 Dec 65	**MOONLIGHT AND ROSES** *RCA RD 7639*	12 1 wk
18 Jun 66	**MOONLIGHT AND ROSES** 2nd re-entry) *RCA RD 7639*	16 5 wks
8 Oct 66	**THE BEST OF JIM REEVES** (re-entry) *RCA RD 7666*	25 1 wk
22 Oct 66	**GOOD 'N' COUNTRY** (2nd re-entry) *RCA Camden CDN 5114*	17 15 wks
22 Oct 66	**MOONLIGHT AND ROSES** (3rd re-entry) *RCA RD 7639*	15 18 wks
29 Oct 66	●**THE BEST OF JIM REEVES** (2nd re-entry) *RCA RD 7666*	8 26 wks
5 Nov 66	●**DISTANT DRUMS** *RCA RD 7814*	2 31 wks
10 Dec 66	**TWELVE SONGS OF CHRISTMAS** (re-entry) *RCA RD 7663*	14 5 wks
28 Dec 68	**DISTANT DRUMS** (re-entry) *RCA RD 7814*	38 3 wks
18 Jan 69	**A TOUCH OF SADNESS** *RCA SF 7978*	27 4 wks
1 Mar 69	**A TOUCH OF SADNESS** (re-entry) *RCA SF 7978*	15 1 wk
5 Jul 69	★**ACCORDING TO MY HEART** *RCA International INTS 1013*	1 14 wks
23 Aug 69	**JIM REEVES AND SOME FRIENDS** *RCA SF 8022*	37 1 wk
6 Sep 69	**JIM REEVES AND SOME FRIENDS** (re-entry) *RCA SF 8022*	24 3 wks
29 Nov 69	**ON STAGE** *RCA SF 8047*	13 2 wks
27 Dec 69	**TWELVE SONGS OF CHRISTMAS** (2nd re-entry) *RCA RD 7663*	15 2 wks

Cliff RICHARD *UK, male vocalist*

Date	Title *Label Number*	Position
2 Jan 60	●**CLIFF** *Columbia 33SX 1147*	10 2 wks
2 Jan 60	●**CLIFF SINGS** *Columbia 33SX 1192*	2 11 wks
2 Apr 60	●**CLIFF SINGS** (re-entry) *Columbia 33SX 1192*	3 17 wks
6 Aug 60	**CLIFF SINGS** (2nd re-entry) *Columbia 33SX 1192*	14 1 wk
15 Oct 60	●**ME AND MY SHADOWS** *Columbia 33SX 1261*	2 33 wks
22 Apr 61	●**LISTEN TO CLIFF** *Columbia 33SX 1320*	2 26 wks
21 Oct 61	★**I'M 21 TODAY** *Columbia 33SX 1368*	1 16 wks
4 Nov 61	**LISTEN TO CLIFF** (re-entry) *Columbia 33SX 1320*	19 1 wk
18 Nov 61	**LISTEN TO CLIFF** (2nd re-entry) *Columbia 33SX 1320*	17 1 wk
23 Dec 61	★**THE YOUNG ONES** (film soundtrack) *Columbia 33SX 1384*	1 42 wks
29 Sep 62	●**32 MINUTES AND 17 SECONDS** *Columbia 33SX 1431*	3 21 wks
26 Jan 63	★**SUMMER HOLIDAY** (film soundtrack) *Columbia 33SX 1472*	1 36 wks
13 Jul 63	●**CLIFF'S HIT ALBUM** *Columbia 33SX 1512*	2 17 wks
28 Sep 63	●**WHEN IN SPAIN** *Columbia 33SX 1541*	8 10 wks
7 Dec 63	**CLIFF'S HIT ALBUM** (re-entry) *Columbia 33SX 1512*	17 1 wk
21 Dec 63	**CLIFF'S HIT ALBUM** (2nd re-entry) *Columbia 33SX 1512*	20 1 wk

Date	Title *Label Number*	Position
11 Jul 64	●**WONDERFUL LIFE** (film soundtrack) *Columbia 33SX 1628*	2 23 wks
9 Jan 65	**ALADDIN** (pantomime) *Columbia 33SX 1676*	13 5 wks
17 Apr 65	●**CLIFF RICHARD** *Columbia 33SX 1709*	9 5 wks
14 Aug 65	**MORE HITS BY CLIFF** *Columbia 33SX 1737*	20 1 wk
8 Jan 66	**LOVE IS FOREVER** *Columbia 33SX 1769*	19 1 wk
21 May 66	●**KINDA LATIN** *Columbia SX 6039*	9 12 wks
17 Dec 66	●**FINDERS KEEPERS** *Columbia SX 6079*	6 18 wks
7 Jan 67	**CINDERELLA** (pantomime) *Columbia SCX 6109*	30 6 wks
15 Apr 67	**DON'T STOP ME NOW . . .** *Columbia SCX 6039*	23 9 wks
11 Nov 67	**GOOD NEWS** *SCX 6167*	37 1 wk
1 Jun 68	**CLIFF IN JAPAN** *Columbia SCX 6244*	29 2 wks
16 Nov 68	**ESTABLISHED 1958** *Columbia SCX 6282*	30 4 wks
12 Jul 69	●**BEST OF CLIFF** *Columbia SCX 6343*	5 9 wks
27 Sep 69	**SINCERELY** *Columbia SCX 6357*	24 3 wks
4 Oct 69	**BEST OF CLIFF** (re-entry) *Columbia SCX 6343*	22 2 wks

Cliff credited to Cliff Richard and the Drifters. The Shadows featured on all or some tracks of the following albums: Cliff Sings, Me And My Shadows, Listen to Cliff, I'm 21 Today, The Young Ones, 32 Minutes and 17 Seconds, Summer Holiday, Cliff's Hit Album, When In Spain, Wonderful Life, Aladdin, More Hits by Cliff, Love is Forever, Finders Keepers, Cinderella, Established 1958, and Best Of Cliff. See also the Shadows.

NELSON RIDDLE — See Shirley BASSEY

Marty ROBBINS *US, male vocalist*

13 Aug 60	**GUNFIGHTER BALLADS** *Fontana TFL 5063*	20 1 wk

Paddy ROBERTS *South Africa, male vocalist*

16 Jan 60	●**STRICTLY FOR GROWN UPS** *Decca LK 1322*	10 1 wk
4 Jun 60	**STRICTLY FOR GROWN UPS** (re-entry) *Decca LK 1322*	20 1 wk
20 Aug 60	**STRICTLY FOR GROWN UPS** (2nd re-entry) *Decca LK 1322*	19 2 wks
17 Sep 60	**PADDY ROBERTS TRIES AGAIN** *Decca LK 4358*	16 1 wk

Clodagh RODGERS *UK, female vocalist*

13 Sep 69	**CLODAGH RODGERS** *RCA SF 8033*	27 1 wk

Ann ROGERS *UK, female vocalist*

8 Mar 69	**SOUND OF MUSIC** *MFP 1255*	30 1 wk

ROCKIN' BERRIES

UK, male vocal/instrumental group

19 Jun 65	**IN TOWN** *Pye NPL 38013*	15 1 wk

ROLLING STONES

UK, male vocal/instrumental group

25 Apr 64	★**ROLLING STONES** *Decca LK 4605*	1 43 wks
23 Jan 65	★**ROLLING STONES NO 2** *Decca LK 4661*	1 37 wks
27 Feb 65	**ROLLING STONES** (re-entry) *Decca LK 4605*	17 2 wks
26 Jun 65	●**ROLLING STONES** (2nd re-entry) *Decca LK 4605*	9 6 wks

Date	Title Label Number	Position	
2 Oct 65	●OUT OF OUR HEADS *Decca LK 4733*	**2**	20 wks
5 Mar 66	OUT OF OUR HEADS (re-entry) *Decca LK 4733*	**12**	4 wks
23 Apr 66	★AFTERMATH *Decca LK 4786*	**1**	28 wks
12 Nov 66	●BIG HITS (HIGH TIDE AND GREEN GRASS) *Decca TXL 101*	**4**	19 wks
28 Jan 67	●BETWEEN THE BUTTONS *Decca SKL 4852*	**3**	22 wks
23 Dec 67	●THEIR SATANIC MAJESTIES REQUEST *Decca TXS 103*	**3**	13 wks
21 Dec 68	●BEGGARS BANQUET *Decca SKL 4955*	**3**	8 wks
26 Jul 69	BEGGARS BANQUET (re-entry) *Decca SKL 4955*	**31**	1 wk
23 Aug 69	BEGGARS BANQUET (2nd re-entry) *Decca SKL 4955*	**31**	2 wks
13 Sep 69	BIG HITS (HIGH TIDE AND GREEN GRASS) (re-entry) *Decca TXL 101*	**31**	2 wks
20 Sep 69	BEGGARS BANQUET (3rd re-entry) *Decca SKL 4955*	**39**	1 wk
27 Sep 69	●THROUGH THE PAST DARKLY (BIG HITS VOL 2) *Decca SKL 5019*	**2**	26 wks
25 Oct 69	BIG HITS (HIGH TIDE AND GREEN GRASS) (2nd re-entry) *Decca TXL 101*	**20**	1 wk
20 Dec 69	★LET IT BLEED *Decca SKL 5025*	**1**	23 wks

Bonny ROSE — See *GUILDFORD CATHEDRAL CHOIR*

Thomas ROUND — See *June BRONHILL and Thomas ROUND*

Diana ROSS and the SUPREMES with the TEMPTATIONS

US, male/female vocal instrumental group

Date	Title Label Number	Position	
25 Jan 69	★DIANA ROSS AND THE SUPREMES JOIN THE TEMPTATIONS *Tamla Motown STML 11096*	**1**	15 wks
28 Jun 69	TCB *Tamla Motown STML 11110*	**11**	9 wks
13 Sep 69	TCB (re-entry) *Tamla Motown STML 11110*	**33**	1 wk

See also the Supremes; Temptations.

Jimmy RUFFIN *US, male vocalist*

Date	Title Label Number	Position	
13 May 67	JIMMY RUFFIN WAY *Tamla Motown STML 11048*	**32**	6 wks

S

SAM and DAVE *US, male vocal duo*

Date	Title Label Number	Position	
21 Jan 67	HOLD ON I'M COMING *Atlantic 588 045*	**35**	7 wks
22 Apr 67	DOUBLE DYNAMITE *Stax 589 003*	**28**	5 wks
23 Mar 68	SOUL MAN *Stax 589 015*	**32**	8 wks

Peter SARSTEDT *UK, male vocalist*

Date	Title Label Number	Position	
15 Mar 69	●PETER SARSTEDT *United Artists SULP 1219*	**8**	4 wks

Band of The SCOTS GUARDS

UK, military band

Date	Title Label Number	Position	
28 Jun 69	BAND OF THE SCOTS GUARDS *Fontana SFXL 54*	**25**	2 wks

Jack SCOTT *US, male vocalist*

Date	Title Label Number	Position	
7 May 60	●I REMEMBER HANK WILLIAMS *Top Rank BUY 034*	**7**	6 wks
26 Jun 60	I REMEMBER HANK WILLIAMS (re-entry) *Top Rank BUY 034*	**13**	5 wks
3 Sep 60	WHAT IN THE WORLD'S COME OVER YOU *Top Rank BUY 25/024*	**11**	1 wk

SEARCHERS *UK, male vocal/instrumental group*

Date	Title Label Number	Position	
10 Aug 63	●MEET THE SEARCHERS *Pye NPL 18086*	**2**	21 wks
16 Nov 63	●SUGAR AND SPICE *Pye NPL 18089*	**5**	13 wks
11 Jan 64	●MEET THE SEARCHERS (re-entry) *Pye NPL 18086*	**5**	23 wks
29 Feb 64	●SUGAR AND SPICE (re-entry) *Pye NPL 18089*	**10**	8 wks
30 May 64	●IT'S THE SEARCHERS *Pye NPL 18092*	**4**	17 wks
27 Mar 65	●SOUNDS LIKE THE SEARCHERS *Pye NPL 18111*	**8**	5 wks

Harry SECOMBE *UK, male vocalist*

Date	Title Label Number	Position	
31 Mar 62	SACRED SONGS *Philips RBL 7501*	**16**	1 wk
22 Apr 67	●SECOMBE'S PERSONAL CHOICE *Philips BETS 707*	**6**	13 wks

See also Harry Secombe, Peter Sellers and Spike Milligan.

Harry SECOMBE, Peter SELLERS and Spike MILLIGAN *UK, comedians*

Date	Title Label Number	Position	
18 Apr 64	HOW TO WIN AN ELECTION *Philips AL 3464*	**20**	1 wk

See also Anthony Newley, Peter Sellers, Joan Collins; Harry Secombe; Peter Sellers; Peter Sellers and Sophia Loren; Spike Milligan.

SEEKERS *Australia, male/female vocal group*

Date	Title Label Number	Position	
3 Jul 65	●A WORLD OF OUR OWN *Columbia 33SX 1722*	**5**	15 wks
3 Jul 65	THE SEEKERS *Decca LK 4694*	**16**	1 wk
25 Dec 65	●A WORLD OF OUR OWN (re-entry) *Columbia 33SK 1722*	**5**	21 wks
19 Nov 66	●COME THE DAY *Columbia SX 6093*	**3**	44 wks
25 Nov 67	SEEKERS-SEEN IN GREEN *Columbia SCX 6193*	**15**	10 wks
20 Jul 68	COME THE DAY (re-entry) *Columbia SX 6093*	**13**	23 wks
14 Sep 68	●LIVE AT THE TALK OF THE TOWN *Columbia SCX 6278*	**2**	22 wks
16 Nov 68	★BEST OF THE SEEKERS *Columbia SCX 6268*	**1**	90 wks
22 Feb 69	LIVE AT THE TALK OF THE TOWN (re-entry) *Columbia SCX 6278*	**12**	3 wks
8 Mar 69	★FOUR AND ONLY *MFP 1301*	**1**	1 wk

Date	Title *Label Number*	Position		Date	Title *Label Number*	Position	

29 Mar 69 ●**LIVE AT THE TALK OF THE TOWN** **4** 4 wks
(2nd re-entry) *Columbia SCX 6278*

24 May 69 **LIVE AT THE TALK OF THE TOWN** **12** 1 wk
(3rd re-entry) *Columbia SCX 6278*

See page 205 for an explanation of the Four And Only *Seekers chart performance.*

Peter SELLERS *UK, male comic vocalist*

2 Jan 60 ●**SONGS FOR SWINGING SELLERS** **3** 10 wks
Parlophone PMC 1111

23 Jan 60 ●**THE BEST OF SELLERS** **6** 5 wks
Parlophone PMD 1069

5 Mar 60 ●**THE BEST OF SELLERS** (re-entry) **10** 1 wk
Parlophone PMD 1069

26 Mar 60 ●**SONGS FOR SWINGING SELLERS** **3** 13 wks
(re-entry) *Parlophone PMC 1111*

2 Jul 60 ●**SONGS FOR SWINGING SELLERS** **10** 3 wks
(2nd re-entry) *Parlophone PMC 1111*

6 Aug 60 **THE BEST OF SELLERS** (2nd re-entry) **11** 2 wks
Parlophone PMD 1069

27 Aug 60 **SONGS FOR SWINGING SELLERS** **12** 3 wks
(3rd re-entry) *Parlophone PMC 1111*

3 Sep 60 ●**THE BEST OF SELLERS** (3rd re-entry) **7** 9 wks
Parlophone PMD 1069

24 Sep 60 **SONGS FOR SWINGING SELLERS** **18** 1 wk
(4th re-entry) *Parlophone PMC 1111*

14 Dec 60 **SONGS FOR SWINGING SELLERS** **17** 1 wk
(5th re-entry) *Parlophone PMC 1111*

3 Jun 61 **THE BEST OF SELLERS** (4th re-entry) **18** 1 wk
Parlophone PMD 1069

See also Anthony Newley, Peter Sellers, Joan Collins; Harry Secombe, Peter Sellers and Spike Milligan; Peter Sellers and Sophia Loren.

Peter SELLERS and Sophia LOREN

UK/Italy male/female comic vocal duo

3 Dec 60 ●**PETER AND SOPHIA** *Parlophone PMC 1131* **5** 17 wks

15 Apr 61 **PETER AND SOPHIA** (re-entry) **16** 1 wk
Parlophone PMC 1131

See also Anthony Newley, Peter Sellers, Joan Collins; Harry Secombe, Peter Sellers and Spike Milligan; Peter Sellers.

SHADOWS *UK, male instrumental group*

16 Sep 61 ★**THE SHADOWS** *Columbia 33SX 1374* **1** 57 wks

13 Oct 62 ★**OUT OF THE SHADOWS** **1** 37 wks
Columbia 33SX 1458

22 Jun 63 ●**GREATEST HITS** *Columbia 33SX 1522* **2** 49 wks

31 Aug 63 **OUT OF THE SHADOWS** (re-entry) **16** 1 wk
Columbia 33SX 1458

9 May 64 ●**DANCE WITH THE SHADOWS** **2** 24 wks
Columbia 33SX 1619

31 Oct 64 **DANCE WITH THE SHADOWS** (re-entry) **15** 3 wks
Columbia 33SX 1619

17 Jul 65 ●**SOUND OF THE SHADOWS** **4** 17 wks
Columbia 33SX 1736

21 May 66 ●**SHADOW MUSIC** *Columbia SX 6041* **5** 17 wks

15 Jul 67 ●**JIGSAW** *Columbia SCX 6148* **8** 16 wks

See also Cliff Richard.

Del SHANNON *US, male vocalist*

11 May 63 ●**HATS OFF TO DEL SHANNON** **9** 13 wks
London HAX 8071

17 Aug 63 **HATS OFF TO DEL SHANNON** (re-entry) **13** 4 wks
London HAX 8071

2 Nov 63 **LITTLE TOWN FLIRT** *London HAX 8091* **15** 5 wks

1 Feb 64 **LITTLE TOWN FLIRT** (re-entry) **19** 1 wk
London HAX 8091

Helen SHAPIRO *UK, female vocalist*

10 Mar 62 ●**TOPS WITH ME** *Columbia 33SX 1397* **2** 25 wks

Sandie SHAW *UK, female vocalist*

6 Mar 65 ●**SANDIE** *Pye NPL 18110* **3** 10 wks

22 May 65 **SANDIE** (re-entry) *Pye NPL 18110* **20** 1 wk

19 Jun 65 **SANDIE** (2nd re-entry) *Pye NPL 18110* **18** 1 wk

3 Jul 65 **SANDIE** (3rd re-entry) *Pye NPL 18110* **19** 1 wk

George SHEARING — See *Nat 'KING' COLE and the George SHEARING QUINTET; Peggy LEE and George SHEARING*

SIMON and GARFUNKEL *US, male vocal duo*

16 Apr 66 **SOUNDS OF SILENCE** *CBS 62690* **13** 6 wks

3 Aug 68 ★**BOOKENDS** *CBS 63101* **1** 28 wks

31 Aug 68 **PARSLEY, SAGE, ROSEMARY AND THYME** *CBS 62860* **15** 24 wks

7 Sep 68 **SOUNDS OF SILENCE** (re-entry) *CBS 62690* **13** 23 wks

26 Oct 68 ●**THE GRADUATE** (Film Soundtrack) **3** 18 wks
CBS 70042

9 Nov 68 **WEDNESDAY MORNING 3 A.M.** **24** 6 wks
CBS 63370

1 Mar 69 **PARSLEY, SAGE, ROSEMARY AND THYME**(re-entry) *CBS 62860* **13** 1 wk

19 Apr 69 ●**BOOKENDS** (re-entry) *CBS 63101* **7** 1 wk

19 Apr 69 ●**THE GRADUATE** (re-entry) *CBS 70042* **7** 4 wks

24 May 69 ●**BOOKENDS** (2nd re-entry) *CBS 63101* **10** 2 wks

24 May 69 **THE GRADUATE** (2nd re-entry) *CBS 70042* **11** 1 wk

31 May 69 **SOUNDS OF SILENCE** (2nd re-entry) **14** 1 wk
CBS 62690

14 Jun 69 **BOOKENDS** (3rd re-entry) *CBS 63101* **13** 7 wks

21 Jun 69 **THE GRADUATE** (3rd re-entry) *CBS 70042* **14** 6 wks

28 Jun 69 **PARSLEY, SAGE, ROSEMARY AND THYME** (2nd re-entry) *CBS 62860* **24** 1 wk

28 Jun 69 **SOUNDS OF SILENCE** (3rd re-entry) **37** 2 wks
CBS 62690

12 Jul 69 **PARSLEY, SAGE, ROSEMARY AND THYME** (3rd re-entry) *CBS 62860* **31** 2 wks

16 Aug 69 **THE GRADUATE** (4th re-entry) *CBS 70042* **20** 5 wks

23 Aug 69 **SOUNDS OF SILENCE** (4th re-entry) **35** 1 wk
CBS 62690

27 Sep 69 **THE GRADUATE** (5th re-entry) *CBS 70042* **32** 1 wk

18 Oct 69 **SOUNDS OF SILENCE** (5th re-entry) **24** 1 wk
CBS 62690

25 Oct 69 **THE GRADUATE** (6th re-entry) *CBS 70042* **23** 1 wk

Nina SIMONE

US, female vocalist/instrumentalist - piano

24 Jul 65 **I PUT A SPELL ON YOU** *Philips BL 7671* **18** 3 wks

15 Feb 69 **'NUFF SAID** *RCA SF 7979* **11** 1 wk

Date	Title *Label Number*	Position	

Frank SINATRA *US, male vocalist*

12 Mar 60	●**SONGS FOR SWINGING LOVERS** *Capitol LCT 6106*	**8**	2 wks
12 Mar 60	●**COME DANCE WITH ME** *Capitol LCT 6179*	**9**	1 wk
2 Apr 60	**SONGS FOR SWINGING LOVERS** (re-entry) *Capitol LCT 6106*	**15**	3 wks
7 May 60	**COME DANCE WITH ME** (re-entry) *Capitol LCT 6179*	**19**	1 wk
11 Jun 60	●**COME BACK TO SORRENTO** *Fontana TFL 5082*	**7**	1 wk
2 Jul 60	**SONGS FOR SWINGING LOVERS** (2nd re-entry) *Capitol LCT 6106*	**17**	1 wk
9 Jul 60	●**COME BACK TO SORRENTO** (re-entry) *Fontana TFL 5082*	**6**	8 wks
29 Oct 60	●**SWING EASY** *Capitol W 587*	**5**	6 wks
24 Dec 60	**SWING EASY** (re-entry) *Capitol W 587*	**14**	2 wks
14 Jan 61	**SWING EASY** (2nd re-entry) *Capitol W 587*	**20**	1 wk
21 Jan 61	●**NICE 'N EASY** *Capitol W 1417*	**4**	27 wks
18 Feb 61	**SWING EASY** (3rd re-entry) *Capitol W 587*	**13**	7 wks
11 Mar 61	**COME DANCE WITH ME** (2nd re-entry) *Capitol LCT 6179*	**14**	1 wk
15 Apr 61	**SWING EASY** (4th re-entry) *Capitol W 587*	**20**	1 wk
15 Jul 61	**SINATRA SOUVENIR** *Fontana TFL 5138*	**18**	1 wk
12 Aug 61	**NICE 'N EASY** (re-entry) *Capitol W 1417*	**19**	1 wk
19 Aug 61	●**WHEN YOUR LOVER HAS GONE** *Encore ENC 101*	**6**	10 wks
23 Sep 61	●**SINATRA'S SWINGING SESSION** *Capitol W 1491*	**6**	5 wks
28 Oct 61	●**SINATRA SWINGS** *Reprise R 1002*	**8**	8 wks
25 Nov 61	●**SINATRA PLUS** *Fontana SET 303*	**7**	9 wks
16 Dec 61	●**RING-A-DING-DING** *Reprise R 1001*	**8**	9 wks
20 Jan 62	**SINATRA'S SWINGING SESSION** (re-entry) *Capitol W 1491*	**20**	1 wk
3 Feb 62	**SINATRA'S SWINGING SESSION** (2nd re-entry) *Capitol W 1491*	**12**	2 wks
17 Feb 62	**COME SWING WITH ME** *Capitol W 1594*	**13**	3 wks
17 Mar 62	**COME SWING WITH ME** (re-entry) *Capitol W 1594*	**17**	1 wk
7 Apr 62	●**I REMEMBER TOMMY** *Reprise R 1003*	**10**	9 wks
9 Jun 62	●**SINATRA AND STRINGS** *Reprise R 1004*	**6**	20 wks
30 Jun 62	**I REMEMBER TOMMY** (re-entry) *Reprise R 1003*	**17**	2 wks
28 Jul 62	**I REMEMBER TOMMY** (2nd re-entry) *Reprise R 1003*	**19**	1 wk
27 Oct 62	**GREAT SONGS FROM GREAT BRITAIN** *Reprise R 1006*	**12**	7 wks
29 Dec 62	**GREAT SONGS FROM GREAT BRITAIN** (re-entry) *Reprise R 1006*	**18**	2 wks
29 Dec 62	**SINATRA WITH SWINGING BRASS** *Reprise R 1005*	**14**	11 wks
27 Jul 63	●**CONCERT SINATRA** *Reprise R 1009*	**8**	16 wks
5 Oct 63	**SINATRA'S SINATRA** *Reprise R 1010*	**16**	1 wk
19 Oct 63	●**SINATRA'S SINATRA** (re-entry) *Reprise R 1010*	**9**	9 wks
21 Dec 63	**CONCERT SINATRA** (re-entry) *Reprise R 1009*	**19**	2 wks
28 Dec 63	**SINATRA'S SINATRA** (2nd re-entry) *Reprise R 1010*	**17**	1 wk
11 Jan 64	**SINATRA'S SINATRA** (3rd re-entry) *Reprise R 1010*	**12**	7 wks
7 Mar 64	**SINATRA'S SINATRA** (4th re-entry) *Reprise R 1010*	**14**	6 wks
19 Sep 64	**IT MIGHT AS WELL BE SWING** *Reprise R 1012*	**17**	1 wk
24 Oct 64	**IT MIGHT AS WELL BE SWING** (re-entry) *Reprise R 1012*	**17**	3 wks
20 Mar 65	**SOFTLY AS I LEAVE YOU** *Reprise R 1013*	**20**	1 wk
22 Jan 66	●**A MAN AND HIS MUSIC** *Reprise R 1016*	**9**	19 wks
21 May 66	**MOONLIGHT SINATRA** *Reprise R 1018*	**18**	8 wks
2 Jul 66	●**STRANGERS IN THE NIGHT** *Reprise R 1017*	**4**	18 wks
1 Oct 66	●**SINATRA AT THE SANDS** *Reprise R 1019*	**7**	18 wks
3 Dec 66	**FRANK SINATRA SINGS SONGS FOR PLEASURE** *MFP 1120*	**26**	2 wks
25 Feb 67	**THAT'S LIFE** *Reprise RSLP 1020*	**22**	12 wks
7 Oct 67	**FRANK SINATRA** *Reprise RSLP 1022*	**28**	5 wks
19 Oct 68	●**GREATEST HITS** *Reprise RSLP 1025*	**8**	17 wks
7 Dec 68	**BEST OF FRANK SINATRA** *Capitol ST 21140*	**17**	10 wks
7 Jun 69	●**MY WAY** *Reprise RSLP 1029*	**2**	9 wks
16 Aug 69	**MY WAY** (re-entry) *Reprise RSLP 1029*	**23**	2 wks
6 Sep 69	**MY WAY** (2nd re-entry) *Reprise RSLP 1029*	**34**	1 wk
20 Sep 69	**MY WAY** (3rd re-entry) *Reprise RSLP 1029*	**37**	1 wk
4 Oct 69	**A MAN ALONE** *Reprise RSLP 1030*	**18**	5 wks
15 Nov 69	**A MAN ALONE** (re-entry) *Reprise RSLP 1030*	**19**	2 wks

See also Frank Sinatra and Count Basie.

Frank SINATRA and Count BASIE

US, male vocalist and male band leader/ instrumentalist - piano

23 Feb 63	●**SINATRA-BASIE** *Reprise R 1008*	**2**	22 wks
3 Aug 63	**SINATRA-BASIE** (re-entry) *Reprise R 1008*	**19**	1 wk

See also Frank Sinatra.

Nancy SINATRA *US, female vocalist*

16 Apr 66	**BOOTS** *Reprise R 6202*	**12**	9 wks
18 Jun 66	**HOW DOES THAT GRAB YOU** *Reprise R 6207*	**17**	3 wks

See also Nancy Sinatra and Lee Hazlewood.

Nancy SINATRA and Lee HAZLEWOOD

US, female/male vocal duo

29 Jun 68	**NANCY AND LEE** *Reprise RSLP 6273*	**17**	12 wks

See also Nancy Sinatra.

SMALL FACES *UK, male vocal/instrumental group*

14 May 66	●**SMALL FACES** *Decca LK 4790*	**3**	25 wks
17 Jun 67	**FROM THE BEGINNING** *Decca LK 4879*	**17**	5 wks
1 Jul 67	**SMALL FACES** *Immediate IMSP 008*	**12**	16 wks
28 Oct 67	**SMALL FACES** (re-entry) *Immediate IMSP 008*	**40**	1 wk
15 Jul 68	★**OGDEN'S NUT GONE FLAKE** *Immediate IMLP 012*	**1**	19 wks

Jimmy SMITH *US, male instrumentalist - organ*

18 Jun 66	**I GOT MY MOJO WORKING** *Verve VLP 912*	**19**	3 wks

Keely SMITH *US, female vocalist*

16 Jan 65	**LENNON-McCARTNEY SCRAPBOOK** *Reprise R 6142*	**12**	7 wks
27 Mar 65	**LENNON-McCARTNEY SCRAPBOOK** (re-entry) *Reprise R 6142*	**20**	1 wk
10 Apr 65	**LENNON-McCARTNEY SCRAPBOOK** (2nd re-entry) *Reprise R 6142*	**19**	1 wk

| Date | Title *Label Number* | Position | |

O. C. SMITH *US, male vocalist*

| 17 Aug 68 | HICKORY HOLLER REVISITED *CBS 63362* | **40** | 1 wk |

SONNY and CHER *US, male/female vocal duo*

16 Oct 65	●LOOK AT US *Atlantic ATL 5036*	**7**	12 wks
16 Apr 66	LOOK AT US (re-entry) *Atlantic ATL 5036*	**25**	1 wk
14 May 66	THE WONDROUS WORLD OF SONNY AND CHER *Atlantic 587 006*	**15**	7 wks

See also Cher.

SOUNDS ORCHESTRAL *UK, orchestra*

| 12 Jun 65 | CAST YOUR FATE TO THE WIND *Piccadilly NPL 38041* | **17** | 1 wk |

SPOTNICKS *Sweden, male instrumental group*

| 9 Feb 63 | OUT-A-SPACE *Oriole PS 40036* | **20** | 1 wk |

Dusty SPRINGFIELD *UK, female vocalist*

25 Apr 64	●A GIRL CALLED DUSTY *Philips BL 7594*	**6**	21 wks
9 Jan 65	A GIRL CALLED DUSTY (re-entry) *Philips BL 7594*	**17**	1 wk
27 Feb 65	A GIRL CALLED DUSTY (2nd re-entry) *Philips BL 7594*	**16**	1 wk
23 Oct 65	●EVERYTHING'S COMING UP DUSTY *Philips RBL 1002*	**6**	12 wks
22 Oct 66	●GOLDEN HITS *Philips BL 7737*	**2**	36 wks
11 Nov 67	WHERE AM I GOING *Philips SBL 7820*	**40**	1 wk
21 Dec 68	DUSTY . . . . DEFINITELY *Philips SBL 7864*	**30**	6 wks

Kay STARR *US, female vocalist*

| 26 Mar 60 | MOVIN' *Capitol T 1254* | **16** | 1 wk |

Cat STEVENS *UK, male vocalist*

| 25 Mar 67 | ●MATTHEW AND SON *Deram SML 1004* | **7** | 16 wks |

Andy STEWART *UK, male vocalist*

| 3 Feb 62 | ANDY STEWART *Top Rank 35 116* | **13** | 2 wks |

STILLS — See *CROSBY, STILLS and NASH*

STORYVILLE JAZZMEN — See *Bob WALLIS and the STORYVILLE JAZZMEN*

Barbra STREISAND *US, female vocalist*

| 22 Jan 66 | ●MY NAME IS BARBRA, TWO *CBS BPG 62603* | **6** | 22 wks |

| Date | Title *Label Number* | Position | |

SUPREMES *US, female vocal group*

5 Dec 64	●MEET THE SUPREMES *Stateside SL 10109*	**8**	6 wks
17 Dec 66	SUPREMES A-GO-GO *Tamla Motown STML 11039*	**15**	21 wks
13 May 67	SUPREMES SING MOTOWN *Tamla Motown STML 11047*	**15**	16 wks
30 Sep 67	SUPREMES SING RODGERS AND HART *Tamla Motown STML 11054*	**25**	7 wks
20 Jan 68	GREATEST HITS *Tamla Motown STML 11063*	**1**	57 wks
30 Mar 68	●LIVE AT THE TALK OF THE TOWN *Tamla Motown STML 11070*	**6**	18 wks
20 Jul 68	REFLECTIONS *Tamla Motown STML 11073*	**30**	2 wks
1 Feb 69	LOVE CHILD *Tamla Motown STML 11095*	**22**	2 wks
22 Feb 69	LOVE CHILD (re-entry) *Tamla Motown STML 11095*	**13**	1 wk
1 Mar 69	●GREATEST HITS (re-entry) *Tamla Motown STML 11063*	**8**	3 wks

Last four albums credited to Diana Ross and the Supremes. See also Diana Ross and the Supremes with the Temptations.

SWINGLE SINGERS

US/France, male/female vocal group

1 Feb 64	JAZZ SEBASTIAN BACH *Philips BL 7572*	**16**	3 wks
9 May 64	JAZZ SEBASTIAN BACH (re-entry) *Philips BL 7572*	**13**	11 wks
1 Aug 64	JAZZ SEBASTIAN BACH (2nd re-entry) *Philips BL 7572*	**20**	2 wks
22 Aug 64	JAZZ SEBASTIAN BACH (3rd re-entry) *Philips BL 7572*	**18**	1 wk
12 Sep 64	JAZZ SEBASTIAN BACH (4th re-entry) *Philips BL 7572*	**17**	1 wk

T

TEMPERANCE SEVEN

UK, male vocal/instrumental group

13 May 61	TEMPERANCE SEVEN PLUS ONE *Argo RG 11*	**19**	1 wk
25 Nov 61	TEMPERANCE SEVEN 1961 *Parlophone PMC 1152*	**11**	4 wks
27 Jan 62	●THE TEMPERANCE SEVEN *Parlophone PMC 1152*	**8**	5 wks

TEMPLE CHURCH CHOIR *UK, choir*

| 16 Dec 61 | ●CHRISTMAS CAROLS *HMV CLP 1309* | **8** | 3 wks |

TEMPTATIONS *US, male vocal group*

24 Dec 66	GETTING READY *Tamla Motown STML 11035*	**40**	2 wks
11 Feb 67	TEMPTATIONS GREATEST HITS *Tamla Motown STML 11042*	**26**	17 wks
22 Jul 67	TEMPTATIONS LIVE *Tamla Motown STML 11053*	**20**	4 wks

Date	Title *Label Number*	Position
18 Nov 67	**TEMPTATIONS WITH A LOT OF SOUL** *Tamla Motown STML 11057*	**19** 18 wks
20 Jan 68	**TEMPTATIONS GREATEST HITS** (re-entry) *Tamla Motown STML 11042*	**17** 23 wks
20 Sep 69	**CLOUD NINE** *Tamla Motown STML 11109*	**32** 1 wk

See also Diana Ross and the Supremes with the Temptations.

TEN YEARS AFTER

UK, male vocal/instrumental group

21 Sep 68	**UNDEAD** *Deram SML 1023*	**26** 7 wks
22 Feb 69	●**STONEDHENGE** *Deram SML 1029*	**6** 5 wks
4 Oct 69	●**SSSSH** *Deram SML 1052*	**4** 7 wks
6 Dec 69	**SSSSH** (re-entry) *Deram SML 1052*	**22** 1 wk

Carla THOMAS — See *Otis REDDING and Carla THOMAS*

TICH — See *Dave DEE, DOZY, BEAKY, MICK and TICH*

TIJUANA BRASS — See *Herb ALPERT and the TIJUANA BRASS*

TRAFFIC *UK, male vocal/instrumental group*

30 Dec 67	**MR FANTASY** *Island ILP 9061*	**16** 8 wks
26 Oct 68	●**TRAFFIC** *Island ILPS 9081 T*	**9** 8 wks

TREMELOES *UK, male vocal/instrumental group*

3 Jun 67	**HERE COMES THE TREMELOES** *CBS SBPG 63017*	**15** 7 wks

TROGGS *UK, male vocal/instrumental group*

30 Jul 66	●**FROM NOWHERE . . . THE TROGGS** *Fontana TL 5355*	**6** 16 wks
25 Feb 67	●**TROGGLODYNAMITE** *Page One POL 001*	**10** 11 wks
5 Aug 67	**BEST OF THE TROGGS** *Page One FOR 001*	**24** 5 wks

Ike and Tina TURNER

US, male instrumentalist - guitar and female vocalist

1 Oct 66	**RIVER DEEP—MOUNTAIN HIGH** *London HAU 8298*	**27** 1 wk

TURTLES *US, male vocal/instrumental group*

22 Jul 67	**HAPPY TOGETHER** *London HAU 8330*	**18** 9 wks

TYRANNOSAURUS REX

UK, male vocal/instrumental duo

13 Jul 68	**MY PEOPLE WERE FAIR AND HAD SKY IN THEIR HAIR BUT NOW THEY'RE CONTENT TO WEAR STARS ON THEIR BROWS** *Regal Zonophone SLRZ 1003*	**15** 9 wks
7 Jun 69	**UNICORN** *Regal Zonophone S 1007*	**12** 1 wk
28 Jun 69	**UNICORN** (re-entry) *Regal Zonophone S 1007*	**22** 2 wks

UNION GAP — See *Gary PUCKETT and the UNION GAP*

V

VANILLA FUDGE

US, male vocal/instrumental group

4 Nov 67	**VANILLA FUDGE** *Atlantic 588-086*	**31** 3 wks

Frankie VAUGHAN *UK, male vocalist*

4 Nov 67	**FRANKIE VAUGHAN SONGBOOK** *Philips DBL 001*	**40** 1 wk
25 Nov 67	**THERE MUST BE A WAY** *Columbia SCX 6200*	**22** 8 wks

Sarah VAUGHAN *US, female vocalist*

26 Mar 60	**NO COUNT-SARAH** *Mercury MMC 14021*	**19** 1 wk

Bobby VEE *US, male vocalist*

24 Feb 62	●**TAKE GOOD CARE OF MY BABY** *London HAG 2428*	**7** 5 wks
31 Mar 62	**HITS OF THE ROCKIN' 50'S** *London HAG 2406*	**20** 1 wk
7 Apr 62	**TAKE GOOD CARE OF MY BABY** (re-entry) *London HAG 2428*	**19** 2 wks
19 May 62	**TAKE GOOD CARE OF MY BABY** (2nd re-entry) *London HAG 2428*	**20** 1 wk
12 Jan 63	●**A BOBBY VEE RECORDING SESSION** *Liberty LBY 1084*	**10** 9 wks
23 Mar 63	**A BOBBY VEE RECORDING SESSION** (re-entry) *Liberty LBY 1084*	**18** 1 wk
20 Apr 63	**A BOBBY VEE RECORDING SESSION** (2nd re-entry) *Liberty LBY 1084*	**15** 1 wk
20 Apr 63	**BOBBY VEE'S GOLDEN GREATS** *Liberty LBY 1112*	**20** 1 wk
4 May 63	**BOBBY VEE'S GOLDEN GREATS** (re-entry) *Liberty LBY 1112*	**12** 3 wks
15 Jun 63	**BOBBY VEE'S GOLDEN GREATS** (2nd re-entry) *Liberty LBY 1112*	**16** 1 wk
29 Jun 63	●**BOBBY VEE'S GOLDEN GREATS** (3rd re-entry) *Liberty LBY 1112*	**10** 9 wks
5 Oct 63	**THE NIGHT HAS A THOUSAND EYES** *Liberty LIB 1139*	**15** 2 wks

See also Bobby Vee and the Crickets.

Bobby VEE and the CRICKETS

US, male vocalist, male and vocal/instrumental group

27 Oct 62	●**BOBBY VEE MEETS THE CRICKETS** *Liberty LBY 1086*	**2** 27 wks

See also the Crickets; Bobby Vee; Buddy Holly and the Crickets.

Date	Title Label Number	Position		Date	Title Label Number	Position	

VIENNA PHILHARMONIC ORCHESTRA
Austria, orchestra

| 8 Mar 69 | ●WORLD OF JOHANN STRAUSS *Decca SD10* | 7 | 1 wk |

Gene VINCENT *US, male vocalist*

| 14 Jul 60 | **CRAZY TIMES** *Capitol T 1342* | 12 | 1 wk |
| 4 Aug 60 | **CRAZY TIMES** (re-entry) *Capitol T 1342* | 19 | 1 wk |

W

Scott WALKER *US, male vocalist*

16 Sep 67	●SCOTT *Philips SBL 7816*	3	17 wks
20 Apr 68	★SCOTT 2 *Philips SBL 7840*	1	18 wks
5 Apr 69	●SCOTT 3 *Philips S 7882*	3	3 wks
5 May 69	**SCOTT 3** (re-entry) *Philips S 7882*	15	1 wk
5 Jul 69	●SONGS FROM HIS TV SERIES *Philips SBL 7900*	7	3 wks

See also Walker Brothers.

WALKER BROTHERS *US, male vocal group*

18 Dec 65	**TAKE IT EASY** *Philips BL 7691*	16	1 wk
8 Jan 66	●TAKE IT EASY (re-entry) *Philips BL 7691*	3	35 wks
3 Sep 66	●PORTRAIT *Philips BL 7691*	3	23 wks
18 Mar 67	●IMAGES *Philips SBL 7770*	6	15 wks
16 Sep 67	●WALKER BROTHERS STORY *Philips DBL 002*	9	19 wks

See also Scott Walker.

Bob WALLIS and his STORYVILLE JAZZMEN *UK, male vocal/instrumental group*

| 11 Jun 60 | **EVERYBODY LOVES SATURDAY NIGHT** *Top Rank BUY 023* | 20 | 1 wk |

Dionne WARWICK *US, female vocalist*

23 May 64	**PRESENTING DIONNE WARWICK** *Pye NPL 28037*	19	1 wk
6 Jun 64	**PRESENTING DIONNE WARWICK** (re-entry) *Pye NPL 28037*	14	3 wks
1 Aug 64	**PRESENTING DIONNE WARWICK** (2nd re-entry) *Pye NPL 28037*	16	3 wks
29 Aug 64	**PRESENTING DIONNE WARWICK** (3rd re-entry) *Pye NPL 28037*	18	3 wks
7 May 66	●BEST OF DIONNE WARWICK *Pye NPL 28078*	8	11 wks
4 Feb 67	**HERE WHERE THERE IS LOVE** *Pye NPL 28096*	39	2 wks
18 May 68	●VALLEY OF THE DOLLS *Pye NSPL 28114*	10	13 wks

Geno WASHINGTON and the RAM JAM BAND *US, male vocalist*

10 Dec 66	●HAND CLAPPIN'—FOOT STOMPIN'— FUNKY BUTT—LIVE! *Piccadilly NPL 38026*	5	31 wks
2 Sep 67	**HAND CLAPPIN'—FOOT STOMPIN'— FUNKY BUTT—LIVE!** (re-entry) *Piccadilly NPL 38026*	17	7 wks
23 Sep 67	●HIPSTERS, FLIPSTERS AND FINGER POPPIN' DADDIES *Picadilly NSPL 38032*	8	13 wks

Ben WEBSTER — See *Gerry MULLIGAN and Ben WEBSTER*

Bert WEEDON *UK, male instrumentalist - guitar*

| 16 Jul 60 | **KING SIZE GUITAR** *Top Rank BUY 026* | 18 | 1 wk |

WHO *UK, male vocal/instrumental group*

25 Dec 65	●MY GENERATION *Brunswick LAT 8616*	5	11 wks
17 Dec 66	●A QUICK ONE *Reaction 593-002*	4	17 wks
13 Jan 68	**THE WHO SELL OUT** *Track 613-002*	13	11 wks
7 Jun 69	●TOMMY *Track 613-013/4*	2	6 wks
2 Aug 69	**TOMMY** (re-entry) *Track 613-013/4*	28	1 wk
16 Aug 69	**TOMMY** (2nd re-entry) *Track 613-013/4*	40	1 wk
27 Sep 69	**TOMMY** (3rd re-entry) *Track 613-013/4*	38	1 wk

Andy WILLIAMS *US, male vocalist*

26 Jun 65	●ALMOST THERE *CBS BPG 62533*	4	46 wks
7 Aug 65	**CAN'T GET USED TO LOSING YOU** *CBS BPG 62146*	16	1 wk
19 Mar 66	**MAY EACH DAY** *CBS BPG 62658*	11	6 wks
30 Apr 66	**GREAT SONGS FROM MY FAIR LADY** *CBS BPG 62430*	30	1 wk
23 Jul 66	**SHADOW OF YOUR SMILE** *CBS 62633*	24	4 wks
29 Jul 67	**BORN FREE** *CBS SBPG 63027*	23	1 wk
19 Aug 67	**BORN FREE** (re-entry) *CBS SBPG 63027*	22	10 wks
11 May 68	**LOVE ANDY** *CBS 63167*	1	22 wks
6 Jul 68	●HONEY *CBS 63311*	4	17 wks
26 Jul 69	**HAPPY HEART** *CBS 63614*	25	2 wks
16 Aug 69	**HAPPY HEART** (re-entry) *CBS 63614*	30	1 wk
30 Aug 69	**HAPPY HEART** (2nd re-entry) *CBS 63614*	24	1 wk
22 Nov 69	**HAPPY HEART** (3rd re-entry) *CBS 63614*	22	1 wk
27 Dec 69	**GET TOGETHER WITH ANDY WILLIAMS** *CBS 63800*	13	3 wks

Sonny Boy WILLIAMSON
US, male vocalist/instrumentalist - guitar

| 20 Jun 64 | **DOWN AND OUT BLUES** *Pye NPL 28036* | 20 | 1 wk |

Stevie WONDER
US, male vocalist/multi-instrumentalist

7 Sep 68	**STEVIE WONDER'S GREATEST HITS** *Tamla Motown STML 11075*	40	1 wk
21 Sep 68	**STEVIE WONDER'S GREATEST HITS** (re-entry) *Tamla Motown STML 11075*	25	9 wks
13 Dec 69	**MY CHERIE AMOUR** *Tamla Motown STML 11128*	17	2 wks

Date	Title *Label Number*	Position		Date	Title *Label Number*	Position

WURZELS — See *Adge CUTLER and the WURZELS*

Y

YARDBIRDS *UK, male vocal/instrumental group*

23 Jul 66	**YARDBIRDS** *Columbia SX 6063*	**20** 8 wks

VARIOUS ARTISTS

ANONYMOUS COVER VERSIONS

29 Feb 64	**BEATLEMANIA** *Top Six TSL 1*	**20** 1 wk
21 Mar 64	**BEATLEMANIA** (re-entry) *Top Six TSL 1*	**19** 1 wk

COMPILATIONS

10 Mar 62	**GREAT MOTION PICTURE THEMES** *HMV CLP 15082*	**19** 1 wk
3 Jun 62	**HONEY HIT PARADE** *Pye GGL 0129*	**13** 3 wks
17 Nov 62	**HONEY HIT PARADE** (re-entry) *Pye GGL 0129*	**15** 3 wks
30 Nov 62	**ALL THE HITS BY ALL THE STARS** *Pye GGL 0162*	**19** 1 wk
22 Dec 62	**ALL THE HITS BY ALL THE STARS** (re-entry) *Pye GGL 0162*	**19** 1 wk
22 Dec 62	**HONEY HIT PARADE** (2nd re-entry) *Pye GGL 0129*	**20** 1 wk
9 Mar 63	●**ALL STAR FESTIVAL** *Philips DL 99500*	**4** 17 wks
13 Jul 63	**ALL STAR FESTIVAL** (re-entry) *Philips DL 99500*	**16** 2 wks
24 Aug 63	**THE MERSEY BEAT Vol 1** *Oriole PS 40047*	**17** 5 wks
7 Sep 63	**HITSVILLE** *Pye GGL 0202*	**11** 5 wks
14 Sep 63	**THE BEST OF RADIO LUXEMBOURG** *Pye GGL 0208*	**14** 2 wks
9 Nov 63	**HITSVILLE** (re-entry) *Pye GGL 0202*	**16** 1 wk
23 Nov 63	**HITSVILLE Vol 2** *Pye GGL 0233*	**20** 1 wk
4 Jan 64	**THE BLUES Vol 1** *Pye NPL 28030*	**20** 1 wk
18 Jan 64	**THE BLUES Vol 1** (re-entry) *Pye NPL 28030*	**15** 1 wk
8 Feb 64	**READY STEADY GO** *Decca LK 4577*	**20** 1 wk
22 Feb 64	**FOLK FESTIVAL OF THE BLUES** *Pye NPL 28033*	**18** 3 wks
2 May 64	**FOLK FESTIVAL OF THE BLUES** (re-entry) *Pye NPL 28033*	**16** 1 wk
16 May 64	**OUT CAME THE BLUES** *Ace Of Hearts AH 72*	**19** 1 wk
23 May 64	**THE BLUES Vol 1** (2nd re-entry) *Pye NPL 28030*	**16** 1 wk
30 May 64	**THE BLUES Vol 2** *Pye NPL 28035*	**16** 3 wks
3 Apr 65	**A COLLECTION OF TAMLA MOTOWN HITS** *Tamla Motown TML 11001*	**16** 2 wks
1 May 65	**A COLLECTION OF TAMLA MOTOWN HITS** (re-entry) *Tamla Motown TML 11001*	**18** 2 wks
2 Apr 66	**SOLID GOLD SOUL** *Atlantic ATL 5048*	**12** 15 wks
11 Sep 66	●**STARS CHARITY FANTASIA** *Save The Childen Fund SCF PL 145*	**6** 12 wks

5 Nov 66	**MIDNIGHT SOUL** *Atlantic 587-021*	**22** 18 wks
10 Dec 66	**SOLID GOLD SOUL** (re-entry) *Atlantic ATL 5048*	**20** 12 wks
10 Dec 66	**STEREO MUSICAL SHOWCASE** *Polydor 104-450*	**26** 2 wks
24 Dec 66	**STARS CHARITY FANTASIA** (re-entry) *Save The Children Fund SCF PL 145*	**26** 4 wks
4 Mar 67	**16 ORIGINAL BIG HITS Vol 4** *Tamla Motown TML 11043*	**33** 3 wks
8 Apr 67	●**HIT THE ROAD STAX** *Stax 589-005*	**10** 14 wks
20 May 67	**THRILL TO THE SENSATIONAL SOUND OF SUPER STEREO** *CBS PR 5*	**32** 6 wks
17 Jun 67	**TAMLA MOTOWN HITS Vol 5** *Tamla Motown TML 11050*	**11** 40 wks
15 Jul 67	**THRILL TO THE SENSATIONAL SOUND OF SUPER STEREO** (re-entry) *CBS PR 5*	**20** 5 wks
5 Aug 67	**HIT THE ROAD STAX** (re-entry) *Stax 589-005*	**40** 2 wks
26 Aug 67	**CLUB SKA '67** *Island ILP 956*	**37** 2 wks
9 Sep 67	**MIDNIGHT SOUL** (re-entry) *Atlantic 587-021*	**38** 1 wk
7 Oct 67	**THRILL TO THE SENSATIONAL SOUND OF SUPER STEREO** (2nd re-entry) *CBS PR 5*	**33** 1 wk
21 Oct 67	●**BREAKTHROUGH** *Studio Two STWO 1*	**2** 19 wks
21 Oct 67	●**BRITISH MOTOWN CHARTBUSTERS** *Tamla Motown TML 11055*	**2** 54 wks
28 Oct 67	**THRILL TO THE SENSATIONAL SOUND OF SUPER STEREO** (3rd re-entry) *CBS PR 5*	**25** 18 wks
10 Feb 68	**MOTOWN MEMORIES** *Tamla Motown TML 11064*	**21** 13 wks
10 Feb 68	**STARS OF '68** *Marble Arch MAL 762*	**23** 3 wks
11 May 68	**BLUES ANYTIME** *Immediate IMLP 014*	**40** 1 wk
24 Aug 68	**TAMLA MOTOWN HITS Vol 6** *Tamla Motown STML 11074*	**32** 2 wks
30 Nov 68	●**BRITISH MOTOWN CHARTBUSTERS Vol 2** *Tamla Motown STML 11082*	**8** 11 wks
8 Mar 69	●**WORLD OF HITS** *Decca SPA 7*	**5** 1 wk
8 Mar 69	**HIT HITS** *MFP 1290*	**13** 1 wk
8 Mar 69	**LIVING PRESENCE STEREO** *SFXL 52*	**17** 1 wk
8 Mar 69	**PHASE FOUR STEREO SAMPLER** *Decca BPS 1*	**23** 1 wk
12 Jun 69	**THE WORLD OF BLUES POWER** (re-entry) *Decca SPA 14*	**40** 1 wk
14 Jun 69	**THIS IS SOUL** *Atlantic 643-301*	**17** 1 wk
14 Jun 69	**YOU CAN ALL JOIN IN** *Island IWPS 2*	**18** 10 wks
21 Jun 69	**IMPACT** *EMI STWO 2*	**15** 4 wks
28 Jun 69	**THE ROCK MACHINE TURNS YOU ON** *CBS SPR 22*	**27** 1 wk
28 Jun 69	**THE WORLD OF BLUES POWER** *Decca SPA 14*	**30** 1 wk
28 Jun 69	**THIS IS SOUL** (re-entry) *Atlantic 643-301*	**16** 12 wks
28 Jun 69	**ROCK MACHINE I LOVE YOU** *CBS SPR 26*	**34** 1 wk
5 Jul 69	**THE WORLD OF BRASS BANDS** *Decca SPA 20*	**13** 8 wks
12 Jul 69	**THE ROCK MACHINE TURNS YOU ON** (re-entry) *CBS SPR 22*	**18** 4 wks
19 Jul 69	**ROCK MACHINE I LOVE YOU** (re-entry) *CBS SPR 26*	**15** 3 wks
26 Jul 69	**IMPACT** (re-entry) *EMI STWO 2*	**15** 4 wks
26 Jul 69	**THE WORLD OF BLUES POWER** (2nd re-entry) *Decca SPA 14*	**24** 2 wks
23 Aug 69	**ROCK MACHINE I LOVE YOU** (2nd re-entry) *CBS SPR 26*	**27** 1 wk
23 Aug 69	**THE ROCK MACHINE TURNS YOU ON** (2nd re-entry) *CBS SPR 22*	**22** 2 wks
30 Aug 69	**IMPACT** (2nd re-entry) *EMI STWO 2*	**28** 2 wks
30 Aug 69	**THE WORLD OF BLUES POWER** (3rd re-entry) *Decca SPA 14*	**32** 2 wks
6 Sep 69	●**THE WORLDS OF HITS Vol 2** *Decca SPA 35*	**7** 5 wks

Date	Title *Label Number*	Position		Date	Title *Label Number*	Position	
13 Sep 69	THE WORLD OF BRASS BANDS (re-entry) *Decca SPA 20*	36	2 wks	11 Mar 61	BEN HUR (re-entry) *MGM C 802*	15	1 wk
20 Sep 69	IMPACT (3rd re-entry) *EMI STWO 2*	19	2 wks	25 Mar 61	BEN HUR (2nd re-entry) *MGM C 802*	19	1 wk
20 Sep 69	THE WORLD OF PHASE 4 STEREO *Decca SPA 32*	29	2 wks	29 Apr 61	●SEVEN BRIDES FOR SEVEN BROTHERS *MGM C 853*	6	21 wks
20 Sep 69	THE WORLD OF PROGRESSIVE MUSIC (Wowie Zowie) *Decca SPA 34*	17	2 wks	6 May 61	CAROUSEL (3rd re-entry) *Capitol LCT 6105*	19	1 wk
27 Sep 69	THIS IS SOUL (2nd re-entry) *Atlantic 643-301*	25	2 wks	3 Jun 61	EXODUS *RCA RD 27201*	17	1 wk
4 Oct 69	THE WORLD OF BRASS BANDS (2nd re-entry) *Decca SPA 20*	28	1 wk	10 Jun 61	CAROUSEL (4th re-entry) *Capitol LCT 6105*	15	1 wk
25 Oct 69	●BRITISH MOTOWN CHARTBUSTERS Vol 3 *Tamla Motown STML 11121*	1	77 wks	29 Jul 61	THE KING AND I (13th re-entry) *Capital LCT 6108*	14	2 wks
				5 Aug 61	CAROUSEL (5th re-entry) *Capitol LCT 6105*	20	1 wk
				19 Aug 61	THE KING AND I (14th re-entry) *Capitol LCT 6108*	19	1 wk

FILM SOUNDTRACKS

Date	Title *Label Number*	Position		Date	Title *Label Number*	Position	
2 Jan 60	●GIGI *MGM C 770*	2	39 wks	7 Oct 61	THE KING AND I (15th re-entry) *Capitol LCT 6108*	16	2 wks
2 Jan 60	★SOUTH PACIFIC *RCA RB 16065*	1	93 wks	14 Oct 61	OKLAHOMA (8th re-entry) *Capitol LCT 6100*	18	1 wk
9 Jan 60	●THE KING AND I *Capitol LCT 6108*	8	1 wk	21 Oct 61	●SOUTH PACIFIC (re-entry) *RCA RB 16065*	2	102 wks
23 Jan 60	●THE FIVE PENNIES *London HAU 2189*	2	8 wks	4 Nov 61	OKLAHOMA (9th re-entry) *Capitol LCT 6100*	18	2 wks
6 Feb 60	●THE KING AND I (re-entry) *Capitol LCT 6108*	8	2 wks	11 Nov 61	GLENN MILLER STORY *Ace Of Hearts AH 12*	12	6 wks
27 Feb 60	●THE KING AND I (2nd re-entry) *Capitol LCT 6108*	9	1 wk	25 Nov 61	THE KING AND I (16th re-entry) *Capitol LCT 6108*	19	1 wk
12 Mar 60	●THE KING AND I (3rd re-entry) *Capitol LCT 6108*	10	1 wk	2 Dec 61	OKLAHOMA (10th re-entry) *Capitol LCT 6100*	19	1 wk
19 Mar 60	●OKLAHOMA *Capital LCT 6100*	6	1 wk	13 Jan 62	SEVEN BRIDES FOR SEVEN BROTHERS (re-entry) *MGM C 853*	17	1 wk
26 Mar 60	●THE KING AND I (4th re-entry) *Capitol LCT 6108*	5	3 wks	27 Jan 62	●THE KING AND I (17th re-entry) *Capitol LCT 6108*	9	1 wk
2 Apr 60	OKLAHOMA (re-entry) *Capitol LCT 6100*	12	1 wk	24 Mar 62	THE KING AND I (18th re-entry) *Capitol LCT 6108*	19	1 wk
9 Apr 60	THE FIVE PENNIES (re-entry) *London HAU 2189*	17	1 wk	24 Mar 62	OKLAHOMA (11th re-entry) *Capitol LCT 6100*	17	1 wk
16 Apr 60	OKLAHOMA (2nd re-entry) *Capitol LCT 6100*	15	2 wks	24 Mar 62	★WEST SIDE STORY *Philips BBL 7530/CBS BPG 62058*	1	163 wks
23 Apr 60	THE FIVE PENNIES (2nd re-entry) *London HAU 2189*	16	1 wk	28 Apr 62	●IT'S TRAD DAD *Colombia 33SX 1412*	3	21 wks
23 Apr 60	THE KING AND I (5th re-entry) *Capitol LCT 6108*	12	3 wks	26 May 62	GLENN MILLER STORY (re-entry) *Ace Of Hearts AH 12*	17	1 wk
7 May 60	●CAN CAN *Capitol W 1301*	2	29 wks	22 Sep 62	THE MUSIC MAN *Warner Bros. WB 4066*	14	9 wks
14 May 60	●OKLAHOMA (3rd re-entry) *Capitol LCT 6100*	5	4 wks	3 Nov 62	PORGY AND BESS *CBS APG 60002*	15	4 wks
21 May 60	CAROUSEL *Capitol LCT 6105*	17	1 wk	8 Dec 62	PORGY AND BESS (re-entry) *CBS APG 60002*	14	3 wks
21 May 60	●THE KING AND I (6th re-entry) *Capitol LCT 6108*	6	3 wks	5 Jan 63	THE KING AND I (19th re-entry) *Capitol LCT 6108*	17	1 wk
28 May 60	PAL JOEY *Capital LCT 6148*	20	1 wk	15 Jun 63	JUST FOR FUN *Decca LK 4524*	20	2 wks
4 Jun 60	CAROUSEL (re-entry) *Capitol LCT 6105*	15	1 wk	12 Oct 63	SOUTH PACIFIC (2nd re-entry) *RCA RB 16065*	14	3 wks
18 Jun 60	●OKLAHOMA (4th re-entry) *Capitol LCT 6100*	4	1 wk	14 Dec 63	●SOUTH PACIFIC (3rd re-entry) *RCA RB 16065*	9	23 wks
18 Jun 60	●THE FIVE PENNIES (3rd re-entry) *London HAU 2189*	4	5 wks	27 Jun 64	SOUTH PACIFIC (4th re-entry) *RCA RB 16065*	16	4 wks
2 Jul 60	OKLAHOMA (5th re-entry) *Capitol LCT 6100*	15	4 wks	31 Oct 64	GOLDFINGER *United Artists ULP 1076*	14	5 wks
16 Jul 60	●OKLAHOMA (6th re-entry) *Capitol LCT 6100*	7	4 wks	31 Oct 64	MY FAIR LADY *CBS BPG 72237*	12	3 wks
16 Jul 60	THE KING AND I (7th re-entry) *Capitol LCT 6108*	19	1 wk	28 Nov 64	MY FAIR LADY (re-entry) *CBS BPG 72237*	16	7 wks
23 Jul 60	HIGH SOCIETY *Capital LCT 6116*	16	1 wk	9 Jan 65	SOUTH PACIFIC (5th re-entry) *RCA RB 16065*	16	1 wk
6 Aug 60	THE KING AND I (8th re-entry) *Capitol LCT 6108*	18	1 wk	16 Jan 65	●MARY POPPINS *HMV CLP 1794*	2	80 wks
20 Aug 60	●OKLAHOMA (7th re-entry) *Capitol LCT 6100*	4	59 wks	20 Feb 65	MY FAIR LADY (2nd re-entry) *CBS BPG 72237*	17	1 wk
27 Aug 60	THE KING AND I (9th re-entry) *Capitol LCT 6108*	15	2 wks	6 Mar 65	MY FAIR LADY (3rd re-entry) *CBS BPG 72237*	17	3 wks
17 Sep 60	CAROUSEL (2nd re-entry) *Capitol LCT 6105*	13	3 wks	3 Apr 65	●MY FAIR LADY (4th re-entry) *CBS BPG 72237*	9	35 wks
17 Sep 60	●THE KING AND I (10th re-entry) *Capitol LCT 6108*	4	12 wks	10 Apr 65	★SOUND OF MUSIC *RCA RB 6616*	1	318 wks
29 Oct 60	GIGI (re-entry) *MGM C 770*	19	1 wk	22 May 65	WEST SIDE STORY (re-entry) *Philips BBL 7530/CBS BPG 62058*	17	2 wks
5 Nov 60	BEN HUR *MGM C 802*	20	1 wk	26 May 65	WEST SIDE STORY (2nd re-entry) *Philips BBL 7530/CBS BPG 62058*	18	1 wk
24 Dec 60	CAN CAN (re-entry) *Capitol W 1301*	19	1 wk	10 Jul 65	WEST SIDE STORY (3rd re-entry) *Philips BBL 7530/CBS BPG 62058*	20	1 wk
7 Jan 61	CAN CAN (2nd re-entry) *Capitol W 1301*	18	1 wk	21 Aug 65	WEST SIDE STORY (4th re-entry) *Philips BBL 7530/CBS BPG 62058*	14	5 wks
21 Jan 61	NEVER ON SUNDAY *London HAT 2309*	17	1 wk	13 Nov 65	WEST SIDE STORY (5th re-entry) *Philips BBL 7530/CBS BPG 62058*	13	3 wks
21 Jan 61	●THE KING AND I (11th re-entry) *Capitol LCT 6108*	9	5 wks	12 Mar 66	MY FAIR LADY (5th re-entry) *CBS BPG 72237*	20	1 wk
18 Feb 61	●SONG WITHOUT END *Pye GGL 30169*	9	10 wks	30 Apr 66	FUNNY GIRL *Capitol W 2059*	19	3 wks
4 Mar 61	●THE KING AND I (12th re-entry) *Capitol LCT 6108*	8	20 wks	27 Aug 66	MARY POPPINS (re-entry) *HMV CLP 1794*	27	2 wks

Date	Title Label Number	Position
11 Sep 66	●DR ZHIVAGO MGM C 8007	3 101 wks
8 Oct 66	MY FAIR LADY (6th re-entry)	27 1 wk
	CBS BPG 72237	
22 Jul 67	CASINO ROYALE RCA Victor SF 7874	35 1 wk
29 Jul 67	A MAN AND A WOMAN	39 1 wk
	United Artists ULP 1155	
16 Sep 67	A MAN AND A WOMAN (re-entry)	35 1 wk
	United Artists ULP 1155	
28 Oct 67	●THOROUGHLY MODERN MILLIE	9 16 wks
	Brunswick STA 8685	
9 Mar 68	●THE JUNGLE BOOK Disney ST 3948	5 4 wks
23 Mar 68	A MAN AND A WOMAN (2nd re-entry)	38 1 wk
	United Artists ULP 1155	
23 Mar 68	THOROUGHLY MODERN MILLIE (re-entry)	38 3 wks
	Brunswick STA 8685	
17 Aug 68	A MAN AND A WOMAN (3rd re-entry)	31 8 wks
	United Artists ULP 1155	
21 Sep 68	STAR Stateside SSL 10233	36 1 wk
12 Oct 68	●THE GOOD, THE BAD AND THE UGLY	2 18 wks
	United Artists SULP 1197	
23 Nov 68	CAMELOT Warner Bros. WS 1712	37 1 wk
20 Feb 65	MY FAIR LADY (2nd re-entry)	17 1 wk
	CBS BPG 72237	
23 Nov 68	OLIVER RCA Victor SB 6777	26 2 wks
8 Feb 69	CHITTY CHITTY BANG BANG	36 1 wk
	United Artists SULP 1200	
15 Feb 69	●OLIVER (re-entry)	7 7 wks
	RCA Victor SB 6777	
1 Mar 69	CHITTY CHITTY BANG BANG (re-entry)	14 2 wks
	United Artists SULP 1200	
12 Apr 69	●OLIVER (2nd re-entry)	4 59 wks
	RCA Victor SB 6777	
10 May 69	FUNNY GIRL CBS 70044	15 1 wk
14 Jun 69	2001 — A SPACE ODYSSEY	12 1 wk
	MGM MGMCS 8078	
28 Jun 69	●2001 — A SPACE ODYSSEY (re-entry)	3 14 wks
	MGM MGMCS 8078	
12 Jul 69	FUNNY GIRL (re-entry) CBS 70044	39 1 wk
18 Oct 69	2001 — A SPACE ODYSSEY (2nd re-entry)	15 2 wks
	MGM MGMCS8078	
6 Dec 69	2001 — A SPACE ODYSSEY (3rd re-entry)	13 2 wks
	MGM MGMCS 8078	
20 Dec 69	EASY RIDER Stateside SSL 5018	11 4 wks
27 Dec 69	THE JUNGLE BOOK (re-entry)	19 2 wks
	Disney ST 3948	

STAGE CAST RECORDINGS

Date	Title Label Number	Position
2 Jan 60	●MY FAIR LADY (Broadway)	3 48 wks
	Philips RBL 1000	
26 Mar 60	●AT THE DROP OF A HAT (London)	9 1 wk
	Parlophone PMC 1033	
26 Mar 60	●FINGS AIN'T WOT THEY USED TO BE	5 11 wks
	(London) Decca LK 4346	
2 Apr 60	●FLOWER DRUM SONG (Broadway)	2 26 wks
	Philips ABL 3302	
7 May 60	●FOLLOW THAT GIRL (London)	5 9 wks
	HMV CLP 1366	
21 May 60	MAKE ME AN OFFER (London)	18 1 wk
	HMV CLP 1333	
21 May 60	●MOST HAPPY FELLA (Broadway)	7 5 wks
	Philips BBL 7374	
28 May 60	FLOWER DRUM SONG (London)	17 1 wk
	HMV CLP 1359	
11 Jun 60	●FLOWER DRUM SONG (London) (re-entry)	10 1 wk
	HMV CLP 1359	
2 Jul 60	●MOST HAPPY FELLA (Broadway) (re-entry)	6 1 wk
	Philips BBL 7374	
9 Jul 60	FLOWER DRUM SONG (London)	15 1 wk
	(2nd re-entry) HMV CLP 1359	

Date	Title Label Number	Position
9 Jul 60	MOST HAPPY FELLA (London)	19 1 wk
	HMV CLP 1365	
30 Jul 60	WEST SIDE STORY (Broadway)	14 1 wk
	Philips SBBL 504	
13 Aug 60	●MOST HAPPY FELLA (Broadway)	10 6 wks
	(2nd re-entry) Philips BBL 7374	
10 Sep 60	●OLIVER (London) Decca LK 4359	6 25 wks
8 Oct 60	FLOWER DRUM SONG (Broadway)	17 1 wk
	(re-entry) Philips ABL 3302	
8 Oct 60	MOST HAPPY FELLA (Broadway)	15 1 wk
	(3rd re-entry) Philips BBL 7374	
11 Mar 61	KING KONG (South Africa) Decca LK 4392	12 7 wks
18 Mar 61	●OLIVER (London) (re-entry) Decca LK 4359	9 6 wks
6 May 61	MUSIC MAN (London) HMV CLP 1444	16 1 wk
13 May 61	●OLIVER (London) (2nd re-entry)	4 59 wks
	Decca LK 4359	
20 May 61	●MUSIC MAN (London) (re-entry)	8 10 wks
	HMV CLP 1444	
25 May 61	KING KONG (South Africa) (re-entry)	13 1 wk
	Decca LK 4392	
3 Jun 61	MY FAIR LADY (Broadway) (re-entry)	15 2 wks
	Philips RBL 1000	
24 Jun 61	MY FAIR LADY (Broadway) (2nd re-entry)	13 10 wks
	Philips RBL 1000	
24 Jun 61	●SOUND OF MUSIC (Broadway)	4 13 wks
	Philips ABL 3370	
22 Jul 61	BEYOND THE FRINGE (London)	15 3 wks
	Parlophone PMC 1145	
22 Jul 61	BYE BYE BIRDIE (Broadway)	17 2 wks
	Philips ABL 3385	
29 Jul 61	●SOUND OF MUSIC (London) HMV CLP 1453	4 65 wks
5 Aug 61	●MUSIC MAN (London) (2nd re-entry)	10 2 wks
	HMV CLP 1444	
12 Aug 61	BYE BYE BIRDIE (re-entry) Philips ABL 3385	18 1 wk
19 Aug 61	BEYOND THE FRINGE (London) (re-entry)	13 4 wks
	Parlophone PMC 1145	
23 Sep 61	BEYOND THE FRINGE (London)	13 9 wks
	(2nd re-entry) Parlophone PMC 1145	
9 Sep 61	●STOP THE WORLD I WANT TO GET OFF	8 10 wks
	(London) Decca LK 4408	
30 Sep 61	SOUND OF MUSIC (Broadway) (re-entry)	16 3 wks
	Philips ABL 3370	
28 Oct 61	SOUND OF MUSIC (Broadway)	19 1 wk
	(2nd re-entry) Philips ABL 3370	
18 Nov 61	MY FAIR LADY (Broadway) (3rd re-entry)	19 1 wk
	Philips RBL 1000	
18 Nov 61	SOUND OF MUSIC (Broadway)	16 1 wk
	(3rd re-entry) Philips ABL 3370	
25 Nov 61	STOP THE WORLD I WANT TO GET OFF	17 4 wks
	(re-entry) Decca LK 4408	
2 Dec 61	SOUND OF MUSIC (Broadway)	17 1 wk
	(4th re-entry) Philips ABL 3370	
19 Dec 61	BEYOND THE FRINGE (London)	20 1 wk
	(3rd re-entry) Parlophone PMC 1145	
31 Mar 62	MY FAIR LADY (Broadway) (4th re-entry)	15 7 wks
	Philips RBL 1000	
30 Jun 62	MY FAIR LADY (Broadway) (5th re-entry)	19 1 wk
	Philips RBL 1000	
14 Jul 62	●BLITZ (London) HMV CLP 1569	7 21 wks
14 Jul 62	OLIVER (London) (3rd re-entry)	16 1 wk
	Decca LK 4359	
15 Dec 62	SOUND OF MUSIC (London) (re-entry)	13 2 wks
	HMV CLP 1453	
9 Mar 63	SOUND OF MUSIC (London) (2nd re-entry)	20 1 wk
	HMV CLP 1453	
18 May 63	HALF A SIXPENCE (London) Decca LK 4521	20 1 wk
1 Jun 63	HALF A SIXPENCE (London) (re-entry)	20 1 wk
	Decca LK 4521	
3 Aug 63	PICKWICK (London) Philips AL 3431	12 7 wks
28 Sep 63	PICKWICK (London) (re-entry)	14 3 wks
	Philips AL 3431	

Date	Title *Label Number*	Position		Date	Title *Label Number*	Position	
4 Jan 64	**MY FAIR LADY** (Broadway) *CBS BPG 68001*	19	1 wk				
22 Feb 64	**AT THE DROP OF ANOTHER HAT** (London) *Parlophone PMC 1216*	12	4 wks		STUDIO CAST RECORDINGS		
18 Apr 64	**AT THE DROP OF ANOTHER HAT** (London) (re-entry) *Parlophone PMC 1216*	17	7 wks	25 Jun 60	**SHOW BOAT** *HMV CLP 1310*	12	1 wk
3 Oct 64	●**CAMELOT** (Broadway) *CBS APG 60001*	10	4 wks		TV SOUNDTRACKS and SPIN-OFFS		
14 Nov 64	**CAMELOT** (Broadway) (re-entry) *CBS APG 60001*	14	8 wks				
16 Jan 65	**CAMELOT** (London) *HMV CLP 1756*	19	1 wk	4 Mar 61	**HUCKLEBERRY HOUND** *Pye GGL 004*	11	1 wk
11 Mar 67	**FIDDLER ON THE ROOF** (London) *CBS SBPG 70030*	14	45 wks	18 Mar 61	●**HUCKLEBERRY HOUND** (re-entry) *Pye GGL 004*	10	9 wks
30 Mar 68	**FIDDLER ON THE ROOF** (London) (re-entry) *CBS SBPG 70030*	30	5 wks	1 Jul 61	**HUCKLEBERRY HOUND** (2nd re-entry) *Pye GGL 004*	12	2 wks
28 Dec 68	●**HAIR** (London) *Polydor 583-043*	8	9 wks	30 Feb 63	**THAT WAS THE WEEK THAT WAS** *Parlophone PMC 1197*	11	9 wks
15 Mar 69	●**HAIR** (London) (re-entry) *Polydor 583-043*	7	1 wk	28 Mar 64	**STARS FROM STARS AND GARTERS** *Pye GGL 0252*	17	2 wks
12 Apr 69	●**HAIR** (London) (2nd re-entry) *Polydor 583-043*	3	13 wks				
19 Jul 69	●**HAIR** (London) (3rd re-entry) *Polydor 583-043*	8	18 wks				
29 Nov 69	**HAIR** (London) (4th re-entry) *Polydor 583-043*	12	23 wks				

ALBUM CHARTS FACTS AND FEATS

First chart of the sixties

1 South Pacific –
   Film Soundtrack
2 Cliff Sings –
   Cliff Richard
3 Time To Celebrate –
   Russ Conway
4 Songs For Swinging Sellers –
   Peter Sellers
5 Gigi –
   Film Soundtrack
6 My Fair Lady –
   Broadway Cast
7 Family Favourites –
   Russ Conway
8 Buddy Holly Story –
   Buddy Holly
9 Cliff –
   Cliff Richard
10 Pack Up Your Troubles –
   Russ Conway

Last chart of the sixties

1 Abbey Road –
   Beatles
2 Let It Bleed –
   Rolling Stones
3 Tom Jones Live In Las Vegas –
   Tom Jones
4 Motown Chartbusters Vol 3 –
   Various Artists
5 Johnny Cash At San Quentin –
   Johnny Cash
6 Engelbert Humperdinck –
   Engelbert Humperdinck
7 To Our Children's Children's
   Children – Moody Blues
8 Sound Of Music –
   Film Soundtrack
9 Led Zeppelin 2 –
   Led Zeppelin
10 Best Of The Seekers –
   Seekers
11 Easy Rider –
   Film Soundtrack
12 Oliver –
   Film Soundtrack
13 Get Together With
   Andy Williams – Andy Williams
14 Hair –
   London Cast
15 Twelve Songs Of Christmas –
   Jim Reeves
16 Best Of Cream –
   Cream
17 Best Of The Bee Gees –
   Bee Gees
18 Going Places –
   Herb Alpert and the Tijuana Brass
19 Jungle Book –
   Film Soundtrack
20 Through The Past Darkly
   (Big Hits Vol 2) – Rolling Stones

Most weeks on chart: by artist

The following list is of all artists who spent 50 or more weeks on the album charts. It is of course possible to be credited with 2 or more chart weeks in the same week owing to simultaneous hits.

	Weeks
Elvis Presley	462
Beatles	435
Frank Sinatra	340
(plus 23 weeks with Count Basie)	
Beach Boys	338
Cliff Richard	337
Jim Reeves	289
George Mitchell Minstrels	278
Bob Dylan	263
Tom Jones	262
Buddy Holly	259
Herb Alpert and the Tijuana Brass	254
Rolling Stones	225
Shadows	221
(plus 305 weeks on various Cliff Richard albums)	
Seekers	203
Otis Redding	192
(plus 17 weeks with Carla Thomas)	
Four Tops	186
Simon and Garfunkel	142
Engelbert Humperdinck	138
Supremes	133
(plus 25 weeks with Diana Ross and the Supremes with the Temptations)	
Cream	131
Val Doonican	119
Roy Orbison	119
Andy Williams	114
Kinks	107
Bachelors	98
Hollies	98
Bert Kaempfert	95
Walker Brothers	93
Monkees	91
Joan Baez	87
Searchers	87

Jimi Hendrix 86
(plus 2 weeks with Curtis Knight)
Animals 83
Frank Ifield 83
John Mayall 82
(plus 17 weeks with Eric Clapton)
Duane Eddy 79
Dubliners 78
Dusty Springfield 78
Ray Conniff 77
Georgie Fame 72
Mantovani 70
Bee Gees 68
James Last 67
Small Faces 66
Temptations 65
(plus 25 weeks with Diana Ross and the Supremes with the Temptations)
Chris Barber and Acker Bilk 61
(Chris Barber has a further 27 weeks as a soloist and in collaboration with Kenny Ball and Acker Bilk; Acker Bilk has a further 72 weeks in similar line ups)
Fleetwood Mac 61
Moody Blues 60
Tony Bennett 59
Manfred Mann 58
Donovan 57
Johnny Cash 51
Gene Pitney 51
Geno Washington 51

Most weeks on chart: Year by Year

1960	Weeks
1 Elvis Presley	51
2 Peter Sellers	48
3 Cliff Richard	43
4 Duane Eddy	32
5 Everly Brothers	31
6 Buddy Holly	29
7 Russ Conway	27
8 101 Strings	25
9 Tony Hancock	24
Mario Lanza	24
Frank Sinatra	24

Note: Peter Sellers 12 more weeks with the Goons. The following film soundtrack albums spent enough weeks on the chart to merit a place in the artists' Top Ten:

SOUTH PACIFIC	53
GIGI	40
OKLAHOMA!	34
CAN CAN	30
THE KING AND I	30

1961	Weeks
1 Elvis Presley	91
2 Frank Sinatra	72

	Weeks
3 George Mitchell Minstrels	63
4 Cliff Richard	62
5 Buddy Holly	52
6 Ray Conniff	40
7 Chris Barber and Acker Bilk	37
8 Adam Faith	29
9 Bob Newhart	21
10 Frankie Lane	20

Note: The following film soundtrack albums spent enough weeks on the chart to merit a place in the artists' Top Ten:

SOUTH PACIFIC	49
OKLAHOMA!	43
THE KING AND I	30
SEVEN BRIDES FOR SEVEN BROTHERS	21

1962	Weeks
1 George Mitchell Minstrels	109
2 Elvis Presley	96
3 Cliff Richard	59
4 Frank Sinatra	57
5 Shadows	53
6 Buddy Holly	48
7 Dorothy Provine	44
8 Mr. Acker Bilk	28
9 Karl Denver	25
Helen Shapiro	25

Note: Acker Bilk 24 more weeks with Chris Barber, and 19 more with Chris Barber and Kenny Ball, total 71 weeks. Helen Shapiro 21 more weeks on It's Trad Dad soundtrack LP.
The following film soundtracks spent enough weeks on the chart to merit a place in the artists' Top Ten:

SOUTH PACIFIC	52
WEST SIDE STORY	41

1963	Weeks
1 Cliff Richard	72
2 Buddy Holly	66
Elvis Presley	66
4 George Mitchell Minstrels	61
5 Shadows	54
6 Frank Ifield	51
7 Beatles	44
8 Frank Sinatra	40
9 Chuck Berry	29
Joe Brown	29
Brenda Lee	29

Note: Frank Sinatra 23 more weeks with Count Basie.
Bobby Vee 27 weeks solo and 17 with the Crickets, total 44 weeks.
The following film soundtracks spent enough weeks on the chart to merit a place in the artists' Top Ten:

WEST SIDE STORY	52
SOUTH PACIFIC	45

1964	Weeks
1 Jim Reeves	115
2 Beatles	104

	Weeks
3 Roy Orbison	59
4 Searchers	54
5 Shadows	48
6 Elvis Presley	44
7 Rolling Stones	36
8 Frank Ifield	31
9 Bachelors	27
10 Hollies	25

Note: The following film soundtrack album spent enough weeks on the chart to merit a place in the artists' Top Ten:

WEST SIDE STORY	52

1965	Weeks
1 Bob Dylan	112
2 Beatles	80
3 Rolling Stones	65
4 Joan Baez	55
5 Jim Reeves	44
6 Animals	39
7 Kinks	32
8 Elvis Presley	30
9 Andy Williams	28
10 Roy Orbison	25

Note: The following film soundtrack albums spent enough weeks on the chart to merit a place in the artists' Top Ten:

MARY POPPINS	50
MY FAIR LADY	41
THE SOUND OF MUSIC	38
WEST SIDE STORY	31

1966	Weeks
1 Beach Boys	95
2 Herb Albert	87
3 Beatles	81
4 Frank Sinatra	61
5 Bert Kaempfert	59
6 Walker Brothers	53
7 Jim Reeves	51
8 Rolling Stones	47
9 Spencer Davis Group	43
10 Kinks	33

Note: The following film soundtrack album spent enough weeks on the chart to merit a place in the artists' Top Ten:

THE SOUND OF MUSIC	52

1967	Weeks
1 Herb Alpert	101
2 Beach Boys	97
3 Monkees	80
4 Tom Jones	75
5 Four Tops	69
6 Beatles	58
Dubliners	58
8 James Last	51
9 Jim Reeves	50
10 Geno Washington	47

Note: The following film soundtrack albums spent enough weeks on the chart to merit a place in the artists' Top Ten:

DOCTOR ZHIVAGO	52
THE SOUND OF MUSIC	52

1968

		Weeks
1	Tom Jones	135
2	Otis Redding	121
3	Beach Boys	116
4	Four Tops	103
5	Engelbert Humperdinck	74
6	Simon and Garfunkel	73
7	Diana Ross and the Supremes	70
8	Herb Alpert	54
9	Cream	50
	Seekers	50

Note: The following film soundtrack album spent enough weeks on the chart to merit a place in the artists' Top Ten:

THE SOUND OF MUSIC	52

1969

		Weeks
1	Seekers	66
2	Simon and Garfunkel	63
3	Cream	57
4	Tom Jones	46
5	Beatles	41
6	Bob Dylan	40
7	Elvis Presley	39
8	Jethro Tull	32
	Led Zeppelin	32
	Moody Blues	32

Note: The following film soundtrack albums spent enough weeks on the chart to merit a place in the artists' Top Ten:

THE SOUND OF MUSIC	52
OLIVER	45

LED ZEPPELIN

Most weeks on chart by disc: consecutively

Weeks

Weeks		Artist
125	The Black And White Minstrel Show	George Mitchell Minstrels
118	Best Of The Beach Boys	Beach Boys
91	Going Places	Herb Alpert and the Tijuana Brass
87	Live At The Talk Of The Town	Tom Jones
72	Four Tops Live!	Four Tops
67	Please Please Me	Beatles
65	Blue Hawaii	Elvis Presley
59	Best Of The Seekers	Seekers
58	Release Me	Engelbert Humperdinck
58	In Dreams	Roy Orbison
57	Shadows	Shadows
57	Greatest Hits	Supremes
56	Greatest Hits	Four Tops
52	Sergeant Pepper's Lonely Hearts Club Band	Beatles
51	GI Blues	Elvis Presley
50	With The Beatles	Beatles

Most weeks on chart by disc: in total

		Weeks	Runs
The Black And White Minstrel Show	George Mitchell Minstrels	142	5
The Buddy Holly Story	Buddy Holly And The Crickets	137	15
Best Of The Beach Boys	Beach Boys	125	5
Going Places	Herb Alpert And The Tijuana Brass	119	5
Live At The Talk Of The Town	Tom Jones	89	3
Otis Blue	Otis Redding	75	4
Four Tops Live!	Four Tops	72	1
Please Please Me	Beatles	70	4
Come The Day	Seekers	67	2
Blue Hawaii	Elvis Presley	65	1
Another Black And White Minstrel Show	George Mitchell Minstrels	64	6
Greatest Hits	Supremes	60	2
Best Of The Seekers	Seekers	59	1
Release Me	Engelbert Humperdinck	58	1
In Dreams	Roy Orbison	58	1
Shadows	Shadows	57	1
Greatest Hits	Four Tops	56	1
GI Blues	Elvis Presley	55	3
Sergeant Pepper's Lonely Hearts Club Band	Beatles	53	2
With The Beatles	Beatles	51	2
Rolling Stones	Rolling Stones	51	3
Greatest Hits	Bob Dylan	51	5

Most hits by artist

The following list is of all artists who have had five or more hits. Re-entries and re-issues do not count as a new hit.

31 Frank Sinatra
(plus one with Count Basie)
29 Elvis Presley
24 Cliff Richard
20 Jim Reeves
13 Beach Boys
13 Beatles
10 Bob Dylan
10 Roy Orbison
10 Rolling Stones
10 Andy Williams
9 Tom Jones
9 John Mayall
(plus one with Eric Clapton)
9 George Mitchell Minstrels
9 Otis Redding
(plus one with Carla Thomas)
8 Herb Alpert and the Tijuana Brass
8 Shirley Bassey
8 Ray Conniff
8 Buddy Holly and the Crickets
8 Bert Kaempfert
8 James Last
8 Mantovani
8 Supremes
(plus two with the Temptations)
7 Bachelors
7 Duane Eddy
7 Hollies
7 Kinks
7 Gene Pitney
7 Shadows
(plus appearances on 18 Cliff Richard albums)
6 Mr Acker Bilk
(plus one with Kenny Ball and Chris Barber, and a further two with Chris Barber)
6 Byrds
6 Johnny Cash
6 Cream
6 Val Doonican
6 Dean Martin
6 Seekers
5 Joan Baez
5 Bee Gees
5 Tony Bennett
5 Chuck Berry
5 Petula Clark
5 Russ Conway
5 Donovan
5 Georgie Fame
5 Four Tops
5 Engelbert Humperdinck
5 Manfred Mann
5 Simon and Garfunkel
5 Temptations
(plus one with Diana Ross and the Supremes)
5 Bobby Vee
(plus one with the Crickets)
5 Dionne Warwick

Most Top Ten hits by artist

The following list is of all artists who have had three or more Top Ten hits. Rules are as for Most Hits but the album must have made the Top Ten for at least one week.

21 Elvis Presley
19 Frank Sinatra
(plus one with Count Basie)
15 Cliff Richard
12 Beatles
10 Beach Boys
10 Jim Reeves
10 Rolling Stones
9 Bob Dylan
7 Tom Jones
7 Shadows
(plus appearances on 12 of Cliff Richard's Top Ten albums)
6 Cream
6 Buddy Holly and the Crickets
6 George Mitchell Minstrels
5 Russ Conway
5 Val Doonican
5 Engelbert Humperdinck
5 Kinks
5 Mantovani
4 Herb Alpert and the Tijuana Brass
4 Animals
4 Joan Baez
4 Four Tops
4 Jimi Hendrix
4 Hollies
4 Frank Ifield
4 Monkees
4 Pink Floyd
4 Searchers
4 Seekers
4 Scott Walker
(plus four with the Walker Brothers)
4 Walker Brothers
3 Bee Gees
3 Chuck Berry
3 Spencer Davis Group
3 Duane Eddy
3 Everly Brothers
3 Fleetwood Mac
3 Mamas and the Papas
3 John Mayall
(plus one with Eric Clapton)
3 Moody Blues
3 101 Strings
3 Roy Orbison
3 Otis Redding
3 Dusty Springfield
3 Supremes
(plus one with the Temptations)
3 Who
3 Andy Williams

Most hits without a Number One hit

31 Frank Sinatra
13 Beach Boys
10 Roy Orbison
9 John Mayall
8 Herb Alpert and the Tijuana Brass
8 Shirley Bassey
8 Buddy Holly and the Crickets
8 Bert Kaempfert
8 James Last
8 Mantovani
7 Bachelors
7 Duane Eddy
7 Kinks
7 Gene Pitney

Most Top Ten hits without a Number One hit

19 Frank Sinatra
10 Beach Boys
6 Buddy Holly and the Crickets
5 Russ Conway
5 Engelbert Humperdinck
5 Kinks
5 Mantovani
4 Herb Alpert and the Tijuana Brass
4 Animals
4 Joan Baez
4 Jimi Hendrix
4 Frank Ifield
4 Pink Floyd

4 Searchers
4 Walker Brothers

Most hits without a Top Ten hit

5 Petula Clark
5 Temptations
4 Louis Armstrong
4 Bo Diddley
3 Chet Atkins
3 Chris Barber
3 David McWilliams
3 Mrs. Mills
3 Peter, Paul and Mary
3 Sam and Dave

Petula CLARK hides behind her singles success. Her five hit albums without a Top Ten placing made her number one in this chart. *Pictorial Press.*

The number one albums

		Number of weeks at number one
1960		
2 Jan	**South Pacific** Film Soundtrack (RCA)	10
12 Mar	**The Explosive Freddy Cannon** Freddy Cannon (Top Rank)	1
19 Mar	**South Pacific** Film Soundtrack (RCA)	19
30 Jul	**Elvis Is Back** Elvis Presley (RCA)	1
6 Aug	**South Pacific** Film Soundtrack (RCA)	5
10 Sep	**Down Drury Lane To Memory Lane** 101 Strings (Pye)	5
15 Oct	**South Pacific** Film Soundtrack (RCA)	13
1961		
14 Jan	**GI Blues** Elvis Presley (RCA)	7
4 Mar	**South Pacific** Film Soundtrack (RCA)	1
11 Mar	**GI Blues** Elvis Presley (RCA)	3
1 Apr	**South Pacific** Film Soundtrack (RCA)	1
8 Apr	**GI Blues** Elvis Presley (RCA)	12
1 Jul	**South Pacific** Film Soundtrack (RCA)	4
29 Jul	**Black And White Minstrel Show** George Mitchell Minstrels (HMV)	4
26 Aug	**South Pacific** Film Soundtrack (RCA)	1
2 Sep	**Black And White Minstrel Show** George Mitchell Minstrels (HMV)	1
9 Sep	**South Pacific** Film Soundtrack (RCA)	1
16 Sep	**Black And White Minstrel Show** George Mitchell Minstrels (HMV)	1
23 Sep	**Shadows** Shadows (Columbia)	4
21 Oct	**Black And White Minstrel Show** George Mitchell Minstrels (HMV)	1
28 Oct	**Shadows** Shadows (Columbia)	1
4 Nov	**I'm 21 Today** Cliff Richard (Columbia)	1
11 Nov	**Another Black And White Minstrel Show** George Mitchell Minstrels (HMV)	8
1962		
6 Jan	**Blue Hawaii** Elvis Presley (RCA)	1
13 Jan	**The Young Ones** Cliff Richard (Columbia)	6
24 Feb	**Blue Hawaii** Elvis Presley (RCA)	17
23 Jun	**West Side Story** Broadway Cast (CBS)	5
28 Jul	**Pot Luck** Elvis Presley (RCA)	5
2 Sep	**West Side Story** Broadway Cast (CBS)	1
8 Sep	**Pot Luck** Elvis Presley (RCA)	1
15 Sep	**West Side Story** Broadway Cast (CBS)	1
22 Sep	**The Best Of Ball, Barber, and Bilk** Kenny Ball, Chris Barber and Acker Bilk (Pye)	1
29 Sep	**West Side Story** Broadway Cast (CBS)	3
20 Oct	**The Best Of Ball, Barber, and Bilk** Kenny Ball, Chris Barber and Acker Bilk (Pye)	1
27 Oct	**Out Of The Shadows** Shadows (Columbia)	3
17 Nov	**West Side Story** Broadway Cast (CBS)	1
24 Nov	**Out Of The Shadows** Shadows (Columbia)	1
1 Dec	**On Stage With The George Mitchell Minstrels** George Mitchell Minstrels (HMV)	2

15 Dec	**West Side Story** Broadway Cast (CBS)	1
22 Dec	**Out Of The Shadows** Shadows (Columbia)	1
29 Dec	**Black And White Minstrel Show** George Mitchell Minstrels (HMV)	2

1963

12 Jan	**West Side Story** Broadway Cast (CBS)	1
19 Jan	**Out Of The Shadows** Shadows (Columbia)	2
2 Feb	**Summer Holiday** Cliff Richard (Columbia)	14
11 May	**Please Please Me** Beatles (Parlophone)	30
7 Dec	**With The Beatles** Beatles (Parlophone)	21

1964

2 May	**Rolling Stones** Rolling Stones (Decca)	12
25 Jul	**A Hard Day's Night** Beatles (Parlophone)	21
19 Dec	**Beatles For Sale** Beatles (Parlophone)	7

1965

6 Feb	**Rolling Stones No. 2** Rolling Stones (Decca)	3
27 Feb	**Beatles For Sale** Beatles (Parlophone)	1
6 Mar	**Rolling Stones No. 2** Rolling Stones (Decca)	6
17 Apr	**Freewheelin' Bob Dylan** Bob Dylan (CBS)	1
24 Apr	**Rolling Stones No. 2** Rolling Stones (Decca)	1
1 May	**Beatles For Sale** Beatles (Parlophone)	3
22 May	**Freewheelin' Bob Dylan** Bob Dylan (CBS)	1
29 May	**Bringing It All Back Home** Bob Dylan (CBS)	1
5 Jun	**Sound Of Music** Film Soundtrack (RCA)	10
14 Aug	**Help** Beatles (Parlophone)	9
16 Oct	**Sound Of Music** Film Soundtrack (RCA)	10
25 Dec	**Rubber Soul** Beatles (Parlophone)	9

1966

19 Feb	**Sound Of Music** Film Soundtrack (RCA)	10
30 Apr	**Aftermath** Rolling Stones (Decca)	8
25 Jun	**Sound Of Music** Film Soundtrack (RCA)	7
13 Aug	**Revolver** Beatles (Parlophone)	7
1 Oct	**Sound Of Music** Film Soundtrack (RCA)	18

1967

4 Feb	**Monkees** Monkees (RCA)	7
25 Mar	**Sound Of Music** Film Soundtrack (RCA)	7
13 May	**More Of The Monkees** Monkees (RCA)	1
20 May	**Sound Of Music** Film Soundtrack (RCA)	1
27 May	**More Of The Monkees** Monkees (RCA)	1
3 Jun	**Sound Of Music** Film Soundtrack (RCA)	1
10 Jun	**Sergeant Pepper's Lonely Hearts Club Band** Beatles (Parlophone)	23
18 Nov	**Sound Of Music** Film Soundtrack (RCA)	1
25 Nov	**Sergeant Pepper's Lonely Hearts Club Band** Beatles (Parlophone)	1

2 Dec	**Sound Of Music** Film Soundtrack (RCA)	3
23 Dec	**Sergeant Pepper's Lonely Hearts Club Band** Beatles (Parlophone)	2

1968

6 Jan	**Val Doonican Rocks But Gently** Val Doonican (Pye)	3
27 Jan	**Sound Of Music** Film Soundtrack (RCA)	1
3 Feb	**Sergeant Pepper's Lonely Hearts Club Band** Beatles (Parlophone)	1
10 Feb	**Greatest Hits** Four Tops (Tamla Motown)	1
17 Feb	**Greatest Hits** Supremes (Tamla Motown)	3
9 Mar	**John Wesley Harding** Bob Dylan (CBS)	10
18 May	**Scott 2** Scott Walker (Philips)	1
25 May	**John Wesley Harding** Bob Dylan (CBS)	3
15 Jun	**Love Andy** Andy Williams (CBS)	1
22 Jun	**Dock Of The Bay** Otis Redding (Stax)	1
29 Jun	**Ogden's Nut Gone Flake** Small Faces (Immediate)	6
10 Aug	**Delilah** Tom Jones (Decca)	1
17 Aug	**Bookends** Simon and Garfunkel (CBS)	5
21 Sep	**Delilah** Tom Jones (Decca)	1
28 Sep	**Bookends** Simon and Garfunkel (CBS)	2
12 Oct	**Greatest Hits** Hollies (Parlophone)	6
23 Nov	**Sound Of Music** Film Soundtrack (RCA)	1
30 Nov	**Greatest Hits** Hollies (Parlophone)	1
7 Dec	**The Beatles** Beatles (Apple)	7

1969

25 Jan	**Best Of The Seekers** Seekers (Columbia)	1
1 Feb	**The Beatles** Beatles (Apple)	1
8 Feb	**Best Of The Seekers** Seekers (Columbia)	1
15 Feb	**Diana Ross and the Supremes Join the Temptations** Diana Ross and the Supremes with the Temptations (Tamla Motown)	3
8 Mar	**Four And Only Seekers** Seekers (MFP)	1
15 Mar	**Goodbye** Cream (Polydor)	2
29 Mar	**Best Of The Seekers** Seekers (Columbia)	2
12 Apr	**Goodbye** Cream (Polydor)	1
19 Apr	**Best Of The Seekers** Seekers (Columbia)	1
26 Apr	**Goodbye** Cream (Polydor)	1
3 May	**Best Of The Seekers** Seekers (Columbia)	1
10 May	**On The Threshold Of A Dream** Moody Blues (Deram)	2
24 May	**Nashville Skyline** Bob Dylan (CBS)	4
21 Jun	**His Orchestra, His Chorus, His Singers, His Sound** Ray Conniff (CBS)	3
12 Jul	**According To My Heart** Jim Reeves (RCA)	4
9 Aug	**Stand Up** Jethro Tull (Island)	3
30 Aug	**From Elvis In Memphis** Elvis Presley (RCA)	1
6 Sep	**Stand Up** Jethro Tull (Island)	2
20 Sep	**Blind Faith** Blind Faith (Polydor)	2
4 Oct	**Abbey Road** Beatles (Apple)	11
20 Dec	**Let It Bleed** Rolling Stones (Decca)	1
27 Dec	**Abbey Road** Beatles (Apple)	1
		(+ 5 in 1970)

Most Number One hits by artist

- 10 Beatles
- 5 Elvis Presley
- 4 Bob Dylan
- 4 Rolling Stones
- 3 George Mitchell Minstrels
- 3 Cliff Richard
- 2 Monkees
- 2 Shadows (plus 3 with Cliff Richard)

Most weeks at Number One by artist

	Weeks
Beatles	154
Cast From The Film 'The Sound Of Music'	70
Cast From The Film 'South Pacific'	55
Elvis Presley	48
Rolling Stones	31
Cliff Richard	21
Bob Dylan	20
George Mitchell Minstrels	19
Cast From The Broadway Staging Of 'West Side Story'	13
Shadows (plus 21 weeks with Cliff Richard)	12

Most weeks at Number One by disc: total

	Weeks
Sound Of Music Film Soundtrack	70
South Pacific Film Soundtrack	55
Please Please Me–Beatles	30
Sergeant Pepper's Lonely Hearts Club Band–Beatles	27
GI Blues–Elvis Presley	22
With The Beatles–Beatles	21
A Hard Day's Night–Beatles	21
Blue Hawaii–Elvis Presley	18
Summer Holiday–Cliff Richard	14
West Side Story–Broadway Cast	13
John Wesley Harding–Bob Dylan	13
Abbey Road–Beatles	12
Rolling Stones–Rolling Stones	12
Beatles For Sale–Beatles	11
Rolling Stones No. 2 – Rolling Stones	10

Most weeks at Number One by disc: consecutively

	Weeks
Please Please Me–Beatles	30
Sergeant Pepper's Lonely Hearts Club Band–Beatles	23
With The Beatles–Beatles	21
A Hard Day's Night–Beatles	21
South Pacific – Film Soundtrack	19
Sound Of Music – Film Soundtrack	18
Blue Hawaii–Elvis Presley	17
Summer Holiday–Cliff Richard	14
South Pacific – Film Soundtrack	13
GI Blues–Elvis Presley	12
Rolling Stones–Rolling Stones	12
Abbey Road–Beatles	11
Sound Of Music – Film Soundtrack	10
Sound Of Music – Film Soundtrack	10
Sound Of Music – Film Soundtrack (Three separate runs of ten weeks each)	10
John Wesley Harding–Bob Dylan	10

Most weeks at Number One in a year: by artist

		Weeks
1960	Cast From The Film 'South Pacific'	46
1961	Elvis Presley	22
1962	Elvis Presley	24
1963	Beatles	34
1964	Beatles	40
1965	Cast From The Film 'The Sound Of Music'	20
1966	Cast From The Film 'The Sound Of Music'	31
1967	Beatles	26
1968	Bob Dylan	13
1969	Beatles	16

Most weeks at Number One in a year: by label

		Weeks
1960	RCA	47
1961	RCA	31
1962	RCA	24
1963	Parlophone	34
1964	Parlophone	40
1965	RCA	20
1966	RCA	31
1967	Parlophone	26
	RCA	26
1968	CBS	20
1969	Apple	16

Most weeks at Number One by label

	Weeks
RCA	186
Parlophone	142
CBS	39
Columbia	39
Decca	33
Apple	20
HMV	19
Pye	10

Most Number Ones by label

- 10 RCA
- 9 Parlophone
- 8 CBS
- 6 Columbia
- 5 Decca

Straight in at Number One

14 Aug 65	Help!	Beatles
13 Aug 66	Revolver	Beatles
7 Dec 68	The Beatles	Beatles
8 Mar 69	Four And Only Seekers	Seekers
15 Mar 69	Goodbye	Cream
21 Jun 69	His Orchestra, His Chorus, His Singers, His Sound	Ray Conniff
9 Aug 69	Stand Up	Jethro Tull
20 Sep 68	Blind Faith	Blind Faith
4 Oct 69	Abbey Road	Beatles
20 Dec 69	Let It Bleed	Rolling Stones